IDENTITIES

IDENTITIES

Edited by Kwame Anthony Appiah

and Henry Louis Gates, Jr.

The University of Chicago Press

Chicago and London

The essays in this volume originally appeared in the journal *Critical Inquiry*. Original publication data can be found on the first page of each essay.

The University of Chicago Press, Chicago, 60637
The University of Chicago Press, Ltd., London

Printed in the United States of America
99 98 97 96 95 5 4 3 2 1

ISBN (cl) 0-226-28438-7
ISBN (pa) 0-226-28439-5

Library of Congress Cataloging-in-Publication Data

Identities / edited by Kwame Anthony Appiah and Henry Louis Gates, Jr.
p. cm.
Includes bibliographical references and index.
ISBN 0-226-28438-7 (cloth).—ISBN 0-226-28439-5 (pbk.)
1. Criticism. 2. Identity in literature. I. Appiah, Anthony II. Gates, Henry Louis.
PN81.I34
809'.93353—dc20 95-39956
CIP

The paper used in this publication meets the minimum requirements of the American National Standard for Information Sciences—Permanence of Paper for Printed Library Materials, ANSI Z39. 48-1984.∞™

Contents

Critical Responses

On the cover: Photo: Big Dog Photography. Fingerprint: Anonymous collection.

Editors' Introduction: Multiplying Identities

Kwame Anthony Appiah
and Henry Louis Gates, Jr.

A literary historian might very well characterize the eighties as the period when race, class, and gender became the holy trinity of literary criticism. *Critical Inquiry*'s contribution to this shift in critical paradigms took the form of two special issues, "Writing and Sexual Difference," and "'Race,' Writing, and Difference." In the 1990s, however, "race," "class," and "gender" threaten to become the regnant clichés of our critical discourse. Our object in this book is to help disrupt the cliché-ridden discourse of identity by exploring the formation of identities and the problem of subjectivity.

Scholars in a variety of disciplines have begun to address what we might call the politics of identity. Their work expands on the evolving anti-essentialist critiques of ethnic, sexual, national, and racial identities, particularly the work of those poststructuralist theorists who have articulated concepts of difference. The calls for a "post-essentialist" reconception of notions of identity have become increasingly common. The powerful resurgence of nationalisms in Eastern Europe provides just one example of the catalysts for such theorizing.

The study of identity crosses a number of disciplines to address such issues as the multiple intersections of race, class, and gender in feminist, lesbian, and gay studies, the interrelations of postcolonialism, nationalism, and ethnicity in ethnic and area studies, and so on. These intersections provide a provocative site for the articulation and discussion of new theories and discourses of identity.

Our original sense that an invitation to speak into this space would elicit thought-provoking responses has, we think, been richly confirmed in the collection of essays that follows. In exploring an astonishing geographical range of cases—from "Gypsies" in the Western imagination, to a mobilization of "the West" in Chinese television, by way of reconceptions of Polynesian and British "cannibalism," of Islam, of "Irishness," and of Arab modernity—we are exposed, above all, to the extraordinary internationalization of the discourses of identity: a process whose history, as Gananath Obeyesekere's paper reminds us, goes back through the processes that Europeans called their "discovery" of the world.

Obeyesekere's paper carries out a careful reading of the history of Captain Cook's encounter with the cultures of the South Pacific, exploring the ways in which ideologies of identity circulate between cultures at their points of meeting. Ideas about cannibalism, he argues, have a centrality in Cook's accounts of the South Pacific because cannibalism matters to Cook, not because cannibalism is either practiced or theorized in all the cultures of the region. But once Cook has introduced the issue to the Hawaiians, for example, they cannot, of course, ignore it; and so it comes to play a role in their understanding of *his* people.

If we want to pick a significance to attach to the Columbian quincentenary, we might as well see it as a point of origin for the extension of European theories of identity into the world; and we might also see in the emblematic "misnaming" of the "Indies" a model of the ways in which the identities of others both impact upon and, at the same time, escape those theories. The lives and understanding of the Caribs and the other inhabitants of the New World were not completely irrelevant to Christopher Columbus's understanding of his discovery; but they can hardly be said to have played a central role in shaping that understanding either.

In the United States ethnic and racial identities have been understood always in terms of differences both internal and external to the American nation. But the internal contrasts have often been figured in terms of outside contrasts because it has always been possible (by occluding the Native American presence) to see America as a "nation of immigrants," whose separateness could be mapped onto their places of origin. Walter Benn Michaels begins with a reading of turn-of-the-century American texts that reflect this process taken, as it were, to the metalevel: he explores Thomas Nelson Page's *Red Rock* and works by Thomas Dixon in

---

Kwame Anthony Appiah, author of *Assertion and Conditionals* (1985), *Truth in Semantics* (1986), and *Necessary Questions* (1989) (an introduction to philosophy), has also published three novels, the latest of which is *Another Death in Venice* (1995). He has recently published essays on politics and identity. **Henry Louis Gates, Jr.** is director of the W. E. B. Du Bois Institute and chair of Harvard University's Afro-American studies department. He is editor of *"Race," Writing, and Difference,* and author of *Figures in Black, The Signifying Monkey, Loose Canons,* and *Colored People.*

which Reconstruction within the United States is modelled implicitly on American imperialism in the world "outside." Here an understanding of the relation of the South to the American state is modelled on the relation of the American empire to the American metropole. Michaels's piece is not, however, merely a reading of these texts. Rather, they are the springboard to a provocative theoretical argument, whose conclusion is that the idea of a culture that is "ours" will always be rooted in an essentialism about who we are. For Michaels, talk of culture is not (as Du Bois so often insisted) an alternative to talk of race, but a continuation of it by other means.

While the United States has always used other places to structure its internal differentiations, it seems to us that we are now witnessing a certain ironical reversal of this pattern. For in recent years and in many places "outside" the United States people have mobilized a figure of America (sometimes under the name of "the West") in order to articulate debates about their "own" identities. Thus, for example, at a recent discussion of civil society and the state at the National Humanities Center, a Czech parliamentarian found himself intervening in U.S. debates about multiculturalism because, having taken the U.S. as a model, he saw in celebrations of African American identity a threatening echo of Slovak "nationalism." Such connections can be deeply illuminating when they are grounded in a knowledge of both ends of the analogy; the irony in this process, however, is that the mobilization of America in these discourses—like the mobilization of "the West" in the Chinese television series "He Shang" (described by Xiaomei Chen)—often has as phantasmic a relation to the empirical United States as American theories of others have often had to their empirical realities.

Ethnic and national identities operate in the lives of individuals by connecting them with some people, dividing them from others. Such identities are often deeply integral to a person's sense of self, defining an "I" by placing it against a background "we." Diana Fuss, in an elegant reading of images of elegance, explores the lesbian identity of the woman's gaze both required by and suppressed in contemporary American magazine fashion photography. More than any of our other pieces, this one explores the role of questions of identity—of gender and sexuality—in the psychic ontogeny of individuals, indeed in the process of individualization. Here theory offers answers to what must surely be seen as a genuine pre-theoretical problem: Why does an image offered up to putatively straight women need to echo the idiom of pornography addressed to putatively straight men? And, if the question of the lesbian does not arise in this context, why does it not arise?

Racial identities, like those along the dimensions of gender and sexuality, are defined in a peculiarly corporeal way: one's identity as an African American is rooted in one's embodiment as a black body. The significance of the body here may sometimes be as profound as it is in our gendered identities, as men and women, gay, straight, bisexual. And it is not surprising that important events occur in the landscape of identity when race and gender compete for and combine in a single body.

Hazel Carby demonstrates this very strikingly in her piece on women blues singers: the regulation of women's bodies is a central theme of discussions of the blues. Her essay is part of an important larger argument about where to locate intellectual leadership in African American culture, in the course of which she is seeking to redefine our understanding of intellectual history.

Carby is turning here towards a focussed local history of an African American discourse of gendered identities, and in so doing she exemplifies a strategy that is advanced by Sara Suleri. Suleri argues that the interplay of questions of gender and of racial embodiment in the broad context of relations among women in the sphere of the "postcolonial" requires considerable attention to local histories. But she also insists that the local histories need to be seen in relation, a point made also, among many others, in a dazzling series of geographical excursions (from Algeria to Bengal to Singapore to Bangladesh to Italy to Canada—where our point of entry will be through someone who is Lebanese) by Gayatri Chakravorty Spivak.

Both Suleri and Spivak attend to questions about women in the sphere of another dimension of identity (one that has been much neglected in recent theory), namely, that of religion. This is, of course, a term that threatens to obscure as much as it illuminates; but it is interesting how these two papers combine with those of Saree Makdisi and Akeel Bilgrami to address Islam. While Makdisi's essay starts as a reading of a particular text—al-Tayyib Salih's *Season of Migration to the North*—and Bilgrami's aims at a more philosophical generality, they concur in understanding the need for history in reconstructing the present. (Makdisi's essay also raises important questions about the role of gender in articulating the opposition of Native and Other, a major theme of Salih's novel.)

Bilgrami is surely right in his insistence that philosophical questions about identity can only be understood within richer histories than much recent philosophy has acknowledged. He also demonstrates how much philosophical illumination (illumination of the particular but also of the general) is to be gained from that immersion in history. And since history is, in the end, a kind of locality, he is here in agreement with points made by Spivak and Suleri.

Phillip Brian Harper's paper explores the politics of address in poetry of the Black Arts movement of the 1960s. Harper shows how a rhetoric that seems explicitly to address a black audience depends for its effects on a recognition that the poems will be heard by a white audience; and he also explores the ways in which the black audience explicitly addressed is often a non-nationalist African American opposed to the poet's nationalist "I." The poetry of the Black Arts movement thus presupposes interracial division and aims to construct intraracial division, Harper argues, reminding us, once more, of the centrality of many levels of difference in the construction of racial identity.

Elizabeth Abel analyzes similar fissures, this time exposed (and created) in the feminist debates about race—within which Carby, Suleri, and Spivak's essays were placed. She explores, in a reading of criticism by white and black feminists, some of the complexities of the relation between black and white feminist writing and reveals at the same time theoretical tensions among deconstructive, psychoanalytic, and materialist forms of reading. The essay's framing exploration of Toni Morrison's "Recitatif" offers a compelling argument for the place of racial and gender identity in the practice of reading.

Conflicting constructions of the body on a less familiar terrain are in evidence in Cheryl Herr's essay, which explores an astonishing range of cultural material—from videos and photographs to Neolithic tumuli—in pursuit of an argument about the erotics of Irishness. Herr explores the ways in which "the represented body has become an anti-fetish in Ireland" (p. 303), which has produced a culture resistant to "*seeing* movement, to recognizing its necessity, and ultimately to sanctioning radical changes of posture" (p. 283). This essay provides a demonstration of the place of culture, high and low, in the construction of national identity; the intersection of nation and gender in the field of representation of the body turns out to be extraordinarily complex in Herr's reading of Irishness.

The body recurs implicitly in Daniel and Jonathan Boyarin's essay on Jewish identity, implied, now, in the corporeal inheritance of a shared genealogy. In their essay, these authors challenge Walter Benn Michaels's provocative argument against the possibility of anti-essentialist accounts of identity. They argue that one root of modern opposition to genealogical notions of group identity—which many now construe, like Michaels, as inescapably racist—lies in St. Paul's attack—exemplified in the well-known passage in Galatians—on the notion that only those literally descended from Abraham are "'heirs according to the promise'" (p. 307). The apparently genial universalism of Paul's position has, they show, a dark underside; the "coercive discourses of sameness" that Étienne Balibar has argued make some forms of universalism racist (p. 319). And they defend a reconstructed notion of Jewish identity that is, in their view, legitimately understood as cultural and not as racial; they argue, generally, that "perhaps the primary function for a critical reconstruction of cultural (or racial or gender or sexual) identity is to construct it in ways that purge it of its elements of domination and oppression" (p. 322).

If we mention Katie Trumpener's paper last it is because it seems appropriate to end with the case that is, in being in some ways least familiar, best able to figure our sense that there is much that is new to be done in the field of identities. For part of what is extraordinary about the people whom the British call "Gypsies" is that their astonishing repression *is* so little known and that the twentieth-century persecutions occurred despite the sentimentalizations of Romani life in so much of nineteenth-century literature (and music). Gypsies in Victorian England managed to serve both as figures of liberty and as models of the human as brute. What we are speaking of here is not, of course, a Romani identity, but the outsider's image of these people. Their own self-understanding is only now coming into the view of the others in Europe and North America among whom they have lived so long. But contemporary Romani identity is, for better or worse, bound up with the history that racist stereotypes created, and it has to face both the sentimentalizing and the brutalizing strands.

In fashioning this book, which began as a special issue of *Critical Inquiry* (Summer 1992), we have added four essays from later issues of the journal, and, at the end, a number of critical responses to the original volume, each of which challenges one or several of the original papers and enlarges and enriches the debate. We are especially grateful to the authors of these responses for the care with which they have taken up issues raised by others and found in them ways to pursue discoveries of their own.

Such internal complexities in our understandings of others reflect (and help to create) the internal tensions in the identities that claim us. One conclusion we may draw from the discourse that this collection of essays both represents and furthers is that we need to attend more to the negotiation of identities by their possessors, recalling always that each identity, however central it is to our self-conceptions, may in some situations simply not be the one we need. In thinking through this issue it is helpful always to be able to draw on a wide range of examples, theorized in a wide range of idioms and through various methods and disciplines. This collection offers, we think, a rich sampler of that necessary variety. In negotiating the myriad complex dimensions of our human identities we surely need all the tools we can borrow or invent.

“British Cannibals”: Contemplation of an Event in the Death and Resurrection of James Cook, Explorer

Gananath Obeyesekere

1. The Dark Side of Being Human

I have recently completed a work entitled *The Apotheosis of Captain Cook: European Mythmaking in the Pacific.*[1] In it I present an alternative view of the events leading to the apotheosis of James Cook by the Hawaiians in 1779 when he first landed there, in effect making the case that the supposed deification of the white civilizer is a Western myth model foisted on the Hawaiians and having a long run in European culture and consciousness. As a result of reading the extensive logs and journals of Cook's voyages, I have become interested in the manner in which “cannibalism” got defined in these voyages. My reading of these texts suggests that statements about cannibalism reveal more about the relations between Euro-

This paper was written during my tenure at the National Humanities Center, North Carolina, in 1989–90 on a senior fellowship awarded by the Mellon Foundation. I am grateful to both these institutions for providing me the time, facilities, and intellectual stimulus to work on a study of James Cook. A version of this paper will appear in a book edited by Gilles Bibeau and Ellen Corin, *The Order of the Text: Asceticism and Violence in the Interpretation of Culture.* The immediate precursor for my work is William Arens, *The Man-Eating Myth: Anthropology and Anthropophagy* (New York, 1979). Unfortunately Arens does not deal with the dialogical nature of cannibalistic discourse, and he does not recognize the possibility that where there is fantasy there could be slippage into reality and from there into human institutions.

1. See Gananath Obeyesekere, *The Apotheosis of Captain Cook: European Mythmaking in the Pacific* (Princeton, N.J., 1992).

This article originally appeared in *Critical Inquiry* 18 (Summer 1992).

peans and Savages during early and late contact than, as ethnographic statements, about the nature of Savage anthropophagy.

Let me begin at the end with the death of Cook in Hawaii during his third and last voyage. It is 1779, but it could be 1996 in another place: one group with their piles of stones and the other with their loaded guns. The ship's officers want genuinely to defuse the tension, but they are not willing to leave till they get the bones of "our dear Captain" for a decent burial at sea. Lieutenant James King, who loved Cook dearly, seems to be in charge. When the Hawaiians are told that if "the body was not brought the next morning, the town should be destroyed," Koah, a chief, a "treacherous fellow" whom King intensely disliked, came aboard to talk about returning Cook's remains.[2] That night two frightened priests, one of whom was the tabu man who accompanied Cook wherever he went, came up; and after loud lamentations about the loss of Lono-Cook, they said they had brought with them whatever remained of him. "He then presented to us a small bundle wrapped up in cloth, which he brought under his arm; and it is impossible to describe the horror which seized us, on finding in it, a piece of human flesh, about nine or ten pounds weight. This, he said, was all that remained of the body" (*V*, 3:68). The rest of Cook they said was cooked in the Hawaiian fashion and distributed among the king and the chiefs, a mode by which Cook was appropriated into the Hawaiian aristocracy. It is in the course of this conversation between King and the priests that the latter came out with the phrase, "When the *Orono* would come again?" (*V*, 3:69). This is of course—at least according to Marshall Sahlins—a reference to the possible return of the god, after his ritual killing and sacrifice at the hands of the Hawaiians, acting out a final phase in a cosmic drama.[3]

Now let me examine the full account of the events by Lieutenant King. Naturally the ship's officers were appalled at the sight of the grisly object, but they soon overcame this, for as the first ethnographers, they were imbued by a scientific curiosity. They could easily change into their white coats, for let it not be forgotten they were representatives of the Royal Society. King reports:

2. James King, vol. 3 of James Cook and King, *A Voyage to the Pacific Ocean*, 3 vols. (Dublin and London, 1784), 3:64, 66; hereafter abbreviated *V*. Cook wrote the first two volumes of this work.

3. See Marshall Sahlins, *Islands of History* (Chicago, 1985), pp. 104–35.

Gananath Obeyesekere is professor of anthropology at Princeton University. He is the author of *The Apotheosis of Captain Cook: European Mythmaking in the Pacific* (1992).

> This [meeting] afforded an opportunity of informing ourselves, whether they were cannibals; and we did not neglect it. We first tried, by many indirect questions, put to each of them apart, to learn in what manner the rest of the bodies had been disposed of; and finding them very constant in one story, that, after the flesh had been cut off, it was all burnt; we at last put the direct question, Whether they had not eat some of it? They immediately shewed as much horror at the idea, as any European would have done; and asked, very naturally, if that was the custom amongst us? They afterward asked us, with great earnestness and apparent apprehension, "When the *Orono* would come again? and what he would do to them on his return?" The same inquiry was frequently made afterward by others; and this idea agrees with the general tenour of their conduct toward him, which shewed, that they considered him as a being of superior nature. [*V,* 3:69]

Thus at least in one instance the famous questions on the return of Lono (Orono) were uttered by the two Hawaiians in the context of a discourse on cannibalism. The "apparent apprehension" of the Hawaiians is converted into "expressions of sorrow" by Sahlins.[4] King interpreted that anxious question as evidence of the Hawaiian belief that they considered Cook to be a "being of superior nature." Elsewhere in the journal King describes Hawaiian attitudes as "adoration," a term of Christian devotionalism. Other British journal writers however interpreted the event in terms consonant with both Hawaiian and European mythic structures: Hawaiians were afraid of the return of Cook's "ghost"!

What was going on in this dialogue between the anxious Hawaiians and the ethnographers? Let me flash back to the first brief visit of Cook to Kauai, one of the Hawaiian islands, the previous year. During that visit James Cook himself asked an identical question. A Hawaiian was carrying "a very small parcel," and since he was anxious to conceal it, Cook insisted it be opened. He saw concealed therein "a thin bit of flesh, about two inches long," and naturally he surmised "it might be human flesh, and that these people might, perhaps, eat their enemies"—a legitimate ethnographic inquiry I might add since Cook says "that this was the practice of some of the natives of the South Sea islands." The questions put to the Hawaiian confirmed the hypothesis, and Cook concluded that "it was their custom to eat those killed in battle."[5]

When Cook tried to confirm his hypothesis of Hawaiian cannibalism the next week (29 January 1778), from a visitor to the ship's gun room he got a different reply. For Cook however this reply was proof of cannibalism:

4. Sahlins, *Historical Metaphors and Mythical Realities: Structure in the Early History of the Sandwich Islands Kingdom* (Ann Arbor, Mich., 1981), p. 24.

5. Cook, *A Voyage to the Pacific Ocean,* 2:209.

> These visiters furnished us with an opportunity of agitating again, this day, the curious inquiry, whether they were cannibals. . . . One of the islanders, who wanted to get in at the gun-room port, was refused; and, at the same time, asked, whether, if he should come in, we could kill and eat him? accompanying this questions with signs so expressive, that there could be no doubt about his meaning. This gave a proper opening to retort the question as to this practice; and a person behind the other, in the canoe, who paid great attention to what was passing, immediately answered, that if we were killed on shore, they would certainly eat us. He spoke with so little emotion, that it appeared plainly to be his meaning, that they would not destroy us for that purpose; but that their eating us would be the consequence of our being at enmity with them. I have availed myself of Mr. Anderson's collections for the decision of this matter; and am sorry to say, that I cannot see the least reason to hesitate in pronouncing it be certain, that the horrid banquet of human flesh, is as much relished here, amidst plenty, as it is in New Zealand.[6]

Something curious was going on here from the very first visit: the British thought that the Hawaiians were cannibals and the Hawaiians thought that it was the British who were out to eat them! Now it is clear that the British inquiry was a legitimate ethnographic hypothesis based on the practice of cannibalism in New Zealand among Maoris and elsewhere. But what about the Hawaiians? How did *their* hypothesis emerge—if one dare call this fear of British cannibalism a hypothesis?

The answer comes from King's journal of the next year (1779). Here a curious event occurred, which Sahlins thinks was due to the anxiety of the Hawaiians to get rid of the god Lono (Cook) who has overstayed his ritual schedule and should, according to the Makahiki calendar, be off to the mythical island of Kahiki whence he and his crew came. King noted: "It was ridiculous enough to see [the Hawaiians] stroking the sides, and patting the bellies, of the sailors (who were certainly much improved in the sleekness of their looks) . . . and telling them, partly by signs, and partly by words, that it was time for them to go." King adds: "if our enormous consumption of hogs and vegetables be considered, it need not be wondered, that they should wish to see us take our leave" (*V*, 3:26). Leave to which place? Brittanee.[7] Thus the home of Lono-Cook known to anthropologists as Kahiki was apparently designated as "Brittanee" by the Hawaiians. What kind of place was this Brittanee though? Let King respond again: "they imagined we came from some country where provisions had failed; and that our visit to

6. Ibid., 2:214–15.

7. The crew were instructed by the admiralty to inform native chiefs who they were and why they were in a particular place. Thus everywhere Polynesians knew they came from "Brittanee." In Hawaii, the priest Koah changed his name to "Brittanee" in honor of the new arrivals.

them was merely for the purpose of filling our bellies. Indeed, the meagre appearance of some of our crew, the hearty appetites with which we sat down to their fresh provisions, and our great anxiety to purchase, and carry off, as much as we were able, led them, naturally enough, to such a conclusion" (*V,* 3:26).

The Hawaiians' hypothesis was based on the pragmatics of common sense. Here were a ragged, filthy, half-starved bunch of people arriving on their island, gorging themselves on food, and asking questions about cannibalism. Since Hawaiians did not know that the British inquiry was a scientific hypothesis, they made the pragmatic inference that these half-starved people were asking questions about cannibalism because they were cannibals themselves and might actually eat the Hawaiians. If the British could ask what seemed to the Hawaiians an absurd question—whether they ate their enemies slain in battle—it is not unreasonable for the Hawaiians to have made a further inference: that since the British had slaughtered so many Hawaiians, it is they who ate their slain enemies. This inference is never explicitly made and does not appear in the journals, but, I think, we must consider at least the fear of the Hawaiians that the British were cannibals before we can interpret the question, When will Lono come again? and the significant words added afterwards, "and what would he do to them on his return?" (*V,* 3:69).

I think the interpretation that the Hawaiians were afraid of Cook's "ghost" is the correct one. The terrible events prior to, and after, Cook's death were well suited to that mythic reality. Remember that these events resulted in the death of at least six Hawaiian chiefs and dozens of ordinary citizens, not to mention the burning of residences. Previous to that, there were constant floggings for theft and the killing of at least one Hawaiian. According to Martha Beckwith, "Hawaiians believe in the power of spirits to return to the scenes they knew on earth in the form in which they appeared while they were alive."[8] One visitation from Cook was enough for the Hawaiians. It should be remembered that the Hawaiian fear of Cook's ghost wasn't without warrant, for soon after this interrogation, British marines burnt villages and some irate sailors chopped off the heads of two natives and displayed them on deck, playing out, as it were, the kind of terror generally attributed to the Savage. These grisly objects inspired terror among the Hawaiians who visited the ship.

It was not only in Hawaii that the queries on cannibalism produced a variety of responses from native peoples. It was the same everywhere. In another South Sea island, Mangaia, in March 1777, Anderson, the ship's doctor, "put the question if they ate human flesh which they answered in the negative with a mixture of indignation and abhorrence."[9] Why then

8. Martha Beckwith, *Hawaiian Mythology* (Honolulu, 1970), p. 164.

9. William Anderson, "A Journal of a Voyage Made in His Majestys Sloop *Resolution,*" in pt. 2 of *The Voyage of the "Resolution" and "Discovery" 1776–1780,* vol. 4 of *The Journals of*

the British preoccupation with cannibalism? One reason it seems to me is clear: cannibalism is what the English reading public wanted to hear. It was their definition of the Savage. Thus in the many places Cook visited, the inevitable question he asked was about cannibalism, and the replies for the most part convinced Cook of its universal prevalence wherever he visited. One month after their visit to Mangaia, Cook came across a number of people in a small Polynesian atoll, Aitutaki, cooking human flesh in an earth oven. Cook's interpreter, the Tahitian Mai, expected "that he and his companions were going to be roasted and eat." The outraged citizens once again protested and responded with the usual retort: "whether [cannibalism] was a custom with us."[10] In fact the human flesh turned out to be a hog, which the sailors gladly consumed. This event brings back a Proustian memory: in my childhood, caretakers told me that it had been told to them that human flesh tastes a bit like pork.

My childhood memory provides a hint that perhaps these dialogues tapped an anxiety on the part of both the British and the indigenous inhabitants—an anxiety that the Other is going to roast and eat us. I call this dark fantasy a psychic structure of long duration and shared by both British and Hawaiians. Not all Polynesians were cannibals; the Hawaiians did not eat the flesh of the human beings they sacrificed. But, I think, those who sacrifice humans carry with them an unconscious wish to partake of that substance. In this situation questions regarding cannibalism can only provoke a terrible anxiety that taps the latent wish and in turn resurrects a childhood dread that the stranger asking these not-so-innocent questions is in fact the cannibal.

But what about the British? Surely these upright people cannot be accused of so vile a fantasy. My answer is that, like the hapless anthropologist, the British were also socialized in their nurseries in the belief in witches and ghosts that ate human flesh. Several decades after Cook's death another malevolent being stalked the European landscape. His name was Napoleon Bonaparte. On his way home from India Thackeray, visiting that man in St. Helena, was told that "he eats three sheep every day and all the little children he can put his hands on."[11] It is no wonder therefore that this short white man was soon converted into a huge black monster of the sort that haunted English nurseries of this period.

Captain James Cook on His Voyages of Discovery, ed. J. C. Beaglehole (Cambridge, 1967), p. 827.

10. Cook, pt. 1 of *The Voyage of the "Resolution" and "Discovery" 1776–1780,* vol. 3 of *The Journals of Captain James Cook on His Voyages of Discovery,* p. 85.

11. Joseph Jacobs, "Little St. Hugh of Lincoln," *The Jewish Historical Society of England* (London, 1893–94), p. 95. I am grateful to Alan Dundes for the Thackeray reference.

Baby, baby, naughty baby
Hush you squalling thing I say
Hush your squalling or it may be
Bonaparte come this way.

Baby, baby, he's a giant
Tall and black as Rouen steeple
And he sups and feeds rely on it
Every day on naughty people[12]

Let me now come back to Hawaii. Underlying the British officers' detached ethnographic hypothesis of cannibalism was the British public's demand for such information; underlying both the hypothesis and the demand is the childhood fantasy. Furthermore, the Hawaiian view of British cannibalism was a rational inference based on British cannibalistic queries and on the Britishers' physical appearance of food deprivation. Underlying both inferences is also a Hawaiian cannibalistic fantasy. These fantasies were reinforced in both parties by events: the fact of British terror, the fact of Hawaiian human sacrifice. The event gets locked into fantasy as the fantasy gets locked into the event. All of these spiral into a variety of crises characterized by what one might legitimately call a temporary "paranoid ethos."[13]

2. *"Mirror on mirror mirrored is all the show"*

—W. B. Yeats, *"The Statues"*

The preceding discussion concerned South Sea societies that did not practice cannibalism. What then occurred in respect of those that did, such as the people of Fiji, the New Hebrides, Marquesas, and New Zealand? Let me deal with the discourse on cannibalism in the British interaction with the Maori. I shall deal with the second voyage of Cook between 1772 and 1775, the voyage of the *Resolution* and the *Adventure.* During this voyage Cook visited New Zealand twice, the first at Dusky Sound briefly in March 1773, and a second more extensive visit in October. When, for the second time, the two ships lost contact with each other, Cook decided to cast anchor in Ship Cove on 3 November to repair his sails and rest his crew. I am interested in an important event that occurred a few weeks later. In his journal entry for 23 November Cook notes that "some of the officers went on shore to amuse themselves among the

12. I am quoting these verses from memory. I have not yet been able to locate the exact reference.

13. Theodore Schwartz, "Cult and Context: The Paranoid Ethos in Melanesia," *Ethos* 1 (Summer 1973): 153–74.

Natives"[14] when they saw an impressive sight: a heart of a youth recently killed was impaled on a forked stick and fixed on the front of the largest canoe. The officers also saw the head and bowels of this unfortunate youth, and Richard Pickersgill, a lieutenant on the *Resolution,* bought the head in exchange for two nails. The tradition of buying Maori heads had already been started in 1770 by Joseph Banks on the very first voyage.[15] No wonder then that the natives of this area had gone up to Admiralty Bay to fight a battle there; this boy's head was from that battle. For according to Reinhold Forster, the scientist of the second voyage, this tribal war was itself provoked by the British demand for "Curiosities."[16] When one group exhausted their supplies, they raided another for heads and other artifacts.

Cook was away during these initial happenings, but when he came back he noted:

> I was informed of the above circumstances and found the quarter deck crowded with the Natives. I now saw the mangled head or rather the remains of it for the under jaw, lip &c were wanting, the scul was broke on the left side just above the temple, the face had all the appearance of a youth about fourteen or fifteen, a peice of the flesh had been broiled and eat by one of the Natives in the presince of most of the officers. [*VRA,* p. 293]

What really had happened was as follows: when Pickersgill brought the head on board, the ship's officers wanted to produce empirical proof of cannibalism among the Maoris. This the despicable Lieutenant Charles Clerke put into effect:

> I ask'd him if he'd eat a peice there directly to which he very chearfully gave his assent. I then cut a peice of carry'd [it] to the fire by his desire and gave it a little broil upon the Grid Iron then deliver'd it to him—he not only eat it but devour'd it most ravenously, and suck'd his fingers 1/2 a dozen times over in raptures: the Captain was at this time absent. [*VRA,* p. 293 n. 2]

When Cook returned he replicated this experimental proof of cannibalism before the ship's crew and the crowded quarter deck of natives (see *VRA,* p. 293).

Meanwhile further proof of Maori cannibalism awaited the crew of

14. Cook, *The Voyage of the "Resolution" and "Adventure" 1772–1775,* vol. 2 of *The Journals of Captain James Cook on His Voyages of Discovery,* p. 292; hereafter abbreviated *VRA.*

15. See Beaglehole, *The Life of Captain James Cook* (London, 1974), p. 213.

16. Johann Reinhold Forster, *The "Resolution" Journal of Johann Reinhold Forster 1772–1775,* ed. Michael E. Hoare, 4 vols. (London, 1982), 3:427; hereafter abbreviated *RJ.*

the *Adventure.* On 9 November 1773, Tobias Furneaux, the commander, took refuge in Tolaga Bay, and seven days later he was back at sea. At Ship Cove Furneaux found a bottle with Cook's instructions to effect a rendezvous. Furneaux now wanted to reestablish contact with Cook at Queen Charlotte Sound (though Cook had already gone there and despaired of regaining contact with the *Adventure*). On 17 December Furneaux sent out the cutter under Master's mate John Rowe for a final load of greens from Grass Cove, but the boat did not return. He therefore sent Lieutenant James Burney in search of them the next day. Burney suspected that some unfortunate accident had occurred rather than hostile action from the Maoris since "I had not the least suspicion of their having received any injury from the Natives, our boats having been frequently higher up and worse provided." Burney and his crew landed in Grass Cove and eventually came upon what seemed indubitable evidence that Rowe and his company were killed and eaten by Maoris. One of Burney's crew found a piece of flesh that Mr. Peter Fannin, the master, thought was dog meat. Later they discovered twenty baskets of human flesh and several belongings and body parts, including the head of Captain Furneaux's black servant.[17] What was especially interesting is that Burney's presence provoked the natives to assemble on the hill nearby "making all the signs of joy imaginable."[18]

Now let me analyze these preceding events in some detail. It is indeed the case that cannibalism is for the British something that defines the Savage as such, an atavistic tendency that even middling civilization cannot overcome. But on the other hand the British scientific curiosity also has a bizarre quality: twice a piece of flesh from a Maori head was cut up and roasted by British officers and then given to a Maori to eat. The latter then consumes it with great relish (or so it seems) as many assembled Maoris and British crew witness the event. Thus on another level we (who think we are outside of it all) sense that both the British and the Maoris are *fascinated* by the same event: the Maoris by the British inquiry about their practice of cannibalism, the British by the fantasy. It is this theme of a common humanity that binds British and Maoris that I want to tentatively explore now, for, following Freud and Jung, one can say that what gives us all a common humanity is not only our higher nature but also a shared dark side of our being.

In probing deeper into the dark bond of cannibalism that united the ship's crew and the Savage as part of their common human nature, one notices an even deeper affinity. It seems that the traditions and practices of cannibalism were not the exclusive preserve of the Savage, and the intuitions of the Polynesians were correct when they asked the British if they were cannibals. The civilized British sailors also had their tradition of can-

17. See James Burney, "Burney's Log," app. 4 of *VRA,* pp. 749–52.

18. Tobias Furneaux, "Furneaux's Narrative," app. 4 of *VRA,* p. 744.

nibalism. These traditions and practices are nicely documented in A. W. Brian Simpson's recent book *Cannibalism and the Common Law.*[19] Though Simpson's study mostly deals with cases that occurred in the middle and late nineteenth century, he does record several remarkable prior instances. He conclusively shows that the traditions of cannibalism were well established by the seventeenth century and seem to have been associated with the expansion of trade and conquest consequent on the European voyages of discovery. The context of cannibalism is also clear: it is almost always associated with survival after a shipwreck.

Simpson argues that cannibalism after shipwreck was so much taken for granted in England that often ordinary innocuous survivors had to *deny* that it had taken place. Public attitudes in seaport towns were, for the most part, in sympathy with the cannibals. Though the law required such cases to be reported, there was not a single case of conviction for cannibalism till the famous case of the *Mignonette* in 1884 (discussed at length by Simpson). On the *Mignonette* the three survivors ate a young man, Richard Parker, since he was closest to dying and also had the least family responsibilities, not being married. What might seem surprising to us today is that the brother of the boy, and indeed the mother herself, did not express any outrage; the former explicitly sided with Captain Dudley and the other survivors. The survivors could calmly talk about the killing and subsequent cannibalism in a matter-of-fact manner, and the executioner kept as a memento the penknife that was used to kill the youth. When the survivors were formally sentenced to prison (only to be pardoned soon after), they expressed resentment and shock at what they felt was legal harassment.

In view of the convention-bound nature of British cannibalism I find it difficult to accept Simpson's argument that cannibalism was entirely based on hunger during shipwreck and related circumstances. The preoccupation with cannibalism existed in British fantasy; hunger was a factor in the origin of the tradition of British cannibalism and a precondition for its continuity and existence. Yet it must be remembered that conditions of starvation (at sea or elsewhere) did not invariably produce cannibalism. This is true of England and anywhere else: there are cultural and psychological conditions that will inhibit cannibalism, especially so when it entails an act of deliberate killing. One might be willing to die rather than kill a fellow human to eat him. These inhibitions might well extend to other tabooed foods, like the Brahmin's repugnance for beef (symbolically analogous to cannibalism). It is the legitimacy of cannibalism, and its convention-bound nature, that fostered and perpetuated it. Thus people who were shipwrecked could in reasonably good conscience eat their ship-

19. See A. W. Brian Simpson, *Cannibalism and the Common Law: The Story of the Tragic Last Voyage of "Mignonette" and the Strange Legal Proceedings to Which It Gave Rise* (Chicago, 1985).

mates since it was a perfectly acceptable, legitimate, normal, and even normative procedure.

The conventions of British cannibalism, insofar as it entailed killing, seem to be both explicit and implicit. The explicit conventions are very clear: First there was to be a drawing of lots, especially to determine the victim. Secondly, the blood of the victim must be drunk to assuage one's thirst. Indeed, in several instances the victim was eaten before he actually died, since only a live victim had enough of the precious fluid left. Two implicit conventions are equally significant. There was a tacit complicity that the alien, the Other, will be the victim, and the lots were manipulated accordingly: hence the Spaniard, the Portuguese, the slave, the black—then to the more problematic case of the boy or unmarried youth or female. The strict employment of the lottery applied only to one's own comrades. Another important implicit convention is the rejection of human extremities that were buried at sea. This especially applied to the head, which was exceptionally repugnant.[20]

The initial choice of the alien or the Other for consumption is based on racial prejudice as well as notions of comradeship that were equivalent to siblingship in respect of one's own fellows. But it is likely that unconscious motivations, triggered in the context of food deprivation, were also operative. In popular thought the black man, the Spaniard, and the Portuguese were highly sexed libidinous creatures. They represented sexuality and life power; by consumption of their flesh one could introject these powers and thus ensure strength and survival value.

3. Hidden Discourses and Practices in Maori-British Cannibalism

Our discussion of British cannibalism helps us understand the manner in which the British *represented* Maori cannibalism in their discursive actions. First let me consider Cook's anthropology of Savage anthropophagy. It seems that the experiment where the flesh from the decapitated head of the Maori was cut into steaks and broiled comes from the discourse of *British* cannibalism. It is interesting that the "experiment" had to be repeated when, of course, this was not necessary. Furthermore the language game imputed to the Savage in fact comes from *British* anthropophagy. Cannibalism is referred to as "the horrid banquet of human flesh" or as "midnight repasts." New Zealanders are supposed to kill their enemies and "feast and gorge themselves on the spot." Their consumption of smaller pieces of human flesh is referred to as a "dainty bit," "steak," and so on. This language is confirmed in later research by New Zealand schol-

20. See ibid., pp. 126, 139, 263.

ars and anthropologists, who attribute "cannibal feasts" to the Maoris in one case with "a meal of six children at once to be cooked to regale [the chief's] friends."[21] The reality of Maori cannibalism is expressed in the practice and fantasy of British cannibalism.

What is called cannibalism at this period is a British discourse about the practice of cannibalism, rather than a description about its practice. This discourse is initiated by British ethnological inquiry and stimulated in turn by the demands of their reading public. This discourse on cannibalism tells us more about the British preoccupation with cannibalism than about Maori cannibalism. The British discourse has to be understood in terms of a larger pervasive fantasy of cannibalism resulting from European socialization of that period and, more narrowly, from a subculture of sailors with a tradition of the practice of cannibalism that in turn gets locked into the primordial fantasy and then, cumulatively, produces shipboard narratives and ballad literature on the subject. These in turn give direction, even form, to the British discourse with Hawaiians and Maoris; it affects their practice of ethnological science such that the experimental proofs of Maori cannibalism are as much science as they are fantasy. Together the discourses, practices, and fantasies that I have outlined constitute a *British* "cannibalistic complex" that must be differentiated from what I think (following Sahlins) is the traditional sacrificial anthropophagy of Polynesian peoples.[22] The British cannibalistic complex is symbolically, contextually, and perhaps even causally related to other practices, for example, the religious practice of holy communion. For my purposes however let me focus on two shipboard practices that show a symbolic affinity with cannibalism.

Dietary Practice

The dietary practice that I want to describe pertains to dog meat. Let me start with a facetious aside made by Banks, the gentleman philosopher, naturalist, and botanist on Cook's first voyage aboard the *Endeavour* in 1769 during their first confrontation with the Maoris. Says Banks: "'I suppose they live intirely upon fish dogs and enemies."[23] Fish, dogs, and enemies, one might say, unified and divided the Maoris and the British. Fish is the flesh that binds both: both eat this as a meat staple. Eating dog meat and one's enemies is of course the practice of the Other. Maoris, like other Polynesian, Melanesian, and South Sea folk, eat dog meat; Maoris also wore dog skins. While the British concern with Maori canine

21. Edward Tregear, *The Maori Race* (Manganni, New Zealand, 1904), p. 357.

22. See Sahlins, "Raw Women, Cooked Men, and Other 'Great Things' of the Fiji Islands," in *The Ethnography of Cannibalism,* ed. Paula Brown and Donald Tuzin (Washington, D.C., 1983), pp. 72–93.

23. Beaglehole, *The Life of Captain James Cook,* p. 213.

carnivorousness was in no way comparable to their interest in Maori cannibalism, the practice was carefully noted in the journals largely to edify and shock their reading public. It is not unlikely that for many Europeans eating dog was much more heinous than cannibalism, since dogs were pets and enemies were not.

The contact with the Maori and other Polynesian people however resulted in the broadening of the British consciousness, for eventually the despised dog meat was consumed by the ship's crew, not the ordinary riff-raff, but by the officers. Dog flesh broke one of the barriers that separated the Savage from the Civilized. The ships had dogs as pets, as hunters, and as consumers of leftovers. Forster emphasized the obvious fact that dogs for the most part were pets for the British and hence full of symbolic and psychic import (see *RJ,* 2:303–5). As pets, dogs were man's best friend and, in the case of lap dogs, objects of love or even surrogate kinsmen or substitutes for children. Thus it would seem that, in the European cultural context, the consumption of dog meat is a horrendous act, exhibiting a symbolic affinity with cannibalism. I think it is likely that the consumption of dog meat by the crew, especially by the ship's officers, was *provoked,* on the unconscious level, by the Savages' consumption of human flesh. What is human flesh for the Savage is dog meat for the English. The ship's officers were tantalized by Savage anthropophagy; it triggered a latent wish, but, since it was impossible to consume human flesh, they chose dog meat. The cutting up of the flesh from the severed head of a Maori youth by the ship's officers and their defining it as steak is not simply a part of an innocuous scientific experiment, but one that seems to tap a latent desire (wish).

Collections

The second shipboard practice that I refer to is that of collections. The young Maori's head that was purchased by Pickersgill was later deposited in the collection of Dr. John Hunter (1728–93), a famous anatomist. Banks and other scientists collected heads and bones of the "victims" of cannibalism. They are as much a part of scientific collections as they are "trophies" for the officers and curios for everyone. Like trophies they were eventually mounted in museums and anthropology departments. For example, the head of the "Irish felon" Alexander Pearce, who escaped from the penal colony at Macquarie harbor on the west coast of Tasmania and then ate his fellow escapee Thomas Cox, found its way into the collection of Dr. Samuel George Morton, an American phrenologist, and later into the University of Pennsylvania Museum.[24] W. Ellis reports for the Nootka: "There was one article of trade which some of these people exposed to sale today, that we never saw before in any country: this was,

24. Simpson, *Cannibalism and the Common Law,* pp. 148–49.

several human skulls and dried hands."[25] And then the usual pantomime on both sides, with the British seamen expressing their fantasies and the Nootka comically parodying them: "Some of our seamen made signs of eating the flesh, which signs they readily made too, probably because they saw us do it; and from this circumstance they were pronounced to be cannibals, though it is not unlikely but that we were too hasty in forming our conjectures" (*AN,* p. 192). Ellis was right: these people were *not* cannibals, only supplying extremities to satisfy European demand. Ellis goes on to say later: "Several skulls and hands were purchased to-day as curiosities, and we bought plenty of fish, but skins of every kind were become scarce" (*AN,* p. 202).

4. The Impact of Historical Context on Cannibalistic Practice and Discourse

The preceding discussion suggests very strongly that the discourse on cannibalism conducted by British officers represented Maori cannibalism in terms of British values, fantasies, and myth models. This means that our anthropological knowledge of the practices of Maori cannibalism eludes us from the very start. There is no doubt that the Maoris practiced cannibalism—not however because they admitted to it, for we know from experiences in Hawaii that people can admit to doing what they don't do, but because there was evidence of cannibalism in the empirical accounts of the British. However slanted the British *representation* of Maori cannibalism might be, there is no denying that Mr. Rowe and his comrades were slain at Grass Cove, their flesh cooked and placed in baskets, and some parts of their anatomies scattered around. But this event in Grass Cove can only partially illuminate Maori cannibalism, for prior to the coming of the Dutch, French, and British, Maoris could not possibly have consumed Europeans. This change in Maori anthropophagous habits and proclivities must be incorporated into our knowledge of Maori cannibalism. It is unlikely that the Maoris simply fitted the British into their preexistent cultural forms and treated them as if they were enemies, since the British were *not* their traditional enemies. New Zealand scholars generally believe that Cook was treated by Maoris as a kind of god (or goblin); if so, it is possible that the crew were also divinized in some form or other. But the problem with this hypothesis is that it also Europeanized Maori cannibalism, for it is virtually certain that the Maoris, unlike the Europeans, did not consume the blood and body of their deity. The coming of the European is a new and traumatic event in their history; British ethnographic

25. W. Ellis, *An Authentic Narrative of a Voyage Performed by Captain Cook and Captain Clerke in His Majesty's Ships "Resolution" and "Discovery" during the Years 1776, 1777, 1778, 1779, and 1780,* 2 vols. (London, 1782), 1:192; hereafter abbreviated *AN.*

inquiries produced a *new* discourse on cannibalism, totally unexpected by the Maori. This discourse, insofar as it occurred in a new historical context of power, domination, and terror, must be located therein. In order to do this we must place the events in Grass Cove and on the deck of the *Resolution* as a historical product that can best be understood in terms of preceding relations between Maoris and Europeans. It must be remembered that the Maori discourse emerged from the British inquiries into cannibalism, and since Maoris did not write about these events as they occurred, their discourse is hidden in the British texts and has to be unraveled by us.

Prior to the events of Cook's second voyage that I have discussed, the Maoris experienced four confrontations: in 1642 a brief visit by Abel Tasman; then the first voyage of James Cook on the *Endeavour* from October 1769 to March 1770 when he circumnavigated New Zealand and mapped its outlines; almost simultaneously a short visit by Jean François Marie de Surville, followed by a fairly extended stay by another Frenchman, Marion du Fresne, in two ships, the *Mascarin* and the *Castries,* from 25 March to 12 July 1772, just over a year before Cook's second voyage. I shall not discuss these voyages in any detail except as they throw light on two features of Maori cannibalism: the discourse and practice whereby they represented *their* cannibalism to the Europeans and the empirical evidence of the emergence of the kind of cannibalism imputed to them by the European. The latter is of course the Maori consumption of Europeans. None of these can be understood outside of the context of domination and terror.

Abel Tasman's visit was the only one in which the Maoris dominated the action. When a group of his men tried to land to seek a safe anchor they were set upon by a group of thirteen Maoris (the bad number) and three sailors were killed. Tasman observed from afar what happened to two of them: one was taken into the canoe, the other thrown into the sea. It is doubtful whether the eating of Europeans was practiced in this particular case, since one of the whites was thrown overboard.

One hundred and twenty-seven years after Tasman's visit Cook came to New Zealand on the *Endeavour.* It is not likely that the Maoris had forgotten the earlier event; it might have been mythologized. On Sunday, 8 October, Cook sighted land and then established contact with the natives the following day. The initial contact at Poverty Bay was dramatic, sudden, and deadly. Cook went ashore with Banks and Daniel Solander and tried to establish contact with the natives, but they went away, only to come back:

> the Coxswain of the pinnace who had the charge of the Boats, seeing this fire'd two musquets over their heads, the first made them stop and look round them, but the 2d they took no notice of upon which a third was fired and killed one of them upon the spot just as he was

> going to dart his spear at the boat; at this the other three stood motionless for a minute or two, seemingly quite surprised wondering no doubt what it was that had thus killed their commorade.[26]

The marines were soon brought in. They landed "to intimidate them and support us in case of necessity." Banks shot at least two people and noted: "we may hope however that neither of them were killd as one of the musquets only was loaded with ball, which I think I saw strike the water without taking effect." Others, including Cook's Polynesian interpreter Tupaia, had better luck in killing and maiming.[27]

Now Cook decided that these people were hopeless and went upstream in search of fresh water and also to try "to surprise some of the natives and to take them on board and by good treatment and presents endeavour to gain their friendship," but this also didn't work (*VE*, p. 170). The following afternoon Cook's journal entry reads:

> I rowed round the head of the Bay but could find no place to land, on account of the great surff which beat every where upon the shore; seeing two boats or Canoes coming in from Sea, I rowed to one of them in order to seize upon the people and came so near before they took notice of us that Tupia called to them to come along side and we would not hurt them, but instead of doing this they endeavoured to get away, upon which I order'd a Musquet to be fire'd over their heads thinking that this would either make them surrender or jump over board, but here I was misstaken for they immidiatly took to thier arms or whatever they had in the boat and began to attack us, this obliged us to fire upon them and unfortunately either two or three were kill'd, and one wounded, and three jumped over board, these last we took up and brought on board, where they were clothed and treated with all immaginable kindness and to the surprise of every body became at once as cheerful and as merry as if they had been with their own friends; they were all three young, the eldest not above 20 years of age and youngest about 10 or 12. [*VE*, pp. 170–71]

Both Banks and Cook felt enormously guilty at this wanton murder.[28] It is however not unsurprising that Cook could not understand that sudden terror followed by unimagined kindness could indeed result in the youth's becoming "cheerful and merry," or, to put it differently, attempting to placate the dreaded aggressor.

The Maori discourse, like the Hawaiian, occurred in the context of uncertainty, fear, and the threat of firepower, and that of European domi-

26. Cook, *The Voyage of the "Endeavour" 1768–1771*, vol. 1 of *The Journals of Captain James Cook on His Voyages of Discovery*, p. 169; hereafter abbreviated *VE*.

27. Sir Joseph Banks, *The "Endeavour" Journal of Joseph Banks 1768–1771*, ed. Beaglehole, 2 vols. (Sydney, 1962), 1:401, 402.

28. See Beaglehole, *The Life of Captain James Cook*, p. 200.

nation. Unlike the Hawaiians the Maoris did practice cannibalism. The Hawaiians, I noted, imputed cannibalism to the British; some also, perhaps more in fun than seriousness, threatened the British with their (feigned) cannibalism. Maoris it seemed employed a similar threat: they admitted their cannibalism, but emphasized and exaggerated it and, like the Hawaiians and the Northwest Coast Indians, seemed to enjoy the European reaction of disgust and fascination. Cannibalistic discourse then was a weapon, one might say, employed by all the parties. Maori discourse on cannibalism was compounded by the ludic and the serious: the ludic, since they seem on occasion, at least, to enjoy the discomfiture of the Europeans; and serious, because it was a weapon to terrify them in the context of unequal power, where their real weapons were nothing in comparison to European guns. The combination of the ludic and the serious comes over neatly during the Frenchman Marion's expedition when Lieutenant Roux, interviewing a Maori on the practice of cannibalism, noted:

> Several of our officers are of my opinion that this is the case, but what completely confirmed what I say on this subject is the fact that one of the chiefs, who well understood what I asked him, told me that after they had killed their enemies, they put them in a fire, and having cooked the corpses, ate them. Seeing that I was greatly disgusted with what he told me, my informant burst into laughter, and proceeded to reaffirm what he had just told me.[29]

The Maori and other Polynesian discourses on cannibalism then seem to be a defense against the European; it is also counterattack, an employment of one form of terror against another. It was Reinhold Forster, of the second voyage, who astutely noted the double uses of the discourse on cannibalism by the people of Tanna, in the New Hebrides: "The Natives are very jealous to let their habitations, wives & Children be seen, & allways desired us not [to] go on, & in order to frighten us, they told if we went on, we should be killed & eaten" (*RJ*, 4:599).

Polynesian people also employed a similar strategy, it seems to me. Consider Cook's first voyage and his initial confirmation of cannibalism by the natives of Queen Charlotte Sound on 13 January 1770:

> Some of us went in the Pinnace into a nother Cove not far from where the Ship lays; in going thether we met with a Woman floating upon the water who to all appearance had not been dead many days. Soon after we landed we met with two or three of the Natives who not long before must have been regailing themselves upon human flesh, for I got from one of them the bone of the fore arm of a Man or a Woman which was quite fresh and the flesh had been but lately pick'd off

29. Le St. Jean Roux, "Journal of the 'Mascarin,'" in *Historical Records of New Zealand*, ed. Robert McNab, 2 vols. (Wellington, 1914), 2:401–2; hereafter abbreviated "J."

> which they told us they had eat, they gave us to understand that but a few days ago they had taken Kill'd and eat a Boats crew of their enemies or strangers, for I beleive that they look upon all strangers as enemies; from what we could learn the Woman we had seen floating upon the water was in this boat and had been drownded in the fray. There was not one of us that had the least doubt but what this people were Canabals but the finding this Bone with part of the sinews fresh upon it was a stronger proof than any we had yet met with, and in order to be fully satisfied of the truth of what they had told us, we told one of them that it was not the bone of a man but that of a Dog, but he with great fervency took hold of his fore-arm and told us again that it was that bone and to convence us that they had eat the flesh he took hold of his own arm with his teeth and make shew of eating.—AM Careen'd scrubed and pay'd the Starboard side of the Ship: While this was doing some of the natives came along side seemingly only to look at us, there was a Woman among them who had her Arms, thighs and legs cut in several places, this was done by way of Mourning for her husband who had very lately been kill'd and eat by some of their enimies as they told us and pointed towards the place where it was done which lay some where to the Eastward. Mr Banks got from one of them a bone of the fore arm much in the same state as the one before mention'd and to shew us that they had eat the flesh they bit a[nd] naw'd the bone and draw'd it thro' their mouth and this in such a manner as plainly shew'd that the flesh to them was a dainty bit. [*VE*, pp. 236–37]

It seems that there is a battle going on here with cannibalism as a weapon. The British view of Polynesian cannibalism is an *imagined* cannibalism, based on a reality that no one seemed to understand. It is also a performance that emerges out of the British discourse; the Maoris are at great pains to prove that not only are they cannibals, but truly horrible ones. The Maori man miming this practice by eating "the flesh . . . of his own arm with his teeth" can be equally well interpreted as a reaction to the British inquiry that elicited information through similar performative actions. So is the bone-chewing act. It is the kind of pantomime that some people might use to scare children, and like many such stories and pantomimes, adults seem to find them funny.

It seems obvious that the Maoris had to cope with the British queries on cannibalism in a variety of ways, soon conventionalized. Cook of course always had the help of Tahitian interpreters: Tupaia, Hitihiti, and Mai (Omai), who managed to converse (imperfectly) with the Maoris and then even more imperfectly translate this into basic Tahitian that Cook (and several other gentlemen) imperfectly knew. But others simply used the language of gestures which, as Tom Dutton shows, was also highly convention-bound and elaborate.[30] An early use of gestural language is

30. See Tom Dutton, "'Successful Intercourse Was Had with the Natives': Aspects of

described beautifully in Robertson's account of the first British contact with the Tahitians during Wallis's expedition of 1767, a year before Cook:

> They seemd all very peaceable for some time, and we made signs to them, to bring of Hogs, Fowls and fruit and showd them coarse cloath Knives sheers Beeds Ribons etc, and made them understand that we was willing to barter with them, the method we took to make them Understand what we wanted was this, some of the men Grunted and Cryd lyke a Hogg then pointed to the shore—oythers crowd Lyke cocks to make them understand that we wanted fowls, this the natives of the country understood and Grunted and Crowd the same as our people, and pointed to the shore and made signs that they would bring off some—We then made signs for them to go in to their canoes and to bring us off what things we wanted—they observed what we meant and some went into their canoes.[31]

This kind of gestural language was the sole means of communication during first contact or with peoples whose language the British did not understand. Thus Reinhold Forster describes a gestural discourse on cannibalism in Tanna, New Hebrides: "It seems that the Islanders eat the people, whom they kill in battle, for they pointed to y[e] Arms, Legs, Thighs etc & and shewed how they roasted & devoured the Meat of them. They showed all this by signs" (*RJ*, 5:595). Again: "They were very eager to undeceive us, and showed, by signs, how they killed a man, cut his limbs asunder, and separated the flesh from the bones. Lastly, they bit their own arms, to express more clearly that they eat human flesh."[32] But this response of the people of Tanna was surely not initiated by them: it is a response to the British inquiry on cannibalism. The British must express themselves exactly as the natives did, that is, "bit their own arms," and so on, since they did not know the native language at all. This too is true, of course, of the Maoris in Queen Charlotte Sound, but it is also clear that the native reaction is a pantomimic response to the British language of gestures.

How would Polynesian peoples respond to this gestural language regarding cannibalism? One reaction is obvious: strange, enigmatic, white

---

European Contact Methods in the Pacific," in *A World of Language: Papers Presented to Professor S. A. Wurm on His 65th Birthday*, ed. Donald C. Laycock and Werner Winter (Canberra, 1987), pp. 153–71.

31. George Robertson, *The Discovery of Tahiti: A Journal of the Second Voyage of H.M.S. "Dolphin" Round the World, under the Command of Captain Wallis, R.N., in the Years 1766, 1767 and 1768* (London, 1948), p. 137; see also Dutton, "'Successful Intercourse Was Had with the Natives,'" p. 158.

32. George Forster, *A Voyage Round the World in His Brittanic Majesty's Sloop, "Resolution," Commanded by Capt. James Cook, during the Years 1772, 3, 4, and 5*, 2 vols. (London, 1777), 2:300.

people inquiring about cannibalism by biting their own bodies and performing other imitative actions could be truly terrifying, activating fears of cannibalistic monsters in childhood socialization. Another reaction, particularly once they became more familiar with the European, is the opposite—the ludicrous. Sometimes the ship's account does not help clear up the issue. For example, take the case of the experiment with cannibal steaks during Cook's second voyage. By this time the Maoris had developed a variety of responses to British queries on cannibalism, but this was an extremely complex one. Remember that Maoris did not eat broiled human steaks, and the whole setting of the ship's quarterdeck would have flouted all Maori conventions of cannibalism. They simply performed another pantomime and joined in the spirit of the game initiated by the British with laughter. What we do not know is the intention behind the Maoris' action in eating the steak with such obvious relish. Perhaps they wanted to prove to the British cannibals that they (the Maori) were even more dreaded ones. But even here the licking of fingers, and so on, is, I think, a Maori imitation of the British expression of relish as they inquired by signs and sounds about the native's relish for human flesh. Once the Polynesians were aware of the British obsession with cannibalism, they were surely going to feed it, either to scare the British or laugh at them or both. Consider the following native scare story noted by Forster: "There circulates on board a Story, made up I believe on purpose, that the Natives told, that a Ship arrived on the Coast of the Northern Isle in a great Storm, & was there broke to pieces. The Men in her were safed on shore, & had an Engagement with the Natives, wherein they killed many Natives, but not being able to keep up a Fire, the Natives came up & killed & devoured them all" (*RJ,* 4:676). This scare story feeds the British fantasy, so that Forster noted that the sailors of the *Resolution* believed that this story portrayed the fate of the crew of the *Adventure* with whom they had lost contact. Forster adds: "the Natives are by no means constant in their story, so that there is little to be depended upon this Tale" (*RJ,* 4:676).

The native populations that did not practice cannibalism had similar standardized reactions to the British imputation of cannibalism. First, there is an outraged denial; second, a feigned playful or eager admission. For Cook and his crew the admission of cannibalism naturally proved its existence. Yet one must ask, Why did Hawaiians on occasion emphatically admit to a practice they did not practice? It seems clear that here also, the false admission of cannibalism must be related to the emergent discourse. Cook's cannibalistic queries provoked the Polynesian counterdiscourse, namely, that they—the Hawaiians—were in fact dreaded cannibals. Then the final response: the alien visitors asking dreadful questions by biting their own bodies and performing other strange gestures and sounds were indeed cannibals themselves. All these reactions are a fallback to fantasy life and its ontogenesis in early childhood of scare stories of man-eating monsters. This is true also of the European sailors: they too had traditions of cannibalism—of a divine figure sacrificed for the well-being of the world whose blood and body is consumed in a highly charged ritual setting, and of a lot of stories of cannibalism circulating in both nurseries and ships. It should be remembered however that in terms of conventional anthropological method, such as the evidence garnered in the Human Relations Area Files, various Polynesian groups are listed as having practiced cannibalism traditionally. By the same methodological token the Europeans too should be included.

Polynesian cannibalism then is constructed out of an extremely complex dialogue between Europeans and Polynesians, a dialogue that makes sense in relation to the history of contact and unequal power relations and the cultural values, fantasies, and the common dark humanity they both share. The discourse on cannibalism, once initiated, affects a variety of cultural practices in which it is embedded; it affects, for example, the early British practice of ethnological science and the late Maori practice of cannibalism. The scientists on board ship were aptly called by the rest of the crew "the experimental gentlemen." The experiment on the Maori head is a product of the discourse on cannibalism and on science. A discourse is not just speech: it is embedded in a historical and cultural context and expressed often in the frame of a scenario or cultural performance. It is about practice: the practice of science, the practice of cannibalism. Insofar as discourse evolves it begins to affect the practice. Since I've already discussed the effect of this discourse on the practice of their science by the ship's "experimental gentlemen," let me now ask a much more controversial question—How did the evolving discourse on cannibalism affect the Maori practice of cannibalism?

The change in Maori practice is probably the most controversial part of my argument. I present my thesis hesitantly, not having yet mastered the literature on Polynesia. Conventional Polynesian ethnography simply constructs an ideal type (or types) of Maori cannibalism from a variety of statements—interviews with older men, myths, missionaries' and magistrates' accounts, and even those of eyewitnesses, but mostly from the middle of the nineteenth century. These sources of information are treated as reality, that is, as a practice of cannibalism rather than a discourse on it. We know that those people who wrote about cannibalism in the nineteenth century were even less sophisticated and self-critical than the experimental gentlemen on Cook's ships. Thus any attempt to construct Maori cannibalism in this fashion is to me extremely dubious, since the discourse is often equated with the practice and the practice itself might get affected by the evolving discourse. For example, the mere fact that eventually the Maoris stopped their practice is proof of the capacity of practice to change.

To put it baldly, let me start with the proposition that not one person in any of Cook's voyages understood anything about Maori cannibalism, outside the knowledge that they were "cannibals." The word itself, derived from Western language games, oriented the lines of inquiry into indiscriminate anthropophagy. The only reasonable evidence of Maori anthropophagy during the earliest contacts was from Maori consumption of white sailors, itself a new practice. The first example of this practice is not from the incident at Grass Cove but from Marion's voyage a year before. Here Marion and his officers and soon after a number of the crew were killed in ambush and in all likelihood eaten, though we do not know in what manner. There was considerable provocation for this by French thieving of important cultural artifacts and by their humiliating imprisonment of an important chief. But Marion himself was a considerate and naively trusting person. His being eaten must be seen in the context of Maori-European power relations.

The Maoris were already acquainted with both Cook (of the first voyage) and de Surville. Their wish to obtain European power had both a pragmatic-rational and a more affect-laden symbolic component. On the rational level Maoris tried to enlist the aid of Cook, de Surville, and Marion himself in their tribal wars. This wasn't successful; they then tried their best to learn the use of firearms. Let Lieutenant Roux from Marion's expedition speak on this matter:

> During the afternoon the chief of the native village on Marion Island came to see me, accompanied by several other natives. They brought me some fish as a present, as is their custom when paying visits. They were very much astonished to see outside my tent the blunderbusses, which I had had put in good order the previous evening, and which were now all mounted on their carriages. As they had not seen this kind of arm before, the chief asked what they were, and how they were used. I explained the use of the weapons to them as well as I could, and made him better understand by taking eight or ten balls and loading a gun with them. He then understood quite well what I told him and showed some alarm, making a sign to me that he considered them very dangerous. . . .
>
> In the afternoon I went shooting with a volunteer. . . . The chief asked me various questions as to the cleaning of our guns. He has seen me kill some birds, but he did not think a man could be killed in the same way. As there are a number of dogs in this country, he made signs to me to shoot one of them that happened to be passing by. I shot at it, and killed it, which completely bewildered the chief. He went and examined the dead animal with the greatest care, so that he could see where the dog had been hit, and then came back to examine the gun with the same minute attention. He then wanted to do what I had done, aiming at another dog, and blew upon the lock of the firearm, thinking that this was the right way to discharge the gun. I did not think it necessary to show him the right way to proceed. On the contrary, I was very glad he did not know in what way we made use of our weapons. ["J," 2:409, 411]

What Roux did not know was that the natives of this bay had already felt the power of Cook's guns on 30 November 1769,[33] and they were now rationally trying to figure out their uses. Roux himself had previously taken charge of the hospital camp where this interaction took place. Troubled by the lack of security in this place, owing to Marion's false confidence, he soon installed new guns and shining blunderbusses outside the tent. This was of course further provocation for the Maoris to find out their uses. There were attempts (mostly unsuccessful) to steal muskets. Hence it seems reasonable for the Maoris (or some groups of them) to wrest these guns and, of course, triumph over their enemies.

These rational political and pragmatic reasons for killing Marion and the crew were balanced by symbolic-affective reasons. They hoped to triumph over the powerful Europeans, humiliate them, and at the same time to identify with them and introject their power, as this seemingly trivial example from Marion's voyage neatly illustrates:

> These natives are greatly given to embracing each other, but they display in these caresses a most noticeable ferocity. They are peculiarly fond of kissing each other, and this they do with great intensity. They were never weary of admiring our skins, especially their whiteness, but when we permitted them to place their lips, either upon our hands or our faces, they sucked the flesh with a surprising greediness. ["J," 2:403]

5. *Conclusion: From Human Sacrifice to Conspicuous Anthropophagy*

I have suggested that a shift in Maori consciousness seems to have occurred, itself provoked by the presence of European power and wealth and the European questions on cannibalism. Maoris were changing their techniques of embracing to introject the color of the European skin and, I think, deeper down, the European himself, symbolically sucking his body to obtain his power. Juxtapose this with the aftermath of the killing of Marion and members of his crew. Both Roux and du Clesmeur repeatedly report that large numbers assembled in jubilant exultation, wearing the clothes and weapons of dead Frenchmen and above all taking turns at wearing Marion's silver pistols; all engaged in conspicuous display. In my view this is the culmination of what occurred as a wish in the acts of kissing and sucking the bodies of the white man: the fantasy is now given a further symbolic extension in the identification with the aggressor, by wearing his clothes and brandishing his pistols and other weapons. Between the two events is the crucial act of eating the Frenchmen; psychoanalytically

33. See *VE,* pp. 214–15, and Beaglehole, *The Life of Captain James Cook,* p. 209.

viewed, it is the introjection of the Other, in this case the power of the aggressor. If my assumption is correct, the consumption of the European resulted in a revitalization of Maori cannibalism and a parallel change in its orientation into a more pronounced anthropophagy. Conditions of mass revitalization, even if temporary, would have meant a greater public participation, actual or vicarious, in dividing and eating the flesh of the powerful aggressor. Consider the event at Grass Cove, a year later, when Englishmen were killed, their flesh cooked and placed, along with fern roots (their "bread" as the ship's crew called them), in twenty or so baskets. If indeed the flesh of the Englishmen were eaten by larger numbers seeking revitalization in the face of a threat to the very existence of their society, one can in fact speak of a change in Maori cannibalism, particularly since the convention of traditional Maori cannibalism (whatever that was) need not apply to the new aliens in their midst. In other words, I am suggesting that large-scale anthropophagy was a reaction to the European presence; it is this that sets the stage for descriptions of Maori "cannibal feasts" of the later historical and anthropological literature. The change in orientation of Maori cannibalism, in some senses, parallels the shift in the orientation of British cannibalism from a generalized fantasy, and a ritualistic act of holy communion symbolically far removed from fantasy, to a tradition of seafaring anthropophagy. With the opening up of the world consequent on the voyages of discovery, shipwrecks and starvation became regular phenomena. Thus in the culture of seafarers the fantasy of cannibalism became a reality, such that sailors began to accept the literal idea of consuming the blood and body of a victim chosen by lots. So among the Maori: the opening up of *their* world consequent on the European voyages of discovery shifted their (sacrificial?) cannibalism into one characterized by pronounced anthropophagy.

There is no account in any of the early texts about precontact cannibalism among the Maori or among any other Polynesian group. My thesis is close to Sahlins's in this regard.[34] Maori cannibalism must be seen in the larger context of human sacrifice common to Polynesian society. It is human sacrifice that is the key institution: in some places like Tahiti and Hawaii human sacrifice is associated with a chief symbolically accepting the eye of the sacrificial victim. I suggest that Polynesians did not practice cannibalism, but instead practiced an anthropophagy (displaced or real) associated with human sacrifice. Pronounced anthropophagy or cannibalism in Polynesia developed with their killing and eating the British; the British discourse on cannibalism produced, in very complicated ways, the Maori practice of cannibalism. In the nineteenth century both the British and the Maoris seem to take for granted Maori cannibalism. And there is plenty of evidence for this, including eyewitness accounts. But almost all

34. See Sahlins, "Raw Women, Cooked Men, and Other 'Great Things' of the Fiji Islands."

of these accounts indicate that cannibalism existed, for the most part, independent of human sacrifice. Furthermore after about 1819 it is the natives, not the British, who are being eaten. This change must also be seen in its historical context. The British presence not only escalated tribal wars, but the availability of guns escalated the killing to a degree unprecedented in Maori history. Elsdon Best refers to missionary accounts that state that by 1840, in a twenty-year period in the northern part of the North Island alone, 80,000 Maoris died in tribal wars.[35] The numbers I think are wildly exaggerated; yet modern warfare did increase the availability of the corpses of enemies chiefly and consequently contributed further to a more general, nonritualized anthropophagy. Thus my conclusion: as a consequence of historical events, both Maori and British cannibalism moved from a highly charged symbolic arena of personal fantasy and religious sacrifice toward the shedding of some of these symbolic attributes for a pattern of conspicuous anthropophagy.[36]

35. See Elsdon Best, *The Maori,* 2 vols. (Wellington, 1924), 2:285.

36. I have written up a detailed account of nineteenth-century warfare in New Zealand entitled "Cannibalism and Anthropology in the Ethnography of the Maori," which I hope to publish in the near future.

Race into Culture: A Critical Genealogy of Cultural Identity

Walter Benn Michaels

Anti-Imperial Americanism

Thomas Nelson Page's *Red Rock* was published in 1898, the year in which the United States annexed Hawaii, went to war in Cuba, seized the Philippines from Spain, and emerged as an imperial power. Needless to say, *Red Rock,* written the year before these events took place and written about events that had themselves taken place some thirty years earlier, is unconcerned with Cuba or the Philippines. But it is not unconcerned with American imperialism; indeed, American imperialism and, above all, the resistance to it, is its main subject. *Red Rock* tells the story of a conquered people, of how they survived under occupation, and of how they eventually "reconquered" what it sometimes refers to as their "country" and sometimes as their "section." It is, in short, an anti-imperialist novel.[1]

In the years immediately after its publication, a good many other similarly anti-imperialist novels appeared, most notably Thomas Dixon's *The Leopard's Spots* (1902) and *The Clansman* (1905).[2] Like *Red Rock,* they are

1. Thomas Nelson Page, *Red Rock: A Chronicle of Reconstruction* (1898; Ridgewood, N.J., 1967), p. vii; hereafter abbreviated *RR.*

2. I characterize *The Leopard's Spots* and the other two novels in *The Trilogy of Reconstruction* (*The Clansman* [New York, 1905]; hereafter abbreviated *C,* and *The Traitor* [New York, 1907]; hereafter abbreviated *T*) as anti-imperialist despite the fact that *The Leopard's Spots* describes the war in Cuba as a triumphant proclamation of "the advent of a giant democracy" (Thomas Dixon, Jr., *The Leopard's Spots: A Romance of the White Man's Burden—1865–1900* [New York, 1902], p. 407; hereafter abbreviated *LS.*) The congressional

This article originally appeared in *Critical Inquiry* 18 (Summer 1992).

set in the Reconstruction South and make no mention of Cuba or the Philippines.[3] But they are nevertheless importantly marked by the anti-

resolution under which the U.S. went to war with Spain had explicitly abjured "sovereignty, jurisdiction, or control" over Cuba, and by 1902, the year in which *The Leopard's Spots* was published, the Platt Amendment had granted the Cubans complete independence. (For accounts of this process, see Ernest R. May, *Imperial Democracy: The Emergence of America as a Great Power* [New York, 1961] and Walter LaFeber, *The New Empire: An Interpretation of American Expansion, 1860–1898* [Ithaca, N.Y., 1963].) Hence it was the invasion and annexation of the Philippines that served as the focus of American anti-imperialism—indeed, some anti-imperialists explicitly distinguished the "war for humanity against the Spanish in Cuba" from "the war for conquest against the Filipinos" (J. Laurence Laughlin, "The Philippine War," speech given at the Chicago Liberty Meeting, 30 Apr. 1899; repr. in *The Anti-Imperialist Reader: A Documentary History of Anti-Imperialism in the United States,* ed. Philip S. Foner and Richard C. Winchester, 2 vols. [New York, 1984, 1986], 1:290–91)—and it is the arguments against annexation of the Philippines that I describe below as playing a central role in Dixon's novels. These arguments tended to take two forms: first, racist assertions that Filipino self-government was the only way to avoid burdening the U.S. with what Mrs. Jefferson Davis called "fresh millions of foreign negroes," even "more ignorant and more degraded" than those at home (Mrs. Jefferson Davis, "Why We Do Not Want the Philippines," *The Arena* 23 [Jan. 1900]:1–4; repr. in *The Anti-Imperialist Reader,* 1:236), and, second, political appeals to the unconstitutionality and, more generally, antirepublican character of imperial acquisition. These latter arguments were sometimes antiracist but even when, as was more often the case, they displayed a certain amount of racial contempt for the Filipinos, that contempt was only incidental to the political point. If, then, anti-imperialist critiques were generally *either* racist *or* constitutional, one way of beginning to understand Dixon's contribution is by noting that in the *Trilogy,* the racial and constitutional arguments against imperial conquest are not only understood as equally important but also (for reasons I give below) as inextricably linked.

The need for something like the preceding paragraph was made clear to me by Amy Kaplan's and Michael Rogin's spirited objections to my characterization of Dixon's anti-imperialism. Although I don't imagine that my response will entirely meet those objections, I am grateful to Kaplan and Rogin for expressing them. This is, perhaps, also the opportunity to thank the other participants (especially Donald Pease) in Dartmouth College's conference on "Cultures of U.S. Imperialism" for which this essay was originally written (a different version of it is forthcoming in the proceedings of the conference to be published by the Duke University Press), and to thank also Frances Ferguson, Michael Fried, Henry Louis Gates, Jr., and the editors of *Critical Inquiry* (especially Arnold I. Davidson) for their critical readings of an earlier draft. Finally, I want to thank Steven Knapp for numerous discussions of the theoretical argument in the third section; if that argument is mistaken, it's as much his fault as it is mine.

3. Ernest Howard Crosby's *Captain Jinks, Hero* (1902; repr. in *The Anti-Imperialist*

Walter Benn Michaels is professor of English and the humanities at The Johns Hopkins University. He is author of *The Gold Standard and the Logic of Naturalism* (1987) and *Our America: Nativism, Modernism, and Pluralism* (1995). His previous contributions to *Critical Inquiry* include "Against Theory" and "Against Theory 2," both written in collaboration with Steven Knapp.

imperialist arguments that had been invoked against McKinley, in particular by the description of the campaign in the Philippines as "a war of conquest" and by the claim that the president had no authority to "govern any person anywhere outside the constitution"[4]: "The constitution," insisted Chicago reformer Edwin Burritt Smith, "makes no provision for the forcible intervention by our government in the affairs of a people who do not form an integral part of our union." More important still, "To the extent we permit our chosen representatives to exercise arbitrary powers, *whether at home or abroad,* we allow them to sap and destroy representative government itself."[5] McKinley's commitment to governing the Philippines "unfettered by constitutional restraint" was thus seen as an attack not merely on Filipino rights but on American rights, on "the very principles for the maintenance of which our fathers pledged their lives."[6] Hence Lincoln, in *The Clansman,* asserting that his first postwar "duty is to reestablish the Constitution as our supreme law over every inch of our soil" (*C,* p. 43), denies that the Civil War was "a war of conquest" (*C,* p. 44)[7] and refuses to establish martial law or to enforce "Negro suffrage" in North Carolina: "The Constitution," he says, "grants to the National Government no power to regulate suffrage, and makes no provision for the control of 'conquered' provinces" (*C,* p. 42). And hence his radical Republican enemy Stoneman (Thaddeus Stevens) wishes to make the "Negro" "the ruler" and condemns the Constitution as "the creation, both in letter and spirit, of the slaveholders of the South" (*C,* p. 43).

Thus, although the major anti-imperialist literature of the turn of the century made no mention of the major imperialist adventures of the turn of the century, it did not fail to address the issues raised by those adventures. Rather it understood those issues as having essentially to do with the nature of American self-government and American citizenship.

Reader, 2:267–394) is virtually the only anti-imperialist text I know that deals explicitly with the events in the Philippines, and *Captain Jinks* is more plausibly described as antimilitarist than as anti-imperialist since it is concerned primarily to burlesque as a "peculiar kind of insanity" the "preoccupation with uniforms and soldiers, and the readiness [of Jinks] to do anything a man in regimentals tells him to" (2:393).

4. "Platform of the Liberty Congress of Anti-Imperialists, Adopted in Indianapolis, August 16," *The Public,* 22 Aug. 1900; repr. in *The Anti-Imperialist Reader,* 2:309.

5. Edwin Burritt Smith, "Liberty or Despotism," speech given at the Chicago Liberty Meeting, 30 Apr. 1899; repr. in *The Anti-Imperialist Reader,* 1:293; my emphasis.

6. "Platform of the Liberty Congress of Anti-Imperialists," 2:309.

7. The phrase "war of conquest" was employed so frequently in anti-imperialist descriptions of the invasion of the Philippines (by people like Bishop Spaulding and Carl Schurz as well as by the anonymous authors of the "Platform" quoted above) that it is difficult not to believe that Dixon intended his audience to hear their voices echoed in the voice of his Lincoln.

"Nation or Empire?" was the question posed by the anti-imperialists.[8] The return to Reconstruction for the answer to this question placed anti-imperialism at the heart of an emerging discourse of American national, racial, and, eventually, cultural identity. Texts like *Red Rock,* I will argue, sought to avoid the perils of empire by avoiding the perils of nationhood first; for Page and for the plantation tradition more generally, the South was a "Region" rather than a political entity. In *Red Rock,* no government can quite be legitimate, and this refusal of legitimacy is connected with a comparative indifference to racial identity (signaled by a feudal identification with the Indian) and an insistence on the importance of the family. For Progressives like Dixon, however, citizenship in the "new nation," produced out of resistance to an "African" empire, became *essentially* racial; the legitimacy of the state (its identity as nation rather than empire) was guaranteed by its whiteness. (This is why in *Red Rock,* where whiteness doesn't yet have any real meaning, the state cannot be legitimated—the choice there is between the illegitimate government and the "tribe.") Then in the 1920s, as whiteness becomes a culture, the Indian and the family reappear, first as models for a nativist Americanism (Willa Cather) and second as models for a pluralism of native cultures (Oliver La Farge, Anzia Yezierska). It is through this pluralism that what I will describe as the rescue of race by culture is made possible. Thus, I will argue first that anti-imperialism promoted racial identity to an essential element of American citizenship; second, that this promotion made possible the emergence of a new cultural and multicultural Americanism; and, third, that our current notion of cultural identity both descends from and extends the earlier notion of racial identity.

In *Red Rock,* by what would come to be Progressive standards, no one is American. *Red Rock* is set in the old South, in a "Region" without a name, referred to as "'the old County,' or, 'the Red Rock section,' or just, 'My country, sir.'" Its heroes are those "aristocrats" who, "subjected to the humiliation" of Reconstruction, eventually "reconquered their section and preserved the civilization of the Anglo-Saxon" (*RR,*

8. "We have come as a people to the parting of the ways. Which shall it be: Nation or Empire? . . . Let us look this imperialism squarely in the face and realize what it means. It means the surrender of American democracy. It means a menace to free American citizenship" (Joseph Henry Crooker, "The Menance to America," *Liberty Tract No. 12* [1900]; repr. in *The Anti-Imperialist Reader,* 1:306–7). This analysis of imperialism as a threat above all to *self*-government tends to be overlooked by those (like Lenin, for whom American anti-imperialists were "the last Mohicans of bourgeois democracy") who criticize what Robert L. Beisner has called the "impotence" of American anti-imperialism and who see them as essentially "conservative" (Robert L. Beisner, *Twelve against Empire: The Anti-Imperialists, 1898–1900* [New York, 1968], p. 222). If we understand American anti-imperialism as committed above all to the revisionary rescue of the concept of American citizenship described in this section, then we must also understand it to have been largely successful and, in its conceptual alliance with what Joel Williamson (in the *Crucible of Race*) calls "radical" racism, hardly conservative.

p. viii). But where, in Dixon, the resistance to Reconstruction will involve not just reconquering the "section" but nationalizing it, making Southern anti-imperialism the basis for the new American nation, in Page the restoration of "the old County" to "the rule of its own citizens" (*RR,* p. 506) is really meant to be just that, a restoration; it's no accident that the "old patrician[s]" of the South use china presented to their "ancestors by Charles the Second" (*RR,* p. 284). And where, in Dixon, what Anglo-Saxon civilization will be saved from is "the Negro," in *Red Rock* it is saved from ambitious "clerks" and "overseers." "Anglo-Saxon" for Dixon will mean "white"; for Page, it means aristocratic. *Red Rock*'s clerks and overseers derisively refer to Page's heroes as "Lords," but the point of the novel is to confirm this identification and to insist on its patriarchal accessories. Thus, in contrast to the social threat posed by the new class of ambitious white men, *Red Rock*'s blacks present no real racial threat and stand instead as a kind of bulwark against the new whites: "'these quality-niggers,'" the scalawag overseer explains to the carpetbagger clerk, are "'just as stuck up as their masters'" (*RR,* p. 129).

The "quality-nigger's" quality derives from membership in a quality family, and it is the family that Page presents as the essential unit of Red Rock society. During the war, slaves behaved "more like clansmen" (*RR,* p. 43), and after the war, they are insulted by the new offer of wages: "'How much does you pay Miss Bessie?'" Mammy Krenda asks her former master, contemptuously analogizing the idea of his Mammy being paid by him to the idea of his wife being paid by him (*RR,* p. 91). In the context of the contemporary critique of marriage as a kind of prostitution (in, say, Charlotte Perkins Gilman), this analogy made a feminist point; in *Red Rock,* however, its purpose is to make it clear that Negroes are "member[s] of the family" (*RR,* p. 90), and that, as such, they cannot be sold or bought—even from themselves. The surest signs of the overseer's degeneracy are his desire to divorce his wife and his history as a "nigger-trader," both understood as assaults on the family.

The transformation in race relations envisioned by Dixon requires the destruction of this essentially multiracial family; it calls for the elimination of the old "Uncles" and "Aunts" of the plantation tradition and a general rewriting of the childhood intimacies with blacks that were supposed to enable white Southerners to understand and appreciate them better. In *The Leopard's Spots,* the lonely Charlie Gaston finds a "playmate and partner in work" in the "ragged little waif" Dick who attaches himself to the Gaston household and even helps to defend it against a "Negro uprising." In plantation versions of this story, Dick, sticking "doggedly to Charlie's heels" (*LS,* p. 99), would count as the loyal Negro in contrast to the new Negroes of Reconstruction and especially of the 1890s. In *The Leopard's Spots,* however, Dick disappears in the early 1870s only to reappear some twenty years later as rapist and murderer of a young white girl. Gaston's attempt to save him from being burned alive is represented here as a feeble and ineffectual deviation from his own white supremacist principles, and Dixon's account of the girl's death doubles the repudiation of the old attachments to blacks by refusing even to allow her to be buried by a black man. The girl's father spurns the grave dug by "old Uncle Reuben Worth" ("the only negro present") and asks "a group of old soldier comrades" to dig him a new one (*LS*, p. 380). Comradeship with white soldiers severs the ties of affection with blacks. The transformation of the friendly little black boy into a savage murderer, a transformation that is revealed rather than explained by the novel since it takes place entirely offstage, is made to stand, precisely because it is unexplained, as a revelation of the truth about blacks. In Dixon, the brutality of the new Negro exposes as a lie the fidelity of the old one.

But this exposure has positive consequences because it is only by means of this confrontation with the new Negro that new ties of affection among whites can be made available: "In a moment the white race had fused into a homogeneous mass of love, sympathy, hate and revenge. The rich and the poor, the learned and the ignorant, the banker and the blacksmith, the great and the small, they were all one now" (*LS*, p. 368). This "fusion" involves to some extent the blurring of lines that might in other contexts seem to divide whites racially among themselves; thus the speech that wins Gaston the gubernatorial nomination characterizes his fellow North Carolinians as descended, " 'by the lineal heritage of blood,' " not only from the "Angle" and the "Saxon" but also from the "Roman," the "Spartan," and the "Celt" (*LS*, p. 442). Out of several possible races, "fusion" creates one "white race." But more important than the elision of potential ethnic differences is the elision of social and political ones. The revolt against Reconstruction succeeds when rebellion against "black rule" melts the South's "furious political passions" into "harmonious unity" by collapsing Whigs and Democrats, Unionists and Secessionists, into a "White Man's Party" arrayed against "the Black Man's Party." And when, in the 1890s, faced with the new problem of the new gap between rich and poor, the old alliance seems exhausted and unable to stand for anything except "the stupid reiteration of the old slogan of white supremacy" (*LS*, p. 197), the threat of the new Negro manages to make even the old slogan new. Listening to Gaston offer as the only plank of the Democratic platform a proclamation that " 'the hour has now come in our history to eliminate the Negro from our life and reëstablish for all time the government of our fathers' " (*LS*, pp. 433–34), the veteran General Worth experiences both nostalgia for "the years of his own daring young manhood" and admiration for "this challenge of the modern world" (*LS*, p. 434). The nostalgia is for the war and the struggle against Reconstruction—both of which Dixon understood as an attempt to unite the nation along racial lines; the admiration is for the renewal and extension of that attempt in the 1890s, the effort to make out of that united nation what Dixon calls a "State."[9]

The target against which Dixon's racial "fusion" is directed is the political "fusion" that successfully united Populists and Republicans against Democrats in the North Carolina elections of 1894 and 1896, and the point of Dixon's "fusion" is to eliminate political differences among whites by transforming them into racial differences between whites and blacks. Politics " 'is a religion,' " according to Charlie Gaston; the " 'Government is the organized virtue of the community' " and " 'the State is . . . the only organ through which the whole people can search for righteousness' " (*LS*, p. 281). What is being imagined here are something like the literal conditions of Progressive nonpartisanship, but what political theorists like Walter Lippmann and Herbert Croly hoped to find in bureaucratic technologies that would turn political issues (that is, conflicts of political interest) into administrative issues (that is, conflicts of expertise), Dixon finds in race. As long as there can be "but one issue—Are you a White Man or a Negro?" (*LS*, p. 159), there can be no partisan divisions between citizens.[10] For the two parties, the Democratic "White Man's Party" and the Populist/Republican "Black Man's Party," represent not a division between citizens but the division between citizens and noncitizens.

9. On the Klan's nationalism and, especially, on the use made of Dixon by D. W. Griffith in *The Birth of a Nation,* see Michael Paul Rogin, " 'The Sword Became a Flashing Vision': D. W. Griffith's *The Birth of a Nation,*" *"Ronald Reagan," the Movie and Other Episodes in Political Demonology* (Berkeley, 1987), pp. 190–235.

10. In fact, after winning the elections of 1894 and 1896, the fusionists were soundly defeated by the Democrats in 1898, and, after the disfranchisement of blacks in 1900, North Carolina followed Louisiana, Mississippi, and South Carolina into the ranks of the solid Democratic South. Charles L. Flynn, Jr., has recently argued that because the southern democracy (he is speaking of Georgia in particular but the argument can be generalized) was held together by "a conspiracy theory of national politics," Democrats were "unable to conceive of legitimate dissent outside of their party" (Charles L. Flynn, Jr., "Procrustean Bedfellows and Populists: An Alternative Hypothesis," in *Race, Class and Politics in Southern History: Essays in Honor of Robert F. Durden,* ed. Jeffrey J. Crow, Paul D. Escott, and Flynn [Baton Rouge, La., 1989], p. 102). Emphasizing the similarity of Populist and Democratic views on fundamental issues, his point is to revise C. Vann Woodward's account of the destruction of radical Populism at the hands of conservative Democrats by suggesting that the ideological differences between the two groups were not as great as the more properly political ones; what the Democrats found most disturbing about the Populists, in effect, was that they were not Democrats. And Flynn traces this nonideological loyalty to the Democratic party back to the Reconstruction identification of Republicans as a "money aristocracy" out to plunder the South. His emphasis on the nonideological character of loyalty to the Democratic party seems to me powerfully suggestive, but I would also argue that it is crucial not to think of this loyalty as simply the continuation of provincial or sectional paranoia. For Progressives (Southern and national), the one-party state could be understood less as a relic of Reconstruction than as a harbinger of the disappearance of partisan politics altogether and of their replacement by (as in Colonel House's *Philip Dru, Administrator*) the "commission"-run, administered state.

It was "'on account of the enfranchisement of the Negro,'" Gaston says, that "'the people of the South had to go into politics'" (*LS*, p. 280). The Negro left in slavery would have left the essentially prepolitical, prenational plantation intact. But—every crisis an opportunity—his enfranchisement brought Southerners into politics in the effort to make the South part of the nation. And now the effort to disfranchise him (an effort that succeeds in *The Leopard's Spots* and that succeeded also in the elections of 1898) makes possible the elevation of politics to a "search for righteousness." For the Progressive Croly's desire to "purify" politics and Dixon's insistence on the "purity" (*LS*, p. 281) of the "State" both require that political differences be understood as moral ones.[11] "The principle of democracy *is* virtue," wrote Croly in *The Promise of American Life* (1909); for democracy to succeed, the "citizen" must aspire to become a "saint."[12] The great triumphs of *The Leopard's Spots* are thus its translation of political fusion into racial "fusion," its representation of a debate between citizens as a debate over who can be a citizen, and its consequent identification of citizenship with "righteousness."

From this perspective, *Red Rock,* with its evocation of the prewar "family, black and white," and its suspicion of the "Government," represents a certain resistance both to the emergence of race as the crucial marker of identity and to the commitment to the state that the primacy of race makes possible. In Dixon, racial ties replace familial ones; the Klan, racially pure in a way that, as I have argued elsewhere, the family can never be, becomes the guarantor of racial identity—its white sheets are whiter than anyone's skin.[13] But in *Red Rock* the Klan's sheets are disparaged as a "'disguise'" for "'blackguards and sneaks'" (*RR,* p. 352), and the familial "clan," in its biological and aristocratic purity, is multiracial. More striking still, *Red Rock*'s repudiation of the Klan is articulated not as respect for the laws the Klan violates but as respect for the code of "honor" that is itself violated by the law. (Think of Judge Driscoll's horror in *Pudd'nhead Wilson* [1894] when he learns that Tom, instead of taking physical revenge for Count Luigi's "assault" on him, has "'crawled to a court of law about it.'")[14] In *Red Rock,* carpetbaggers embody the law, walking about, literally, with copies of "The Statutes of the United States" clasped under their arms, whereas Southern gentlemen, black and white, are bound by "honor" not to betray each other to the "Government." In Dixon, however, both the forming of the Klan and its disbanding are attempts to replace blood and honor with law and order.

11. Herbert Croly, *The Promise of American Life* (1909; New York, 1963), p. 340.

12. Ibid., p. 454. Croly is quoting and endorsing Santayana, who is himself quoting Montesquieu.

13. See Walter Benn Michaels, "The Souls of White Folk," in *Literature and the Body: Essays on Populations and Persons,* ed. Elaine Scarry (Baltimore, 1988), pp. 185–209.

14. Mark Twain, *Pudd'nhead Wilson and Those Extraordinary Twins,* ed. Sidney E. Berger (New York, 1980), p. 60.

This is most obviously true in the last volume of the trilogy, *The Traitor,* which, although it is sometimes described as Dixon's attempt to back away from the positions he had taken so strongly in the first two volumes, is, in fact, an extension rather than a repudiation of them. Its hero, John Graham, is the leader of the Klan in North Carolina and so of the resistance to the "African Government," but as the Klan degenerates and becomes increasingly identified with "lawlessness," he will become increasingly reluctant to participate in its activities and will eventually seek to disband it. When he is nonetheless arrested for a murder (actually committed by a carpetbagger), he rejects the possibility of escape, proclaiming, "'I'm done with lawlessness. . . . I've led a successful revolution . . . and now with silent lips I'll face my accusers'" (*T,* p. 266). But while it is true that rejection of escape is somewhat anomalous in Dixon, the rejection of lawlessness and the proclamation of the "successful revolution" suggest the ways in which *The Traitor* continues the commitments of its predecessors. For insofar as the real effort of these books is to replace an illegitimate ("African") state with a legitimate one, "lawlessness" can never be countenanced. Indeed, Graham's submission to and eventual redemption by authority is here contrasted to the refusal of authority embodied in the "African Government" itself. For that government, making the Klan illegal, suspending *habeas corpus,* proclaiming martial law in the South, and placing Graham's home "county of Independence under military government," stands "in violation of the Constitution" (*T,* p. 330). And Graham's threat to take his case all the way to the Supreme Court, "the last bulwark of American liberties," produces a hasty pardon from those "little politicians" who finally "do not dare to allow the Supreme Court to overwhelm them with infamy." The point, then, is that Graham's is the true commitment to "the process of the law" (*T,* p. 61) and to the Constitution that is both the ultimate law of the land and the originating document of the state.

In sum, anti-imperialism here becomes synonymous with a certain Constitutionalism. Just as the enemy throughout the trilogy is the imperial "African," usurping the Constitution, the hero is inevitably a defender of the Constitution and a creature of the state. In Page, the "clan" was saved from the state (loyal blacks supporting honorable whites against the corrupt administrators of the "Statutes"); in Dixon, the state is saved by the Klan ("'We have rescued our state from Negro rule,'" Graham tells his fellow Klansmen [*T,* p. 53]). Or rather, since Dixon actually imagines no preexisting state to be saved from the empire by the Klan, the state is *constituted* or *prefigured* by the Klan, which offers racial identity as a kind of rehearsal for the collective identity required by the new modes of national citizenship. Making it white, Dixon distinguishes the nation from the family and chooses it over the empire, indeed, creates it out of resistance to the empire. His point, then, is not the defence of the white state but the creation of the state through whiteness.

Culture as an Object of Pathos

I have suggested above that the refusal to name the "country" where Red Rock the plantation is located and *Red Rock* the novel takes place involves a refusal to understand it as part of a "nation," and even the etiology of the name "Red Rock"—the rock is supposed to have been made red by "the blood of the Indian chief" who killed the first settler's wife and was in turn killed by him—represents a kind of solidarity with those who, like the Confederacy, resist the imperial power of the United States. For if the "Lords" of Red Rock have always been "Indian-killer[s]" (that's what the first one was called and, at the end of the novel, that's what the last one is out West doing), they are also in a way Indians themselves: young Rupert is a "volunteer scout" (*RR,* p. 473), which is to say that although he fights Indians, he serves with that branch of the Army that was made up mainly of Indians; and it is said of the Red Rock "aristocrats" generally that "they stick together like Indians," so that, the overseer complains to his carpetbagger ally, "'if one of 'em got hurt, the whole tribe would come down on me like hornets.'" To which the carpetbagger's reply, "'We'll be more than a match for the whole tribe. Wait till I get in the Legislature; I'll pass some laws that will settle 'em,'" represents precisely the opposition (between family and state [as tribe and law]) that Dixonian or Progressive racism sought to overcome (*RR,* p. 206).

But if identification with the Indian could function at the turn of the century as a *refusal* of American identity, it would come to function by the early 1920s as an *assertion* of American identity. Perhaps the most powerful literary instance of this process is the production of Tom Outland as the descendant of Colorado cliff dwellers in Willa Cather's *The Professor's House* (1925), but Cather's earlier novel *A Lost Lady* (1923) provides an even clearer outline of how the old regionalist resistance to the American state could begin to be transformed into the defence not of that state but, instead, of what might provisionally be called an American culture.[15] The Indian-identified "aristocratic" family that in Page resisted subsumption by the Progressive American "nation," in Cather provides the technology enabling an Americanism that will go beyond the merely national American citizenship offered by the state. But to provide this technology the family must itself be altered; it must in particular cease to be the site of a certain indifference to racial difference (the family "black and white") and must be made instead into the unequivocal source of racial difference.

In *A Lost Lady,* the family in question is Captain Forrester's, and Forrester himself is both a member of what Cather calls the "railroad aris-

15. See Willa Cather, *A Lost Lady* (New York, 1923); hereafter abbreviated *LL.* For extended discussion of *The Professor's House* in relation both to the Johnson Immigration Act of 1924 and the Indian Citizenship Act of the same year, see Michaels, "The Vanishing American," *American Literary History* 2 (Summer 1990): 220–41.

tocracy" (*LL,* p. 9) and—through his status as one of the "pioneers" whose "dreams" settled the West—an Indian. "'All our great West has been developed from . . . dreams,'" Captain Forrester says, but his account of those dreams (and of the disappearance of the aristocratic pioneers) culminates in a "grunt" that Cather describes as "the lonely, defiant note that is so often heard in the voices of old Indians" (*LL,* p. 55). In one sense, of course, this identification is exceptionally misleading; after all, it was the pioneers and railroad men who made the Indians disappear. But in Cather, as in Page, killing Indians is no obstacle to being Indian, and the fact that the pioneers are now themselves a vanishing race only confirms the identification. The "Old West had been settled by dreamers, great-hearted adventurers . . . a courteous brotherhood," but it is now "at the mercy of men like Ivy Peters, who . . . never dared anything, never risked anything" (*LL,* p. 106). Ivy Peters makes his fortune by "'cheat[ing] Indians.'" ("'He gets splendid land from the Indians some way, for next to nothing'" [*LL,* pp. 124, 123].) Which is to say also, by exploiting men like Captain Forrester. And in this he is like Forrester's own partners who, after their bank has failed, refuse to "come up to the scratch and pay their losses like gentlemen" (*LL,* p. 90). "'In my day,'" the Captain's aristocratic lawyer exclaims, "'the difference between a business man and a scoundrel was bigger than the difference between a white man and a nigger'" (*LL,* p. 92). Now that the difference between businessmen and scoundrels is disappearing, the difference between white men and "niggers" must be preserved. The reason that Ivy Peters can't properly succeed Captain Forrester is that he's more like a "nigger" than he is like an Indian.

In *The Great Gatsby,* published two years after *A Lost Lady,* Gatsby's relation to Daisy seems, at least to Tom, a kind of miscegenation, a threat to the difference between white men and "niggers." Fitzgerald had read and admired *A Lost Lady* while working on *Gatsby* and subsequently wrote Cather a famous note, apologizing for what he described as an act of "apparent plagiarism," an unintentional similarity between descriptions of Mrs. Forrester and Daisy. How similar the descriptions actually are is a nice question,[16] but the connection—with respect to miscegenation—

16. F. Scott Fitzgerald, letter to Cather, late Mar. / early Apr. 1925, *Correspondence of F. Scott Fitzgerald,* ed. Matthew J. Bruccoli and Margaret M. Duggan (New York, 1980), p. 155. Cather thought there was no duplication and wrote him that, even if there were, any possible debt had been more than repaid by the pleasure she experienced reading *Gatsby,* but many readers have been struck by a certain resemblance between the texts. James Woodress, for example, noting that the first draft of *The Great Gatsby* is narrated by an omniscient author, suggests that Fitzgerald "may have invented Nick Carraway, his point-of-view-character" after the model of *A Lost Lady*'s Niel, and the comparison between Nick and Niel (especially if, as I have argued in "The Souls of White Folk," Nick is to be understood as a tolerant Tom) is an apt one (James Woodress, *Willa Cather: A Literary Life* [Lincoln, Nebr., 1987], pp. 351–52). Both *The Great Gatsby* and *A Lost Lady* produce the threat of miscegenation and both find ways of rescuing themselves from it at the end. Tom and Daisy are restored to each other and Nick is restored to an America that tries to make

between the Captain's wife Marian and Daisy Buchanan is real enough. Though married to an aristocrat, Marian reveals herself, in sleeping with Ivy Peters, to be nothing but "a common woman" (*LL,* p. 170). What gets "betrayed" by this affair is not exactly the Captain, since he's dead, but the "quality" the Captain and Mrs. Forrester herself supposedly embodied. This is what makes it, like Daisy's affair with James Gatz, a kind of miscegenation. Mrs. Forrester is untrue to something more than her husband: "she was not willing to immolate herself, like the widow of all these great men, and die with the pioneer period to which she belonged" (*LL,* p. 169). The great men, like Indians, had died rather than adjust to changing conditions; Mrs. Forrester "preferred life on any terms" (*LL,* p. 169). She is like an Indian who has somehow consented to change; what she betrays is not so much a husband as a race.

The racial meaning of this betrayal is clarified by the substitution two years later in *The Professor's House* of the Jewish Louie Marsellus for the merely unscrupulous Ivy Peters (as well as by Gatsby's association with Meyer Wolfsheim and Brett Ashley's affair with Robert Cohn). Marian Forrester's affair with Ivy Peters counts as a kind of miscegenation, one might say, not because he's black but because he's a proto-Jew. At the same time, then, that *A Lost Lady* asserts the importance of the difference between the "white man" and the "nigger," it also begins to rewrite that difference as the difference between an Indian and a Jew. And this rewriting can hardly be read as the adjustment of an older racist structure to new racial tensions: for one thing, racial conflict between Indians and

---

Gatsby himself almost indigenous. Marian Forrester is finally, almost as an afterthought, saved by "the right man," an "old Englishman" who carries her off to Buenos Aires. But, especially in Cather, the "right man" can never be right enough, at least for a woman. As long as women are charged with the responsibility of "keeping everyone in his proper place," people are likely to get out of place because the feminine preference for "life on any terms" can lead to a loss of the crucial "faculty of discrimination" (*LL,* p. 153); hence Daisy's interest in Gatsby (see also Fitzgerald's "The Last of the Belles") and Mrs. Forrester's in Ivy Peters. Cather's defence against such deracination is to construct families without women and almost without any need for women. Niel's mother is dead; he lives shabbily with his father and Cousin Sadie, hating "to have any one come to see them" and clinging, first in his imagination and then in reality, to his "bachelor" uncle, Judge Pommeroy (*LL,* p. 30). The judge is his true family, and when Niel, "glad to be rid of his cousin and her inconsequential housewifery," resolves to be a bachelor himself and sets up "monastic" housekeeping in his uncle's quarters, what Cather seems to propose (as if heterosexuality as such were a form of miscegenation) is a vision of the family as a series of bachelors, independent of and so unthreatened by the deracinating potential of femininity (*LL,* p. 33). This vision is imagined more fully in *The Professor's House* where it serves to link Tom and Roddy to the extinct cliff dwellers but, as Jared Gardner has shown (in an essay forthcoming in *American Quarterly*), it achieves what is probably its most complete articulation in Hart Crane's *The Bridge* (1930) where, because the homosexual is identified with the Indian, the founding moment of American identity is conceived to be doubly secured—it's as if Captain Forrester had married an Indian man instead of an inevitably lost white lady.

Jews was hardly a social phenomenon of even observable magnitude; and, for another, the older racist structure is not perpetuated with a new content; rather, it is altered. For the new valorization of the Indian points toward an interest in an essentially *pre*national (that is, prerevolutionary or, in Dixonian terms, pre–Civil War) America, an interest that one finds everywhere in the 1920s from Cather to Calvin Coolidge (the end of *Gatsby* is, perhaps, the most obvious example) and that repudiates the political nationalism of the Progressives: Americanism would now be understood as something more than and different from the American citizenship that so many aliens had so easily achieved.

Indeed the substitution of the Jew for the "nigger" makes the point even more strongly. When, in Dixon, the outlaw remnants of the disbanded Klan set out to raid "old Sam Nickaroshinski, the Jew storekeeper, and rob 'im ter-night," the act of robbery as such is a sure sign of the "new" Klan's renegade status, its identification with the "lawlessness" that in *The Traitor* is essentially "African." But robbing a Jew is even more damning, for if the Jew in the twenties will be a problematic figure for the Klan, the Jew in Dixon is a fellow revolutionary: "A refugee from Poland, his instinctive sympathies had always been with the oppressed people of the South" (*T*, p. 107). The Jew has a place in the anti-African revolutionary American state that he will not have in American culture. When Graham is led through the streets to be carried away to the penitentiary (in a chapter Dixon calls "The Day of Atonement"), it is Nickaroshinski who slips him a hundred dollars and whispers, "don't you vorry, me poy, ve'll puild a monumendt to you in de public squvare yedt" (*T*, p. 328).[17] In 1924, however, the Jew's "instinctive sympathies" make him not an anti-imperialist Southerner, but "a Jew." The Jew is "by primal instinct a Jew," according

17. The idea that Jewish refugees made exemplary Americans was by no means unique to Dixon; Mary Antin's *The Promised Land* (Boston, 1912) makes clear the suitability of the Jew for American citizenship. In Russia, according to Antin, the Jew is utterly resistant to assimilation: "he was a Jew, and nothing would make him change" (p. 11). In America, however, the Jew, exemplified by Antin herself, instantaneously becomes an American, writing poems in honor of George Washington and celebrating his birthday with her "Fellow Citizens." What makes this transformation possible is that where Jewish assimilation in Russia requires "apostasy" (the Jew is required to stop being a Jew and become a Gentile), Jewish assimilation in America is national rather than religious. The Jews in Russia were never Russians, Antin writes, they were "a people without a country." Hence becoming American for them in no way involves giving up one nation for another; on the contrary, it involves, as it does for Dixon's unreconstructed Southerners, their first experience of "a spirit of nationalism." Americanization in Antin, as her title suggests, is almost a kind of Zionism, insofar, at least, as Zionism is understood as the fulfillment of the "national expectations" of a people in "exile" (p. 227). *The Promised Land,* like the *Trilogy of the Clan,* thus tells the story of a people achieving nationality and becoming citizens, and Mary Antin, with her hatred for the czar, is a fitting compatriot of Sam Nickaroshinski, with his hatred for the "African empire." In the 1920s, however, as political/racial identity gives way to cultural/racial identity, Jewish life in exile is reinterpreted as the refusal of national ambitions and the embrace of a nonnational cultural identity.

to Dr. H. W. Evans, the Imperial Wizard of the Klan; he is "a stranger to the emotion of patriotism as the Anglo-Saxon feels it."[18] Which does not mean that the Jew in relation to the Klan of 1924 occupies the position occupied by the black in relation to Dixon's Klan. On the contrary, not even the black occupies that position any longer. For the slogan of the Klan, as an Indiana colleague of Dr. Evans puts it, is "Difference Not Inferiority": the "implications" of "Ku Kluxism" are "not those of inferiority, but those of difference; and it cherishes no hostility to Catholics, Jews, negroes or foreigners as such" (*KKK*, p. 51).

It should not be thought, however, that the declared absence of "hostility" and commitment to difference represent any diminution of racism. After all, the numerous whippings and occasional lynchings carried out by the Klan in the early twenties make it clear that a good deal of racial hostility continued to be felt. But, even setting these incidents aside, the commitment to difference itself represents a theoretical intensification of racism, an intensification that has nothing to do with feelings of tolerance or intolerance toward other races and everything to do with the conceptual apparatus of pluralist racism.[19] For insofar as the Dixonian commitment to a hierarchical ranking of the races survived into the twenties, it was seen to require a common scale of measurement; thus Frank H. Hankins, a critic of pluralism, argued that, since racial identity consisted in a set of "distinctive hereditary traits" distributed within each race on a bell-shaped curve, there was, on the one hand, no "discontinuity" between the races and, on the other hand, no equality. There could be no discontinuity because all the traits of all the races could be plotted somewhere along the curve; hence racial differences were necessarily "not those of kind but those of degree; not those of quality but of quantity."[20] There

18. *Is the Ku Klux Klan Constructive or Destructive? A Debate between Imperial Wizard Evans, Israel Zangwill and Others*, ed. E. Haldeman-Julius (Girard, Kans., 1924), p. 14; hereafter abbreviated *KKK*.

19. The most important recent (literary) critic of pluralism has been Werner Sollors; see his *Beyond Ethnicity: Consent and Descent in American Culture* (New York, 1986), and, especially, "A Critique of Pure Pluralism," in *Reconstructing American Literary History*, ed. Sacvan Bercovitch (Cambridge, Mass., 1986), pp. 250–79. In the latter, citing Horace Kallen's 1924 description of the choice facing Americans as one between "'Kultur Klux Klan and Cultural Pluralism,'" Sollors calls attention to the "notion of the eternal power of descent, birth, *natio*, and race" (pp. 258, 260) that Kallen shares with his racist opponents. Students of cultural identity (especially the skeptical ones) owe Sollors a great debt. It is essential to see, however, that pluralism can no more be thought of as a simple extension of racism than it can be thought of as a repudiation of racism since, as I argue in the text, it produces a fundamental change in what racism is. And it's important also to note, as I've suggested in the closing pages of "The Vanishing American" and as I argue in the last section of this essay, that the substitution of culture for race (the idea that ethnic identity is culturally rather than genetically transmitted) can never, as long as cultural identity counts as anything more than a description, be complete.

20. Frank H. Hankins, *The Racial Basis of Civilization: A Critique of the Nordic Doctrine*, rev. ed. (1926; New York, 1931), p. 293.

could be no equality because if the distribution of traits in one race exactly matched the distribution in another, there would be no grounds for distinguishing between the two races. Hankins's denial that racial differences are differences "of kind" thus amounts to an insistence on racial inequality—if there are races, they must be unequal. And, by the same token, the pluralist denial of racial inequality amounts to an insistence that, since they can't be "of degree," racial differences must be "of kind." Pluralism requires the assertion of differences in "quality," not just "quantity." Where Hankins's commitment to white supremacy required that races be different from each other only insofar as one had more or less of what the others also had, the antisupremacist or pluralist commitment to difference without hierarchy made races essentially different rather than more or less like each other. It was only, in other words, the pluralist denial of hierarchy that made possible the escape from the common scale and the emergence of an unmeasurable and hence incomparable racial essence.

The transformation of the Progressive opposition between "white man" and "nigger" into the new opposition between Indian and Jew thus signals at least two changes in racist discourse: first, a change in the sense of what is being preferred and, second, a change in the sense of why it is being preferred.[21] In Progressive racism, Confederate comrades in arms offer the image of a racial entity that breaks the organic bonds of the (multiracial) family and substitutes for them the superorganic bonds of the white "State"; in the 1920s, the Indian embodies a racial entity that finds through the family a "heritage" or "culture" that transcends the (multiracial) state. In Progressive racism, the "nigger" is essentially inferior; the difference between races must be maintained so that the lower will not contaminate the higher. What emerges in the twenties, however, is a racial pluralism: one prefers one's own race not because it is superior but because it is one's own.

It would be a mistake, however, to think that these changes took place neatly or all at once. As late as 1927, for example, the poet Stephen Vincent Benét could choose the Civil War as his subject for an American epic, and as late as 1928, the critic Henry Seidel Canby could praise Benét for being (along with Sinclair Lewis) the first American writer "concerned with the great theme of a national life."[22] Indeed, it was precisely Benét's treatment of the war that marked for Canby his originality. According to Canby, a true understanding of the Civil War had not been possible until the Great War because it took the Great War to make us see that the Civil

21. It signals also a narrowing of the category "white" and an expansion of "nigger": the Klan flogged a Greek for going out with a "white" woman, ordered all Syrians expelled from Macon, Georgia, and boycotted Italian storekeepers in Illinois. See David M. Chalmers, *Hooded Americanism: The History of the Ku Klux Klan* (New York, 1981), p. 110.

22. Henry Seidel Canby, introduction, in Stephen Vincent Benét, *John Brown's Body* (Chicago, 1990), p. ix; hereafter abbreviated "I."

War had been the first truly "modern" war, modern in the sense that it was "a people's war." Previous treatments of the war, Canby wrote, had been "content either with odes on the North and paeans on the South, or with local color sketches like Stephen Crane's *The Red Badge of Courage*" ("I," p. x). In other words, from the standpoint of what Canby praises as the "intense nationalism" of *John Brown's Body* (p. xiii), previous treatments had been insufficiently *national,* devoted, almost as if the war had never taken place, to one side or the other ("odes on the North and paeans on the South") or, if not actually taking sides between the two regions, to the idea of regionalism itself (*The Red Badge of Courage* as "local color"). For Canby, then, Benét is the first truly national writer because he is the first to see what the Civil War created, the first to see the Civil War as the origin of the American nation.

There is, of course, an important sense in which this claim is obviously false: the whole point of the Civil War for a writer like Dixon was that, freeing racism from slavery, it dissolved the sectional differences between North and South and replaced them with the racial difference between black and white, thus making possible the transsectional, white nation. But there are important senses also in which Canby's sense of the novelty, if not exactly the originality, of *John Brown's Body* is appropriate. For one thing, it is true that the major writers of the Progressive period—Dreiser, Wharton, London—were comparatively indifferent to the question of American national identity: even in Dreiser's major work of the postwar period, *An American Tragedy,* "American" signifies a certain set of social and economic conditions rather than a political entity or cultural heritage. It is as if, during the period when industrial America was devoted to assimilating and "Americanizing" its immigrants as quickly and thoroughly as possible, only those confronted with what seemed to them the unassimilable "Negro" were compelled to produce an account of the constitutive boundaries of the American. It is from this standpoint that a book like *The Leopard's Spots*—without any literary merit or, for that matter, any real literary ambition—can count as a rehearsal for the major literary achievements of Cather, Fitzgerald, Hemingway, and others.

In addition to the fact that Benét's literary ambitions are closer to Cather's than to Dixon's, there are important differences between *John Brown's Body* and its nationalist predecessors. If, for Dixon (and even for Canby), the alternative to "American" is sectional—Northern or Southern, "local"—for Benét it is "foreign" ("This flesh was seeded from no foreign grain / But Pennsylvania and Kentucky wheat") or "alien" ("To strive at last, against an alien proof").[23] The "American thing" (*JBB,* p. 5) in Benét is not the state that subsumes local differences and that (as embodied in the various Progressive projects of Americanization) converts aliens into Americans; it is the "native" ("As native as the shape of

23. Benét, *John Brown's Body,* p. 7; hereafter abbreviated *JBB.*

Navajo quivers" [*JBB*, p. 3]) that insists on its difference from the "alien." Benét's nationalism, in other words, is a kind of (tolerant) nativism, committed not to turning the alien into an American but to distinguishing between the alien and the American. And this anti-Progressive, anti-Americanization shows up even in his treatment of racial difference: "Oh, blackskinned epic, epic with the black spear, / I cannot sing you, having too white a heart" (*JBB*, p. 308). Canby says (amazingly) that Benét's "Negroes are the truest I know in American poetry" ("I," p. xiv), but Benét's essentially pluralistic nationalism commits him more truly to denying that he can represent the Negro at all than to representing him well. The discovery of "the American thing" thus appears most certainly in the assertion of what the "American Muse" *can't* sing: the Negro, the alien. The inability of the American Muse to sing it is the proof that she's American.

It is, in other words, as nationalism turns into nativism that it becomes also a kind of pluralism. From the standpoint of the Indianized American, the "native," this must involve the repudiation of the "alien's" efforts of Americanization, where Americanization is understood no longer as the alien's attempt to become a citizen but instead as his attempt to join the family. Tom Outland could marry the Professor's daughter because Tom is already imagined by *The Professor's House* as his son (incestuous marriages bring no one into the family). But marriage to Louie Marsellus compromises the family; indeed, it compromises *two* families. The Jew is, by "deliberate election," "unassimilable," writes the Klan's Dr. Evans; "He rejects intermarriage" (*KKK*, p. 14). A thoroughgoing pluralism would cast Louie Marsellus's father in the same position as the Professor, in opposition to a marriage that will eliminate differences rather than preserve them.

Of course, the self-appointed spokesman for the Jew here is the Imperial Wizard of the Ku Klux Klan and, when asked to comment on these remarks, Israel Zangwill, the author of *The Melting Pot*, disputed him, claiming that intermarriage of Jews with Gentiles was frequent, more frequent than intermarriage of "protestants with Catholics" (*KKK*, p. 32). But it's hardly as if nativist pluralism went unarticulated among Jews. Anzia Yezierska's *Bread Givers*, for example (published, like *Gatsby* and *The Professor's House*, in 1925), presents itself as a first-person narrative of the attempt to assimilate, almost as if a suitably reconfigured *The Professor's House* had been written from the standpoint of a lower-class Louie Marsellus. But the central conflict is not between assimilating aliens and Americans who unjustly reject them; it is between Sara, whose desire to become one of the "real Americans"[24] is so intense that successful Americanization seems to her the equivalent of being "changed into a person"

24. Anzia Yezierska, *Bread Givers* (1925; New York, 1975), p. 210; hereafter abbreviated *BG*.

(*BG*, p. 237), and her father, whose embodiment of the Jewish "race" is so absolute that he seems to his family "an ancient prophet that had just stepped out of the Bible" (*BG*, p. 125). Insofar as Sara is like a "pioneer," compared by a sympathetic Dean at her "real American" college to his own "grandmother" contending with the "wilderness" (*BG*, p. 232), her father, Reb Smolinski, is an Indian: "In a world where all is changed, he alone remained unchanged—as tragically isolate as the rocks" (*BG*, p. 296). From this standpoint, from the Jewish as opposed to the American standpoint, Sara is less like Louie Marsellus than like the woman he marries, the Professor's daughter Rosamond; as Rosie betrays her family by marrying a Jew, Sara wants to marry "an American-born man" (*BG*, p. 66). And her father is like the Professor; indeed, to reproduce in *Bread Givers* not just the thematic but the *affective* structure of *The Professor's House*, one need only imagine it written from the point of view of Reb Smolinski: *The Rabbi's House*. But the goal here, of course, is not simply to find ways of mapping these two texts onto each other; it is to suggest instead (in part, through such a mapping) that the nativist's vanishing Indian could function simultaneously as the alien's vanishing Jew: assimilation could be repudiated from both sides.

The opposition between "Indian" and "Jew" is not in this way undone, it is just, like the *Bread Givers* imagined above, reconfigured. The Indian who in Cather (and elsewhere: see, for example, Zane Grey's *The Vanishing American* [1925] or Hart Crane's *The Bridge* [1930]) embodies the nativist American is made instead to embody the nativist ethnic and in both positions resists assimilation. This is made most explicit in Oliver La Farge's *Laughing Boy* (1929), where the Indians really are Indians and the "foreigners" or "aliens" are the Americans. La Farge's Slim Girl (like Grey's Carlisle Indian, Nophaie) has been sent to an American-run school and the Navajos think of her as no longer Navajo: "She is a school-girl. . . . She is not of the People any more, she is American."[25] But where *The Vanishing American* works to narrativize the opposition between Indian and American so that, by the text's end, the Indian can melt into the American, becoming not his antagonist but his ancestor, *Laughing Boy* insists on the antagonism. Nophaie marries an American, but Slim Girl, having been seduced and prostituted by Americans, turns the act of prostitution into an act of war—when she returns from sleeping with her American, she has the "look," La Farge says, "of a man who has just killed and scalped a hated enemy" (*LB*, p. 88)—and seeks to restore herself to the Navajos by marrying one: "he was the means of returning to the good things of the Navajo, the good things of life" (*LB*, p. 109). Thus where the Indians in *The Vanishing American*, as in *The Professor's House*, are foundational for a distinctly *American* cultural identity, in *Laughing Boy* they have become a

25. Oliver La Farge, *Laughing Boy* (1929; New York, 1971), p. 33; hereafter abbreviated *LB*.

culture of their own, no longer deployed in opposition to the ethnics but as one of them.

But the point embodied in Slim Girl involves more than insisting on the difference between Navajos and Americans by repudiating intermarriage between them. For while miscegenation counts in itself as the betrayal of the racial family, simply ceasing to sleep with Americans cannot restore Slim Girl to "the People." Navajo identity in *Laughing Boy* involves something more than biological fidelity to the Navajo race; to be a Navajo, in this text, is not only to be born a Navajo but to behave like a Navajo. Biology is an essential but not a sufficient condition of what here emerges as a specifically cultural identity, an identity that can be embraced or rejected. Thus Slim Girl's learning to weave, to ride, and to sleep out under the stars are represented by the text as her attempt to exercise a "right" (*LB,* p. 62) granted her by birth but requiring at the same time that she lay claim to it. *Laughing Boy* enacts, in other words, the project of becoming Navajo, a project made possible only by the fact that there's a sense in which Slim Girl isn't a Navajo and made fulfillable only by the fact that there's a sense in which she is.

Laughing Boy was written by an American who had done anthropological work among the Navajos, and La Farge's admiration for them is obvious throughout. But the particular ingenuity of the book is in its translation of the American anthropologist's affection for Navajo culture into what amounts to a Navajo affection for Navajo culture. That is, by provisionally depriving Slim Girl of her "heritage," La Farge is able not only to depict a heritage as essentially the kind of thing (unlike one's racial identity or one's social practices) that you can get separated from but also to make that thing potentially an object of affect. Thus when Slim Girl camps out, she takes pleasure not in the act of camping out as such and not even in her perception of the night as "beautiful with stars" but in her sense that "camping . . . was a part of her people's heritage. She was doing a Navajo thing" (*LB,* p. 99). What this involves is the representation of your culture not as the things you love to do but as the things you love to do because they are your culture. The drama of the schoolgirl's separation thus makes two points: that your cultural practices are yours even if you don't practice them—this is what it means for Slim Girl to have a "right" to weaving even when she can't weave—and that cultural practices are attractive to you insofar as they are yours—this is what it means for her to like "doing a Navajo thing."

The attractions of Navajo things thus consist in the fact of their being Navajo; authenticity becomes a crucial aesthetic concept.[26] Laughing

26. Thus Houston A. Baker, Jr., praising the "genuine cultural authenticity" of certain black cultural performances, distinguishes between the authenticity that connotes "powers of certification and invoke[s] a world of rarefied connoisseurship—and a desire, as well, for only the genuine and the original" and an authenticity that is the product of the "everyday

Boy's turquoise and silver jewelry, for example, is admired because it is "strong, pure stuff, real Northern Navajo work, untouched by European influence" (*LB,* p. 79). And the mark of its purity is that not only tourists but "other Indians" buy it. In *Laughing Boy,* Navajos are represented as a people with a powerful aesthetic sense, concerned above all with doing things "in a beautiful way" (*LB,* p. 64), and Laughing Boy himself is presented as desiring to make his every action beautiful: "He was thinking hard about what he was doing; he was putting forth every effort to make it good and beautiful" (*LB,* p. 63). But what the invocation of purity makes clear is that Navajo culture is the criterion as well as the instantiation of beauty; Navajo things are beautiful insofar as they are Navajo. This is, of course, a characteristically anthropological view but, again, it is part of the originality of *Laughing Boy* that it here appears as a Navajo view. The Navajos in *Laughing Boy* understand their behavior not as constituting their culture but as representing it. And this understanding, insofar as it makes possible a discrepancy between behavior and culture, also makes possible both the mistake of straying from your culture and the project of returning to it.

"He was the Old World. I was the New," Sara Smolinski says of her father and herself in *Bread Givers.* But the claim to belong to the New World by virtue of your distance from the Old was becoming obsolete as she spoke; even *Bread Givers* ends with Sara and her father reconciled. Furthermore, although Sara is compelled to recognize the "oneness of the flesh that's in him and me" (*BG,* p. 286), that oneness is not in itself sufficient for their reunion. This can only be effected through the medium of her new husband, Hugo, who is at once an American, an expert in English pronunciation, and a "'*landsleute*'" (*BG,* p. 277), from the same part of Poland. "We talked one language. We had sprung from one soil" (*BG,* p. 278). Through Hugo, Sara begins to experience her affection for her father as an affection for the old ways, and Hugo's desire to have her father teach him Hebrew ("'An American young man, a principal, and

---

world occupied by our grand, great-grand, and immediate parents—our traceable ancestry that judged certain select sounds appealing and considered them efficacious in the office of a liberating advancement of THE RACE" (Houston A. Baker, Jr., *Modernism and the Harlem Renaissance* [Chicago, 1987], p. 100). The authenticity that accompanies connoisseurship is an artifact of an earlier (but, obviously, surviving) sense of culture as the characteristic aesthetic activities of an advanced civilization; the authenticity of the ancestral "everyday world" is an artifact of the more modern, anthropologized sense of culture as the totality of the beliefs and practices of any given people. The original and the genuine are valued in both conceptions, but what is meant by original and genuine change. The original on the connoisseurship model is opposed to the derivative; on the anthropological model, it is opposed to the debased or impure. Laughing Boy's jewelry is valued not because it is different from (more original than) the work of other real Navajos but because it is different from the work of those Navajos whose taste has been corrupted by exposure to whites—its originality consists in its being *just like* the work of other real Navajos.

wants to learn Hebrew?' " [*BG,* p. 293]) makes explicit the emergence of ethnicity as something to be reclaimed (or repudiated) rather than simply embodied. To resume for a second the analogy with *The Professor's House,* Hugo plays the role of Tom Outland; his learning Hebrew from Reb Smolinsky will be like Tom's learning Latin on the Blue Mesa, an act of filial piety. Thus Hugo's willingness to accept Reb Smolinski into his home restores Sara to her father and reconstitutes the Jewish family, but with a difference: learning Hebrew, doing a Jewish thing, the family becomes a culture.

(Anti-)Identities

"What is Africa to me?" is the initiating question of Countée Cullen's "Heritage," asked in a spirit of skepticism that the poem will seek to eliminate but that has nonetheless prompted Arthur Schlesinger, Jr., recently to cite "Heritage" as evidence of a traditional African-American indifference to Africa.[27] Schlesinger presumably hasn't read past the poem's first ten lines, but an essay that appears some hundred pages after "Heritage" in Alain Locke's *The New Negro* (1925) does provide some support for Schlesinger's anti-Afrocentrism. The Negro represents "a case of complete acculturation," Melville J. Herskovits wrote in "The Negro's Americanism."[28] Denying the idea of a "cultural genius" that could be identified with any "innate" or racially "African" characteristics, Herskovits denies also that any of the "customs" of "ancestral Africa" have survived in America ("NA," p. 356). Insofar as there is anything in Harlem different from the "white culture" that surrounds it, that difference can best be explained, Herskovits argues, as "a remnant from the peasant days in the South" ("NA," p. 359). For, "one three centuries removed / From the scenes his fathers loved," Herskovits's answer to the question, "What is Africa to me?" is nothing: the Negro has become completely "Americanized, "of the African culture, not a trace" ("NA," p. 359).

But in "Heritage," of course, that answer is not allowed to stand. For although the scenes the father loved are initially presented as "unremembered" by the son, the tendency to *forget* (as if Africa were too distant to matter) is immediately reinterpreted as a requirement to *repress* (as if Africa were too near to be forgotten): "One thing only I must do / Quench my pride and cool my blood, / Lest I perish in their flood, . . .

27. Countée Cullen, "Heritage," in *The New Negro: An Interpretation,* ed. Alain Locke (New York, 1925), p. 250; hereafter abbreviated "H." See Arthur M. Schlesinger, Jr., *The Disuniting of America: Reflections on a Multicultural Society* (New York, 1991), p. 84; hereafter abbreviated *DA.*

28. Melville J. Herskovits, "The Negro's Americanism," in *The New Negro,* p. 360; hereafter abbreviated "NA."

Lest the grave restore its dead" ("H," pp. 250–51), lest an apparently lost ancestral Africa turn out not only to be present but to be a force as strong or stronger than the Negro's Americanization. And this attempt to repress the African past is now presented as a failure, since the metaphor through which Africa is supposed to be kept out—"Though I cram against my ear / Both my thumbs, and keep them there"—is in fact the technique through which it is discovered that Africa is already inside—"So I lie, who always hear . . . Great drums beating through the air" ("H," p. 251). Trying not to hear the drums outside involves hearing instead the drums inside, the circulation of one's own "dark blood." Thus Africa is, in the end, triumphantly, not only "remembered" but repeated; in *The New Negro,* "Heritage" appears, not in the "Poetry" section (with Cullen's other poems), but in a section entitled "The Negro Digs Up His Past."

In *The New Negro,* then, Herskovits's view of the Negro as completely assimilated was anomalous; in the scholarly world more generally, however, as the citations in his own *The Myth of the Negro Past* (1941) make clear, it was widely held. Herskovits quotes Robert Park's claim that it is "very difficult to find in the South today anything that can be traced directly back to Africa"; Cleanth Brooks's declaration that for the purposes of linguistic study "the speech of the negro and of the white" should be "considered as one"; E. F. Frazier's description of the Negro people as "stripped of its social heritage"; and Charles S. Johnson's description of the Negro's "cultural heritage" as "completely broken."[29] But by 1941 (and even, in his private correspondence, as early as 1927), Herskovits himself had come to see things very differently.[30] In 1925 he had argued that "all racial and social elements in our population who live here long enough become acculturated, Americanized in the truest sense of the word, eventually" ("NA," p. 360), and that the Negro was no exception; in 1941, he argued that the distinguishing traits of "Italians or Germans or Old Americans or Jews or Irish or Mexicans or Swedes" could not be understood "without a reference to a preceding cultural heritage" (*M,* p. 299) and, again, that the Negro was no exception. What he had seen in 1925 as the Negro's likeness to other groups in becoming acculturated, he now saw as the Negro's likeness to other groups in *not* becoming acculturated.

The myth of the Negro past, in other words, was that he had none, that he was either completely a creature of the culture imposed upon him in slavery or that he had no culture at all, and, insofar as Negroes were themselves brought to accept this view, Herskovits regarded them as the

29. Quoted in Herskovits, *The Myth of the Negro Past* (1941; Boston, 1990), pp. 3,5,3,4; hereafter abbreviated *M.*

30. For an account of Herskovits's career, see Walter Jackson, "Melville Herskovits and the Search for Afro-American Culture," in *Malinowski, Rivers, Benedict and Others: Essays on Culture and Personality,* ed. G. W. Stocking, Jr. (Madison, Wis., 1986), pp. 95–126.

victims of cultural imperialism. *Native Son*'s (1940) Bigger Thomas, for example, is described by Richard Wright as "bereft of a culture." "The Negro," according to Wright, "possessed a rich and complex culture when he was brought to these alien shores" but it was "taken from" him.[31] Herskovits's argument in *The Myth of the Negro Past* was that it had *not* been taken from him, and that the myth of the Negro's unique cultural "pliancy" was a function of "racial prejudice." His point, then, was to show both that the Negro did have a past and that, like other groups, he had clung to it. The "stereotype of the pliant Negro . . . which contrasts him to the Indian, who is held to have died rather than suffer enslavement" is false, Herskovits claimed (*M,* p. 90). The Indian who died to show his "cultural tenacity" now becomes the model not only for "Old Americans" like Tom Outland and old Jews like Reb Smolinski but for the newly historicized Negro whose "pre-American traditions" make him an ethnic like the others (*M,* p. 293).

Precipitated out of the family "black and white" as the first American race, the Negro—filtered through the Indian—now becomes the last American culture. But here Herskovits is not simply catching up to the twenties, he is advancing the argument. For cultural identity in the twenties required, as we have seen, the anticipation of culture by race: to be a Navajo you have to do Navajo things, but you can't really count as doing Navajo things unless you already are a Navajo. For Herskovits, however (and here *The Myth of the Negro Past* is consistent with "The Negro's Americanism"), racial identity plays no role in the constitution of cultural identity; his "analysis is consistently held to the plane of learned behavior, so that whatever role innate endowment may play, it is not permitted to confuse the issues of the research" (*M,* p. 14). Thus where Countée Cullen identified the African heritage genealogically, finding it in the body's "black blood," Herskovits saw the distinctive "Africanisms" of the body as "cultural" rather than "biological": his research assistant, Zora Neale Hurston, he noted, was "more White than Negro in her ancestry" but her "motor behavior" was "typically Negro."[32]

When Herskovits sought to prove that the Negro was not a man "without a past," then, the past he sought to give him was entirely cultural (*M,* p. 31). The idea was to show that many aspects of contemporary Negro behavior could be traced back to African beliefs and practices, and the point in doing this was to help the Negro toward a proper "appreciation of his past," for a "people that denies its past cannot escape being a prey to doubt of its value today" (*M,* p. 32). When, in *Native Son,* Bigger goes to the double feature the movies he sees are *The Gay Woman* and

31. Richard Wright, "I Bite the Hand That Feeds Me," *Atlantic Monthly* 165 (June 1940): 828, 827.

32. Quoted in Jackson, "Melville Herskovits and the Search for Afro-American Culture," p. 107.

Trader Horn. The Gay Woman, as Wright describes it, is about "rich white people," "dancing, golfing, swimming, and spinning roulette wheels;"[33] *Trader Horn* is about "black men and women dancing free and wild, men and women who were adjusted to their soil and at home in their world" (*NS,* p. 36). *Trader Horn,* in Herskovits's terms, presents Bigger with the spectacle of an African culture that should be his—a display of those "distinctive" "motor habits" (*M,* p. 148) that he is supposed to have brought with him from Africa. But it is a spectacle that Bigger himself cannot see. "He looked at *Trader Horn* unfold . . . and then gradually the African scene changed and was replaced by images in his own mind of white men and women dressed in black and white clothes, laughing, talking, drinking and dancing" (*NS,* pp. 35–36). The white world from which he is shut out is more alluring than the African world with which Herskovits wishes to reconnect him. This, from the standpoint of Herskovits, is what it means to belong to a people that denies its past.[34]

But Bigger's indifference may perhaps be more easily understood as a critique of Herskovits than as a failure to live up to his ideals, and what seems to Herskovits at best the Negro's inability to recognize his past and at worst his commitment to denying his past may be read instead as a question about why the past in question is his. For in his identification of the Negro "people" and, more particularly, in his characterization of African customs as part of that people's past, Herskovits turns out to lean more heavily on the concept of racial identity than his culturalist rhetoric sug-

33. Wright, *Native Son* (1940; New York, 1966), p. 33; hereafter abbreviated *NS.*

34. This also is a central aspect of James Baldwin's critique of *Native Son* in "Everybody's Protest Novel" and "Many Thousands Gone," with, however, Bigger's repudiation of African culture read as Wright's inability to express the "tradition" of the American Negro: "the fact is not that the Negro has no tradition but there has as yet arrived no sensibility sufficiently profound and tough to make this tradition articulate. For a tradition expresses, after all, nothing more than the long and painful experience of a people; it comes out of the battle waged to maintain their integrity" (James Baldwin, "Many Thousands Gone," *Notes of a Native Son* [Boston, 1990], p. 36). Some recent critics have sought to defend Wright against Baldwin, arguing that "a genuine folk heritage shines forth" from *Native Son* (Baker, "Racial Wisdom and Richard Wright's *Native Son,*" in *Critical Essays on Richard Wright,* ed. Yoshinobu Hakutani [Boston, 1982], p. 74), but the role of supplying such a heritage has, of course, been much more frequently assigned to Hurston. For an important critique of this use of Hurston, however, see Hazel V. Carby, "The Politics of Fiction, Anthropology, and the Folk: Zora Neale Hurston," in *New Essays on "Their Eyes Were Watching God,"* ed. Michael Awkward (Cambridge, 1990), pp. 71–93. Asking why "*Their Eyes Were Watching God* has become such a privileged text," Carby goes on to wonder why it is "considered necessary that the novel produce cultural meanings of authenticity" and how "cultural authenticity come[s] to be situated so exclusively in the rural folk" (p. 89). It should be pointed out, however, that her answer to these very useful questions—in essence, that the contemporary critical commitment to Hurston is a response to the current crisis in "black urban America"—speaks more clearly to the question of why authenticity gets located in the folk than it does to the question of the novel's relation to cultural authenticity as such.

gests. Indeed, how else can an American Negro of the twentieth century be said to be denying his or her past in denying that his or her practices have their roots in Africa?[35]

In *Laughing Boy,* Slim Girl's *actual* past, the things she has herself done (her American education, her conversion to Christianity, her love affair with an American), are regarded as less crucial to her identity than her people's past, the things her mother and father used to do. "Her past" is "dead," Laughing Boy thinks, and, indeed, he himself represents to her "an axe with which to hew down the past" and "a light with which to see her way back to her people" (*LB,* p. 45). The way to beliefs she has never held and to customs she has never practiced can seem a way *back* in *Laughing Boy* because race provides the necessary (but, crucially, not sufficient) ground of Slim Girl's identity. Neither what she was born nor what she has done is sufficient to confer cultural identity; she can make herself a Navajo only by doubling Navajo birth with the doing of Navajo things. The discrepancy between Slim Girl's actual past and her people's past is thus the enabling condition for the appearance of cultural identity as a project, the project of lining up her practices with her genealogy. Herskovits, however, cannot afford such a discrepancy between what people do and what their ancestors did. Since his analysis is committed only to a genealogy of "learned behavior," a break in that genealogy (a failure actually to do yourself what your ancestors did) can only count as a complete rupture with the past; there can be no appeal to racial continuity.

Thus Herskovits is required to explain, for example, how the "retention of Africanisms" was possible for house slaves and others "in close contact with whites" (*M,* p. 133). Such people, despite being thoroughly trained in white ways and encouraged in the "adoption of white values" (M, p. 132), could "reabsorb Africanisms" during the periods when they were released from their duties and could mingle with field hands whose practices had been left relatively untouched or, even better, he suggests, with "newly arrived Africans" whose practices were completely untouched (*M,* p. 133). Whatever the historical plausibility of this explanation, and even though the movement from retention to reabsorption suggests a certain slippage (if you were trained as a house slave, why would absorbing Africanisms count as reabsorbing them?), its theoretical purpose is clear:

35. Where Herskovits wished to attack the idea of racial identity by substituting for it the idea of historical identity, other writers have sought to *save* the idea of racial identity by redescribing it as historical identity. For a brilliant critique of this effort, one that has influenced my critique of cultural identity, see Anthony Appiah, "The Uncompleted Argument: Du Bois and the Illusion of Race," in *"Race," Writing, and Difference,* ed. Henry Louis Gates, Jr. (Chicago, 1986), pp. 21–37. It is unclear to me, however, to what extent Appiah's own "hermeneutic" conception of cultures as "communities of meaning, shading variously into each other in the rich structure of the social world" is meant to do the racial work that I criticize in the remainder of this section (p. 36).

to guarantee an unbroken chain of (cultural) Africanisms and so avoid any appeal to "innate endowment."

In fact, however, the appearance of a break in the cultural chain only makes visible what must already be present for the "retention of Africanisms" to count as the acquisition of a "past." For the fact that some people before you did some things that you do does not in itself make what they did part of your past. To make what *they* did part of *your* past, there must be some prior assumption of identity between you and them, and this assumption is as racial in Herskovits as it is in Cullen or La Farge. The things the African Negro used to do count as the American Negro's past only because both the African and the American are "the Negro." Herskovits's anti-racist culturalism can only be articulated through a commitment to racial identity.[36]

"What is Africa to me?" The answer, if you are Herskovits's Negro, is "my past." Schlesinger, as I noted earlier, cites that question as an instance of the rejection by black Americans of the idea that their past is African. But this rejection involves for him only a denial of the Africanness of their past, not a rejection of the idea that black Americans as such have a past or of what he calls the "right" of black Americans "to seek an affirmative definition of their past" (*DA,* p. 30). He does not, in other words, reject the idea of our past as something more than our personal or actual past. On

36. Nervous about Herskovits-style claims for continuous cultural descent, anthropologists have recently begun to criticize the idea of culture precisely because of what they take to be "its bias toward wholeness, continuity, and growth" (James Clifford, *The Predicament of Culture: Twentieth-Century Ethnography, Literature, and Art* [Cambridge, Mass., 1988], p. 338). According to Clifford, it "does not tolerate radical breaks in historical continuity"; thus the only two available narratives about cultures imagine them either dying or surviving, and these narratives cannot account for the discovery of "new ways to be different," for "complex historical processes of appropriation, compromise, subversion, masking, invention, and revival" (p. 338). Hence, with respect to problems like the legal determination of Indian identity (the particular example is a trial to determine whether the Mashpee Indians can be counted as a "tribe"), Clifford finds the "organicist" criterion of culture irrelevant. While it is true, he argues, that participation in "traditional" Indian practices was intermittent so that Indian culture (understood as the continual participation in these practices) could not be said to have "survived," it was also true that "Indianness" had been continually "reinvented." In court, and according to the anthropological understanding of culture, such reinventions could not be accepted: "An identity could not die and come back to life" (p. 341). In fact, however, it is precisely through such reinventions that "collective structures" "reproduce themselves." "Their wholeness is as much a matter of reinvention and encounter as it is of continuity and survival" (p. 341).

But the opposition here between "reinvention" and "continuity" is problematic. Clifford argues that "any part of a tradition" that can be "remembered, even generations later" and "caught up in a present dynamism" cannot be understood as "lost" (p. 342). It is this kind of reinvention that constitutes Mashpee identity. The appeal to memory makes it clear that the resumption of a discontinued Indian practice cannot in itself count as a marker of Indian identity; going to powwows, taking up drumming, and starting to wear "regalia" wouldn't turn a New York Jew into a Mashpee Indian. The point of "remembered" as opposed to discovered (or of "reinvented" as opposed to invented) is to identify

the contrary, his goal in *The Disuniting of America* is to reclaim the past from Afrocentrists and others who threaten his vision of who we are and what our past is. And, in this, Schlesinger and his opponents stand on the same ground. For if American historians study what is meant to seem to us, if we are Americans, "our" past ("For history is to the nation rather as memory is to the individual" [*DA*, p. 45], Schlesinger says),[37] nothing is

---

the traditions in question as appropriate to (already in some sense belonging to) the person who (re)involves himself in them. It is a mistake, then, to think that there is no appeal here to either "continuity" or "survival." On the contrary, it is only the (implied) assertion of continuity between the person who originally practiced, say, drumming, then discontinued the practice and has now once again begun to drum that makes sense of the notion that the practice of drumming is being remembered rather than invented.

But this assertion is, of course, false. The reason there is a question about Mashpee identity in the first place is because there is no such person. But, since there is no such person, it is difficult to see why taking up drumming should be understood as remembering part of a lost tradition. If, then, the criteria of Mashpee identity are drumming, dressing in "regalia," and so on, it should be the case that anyone who meets these criteria counts as a Mashpee. But if these criteria aren't sufficient, then some other criterion must be invoked. Clifford rejects culture as a mark of identity because culture tolerates no discontinuities. But he himself can tolerate discontinuity only if it is grounded in a continuity that runs much deeper than culture: drumming will make you a Mashpee not because anyone who drums gets to be a Mashpee but because, insofar as your drumming counts as remembering a lost tradition, it shows that you already *are* a Mashpee. The point here is not that Clifford is secretly depending on some notion of racial identity but that his rejection of cultural identity gets him no further away from racial identity than does the more usual insistence on cultural identity. The problem, in other words, is with the claim for identity.

When the object of anthropological attention is "ethnicity" instead of "culture," the effort to avoid race is even more obviously a failure. Like Clifford, Michael M. J. Fischer seeks to emphasize the creative discontinuities in the transmission of ethnicity—it is "reinvented and reinterpreted" rather than "simply passed on from generation to generation, taught and learned" (Michael M. J. Fischer, "Ethnicity and the Post-Modern Arts of Memory," in *Writing Culture: The Poetics and Politics of Ethnography,* ed. Clifford and George E. Marcus [Berkeley, 1986], p. 195). The point here is that ethnicity does not consist in simply following the traditional practices of the ethnic group in question. Rather, ethnicity is "something dynamic, often unsuccessfully repressed or avoided" (p. 195), a "recognition of something about one's essential being [that] seems to stem from outside one's immediate consciousness and control, and yet requires an effort of self-definition" (pp. 196–97). Ethnicity here is by no means simply biological (indeed, Fischer never mentions biology, and it is difficult to see how a biological ethnicity could be "reinvented" or "repressed" as opposed to just embodied), but it is by no means simply transmitted through what Fischer contemptuously refers to as "socialization" either (if it were it could hardly be described as "a sense of the buried coming to the surface" and analogized to the Freudian id [p. 196]). In fact, in order to convert ethnicity into something other than socialization, Fischer has no choice but to rely on biology as a necessary but not sufficient condition of ethnic identity, necessary because it confers on the ethnic subject a mark of identity that transcends one's actual practices and experiences, insufficient because without eventual recourse to the appropriate practices and experiences, there can be no reinvention or return of the repressed.

37. The description of historical understanding as "remembering" is, in general, tendentious. Why should learning something about the past that we have never known be described as remembering it? The remembering subject (in order to count as remember-

more common today than the challenge to this description that takes the form of asking who "we" are and demanding that our past be pluralized in response to that question, that the "American" past be understood instead as the native-American past, the African-American past, the Jewish-American past, and so on.

But why does it matter who we are? The answer can't just be the epistemological truism that our account of the past may be partially determined by our own identity, for, of course, this description of the conditions under which we know the past makes no logical difference to the truth or falsity of what we know. It must be instead the ontological claim that we need to know who we are in order to know which past is ours. The real question, however, is not *which* past should count as ours but why *any* past should count as ours. Virtually all the events and actions that we study did not happen to us and were not done by us. In this sense, the history we study is never our own; it is always the history of people who were in some respects like us and in other respects different. When, however, we claim it as ours, we commit ourselves to the ontology of "the Negro," to the identity of "we" and "they," and the primacy of race.[38]

This is not to say, of course, that all accounts of cultural identity require a racial component; it is only to say that the accounts of cultural identity that do any cultural work require a racial component. For insofar as our culture remains nothing more than what we do and believe, it is impotently descriptive. The fact, in other words, that something belongs to

---

ing) must once have known and then forgotten what it now comes to know *again* (and so remembers). But who is this subject? This is the question Schlesinger answers when he says that "history is to the nation rather as memory is to the individual" (*DA*, p. 45). He subsequently warns against the "corruption of history by nationalism" (by which he means the tendency of some historians to subordinate the truth to the "nurture of a nation" [*DA*, p. 47]), but nationalism in his own account plays a more crucial role in the constitution of history than in its corruption. For history to serve as the nation's memory, the nation must become a subject; without nationalism, history could never become memory. Of course, it is more or less a truism to point out the connection between historical study and nationalism. My point here is only to emphasize that the links between history and nationalism do not depend on the historian's tendency to produce nationally biased accounts of his or her country's past; it is built into the account of his or her activity as an attempt to *remember* that past. And my further point is that this construction of the historical or remembering subject need not be limited to the nation. Rather, it is part of the argument of this essay that at certain moments the notion of *cultural* memory has importantly supplemented or replaced the notion of national memory.

38. For criticism of the (nonracist) models of collective identity required to make events in which we did not personally participate part of "our" past, see Steven Knapp, "Collective Memory and the Actual Past," *Representations*, no. 26 (Spring 1989): 123–49. (Whether racial identity, even if admitted, can provide such a model remains an open question; my interest here is only in those who do not wish to—but, I claim, nevertheless must—appeal to race.) The argument in this section relies also on an unpublished draft of an essay on race and culture written in collaboration by Knapp and Michaels.

our culture, cannot count as a motive for our doing it since, if it *does* belong to our culture we *already* do it and if we don't do it (if we've stopped or haven't yet started doing it) it doesn't belong to our culture. (It makes no sense, for example, to claim that we shouldn't teach Shakespeare because he isn't part of our culture since to teach him will immediately *make* him part of our culture, but it also makes no sense to claim that we should teach him because he is part of our culture since, if we stop teaching him, he won't be any longer.) It is only if we think that our culture is not whatever beliefs and practices we actually happen to have but is instead the beliefs and practices that should properly go with the sort of people we happen to be that the fact of something belonging to our culture can count as a reason for doing it. But to think this is to appeal to something that must be beyond culture and that cannot be derived from culture precisely because our sense of which culture is properly ours must be derived from it. This has been the function of race. Just as it is only the presumed racial identity between Herskovits's Negroes and their African ancestors that makes what the Africans did part of the Negroes' past, so it is only the idea that the appropriateness of culture can be derived from race that makes it possible to think that a certain culture is the right one for a certain people. The modern concept of culture is not, in other words, a critique of racism; it is a form of racism.

This emerges most clearly in the logic of cultural pluralism. As Schlesinger puts it, defending American values, "We don't have to believe that our values are absolutely better than the next fellow's or the next country's, but we have no doubt that they are better *for us,* reared as we are—and are worth living by and worth dying for" (*DA,* p. 137). The move to pluralism is built into the distinction between "better" and "better for us." It is easy to see why we should continue to hold the values we hold if we regard them as better than other values, more difficult to see why we should continue to hold them if we don't. If they are not just better but are just better "for us," then our reason for holding them can only be that they are ours. But, insofar as what we mean by calling them "ours" is that they are what we believe, the fact that they are what we believe is obviously not in itself a sufficient reason for continuing to believe them—we often stop believing some things and start believing others precisely because the new beliefs seem to us better than the old ones. So the claim that our beliefs are better "for us" involves something stronger than the claim that our beliefs are ours insofar as they are the beliefs we actually hold. The pluralist gesture toward tolerance (not "better" but "better for us") requires an essentialist assertion of identity; instead of who we are being constituted by what we do, what we do is justified by who we are. In cultural pluralism, culture does not make up identity, it reflects it.[39]

39. "Cultural pluralism" is an oxymoron; its commitment to culture is contradicted by its commitment to pluralism. For, on the one hand, the pluralist claim that our practices are justified only because they are better for us requires us to be able to say who we are inde-

Part of what I have tried to show in this essay is that the "something stronger" required to derive our beliefs and practices from our identity—required to connect who we are with how we should behave—has historically taken the form of race. But, of course, the fact that the origins of cultural pluralism in America are so deeply intertwined with conceptual advances in racism—in particular with the repudiation of ideas of racial inferiority (which implied a common scale) and their replacement by ideas of racial difference (which relied upon the assertion of incommensurability)—does not mean that contemporary cultural pluralism must also rest on an essentially racial base. I have also tried to show, however, that it does rest on such a base. When, for example, people dispute Schlesinger-style claims about the values we ought to hold by asking who "we" are, they assume that the answer to the question of which values are appropriate for us depends on identifying which culture we belong to. But if, as I have argued, our culture can only function as a justification of our values insofar as it is transformed into something more than a description of them, then the question of which culture we belong to is relevant only if culture is anchored in race.[40]

Our sense of culture is characteristically meant to displace race, but part of the argument of this essay has been that culture has turned out to be a way of continuing rather than repudiating racial thought. It is only

---

pendent of those practices and so requires us to produce our racial identity. But, on the other hand, the cultural claim denies the relevance of race and so leaves us unable to appeal to facts about who we are as justifications for what we do. To be a cultural pluralist, then, is to be required to choose between culture and pluralism, which is to say, between culture and race. And the debate over multiculturalism has been framed in such a way that every participant in it, merely by participating in it, chooses pluralism, chooses race.

Furthermore, it is important to stress that this essentialist commitment to the primacy of identity is in no way avoided by what are hopefully described as anti-essentialist accounts of identity, accounts that emphasize the complex, conflicted, mobile, and so on nature of identity. There are no anti-essentialist accounts of identity. The reason for this is that the essentialism inheres not in the description of the identity but in the attempt to derive the practices from the identity—we *do* this because we *are* this. Hence anti-essentialism with respect to cultural identity must take the form not of producing more sophisticated accounts of identity (that is, more sophisticated essentialisms) but of ceasing to explain what people do or should do by reference to who they are and/or what culture they belong to. (Needless to say, and for the same reason, making the *culture* more complex, contradictory, discontinuous, and so on is also just another turn of the essentialist screw.)

40. My point here is not that Schlesinger and his multiculturalist opponents are racists; it is instead that their nonracist appeals to culture carry no weight except as disguised appeals to race. If the Progressive Era saw, in the separation of race from family, a certain liberation of racism from biology in the service of the state; and if the twenties saw, in the doubling of race by culture, the dissemination of racial essences in the service of a plural nativism; what we are seeing now, we might say, is—through the transformation of race into culture—the rescue of racism from racists. To what purposes a racism without racists may be put, however, we don't yet know.

the appeal to race that makes culture an object of affect and that gives notions like losing our culture, preserving it, stealing someone else's culture, restoring people's culture to them, and so on, their pathos. Our race identifies the culture to which we have a right, a right that may be violated or defended, repudiated or recovered. Race transforms people who learn to do what we do into the thieves of our culture and people who teach us to do what they do into the destroyers of our culture; it makes assimilation into a kind of betrayal and the refusal to assimilate into a form of heroism. Without race, losing our culture can mean no more than doing things differently from the way we now do them and preserving our culture can mean no more than doing things the same—the melodrama of assimilation disappears.[41] If, of course, doing things differently turns out to mean doing them worse, then the change will seem regrettable. But it's not the loss of our culture that will make it regrettable; it's the fact that the culture that will then be ours will be worse than the culture that used to be ours. It is, of course, always possible and often likely that things will get worse; abandoning our idea of culture, however, will not make them worse.

41. Needless to say, the situation is entirely different with respect to compulsory assimilation; what puts the pathos back is precisely the element of compulsion.

Occidentalism as Counterdiscourse: "He Shang" in Post-Mao China

Xiaomei Chen

1

In the years since its introduction, Edward Said's celebrated study *Orientalism* has acquired a near-paradigmatic status as a model of the relationships between Western and non-Western cultures. Said seeks to show how Western imperialist images of its colonial others—images that, of course, are inevitably and sharply at odds with the self-understanding of the indigenous non-Western cultures they purport to represent—not only govern the West's hegemonic policies, but were imported into the West's political and cultural colonies where they affected native points of view and thus served as instruments of domination themselves. Said's focus is on the Near East, but his critics and supporters alike have extended his model far beyond the confines of that part of the world. Despite the popularity of Said's model, however, comparatists and sinologists have yet to make extensive use of it in their attempts to define

I wish to thank Ci Jiwei, C. Clifford Flanigan, Arif Dirlik, Lyman P. Van Slyke, Eugene C. Eoyang, and an anonymous reader for *Critical Inquiry* for reading and commenting extensively on earlier drafts of this essay. I am indebted to the Stanford Humanities Center, whose Andrew W. Mellon Fellowship made possible my research and writing at the Hoover Institution, and to the Second Walter H. Shorenstein Conference in East Asian Studies for providing a forum for this paper. I am also grateful to my colleagues in the Division of Comparative Studies at Ohio State University, whose group discussions on this paper provided valuable suggestions.

All translations from the Chinese are mine unless otherwise noted.

This article originally appeared in *Critical Inquiry* 18 (Summer 1992).

China's self-image or the nature of Sino-Western social, cultural, and political relationships.

On first consideration, this neglect of Said's work seems justified. Throughout this century, and especially recently, the People's Republic of China and its political forebears have emphasized their unique and "Chinese" way of doing things. Yet, as Said's book warns us, such talk can be deceptive. Indeed it seems clear that when Mao Tse-tung and Deng Xiaoping advocated a "particular Chinese road to socialism and communism," their "Chineseness" was not merely the product of how the Chinese understood their unique political and cultural circumstances. Rather, just as Said's model suggests, the "pure Chinese" self-understanding advocated by such belated figures had already been historically "contaminated" and even constructed by cultural and cross-cultural appropriations that belong to the whole of Chinese-Western relationships, which to a marked degree have been determined—and overdetermined—by the way that the West has understood itself and China. Most recently, for instance, in announcing its cultural uniqueness, the advocates of a culturally pure China have declared their nation as "the last banner of socialism." Such claims seek to have hortatory as much as descriptive content, since they take as their priority the national campaign against "the foreign imperialists' dream of a peaceful transformation to capitalism in China," especially in view of the recent disintegration of the Soviet Union, which had "tragically regressed to the road of capitalism."

Indeed, as this remark suggests, nowhere is the phenomenon of a pervasive Orientalism in modern China more visible than in the history of the Chinese revolution. One might well argue that to a large extent all elite discourses of antitraditionalism in modern China, from the May Fourth movement to the 1989 Tiananmen student demonstration, have been extensively orientalized. This at least partially self-imposed Orientalism is quintessentially reflected, for example, in Chinese appropriations of the idea of history as progress and teleology, notions derived from the Western Enlightenment and from various schools of Western utopian thinking that, of course, found their most potent expression in the ideas of Karl Marx. Indeed, as Arif Dirlik has succinctly pointed out, Chinese Marxism has been greatly influenced by a Marxist globalized historical consciousness that takes unilinear European history as the

---

Xiaomei Chen is associate professor of Chinese and comparative literature at Ohio State University. She is author of *Occidentalism: A Theory of Counter-Discourse in Post-Mao China* (1995) and is currently working on a book entitled *Acting the Part: The Politics of Theater in the Age after Mao*.

model to represent China's past in order to attain its admission into universal history.[1]

Yet for all of this it would not be accurate to say that Chinese political and intellectual culture is nothing more than an outpost of mindlessly replicated Western thought. However Western these "Chinese" ideas may be in their origins, it is undeniable that their mere utterance in a non-Western context inevitably creates a modification of their form and content. In such modifications of Western Marxist thought we see examples of the way that in China—and perhaps elsewhere—Orientalism, or the Western construction of the Orient, has been accompanied by instances of what might be termed Occidentalism, a discursive practice that, by constructing its Western Other, has allowed the Orient to participate actively and with indigenous creativity in the process of self-appropriation, even after being appropriated and constructed by Western others. As a result of constantly revising and manipulating imperialistically imposed Western theories and practices, the Chinese Orient has produced a new discourse marked by a particular combination of the Western construction of China with the Chinese construction of the West, with both of these components interacting and interpenetrating each other. This seemingly unified discursive practice of Occidentalism exists in a paradoxical relationship to the discursive practices of Orientalism, and in fact shares with it many ideological techniques and strategies. Despite these similarities, however, Chinese Occidentalism has mainly served an ideological function quite different from that of Orientalism. Orientalism, in Said's account, is a strategy of Western world domination, whereas, as the rest of this essay seeks to show, Chinese Occidentalism is primarily a discourse that has been evoked by various and competing groups within Chinese society for a variety of different ends, largely, though not exclusively, within domestic Chinese politics. As such, it has been both a discourse of oppression and a discourse of liberation.

Chinese Occidentalism might be regarded as two related yet separate discursive practices, or perhaps two different appropriations of the same discourse for strikingly different political ends. In the first, which I term official Occidentalism, the Chinese government uses the essentialization of the West as a means for supporting a nationalism that effects the internal suppression of its own people. In this process, the Western Other is construed by a Chinese imagination, not for the purpose of dominating it, but in order to discipline, and ultimately to dominate, the Chinese self at home. This variety of official Occidentalism perhaps found its best expression in Mao Tse-tung's theory of three worlds in which he asserted that the First World superpowers—the Soviet Union and the United

1. See Arif Dirlik, "Marxism and Chinese History: The Globalization of Marxist Historical Discourse and the Problem of Hegemony in Marxism," *Journal of Third World Studies* 4 (1987): 151–64, esp. p. 158.

States—invariably exploit and oppress the Third World countries in Asia, Africa, and Latin America. This theory was to a great extent a product of the radical cultural revolutionary ideology that, despite its expressed concern for the non-Chinese oppressed of the world, had as its chief interest the domestic legitimization of Mao as the "great leader" of the Third World. It thus was a strategy to consolidate Mao's shaky and increasingly problematic position within the Chinese Communist party. At the dawn of the Cultural Revolution in 1965, Lin Biao, Mao's chosen successor at the time, advocated the application of Mao's theory of "establishing revolutionary base areas in the rural districts and encircling the cities from the countryside"—a theory that was said to have brought about the victory of the Chinese revolutionary—to the international arena of the Third World countries in their struggle against "aggression and enslavement on a serious scale by the imperialists headed by the United States and their lackeys."[2] We can see these concerns in Lin's *Long Live the Victory of People's War!* first published in *People's Daily* on 3 September 1965 "in commemoration of the twentieth anniversary of victory in the Chinese people's war of resistance against Japan":

> Taking the entire globe, if North America and Western Europe can be called "the cities of the world," then Asia, Africa and Latin America constitute "the rural areas of the world." Since World War II, the proletarian revolutionary movement has for various reasons been temporarily held back in the North American and West European capitalist countries, while the people's revolutionary movement in Asia, Africa, and Latin America has been growing vigorously. In a sense, the contemporary world revolution also presents a picture of the encirclement of cities by the rural areas. In the final analysis, the whole cause of world revolution hinges on the revolutionary struggles of the Asian, African, and Latin American peoples who make up the overwhelming majority of the world's population. The socialist countries should regard it as their internationalist duty to support the people's revolutionary struggles in Asia, Africa, and Latin America.[3]

As has subsequently become clear, Lin's discourse, although seemingly directed to Third World countries against Western imperialist policies, was part and parcel of his radical anti-Western and antibourgeois ideology advanced in an attempt to advocate the Cultural Revolution for decidedly internal and domestic political ends. The most direct impact of his book was to initiate and promote a Maoist cult, which reached its peak at the beginning of the Cultural Revolution, under the pretext of spreading "Mao Tse-tung Thought" as the supreme principle and living gospel of

2. Lin Biao, *Long Live the Victory of People's War! In Commemoration of the Twentieth Anniversary of Victory in the Chinese People's War of Resistance against Japan* (Beijing, 1965), p. 48.
3. Ibid., pp. 48–49.

Marxism and Leninism. We seem to have here an Occidentalism wholly Chinese in its content and purpose.

Yet matters are more complicated than they might at first appear. Even the brief quotations given above suggest the complex relationship between Chinese Occidentalism and Western Orientalism. Lin cleverly elaborated Mao's supposedly Chinese theory of the dichotomy between the town and the country—a dichotomy that had served a strategic function in the triumph of the Chinese revolution—into a larger context of world revolution, in which the Third World "countryside" was expected to surround and finally overcome the "cities" of the imperialist Western superpowers. Beneath these claims lies a pervasive modern Chinese antiurbanism that, as Maurice Meisner has pointed out, reveals a key element of Maoist thought characterized by "a deep emotional attachment to the rural ideal of 'the unity of living and working'" and a profound distrust of the cities as sites of foreign dominators and their servants, urban intellectuals. Mao presented these notions as products of a specifically Chinese experience, as indigenous insights far removed from Western thought. Yet obviously this supposedly uniquely Chinese Maoist antiurbanism shared "certain similarities with a strain in the Western intellectual tradition, partly derived from Rousseau, which viewed the city as the embodiment of all social evils and moral corruptions, as a monolith threatening to crush the natural purity of the countryside."[4] In this regard Maoist Occidentalism seems dependent on the very Western predecessors with which it disavows any connection. Like its Orientalist counterpart, it seeks to construe its other by asserting a distorted and ultimately anxious image of its own uniqueness. In addition, the apparent aim of this discourse seems, again like its Western counterpart, to be directed toward an imperialist strategy: it is China that will lead the rural Third World to its liberation because it is China, at least in the period since the end of the Second World War, that seems uniquely suited for this task. Yet it must be strongly emphasized that the ultimate aim of this Occidentalist practice was not primarily Chinese hegemony in the Third World but the consolidation of a particular group within domestic politics. It is possible to overemphasize this point, of course. Concerns with domestic politics are seldom absent from the exercise of Western Orientalism. But if we historically compare Western Orientalism with Maoist Occidentalism, it seems clear that the primary aim of the Chinese discourse has been domestic oppression of political opponents rather than world domination, while the inverse has been true in the West. Such a difference, obviously, does not arise out of the moral superiority or even the ultimate political aims of the Chinese practitioners of Occidentalism; after all, China has a history of imperialist longings and practices that is at least as old as its counterparts in the West.

4. Maurice Meisner, *Marxism, Maoism, and Utopianism: Eight Essays* (Madison, Wis., 1982), pp. 98, 100.

Rather this difference reflects the historical moment in which Western imperialism, aided in large measure by its Orientalist discourse, was at or near its apogee and in various ways presented a threat even to the prevailing Chinese political order. In this sense, Chinese Occidentalism is the product of Western Orientalism, even if its aims are largely and specifically Chinese.

This official Occidentalism—Chinese in purpose yet in paradoxical ways dependent on Western ideas—is pervasive in contemporary Chinese culture and life. But Chinese Occidentalism is by no means confined to this official use. Alongside it we can readily find examples of what we might term anti-official Occidentalism, since its purveyors are not the established government or party apparatus but the opponents of those institutions, especially among the intelligentsia. Although impoverished in political power and material wealth, the Chinese intelligentsia has nevertheless always been blessed with knowledge and literacy, qualities that repeatedly have been ingeniously maneuvered into its own practice of power against the "powerful" status quo. Throughout Chinese history, literary and political texts have often been composed by the intelligentsia as deliberate endeavors of anti-official discourse. The ability to write, especially as it enables the production of anti-official agendas, points to an obvious advantage of the urban intellectuals over the peasants, the majority of whom have remained illiterate even in postrevolutionary China. Indeed the very act of public writing is itself a form of anti-official Occidentalism and thus a critique of Mao's anti-urbanism, which, as we have seen, is itself a result of and a reaction to Chinese Orientalism.

Yet the creation of an anti-official Occidentalism by the Chinese intelligentsia is more than a coincidental product of its literacy. It was preconditioned by the parameters of Maoist political discourse, which categorized anything opposed to its political dominance as "Western" or "Westernized." To prevent China from being "Westernized" or "capitalized," for instance, was commonly advanced as the reason for starting the Cultural Revolution and for persecuting numerous intellectuals. In this situation, the adoption of an Occidentalist discourse was a strategic move by dissenting intellectuals. Accused of being "Western" both by virtue of their cultural status and their political sympathies, they had little choice but to assert that the Western Other was in fact superior to the Chinese Self. By thus accepting the inevitable official critique raised against them, whether or not it was "factually" always the case, they strengthened their anti-official status. By suggesting that the West is politically and culturally superior to China, they defended their opposition to established "truths" and institutions. In the process, these urban intellectuals created a form of anti-official Occidentalism that stands in the sharpest contrast to the official Occidentalism pervasive in government and party propaganda in contemporary China.

Nowhere is this anti-official Occidentalism more evident than in the controversial 1988 television series "He Shang" ["River Elegy"]; indeed, as we shall see, the critical debate that this series engendered can serve as an especially revealing example of the character and function of anti-official Occidentalist discourse. "He Shang" was widely noted even in the West for its positive image of a scientific and modern West, indeed for its almost embarrassingly positive evaluation of all things Western. Given this apparent celebration it would be easy—though facile and mistaken—to dismiss the series as an especially overt example of Western "cultural imperialism," as that term is now defined in postcolonial and Third World discourses. Seen from such a limited and mistaken perspective, "He Shang" appears as but another potent example of the ideological power wielded by the West in Said's account of Orientalism. Yet if considered within the cultural and historical context of post-Mao society, "He Shang" can be seen more profitably as a product of anti-official Occidentalism. From this perspective it can be best understood neither as an example of Chinese naivete nor Western imperialism, but as an anti-official discourse that was powerfully and skillfully employed by the Chinese intelligentsia to express what was otherwise politically impossible and ideologically inconceivable.

Before turning to the details of "He Shang," however, it is important to notice that it offers a paradigm for a number of more general and pressing theoretical and political issues, and that it thus has a cross-cultural significance that reaches beyond contemporary China and the authorized and unauthorized discourses associated with it. One difficulty in the ongoing debates concerning Third World and anticolonial discourses is that some critics seem to have interpreted Said's book as asserting that any kind of indigenous cultural appropriation of the Other has necessarily negative effects, being either an act of imperialistic colonialization when performed by the "superior" culture, or one of self-colonialization when carried on by the "inferior" culture in the context of global domination. Such a charge, for example, has recently been brought against Peter Brook's production of the Indian epic *The Mahabharata.* While not in total disagreement with Brook's intertextual reading, which relates *The Mahabharata* to various Shakespearean themes, Gautam Dasgupta believes that "one should not, under cover of universality of theme or character, undercut the intrinsic core of how *The Mahabharata*'s characters function within the world of which they are a part."[5] Here we see a privileging of the "intrinsic core" of an original text and the culture of which it is a part, understood from "the native's point of view," over the alien specificities of a receiving culture that necessitate cross-cultural communications in the first place.

In order to take account of such arguments against cross-cultural

5. Gautam Dasgupta, "*The Mahabharata:* Peter Brook's 'Orientalism,'" *Performing Arts Journal,* no. 30 (1987): 14.

appropriations—that they are demeaning and perpetuate potentially harmful "misconceptions" about the Other—I hope to make clear by this study of "He Shang" that ideas or ideological concepts, whether they stem from a politically dominant or subordinate culture, are never intrinsically oppressive or liberating. Certainly the appropriation of the image of the West, when put into critical use against the domestic hegemony of the ruling ideology, as is the case with "He Shang," can rightly be viewed as positive, liberating, and even desirable. Seen from this perspective, "He Shang" is above all else an anti-official discourse that employs the Occidental Other as a cultural and ideological absence that critiques the oppressive presence of official ideology. Its depiction of the West is not offered as mimesis but as an oppositional and supplementary Other and as a counterdiscourse that seeks to subvert the dominant and official Orientalism and Occidentalism prevalent throughout Chinese culture. Thus the account of "He Shang" that follows argues against the essentializing of any cultural discourse, Western or Eastern, and offers a prime example of how superficially similar sign systems can be manipulated for very different ideological ends.

2

Initially broadcast 11 June 1988, the six-part documentary television series "He Shang" roused perhaps the greatest national sensation in the history of the PRC television industry. Immediately after its premiere, the show's writers received thousands of letters from audiences in all walks of life unanimously expressing their deep gratitude for an excellent TV program and requesting a copy of the script in order to study its "profound messages."[6] As a result, "He Shang" was (unprecedentedly) rebroadcast two months later in prime time and in spite of official efforts to ban it as a vilification of Chinese culture.[7]

One of the "profound messages" of "He Shang," surprisingly, can be found in its total rejection of traditional Chinese cultural fetishes. Contrary to its conventional image as the cradle of the Chinese civilization, the Yellow River is portrayed as a source of poverty and disaster. In fact, it is depicted almost as if it were a willful human being, violent, brutal, tyrannical, periodically sweeping away millions of people and their livelihoods. It seems likely that such an image of the river could not help but remind

6. Wang Dan, "Biyoade bianhu" ["A Necessary Defense"], in *He shang lun* [*About "He Shang"*], ed. Cui Wenhua (Beijing, 1988), p. 205.

7. "He Shang" was produced by Xia Jun, then a twenty-six-year-old television director and journalist. The principal scriptwriters were Su Xiaokang, Wang Luxiang, Zhang Gang, Xie Xuanjun, and Yuan Zhiming. For an insightful summary, analysis, and review in English, see Frederic Wakeman, Jr., "All the Rage in China," *New York Review of Books,* 2 Mar. 1989, pp. 19–21.

many Chinese people of their traumatic experiences during the Cultural Revolution. In the television series, the river is personified as a dying old man, alone and desolate, "stubbornly waiting to die in his devastated homeland," "deserted by God."[8] This characterization certainly defamiliarizes the common presentation of the Yellow River as a revolutionary symbol of national resistance such as we find it, for example, in Xian Xinghai's "The Yellow River Chorus." Composed in 1939 during the Sino-Japanese War, this musical piece has been interpreted as eulogizing the "gigantic image of the Chinese nation, whose glory, diligence, and courageousness are depicted in the battlefields on either side of the Yellow River against Japanese invaders."[9] Its repeated performances at crucial historical moments after the war, such as the one after the arrest of the Gang of Four, preserved its function as an inspiration for the Chinese people's commitment to socialism, especially in hard times. In addition to deviating from this earlier association of the Yellow River with China's revolutionary tradition, "He Shang" also rejected an earlier television depiction of the river in a series of documentary programs in 1988 on Chinese landscapes; here the river was idealized for its "beauty," "grandeur," and its personification of the "resourcefulness" of the motherland.[10]

As if such blasphemy of China's "cultural roots" were not enough, "He Shang" also deconstructs other quintessential national symbols. The dragon and the Yellow Earth are interpreted as representing cynicism, parochialism, conservatism, confinement, and land and ancestry worship in Chinese culture. The Great Wall, China's most famous tourist attraction and historical site, is also singled out for ridicule as a defense mechanism that secluded China from the rest of the world. "If the Great Wall could speak for itself," the narrator in "He Shang" assures us, "it would have honestly told Chinese offspring that it is a huge monument of tragedy constructed by the fate of history," not a symbol of the strength, glory, and enterprising spirit of the Chinese nation.[11] As a kind of culmination, all of the negative aspects of Chinese culture are finally traced to Confucian ideology, whose monolithic social system resists plurality and change. "He Shang" thus concludes that the Yellow Earth and the Yellow River cannot teach contemporary Chinese much about the spirits of science and

8. Su, "Longnian de beicang-guanyu He Shang de zhaji" ["The Sorrow of the Year of the Dragon-Scratches from 'He Shang' on Location"], *Su Xiaokang baogaowenxue jingxuan* [*Memoir on Freedom: Selected Works of Su Xiaokang's Reportage*] (Hong Kong, 1989), p. 270; hereafter abbreviated "S."

9. *Cihai* [*Chinese Encyclopedia*], 1979 ed., s.v. "Huanghe dahechang" ["The Yellow River Chorus"].

10. Examples of these television programs include "Tangfan gudao" ["The Ancient Route to the West in Tang Dynasty"], "Huashuo Changjiang" ["On the Yangtze River"], "Huashuo Yunhe" ["On the Grand Canal"], and "Huanghe" ["The Yellow River"].

11. Su et al., "He Shang" ["River Elegy"], in *About "He Shang,"* p. 24; hereafter abbreviated "HS."

democracy, both of which are necessary for life at the end of the twentieth century. Similarly, these traditional cultural monuments, it is suggested, will not provide the Chinese people with the "nourishment and energy for the invention of a new culture" ("HS," p. 71).

The most critical and adversarial comment that the television series makes about Chinese culture, however, is presented in its very title.[12] The word *he* [river] refers to the Yellow River civilization and, by extension, to other primitive agricultural civilizations such as those in India and Egypt. The word *shang* means "dying before one comes of age." According to Su Xiaokang, one of the principal screenwriters of "He Shang," the term suggests the stagnation of the characteristic Asian mode of production, which "had matured too early, which resulted in an early stagnancy" ("S," p. 273). The word *shang* also suggests a survivor's mourning for the martyrs who had sacrificed their lives for their country, as evidenced in Qu Yuan's (340 B.C.–278 B.C.) poem, "Guo Shang," in his *Elegies of Chu.* Thus *he* and *shang* together "crystallized the ambiguous feelings of Chinese intellectuals"—the more deeply they love their country, the more eagerly they long for its rebirth.[13] Using the elegy of the Yellow River as a central image, "He Shang" "meditates, in all aspects, on the history, civilization, and destiny of the Chinese nation," foregrounding the imperativeness of "economic and political reforms."[14] To the inhabitants of the PRC, who are necessarily accustomed to reading between the lines in a strictly censored media, such statements were clear cries of protest against the current regime, which is fundamentally opposed to political reform.

In addition to unsettling its Chinese viewers with its depictions of a dying and declining Orient, "He Shang" further shocked its audiences with a passionate account of an Occidental Other, which, it suggests, represents youthfulness, adventure, energy, power, technology, and modernity. The West is characterized as an "ocean civilization," "blue," transparent, openly embracing the outside world and "simultaneously transporting the hope of science and democracy" across the oceans ("HS," p. 70). Even the major successes of the West are attributed to its "right" attitude toward the sea. The rise of Athens as a marine power is viewed as having paved the way for "a democratic revolution" "in ancient Greece" ("HS," p. 70). Columbus's discovery of the New World and Magellan's journey in 1519 across the ocean, the program claims, established among other things the foundations for a bourgeois revolution. Even the history of science and technology in the West is closely related to mankind's fate on the ocean. The urgent need for building bigger and better oceangoing

12. See Huo Xiangwen, "Guanyu He Shang timing dawen" ["Reply to a Reader's Letter on the Title of 'He Shang,'" *Renmin ribao* [*People's Daily*], 26 Sept. 1988, p. 8.

13. Ibid.

14. Su, "Huhuan quan minzu fanxing yishi" ["Calling on the Self-reflective Consciousness of the Chinese Nation"], in *About "He Shang,"* p. 1.

ships for world trade and colonialism, for example, "demanded a further development of mathematics, physics, technology, and science." This was the reason why, according to "He Shang," "Galileo published his *Dialogue concerning Two New Sciences* in 1636, which was conducted," not incidentally, "in a ship-yard" ("HS," p. 71).[15]

"He Shang" persistently laments the historical opportunities that, it suggests, the Chinese people had lost, often by failing to heed the "advice" of Western men of letters. While Magellan was sailing across the oceans, "He Shang" notes with regret, the Chinese emperor Jiajing (Ming dynasty) declared a "closed-door" policy after a quarrel with a Japanese official over Japan's "tribute" to China ("HS," p. 71). The Chinese people "did not hear in time" what Adam Smith had to say in 1776 about Chinese culture in his *The Wealth of Nations,* where he declared that Chinese culture "suffered from stagnation as a result of neglecting overseas trade." History, the program declares, has proved correct this Westerner's view that to "close oneself up amounts to suicide" ("HS," p. 71). As another instance of the neglect of salutary components of Western culture, the program alludes to the case of Yan Fu (1853–1921), an important Chinese thinker and translator, who believed that Western notions such as the social contract and the will to power were useful "balance mechanisms" that could fully tap human potential, thus bringing about new forms of culture with vigor and vitality. Yet the conservative resistance to Western ideas was so strong in China that in his old age, Yan Fu was forced to surrender to Confucianism at the very historical moment when Ito Hirobumi (1841–1909), his former Japanese schoolmate in a British naval college, was successfully leading Japan's rapid advance to a position as a world power while serving as the Japanese prime minister ("HS," pp. 72–73).[16] Here, then, a Japanese imperialist, known in Chinese history books to have been responsible for the seizure of Taiwan from China and the imposition of Japanese colonial rule in Korea, is paradoxically presented as a superior and senior Other who is contrasted with an inferior and impoverished Chinese Self. It is worth noting that in "He Shang" this Other is alien even though he would seem to a non-Chinese viewer as Oriental, if not Chinese.

The details cited here are merely representative. "He Shang"

15. I am aware that the actual date for Galileo's *Dialogue concerning Two New Sciences* is 1638. This kind of factual error is typical in "He Shang."

16. A post-Tiananmen massacre article, which accused the "He Shang" writers of taking a "reactionary political attitude," pointed out that when Ito Hirobumi went to England to study naval military technology, Yan Fu was only nine years old; they could not possibly have been schoolmates. Such corrections of factual errors dominate the official critique of "He Shang." Starting on 9 August 1989, the *Beijing Evening Post* [*Beijing wanbao*] ran a special column entitled "The Many Errors in 'He Shang' "; a total of 101 articles appeared in this corrective series. See also " 'He Shang' Is Riddled with Errors," *National Affairs,* 26 Jan. 1990, pp. 25–31.

abounds in problematic images of China and its others, and many of these images are even richer and more complex than the examples I have given here. Indeed "He Shang" amounts to no less than a rewriting of the usual Chinese versions of world history. Included are references to such events in Western history as the rise of the Roman Empire, the British Industrial Revolution, the French Revolution, and the Russian Revolution—almost all of which paint the West in favorable colors. Western thinkers are also approvingly evoked, among them Hegel, Marx, Plekhanov, Francis Bacon, Joseph Needham, and Arnold Toynbee. It seems clear that such an extremely and even one-sidedly favorable treatment of these people and events can only serve to establish a non-Chinese paradigm that can then be employed to critique things Chinese.

Naturally such a presentation drew many outraged cries of disagreement. It was reported, for instance, that "Vice-President Wang Zhen condemned 'He Shang' as a 'vilification' of Chinese culture and barred videotapes of the program from leaving the country."[17] In a literary journal, Chen Zhi-ang also observed that although "He Shang" aimed at "an all-around meditation on Chinese history, civilization, and destiny," as one of its authors, Su Xiaokang, had claimed, it amounted in effect to a meditation on the negative aspects of the Chinese culture, which are set in sharp contrast, whenever possible, with the positive elements of the Western cultures. Quoting Lenin's remarks on the dual possibilities to be found in any cultural heritage, Chen argued that an all-around meditation on any single culture, be it Chinese or Western, must include analysis of both the negative and the positive sides. Only in this way, he claimed, could it become dialectical and hence convincing.

Other academics, of course, focused on factual mistakes in "He Shang." Gao Wangling noted that "He Shang" expressed an "unbalanced view" of Chinese history by "hallucinating" an idealized Western Other. Using outdated "research materials from the fifties to express their sentiments in the eighties," Gao argued, the show's screenwriters created "acts of misunderstanding" in their proclamation of an "oceanic myth," which viewed the lack of a navigational culture as the root of China's stagnation. Yet for a long time, Gao pointed out, navigation in the West was indeed limited within the "small bathtub" of the Mediterranean. Its "cultural expansion" cannot possibly be compared to that of China in the same historical period when the latter reached out to the world on a much larger scale both by sea and by land. Neither is the Yellow Earth a particular

17. See Lai Pui-yee, "Intellectuals Alarmed by Film Series Clampdown," *Morning Post,* 17 Oct. 1988, p. 9.

18. See Chen Zhi-ang, "'He Shang' zhi shang" ["The Elegy of 'He Shang'"], *Wenyi lilun yu piping* [*Theory and Criticism of Literature and Art*] 1 (1989): 54–60, esp. p. 54.

Chinese phenomenon. The West, too, has developed an inland agricultural civilization.[19]

As if to further support Gao's view, Pan Qun observed that in at least two periods in Chinese history—during the early Qin dynasty and again before the Song and Yuan dynasties—China had developed much more advanced navigational enterprises than any country in the West. Zheng He's seven journeys to the West across the Pacific Ocean and Indian Ocean—journeys that began in 1405 and lasted for the next twenty-eight years—were results of the open-door policies of the imperial courts. At least at one time or another, China, too, enjoyed a hegemony over the "blue ocean." The subsequent stagnation of Chinese society, Pan Qun conceded, was brought about by the closed-door policy of the Qing dynasty in a much later period; thus, he claimed, it had nothing to do with an absence of a "blue culture."[20] Commenting further on "He Shang"'s oversimplification of Occidental-blue/Oriental-yellow civilizations, Yan Tao stated that if it were true that the ancient Greeks were a "blue-ocean culture," as "He Shang" claimed, then the medieval millennium certainly had nothing to do with this "blueness." The Middle Ages were indeed much "darker" and more isolated from the rest of the world than was Chinese culture during this period ("N," p. 3). As for the Great Wall as a symbol of China's defensiveness toward the outside world, Ji Ren noted to the contrary that in the Han dynasty, Emperor Wu extended the Great Wall to what is now the Xinjiang Autonomous Region for the sole purpose of protecting the Silk Road, the only trade route between China and what was then known as the Western Region. Thus the Great Wall significantly contributed to cultural and economic exchanges between China and the West. It therefore had nothing to do with China's "cowardice," "parochialism," and "self-isolation" as "He Shang" had claimed.[21]

In all of this it seems clear that "He Shang" created and propagated a misleading image of the alien West, which might well be termed Occidentalism since it provides a politically and culturally motivated image of the cultural Other. This Occidentalist discourse in "He Shang" becomes even more striking when viewed in the context of much current Third World discourse against a claimed Eurocentric Western domination. For example, citing Martin Bernal's argument in *Black Athena* con-

19. Gao Wangling and Wu Xin, "'He Shang' fanying le yizhong shitai xintai" ["'He Shang' Reflects an Unbalanced Cultural Mentality"], in *About "He Shang,"* pp. 186, 181, 181–82.

20. "Nanjing Daxue zhongguo sixiangjia yanjiu zhongxin juxing 'He Shang' zuotanhui" ["Nanjing University's Research Center for Chinese Thinkers Held Seminar on 'He Shang'"], *Guangming ribao* [*Guangming Daily*], 20 Nov. 1988, p. 3; hereafter abbreviated "N."

21. Ji Ren, "Wanli changcheng shi fengbide xiangzheng ma?" ["Is the Great Wall a Symbol of Closed-Door Policy?"], *Renmin ribao,* 15 Aug. 1989, p. 6.

cerning the "fabrication of Ancient Greece," Samir Amin observed that the Western ideology of Eurocentrism was based on cultural, religious, literary, and linguistic reconstructions of a Hellenist myth with a false "annexation of Greece by Europe" from the ancient Orient.[22] Set against such a perspective, "He Shang" seems to voluntarily import such a "Eurocentrism" rather than reject it as much of the Third World seeks to do. At least on first consideration, "He Shang" seems to fortify what Amin calls an "eternal West" (*E*, p. 89) with its repeated claims that a combination of the best cultural heritage of Greek civilization and Western industrialization accounts for the rapid emergence of a modern Europe. Such an image of an "annexed" Athens as the "cultural capital" of Europe (*E*, p. 93) is most typically underscored in "He Shang"'s glorifications of the rise of Hellenism, the conquest of Alexander the Great, the discovery of the New World, and the triumph of colonialism and imperialism. Advocating in the East an Orientalism that Third World intellectuals like Amin consider a distorted view of both the East and the West, "He Shang" can be seen as an Oriental fabrication of the Occidental Other whose centrality is ultimately celebrated in a historical "progression from Ancient Greece to Rome to feudal Christian Europe to capitalist Europe—one of the most popular of received ideas" in the West (*E*, pp. 89–90).

Moreover, "He Shang"'s sympathetic portrayal of the Italian missionary Matteo Ricci—the first Westerner who brought scientific works to the Chinese and "informed them that they did not live in the center of the world, but live somewhere in the Northern Hemisphere"—can be seen as a Chinese postcolonial affirmation of an earlier act of European cultural imperialism. This is indeed a shocking departure from what conventionally has been taught in standard Chinese history books on the imperialist nature of Western missionary activities, which are usually described as being conducted hand in glove with Western military aggression. It is thus not surprising that "He Shang" mentions only in passing the humiliating Opium War, which resulted in a series of treaties and agreements—and the 1842 Treaty of Nanjing in particular—by which China was forced to pay an indemnity of $21 million to cede Hong Kong and to open Guangzhou, Fuzhou, Xiamen, Ningpo, and Shanghai to foreign trade with most-favored-nation treatment.[23] Furthermore, the claims that the Yellow River and the Great Wall symbolize an "inward-looking," agricultural society seem to inflict a Western "geographic racism" that, following the failure of "genetic racism," still attempts to explain an underdevel-

22. Samir Amin, *Eurocentrism*, trans. Russell Moore (New York, 1989), p. 93; hereafter abbreviated *E*. See also Martin Bernal, *Black Athena: The Afroasiatic Roots of Classical Civilization*, vol. 1 of *The Fabrication of Ancient Greece, 1785–1985* (New Brunswick, N.J., 1987).

23. For a classic account of imperialism and a standard textbook used in Chinese universities, see Hu Sheng, *Imperialism and Chinese Politics*, trans. Foreign Languages Press (Beijing, 1955).

oped and conquered Orient by locating "acquired and transmissible traits produced by the geographic milieu" without any "scientific value whatsoever" (*E,* p. 96).

A comparison of "He Shang" with such a Third World critique of it points to a number of striking paradoxes between Amin's rather typical anti-Eurocentrism and "He Shang"'s Occidentalism. Whereas Amin criticizes the West for regarding itself as "Promethean *par excellence,* in contrast with other civilizations" (*E,* p. 99), "He Shang" laments over the profound tragedy of the Chinese literati, who failed to bring into China "the spirit of Prometheus and Faustus" ("HS," p. 72). Moreover, Amin would indeed be surprised to learn that "He Shang" did not depreciate the image of China alone; it sounds like an elegiac criticism of Oriental traditions as a whole. Recalling Marx's theory of an Asian mode of production, "He Shang" claims that although in ancient Semitic languages *Asian* means "the region where the sun rises," five thousand years later the "Asian sun" has finally set—the ancient civilizations in the Orient have declined one after another for the simple reason that they have depended too heavily, and for too long, on an agricultural mode of production.

Perhaps the greatest paradox to be found in "He Shang" concerns its "misreadings" of Arnold Toynbee, whose early theory of challenge and response is cited as if it were uttered by a universally acknowledged great authority. Quoting Toynbee's view that the hostile physical surroundings along the lower Yellow River valley engendered Chinese civilization, "He Shang" calls on the Chinese people to confront the hard facts of history, which, according to Toynbee's *A Study of History,* chronicle the extinction of fourteen civilizations and the decline of six, including those of the Euphrates, the Nile, and the Yellow River. The critics of "He Shang" were, not surprisingly, quick to point out that this early theory was already considered passé in Western scholarship and that Toynbee himself had corrected these views in the 1970s: he no longer assumed that Chinese civilization was isolated and backward, but argued instead that China's "Ecumenical spirit" will play a major role in shaping the future of the world.[24] Indeed, in *The Toynbee-Ikeda Dialogue,* Toynbee completely turned around the "success story" of the West—which the "He Shang" screenwriters borrowed from his early works—a West that in the late seventies he saw disintegrating. Toynbee's prediction that "the future unifier of the world will not be a Western or Westernized country but will be China" is obviously unheard—or deliberately ignored—by his Chinese disciples, who wished to eradicate from Chinese society those

24. "He Shang weixin zhuyi lishiguan pouxi: Shoudu bufen shixue gongzuozhe pipan He Shang jiyao" ["On a Metaphysical View of History in 'He Shang': Minutes of a Critique of 'He Shang' by Some Historians in Beijing"], ed. Dong Yue and Liu Jun, *Renmin ribao,* 23 Oct. 1989, p. 6.

very qualifications to which Toynbee had appealed as a "better" model in the West.[25]

Yet perhaps Toynbee and the "He Shang" screenwriters have yet other things in common as well. Just as Toynbee sought to write a philosophy of history that sometimes plays a bit freely with historical facts, so did the "He Shang" screenwriters, who sought a political statement that was not intended to be accurate about the historical events it reported. Both Toynbee and the "He Shang" writers were seeking a macrohistorical model in order to come to terms with a teleology of their contemporary societies, be it in the East after the chaotic Cultural Revolution or in the West after the disastrous world war. Indeed, "He Shang" was never meant to be a scholarly essay. As Yuan Zhiming, one of the screenwriters, has rightly said, "'He Shang' can never be qualified as an academic work; it did not even claim to address specific issues either in history or in contemporary society."[26] Thus "He Shang" might be regarded more profitably as a poetic text rather than a historical one, a text that expresses a younger generation's mythic vision of the world. It is also a political text that reflects Chinese intellectuals' own vision of "truth" and "knowledge." Or, seen from yet another angle, the "He Shang" screenwriters *did* attempt to be accurate, but in the production of their program they singled out only those historical facts and data that supported their thesis. In the final analysis, whether these "facts" are accurate is not ultimately important. What is important is their critical use.

Indeed the debate on whether "He Shang" is a "historical" or a "literary" text is quite beside the point. "He Shang" cleverly interweaves two levels of discourse—the factual and the symbolic. By appealing to historical "facts"—which its writers selected and emphasized in order to support the polemical thrust of their documentary—"He Shang" proceeds as if it were based on solid factual data and is hence empirically rather than merely rhetorically convincing. Yet these "hard facts" were, to a great extent, manipulated in order to appeal to the emotions of the contemporary Chinese audience against the ruling ideology. Thus from its very outset, the critique of "He Shang" was problematic since it is predicated on a fundamental confusion about genre. If "He Shang" were considered as literature, its detractors were mistaken in their critique of its nonfactuality; if it were treated as history, however, one could not account for the appeal of its rhetorical and symbolic dimension, which disqualifies it as history. Indeed, "He Shang" struck a chord in the national sensibility by glossing over the jump from the factual to the symbolic. It was the rhetorical power and emotional appeal of "He Shang" that encouraged its willing audiences

25. Arnold J. Toynbee and Daisaku Ikeda, *The Toynbee-Ikeda Dialogue: Man Himself Must Choose* (Tokyo, 1976), p. 233.

26. Yuan Zhiming, "He Shang yu gaoji laosao" ["'He Shang' and the So-Called Sophisticated Complaint"], *Guangming ribao*, 18 Aug. 1988, p. 3.

to overlook the missing links and fill in the gaps between the historical and the symbolic with their own imagination, a faculty that at the moment "He Shang" was aired was dominated by its strong predisposition against the official ideology. There was no real engagement in the debate about the factuality in "He Shang"—both its writers and supporters admitted that it would not pass muster as history. What was at stake was the ideological thrust of the series, which was both more and less than history. The rhetorical force of "He Shang," therefore, lies in the intricate interplay between history, poetry, and politics, having to do, for the most part, with the symbolic rather than with the factual. To single out any one of its three dimensions for critique is to miss the better part of the picture.

This characterization can perhaps explain the reason why, in spite of its expressed Occidentalism accompanied by "self-degradation," "He Shang"—a seemingly "colonialist" television series with otherwise dry facts, figures, and philosophical and political jargon, and without any sexual or violent content—could touch millions of Chinese from all walks of life. In fact, as Gong Suyi has observed, there emerged in the China of 1988 a "'He Shang' phenomenon" in which philosophers and scholars "walked out of their studies and salons to initiate a dialogue on television screens with a national audience" concerning China's past, present, and future. "He Shang" was thus hailed as a successful combination of both popular-cultural media and "elite," "scholarly" discourse. It is interesting to note here that the image of the West is so predominant and paradoxical in contemporary China that even in the act of appreciating a heavily Eurocentric "He Shang," the Chinese critics did not forget to mention the difference between China and the West in "television culture" "as products of various historical conditions. . . . We should therefore not blindly accept the Western concept that sees television as popular culture; under the specific circumstances in China, an elite cultural discourse [such as "He Shang"] can become the soul of television." Popular culture thus means the "popularity of a particular work among the ordinary people."[27] One finds in this remark an example of a deeply rooted practice of alluding to the Occident as a contrasting Other in order to define whatever one believes to be distinctively "Chinese."

The favorable reception of "He Shang" can be seen from yet another angle. Immediately after its premiere, "He Shang" became so popular that many prestigious newspapers competed with one another in publishing the narrative script. Furthermore, viewers and readers hand-copied and circulated the script among themselves. These actions significantly transformed "He Shang" from a media event into a literary text, and an

27. Gong Suyi, "Shoudu bufen zhuanjia xuezhe zuotan: Cong He Shang xianxiang kan dianshi wenhua jianshe" ["Experts and Scholars in Beijing Discussing 'He Shang': From the 'He Shang' Phenomenon to a Construction of Television Culture"], *Guangming ribao,* 16 Aug. 1988, p. 1.

exceedingly popular text at that. Especially worth noting is its warm reception among high school students, usually a disillusioned generation that in recent years has shown little interest in the fate of their country. A high school student reported to the "He Shang" writers that her graduating class sacrificed their "precious" preparation hours for college entrance examinations in order to study the "He Shang" script together in class. "When our teacher read aloud the passage in which the Great Wall is depicted as a huge monument of national tragedy, we all applauded with excitement!" ("S," p. 284). A senior high school student from a poor Henan village told the "He Shang" writers that since television sets are still a luxury item in some remote country locations he had to walk a long distance, twice a week, in order to watch every single part of the series in another village ("S," p. 284). High school students were by no means the only group that received "He Shang" with excitement and fervor. Even the elder generation took it personally and seriously. An old "revolutionary," who fought in the war at the age of sixteen, lost sleep after watching "He Shang," pondering over the meaning of her "glorious" life stories—"How many of them were indeed mistakes?" "How would later generations evaluate my revolutionary career?"[28] It seems clear that to a large extent the success of "He Shang" can be attributed to its fundamental challenge of Chinese conventional value systems and worldview.

Such an outlet of anti-official sentiments among the Chinese people inevitably drew automatic defenses from China's "revolutionary tradition" by those who saw the message of "He Shang" as representing "anti-Marxist" and "counterrevolutionary political programs."[29] Others were disturbed by the fact that the "sacred" places along the Yellow River, such as Yenan, where Mao Tse-tung rallied his revolutionary forces in the thirties, were dismissed and even profaned as poverty stricken. Confronted with such criticism, Su Xiaokang explained that while on location, his crews did go to "pay their respects" to the "revolutionary relics" in Yenan. The "white-washed, tidy, and well-kept" cave dwellings of the party leaders in the thirties did arouse in them a sense of admiration. Yet when looking closer at the names in front of each cave dwelling, Su recalls, their hearts "saddened at once when ruminating on the tragic endings of, or the relationships between," most of the former revolutionary leaders, "such as Mao Tse-tung, Zhang Wentian, Liu Shaoqi, Zhou Enlai, Zhu De, and Ren Bishi." As a result, Su and his crews left with heavy hearts "without shooting a single scene" in Yenan, the so-called cradle and beacon of the Chinese revolution ("S," p. 276).

At their next stop in Kaifeng in Henan province, Su tells us, his crews went straight to the small, dark room in a tightly secured bank office

28. Xiu Xinmin expressed her afterthoughts on "He Shang" in a letter to the director of the Central Television Station, 19 June 1988, in *About "He Shang,"* pp. 113–14.

29. "On a Metaphysical View of History in 'He Shang,'" p. 6.

where Liu Shaoqi, the first president of the People's Republic, was detained for the twenty-eight days before his tragic death during the Cultural Revolution. It was Liu who supervised the implementation of the first constitution of the People's Republic in 1955. Yet, as Su has rightly pointed out, as an architect of PRC legislation, Liu could not even protect his own rights as a citizen, let alone those of the president of the Republic, who was, ironically, elected by the Chinese people according to the letter and spirit of their constitution. Liu was persecuted without any trial or legal procedure. He died in that desolate room, alone and in agony, Su emphasizes, adding the detail that his unattended white hair was reported to be more than a foot long.

Su could not help but compare this "horror room" with Liu's "honorable" room in Yenan. He perceived in them a historical connection and the inevitable tragedy of not just one individual but of "the entire generation of Chinese communists." For Su and his crews, the "sacred" places along the Yellow River region could not teach them about the "gigantic revolutionary spirit," nor could it inspire in them a sense of national pride and grandeur. It merely offered them a vivid lesson on ignorance, self-deception, and autocracy. It is high time, Su insists, that we open our eyes to the outside world and stop considering China as still "number one." It is high time that we catch up. For him, this is perhaps one of the most important messages in the entire Occidental discourse of the "He Shang" series.

Such a remark seems to offer a perspective from which we can begin to make sense of the "He Shang" phenomenon. Whatever else it might be, "He Shang" is without a doubt an expression of an anti-official discourse prevalent in China at the end of the 1980s, which painted the Occident as an oppositional and supplementary Other. Clearly such a discourse served above all as a counterdiscourse that aimed at subverting the ruling and official ideology. Thus the majority of the audience did not care whether the historical facts were "correct." They read into the contrasting Other a hope for remodeling and rescuing their own country and their own selves. Realizing this can help explain why even academics, who had earlier questioned the scholarly soundness of "He Shang," began to defend it politically after party tyrants such as Wang Zhen threatened to denounce it as "counterrevolutionary." The critical point that seemed to have been driven home among the critics and viewers was that it is not the Chinese people who are ultimately depicted as inferior to their Western counterparts. The "inferior" China presented in the program is part of a strategy for exposing the inferiority of a monologic, one-party system. The depiction in "He Shang" of a problematic cultural past and a progressive Occidental Other are merely pretexts to debunk current official ideology.

3

This observation is central for any understanding of "He Shang," but it also needs to be set in a broader framework. To Westerners unfamiliar with the history of twentieth-century China, "He Shang"'s Occidentalism may seem striking and innovative. Perhaps to a certain degree it is. But it is important to recognize that Occidentalism has frequently been employed by the ruling classes in modern China for their own political agendas. No one can dismiss the undeniable fact, for instance, that ever since the founding of the PRC, both Mao Tse-tung and Deng Xiaoping have "successfully" used anti-imperialist discourse to stunt anti-official voices at home. During the Cultural Revolution, even Mao's former comrades-in-arms were persecuted as *di-te-pan*—enemies, spies, and traitors—who allegedly aligned themselves with Western powers and their nationalist followers; such an association with the West was even more strongly—and fictionally—created for those dissidents who openly challenged Mao's ideology. Liu Shaoqi was publicly humiliated during the Cultural Revolution for his pro-Western and procapitalist stance, and his wife, Wang Guangmei, was accused of adopting a Western, and hence rotten, life-style. One should not, of course, idealize Liu, one of the top party leaders up to 1966, who was also deeply involved in the policy formation concerning China's involvement in the Korean War and other anti-Western movements. Yet the very fact that even an anti-Western president of the PRC was accused of being pro-Western, and hence counter-Marxist and counterrevolutionary, demonstrates the powerful role that Occidentalism plays in the political drama of contemporary China.

The same is true even for Deng Xiaoping, who was himself removed more than once from the top party apparatus for the sole "crime" of introducing Western technology. It thus seemed natural for Deng to use his own brand of Occidentalism at the beginning of the post-Mao years to attack Mao's Cultural Revolution, his political purges, and his closed-door policies. Yet it is ironic to note that in January 1979, when Deng was visiting the United States as the first major party leader to do so in thirty years—performing his "epoch-making," pro-Western drama—he had already started in China a large-scale government crackdown on the Democratic Wall movement, just as soon as his own political power was secured after Mao's death. Wei Jingsheng, the movement's leader, was sentenced to fifteen years in prison for his alleged spying activities—for providing information on the Sino-Vietnamese War to a Western journalist.

Likewise, the official reason for the 1989 Tiananmen student massacre, announced by Deng Xiaoping himself, was that it was a "counterrevolutionary rebellion" that was caused, not incidentally, by "an international and domestic climate" in an attempt to "overthrow the Communist Party and socialist system" and to "establish a bourgeois republic entirely dependent on the West."[30] The ensuing event, in which Fang Lizhi took refuge in the U.S. embassy, was manipulated to further testify to the official view that the student movement was indeed plotted by a "traitor" who ran into the open arms of American imperialists. Seen from these political and ideological perspectives, such events enable one to argue that it is this "Western devil" and its professed ideology—although seriously and justly critiqued by its own people in the West—that has paradoxically kept alive a myth of democracy and human rights in post-Mao China. Indeed, Deng himself is a master in annexing the Occident: he wants only Western science and technology for his economic reform, while wholly rejecting Western political and legal systems. Such contradictions inevitably led to the Tiananmen massacre, which signifies, among other things, the end of Deng's pro-Western era and the beginning of a closed-door policy once again.

In view of the domestic politics in Dengist China, it is important to point out that it was almost accidental that a polemical treatise such as "He Shang" could be allowed even a short life. Cui Wenhua has explained the accidental appearance of "He Shang" within the limitations of a strict censorship system. According to Cui, both Chen Hanyuan, the deputy director of the Central Television Station, and Wang Feng, the vice minister of broadcasting, cinema, and television, could have vetoed any film or television show at any point by simply questioning its "political healthiness." Yet, to everyone's surprise, they both minimized their power "as the ultimate censor" and did not even suggest any changes for the script. Had either one of them chosen to play his "proper" role as the "representative of the Ideological State Apparatus"—whose job is to "purify" and unify people's way of thinking—"we would probably have never seen 'He Shang'" at all. Its appearance, Cui argued forcefully, does not testify to the soundness of the Chinese television industry; it illustrates, rather, how a few people's "free will" could have instantly killed numerous movies and television programs in spite of the fact that they were the products of many people's talents and hard labor.[31] In addition to the fact that a controversial program like "He Shang" was inevitably in constant political danger in the PRC's highly centralized and tightly controlled media, it is also true, in my view, that all key persons involved in the "He Shang" affair may well have had accounts to settle with the ruling ideology. It is at least possible that the ministers may have deliberately looked the other way because they, too, for a variety of possible motives, wanted this counterdiscourse to appear. At any rate, their neglect of duty testifies to the popularity of the provoca-

30. Deng Xiaoping, speech at reception for army commanders of Beijing troops carrying out martial law, in *Renmin ribao,* 28 July 1989, p. 1.

31. Cui, "He Shang dui zhongguo dianshide qishi hezai?" ["What Does 'He Shang' Tell Us about Chinese Television?"], in *About "He Shang,"* p. 133.

tive "He Shang," which to a large extent represented the anti-official sentiments that culminated in the student movement of the following year.

The "accidental" appearance of "He Shang" can also be better comprehended when placed in the context of the power struggle within the Communist party: without the support of Zhao Ziyang, then the Communist party secretary, "He Shang" would have been severely criticized for its pro-Western, antisocialist, and anti-Party stance, even after seeing the light of day, as has often happened to many films and literary works after 1949. The importance of Zhao's support was underscored in an official Chinese report after he was ousted as a scapegoat for the Tiananmen students' protest of 1989. Jin Ren points out, for example, that soon after its appearance, Zhao encouraged his "elite-cultural activists" to write positive and even "flattering" reviews despite the fact that some academics questioned the soundness of its scholarship. Zhao even asked that five hundred videotape copies of the program be distributed around the country. In late September 1988, as General Party Secretary, Zhao ignored Wang Zhen's request that "He Shang" be criticized for its antisocialist content during the third plenary session of the Thirteenth Congress of the CCP Central Committee.[32] Although Jin's account can be seen as part of another political campaign against Zhao and hence highly questionable in its cited "facts," it at least tells us how polemical a role "He Shang"—or any other work of literature or art—can play in the political dramas of the PRC—and that "He Shang" was part of that polemical drama is beyond doubt.

To a large extent, then, the screenwriters' initial anti-official efforts to interfere with everyday reality were subsequently used by reformist Party officials like Zhao to discredit his conservative opponents within the Chinese Communist party. This was an accidental—but crucial—circumstance that allowed "He Shang" a temporary but highly political life. The very act of attempting to transform the ideological state apparatus was nevertheless appropriated by a different faction within the ruling ideology for consolidating its own power. Seen in this light, the anti-official Occidentalism of the program was in turn manipulated by the ruling clique itself, which, as in the case of Zhao, collaborated with the anti-official Occidentalism in order to achieve its own practical goals in Party politics. It was to be expected, therefore, that "He Shang" became an immediate target for another political campaign against "cultural imperialism" in post-1989 China, a campaign that accused writers, producers, and supporters of "He Shang" of being pro-Western and hence anti-Chinese-"nationalistic."

At this point I must finally address the issue of nationalism, a confus-

32. Jin Ren, "Zhao Ziyang tongzhi de jierushuo he He Shang de 'xinjiyuan'" ["Comrade Zhao Ziyang's Theory of 'Interference' and 'He Shang''s 'New Epoch'"], *Renmin ribao,* 15 Aug. 1989, p. 4.

ing term that frequently surfaced in the "He Shang" debates. "He Shang" was on many occasions criticized for its "cultural nihilism" and its lack of the patriotism that is said to have stimulated masterpieces of literature and art in the past, inspiring many people to sacrifice their lives for the dignity and integrity of the motherland. Chinese-American Nobelist T. D. Lee, for example, warned the "He Shang" writers that "a nation that depends entirely on its past has no future; neither does it have any future if it totally rejects its own ancestors."[33] Its defenders argued, on the contrary, that "He Shang" expresses a deeper and more profound nationalism, the very strength of which lies in the rejection of the negative elements of a cultural tradition in order to better preserve that tradition ("N," p. 3).

It is interesting to note that both sides cling firmly to the notions of nation, nationness, and nationhood, as if they were politically and ideologically neutral terms. According to Benedict Anderson's celebrated study of nationalism, however, such notions are nothing but "cultural artefacts of a particular kind" that are "capable of being transplanted, with varying degrees of self-consciousness, to a great variety of social terrains, to merge and be merged with a correspondingly wide variety of political and ideological constellations." Seen from this perspective, much of the political and intellectual history of modern China appears as the result of deliberate maneuverings of what Anderson terms an "official nationalism" that combines "naturalization with retention of dynastic power" in order to stretch "the short, tight, skin of nation over the gigantic body of the empire."[34] The deceptive power of such "official nationalism" was particularly telling in the civil war between the Chinese Communist party and the Kuomingdang nationalists, in which both sides claimed to be "patriots," thus "inspiring" millions of supporters from each camp to give up their lives for their diametrically opposed "glorious causes." It is this same kind of "official nationalism," with only slight variations in form, that justified China's territorial disputes and military clashes with India, the Soviet Union, and Vietnam, and for the numerous political campaigns against pro-Western "counterrevolutionaries" and "foreign spies" in various ideological movements of the PRC "dynasty." Joseph Levenson was thus insightful when he remarked twenty years ago that in the PRC, "class-struggle provided the motor: Marxism, especially Leninist anti-imperialism, would implement Chinese nationalism. Marxist and national fervour seemed to reinforce each other."[35]

33. T. D. Lee, "Du He Shang yougan" ["Afterthought on 'He Shang'"], *Renmin ribao,* 4 Nov. 1988, p. 3.

34. Benedict Anderson, *Imagined Communities: Reflections on the Origin and Spread of Nationalism* (New York, 1983), pp. 13–14, 82.

35. Joseph R. Levenson, "The Past and Future of Nationalism in China," *Modern China: An Interpretive Anthology* (London, 1971), p. 9.

The most intriguing "official nationalism" of its kind—since it has a strong appeal among the Chinese people even today—finds its expression in the military and religious suppression of "national minorities" such as Tibetans, Uighurs, and Mongolians, with the justification of "national territorial integrity." This is an example of what I call national-cultural imperialism by which a Third World country such as China can legitimate and exercise its own central, imperial hegemony over regional or ethnic groups in all spheres. Seen from this perspective, then, attacks on "He Shang" can be viewed as yet another ideological posture in which the official claim to Chinese nationalism protects the vested interests of the conservative ruling group. Thus the so-called antinationalism of "He Shang" can be "a means of self-definition" against the status quo in the guise of Occidentalism.[36] Its use of Occidentalism is thus a self-conscious subversion of the centrality of the official culture by moving into the very center of its own discourse a redefined and re-presented Western Other. Ironically, this is the same Other that, in the culture of its origin, has used Orientalism to enlarge its own cultural space, as Edward Said has so forcefully pointed out. Yet, as I hope this essay has made clear, it would be a serious mistake to claim that a native self-understanding is by nature more liberating or "truer" than the view of it constructed by its Other. And it would be equally misleading to argue that Occidentalist discourse is less tied to power relationships and strategies of domination than its Orientalist counterpart. As Michel Foucault has forcefully taught us, no discursive practice is ever free from a will to power.[37]

It is from this perspective that we can finally address the issue of hegemony and its relationship to Orientalist or Occidentalist discourse. On the one hand, it is crucial to analyze the function of an imperialist discourse such as Orientalism that imposes on the colonial Other an economic and political hegemony. On the other hand, such a hegemony in

36. In a different context, Nasrin Rahimieh explores how the coming to terms with the Occident on the part of Egyptian, Palestinian, Iranian, Iraqi, North African, Turkish, and Indian Writers "can be a means to self-definition" (Nasrin Rahimieh, "Responses to Orientalism in Modern Eastern Fiction and Scholarship," *Dissertations Abstract International* 49/05A, University of Alberta, 1988).

37. One way in which Orientalist discourse has been exploited for power relationships and strategies of exclusion has been studied by John Wixted. Raising a cry of "reverse orientalism," Wixted challenges "a fundamental view" of ethnically Oriental scholars toward Western scholars—that only "we the Chinese" or "we the Japanese" can understand Chinese or Japanese culture and people. Wixted considers these attitudes expressions of "culturalism, nationalism, and a kind of 'ethnic racism.'" He argues that although Said specifically disclaims "the view that only Blacks can talk with validity about Blacks, only women can talk with authority about women, etc.," Said nevertheless "feels that what Palestinians have to say about Palestine, or Muslims about Islam, has a special, even privileged validity. I think there is an element of having-your-cake-and-eating-it-too in [Said's] own praxis" (John Timothy Wixted, "Reverse Orientalism," *Sino-Japanese Studies* 2 [Dec. 1989]: 19, 23).

the international arena, when situated in different cultural and historical circumstances, may also subvert a domestic hegemony within a particular culture. Thus Orientalism and Occidentalism must be seen as signifying practices that have no permanent or essential content. Given their socioeconomic and political status in relationship to the West, Third World countries have rightly decried their Western Other in Occidentalist discourse. But Third World countries have an equal right to employ discourses of Occidentalism for contrary purposes, to use, misuse, present, re-present, distort, and restore the Western Other, exploiting it as a counterstructure against the monolithic order of things at home. Thus a so-called Third World discourse, although historically significant in the international arena in a postcolonial age, can be reduced to or appropriated as a domestic imperialist discourse for the ulterior motive of maintaining an imperial dynasty at home. It is thus one-sided to claim that misconceptions of the Other, such as Orientalism or Occidentalism, are necessarily imperialistic acts. It is the use to which they are put by those who articulate them, and by those who hear and receive them, that determines their social—and literary—effects.

The claim against imperialistic discourse can thus go both ways: if it is imperialistic for the Occident to "misrepresent" the Orient, then the Orient can also anti-imperialistically use the Occident to achieve its own political aims at home. It is by such a political end that the "He Shang" screenwriters could justify the anti-imperialistic means with which they ingeniously fragmented and pluralized the official culture in their very invention of a West. In this case, both Orientalism and Occidentalism of whatever form never refer to a "thing in itself," but to a power relationship. Whether this projection into the Other is a positive or negative one depends, of course, on the problematic and often paradoxical social, political, and economic conditions in the indigenous culture in question—and on one's own place in structures of power. Indeed, if Trinh Minh-ha is correct in observing that in the twentieth century "the West is painfully made to realize the existence of a Third World in the First World," we can say by the same token that there also exists a First World whose master-slave relationship with its own people is being fundamentally challenged by a Third World discourse against the predominant ruling ideology within a Third World country itself.[38] Seen in this light, both Third World and First World need to learn to stop feeling privileged as the Other. Only in this way can either world even hope for a corrective and critical movement in which neither a Western vision nor a non-Western vision is ultimately exempted from its own historical conditions.

Having thus argued for the politically positive implications of Occidentalism in contemporary Chinese life, however, it seems salutary—

38. Trinh T. Minh-ha, *Woman, Native, Other: Writing Postcoloniality and Feminism* (Bloomington, Ind., 1989), p. 98.

and necessary—to offer as a coda a brief consideration of the potential danger of such a discourse. I hope I have made it clear by now that "He Shang" does not celebrate the geographical West as a kind of timeless and present historical reality. It is rather the West's value systems, imagined and fictionalized, that are used to create a cultural message put forth in opposition to the official Chinese Other. Yet to foresee the future of China, one has to raise the question of what happens after the domestic hegemony is overthrown. Will China then incorporate the West with its values and systems, ultimately and inevitably to be culturally overwhelmed by it? Were this to happen, it would likely result in the repetition of the unsuccessful history of the May Fourth movement with its attempt to modernize China according to Western models. Certainly there is a danger in the present Chinese fascination and even appropriation of things Western, an appropriation that, in spite of its usefulness as a discourse of antidomestic hegemony at the moment, seems destined to mislead the Chinese public at large.

To recognize this is to admit that both official and anti-official Occidentalism have one thing in common: a teleological worldview and a unilinear and universal historiography. Indeed, one might argue that the only fundamental difference between them has to do with the ends of history. Influenced by bourgeois liberalism, Su Xiaokang and other "He Shang" writers identified capitalism as the alternative future of China, while Maoists and Dengists who still cling to the ideological standpoint of classical Marxism view communism as China's destiny. It is only by reason of the positive value judgment assigned to the West for the purpose of establishing an anti-official discourse that we are able to say that "He Shang"'s essentialization of the West is qualitatively different from that of its official opposite. For it remains unavoidably and painfully true that once it is cast under the spell of a West invented by anti-official Occidentalism, the Chinese public will be seriously disillusioned when in some inescapable moment it discovers the "real" West, an illiberal and inequitable world severely criticized by its own people. To a large extent, "He Shang" can be seen as building up expectations for utopia, even in the very act of acknowledging that what it has presented is and can only be a utopia in the etymological sense of that word. Thus, the anti-official movement of "He Shang," like every human utterance caught within the prison house of language, contains the seeds of its own destruction and has from the very moment of its outset. Once the short-term purpose of antidomestic hegemony is achieved, its very success will produce a new obstacle.

Furthermore, in the context of cross-cultural politics, one has to stress the fact that the critical position of Occidentalism is taken by the "He Shang" writers with a high cost: the willing acceptance of Euro-American ideological hegemony and of all its premises of Orientalism concerning the Third World and Europe. The very existence of a Chinese

Occidentalism seems tacitly to have admitted that "the Third World is incapable of presenting an independent critique of the past and the West, which puts us within the iron cage of modern Western dominance."[39] Seen from this perspective, Taiwanese journalist Yin Yunpeng is correct in pointing to the irony of the situation in which "He Shang" affirms an "ocean-culture" in order to catch up with the Western world at the very moment when Western scholars have proposed to draw lessons from the economic successes of the "four Asian dragons"—Taiwan, South Korea, Singapore, and Hong Kong—whose economic miracles testify to the potential of Confucianism to offer a new model for an affluent society.[40] The theory and practice of the human sciences in recent times—both in their more historical and more formalist phases—have taught us that such dialectical swings are not only to be expected, but are unavoidable. But if such reflections are to affect in a positive way the life of all of us enmeshed in the real and the historical—as well as the imagined and imaginary—conditions of the present and the future, it seems imperative that we at least attempt to find a reasonable balance between Self and Other, between East and West, so that no culture is fundamentally privileged over its Others. Perhaps the realities of history cannot allow such a balance to be fully realized. Indeed, it is even necessary to affirm that these master tropes are necessarily veiled by the fictional. What must be stressed here is that even imagining such a balance—surely one of the first requirements of a new order of things—can never be possible without each Self being confronted by an Other, or by the Other being approached from the point of view of the Self in its own specific historical and cultural conditions.

39. Quoted from Arif Dirlik's comments on an earlier version of this essay.

40. Yin Yunpeng, "Jingji kaifang bushi wanglingyao" ["Economic Reform Is Not an Elixir"], in *Haiwai He Shang da taolun* [*Overseas Debates on "He Shang"*] (Haerbin, 1988), p. 49.

Fashion and the Homospectatorial Look

Diana Fuss

Women's fashion photography, and the industries of mass clothing production and commercial advertising it supports, all presume and indeed participate in the construction of a heterosexual viewing subject. This "photographic contract," like the "cinematic contract,"[1] appears to operate as a cultural mechanism for producing and securing a female subject who desires to be desired by men—the ideal, fully oedipalized, heterosexual woman. Playing on the considerable social significance attributed to a woman's value on the heterosexual marketplace, women's fashion photography scopophilically poses its models as sexually irresistible subjects, inviting its female viewers to consume the product by (over)identifying with the image. But this "concealed" ideological project—to fashion female viewers into properly heterosexualized women—stands in direct tension with (and appears to work against) its own surface formalist structure and mode of address, which together present eroticized images of the female body for the explicit appreciation and consumption by a female audience. In fact, the entire fashion industry operates as one of the few institutionalized spaces where women can look at other women with cultural impunity. It provides a socially sanctioned structure in which women are encouraged to *consume*, in voyeuristic if not vampiristic fashion, the images of other women, frequently represented in classically exhibitionist

1. The contractual metaphor is Teresa de Lauretis's; see her *Technologies of Gender: Essays on Theory, Film, and Fiction* (Bloomington, Ind., 1987), p. 105.

This article originally appeared in *Critical Inquiry* 18 (Summer 1992).

and sexually provocative poses. To look straight *at* women, it appears, straight women must look *as* lesbians.

Sometimes the exhibitionism is coy, as in the ad for "knockout knits" (fig. 1) in which the model playfully clutches the bottom hem of her knitted dress, ostensibly concealing and protecting the triangular zone of the genital area from the viewer's intrusive gaze, but, in so doing, drawing our attention more irresistibly to it. The genital zone (for Freud, of course, the infamous biologistic site of women's talent for "plaiting and weaving") is not occluded so much as framed, given shape, and magnified by the inverted triangle of the model's arms, the V-shape of her cleavage, and the curve of her own body. Other typical shots in women's fashion photography are even more explicitly erotic, presenting to the female spectator an image typically found in straight male pornography: the image of an all too receptive, quite nearly orgasmic woman waiting to be taken by more than a camera (fig. 2). Even the covers of magazines like *Vogue, Elle, Glamour,* or in this case *Cosmopolitan,*[2] could be mistaken for the covers of some skin magazines commercially produced and marketed for consumption by heterosexual men were it not for the teasers running down the side that tell us that the image of this woman is intended to function for its female audience not as an object of desire but rather a point of identification.

2. Since desire and the structures of fantasy, not to mention the very formations of subjectivity, change and transmogrify under the weight of historical pressures, I will further limit the focus of this essay to the fashion codes of late twentieth-century postindustrial capitalism. The photographs that form the basis of the present reading are all culled from recent issues (1989–90) of the currently most widely marketed women's fashion magazines in the United States: *Vogue, Elle, Glamour,* and *Cosmopolitan.* Readers interested in analyses of the fashion system based on the history of Western fashion, its role in a consumer culture oriented toward women, or its privileged if problematic status in the debates on postmodernism might wish to consult the following: J. C. Flügel, *The Psychology of Clothes* (London, 1930); Anne Hollander, *Seeing through Clothes* (New York, 1978); Alison Lurie, *The Language of Clothes* (London, 1981); David Kunzle, *Fashion and Fetishism: A Social History of the Corset, Tight-Lacing, and Other Forms of Body-Sculpture in the West* (Totowa, N.J., 1982); Rosalind Coward, *Female Desires: How They Are Sought, Bought and Packaged* (New York, 1985); Valerie Steele, *Fashion and Eroticism: Ideals of Feminine Beauty from the Victorian Era to the Jazz Age* (New York, 1985); Kaja Silverman, "Fragments of a Fashionable Discourse," in *Studies in Entertainment: Critical Approaches to Mass Culture,* ed. Tania Modleski (Bloomington, Ind., 1986), pp. 139–52; *Fabrications: Costume and the Female Body,* ed. Jane Gaines and Charlotte Herzog (New York, 1990); and Cathy Griggers, "A Certain Tension in the Visual/Cultural Field: Helmut Newton, Deborah Turbeville, and the *VOGUE* Fashion Layout," *Differences* 2 (Summer 1990): 76–104. My own investigation seeks to redress a symptomatic aporia in all of these important studies, namely, the fashion system's institutionalization of a homospectatorial look.

Diana Fuss is associate professor of English at Princeton University. She is the author of *Essentially Speaking: Feminism, Nature, and Difference* (1989) and *Identification Papers* (1995) and the editor of *Inside / Out: Lesbian Theories, Gay Theories* (1991) and *Human, All Too Human* (1995).

FIG. 1.—Advertisement, *Cosmopolitan* (Aug. 1989). Photo: Barry Hollywood; reproduced through the courtesy of *Cosmopolitan*.

Presumably, the readers of these magazines are to desire to *be* the woman, not to *have* her.

The project of this essay is to begin to decode the complicated operations of identification and desire, of being and having, that are at work in the social production of female spectatorial subjectivity. In an attempt to account psychoanalytically for the enduring fascination that commercial fashion photography holds for its female viewers, I will draw on Freud's theories of primary and secondary identification, Lacan's readings of specularity and subjectivity in relation to the preoedipal mirror stage, and Kristeva's notions of abjection and the "homosexual-maternal facet." Throughout I will be attempting to demonstrate, through a narrowly delimited reading of contemporary signifying codes of fashion photography,[3] that "identities" can never be isolated from or adequately understood outside the institutions of identification that work to produce them in the first place. Identity, because it is never in a moment of critical repose, because it resists the forces of suspension or negation, and because it neither begins nor ends at a point of total immobility, draws its very lifeblood from the restless operations of identification, one of the most powerful but least understood mechanisms of cultural self-fashioning.

Fashion Fetishism

The Lacanian subject is a subject fashioned in and by identifications, a subject that comes-into-being [*devenir*] through the agency of a complex network of identificatory processes—narcissism, aggressivity, misrecognition, and objectification—all working variously with and against each other at different moments in the child's psychical development and continuing on into adulthood. The importance Lacanian psychoanalysis attributes to specularity and identification in the formation of the sexed subject suggests several points of entry to the psychical geography traversed and bounded by the arena of women's commercial fashion photography. I will argue that these photographs work as post-mirror phase images that create fascination precisely through a cultural staging of pre-mirror phase fantasies; they, in effect, mirror the pre-mirror stage, directing our gaze solipsistically back to our own specular and fictive origins.

3. The study with which any reading of fashion photography may immediately invite comparison is Roland Barthes, *The Fashion System,* trans. Matthew Ward and Richard Howard (1967; New York, 1983). Whereas Barthes's structuralist analysis is limited to the decoding of articles about fashion in commercial magazines, my own post-structuralist analysis is largely based on a reading of the photographic images. Both are at best partial and severely circumscribed investigations into the "fashion system."

FIG. 2.—Cover, *Cosmopolitan* (Sept. 1989). Photo: Francesco Scavullo; reproduced through the courtesy of *Cosmopolitan.*

Through *secondary* identification(s) with the sequence of images that fashion photography serially displays, the female subject is positioned by the photographic codes of framing, color, lighting, focus, and pose to rehearse repetitiously the introjection of the (m)other's imago, which is itself a complex rehearsal of the infant's primary identification or absorption with the (m)other.[4] These images of the female body reenact, obsessively, the moment of the female subject's earliest self-awareness, as if to suggest the subject's profound uncertainty over whether her own subjectivity "took." This subject is compelled to verify herself endlessly, to identify all her bodily parts, and to fashion continually from this corporeal and psychical jigsaw puzzle a total picture, an imago of her own body.

The specular image of the body that women's fashion photography constructs is a reimaging of the body in pieces [*le corps morcelé*], the fragmented and dispersed body image that Lacan posits as the infant's pre-mirror experience of its amorphous self. These photographs recall Lacan's identification in "Aggressivity in Psychoanalysis" of a group of images categorized as "*imagos of the fragmented body*": "images of castration, mutilation, dismemberment, dislocation, evisceration, devouring, bursting open of the body."[5] Some of the most common and prevalent shots of female bodies in women's fashion photography are those of decapitation and dismemberment—in particular headless torsos and severed heads. In a L'Oréal ad for waterproof makeup (fig. 3), a woman's head floats above the water, her face, framed in medium close-up, detached from any visible body, supported only by her reflection in the water below. This very reflection is an extension of the body: woman as mirror is all face. But more terrifying than an economy of looking that overinvests the woman's face as the primary site of subjectivity is the flip side of this same scopic economy that divests the woman of subjectivity altogether. A Chanel ad, for example, phantasmically constructs an unthinkable body—a body without identity, a body without face or surface to convey any distinctive identifying features beyond the class- and gender-inflected signifiers of the clothes themselves. By "amputating" the model's head and legs, and by rendering invisible any flesh or skin tones, the camera presents to the viewer the fantasy not of a body without organs but a body without a subject. The terror and fascination evoked by the Chanel ad is that of the complete erasure of subjectivity. But then, the

4. *Imago* is a term Lacan borrows from Freud's famous distinction between two different kinds of identifications: primary identification, which signifies the child's preoedipal state of nondifferentiation with the mother, and secondary identification, which signifies the child's oedipal introjection of the imago of the same-sex parent. Freud's primary and secondary identifications correspond roughly to Lacan's pre-mirror and mirror stages, thus predating the subject's oedipal drama and situating the roots of identification and desire firmly in the presubject's imaginary relation to the mother.

5. Jacques Lacan, *Écrits: A Selection*, trans. Alan Sheridan (New York, 1977), p. 11.

FIG. 3.—Advertisement, *Glamour* (July 1989). Photo: Ken Browar; reproduced through the courtesy of *Glamour.* © 1989 by The Condé Nast Publications, Inc.

floating head and the headless torso offer only apparently different "takes" on the female subject, for overpresence figures a kind of absence, and to be the mirror is simultaneously to be without a self-image of one's own.

This representational body in pieces also functions for the female spectator as a cultural reminder of her fetishization, of the "part" she plays in the disavowal of the mother's castration. A fetish (typically a woman's legs, breasts, face, or other body part) is a substitute for the missing maternal phallus, a prop or accessory fashioned to veil its terrifying absence. In a patriarchal Symbolic a fetishist is one who continually strives to deny the "truth" of the mother's castration by registering the phallus elsewhere, seeking to resecure and to hold in suspense the early imaginary attachment to the phallic mother that was lost with the subject's entry into the Symbolic and its subjugation to the law of the father.[6] Photography, which similarly seeks to fix an image in an eternal moment of suspense, comes to function not merely as a technological analog for the psychical workings of fetishism but as one of its internal properties—that is, the fetish itself has "the frozen, arrested quality of a photograph."[7] This intimate co-dependency of fashion, fetishism, photography, and femininity suggests that in the dominant regime of fashion photography, femininity is itself an accessory: it operates as a repository for culture's representational waste. Images of waste and refuse make visible the Symbolic representations of femininity, which Luce Irigaray identifies as the "shards," the "scraps," the "uncollected debris," the "scattered remnants of a violated sexuality."[8] While it is the incorporation *and expurgation* of the feminine that constitutes the founding order of subjectivity for both boy and girl, only the girl attains subjectivity by becoming "the negative image of the subject,"[9] the photographic inversion, the materials of the mirror itself, its scattered shards. Juliet MacCannell's metaphor of the "trash can" to describe female subjectivity is thus entirely relevant to this discussion of fashion and fetishism. "'Woman' as generality," she writes, "is only seen in pieces (in part-objects, in the 'trash can' of overvalued zones of her body—breast, eyebrow, ankle, smile): any part that can be 'phallicised' or made, as a single part, into a metaphor for a wholeness that the woman lacks."[10] All of this is simply to suggest that it is possible to read fashion fetishism in

6. For a particularly precise and detailed reading of fetishism, as contrasted with psychosis, to which my own understanding of these psychical mechanisms is partially indebted, see Elizabeth Grosz, *Sexual Subversions: Three French Feminists* (Sydney, 1989), pp. 56–59.

7. Parveen Adams, "Of Female Bondage," in *Between Feminism and Psychoanalysis,* ed. Teresa Brennan (London, 1989), p. 252.

8. Luce Irigaray, *This Sex Which Is Not One,* trans. Catherine Porter and Carolyn Burke (1977; Ithaca, N.Y., 1985), p. 30.

9. Ibid., p. 78.

10. Juliet Flower MacCannell, *Figuring Lacan: Criticism and the Cultural Unconscious* (Lincoln, Nebr., 1986), p. 108.

photography in the same way that film theorist Kaja Silverman has read commodity fetishism in Orson Welles's *Citizen Kane:* as "a vain attempt to compensate for the divisions and separations upon which subjectivity is based."[11]

The Homosexual-Maternal Face(t)

So far, this reading of fashion photography has only suggested the *discomfort* these images may be assumed to provoke for their female viewers—specifically the fear and anxiety generated by (over)exposed fragmented body parts, remnants of an abjected existence prior to the mirror stage formulation of an economy of subjects and objects. It may be helpful here to turn directly to the work of Julia Kristeva, the writer perhaps most often associated with the difficult enterprise of theorizing the mechanisms of primary identification, primary narcissism, and abjection. Buried within a theory of sexuality noted for its persistent heterocentrism and its tendency toward maternalism[12] is a concept nonetheless particularly suggestive for understanding the endless fascination that fashion photography holds for its female spectators—suggestive precisely *because* of its insights into the Symbolic privileging of the maternal in the cultural production of feminine subjectivity. Kristeva's notion of the "homosexual-maternal facet"[13] posits a fundamental female homosexuality in the daughter's preoedipal identification with the mother, thus posing the larger question of the role that homosexuality plays (its repression and/or its mobilization) in the psychosocial constitution of *any* female subject. This homosexual-maternal facet is for Kristeva a particular modality of the semiotic *chora,* that period and place of indistinction prior to the various splittings (subject/object, self/other, mother/child) initiated by the mirror stage. In the pre-mirror stage, the still to be gendered presubject is "face to face with primary narcissism" (*D,* p. 265), caught in a primary identification with the mother that, for the girl, positions her along with the mother on a homosexual continuum. Importantly, it is the mother's face that functions as a screen providing the child with its first mirror image and facilitating the process of the *child's* identity formation by *ef*facing itself: the mother's face becomes a lost object. At the very point

11. Silverman, *The Acoustic Mirror: The Female Voice in Psychoanalysis and Cinema* (Bloomington, Ind., 1988), p. 86.

12. See for example Judith Butler, *Gender Trouble: Feminism and the Subversion of Identity* (New York, 1990), chap. 3; Silverman, *The Acoustic Mirror,* chap. 4; and Jennifer Stone, "The Horrors of Power: A Critique of 'Kristeva,'" in *The Politics of Theory,* ed. Francis Barker et al. (Colchester, 1983), pp. 38–48.

13. Julia Kristeva, *Desire in Language: A Semiotic Approach to Literature and Art,* trans. Thomas Gora, Alice Jardine, and Leon S. Roudiez, ed. Roudiez (New York, 1980), p. 239; hereafter abbreviated *D.*

the mother's face reflects the child's image back to him/her, this screen is itself "lost," eclipsed by its own reflective properties. For the girl, such a loss is a double deprivation since the mother's image is, simultaneously, her own.

The prevalence of close-ups of the woman's face in fashion photography would seem to suggest that one possible explanation for the fascination these images hold for women involves the pleasures evoked by the potential restitution of the lost object—specifically the reconstitution of the mother's face. A Revlon ad (fig. 4) for an antiageing moisturizer is surprisingly self-conscious about the psychical processes it so powerfully puts into play; it works its appeal by way of an imperative, commanding the spectator to "recover" the lost object in order to "discover" eternal youth. In its soft-focus lighting and languid radiance, the black-and-white image is strikingly reminiscent of a cinematic close-up of Greta Garbo or Claudette Colbert. The spectatorial appeal of the Revlon ad is much the same as that of a film close-up, perhaps even heightened by the immobility of the photographic image—its unrelenting overexposure to the viewer. Mary Ann Doane's comments on the cinematic close-up may help explain its analogous appeal in fashion photography:

> At moments it almost seems as though all the fetishism of the cinema were condensed onto the image of the face, the female face in particular. . . . The face is that bodily part not accessible to the subject's own gaze (or accessible only as a virtual image in a mirror)—hence its overrepresentation as *the* instance of subjectivity.[14]

The female subject, whose hold on subjectivity is always a precarious one, may derive a special pleasure from this "face-to-face" encounter with a shimmering, luminous, reconstituted image of the mythic "Mother";[15] the photograph's structure of visualization stages a homosexual-maternal encounter by symbolically imagining for the spectator a fantasized preoedipal relation with the face of the maternal. As one of the earliest planes of psychical organization, the mother's face is refigured by the

14. Mary Ann Doane, "Veiling over Desire: Close-ups of the Woman," in *Feminism and Psychoanalysis,* ed. Richard Feldstein and Judith Roof (Ithaca, N.Y., 1989), p. 108. Peter Matthews, in his absorbing reading of Greta Garbo as gay male icon, also reads the face as fetish, arguing that the feminine face is the site where spectators immerse themselves and momentarily relinquish their subjectivity. See Peter Matthews, "Garbo and Phallic Motherhood: A 'Homosexual' Visual Economy," *Screen* 29 (Summer 1988): 27.

15. In figure 5 (see p. 725) we are presented with an image of the "Great White Mother," a racially marked iconography of feminine beauty that betrays a Western nostalgia for the "recovery" of racial "purity." Commercial fashion photography persistently plays out such fantasies of racial purification through its calculated matching of products with models; after surveying thousands of images, I was struck by the overwhelming predominance of *white* women's faces in those advertisements selling specifically skin creams, makeup, facial cleansers, and other skin care products.

FIG. 4.—Advertisement, *Cosmopolitan* (Aug. 1989). Reproduced through the courtesy of Revlon, Inc. © 1989.

photographic apparatus as eternally present—fashioned, fetishized, and fixed by the gaze of the desiring subject. These images instill pleasure in the viewer by at once constructing and evoking the memory of a choric union; they bear "the imprint of an archaic moment" (*D,* p. 283)[16] achieved through the technological simulation of a past event. Often in these shots of a severed woman's head we see the face from the distance and perspective that an infant might see it. For example, in figure 5 the face wells up in front of us, its charged presence almost too large for the frame to hold, while in figure 6 the face is more indistinct, shadowy, blurred, remote. The lighting in both cases (orange-yellow, pink-black) is never quite "natural," as if these images were always either under- or over-exposed. The closeness of the faces to the viewer and the awkward play of light and shadow in both shots further suggest that no camera produced these particular images, and indeed they belong to a second-order genre in advertising based on the *simulated photograph:* drawings that mimic the immediacy and referentiality of a photographic copy and, in so doing, draw attention to the status of the photograph itself as a product of representation, a cultural simulation.

The reproduction of photographic codes in these imitative drawings function as a reminder of the phantasmic intensity of their subject (the mother's frozen face), as if the machinery of photographic representation cannot bear such close proximity to the object of desire whose reflective properties it so jealously seeks to capture and to refine. Clearly we are operating fully within the realm of fantasy here, for the choric reunion evoked by these images can only ever have the status of a fantasized memory and can only be purchased, paradoxically, at the price of disabling the very identity this fantasy purportedly seeks to secure in the first place. Any return to the semiotic *chora* and the homosexual-maternal continuum involves a regression to primary narcissism and thus to the moment before the formation of the subject's identity as subject. Kristeva's "ravishing maternal jouissance"—which constitutes the powerful lure of the "choric fantasy"[17]—is balanced and set against the equally powerful repulsion of its "terrorizing aggressivity" (*D,* p. 263). One of Kristeva's most important contributions to psychoanalytic theories of subject formation may well be her insistence that the "idyllic" dual relationship Freud identified between mother and child—the "soothing" symbiosis of the imaginary relation—represents in fact Freud's own defensive negation of the knowledge that the mother-child relation is anything but

16. It should be clear by now that this reading of the woman's face as maternal icon relies heavily on that body of work in feminist art history that insists that "the body to which representation refers is always, however specific the representation, the maternal body" (Griselda Pollock, "Missing Women: Rethinking Early Thoughts on Images of Women," in *The Critical Image: Essays on Contemporary Photography,* ed. Carol Squiers [Seattle, 1990], p. 211).

17. I take this especially useful term from Silverman, *The Acoustic Mirror,* p. 101.

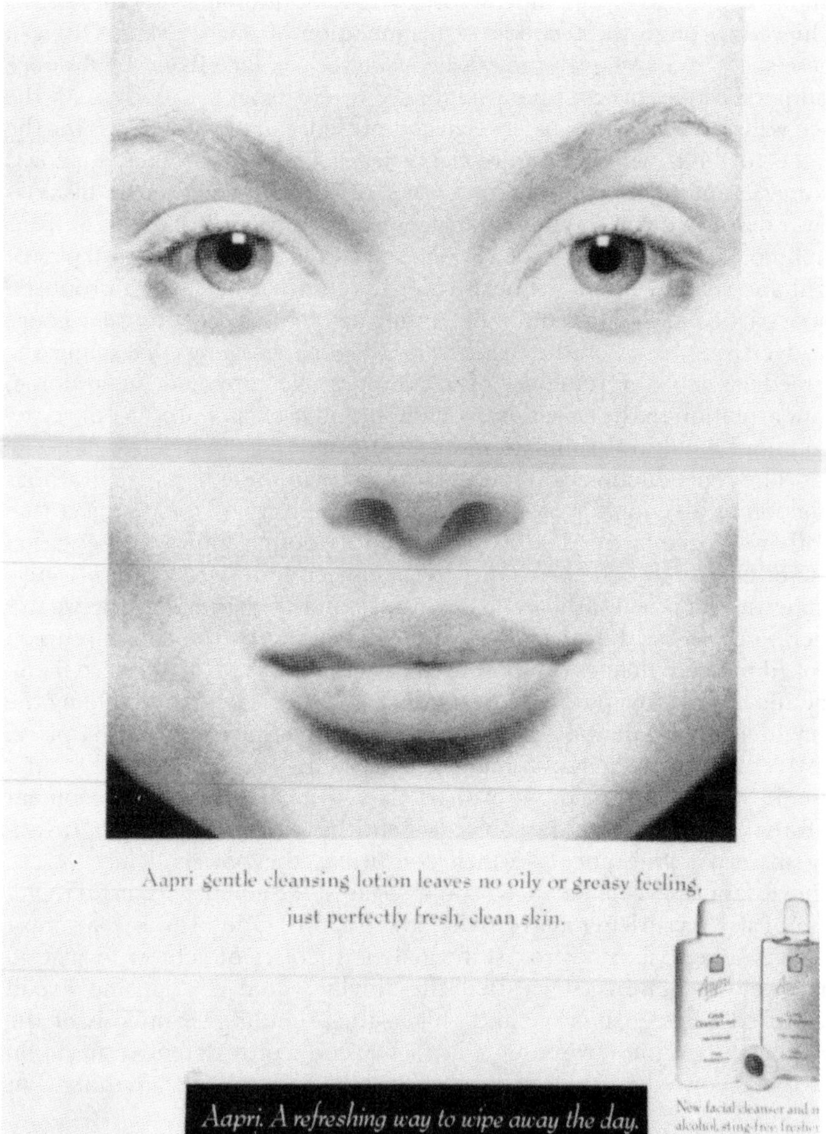

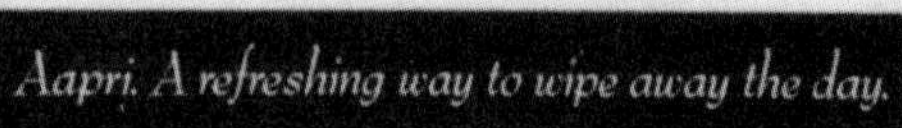

FIG. 5.—Advertisement, *Elle* (July 1989).

FIG. 6.—Advertisement, *Elle* (Oct. 1989). Reproduced through the courtesy of the Swiss Watch Corporation.

utopic. The primary narcissism implied by the homosexual-maternal facet is weighted with hostility and laden with uncertainty: "the archaic relation to the mother, narcissistic though it may be, is . . . of no solace to the protagonists and even less so to Narcissus." Primary narcissism, by erasing the borders between subject and object and immersing both mother and child in abjection, "threatens" the ego and "menaces" subjective identity.[18] In opposition then to a psychoanalytic understanding of female film spectatorship, which reads the woman's fascination with her image as a symptom of her "predisposition" to (primary) narcissism, I am suggesting that the female spectator's fascination with her etherealized image in fashion photography operates not as an Imaginary *effect of* primary narcissism but as a Symbolic *defense against* it—against all the terrors primary identification with the mother holds for the always imperfectly oedipalized woman. What these angelic images of the mother's face provide for the female spectator is a *negation* of the uncertainty that disturbs her psychic borders and a *disavowal* of the pain born out of her primary identification with the (m)other—a negation and a disavowal made visible through a representational excess (which is always a kind of waste): namely, the cosmetic beautification and beatification of the mother's face.

One thinks here of Georges Bataille, perhaps the preeminent theorist of waste, refuse, and the violence of refusal, which he sees as the very precondition of desire. To possess the object of desire—to "take" it, like a photograph—would be simultaneously to *take away* the motivation for the desire and thus desire itself. However, for Bataille, woman's cultural utility as repository of beauty operates to disguise the animal nature of heterosexual intercourse and further to mask what he terms the "ugliness" and crudity of the sexual organs. In Bataille's "vision of excess,"[19] it is specifically the woman's face—heavily adorned and meticulously masqueraded—that attracts the male subject's gaze away from the sex organs and toward a more luminous surface. Bataille's theoretical figuration of the female face as "beautiful" enacts a slight shift in registers from *re*flection to *de*flection: the fashionable face (the female face on display) has the power to send the look through a circuitous route, from the vertical lips to the horizontal lips, not to effect an eclipse of the genital by the facial but

18. Kristeva, *Powers of Horror: An Essay on Abjection,* trans. Roudiez (New York, 1982), p. 63. For an interesting and suggestive discussion of the *mother's* abjection, and a theory of subject formation based on identification with the desire *of* the mother rather than with a desire *for* her, see Cynthia Chase, "Desire and Identification in Lacan and Kristeva," in *Feminism and Psychoanalysis,* pp. 65–83, and "Primary Narcissism and the Giving of Figure: Kristeva with Hertz and de Man," in *Abjection, Melancholia, and Love: The Work of Julia Kristeva,* ed. John Fletcher and Andrew Benjamin (New York, 1990), pp. 124–36.

19. Georges Bataille, *Erotism: Death and Sensuality,* trans. Mary Dalwood (San Francisco, 1986), p. 129–46. In Bataille's erotics of waste and refuse, "beauty is desired in order that it may be befouled" (p. 144). See also Bataille's *Visions of Excess: Selected Writings, 1927–1939,* trans. and ed. Allan Stoekl (Minneapolis, 1985).

rather to collapse one bodily site onto the other.[20] This is not a new or perhaps even very interesting story: Freud's reading of the terrifying decapitated head of Medusa as a representation of the female genitals (specifically, the mother's genitals)[21] similarly insists on the symbolic connection between female face and female genitalia. These two cultural readings (Bataille's and Freud's) of the iconic power of a woman's face tell us less about a woman's complex relation to her private body parts than about the parts her privates have been made to play in the history of Western representations of *male* subjectivity. To understand the fear and fascination the mother's face holds for a *female* subject, one needs to turn away from Medusa.

Vampiric Identification

Disavowal, as is its wont, simultaneously involves for the subject in discord both a denial *and* a recognition of the source of its pain. It is, after all, the very immobility of the photographic image of the mother's face that threatens to capture and overwhelm the subject in the archaic confusion of its own libidinous drives. If the high cost of regression to the pre-Symbolic is psychosis, which Kristeva defines in an eloquent turn of phrase as "the panicking at the loss of all reference" (*D,* p. 139), then the photographic apparatus itself comes to function as a paradigm for the workings of psychosis, a loss of reference triggered by the face-to-face encounter with primary narcissism and the possibility of both plenitude and loss reflected in and by the mother's magnified, beatific face. On the one hand, photography, unlike other systems of representation, can never deny the existence of the referent—the "that-has-been" status, as Roland Barthes puts it, of the lost object.[22] On the other hand, photography never

20. For an alternative use of Bataille's erotics of waste that is read through the discourse of fashion, see Peter Wollen, "Fashion/Orientalism/The Body," *New Formations,* no. 1 (Spring 1987): 5–33. Wollen accurately points out that for Bataille the general economy of waste, of excess spent without return, is the very domain of the erotic. It is also, I would add, the domain of Irigaray's "feminine."

21. See Sigmund Freud, "Medusa's Head" (1922), *The Standard Edition of the Complete Psychological Works of Sigmund Freud,* trans. and ed. James Strachey, 24 vols. (London, 1953–74), 18:273–74.

22. Barthes has this to say about the specificity of photography:

> Photography's Referent is not the same as the referent of other systems of representation. I call "photographic referent" not the *optionally* real thing to which an image or a sign refers but the *necessarily* real thing which has been placed before the lens, without which there would be no photograph. Painting can feign reality without having seen it. Discourse combines signs which have referents, of course, but these referents can be and are most often "chimeras." Contrary to these imitations, in Photography I can never deny that *the thing has been there.* [Barthes, *Camera Lucida: Reflections on Photography,* trans. Howard (New York, 1981), p. 76]

ceases in its attempt to restore the lost object, the referent that has been but is no longer.[23] Like the mother's face, the photographic image is the place of both a constitution and a fading of subjectivity: both are "screens" that operate for the subject as sites where identity emerges *and* recedes. Photography simulates and mechanizes the reflective properties of the mother's look, suggesting that if the mother's face operates as the primary "plane" of abjection, photography may represent its most perfect science. Abjection, defined by Kristeva as that boundary where "'subject' and 'object' push each other away, confront each other, collapse, and start again,"[24] is the psychical equivalent of photography's mechanical transformation of subjects into objects. Barthes writes "the Photograph . . . represents that very subtle moment when . . . I am neither subject nor object but a subject who feels he is becoming an object: I then experience a micro-version of death (of parenthesis): I am truly becoming a specter."[25] Photography, the very technology of abjection, functions as a mass producer of corpses, embalming each subject by captivating and fixing its image. Along with vampirism and psychoanalysis, photography can be seen as yet another of the "rival sciences of the undead."[26]

This idea of the undead, when combined with the spectacle of women "feeding off" the images of other women, points toward a vampiric structure of the look in women's fashion photography. The vampirism of the gaze is directly thematized through the prevalence of neck shots: images of women with their heads thrown back, their eyes closed, their lips slightly parted, their necks extended and exposed (figs. 7 and 8). This is, of course, the classic pose of sexual ecstasy for the woman, a pose that visually demonstrates how a woman's very vulnerability and passivity are culturally eroticized. Only this time it is women themselves who are invited to actively consume the image—female spectators who are constrained to assume the position of lesbian vampires. Laura Mulvey, in her well-known reading of the narrative codes of classical Hollywood cinema, theorizes two possible spectatorial relations to the image on the screen: scopophilia, which implies "a separation of the erotic identity of the subject from the object on the screen," and narcissism, which demands "identification of the ego with the object on the screen through the spectator's fascination

23. A reminder of the precise psychoanalytic definition of psychosis might help clarify the relation I am positing here between this psychical mechanism and photographic technology. Psychosis is "a primary disturbance of the libidinal relation to reality"; its "manifest symptoms . . . are accordingly treated as secondary attempts to restore the link with objects" (Jean Laplanche and J.-B. Pontalis, *The Language of Psycho-analysis,* trans. Donald Nicholson-Smith [1967; New York, 1973], p. 370).

24. Kristeva, *Powers of Horror,* p. 18.

25. Barthes, *Camera Lucida,* p. 14.

26. Laurence A. Rickels, *Aberrations of Mourning: Writing on German Crypts* (Detroit, 1988), p. 318.

with and recognition of his like."[27] Vampirism, I would like to suggest, marks a third possible mode of looking, a position that demands both separation and identification, both a having and a becoming—indeed, a having *through* a becoming. The spectatorial relation of the woman to her image serially displayed across the pages of the fashion magazine is structurally vampiric, involving neither immediate identification nor unmediated desire but rather a complicated and unstable exchange between already mediated forms.

Becoming the other by feeding off the other presents a tropological way of understanding identification that is not without precedent in psychoanalysis. In Freud's understanding of the process of secondary identification, introjection of the imago works specifically through "the oral, cannibalistic incorporation of the other person,"[28] an act of consumption that seeks to satisfy the ego's insatiable desire to become the other by devouring it whole. But as a cultural figure for the psychical process of identification, vampirism differs from cannibalism in that the vampire does more than incorporate the alterity of the other in her erotic feedings; she also creates a shadow or reflection of herself by transforming her "victims" into fellow vampires. Vampirism works more like an inverted form of identification—identification pulled inside out—where the subject, in the act of interiorizing the other, simultaneously reproduces itself externally in that other. Vampirism is both other-incorporating and self-reproducing; it delimits a more ambiguous space where desire and identification appear less opposed than coterminous, where the desire to be the other (identification) draws its very sustenance from the desire to have the other. Vampiric identification operates in the fashion system in the way that the photographic apparatus positions the spectator to identify with the woman precisely so as not to desire her, or to put it another way, to desire to be the woman so as to preclude having her. But in order to eradicate or evacuate the homoerotic desire, the visual field must first *produce* it, thereby permitting, in socially regulated form, the articulation of lesbian desire within the identificatory move itself.

The vampire—and, I would propose, the lesbian vampire specific-

27. Laura Mulvey, "Visual Pleasure and Narrative Cinema," in *Feminism and Film Theory,* ed. Constance Penley (New York, 1988), p. 61.

28. Freud, *New Introductory Lectures on Psycho-analysis* (1932), *Standard Edition,* 22: 63. See Freud's discussion of the primal father's murder and cannibalism by the sons in *Totem and Taboo* (1912–13), *Standard Edition,* 13:vii–162, and his association of identification with the earliest phase of infantile sexuality, the libidinal oral phase, in which the ego incorporates the object by devouring it, a process described both in *Group Psychology and the Analysis of the Ego* (1921), *Standard Edition,* 18:69–143, and in "Mourning and Melancholia" (1915), *Standard Edition,* 14:243–58. On eating as a figure for the interiorization of the other, see also Jacques Derrida, "Subverting the Signature: A Theory of the Parasite," *Blast* 1 (1990): 16–21, and "'Eating Well,' or the Calculation of the Subject: An Interview with Jacques Derrida," interviewed by Jean-Luc Nancy, in *Who Comes after the Subject?* ed. Eduardo Cadava, Peter Connor, and Nancy (New York, 1990), pp. 96–119.

FIG. 7.—Advertisement, *Vogue* (Oct. 1989). Photo: Skrebneski; reproduced through the courtesy of Flemington Furs, Flemington, N.J.

ally—represents the perfect trope for allegorizing the activity of fashion photography's voracious female spectators. A rare, explicit acknowledgment of how the fashion system works through vampiric identifications is presented by a striking ad for Italian clothing designer Moschino (fig. 9). Assuming the form of a rough sketch rather than a glossy photograph, this antifashion fashion statement crosses out not simply any woman's face but a vampire's face. Red splotches connote both the red paint of the *X* and the red blood dripping from the vampire's fangs. Eyes, nose, and mouth are all blocked out: this woman sees red, but, as a vampire, she also smells it and tastes it. The violence of the image lies in its refusal of what I have argued is the spectatorial position that the fashion system constructs for its female viewers, namely, lesbian vampirism. Female spectatorial subjectivity is precisely what is denied by the injunction to "**STOP** THE FASHION SYSTEM!" Yet the subtle play with spacing and typography in the visual presentation of "**STOP** THE FASHION SYSTEM!" suggests a possible counter-reading: if we place the emphasis on the imperative—**STOP**—as the word's size and placement on the page encourage us to do, we can then gloss the line as a different kind of command: a bid for our attention, an alert to **STOP** and to take notice of THE FASHION SYSTEM. The connotative ambiguity encoded by the text permits a second order of meaning that significantly complicates the first, suggesting perhaps that the point we really should register here is the fashion system's ability to renew and to perpetuate itself by continually invoking the specter of its death or obsolescence—in much the same way, it could be argued, that heterosexuality secures its identity by at once disavowing and perpetually calling attention to its abject, interiorized, and ghostly other, homosexuality.[29]

A psychoanalytic reading of heterosexuality needs to look beyond the standard repression hypothesis of sexuality in order to fully account for the way in which heterosexuality, far from constituting itself through the simple sublimation of homosexuality, works through and by the dialectic of its continual activation and disavowal. Homosexuality is "repressed" to the degree that the structure it provides for the formation of the heterosexual subject is so apparent that it becomes transparent; the very obviousness of the lesbian eroticism evoked by women's fashion photography simultaneously produces and occludes the homoerotic structure of the look.[30] Fashion photography works to ensure the formation of a subject's heterosexual object-choices through the stimulation and control of its "homopathic" identifications; the same-sex desire one might imagine to

29. Another aspect of the vampire trope that seems relevant here is the absence of the vampire's reflection in the mirror. The vacant mirror names the subjectless subject discussed earlier in this essay, specifically in regard to the eclipsing of the mother's face.

30. Or, as Butler incisively phrases the problem, "homosexuality emerges as a desire which must be produced in order to remain repressed" (Butler, *Gender Trouble,* p. 77).

FIG. 8.—Advertisement, *Elle* (Sept. 1989). Photo: Gideon Lewin for Martha International.

be triggered by the erotically charged images of women's bodies is sublimated into the camera's insistence on same-sex identification (being rather than having the woman). Yet these structural identifications, while harnessing the tabooed desire, nonetheless give it a certain play, licensing the desire as that which must be routinely managed and contained. Desire operates *within* identification, destabilizing the grounds of a heterosexual identity formation and undermining its defensive claims to a "pure" or "uncontaminated" sexuality. This play of homosexual desire within a homophilic identification may explain the fashion photograph's greatest lure: the pull of a forbidden desire, there (if only) for the taking.

Images of the female form—and, in particular, the woman's face—in contemporary fashion photography inspire in the viewing subject a certain "preoedipal nostalgia." That is not to suggest, however, that the power and attraction of these images derive from any simple evocation of early childhood memories. Rather, the "memory" these ads seem to "tap into" are contemporary fictional constructs projected back into the subject's preconscious to function as screens to protect against an all too present pain: the cultural repression of same-sex desire. In this regard, each photograph achieves the status of Freud's earliest understanding of a "screen memory"—a "memory" (for example, of maternal plenitude, the beatific face) manufactured and mapped onto the past in order to disguise a present anxiety (the subject's painfully distant relation to that face and the disavowal of homosexual desire). Actually, Freud offers us two ways to theorize a screen memory: first, as an early impression utilized as a screen for a much later event, and second, as a later impression used to disguise an early childhood event.[31] The images offered by fashion photography operate both ways: as defenses (or screens) against the early interruption of the homosexual-maternal continuum, but also and more importantly as defenses against the pain that this psychical rupture continues to inflict on the adult subject. In other words, these images function as countermemories that tell us as much about the subject's current history as they do about her already shadowy prehistory, perhaps even more. What they tell us is that heterosexuality is profoundly unstable, tenuous, and precarious, and therefore must be continually reinforced and resecured. Nostalgia for the preoedipal, *itself a construction of the oedipal,* works as a psychical mechanism for strengthening the homopathic identification so that the socially sanctioned heterosexual object-choice can be perpetually sustained. In constant threat of dissolution, female heterosexuality must

31. Freud develops the first of these theories in "Screen Memories" (1899), *Standard Edition,* 3: 299–322, and the second, more common understanding in *The Psychopathology of Everyday Life* (1901), *Standard Edition,* vol. 6. In "Screen Memories" Freud provides a further reason for casting suspicion on the efficacy of reading representational images simply as evocations of early childhood memories: "It may indeed be questioned whether we have any memories at all *from* our childhood: memories *relating to* our childhood may be all that we possess" (3:322).

FIG. 9.—Advertisement, *Elle* (Mar. 1990). Reproduced through the courtesy of Moda and Company.

be critically maintained through the cultural institutionalization of the homosexual look. This strategic deployment of a homospectatorial look may partially account for what has long been a puzzling contradiction: how is it that, in the dominant sexual Symbolic, there can be homosexual looks but no homosexuals?

Even Freud eventually came to recognize that a daughter's unconscious preoedipal homosexual desire for the mother continually impacts upon her conscious adult life; it is precisely this same-sex desire that is evoked, which is to say *pro*voked, by photographic images of the female body—powerfully activated, mobilized, and channeled (or *Chanel*led, as it were). The problem, of course, is that any female subject *as subject* is already situated in the Symbolic, and no matter how uncertain this symbolization is for the woman, the mother's face as lost object is fundamentally irrecuperable. Still, the *fantasy* of repossessing the lost object, the *promise* these photographic images hold of reconnecting (re-fusing?) the homosexual-maternal relation, goes a long way toward explaining the enduring fascination that fashion photography holds for its female viewers, the pleasures it seeks to provide, as well as the discomforts it may inadvertently summon.

Conclusion

The lesbian-looks coded by fashion photography radically de-essentialize conventional notions of the identity of the viewing subject that posit desire in the viewer, prior to any operations of spectatorial identification. We need to theorize "homoerotic looks" not in terms of anything inherent to the viewing subject but in terms of a visual structuring and identification that participates in organizing the sexual identity of *any* social subject. One question I have not addressed is how lesbian viewers might consume these images.[32] What is at issue in this reading, however, is not "homosexual" versus "heterosexual" spectatorship but the homosexualization of the viewing position itself as created by the contemporary codes of women's fashion photography. This is not to deny that more work needs to be done on how spectators from different gendered, racial, ethnic, economic, national, and historical backgrounds might appropriate or resist these images,[33] but only to insist that if subjects look differently, it is the

32. One recent attempt to do just this is Danae Clark, "Commodity Lesbianism," *Camera Obscura* 25–26 (Jan.–May 1991): 181–201.

33. I have in mind the kind of work showcased by a recent collection of essays on "The Spectatrix," ed. Janet Bergstrom and Doane, *Camera Obscura,* nos. 20–21 (May–Sept. 1990). See also "The Last 'Special Issue' on Race?" ed. Isaac Julien and Kobena Mercer, *Screen* 29 (Autumn 1988), and a collection on "(Un)Naming Cultures," ed. Trinh T. Minh-ha, *Discourse* 11 (Spring–Summer 1989).

enculturating mechanisms of the look that instantiate and regulate these differences in the first place.

A second implication of a study like this one, which draws heavily on recent film theory, is a recognition nonetheless of the limited uses to which this theory can be put in the critical analyses of photography. Photography differs from film in its organization of both spatial and temporal orders and in its relation to referentiality and alterity.[34] In its frozen time and circumscribed space, the photograph constitutes another frame of reference, a different structure of visualization, an alternative field of vision. And, especially important for this particular investigation of photography, the photograph constructs an entirely other identificatory structure from that described by Mulvey, for whom the spectatorial look produced by the classical film apparatus is masculine, heterosexual, and oedipal. I have suggested in this essay that the spectatorial position mapped by contemporary commercial fashion photography can be read, by contrast, as feminine, homosexual, and preoedipal.

Finally, we need to rethink the always-complicated relation between desire and identification in the formation of the subject's identity. For Freud, Lacan, and Kristeva, desire and identification are mutually interdependent but counterdirectional trajectories in which identifying with one sex is the necessary condition for desiring the other. To identify with *and* to desire a person of the same sex is, in this logic, a structural impossibility. But such a symmetrical, rigid, chiasmatic relation between terms may disguise the ways in which any identification *with* an other is secured through a simultaneous and continuing desire *for* that other. In Freud's only case study of a female paranoiac, he insists that the analysand can "free" herself of her homosexual "dependence" on her mother only by becoming her mother through renewed secondary identifications.[35] This becoming is presumed to erase all desire, or rather to reroute the desire toward a wholly different love object. But the desire to be *like* can itself be motivated and sustained by the desire to *possess:* being can be the most radical form of having. Identification may well operate in the end not as a foreclosure of desire but as its most perfect, and most *ruthless,* fulfillment.

34. For a lengthier discussion of the differences between cinema and photography, see Derrida, afterword in Marie-Françoise Plissart, *Droit de regards* (Paris, 1985).

35. See Freud, "A Case of Paranoia Running Counter to the Psychoanalytic Theory of the Disease" (1915), *Standard Edition,* 14: 263–72.

Policing the Black Woman's Body in an Urban Context

Hazel V. Carby

> The problem of the unemployed negro woman in New York city is probably more serious than that of any other class of worker. She is unquestionably shut out from many lines of occupation, and through her increasing inefficiency and desire to avoid hard work, the best households and hotels and restaurants are gradually supplanting her with whites. This means in many instances that she must rely upon odd jobs and employment in the questionable house. . . .
>
> Negro women who are led into immoral habits, vice and laziness, have in too many instances received their initiative from questionable employment agencies. . . . Some preventive measure must be taken for the colored girl going to work for the first time, and for the green helpless negro woman brought up here from the South—on promises of "easy work, lots of money and good times."
>
> —Frances A. Kellor, "Southern Colored Girls in the North"

The migration of black people to cities outside of the Secessionist states of the South in the first half of the twentieth century transformed America socially, politically, and culturally. Of course, the migration of black people is not a twentieth-century phenomenon. In the antebellum period the underground railroad was the primary conduit out of the slave-holding states; in the late 1870s there was significant black migration to Kansas and in the 1880s to Oklahoma. Before 1910 there were major changes in the distribution of the black population between rural and urban areas within the South. The proportion of black people in southern cities more than doubled between 1870 and 1910 and, consequently, the

This article originally appeared in *Critical Inquiry* 18 (Summer 1992).

proportion of the black population that continued to live in rural areas decreased significantly from 81 to 70 percent.[1] Historians and demographers seem to agree that what is now called the Great Migration needs to be viewed in the context of these earlier migratory patterns and in light of the fact that black people were becoming increasingly urbanized before they left for northern cities.

When considering the complex cultural transformations that not only accompany but are an integral part of these demographic shifts, it is important to challenge simplistic mythologies of how a rural black folk without the necessary industrial skills, untutored in the ways of the city, "green" and ignorant, in Frances Kellor's opinion, were exploitable fodder for the streets of New York, Chicago, Detroit, Cleveland, Philadelphia, and Pittsburgh.[2] Certainly, male and female black migrants suffered economic and political exploitation, but it is important to separate the structural forces of exploitation from the ways in which black migrants came to be regarded as easily victimized subjects who quickly succumbed to the forces of vice and degradation.

I am going to argue that the complex processes of urbanization had gender-specific and class-specific consequences for the production of African-American culture, in general, and for the cultural representation of black women, in particular. The movement of black women between rural and urban areas and between southern and northern cities generated a series of moral panics. One serious consequence was that the behavior of black female migrants was characterized as sexually degenerate and, therefore, socially dangerous. By using the phrase "moral panic" I am attempting to describe and to connect a series of responses, from institu-

1. See Daniel M. Johnson and Rex R. Campbell, *Black Migration in America: A Social Demographic History* (Durham, N. C., 1981).

2. Carole Marks argues two important points in her recent book. The first is that the majority of migrants at this stage of migration were from urban areas and left not just to "raise their wages but because they were the displaced mudsills of southern industrial development." Second, the level of a laborer's skill was less important "than institutional barriers in determining migrant assimilation and mobility." While there is a dispute about whether the majority of migrants were from rural or urban areas in the South it is clear that a significant number of migrants were urbanized and had previous experience of wage labor, skilled and unskilled, and that a number were professionals following their clients (Carole Marks, *Farewell—We're Good and Gone: The Great Black Migration* [Bloomington, Ind., 1989], p. 3). See also Johnson and Campbell, *Black Migration in America,* p. 79.

Hazel V. Carby is professor of African American and American studies at Yale University. Her books include *Reconstructing Womanhood: The Emergence of the African-American Woman Novelist* (1987) and *Race Men: Genealogies of Race, Nation, and Masculinity* (forthcoming). This essay is part of a larger work entitled *Women, Migration, and the Formation of a Blues Culture* (forthcoming).

tions and from individuals, that identified the behavior of these migrating women as a social and political problem, a problem that had to be rectified in order to restore a moral social order.[3] These responses were an active part of a 1920s bourgeois ideology that not only identified this moral crisis but also produced a language that provided a framework of interpretation and referentiality that appeared to be able to explain for all time the behavior of black women in an urban environment. Kellor's indictment of the sexual behavior of black migrant women registers the emergence of what would rapidly become a widely shared discourse of what was wrong with black urban life.

Frances Kellor was the general director of the Inter-Municipal Committee on Household Research in New York City, and her "Southern Colored Girls in the North" appeared in *Charities,* "A Review of Local and General Philanthropy." Her article provides important evidence that as early as 1905 the major discursive elements were already in place that would define black female urban behavior throughout the teens and twenties as pathological.[4] The subjects of Kellor's article are migrating black women who are looking for work, and she implicitly assumes that these women are alone, either single or, at least, without men. Therefore, according to Kellor, they need "protection." On the surface, it looks as if Kellor is inciting moral alarm in defence of the rather abstract quality of female virtue, but it is quickly evident that she does not believe that black women have any moral fiber or will of their own that can be mobilized in the defence of their own interests. On the contrary, she believes that they become prostitutes because they are unable to protect themselves. Kellor's report makes a strong case for the creation of an alternative set of institutions to police the actual bodies of migrating black women. While Kellor is apparently condemning the existence of employment agencies that create a situation of economic dependency and exploitation in order to channel black women into houses of prostitution, she is actually identi-

3. See Stuart Hall et al., *Policing the Crisis: Mugging, the State, and Law and Order* (London, 1978), pp. 16–20. Hall and his coauthors draw on the work of Stanley Cohen, who argues that

> societies appear to be subject, every now and then, to periods of moral panic. A condition, episode, person or group of persons emerges to become defined as a threat to societal values and interests; its nature is presented in a stylized and stereotypical fashion by the mass media; the moral barricades are manned by editors, bishops, politicians and other right-thinking people; socially accredited experts pronounce their diagnoses and solutions; ways of coping are evolved or (more often) resorted to; the condition then disappears, submerges or deteriorates and becomes more visible. Sometimes the object of the panic is quite novel and at other times it is something which has been in existence long enough, but suddenly appears in the limelight. [Stanley Cohen, *Folk Devils and Moral Panics: The Creation of the Mods and Rockers* (London, 1972), p. 9]

4. See Frances A. Kellor, "Southern Colored Girls in the North: The Problem of Their Protection," *Charities,* 18 Mar. 1905, pp. 584–85.

fying the "increasing inefficiency and desire [of black women] to avoid hard work" as the primary cause of the "problem."

Kellor has three major recommendations to make in addition to the establishment of more respectable and law-abiding agencies. First, she suggests the use of "practical and sympathetic women," like those on Ellis Island "who guide and direct the immigrant women," to "befriend" and act as "missionaries" toward black women when they arrive from the South. Second, she advocates the institution of a controlled system of lodging houses where black women can be sent at night and kept from going off on their own into the streets. Finally, she argues for the creation of training schools to make black women "more efficient."[5] This discourse, however, establishes a direct relationship between the social supervision of black women migrants and the control of their moral and sexual behavior, between the morally unacceptable economics of sex for sale and a morally acceptable policing of black female sexuality. In other words, Kellor characterizes the situation not as the lack of job possibilities for black women with the consequent conclusion that the employment market should be rigorously controlled, but, on the contrary, as a problem located in black women themselves, who, given the limited employment available to them and their "desire to avoid hard work," will sell their bodies.[6] Therefore, the logic of her argument dictates that bodies, not economic markets, need stringent surveillance.

The need to police and discipline the behavior of black women in cities, however, was not only a premise of white agencies and institutions but also a perception of black institutions and organizations, and the black middle class. The moral panic about the urban presence of apparently uncontrolled black women was symptomatic of and referenced aspects of the more general crises of social displacement and dislocation that were caused by migration. White and black intellectuals used and elaborated this discourse so that when they referred to the association between black women and vice, or immoral behavior, their references carried connotations of other crises of the black urban environment. Thus the migrating black woman could be variously situated as a threat to the progress of the race; as a threat to the establishment of a respectable urban black middle class; as a threat to congenial black and white middle-class relations; and as a threat to the formation of black masculinity in an urban environment.

Jane Edna Hunter, who was born in 1882 on the Woodburn plantation in South Carolina and trained as a nurse in Charleston and then at the Hampton Institute, arrived in Cleveland in May 1905 with little money. In an attempt to find accommodations she mistakenly arrived at a brothel, and her search for a place to live, she says, gave her an insight into the con-

5. Ibid., p. 585.

6. Another unspoken assumption here, of course, is that selling sex is not hard but easy work.

ditions that a black girl, "friendless and alone," had to face.[7] Hunter reflects that at home on the plantation she was well aware that some girls had been seduced, but she was totally unaware of what she calls a "wholesale organized traffic in black flesh" (*NP,* p. 68). When she goes to a dance she is shocked to see that the saloon on the first floor of Woodluff Hall is "the resort of bad women," and that the Hamilton Avenue area is the home of "vice." Hunter's discovery of what she identifies and criticizes as organized vice is interspersed with a description of her own difficult search for legitimate employment. Although highly trained she cannot find a doctor who wants to employ a black nurse, and she depends on a cousin to find cleaning jobs for her.[8] Eventually, Hunter alternates work as a domestic with temporary nursing assignments until she finds a permanent position in the office of a group of doctors.

In her autobiography, *A Nickel and a Prayer,* Hunter states that her experiences led her to conclude that "a girl alone in a large city must needs know the dangers and pitfalls awaiting her" (*NP,* p. 77). While Hunter never situates herself as a helpless victim she carefully creates a narrative that identifies and appears to account for the helplessness of other black migrating women, and as she does so she incorporates Kellor's analysis, strategies, and conclusions. Hunter turned the death of her mother, from whom she had become estranged, into a catalyst to devote her life to political and social activity on behalf of the black women she designated as helpless. As a young woman Hunter was forbidden to see the man she loved, and she blamed her mother for forcing her into marriage with a man forty years older than herself. However, she walked out of the marriage fifteen months later and went to Charleston to find work, declaring that "a great weight rolled from my mind as I left him, determined to find and keep the freedom which I so ardently desired" (*NP,* p. 50). Hunter's mother died in 1911, after Hunter had lived in Cleveland for four years, and the realization that reconciliation was now impossible occasioned deep despair. In the midst of contemplating suicide Hunter found herself asking the question: "how could I best give to the world what I had failed to give her?" (*NP,* p. 81). Hunter's self-interrogation resulted in her making her mother, rather than herself, a symbol for the helplessness of all migrant women. Hunter characterized her mother as both "immature and impulsive" and imagined that her mother would have been totally helpless if she had been a migrant. What Hunter cannot explicitly acknowledge is that a figure of such helplessness stands in direct contrast to the way she writes with confidence and self-determination about her own need to gain and

7. Jane Edna Hunter, *A Nickel and a Prayer* (Cleveland, 1940), p. 67; hereafter abbreviated *NP.* I am very grateful to Darlene Clark Hine for telling me about Hunter, her autobiography, and her papers.

8. Hunter maintains that she was one of only two black professional nurses in Cleveland. See *NP,* p. 87.

retain her freedom through urban migration. But the designation of her mother as helpless enables Hunter to occupy the absent maternal space. The daughter becomes mother as Hunter listens to the strains of a spiritual and is moved by the words, "ah feels like a motherless child." At this moment she decided on her "supreme work," dedicating her life to helping "the young Negro girl pushed from the nest by economic pressure, alone and friendless in a northern city; reduced to squalor, starvation; helpless against temptation and degradation" (*NP,* p. 83).

The fruit of Hunter's labors and the institutionalization of her maternal role into that of a matriarch is the formation of the Working Girls' Home Association, which later became the Phillis Wheatley Association, with Hunter as president. The Phillis Wheatley Association was the equivalent of the "controlled system of lodging houses" that Kellor recommended in her report, but under black not white control. In cooperation with the National Association of Colored Women other similar institutions were established in cities across the country with Hunter as chair of the Phillis Wheatley department of the NACW. The board that was established in 1913 to oversee the home included white as well as black patrons, and Hunter argued that the Phillis Wheatley Association was "one of the strongest ties between the Negro and white races in America"(*NP,* p. 165). It was not only at the level of management, however, that Hunter was proud of the association as a model of interracial cooperation. The home was a training ground to prepare young black women for domestic service, and one of Hunter's aims was to improve relations between white mistress and maid by producing a happy and efficient servant. As Hunter states:

> The most important factor in successful domestic service is a happy and human relation between the lady of the house and the maid—on the part of the maid, respect and affectionate regard for her employer; on the part of the employer, sympathy and imagination. Perhaps it is not going too far to say that the lady of the house should stand in the relation of a foster mother to the young woman who assists her in the household tasks. . . .
>
> The girl who is fairly well-trained and well-disposed will become interested in the life of the family that she serves, and will be devoted to its happiness. [*NP,* pp. 161–62]

Hunter asserted that the Phillis Wheatley Association was "an instrument for [the] social and moral redemption" of young black women (*NP,* p. 157). A prerequisite for this redemption, Hunter maintained, was surveillance over all aspects of the lives of the girls in the home:

> In fact it was necessary at all times to guard our girls from evil surroundings. I kept a vigilant ear at the switchboard in my office to catch conversations of a doubtful character, and to intercept assigna-

> tions. No effort we made to restrict tenancy to girls of good character could exclude the ignorant, the foolish, and the weak, for these had to be protected as well. In the company of a policeman whom I could trust, I would sometimes follow couples to places of assignation, rescue the girl, and assist in the arrest of her would-be seducer. [*NP*, pp. 128–29]

There are extraordinary contradictions present in this narrative reconstructing the life of a woman who when young had declared her independence from both the patriarchal power of her husband and the maternal power of her mother by walking away from both of them to "find and keep the freedom [she] so ardently desired," only to find herself in her mature years thwarting the desires of other young women by lurking in hallways to eavesdrop on their telephone calls and marching off into the night accompanied by the police to have their lovers arrested. And, yet, Hunter clearly tries to establish a maternal framework to disguise and legitimate what are actually exploitative relations of power. Exploitation becomes nurturance when Hunter describes the white mistress acting as a "foster mother" to a young black domestic worker and when she herself dominates the lives of her charges in the Phyllis Wheatley Association. Hunter, remembering her own mother as weak and helpless, created the association as a matriarchy that allowed her to institutionalize and occupy a space of overwhelming matriarchal power over younger black women.

Although Hunter is uncritical of and, indeed, manipulates and abuses the possibilities of matriarchal power, she is explicit in her criticism of the ways in which an abusive patriarchal power becomes embedded in the corrupt legal and political machinery of city governance. Hunter is trenchant in her analysis of the mutually beneficial relations between "unscrupulous politicians," the "rapacity of realtors," the creation of the segregated ghetto, and organized vice in Cleveland. But urban blacks are situated as merely the victims of the forces of corruption: the politicians, Hunter felt, played "upon the ignorance of the Negro voter to entrench themselves in office, and then deliver[ed] the Negro over to every force of greed and vice which stalked around him" (*NP*, p. 121).

Hunter utilizes the forces of matriarchal power to declare war on what she feels to be her most formidable enemy, "commercialized vice." She describes her battle in the most epic of biblical language, a battle in which she joins with a "dreadful monster . . . spawned by greed and ignorance . . . hideous to behold. 'Out of its belly came fire and smoke, and its mouth was as the mouth of a lion . . . and its wages were death'" (*NP*, p. 120). Corrupt city politics enables and maintains the monstrous network that feeds on the young female souls in Hunter's charge, but at its heart is a single patriarchal figure whom she refers to only as "Starlight."[9] If

9. This figure was Albert D. "Starlight" Boyd, whom Katrina Hazzard-Gordon refers

Hunter sees herself as the matriarchal savior of young black women, she describes "Starlight" as the "'Great Mogul' of organized vice." He is the epitome of the seducer of young black women whom he manipulates, betrays, and then drags as "prisoners" down into the depths of "shame and degradation" (*NP*, p. 122). But, although the war is figuratively between these forces of patriarchal power and maternal influence, Hunter's matriarchal power is aimed directly at other women. Black female sexual behavior, because according to Hunter it is degenerate, threatens the progress of the race: threatens to "tumble gutterward," in her words, the "headway which the Negro had made toward the state of good citizenship" (*NP*, p. 126).

Dance halls and nightclubs are particular targets of Hunter's reformist zeal, and she identifies these cultural spaces, located in the "heart of [the] newly created Negro slum district[s]," as the site of the production of vice as spectacle: "Here, to the tune of St. Louis voodoo blues, half-naked Negro girls dance shameless dances with men in Spanish costumes. . . . The whole atmosphere is one of unrestrained animality, the jungle faintly veneered with civilized trappings" (*NP*, pp. 132–33). Places of amusement and of recreation for black people are condemned as morally dangerous and described as being filled with "lewd men and wretched women" (*NP*, p. 132). Nightclubs where black women perform for a white audience threaten the very foundations of Hunter's definitions of acceptable interracial relations:

> Interracial co-operation built the Phillis Wheatley Association and is carrying on its work; a co-operation of Negroes and whites for worthy purposes; which can gauge the spiritual contribution the Negro has made to American life, since his arrival in America. But in the meeting of blacks and whites in night clubs . . . there is to be found only cause for regret and head-hanging by both races. On the one side an exhibition of unbridled animality, on the other a blase quest for novel sensations, a vicarious gratification of the dark and violent desires of man's nature, a voluntary return to the jungle. [*NP*, p. 133]

There are deep fears being expressed in this passage in which the exploitation of black women is only one concern among many. These fears haunt the entire narrative and are also embedded in Kellor's account of young, black migrating women: fears of a rampant and uncontrolled female sexu-

---

to as a "political strongman." He owned and operated Woodluff Hall, the dance hall that Hunter felt was so disreputable, and the Starlight Café. Boyd had numerous estate holdings and links to prostitution and gambling and helped to deliver the black votes of the Eleventh Ward to the Republican boss Maurice Maschke (Katrina Hazzard-Gordon, *Jookin': The Rise of Social Dance Formations in African-American Culture* [Philadelphia, 1990], p. 127; see also pp. 128, 130–32, and 136–37).

ality; fears of miscegenation; and fears of the assertion of an independent black female desire that has been unleashed through migration. If a black woman can claim her freedom and migrate to an urban environment, what is to keep her from negotiating her own path through its streets? What are the consequences of the female self-determination evident in such a journey for the establishment of a socially acceptable moral order that defines the boundaries of respectable sexual relations? What, indeed, is to be the framework of discipline and strategies of policing that can contain and limit black female sexuality? These are the grounds of contestation in which black women became the primary targets for the moral panic about urban immorality.

St. Clair Drake and Horace Cayton in their history of Chicago, *Black Metropolis,* describe how the existence of residential restrictive convenants made middle-class neighborhoods in Bronzeville "the beach upon which broke the human flotsam which was tossed into the city streets by successive waves of migration from the South."[10] They also describe the deep ambivalence in the attitudes of the black middle class toward the black working class who, as Drake and Cayton insist, perform "the essential digging, sweeping, and serving which make Metropolitan life tolerable" (*BM,* p. 523). This ambivalence, they argue, caused the black upper class to live a contradictory existence. On the one hand they defined their social position by emphasizing their *differentness* from the lower class:

> But, as Race Leaders, the upper class must [also] identify itself psychologically with "The Race," and The Race includes a lot of people who would never be accepted socially. Upper-class Negroes, too, depend upon the Negro masses for their support if they are business or professional men. The whole orientation of the Negro upper class thus becomes one of trying to speed up the processes by which the lower class can be transformed from a poverty-stricken group, isolated from the general stream of American life, into a counterpart of middle-class America. [*BM,* p. 563]

Hunter, clearly, lives this contradiction: her self-definition and her right to control her own behavioral boundaries are beyond question. But, by positioning herself as part of the emergent black bourgeoisie, Hunter secures her personal autonomy in the process of claiming the right to circumscribe the rights of young black working-class women and to transform their behavior on the grounds of nurturing the progress of the race as a whole.

What Drake and Cayton fail to recognize, however, is the extent to which the behavioral transformation of this lower class was thought to be

10. St. Clair Drake and Horace R. Cayton, *Black Metropolis: A Study of Negro Life in a Northern City* (New York, 1946), p. 577; hereafter abbreviated *BM.*

about transforming the behavior of black working-class women. Hunter's accounts of the women who represented the success stories of the Phillis Wheatley Association, for example, are narratives of the transformation of the behavior of migrant working-class black women to conform to middle-class norms of acceptable sexual behavior while actually being confirmed in their subordinate, working-class status as female domestics. These success stories represented the triumphant fulfilment of the mission of the Phillis Wheatley Association, a mission that declared itself to be "to discover, protect, cherish, and perpetuate the beauty and power of Negro Womanhood," but which was primarily concerned with shaping and disciplining a quiescent urban, black, female, working-class population.

The texts that draw on aspects of this discourse of black female sexuality as a way to respond to northern urban migration are multiple and varied. In two important novels about Harlem during the twenties, Carl Van Vechten's *Nigger Heaven* (1926) and Claude McKay's *Home to Harlem* (1928), both authors use their female characters as the terrain on which to map a relation between the sexual and class politics of urban black life.[11] While neither author appears to be overtly interested in prescribing a program of social engineering, both novels are fictions of black urban classes in formation. Central to the success of the emergent black middle class in these two novels is the evolution of urban codes of black masculinity. In each text representations of urban black women are used as both the means by which male protagonists will achieve or will fail to achieve social mobility and as signs of various possible threats to the emergence of the wholesome black masculinity necessary for the establishment of an acceptable black male citizenship in the American social order.

The first part of *Nigger Heaven* focuses on Mary Love, a figure of virginal purity. The failure of Byron Kasson, the male protagonist, to recognize the worth of Mary to the social security of his own future leads directly to his social disintegration. Van Vechten, a white patron of black culture and black artists, describes Mary as "cold":

> She had an instinctive horror of promiscuity, of being handled, even touched, by a man who did not mean a good deal to her. This might, she sometimes argued with herself, have something to do with her white inheritance, but Olive [her friend], who was far whiter, was lacking in this inherent sense of prudery. At any rate, whatever the cause, Mary realized that she was different in this respect from most of the other girls she knew. The Negro blood was there, warm and passionately earnest: all her preferences and prejudices were on the side of the race into which she had been born. She was as capable, she

11. See Carl Van Vechten, *Nigger Heaven* (New York, 1926), hereafter abbreviated *NH;* and Claude McKay, *Home to Harlem* (1928; New York, 1987), hereafter abbreviated *HH.*

> was convinced, of amorous emotion, as any of her friends, but the fact remained that she was more selective. Oh, the others were respectable enough; they did not involve themselves too deeply. On the other hand, they did not flee from a kiss in the dark. A casual kiss in the dark was a repellent idea to Mary. What she wanted was a kiss in the light. [*NH,* p. 54]

Van Vechten appears to dismiss, or put in doubt, the classic nineteenth-century literary explanation of blood "admixture" for these opposing aspects of Mary's fictional personality in favor of using a more contemporary, and urban, explanation that uses Mary's "horror of promiscuity" as a sign of her secure class position.

Mary's middle-class existence is initially defined through her job; she works as a museum curator gathering together collections of African art. But Van Vechten also carefully defines her differentness from migrant and working-class black women in a variety of more complex ways. When Mary attends a rent party, for example, she is figuratively defiled by the gin and juice that is spilled over her and stains her clothes. When she regretfully wonders why she danced at this party until two in the morning Van Vechten has her mentally discipline herself by reflecting on a long, directly quoted passage from Gertrude Stein's "Melanctha." The passage is an extended reflection on the dangers of "colored people" getting excited and "running around and . . . drinking and doing everything bad they can think of" instead of "working hard and caring about their working and living regular with their families and saving up all their money, so they will have some to bring their children up better" (*NH,* p. 57). Mary carefully differentiates herself culturally and ideologically from the black working class. On the one hand, she defines spirituals, which deeply affect her, as a cultural form produced from "real faith," which has the power to "touch most of us . . . and make us want to cry or shout." But on the other hand, she sees the culture of "servant girls and the poor" as being very different. The latter, she is convinced, don't really "feel faith—except as an escape from the drudgery of their lives. They don't really stop playing Numbers or dancing on Sunday or anything else that their religion forbids them to do. They enjoy themselves in church on Sunday as they do in the cabarets on week-days" (*NH,* pp. 60, 59). Mary's disdain of sexual promiscuity is firmly embedded, by Van Vechten, in a middle-class ideology of endlessly deferred gratification.

The counterpoint to Mary is a character called Lasca Sartoris, who uses her sexuality to negotiate her way through her life. Unlike Mary, who has never even been to the South, Lasca, the daughter of a country preacher, "began by teaching school in the backwoods down in Louisiana" and then migrated north when an uncle left her an inheritance. In the city Lasca is said to "cut loose" dancing, playing the piano, and singing in Harlem clubs all night (*NH,* pp. 83–84). Lasca's sexuality ensnares a rich and much older husband whose death leaves her a rich heiress. Van Vechten uses Lasca as a figure of overt and degenerate sexuality whose behavior is absolutely outside of all moral boundaries. She attracts, then physically and emotionally destroys and discards a series of male lovers, including Byron Kasson, having embroiled them in an intense bacchanalia of alchoholic, drug, and sexual abuse. For Byron, the would-be intellectual and writer, his choice of the influence of Lasca, rather than Mary, brings a certain end to all his hopes and ambition.

Claude McKay has a rather more subtle but, for women, an equally damning approach to the relation between black sexual politics, masculinity, and the securing of social position. McKay's protagonist, Jake, is ultimately saved by Felice, the woman he loves, in an interesting narrative sleight of hand that transforms Felice from the position of prostitute to a figure of wholesome sexuality. Jake arrives in Harlem and meets Felice in a bar. He spends the night with her, pays her, and leaves the following morning thinking he will never see her again. Wondering if he can afford breakfast Jake discovers that Felice has returned all his money to his pocket, thus proving that her sex is not for sale. This gesture convinces Jake that he must return to Felice, but he is quickly lost in the unfamiliar city streets, and it takes the whole course of the novel for him to find her again. On the journey back toward this "true" woman, however, Jake has to negotiate the vice and temptations of the city, which are embodied in a series of other women that he meets.

McKay has a much deeper, richer, and more complex understanding of the cultural forms of the black urban landscape on which he draws than Van Vechten. But, despite this formal complexity, McKay situates his female figures in a very simplistic manner in various degrees of approximation to an uncontrolled and, therefore, problematic sexual behavior. For Jake's journey is not just a journey to find the right woman; it is, primarily, a journey of black masculinity in formation, a sort of *Pilgrim's Progress* in which a number of threatening embodiments of the female and the feminine have to be negotiated. The most significant of these female figures is Rose, a nightclub singer at a cabaret called the Congo. As its name implies, the Congo is "a real throbbing little Africa in New York. It was an amusement place entirely for the unwashed of the Black Belt. . . . Girls coming from the South to try their future in New York," McKay stresses, "always reached the Congo first" (*HH,* pp. 29–30). These "chippies [that] come up from down home," a male friend of Jake's advises him, represent "the best pickings" in Harlem (*HH,* p. 35). Felice, of course, is never seen there. At the heart of what McKay describes as the "thick, dark-colorful, and fascinating" Congo, he situates the blues and Rose, the blues singer (*HH,* p. 36). As far as Jake is concerned, Rose is "a wonderful tissue of throbbing flesh," though he neither loves nor feels "any deep desire for her" (*HH,* pp. 42, 114). The assumption of the novel is that male love and desire could not be generated for, or be sustained by, a woman like Rose, who is characterized as bisexual because she lacks the acceptable feminine qualities of "tenderness . . . timidity . . . [and] aloofness." Indeed, Rose's sexual ambiguity is positioned as a threat to the very existence of black masculinity, reducing Jake to the role of a "big, good slave" (*HH,* pp. 42, 41). McKay proposes that only a pathological and distorted form of masculine power could exist in such a relationship when Rose makes masochistic demands that Jake brutalize her, confirming his belief "that a woman could always go further than a man in coarseness, depravity, and sheer cupidity" (*HH,* p. 69). Jake's refusal to beat Rose is a triumph of wholesome masculinity over the degenerate female element and allows Jake to proceed on his journey to become a man.

The dance hall and the cabaret, in the texts that I have been discussing, are the most frequently referenced landscapes in which black female promiscuity and sexual degeneracy were described. In William H. Jones's sociological study of black urban recreation and amusement (1927), the dance hall was a complex and a contested social space. Jones could not condemn the dance hall as an "essentially antisocial institution" because it was possible that a dance hall could be a place in which "romantic love of the most idealistic type" could blossom. But dance halls encouraged a quick intimacy that could also lead the young "on the downward path to crime."[12] What Jones condemned without compromise was the dancing that took place in the dance halls. He saw modern dances as nothing more than "sexual pantomimes. They are similar to many of the ancient and primitive methods of publicly arousing human passions in preparation for lascivious orgies." He asserted that the results of his "careful investigation disclosed the fact that . . . a large amount of illicit sex behavior is unquestionably the natural sequence of certain modern forms of dancing" (*RA,* p. 122).

Jones reserved his greatest vehemence for the cabaret, where

> excess in dancing, jungle laughter, and semi-alcoholic beverages are characteristic features of their life. Here, jazz music is carried to extremes. In general, there is more abandon achieved by the dancers than in the formal dance hall, and more of a tendency toward nakedness on the part of the female entertainers. [*RA,* p. 131]

What Jones particularly feared was what he called "social demoralization." He designated these recreational social spaces as places where "the most powerful human impulses and emotions are functioning," impulses and emotions that threatened the deterioration of the fragile social fabric of the black urban community (*RA,* p. 122).

12. William H. Jones, *Recreation and Amusement among Negroes in Washington, D. C.: A Sociological Analysis of the Negro in an Urban Environment* (Washington, D. C., 1927), p. 121; hereafter abbreviated *RA.*

The existence of dance halls and cabarets was particularly dangerous to the moral health of the black middle class, Jones maintained, because of "the rapidity and ease with which the anti-social forms of dancing spread upwards into and engross the so-called higher classes." He viewed the social fabric of the black urban community as fragile because of the lack of "adequate bulwarks against the encroachment of such behavior forms upon the life of the more advanced groups of Negroes" (*RA*, p. 122). "Class stratification" within the black community, Jones continued, only "seems to be strong." If black middle-class public opinion could generate disapproval of "the vulgar, sexually-suggestive modern dances . . . they would be compelled to confine themselves to the lower anti-social cultural groups in which they originated" (*RA*, p. 123). His appeal to the mobilization of social disapproval appears to be as much about generating a black middle-class ideology of solidarity and coexistence as about challenging threats to the social mores of that group. If middle-class hegemony could be established in the black community it could more effectively discipline the black working class through the implementation of what Jones refers to as "mechanisms of control whereby forces which tend to disintegrate and demoralize the higher forms of culture may be excluded or annihilated" (*RA*, p. 123).

Between Kellor's report for *Charities* and Jones's book the moral panic about the lack of control over the sexual behavior of black women had become absorbed into the fundamental assumptions of the sociological analysis of urban black culture, which thus designated many of its forms of entertainment and leisure "pathological" and in need of greater institutional control.[13] Kathy Peiss, in her recent analysis of white working-women's leisure and recreation in New York, describes how white reformers in the early decades of the twentieth century believed that "the primary purpose of reform for working women was to inculcate standards of respectable behavior." Perceptions of "a rising tide of promiscuity and immorality" and panics over "white slavery and commercialized prostitution," she argues, motivated Progressive reformers whose prime target was increasingly "the growing menace of commercial amusements."[14] But the black urban community was constructed as pathological in very specific ways. Black urban life was viewed as being intimately associated with commercialized vice because black migrants to

13. Jones acknowledged his greatest debt to Robert E. Park and others of the Department of Sociology at the University of Chicago.

14. Kathy Peiss, *Cheap Amusements: Working Women and Leisure in Turn-of-the-Century New York* (Philadelphia, 1986), pp. 178–79. The focus of my analysis is rather different than Peiss's. She describes her book as "a study of young working women's culture in turn-of-the-century New York City—the customs, values, public styles, and ritualized interactions—expressed in leisure time" (p. 3). Not only am I concentrating on black women rather than white women, but also I am most interested here in the black women for whom the site of leisure was a place of work rather than recreation.

cities were forced to live in or adjacent to areas previously established as red-light districts in which prostitution and gambling had been contained. The existence of restrictive convenants enforced black residential segregation and limited the expansion of what became identified as black urban ghettos.[15] It was within the confines of East St. Louis, the south side of Chicago, the tenderloin in Kansas City, and Harlem in New York that an entertainment industry that served both a white and a black clientele was located and from which an urban blues culture emerged.

On the eve of the depression black women who had migrated to urban areas were still overwhelmingly limited to employment in domestic service and as laundresses. In Chicago, for example, between the First World War and the onset of the depression, over 40 percent of white women workers but only 5 percent of black women workers who entered the labor force obtained "clean" work (see *BM,* pp. 220–29). The category "clean" work referred to jobs like office secretary and department store clerk; "clean" work was the type of employment from which black women were rigorously excluded. From the biographies and autobiographies of the black women who eventually became entertainers it is clear that joining a touring vaudeville troupe or tent show was an important avenue of geographic mobility for young black women who were too poor to pay for train fares and for whom hopping a freight car was dangerous. In addition, being a member of a vaudeville show or performing in a nightclub was not attractive primarily because it offered a mythic life of glamor but because it was a rare opportunity to do "clean" work and to reject the life of a domestic servant.

When she was eight years old Josephine Baker started her first job and discovered that working as a maid for a white mistress was not "the happy and human relation" that Jane Edna Hunter maintained it should be. Baker was assured by her mistress, Mrs. Keiser, that she loved children, and she promised Baker the shoes and a coat that her own family were too poor to provide. However, Baker had to start to work at five in the morning so she could be at school by nine, and when she arrived home in the afternoon she had to work again until ten o'clock at night when she was sent to bed in the cellar to sleep with the dog. One day when Baker made a mistake Mrs. Keiser punished her by plunging the little girl's arms into boiling water. This story and Baker's account of how she watched white people murder and torture her relatives and neighbors during the East St. Louis riot of 1917 are situated in her autobiography as the preface to her decision to leave St. Louis when she was thirteen years old and get on a train with a vaudeville troupe called the Dixie Steppers.[16]

15. See William Barlow, *"Looking Up at Down": The Emergence of Blues Culture* (Philadelphia, 1989), pp. 240–43 (on Kansas City), 250–51 (on St. Louis), and 287–92 (on Chicago). See also *BM,* pp. 174–213.

16. See Josephine Baker and Jo Bouillon, *Josephine,* trans. Mariana Fitzpatrick (New

Alberta Hunter left Memphis when she was thirteen because she had heard that young girls in Chicago were being paid ten dollars a week to sing.[17] In 1912 she started working in a club called Dago Frank's, singing to an audience of pimps and prostitutes, and then moved to Hugh Hoskins, a club for "confidence men and their girls who were pickpockets." In many ways Alberta Hunter's story of her early years in Chicago epitomizes the life from which Jane Edna Hunter wanted to save young black women in the name of maternal protection. But Alberta Hunter emphasizes how she found maternal care and nurturance from the prostitutes in her audience and describes how "the prostitutes were so wonderful, they'd always make the 'Johns' give me money you know. . . . They'd go out and buy me little dresses and things to put on me so I'd look nice."[18]

Ethel Waters agreed to join the act of two vaudevillians she met in a Philadelphia saloon because she was offered ten dollars a week playing the Lincoln Theatre when she was "getting three fifty a week as a scullion and chambermaid [at the Harrod Apartments] and a dollar and a quarter more for taking home some of the guests' laundry."[19] Waters grew up in the red-light districts of Philadelphia, and in her autobiography she asserts that she "always had great respect for whores" (*H,* p. 17). Like Alberta Hunter she utilizes the language of maternal nurturance when she describes how her friendship with a young prostitute blossomed:

> Being hardly more than a child herself, Blanche often played with me, read me stories, and sang little songs with me. Her beauty fascinated me. I loved her. There was a great camaraderie between us, and that young prostitute gave me some of the attention and warm affection I was starving for. Whenever I tipped off the sporting world that the cops were just around the corner I felt I was doing it for Blanche and her friends. [*H,* p. 18]

Waters reveals a consciousness of being part of a world in which women were under surveillance and has little hesitation in declaring her allegiance. The images and figures of the sources of both exploitation and nurturance in the lives of these young black women are in direct contrast to and, indeed, in direct conflict with the attempts of the black middle class to police and discipline female sexuality.

York, 1977), pp. 3–4. See also Phyllis Rose, *Jazz Cleopatra: Josephine Baker in Her Time* (New York, 1989), p. 12.

17. See Frank C. Taylor and Gerald Cook, *Alberta Hunter: A Celebration in Blues* (New York, 1987), pp. 20–23.

18. Alberta Hunter, quoted in Stuart Goldman (producer), *Alberta Hunter: My Castle's Rockin'* (1988).

19. Ethel Waters and Charles Samuels, *His Eye Is on the Sparrow* (New York, 1951), p. 72; hereafter abbreviated *H.*

Black women blues singers, musicians, and performers dominated the black recording industry and vaudeville circuit throughout the twenties, and they are the central figures in the emergence and establishment of an urban blues culture. However, in order to acknowledge their roles as the primary cultural mediators of the conditions of transition and the producers of a culture of migration we have to challenge the contemporary histories of the formation of a black urban culture as a history of the black middle class. The dominance of the conceptual paradigm of the Harlem Renaissance with its emphasis on the practices of literature and fine art relies on a belief that the black middle class did, in fact, accomplish and secure its own cultural and political dominance within black America. However, as Houston A. Baker, Jr., argues, what is called the Renaissance actually marks the historical moment of the failure of the black bourgeoisie to achieve cultural hegemony and to become a dominant social force.[20]

The contradictory nature of the culture that was produced in black urban America between the teens and the depression has not been retained or absorbed within black urban cultural histories. The twenties must be viewed as a period of ideological, political, and cultural contestation between an emergent black bourgeoisie and an emerging urban black working class. The cultural revolution or successful renaissance that did occur stemmed from this terrain of conflict in which the black women who were so central to the formation of an urban blues culture created a web of connections among working-class migrants. The possibilities of both black female liberation and oppression were voiced through a music that spoke to the desires which were released in the dramatic shift in social relations that occurred in a historical moment of crisis and dislocation.[21]

Women's blues was not only a central mechanism of cultural mediation but also the primary means of the expression of the disrupted social relations associated with urban migration. The blues women did not pas-

20. See Houston A. Baker, Jr., *Modernism and the Harlem Renaissance* (Chicago, 1987).

21. Virginia Yans-McLaughlin argues that the new scholarship in immigration and migration studies has moved away from questions about

> individual and group agency toward the social relations of exchange. So, instead of individuals assimilating or achieving, we have group strategies and networks. What we might call a network-exchange theory seems to be emerging as a potential alternative to assimilation and human-capital theory. In network-exchange theory, an ethnic group's human capital is not simply transported from one place to another by individuals who fold their riches into the American system. Although it is true that the groups are sometimes portrayed as holders of assets, these are transformed to new purposes; indeed, immigrant groups seem capable of creating new advantages for themselves. The network structure that originally functioned as the grid connecting Old World kin might, for example, transform itself in ethnic subeconomies to provide jobs, housing, or even business opportunities. [Virginia Yans-McLaughlin, introduction, *Immigration Reconsidered: History, Sociology, and Politics*, ed. Yans-McLaughlin (New York, 1990), p. 12]

Using such a methodology Suzanne Model argues that because of their very limited access

sively reflect the vast social changes of their time; they provided new ways of thinking about these changes, alternative conceptions of the physical and social world for their audience of migrating and urban women and men, and social models for women who aspired to escape from and improve their conditions of existence. I have already described how hopping freight cars, because of the inherent dangers associated with that form of travel, was not a viable option for women and that travelling tent shows and vaudeville on the Theater Owner's Booking Association circuit (TOBA) offered an alternative way to achieve mobility for young women—Mamie Smith, for example, started dancing when she was ten, and Ida Cox left home to join the Black and Tan Minstrel Show when she was fourteen. This increase in their physical mobility parallels their musical challenges to sexual conventions and gendered social roles. However, the field of blues history is dominated by the assumption that "authentic" blues forms are entirely rural in origin and are produced by the figure of the wandering, lone male. Thus the formation of mythologies of blues masculinity, which depend on this popular image, have obscured the ways in which the gendering of women was challenged in the blues. The blues women of the twenties, who recorded primarily in urban centers but who employed and modified the full range of rural and urban blues styles, have come to be regarded as professionalized aberrations who commercialized and adulterated "pure" blues forms. But as Chris Albertson insists, the blues "women were all aggressive women [who] knew what they wanted and went after it."[22] The blues women brought to the black, urban, working class an awareness of its social existence and acted creatively to vocalize the contradictions and tensions of the terrain of sexual politics in the relation of black working-class culture to the culture of the emergent black middle class.[23] In doing so they inspired other women to claim the "freedom [they] so ardently desired."

---

to the job market black migrants were unable, or failed to establish such a system of mutual assistance. Although it is clear that networks of exchange did indeed exist within black urban migrant enclaves my argument here is that network-exchange theory is unnecessarily limited if it is applied only to access to the labor market and to alternative economies that existed within migrant communities. I would argue that urban blues culture could profitably be regarded as a network of exchange or web of connection rather than as a conglomeration of individual achievement. See Suzanne W. Model, "Work and Family: Blacks and Immigrants from South and East Europe," in ibid., pp. 130–59. It would seem to me that the role of the *Chicago Defender* would be important in writing a history that documented the system of mutual exchange in black communities that provided information about and access to the job market. See, for example, Emmett J. Scott, "Letters of Negro Migrants of 1916–1918," *Journal of Negro History* 4 (July 1919): 290–340, and "Additional Letters of Negro Migrants of 1916–1918," *Journal of Negro History* 4 (Oct. 1919):412–65.

22. Chris Albertson, quoted in Carole van Falkenburg and Christine Dall (producers), *Wild Women Don't Have the Blues* (1989).

23. See my forthcoming book, *Women, Migration, and the Formation of a Blues Culture.*

Woman Skin Deep: Feminism and the Postcolonial Condition

Sara Suleri

Given the current climate of rampant and gleeful anti-intellectualism that has overtaken the mass media at the present time, both literary and cultural interpretive practitioners have more than ample reason to reassess, to reexamine, and to reassert those theoretical concerns that constitute or question the identity of each putatively marginal group. There are dreary reiterations that must be made, and even more dreary navigations between the Scylla and Charybdis so easily identified in journalism as a conflict between the "thought police" on the one hand and the proponents of "multiculturalism" on the other. As readers of mass culture, let us note by way of example the astonishing attention that the media has accorded the academy: the Gulf War took up three months of their time, whereas we have been granted over a year of headlines and glossy magazine newsworthiness. Is our anathema, then, more pervasive than that of Saddam Hussein? In what fashion is the academy now to be read as one of the greatest sources of sedition against the new world order? The moment demands urgent consideration of how the outsideness of cultural criticism is being translated into that most tedious dichotomy that pits the "academy" against the "real world." While I am somewhat embarrassed by the prospect of having to contemplate such a simplistic binarism, this essay seeks to question its own cultural parameters by situating both its knowledge and its ignorance in relation to the devastating rhetoric of "us and them" that beleaguers issues of identity formation today. Grant me the luxury, then, of not having to supply quotation marks around several of

This article originally appeared in *Critical Inquiry* 18 (Summer 1992).

the terms employed, and—since the time of life is short—an acknowledgement that the "we" to which I am forced to take recourse is indeed very, very wee.

The sustained and trivializing attack on what is represented as academic self-censorship cannot be segregated from current reformulations of cultural identities: the former will continue to misconstrue deliberately questions of marginality into solutions of frivolity, or cultural criticism into tyrannical cliches about the political correctness of the thought police. And, if the debate on multiculturalism simply degenerates into a misplaced desire for the institution of rainbow coalition curricula, its shadow will fall in all heaviness on those disciplines most responsible for producing the kind of rhetoric that is presently castigated for its political rectitude. Discursive formations that question canonical and cultural censors, in other words, are precisely the ones to be singled out as demonstrative of the academy's spinelessly promiscuous submission to "correctness." The list of public enemies thus produced is hardly surprising: our prostitution is repeatedly characterized by intellectual allegiances to the identity of postcolonialism, of gender, of gay and lesbian studies, and finally, of the body. The academy has subcultured itself out of viable existence, we are told, and the subtextual moral that attends such journalistic cautionary tales is almost too obvious to merit articulation: if thy left hand offendeth thee, cut it off.

Since none of us are partial to being lopped, the only resort appears to be a two-tiered response to the anti-intellectualism that is our "fin de siècle" fate. First—as has been clear for at least the last year—the world lies all before us; we have and must continue to respond. While much of the material that has appeared in the popular press is so low-grade as to disqualify itself as discourse, the academy must persist in making a resolute attempt to present some firm alternative opinions within those very columns. On a very simplistic and pragmatic level, if we must be freaks, let us be freaks with a voice. It may well be that this effort at articulation will yield some useful readings of the peculiar identity of the professional academic: how plural are we in our constructions of singularity; and how singular in our apprehensions of the plural? The second tier of any sustained response consists of an attempt to engender within the academy an overdue exchange about the excesses and the limitations that marginal discourses must inevitably accrue, even as they seek to map the ultimate obsolescence of the dichotomy between margin and center. For until the participants in marginal discourses learn how best to critique the intellec-

---

Sara Suleri is professor of English at Yale University. She is the author of *Meatless Days* (1989) and *The Rhetoric of English India* (1992).

tual errors that inevitably accompany the provisional discursivity of the margin, the monolithic and untheorized identity of the center will always be on them. The following readings seek an alignment with the second strategic tier to contain anti-intellectualism—that is, an essay into the methodology through which contemporary academic discourse seeks to decontaminate itself of territorial affiliations and attempts instead to establish the proliferating and shifting locations of the margins of cultural identities.

1

The specific margin that is my subject is one most virulently subjected to popular parodies and to the label of irrational rectitude: the work conducted around theoretical intersections of feminism and gender studies. It would be unproductive to demonstrate that journalists are shoddy readers, or that the "elevation" of Camille Paglia's words to the pages of a soft-core porn magazine is in fact quite apposite with her discourse. An alternative margin might be found in the tensions incipient within the critical practice itself: are the easy pieties that emanate from the anti-thought-police press in any way implicit in academic discourse on this keen cultural problem? Is girl talk with a difference, in other words, at all responsible for the parodic replays that it has engendered in the scurrilous imaginations of North American magazines? If the academy chooses to be the unseen legislator through which cultural difference is regulated into grouped identities of the marginal, then an urgent intellectual duty would surely be to subject not merely our others but ourselves to the rigors of revisionary scrutiny.

If you will allow me some further space-clearing generalizations, I would claim that while current feminist discourse remains vexed by questions of identity formation and the concomitant debates between essentialism and constructivism, or distinctions between situated and universal knowledge, it is still prepared to grant an uneasy selfhood to a voice that is best described as the property of "postcolonial Woman." Whether this voice represents perspectives as divergent as the African-American or the postcolonial cultural location, its imbrications of race and gender are accorded an iconicity that is altogether too good to be true. Even though the marriage of two margins should not necessarily lead to the construction of that contradiction in terms, a "feminist center," the embarrassed privilege granted to racially encoded feminism does indeed suggest a rectitude that could be its own theoretical undoing. The concept of the postcolonial itself is too frequently robbed of historical specificity in order to function as a preapproved allegory for any mode of discursive contestation. The coupling of *postcolonial* with *woman*, however, almost inevitably leads to the simplicities that underlie unthinking celebrations of oppression, elevating the racially female voice into a metaphor for "the good." Such metaphoricity cannot exactly be called essentialist, but it certainly functions as an impediment to a reading that attempts to look beyond obvious questions of good and evil. In seeking to dismantle the iconic status of postcolonial feminism, I will attempt here to address the following questions: within the tautological margins of such a discourse, which comes first, gender or race? How, furthermore, can the issue of chronology lead to some preliminary articulation of the productive superficiality of race?

Before such questions can be raised, however, it is necessary to pay some critical attention to the mobility that has accrued in the category of postcolonialism. Where the term once referred exclusively to the discursive practices produced by the historical fact of prior colonization in certain geographically specific segments of the world, it is now more of an abstraction available for figurative deployment in any strategic redefinition of marginality. For example, when James Clifford elaborated his position on travelling theory during a recent seminar, he invariably substituted the metaphoric condition of postcoloniality for the obsolete binarism between anthropologist and native.[1] As with the decentering of any discourse, however, this reimaging of the postcolonial closes as many epistemological possibilities as it opens. On the one hand, it allows for a vocabulary of cultural migrancy, which helpfully derails the postcolonial condition from the strictures of national histories, and thus makes way for the theoretical articulations best typified by Homi Bhabha's recent anthology, *Nation and Narration.*[2] On the other hand, the current metaphorization of postcolonialism threatens to become so amorphous as to repudiate any locality for cultural thickness. A symptom of this terminological and theoretical dilemma is astutely read in Kwame Anthony Appiah's essay, "Is the Post- in Postmodernism the Post- in Postcolonial?"[3] Appiah argues for a discursive space-clearing that allows postcolonial discourse a figurative flexibility and at the same time reaffirms its radical locality within historical exigencies. His discreet but firm segregation of the postcolonial from the postmodern is indeed pertinent to the dangerous democracy accorded the coalition between postcolonial and feminist theories, in which each term serves to reify the potential pietism of the other.

In the context of contemporary feminist discourse, I would argue, the category of postcolonialism must be read both as a free-floating metaphor for cultural embattlement and as an almost obsolete signifier for the

1. James Clifford's course, "Travel and Identity in Twentieth-Century Interculture," was given as the Henry Luce Seminar at Yale University, fall 1990.

2. See *Nation and Narration,* ed. Homi K. Bhabha (New York, 1990).

3. See Kwame Anthony Appiah, "Is the Post- in Postmodernism the Post- in Postcolonial?" *Critical Inquiry* 17 (Winter 1991): 336–57.

historicity of race. There is no available dichotomy that could neatly classify the ways in which such a redefinition of postcoloniality is necessarily a secret sharer in similar reconfigurations of feminism's most vocal articulation of marginality, or the obsessive attention it has recently paid to the racial body. Is the body in race subject or object, or is it more dangerously an objectification of a methodology that aims for radical subjectivity? Here, the binarism that informs Chandra Mohanty's paradigmatic essay, "Under Western Eyes: Feminist Scholarship and Colonial Discourses," deserves particular consideration. Where Mohanty engages in a particular critique of "Third World Woman" as a monolithic object in the texts of Western feminism, her argument is premised on the irreconcilability of gender as history and gender as culture. "What happens," queries Mohanty, "when [an] assumption of 'women as an oppressed group' is situated in the context of Western feminist writing about third world women?" What happens, apparently, begs her question. In contesting what she claims is a "colonialist move," Mohanty proceeds to argue that "Western feminists alone become the true 'subjects' of this counter-history. Third World women, on the other hand, never rise above the debilitating generality of their 'object' status."[4] A very literal ethic underlies such a dichotomy, one that demands attention to its very obviousness: how is this objectivism to be avoided? How will the ethnic voice of womanhood counteract the cultural articulation that Mohanty too easily dubs as the exegesis of Western feminism? The claim to authenticity—only a black can speak for a black; only a postcolonial subcontinental feminist can adequately represent the lived experience of that culture—points to the great difficulty posited by the "authenticity" of female racial voices in the great game that claims to be the first narrative of what the ethnically constructed woman is deemed to want.

This desire all too often takes its theoretical form in a will to subjectivity that claims a theoretical basis most clearly contravened by the process of its analysis. An example of this point is Trinh Minh-ha's treatise, *Woman, Native, Other,*[5] which seeks to posit an alternative to the anthropological twist that constitutes the archaism through which nativism has been apprehended. Subtitled *Writing Postcoloniality and Feminism,* Trinh's book is a paradigmatic meditation that can be essentialized into a simple but crucial question: how can feminist discourse represent the categories of "woman" and "race" at the same time? If the languages of feminism and ethnicity are to escape an abrasive mutual contestation, what novel idiom can freshly articulate their radical inseparability? Trinh's strategy is to

4. Chandra Talpade Mohanty, "Under Western Eyes: Feminist Scholarship and Colonial Discourses," *Third World Women and the Politics of Feminism,* ed. Mohanty, Ann Russo, and Lourdes Torres (Bloomington, Ind., 1991), p. 71.

5. See Trinh T. Minh-ha, *Woman, Native, Other: Writing Postcoloniality and Feminism* (Bloomington, Ind., 1989); hereafter abbreviated *WNO.*

relocate her gendering of ethnic realities on the inevitable territory of postfeminism, which underscores her desire to represent discourse formation as always taking place after the fact of discourse. It further confirms my belief that had I any veto power over prefixes, *post-* would be the first to go—but that is doubtless tangential to the issue at hand. In the context of Trinh's methodology, the shape of the book itself illuminates what may best be called the endemic ill that effects a certain temporal derangement between the work's originary questions and the narratives that they engender. *Woman, Native, Other* consists of four loosely related chapters, each of which opens with an abstraction and ends with an anecdote. While there is a self-pronounced difference between the preliminary thesis outlined in the chapter "Commitment from the Mirror-Writing Box" to the concluding claims in "Grandma's Story," such a discursive distance is not matched with any logical or theoretical consistency. Instead, a work that is impelled by an impassioned need to question the lines of demarcation between race and gender concludes by falling into a predictable biological fallacy in which sexuality is reduced to the literal structure of the racial body, and theoretical interventions within this trajectory become minimalized into the naked category of lived experience.

When feminism turns to lived experience as an alternative mode of radical subjectivity, it only rehearses the objectification of its proper subject. While lived experience can hardly be discounted as a critical resource for an apprehension of the gendering of race, neither should such data serve as the evacuating principle for both historical and theoretical contexts alike. "Radical subjectivity" too frequently translates into a low-grade romanticism that cannot recognize its discursive status as *pre-* rather than *post-*. In the concluding chapter of Trinh's text, for example, a section titled "Truth and Fact: Story and History" delineates the skewed idiom that marginal subjectivities produce. In attempting to proclaim an alternative to male-identified objectivism, Trinh-as-anthropologist can only produce an equally objectifying idiom of joy:

> Let me tell you a story. For all I have is a story. Story passed on from generation to generation, named Joy. Told for the joy it gives the storyteller and the listener. Joy inherent in the process of storytelling. Whoever understands it also understands that a story, as distressing as it can be in its joy, never takes anything away from anybody. [*WNO*, p. 119]

Given that I find myself in a more acerbic relation both to the question of the constitution of specific postcolonialisms and of a more metaphoric postcolonial feminism, such a jointly universalist and individualist "joy" is not a term that I would ordinarily welcome into my discursive lexicon. On one level, its manipulation of lived experience into a somewhat fallacious allegory for the reconstitution of gendered race bespeaks a transcendence—and an attendant evasion—of the crucial cultural issues at hand. On a more dangerous level, however, such an assumption serves as a mirror image of the analyses produced by the critics of political rectitude. For both parties, "life" remains the ultimate answer to "discourse." The subject of race, in other words, cannot cohabit with the detail of a feminist language.

Trinh's transcendent idiom, of course, emanates from her somewhat free-floating understanding of "postcoloniality": is it an abstraction into which all historical specificity may be subsumed, or is it a figure for a vaguely defined ontological marginality that is equally applicable to all "minority" discourses? In either case, both the categories of "woman" and "race" assume the status of metaphors, so that each rhetoric of oppression can serve equally as a mirrored allegory for the other. Here, *Woman, Native, Other* is paradigmatic of the methodological blurring that dictates much of the discourse on identity formation in the coloring of feminist discourse. To privilege the racial body in the absence of historical context is indeed to generate an idiom that tends to waver with impressionistic haste between the abstractions of postcoloniality and the anecdotal literalism of what it means to articulate an "identity" for a woman writer of color. Despite its proclaimed location within contemporary theoretical—not to mention post-theoretical—discourse, such an idiom poignantly illustrates the hidden and unnecessary desire to resuscitate the "self."

What is most striking about such discursive practices is their failure to confront what may be characterized best as a great enamorment with the "real." Theories of postcolonial feminism eminently lend themselves to a reopening of the continued dialogue that literary and cultural studies have—and will continue to have—with the perplexing category known as realism, but at present the former discourse chooses to remain too precariously parochial to recognize the bounty that is surely its to give. Realism, however, is too dangerous a term for an idiom that seeks to raise identity to the power of theory. While both may be windmills to the quixotic urge to supply black feminism with some version of the "real," Trinh's musings on this subject add a mordantly pragmatic option to my initial question: "what comes first, race or gender?" Perhaps the query would be more finely calibrated if it were rephrased to ask, "What comes first, race, gender, or profession?" And what, in our sorry dealings with such realisms, is the most phantasmagoric category of all?

According to *Woman, Native, Other,* such a triple bind can be articulated only in order to declare that bonding is all. An opening section of that text is in fact titled "The Triple Bind"; it attempts to outline the alternative realism still to be claimed by the postcolonial feminist mentality:

> Today, the growing ethnic-feminist consciousness has made it increasingly difficult for [the woman of color who writes] to turn a blind eye

> not only to the specification of the writer as historical subject . . . but also to writing itself as a practice located at the intersection of subject and history—a literary practice that involves the possible knowledge (linguistical and ideological) of itself as such. [*WNO,* p. 6]

Here the text evades the threat of realism by taking recourse to the "peaceable" territory of writing, on which all wars may be fought with each discursive contingency in deployment. While writing may serve as a surrogate for the distance between subject (read self) and history, Trinh unwittingly makes clear her academic appreciation of alterity: the female writer, or the third person "she" that haunts her text, "is made to feel she must choose from among three conflicting identities. Writer of color? Woman writer? Or woman of color? Which comes first? Where does she place her loyalties?" (*WNO,* p. 6). The hierarchy of loyalties thus listed illustrates the danger inherent in such cultural lists: the uneasy proclamation with which *Woman, Native, Other* sets out to be the "first full-length study of post-feminism" (according to the book's jacket) is a self-defeating project, for feminism has surely long since laid aside the issue of an individualized female loyalty as its originating assumption. If race is to complicate the project of divergent feminisms, in other words, it cannot take recourse to biologism, nor to the incipient menace of rewriting alterity into the ambiguous shape of the exotic body.

The body that serves as testimony for lived experience, however, has received sufficient interrogation from more considered perspectives on the cultural problems generated by the dialogue between gender and race, along with the hyperrealist idiom it may generate. Hazel Carby helpfully advocates that

> black feminist criticism [should] be regarded critically as a problem, not a solution, as a sign that should be interrogated, a locus of contradictions. Black feminist criticism has its source and its primary motivation in academic legitimation, placement within a framework of bourgeois humanistic discourse.[6]

The concomitant question that such a problem raises is whether the signification of gendered race necessarily returns to the realism that it most seeks to disavow. If realism is the Eurocentric and patriarchal pattern of adjudicating between disparate cultural and ethnic realities, then it is surely the task of radical feminism to provide an alternative perspective. In the vociferous discourse that such a task has produced, however, the question of alternativism is all too greatly subsumed either into the radical strategies that are designed to dictate the course of situated experience, or

6. Hazel V. Carby, *Reconstructing Womanhood: The Emergence of the Afro-American Woman Novelist* (New York, 1987), p. 15.

into the methodological imperatives that impell a work related to *Woman, Native, Other* such as bell hooks's *Talking Back: Thinking Feminist, Thinking Black.*

While the concept of "talking back" may appear to be both invigorating and empowering to a discourse interested in the reading of gendered race, the text *Talking Back* is curiously engaged in talking to itself; in rejecting Caliban's mode of protest, its critique of colonization is quietly narcissistic in its projection of what a black and thinking female body may appear to be, particularly in the context of its repudiation of the genre of realism. Yet this is the genre, after all, in which African-American feminism continues to seek legitimation: hooks's study is predicated on the anecdotes of lived experience and their capacity to provide an alternative to the discourse of what she terms patriarchal rationalism. Here the unmediated quality of a local voice serves as a substitute for any theoretical agenda that can make more than a cursory connection between the condition of postcolonialism and the question of gendered race. Where hooks claims to speak beyond binarism, her discourse keeps returning to the banality of easy dichotomies: "Dare I speak to oppressed and oppressor in the same voice? Dare I speak to you in a language that will take us away from the boundaries of domination, a language that will not fence you in, bind you, or hold you? Language is also a place of struggle."[7] The acute embarrassment generated by such an idiom could possibly be regarded as a radical rhetorical strategy designed to induce racial discomfort in its audience, but it more frequently registers as black feminism's failure to move beyond the proprietary rights that can be claimed by any oppressed discourse.

As does Trinh's text, hooks's claims that personal narrative is the only salve to the rude abrasions that Western feminist theory has inflicted on the body of ethnicity. The tales of lived experience, however, cannot function as a sufficient alternative, particularly when they are predicated on dangerously literal professions of postcolonialism. *Yearning: Race, Gender, and Cultural Politics,* hooks's more recent work, rehearses a postcolonial fallacy in order to conduct some highly misguided readings of competing feminisms within the context of racial experience. She establishes a hierarchy of color that depressingly segregates divergent racial perspectives into a complete absence of intellectual exchange. The competition is framed in terms of hooks's sense of the hostility between African-American and Third World feminisms:

> The current popularity of post-colonial discourse that implicates solely the West often obscures the colonizing relationship of the East in relation to Africa and other parts of the Third World. We often

7. bell hooks [Gloria Watkins], "On Self-Recovery," *Talking Back: Thinking Feminist, Thinking Black* (Boston, 1989), p. 28.

> forget that many Third World nationals bring to this country the same kind of contempt and disrespect for blackness that is most frequently associated with white western imperialism. . . . Within feminist movements Third World nationals often assume the role of mediator or interpreter, explaining the "bad" black people to their white colleagues or helping the "naive" black people to understand whiteness. . . . Unwittingly assuming the role of go-between, of mediator, she re-inscribes a colonial paradigm.

What is astonishing about such a claim is its continued obsession with a white academy, with race as a professional attribute that can only reconfigure itself around an originary concept of whiteness. Its feminism is necessarily skin deep in that the pigment of its imagination cannot break out of a strictly biological reading of race. Rather than extending an inquiry into the discursive possibilities represented by the intersection of gender and race, feminist intellectuals like hooks misuse their status as minority voices by enacting strategies of belligerence that at this time are more divisive than informative. Such claims to radical revisionism take refuge in the political untouchability that is accorded the category of Third World Woman, and in the process sully the crucial knowledge that such a category has still to offer to the dialogue of feminism today.

The dangers represented by feminists such as hooks and Trinh is that finally they will represent the profession as both their last court of appeal and the anthropological ground on which they conduct their field work. The alternative that they offer, therefore, is conceptually parochial and scales down the postcolonial condition in order to encompass it within North American academic terms. As a consequence, their discourse cannot but fuel the criticism of those who police the so-called thought police, nor is it able to address the historically risky compartmentalization of otherness that masquerades under the title of multiculturalism. Here it is useful to turn to one of the more brilliant observations that pepper Gayatri Spivak's *The Post-Colonial Critic.* In concluding an interview on multiculturalism, Spivak casually reminds her audience that

> if one looks at the history of post-Enlightenment theory, the major problem has been the problem of autobiography: how subjective structures can, in fact, give objective truth. During these same centuries, the Native Informant [was] treated as the objective evidence for the founding of the so-called sciences like ethnography, ethnolinguistics, comparative religion, and so on. So that, once again, the theoretical problems only relate to the person who knows. The person who *knows* has all of the problems of selfhood. The person who is *known,* somehow seems not to have a problematic self.[9]

8. hooks, *Yearning: Race, Gender, and Cultural Politics* (Boston, 1990), pp. 93–94.

9. Gayatri Chakravorty Spivak, "Questions of Multiculturalism," interview by Sneja

Lived experience, in other words, serves as fodder for the continuation of another's epistemology, even when it is recorded in a "contestatory" position to its relation to realism and to the overarching structure of the profession.

While cultural criticism could never pretend that the profession does not exist, its various voices must surely question any conflation of the professional model with one universal and world historical. The relation between local and given knowledge is obviously too problematic to allow for such an easy slippage, which is furthermore the ground on which the postcolonial can be abused to become an allegory for any one of the pigeonholes constructed for multiculturalism. Allow me to turn as a consequence to a local example of how realism locates its language within the postcolonial condition, and to suggest that lived experience does not achieve its articulation through autobiography, but through that other third-person narrative known as the law.

2

I proffer life in Pakistan as an example of such a postcolonial and lived experience. Pakistani laws, in fact, pertain more to the discourse of a petrifying realism than do any of the feminist critics whom I have cited thus far. The example at hand takes a convoluted postcolonial point and renders it nationally simple: if a postcolonial nation chooses to embark on an official program of Islamization, the inevitable result in a Muslim state will be legislation that curtails women's rights and institutes in writing what has thus far functioned as the law of the passing word. The Hudood Ordinances in Pakistan were promulgated in 1979 and legislated in 1980, under the military dictatorship of General Mohammad Zia-ul-Haq. They added five new criminal laws to the existing system of Pakistani legal pronouncements, of which the second ordinance—against *Zina* (that is, adultery as well as fornication)—is of the greatest import. An additional piece of legislation concerns the law of evidence, which rules that a woman's testimony constitutes half of a man's. While such infamous laws raise many historical and legal questions, they remain the body through which the feminist movement in Pakistan—the Women's Action Forum—must organize itself.

It is important to keep in mind that the formulation of the Hudood Ordinances was based on a multicultural premise, even though they were multicultural from the dark side of the moon. These laws were premised on a Muslim notion of *Hadd* and were designed to interfere in a

---

Gunew (30 Aug. 1986), *The Post-Colonial Critic: Interviews, Strategies, Dialogues,* ed. Sarah Harasym (New York, 1990), p. 66.

postcolonial criminal legal system that was founded on Anglo-Saxon jurisprudence. According to feminist lawyer Asma Jahangir,

> the Hudood Ordinances were promulgated to bring the criminal legal system of Pakistan in conformity with the injunctions of Islam. . . . Two levels of punishments are introduced in the Ordinances. Two levels of punishment and, correspondingly, two separate sets of rules of evidence are prescribed. The first level or category is the one called the "Hadd" which literally means the "limit" and the other "Tazir", which means "to punish".[10]

The significance of the *Hadd* category is that it delineates immutable sentences: *Tazir* serves only as a safety net in case the accused is not convicted under *Hadd.* These fixed rules are in themselves not very pretty: *Hadd* for theft is amputation of a hand; for armed robbery, amputation of a foot; for rape or adultery committed by married Muslims, death by stoning; for rape or adultery committed by non-Muslims or unmarried Muslims, a hundred public lashes (see *HO,* p. 24). While I am happy to report that the *Hadd* has not yet been executed, the laws remain intact and await their application.

The applicability of these sentences is rendered more murderous and even obscenely ludicrous when the immutability of the *Hadd* punishments is juxtaposed with the contingency of the laws of evidence. If a man is seen stealing a thousand rupees by two adult Muslim males, he could be punished by *Hadd* and his hand would be amputated. If an adult Muslim stole several million rupees and the only available witnesses were women and non-Muslims, he would not qualify for a *Hadd* category and would be tried under the more free-floating *Tazir* instead. "A gang of men can thus rape all the residents of a women's hostel," claims Jahangir with understandable outrage, "but [the] lack of ocular evidence of four Muslim males will rule out the imposition of a Hadd punishment" (*HO,* p. 49). Such a statement, unfortunately, is not the terrain of rhetoric alone, since the post-Hudood Ordinance application of the *Tazir* has made the definition of rape an extremely messy business indeed.

Here, then, we turn to *Zina,* and its implications for the Pakistani female body. The Hudood Ordinances have allowed for all too many openings in the boundaries that define rape. Women can now be accused of rape, as can children; laws of mutual consent may easily convert a case of child abuse into a prosecution of the child for *Zina,* for fornication. Furthermore, unmarried men and women can be convicted of having committed rape against each other, since a subsection of the *Zina* offense defines rape as "one where a man or a woman have illicit sex knowing

10. Asma Jahangir and Hina Jilani, *The Hudood Ordinances: A Divine Sanction?* (Lahore, Pakistan, 1990), p. 24; hereafter abbreviated *HO.*

that they are not validly married to each other" (quoted in *HO,* p. 58). In other words, fornication is all, and the statistics of the past few years grimly indicate that the real victims of the Hudood Ordinances are women and children, most specifically those who have no access to legal counsel and whose economic status renders them ignorant of their human rights.

Jahangir cites the example of a fifteen-year-old woman, Jehan Mina, who, after her father's death, was raped by her aunt's husband and son. Once her pregnancy was discovered, another relative filed a police report alleging rape. During the trial, however, the accused led no defense, and Mina's testimony alone was sufficient to get her convicted for fornication and sentenced to one hundred public lashes. That child's story is paradigmatic of the untold miseries of those who suffer sentences in Muslim jails.

Let me state the obvious: I cite these alternative realisms and constructions of identity in order to reiterate the problem endemic to postcolonial feminist criticism. It is not the terrors of Islam that have unleashed the Hudood Ordinances on Pakistan, but more probably the United States government's economic and ideological support of a military regime during that bloody but eminently forgotten decade marked by the "liberation" of Afghanistan. Jehan Mina's story is therefore not so far removed from our current assessment of what it means to be multicultural. How are we to connect her lived experience with the overwhelming realism of the law? In what ways does her testimony force postcolonial and feminist discourse into an acknowledgement of the inherent parochialism and professionalism of our claims?

I will offer a weak bridge between the two poles of my rhetorical question: a poem by the feminist Pakistani writer, Kishwar Naheed. Her writing has been perceived as inflammatory, and she has been accused of obscenity more than once. The obscenity laws, or the Fahashi laws, are another story altogether. Once they were passed, they could not be put in print because the powers that be declared them to be too obscene. The poem below, however, is one that could easily earn the poet a prison sentence in contemporary Pakistan:

It is we sinful women
who are not awed by the grandeur of those who wear gowns
who don't sell our lives
who don't bow our heads
who don't fold our hands together.

It is we sinful women
while those who sell the harvests of our bodies
become exalted
become distinguished
become the just princes of the material world.

It is we sinful women
who come out raising the banner of truth
up against barricades of lies on the highways
who find stories of persecution piled on each threshold
who find the tongues which could speak have been severed.

It is we sinful women.
Now, even if the night gives chase
these eyes shall not be put out.
For the wall which has been razed
don't insist now on raising it again.

It is we sinful women.
who are not awed by the grandeur of those who wear gowns
who don't sell our bodies
who don't bow our heads
who don't fold our hands together.[11]

We should remember that there remains unseen legislation against such poetry, and that the *Hadd*—the limit—is precisely the realism against which our lived experience can serve as a metaphor, and against which we must continue to write. If we allow the identity formation of postcolonialism to construe itself only in terms of nationalism and parochialism, or of gender politics at its most narcissistically ahistorical, then let us assume that the media has won its battle, and the law of the limit is upon us.

11. Kishwar Naheed, "We Sinful Women," in *Beyond Belief: Contemporary Feminist Urdu Poetry,* trans. Rukhsana Ahmad (Lahore, Pakistan, 1990), pp. 22–23.

Acting Bits/Identity Talk

Gayatri Chakravorty Spivak

In *Fantasia: An Algerian Cavalcade,* Assia Djebar places herself with great autobiographers: Augustine, the Berber who wrote not only his theology but his *Confessions* in the language of Rome; and Ibn Khaldûn, son of a family that fled southern Arabia, who wrote not only his history but his *Ta'arif* [identity] in Arabic. Staging herself as an Algerian Muslim woman, she gives a fragmented version of the graph-ing of her bio in French, of which I quote the following fragments:

> The overlay of my oral culture wearing dangerously thin. . . . Writing of the most anodyne of childhood memories leads back to a body bereft of voice. To attempt an autobiography in French words alone is to show more than its skin under the slow scalpel of a live autopsy. Its flesh peels off and with it, seemingly, the speaking of childhood which can no longer be written is torn to shreds. Wounds are reopened, veins weep, the blood of the self flows and that of others, a blood which has never dried.[1]

Identity as a wound, exposed by the historically hegemonic languages, for those who have learned the double-binding "practice of [their] writing" (*F,* p. 181). I accept this difficult definition, to present a series of citations of "myself" engaged in identity talk.

I think one of the major motifs of *Fantasia* is a meditation on the pos-

1. Assia Djebar, *Fantasia: An Algerian Cavalcade,* trans. Dorothy S. Blair (London, 1985), p. 156; hereafter abbreviated *F;* translation occasionally modified. For details on Ibn Khaldûn, see Albert Hourani, *A History of the Arab Peoples* (Cambridge, 1991), p. 1.

This article originally appeared in *Critical Inquiry* 18 (Summer 1992).

sibility that to achieve autobiography in the double bind of the practice of the conqueror's writing is to learn to be taken seriously by the gendered subaltern who has not mastered that practice. And therefore, hidden in the many-sectioned third part of the book, there is the single episode where the narrator speaks in the ethical singularity of the *tu-toi* to Zohra, an eighty-year-old rural *mujahida* [female freedom fighter] who has been devastated both by her participation in the Nationalist struggle and by the neglect of women's claims in decolonized Algeria.[2] The achievement of the autobiographer-in-fiction is to be fully fledged as a storyteller for this intimate interlocutor: to tell not one's own story, but the animation of the story of two nineteenth-century Algerian prostitutes, Fatma and Meriem, included in Eugène Fromentin's *Un Été au Sahara.* And to succeed, for Zohra's curiosity flares up, "'And Fatma? And Meriem?' Lla Zhora interrupted, catching herself following the story as if it were a legend recounted by a bard. 'Where did you hear this story?' she went on, impatiently." The "I" (now at last articulated because related and responsible to "you") replies simply: "'I read it!' I retorted. 'An eye-witness told it to a friend who wrote it down'" (*F,* p. 166).

The relationship between the texts of the conqueror and the autobiographer is part of the spectacular "arabesques" of *Fantasia.* This unemphatic section ends simply, "I, your cousin, translate this account into the mother tongue, and report it to you. So I try my self out, as ephemeral teller, close to you little mother, in front of your vegetable patch" (*F,* p. 167). She shares her mother tongue as instrument of translation with the other woman.

This is the divided field of identity, that a feminist-in-decolonization—as the sign of a(n) (l)earned perspective, not an autobiographical identity—can uncover between books 9 and 10 of the *Confessions,* in Khaldûn's "sudden . . . yearning to turn back on himself . . . [to] become . . . the subject and object of a dispassionate autopsy" (*F,* p. 216).

In the rift of this divided field, the tale shared in the mother tongue is forever present (in every act of reading) and forever absent, for it is in the mother tongue. The authority of the "now" inaugurates this absent autobiography in every "here" of the book: The fleeting framed moment

2. For a discussion of the singular *tu-toi* in Hélène Cixous, see Gayatri Chakravorty Spivak, "French Feminism Revisited: Ethics and Politics," in *Feminists Theorize the Political,* ed. Judith Butler and Joan Scott (New York, 1992).

Gayatri Chakravorty Spivak is professor of English and comparative literature at Columbia University. She is the translator of Jacques Derrida's *Of Grammatology* (1976) and of three stories by Mahasweta Devi, *Imaginary Maps* (1995). Her books include *In Other Worlds* (1987) and *Outside in the Teaching Machine* (1993).

undoes the "blank [*blanc*] in the memory" of her personal childhood, which only yields the image of an old crone whose muttered Quranic curses could not be understood (*F,* p. 10).

The language and education policies of the French in Algeria and those of the British in India are rather different.[3] The articulation of patriarchy with Hinduism and with Islam is also significantly different. Yet there is a strong structural bond between the delicacy of Djebar's staging of temporary storytelling, and my position, some nine months before I read *Fantasia,* lecturing in my mother tongue, in Calcutta, on the subject of "Deconstruction-Translation," in front of a university audience, many of the senior members of whom were my former fellow students. It was a situation of the public acknowledgement of the responsibility of Bengali identity among Bengalis in their felicitous habitat. Calcutta is the capital of West Bengal, the center of Indian Bengali high culture. It was also a situation of the testing of the expatriate by the locals—a presentation of an identity card as it were. The locals were ferociously well-prepared in deconstructive matters as well as its humanist critique. Any suspected patronizing (I was terrified) would have been not only an error of judgment but a betrayal precisely of the contamination of my identity by prolonged contact with the United States. (In the event, the patronage came from the other side. In the Sunday supplement of *Ananda Bazar Patrika,* the Bengali-language daily with the largest circulation, my identity was validated. I was hailed as a "daughter of Bengal," but also embarrassingly complimented on my control over my native language.)

For me the most interesting thing, in retrospect, about my careful exercise on "Deconstruction-Translation" was that I could get into it only by staging an error in a dictionary definition of *identity,* the English word. I will again turn to Assia Djebar before I advance my argument.

The final movement of *Fantasia* is in three short bits, what remains of an autobiography when it has been unravelled strand by strand. First a tribute to Pauline Rolland, the French revolutionary of 1848, exiled in Algeria, as the true ancestress of the *mujahidat.* Revolutionary discourse for women cannot rely on indigenous cultural production. If the tale told to Zohra is a divided moment of access to autobiography as the telling of an absent story, here autobiography is the possibility of writing or giving writing to the other, identifiable only as a mutilated metonym of violence, as part-object. The source is, once again, Eugène Fromentin. There is one unexplained Arabic word in the following passage, a word that means, in fact, "pen":

3. See David Prochaska, *Making Algeria French: Colonialism in Bône 1870–1920* (Cambridge, 1990), and David Kopf, *British Orientalism and the Bengal Renaissance: The Dynamics of Indian Modernization, 1775–1835* (Berkeley, 1969).

> Eugène Fromentin offers me an unexpected hand—the hand of an unknown woman he was never able to draw. . . . He describes in sinister detail: as he is leaving the oasis which six months after the massacre is still filled with its stench, Fromentin picks up out of the dust the severed hand of an anonymous Algerian woman. He throws it down again in his path.
>
> Later, I seize on this living hand, hand of mutilation and of memory, and I attempt to bring it the *qalam* [*F*, p. 226].

This fragmentary finale begins with two French dictionary entries about a term signifying an item in the rhetoric of the Algerian woman's body. The entries read the figure in two opposed ways. One says that *tzarl-rit* means "to utter cries of *joy* while smacking the lips with the hands (of women)." The other says that the same word means "shout, vociferate (of women when some *misfortune* befalls them)" (*F*, p. 221; my emphasis).

Structurally, although not in expressed affective character, I can find something like a relationship between this inauguration of the bestowal of writing through a European's mutilation/memory by way of an example of the limits of European lexicography and, as the second element, my own opening of the translation of Derrida's writing (on) translation by way of an example of the limits of the lexicography of English. There, women's corporeal rhetoric: *tzarl-rit;* here, men's transcendental logic: "identity" itself.

(I am, of course, somewhat absurdly straining to share the field of identity with Assia Djebar, rather than some identically produced, rooted Indian sister. Who, she? Is there some pertinence to the fact that what I self-cite below is an example of the very first time that I have translated my own Bengali prose into my own English? But am I not always doing that, in a way that I cannot fathom? There, then, women's corporeal rhetoric; here, below, men's transcendental logic—mistakes in dictionaries.) I quote:

In the field of rational analysis, a feeling of recognized kinship is more desirable than nationalism. Therefore I have started with the family resemblances between deconstruction and Bhartrhari-Nagarjuna.[4] So that I can tangle deconstruction with our own *idamvada*.[5] *Idamvada* is a weird translation of the word *identity*. Usually we translate identity as *vyaktisatva, svarupa, ekarupata,* and the like. The other day in the United

4. For a discussion of the work of these two philosopher-linguists, see Bimal Krishna Matilal, *Word and the World: India's Contribution to the Study of Language* (Delhi, 1990).

5. All the "Indian" words that follow are spelled according to the transcription of Sanskrit orthography, although in the Bengali pronunciation they sound quite different, and the Bengali alphabet is quite different from the Sanskrit *devanāgari* alphabet, although descended from it. Another rift of history that English obliterates.

States I saw in a students' English dictionary that the source of the word was given as Latin *idem* or Sanskrit *idam* and both were cited as meaning "same." Now the meaning of the Latin word *idem* is not exactly "same" in the sense of one, but rather "same" in the sense of multitudes or repetitions. That is to say, that which is primordial [*anādi*] and unique [*ekamevadvītiam*] is not *idem,* but rather that which can be cited through many re-citations, that is *idem.* To make these two meanings one is that clandestine patching up of a loose part of the fabric of which I have already spoken. At least from the outside it seems that in our solemn recitation of *Hindutva* [Hindu-ness, a key word of Hindu fundamentalism] this clan-destiny or ruse is at work. The little Sanskrit that I learnt under the able guidance of Miss Nilima Pyne at the Diocesan School in Calcutta [I beg the U.S. reader not to lose sight of the social textile here] allowed me to suspect that the Sanskrit *idam* is also not the undiminishing singly manifest [*akshaya ekarūpa*]. Then I looked at the dictionary. *Idam* is not only not the undiminishing selfsame, as a pronoun it does not even have the dignity of a noun, and it is always enclitic or inclined towards the noun, always dependent on the proximity of a particular self, for *idam* must remain monstrative, indexed. All over the world today identity politics (that is to say, a separation in the name of the undifferentiated identity of religion, nation, or subnation) is big news and almost everywhere bad news.[6] The unremarkable and unremarked ruse in the United States students' dictionary [Merriam-Webster's college edition, I think] makes visible the fraud at the heart of identity politics. As a memorial to that publication I submit this outlandish deconstructed translation of *identity,* only for this occasion—not *ahamvāda* [ego-ism as ipse-ism] but *idamvāda.* Deconstruction-work shakes the stakes of the spirit's *ahamvāda* to show *idamvāda,* and therefore we protect ourselves in the name of a specific national identity; we do not want to know it, we dis-pose of it rather than pro-pose it.[7]

Here then am I, Gayatri Chakravorty (the newspaper dropped the Spivak), speaking on identity as a Bengali ("daughter of Bengal") to Bengalis. As I have remarked in footnote 5, all the terminology is general Indic (although the matrix language, here English, is Bengali) rather than specifically Bengali. (The identity of the language drops off not only in translation, but even in transcription.) I *am* Indian, and there is another

6. I will, later in the paper, disassociate myself from the view that U.S. multiculturalism is, according to Arthur M. Schlesinger, Jr., "the disuniting of America." See his *The Disuniting of America: Reflections on a Multicultural Society* (New York, 1992). In the Indian context, however, I felt that I must speak out against separatism. I am not a situational relativist. One must take account of situations because one acts according to imperatives.

7. "Pro-pose" takes me back to an earlier discussion in my paper of the famous line of Nagarjuna: "Nāsti ca mama kācana pratijnā" [roughly, "My proposition is not there at all"].

Bengal, the Eastern part of the land mass, another nation-state, Bangladesh. The next fragment of identity comes from Gayatri Chakravorty Spivak, an Indian in Bangladesh. The language is the same. The fragment is, in a sense, doubly cited, for it is an account of something that happened in Bangladesh that I presented at a conference on Institutions of Culture at the National University of Singapore, again an academic among academics, speaking of another place, an Asian among, largely, Asians. (A colleague from the Asian Pacific was reported as complaining, after what follows, "this sort of theory can't lead to practice." If he should read these pages, and he well might, I would gently respond that even if the relationship between theory and practice were vectored—which I cannot for a moment credit—the vector is the other way here—theory desperately attempting to digest practice.) I quote:

(*Preamble*—I start from the assumption that men and women occupy different positions in the making of culture. Any discussion of culture that does not take this into consideration is symptom more than explanation. Women are either silenced or ventriloquial, not-quite-subjects who hold up the culture or, if conscientized, resist.

For the last few days we have been talking about the cognitive mapping of unisex cultures. But institutions *in* culture must precomprehend an institution or instituting *of* culture, not simply as a chronologically prior event but as a philosophically subtending layer. In fact at this level, continuous with the possibility of being in the world, "culture" is one of the many names that one bestows upon the trace of being othered from nature, and by so naming, effaces the trace. This intimate proximate level is already sexed and ready for the supplement of gender, like that other most intimately distanced text of culture, the so-called experience of the inside of the body. However we narrativize the difference-deferment of cultural identity or the subjectship of culture, in this place *culture* is a word like *value* in Marx, simple and contentless, immediately codable as ground of difference.

What I have liked about Derrida over the years is the obstinate naïveté that makes him repeat the necessary but impossible questions beginning with "What is . . . ." The one that has engaged me most for the last couple of years is: What is it to learn? Particularly because the subjectship of ethics and the subjectship of culture, past the threshold of naming, in and out of claims to alterity, is in the hands of only those who can enter or counter globality. I am frustrated that I cannot hear the subaltern, if that is a name of culturing apart. "What *is* it to learn, these lessons, otherwise?" I am not interested, in other words, in legitimizing the global by reversing it into the local. I am interested in tracking the exorbitant as it institutes its culture.

This is a question I can neither answer nor stop asking. And as an effect of this predicament, or an adjunct to it, perhaps even a companion to it, or perhaps to shut it out, I find myself turning fragments of the institution of culture, conventionally primary *or* secondary, into cases. Cases of exorbitant normality rather than diseases; cases of confounding the instituted laws. I want to be able to give you four of these cases in the following pages. But let me tell you first why I think of these slippery things as cases. Because I do not want them to prove a theory by becoming *post*-dictions and making the theory pre-dictive metaleptically; but perhaps they do? I do not want them to be illustrations of our arguments. But perhaps they are? At any rate, these case reports inevitably produce a series of failures, working analyses and descriptions, in other words, that seem to lead somewhere.

How do I know a case is a case? Simon During asked. I cannot say, for I see a shaped outline in a fragment, it begins to make sense, and it fits into a case. And then, what is it a case of? This has not yet been a thing I have worried about in my project of unlearning learning in order to ask: What is it to learn? But, for the moment, since a question generates an answer, let me say cases of subject-ing, cases of agent-ing, thus cases of identifying, cases of the staging of culture as the originary synthesis with the absolute other; everything that we leap over when we *start* with the object of cultural studies or the politics of culture. But the real answer is *you* tell *me,* when you have read these pages.

The first case is just an account of a conversation, a fragile exchange that I have no business setting down here.)

I was at the top of this bit of coast before I came to Singapore, on the edge of the armpit of the Bay of Bengal, the waterlogged islands of Kutubdia and Maheshkhāli and the town of Cox's Bazar, the places hit by the cyclone and tidal wave of 29 April 1991. Every act of life there is a major effort. I did not think *of* these efforts and encounters while I was there except to reflect repeatedly and bitterly upon the contrast between the cheerful relief and rehabilitation efforts of grass roots workers, mostly women, in the area, and the hyperreal videographic image of the absolutely abject and dependent victim. These places are not outside of globality; in another context I could tell the story of the presence there of the U.S. task force and its tremendous *popular* critique as one episode in a serial narrative.[8]

8. A popular critique quite at odds with the official view of the government. I offer here an excerpt from my personal copy of a long letter written on 6 June 1991, to the Commander of the Joint Task Force by the Sub-Zonal Relief Coordinator. (The only air-conditioned interior I entered in the area was the spacious room of the old British Circuit House, now his office.)

> Excellency, as you passed from bondage to freedom and independence, we passed from independence to slavery and bondage, and we were a nation lost. It was through and after long years of struggle and sacrifice that, we were finally able to throw off our chains and fetters. Today, democracy in our country is reborn. It is young, hardly a few

When I returned to the capital city of Dhaka, Farhad Mazhar, a male activist, a pharmacist-poet who knows his Marx and Hegel, asked me: "What did you see?" I had not thought of this yet. But, since a question generates an answer, I scrambled to legitimize myself with this man of work. Beside me were sitting a woman, a high school graduate from a country town who is a teacher at a barefoot school (not a player in the culture of the coastal islands), and a woman law graduate, considerably more articulate but less of a worker, just beginning to worry about the problems of Bangladeshi rape law. I knew that what I was saying was over the women's heads, and it was my problem, not theirs. But the case got made nonetheless.

I had seen, I said, that life and death are in the rhythm of water and land for these coastal peoples—I implore the U.S. reader not to confuse this with an identikit for all Bangladeshis—and not only for the very poor among them. They build in the expectation of obliteration, planned obsolescence at the other end. *Everyone,* including the health and relief workers from other parts of Bangladesh, half a notch above the lowest of them in class, remarks on the fact that loss of land and kin seems to leave a noticeably impermanent mark on the inhabitants of this area. Yet they are not "fatalists," they grieve and want relief, to rebuild in the face of certain loss, yet again. This is an eco-logical sense of being-in-the-world. The way I found myself putting the case was in terms of the young Marx's perception of species-life rather than species-being, where human life and death

---

> months old. But within these few months it has had its baptism of fire, with the fateful and devastating Cyclone and Tidal surge of 29 April, 1991, which rocked our people to their roots and caused devastation on a scale hitherto unknown, and left them in a state of complete shock and bewilderment.
>
> But our people are resilient, they are born in cyclones and tidal bores, and they grow and live with them. For them, cyclones and tidal bores are almost so to say a natural habitat. With fortitude, and indomitable courage our people withstood the scourge of the cyclone which was like a holocaust. Inspiration and unshakable assistance from friends like you helped to get us back on our feet sooner than later, and move boldly ahead. You and your sea angels, helped, facilitated and expedited the process of our recovery. For this, we will remain indebted. We have no words adequate to express our gratitude.
>
> But above all, it was your conduct your Excellency, which perhaps was the wellspring of inspiration and hope. Your memorable words still echo and ring in our ears. These have left an indelible imprint on hearts and minds. You likened democracy in our country to a young plant which needed extreme care and attention to flower and blossom. You had as you said, come to nurture and water the roots of this young plant, for according to there could be no humanity without democracy. Your words and action have once again, convinced us that our road to progress and development was only one—the road of democracy.

No comment is surely needed here about the fracture between claimed "national identity" and the alignment with another "nation"—the United States—on the one hand and being-in-the-land on the other.

is no more than Nature breathing in and out.[9] Marx was obliged to narrativize the case in both a logical and a historical way: for him, both logically and historically, this space was a determination where revolution or planning would not take. And in the understanding of history as sequence, knowing how to help presumed knowing what should be wanted, easier within a mere scientific vision of the formation of class, but not possible on this coastline. Here the cultural rather than the class subject was repeatedly being instituted, or instituting itself in an eco-logy, a logic of a greater household or *oikos,* where the subject of the logic is not necessarily "worlded" as human in the common individualist sense. For my interlocutor, Mazhar, this was *proof* that, after the critique of consciousness as appropriation, Marx had not theorized property adequately, and that the *task* of alternative strategies of development that respected subaltern agencies of the institution of culture is to learn to rethink property. I had no such confidence; I was stalled at "what is it to learn" and offered a contradiction that I had also seen.

If this was an eco-logic where the unlikely material subject was the pulse of the tide and the rhythm of the waterlogging of wind, I was in no way ready, daily encountering these very people's savvy discussion of the U.S. task force—that had taken its helicopters back home, that had dropped supplies already available and moving "in much larger quantities" in the slow-moving trawlers, that had created more trouble in their medical facilities because they could not communicate, that had been contemptuous to the locals, all comments heard from these very people—simply to narrativize them as an earlier pre-scientific stage where the proper help was to control nature so that these people could be redefined as passive and graduate to a more or less remote commitment to, *or* critique of, capitalism. What would it be to learn otherwise, here? Better offer the contradiction: they will not move except as unwilling refugees.

It is commonplace now to say that the expansion of colonialism transformed habitation or land from its status as reference for the dominant subject, so that space could become a signifier for the colonizer: and through "nation" into empire. It is becoming commonplace to say that, for the migrant or nomad or yet hybrid, land or space is now being transformed into a script or graph, not a containing system of signs. Smadar Lavie has written on Israeli holding action, in the face of this script, energetically defining an "identity" for the Bedouin, that master nomad, since the late sixties.[10] But this tenacious clinging to land seemed something else: a postponement of the eco-logic that otherwise instituted the cultural moment for these people. What was it to learn to help, here? I could

9. See Karl Marx, *Early Writings,* trans. Rodney Livingstone and Gregor Benton (Harmondsworth, 1975), p. 328.

10. See Smadar Lavie, *The Poetics of Military Occupation: Mzeina Allegories of Bedouin Identity under Israeli and Egyptian Rule* (Berkeley, 1990).

respect the relief workers' bemused on-the-spot decision that this other kind of resistance to rehabilitation must not be allowed to develop into an aporia. The work of rehab must continue. But with the vestiges of intellectual sophistication I possessed, I saw through with distaste the long-distance theorist's dismissal of the aporia as anachrony or his embracing of it as the saving grace of a-chrony. I was adrift. I knew the ways of cutting the drift or *dérive,* of course. Silence the subaltern by talking too much. Describe, account, print.

I cannot close this case. I will go back, asking again: "What is it to learn?" In a minute I will make an enormous leap into the much more comfortable and recognizably political arena of the institution of culture in hyphenated art in the First World: Lebanese-Canadian. But I cannot leave this case without reminding myself that even in this liminal culture, by religious naming, Muslim-Hindu and Buddhist, women have an ironic relationship to both eco-logic and the positing of land as its postponement. In exogamy, these women shift their loyalty from father's land to husband's, quite as our female colleagues do. In reproductive culture, these girls' knees scissor in at adolescence and slowly open wider and wider as the rhythm of childbearing *in* the rhythm of tide and wind is seen as the definitive predication of gendering. Perhaps deconstruction rewrites Marxism for me by the fearful sense that even species-*life,* the Realm of Freedom, *Stoffwechsel* as Marx called it, or material alteration of nature, cannot be without gendering if disclosed in the institution of culture. The move into globality here is either the utter dehumanizing of reproductive engineering or the processing zones of post-Fordist export. Chittagong, the biggest town in the area, is also a port. There are plans to transform Cox's Bazar into a serious port as well.

If the previous part was written in the wake of the U.S. task force, the following bit was written in the shadow of a war as intercultural performance, where an old politics of identity successfully managed an absolute politics of culture.

In February of 1991, I was in a pretty villa on Lake Como, owned by the Rockefeller Foundation, where I hope to be again. We were conferring on intercultural performance. I flew back to Toronto, to read a paper, on my birthday. I was musing on identity, thinking that my entry into identity had been "experienced" by my mother as pain, relief, attachment; that the famous birth trauma, opening the ontic, remained inaccessible to "experience," to onto-logy as auto-bio-graphy. I was considering how powerfully this is used for an ethics of sexual difference by Luce Irigaray in her "Fecundity of the Caress."[11] The man behind me started up

11. See Luce Irigaray, "The Fecundity of the Caress: A Reading of Levinas, *Totality and Infinity,* Section IV, B, 'The Phenomenology of Eros,'" in *Face to Face with Levinas,* ed.

a conversation. He told me with considerable relish that we had started the ground war in Iraq.

I felt the force of that shared "we" so strongly that I knew that I would start with talk of war that evening in Toronto. This identification, in the most colloquial sense, can only be described through the political affect of the green (no longer phenomenally so) or alien registration (identity) card—an unnameable identity, named only as "alien," yet strong enough, again, for public self-identification with protesters in the nation. I quote:

I have been struck by the extent of a certain kind of Judeo-Christian religiosity and patriotism on both sides of the war in the United States: Because we are good Jews and good Christians, and because we are Americans, we must punish Saddam for misbehaving and kill the people of Iraq; or, because we are good Jews and good Christians, and because we are Americans, the people of Iraq are our brothers and sisters, however devilish or clownish Saddam might be.

To put it in code: "legitimation by reversal," of a war, of the new imperialism. Millennially, whenever there has been a certain kind of classic victory, the imperialist powers have reshuffled what remains in order to create a new empire. The apparent winning of the cold war and the dissolution of the Warsaw Pact had to be organized by the United States so that the positions could be reshuffled, so that we could have a new world order before the European Economic Community could become the United States of Europe.

In the context of the Eighteenth Brumaire of the Bolshevik Revolution, these words relating to cultural politics are already out of date. Economic abstractions have a slower tempo, and hence the following passage still retains a certain pertinence:

> The Western powers will be kind enough to destroy their lands, and those whose lands are destroyed will be made to pay the cost of destruction. But the Western powers will be equally kind enough to engage in the reconstruction of the prostrate, devastated lands, for which the victims of devastation will have to fork out money a second time around. . . . The opportunities, as currently assembled, are so tempting that a scramble is already on among contractors and engineers hailing from different Western countries. They have not the least doubt that whatever the temporary difficulties, that beast,

---

Richard A. Cohen (Albany, N.Y., 1986), p. 232.

> Saddam, is bound to receive his just deserts, and Kuwait and its oil will be regained for the West.[12]

The most frightening thing about imperialism, its long-term toxic effect, what secures it, what cements it, is the benevolent self-representation of the imperialist as savior.

Therefore, listening to the United States protest movement as well as the voice of the new patriotism, some noticed how difficult, even impossible, it would be to transform that cement into an international voice that acknowledges global cultural diversity with respect rather than mere benevolence. Some were reminded over and over again of the lessons that we learned in our lives, about the sense of mission that secures and cements imperialist victories in the economic and the political fields by persuading the victim to produce assent.

What we call experience is a staging of experience, sometimes on the small screen. In this sense, an earlier experience is being staged in this new, displaced imperialist scene: the horror of an absolute act of intercultural performance. One of the many tasks of the activist intellectual is to offer scrupulous and plausible accounts of the mechanics of staging. A most tenacious name, as well as the strongest account of the agency or mechanics of the staging of experience-in-identity is "origin": "I perform my life this way because my origin stages me so." National origin, ethnic origin. And, more pernicious: "You cannot help acting this way because your origin stages you so."

The notion of origin is as broad and robust and full of affect as it is imprecise. "History lurks in it somewhere," I had written, but now I think that sentence would have to be revised: History slouches in it, ready to comfort *and* kill. Yet to feel one is from an origin is not a pathology. It belongs to that group of grounding mistakes that enable us to make sense of our lives. But the only way to argue for origins is to look for institutions, inscriptions and then to surmise the mechanics by which such institutions and inscriptions can stage such a particular style of performance. This preserves and secures the minority voice in Anglo cultures and also reveals the manipulation of the very same minorities into superpower identification in the violent management of global cultural politics.

In a crisis the intellectual as activist does not always stop to divide a fully mobilized unity. Stands get taken on both sides because, at ground level, democracy is counting bodies—the more the better. That is how changes in agency are inaugurated, higher lawmaking is pushed by bodies mobilized into "the same voice." At a moment of crisis one does not speak up against the absolute intercultural translation that may be cementing both protest and blind patriotism. Even if one knows from the staging of the experience of history that this absolute interculturalism is also that

12. A.M., "Calcutta Diary," *Economic and Political Weekly*, 23 Feb. 1991, p. 403.

which cements imperialist malevolence, one does not speak up, one joins. In a crisis, no hand is clean. Analysis is action there, performance is art. One does not speak of art there as a specific terrain, and does not mention the possibility that rights as written by Law are not "experienced" as such by an individual-in-identity, but rather animate an abstract agent-in-experience.

When I speak of art specifically, away from the scene of crisis, my take is a schoolteacher's take: art and literature and music for me are audiovisual teaching aids in the construction of cases. Naïve but useful if one is groping to state the question: what is it to learn? In this view, art also performs the short-haul/long-haul two-step I have just described in terms of the performance of protest. The videographic performance of war and its aftermath pretends to be analytic as well as performative. It tries to fluff the important difference and relationship between the short haul joining together for body count and the long haul speaking up to displace the legitimation by reversal.

Let us now consider a few bits of visual production that intervene in various ways to confuse the possibility of an absolute translation of a politics of identity into cultural performance. In doing so they blur the identity among minority voices without creating a monolithic solidarity. Let us consider a piece by the Lebanese-Canadian artist Jamelie Hassan. We will look briefly at her installation called *Midnight's Children,* part of a mixed-media show called *Inscription.*[13] This particular installation is a treatment of Salman Rushdie's novel of the same name. In this particular installation Hassan powerfully wrenches the title of Rushdie's novel from its context. She is working to confuse the possibility of absolute translations, in the field of identity as well as performance.

Like Rushdie, I am from the Indo-Pakistani subcontinent. We are, then, talking about my own context, productive of my own identity as decolonized subcontinental. I applaud Jamelie Hassan's feeling for "becoming involved and taking a stand on issues that may not necessarily affect you directly," especially in the face of the fierce turf battles in radical cultural studies in multiracial cultures as well as on the geo-graphed globe, where the only possible politics seems sometimes to be the politics of identity in the name of *being* the Other.[14]

But, although I applaud this, *Midnight's Children* is on my own turf. By relocating it, Hassan puts my own identity in parentheses, shows that

13. The following seventeen paragraphs are excerpted and modified from Spivak, "Inscriptions of Truth to Size," in *Inscription* (exhibition catalogue, Dunlop Art Gallery, Regina, Saskatchewan, 15 Sept.–21 Oct. 1990), pp. 9–11, 14–15.

14. Hassan, quoted in *Inscription,* p. 18. On the situation of current identity politics, see Edward W. Said, "The Politics of Knowledge," *Raritan* 11 (Summer 1991): 17–31. I remain saddened by his impatience with deconstruction and his refusal to understand the robust sense of "text." I have written so much about it elsewhere, that I will simply record this melancholy here.

FIG. 1.—Jamelie Hassan, *Midnight's Children.* Detail. Photo: Jamelie Hassan.

"my" context is also unsaturated and open, like all contexts. The effort at fracturing my identity is precisely not to sanctify the memory that I was awake, as a child, on that midnight, between the 14th and 15th of August 1947, when an India divided into India and Pakistan became independent. Hassan makes me learn the ropes. She has unmoored the date, away from Rushdie's India and Pakistan, and given it over to the children of Egypt—who seem, to most sympathetic spectators in North America, and they are in a minority, to be the children of Palestine. And I say, it's all right.

On the wall, flanked by the photographs of children, is a large brass plate by Aly-Aly Hassan, an Egyptian artisan, inscribed "Midnight's Children" in English and Arabic, with "Salman" in Arabic in the center. The final sentence of *Midnight's Children,* written in a spiral on the wall, now speaks the fate of the dispossessed children who lost their country in 1948,

FIG. 2.—Jamelie Hassan, *Midnight's Children.* Installation. Photo: Douglas Clark.

although neither photograph nor novel represents them, since the children in the novel are Indian and Pakistani citizens, and the actual children in the photograph are Egyptian. This is a strange feeling that you may not share unless you are subcontinental by "origin." In the staging of my identity, the idea of that midnight is solidly established as historically belonging only to my own access to postcoloniality. This, after all, is a more publicly accessible field of self-recognition than standing before my classmates, our teachers, and their students, in my hometown, speaking in the mother tongue about uneasy Theory, or hanging out in wind and water, learning not to transcode too quickly. I stood in front of the installation stripped, precisely, of my "identity." This is the kind of stripping that must be undertaken together if ethnic identities in the so-called First World are to become culturally and politically productive.

A year later, having had my first lesson, I was adrift in Djebar.

This is the constructed base from which one can emphasize the new American and place her with the Africans and the American nations that built today's America in unacknowledged blood. To create the new American out of the pipe dream of "We, the People," or out of the bogus concept of the world's policeman, or to give democratic ideals a kind of moral luck is to forget the violence at the origin. When we engage in identity turf battles, we forget this unacknowledged heritage; we accept the staging of the U.S. as enlightened white and behave as if the ethnic scene in the United States represents the globe. This representation is a version of the dream of white America.

Think of it this way: what we *call* culture, at many removes from that vestigial originary space I grappled with in the case of coastal Bangladesh, may be shorthand for an unacknowledged system of representations that allows you a *self*-representation that you believe is true. Then the culture of the United States, even before the establishment of the United States as such (the kind of place that, say, Goethe looks forward to at the end of *Wilhelm Meister,* the dream of old Europe come true) *is,* in that understanding, the dream of interculturalism: benevolent, hierarchized, malevolent, in principle homogenizing, but culturally heterogeneous. And that particular hegemonic U.S. cultural system of self-representation, abundantly available in and for the socius, begins to usurp, for the U.S., the entire globe. And the fact that every national origin is written with a hyphen before the word *American* tends to get forgotten. The next step is Arthur Schlesinger and Lynne Cheney, armed with *The Disuniting of America.* But not every artist performs that way.

Here is another example from Jamelie Hassan's work that represents the new American, speaking. I want to walk over to another installation piece called *Meeting Nasser.*

Jamelie Hassan, whose parents came to Canada in 1914 and 1939 from Lebanon, grew up in an Arabic-speaking household. Yet she is not

FIG. 3.—Jamelie Hassan, *Meeting Nasser, 1985–86.* Installation. Collection: Canada Council Art Bank, Ottawa. Photo: National Gallery of Canada, Ottawa.

FIG. 4.—*Meeting Nasser.* Original found image.

merely nostalgic about her place of origin. She sees it as a place in the history of the present, not just in the history of her own displaced migration. This installation is a "texting"—a weaving, as in textile—of that seeing. Hassan sees the place of Gamal Abdel Nasser, the "liberator" of Egypt, through the writing of Naguib Mahfouz, one of the writers censored by him. The child in the video monitor in the installation reads a passage from Mahfouz, *on* censorship, *in* English translation.

This is a text about the restitution of truth to history through rememoration. Because Hassan recognizes the place of origin as a place other than simply an endorsement for herself as cross-cultural North American Other, she can respect the immigrant as agent of historical rememoration. The immigrant is becoming the agent of the history of the metropolitan country in the coarse grain of the law as well as in the paradox of language. The photographs lining the walls in this installation were found in her family album. An extremely strong statement of the politicization of the personal.

Who is the little girl presenting the bouquet to Nasser in the blown-up photo on the wall, overshadowed by grinning men? Is it a younger Jamelie Hassan? We cannot know; nor can she. All we have is another blown-up snapshot on the wall, of herself full face, without Nasser.

With Nasser the little girl's back is turned to the camera: a simple sign—nothing as heavy as a metaphor or a symbol—of the recovery of identity in politics, or the loss of reference in the graph. You cannot have a true fit of identity in the political. The little girl with Jamelie and the little girl in the picture are not the same, just the approximate size, a hand-me-down, to others who must stage the same collective origin as yourself.

The video monitor mimes the scene or stage of the writing of history. This girl, dressed quite like the girl in the photo, faces us. She is Elizabeth Hassan, Jamelie's niece. The photo of meeting Nasser is behind her on the small screen, as well as blown up on the wall of the gallery. Again and again, this agent of rememorating history, this little girl, turns her back and enters the picture in the picture, though the superimposition is never adequate. Again and again she moves forward and reads the lines.

The ethnic American—who is the nonethnic American?—has her face turned back *and* front. She must understand the place of origin as politically present *without* her. She must also speak that politics to the metropolis, in the words censored in that other space, but translated into the metropolitan language. The child reads an adaptation into English. The child as agent is reading a history written elsewhere; this too is the politics of culture and translation, the fabrication of a strong identity. The child as agent of reading a history written elsewhere *for* this space, the proper pronunciation for the big words prompted by the artist's audible

FIG. 5.—Jamelie Hassan, *Meeting Nasser, 1985–86.* Detail from video. Collection: Canada Council Art Bank, Ottawa. Photo: Wyn Geleynse.

whispers (in the installation there is a soundtrack): "imagination," as she is stumbling; "event"; "mysterious."

This is a much more complex and overdetermined scenario than claiming Otherness. But the agent of history has her own lesson to teach: it is a lesson about learning. After "an act of liberation," says Michel Foucault, learning "the practices of liberty."[15] Little Elizabeth Hassan tells her artist foremother confidently why she still needs prompting. She says she can still only read big letters, in English of course. She has stepped off the staged origin. She is a Canadian, the agent of new Canadian history.

I want to dwell on this apparently minor moment about the size of letters in this exhibit about the written word entitled *Inscription.* The child, as reader of writing, speaks again and again of the size of letters on the electronic stage: a simulacrum of the opening-up of history, for the telematic hyperreal small screen has speeded up the tempo of the translation of cultures since the mid-seventies.

It is interesting that she might be making a mistake. She might be meaning the size of words. This measure of the unit of learning, even mistaken, by the child who is learning the size of letters may be the place of the *techne* or art of art and history. We learn identity letter by letter. The child's repetitiveness in the work of art "makes the expert speak [—without repetition—the expert] who will not take long to say" the work "speaks" the texting of history.[16] I speak too quickly: *she* is learning, letter by letter. What is it to learn?

If we believe that we can restore the personal, political, historical, and cross-cultural truth of art, we are silenced by the child apprentice in cultural politics as art and the performance of life: the new immigrant. The great divide between the mother and child, the mother and daughter, in the new immigrant family, is one of the most instructive things to meditate on for any student of cultural politics. We on the outside, on the other hand—somewhat older immigrants in the intellectual scene—if we believe we can restore the personal, political, historical, cross-cultural truth of art, we are silenced by the child apprentice in the art of history, who reminds us that we learn the inscription of identity letter by letter.

Therefore one must think of restitution, not of truth in art, *peinture,* but size, *pointure.* I am referring to Derrida's long piece on the debate between Heidegger and Schapiro about a Van Gogh painting, which is called precisely "vérité en pointure." The installation is becoming a case. One must think, then, of restitution, not of truth in art, *peinture,* but of size, *pointure.* One must think of restitutions of truth to size, which means,

15. See Michel Foucault, "The Ethic of Care for the Self as a Practice of Freedom: An Interview," trans. J. D. Gauthier, in *The Final Foucault,* ed. James Bernauer and David Rasmussen (Cambridge, Mass., 1988), p. 3.

16. Jacques Derrida, "Restitutions of the Truth in Pointing [*pointure*]," *The Truth in Painting,* trans. Geoff Bennington and Ian McLeod (Chicago, 1987), p. 314.

in this case, the number of stitches. The painting in question is Van Gogh's *Old Shoes with Laces.* And size is the number of stitches in a shoe or a pair of gloves. "But truth," and this is Van Gogh, "is so dear to me . . . that indeed I believe, I believe I would still rather be a cobbler than a musician with colors."[17]

Restitutions of truth to size of letters. How different to learn the agency of reading the *borrowed* script of history by the new immigrant—how different it is from *talking* about learning, or being *grounded* in an ethnic reality.

The other kind of emphasis on being a new American is not at all so benign. It is what is called, these days, "border culture." This stops the easy traffic in ethnicity where the sign system in use, English, belongs to the master. Here are some words from "Border Notebook" by Guillermo Gomez Peña, the Chicarrican artist from Tijuana-San Diego:

> I dreamt the U.S. had become a totalitarian state controlled by satellites and computers. I dreamt that in this strange society poets and artists had no public voice whatsoever. Thank God it was just a dream. In English. English only. Just a dream. Not a memory. Repeat with me: *Vivir en estado del sitio* is a translatable statement; to live in a state of siege *es suseptibile de traduccion.* In Mexican in San Diego, in Puerto Rican in New York City, in Moroccan in Paris, in Pakistani in London. Definitely, a translatable statement. *Vivir en estado de alerta* is also translatable, my dear. To live in a state of alert, with your wings ready to flap and your eyes ready to question. Why? Why? A child of the Mexican crisis, a new foreigner in the art world, out to exhibit his wounds in immaculate neon coffins. Why? Why? Why? Why? Why? Why? San Diego Channel 10. Super Mojado loses his cool in middle of an interview. The producers are crapping their pants. Yeah.[18]

I wrench together this anguish with a short passage from Toni Morrison's *Beloved,* the most extreme example of the withholding of translation. Let us look at the scene of the mother tongue changing from mother to daughter, the institution of a culture that will yield Toni Morrison. (We have to remember that chattel slavery is matrilineal.) The scene in the novel is not of a change, but a loss. For the narrative is not of immigration but of slavery. Sethe, the central character of the novel, remembers "what Nan"—her mother's fellow slave and friend—"told her she had forgotten, along with the language she told it in. The same language her ma'am spoke"—the African language—"and which would

17. Quoted in ibid., p. 255.
18. Guillermo Gomez Peña, performance tape.

never come back. But the message—that was and had been there all along."[19]

Yet the representation of this message, as it passes through the forgetfulness of death, to Sethe's ghostly daughter Beloved, is of a withholding. Morrison writes, "This is not a story to pass on" (*B*, p. 275). Even between mother and daughter, a certain historical withholding intervenes. If the situation between the new immigrant mother and daughter—when the mother talks protecting honor and the daughter talks reproductive rights—if this situation provokes the question as to whether it is the birth or death of translation, here the author represents, *with* violence, a certain birth *in* death.

A death in the birth of a story that is not to translate or pass on. Strictly speaking, therefore, an aporia or unbridgeable gulf. And yet it *is* passed on, with the mark of untranslatability on it, in the bound book *Beloved* that we hold in our hands. The most extreme case.

Contrast this case with one's confidence in accessibility in the house of power, ministry of culture, or official feminism, where history is waiting to be restored. The scene of violence between mother and daughter reported and passed on by the daughter Sethe, a former slave, to her daughter Denver, who carries the name of a white-trash girl in partial acknowledgement of women's solidarity in birthing, is the condition of impossibility of the book *Beloved*. It celebrates its own impossibility in this tragic way. Here is Sethe telling the story of that impossibility to her daughter: "She picked me up and carried me behind the smokehouse"—her slave mother whose language she could no longer speak:

> Back there she opened up her dress front and lifted her breast and pointed under it. Right on her rib was a circle and a cross burnt right in the skin. She said, "This is your ma'am. This," and she pointed. . . . "Yes Ma'am," I said. "But how will you know me? . . . Mark me, too," I said. . . .
>
> "Did she?" asked Denver.
>
> "She slapped my face."
>
> "What for?" [the daughter now asks this mother]
>
> "I didn't understand it then. Not till I had a mark of my own." [*B*, p. 61]

That would of course be a different mark because the owner is different. This scene, of claiming the brand of the owner as my own, is what we are talking about. On the other side is a resistance that cannot speak itself *as* resistance. An example, if the reader's attention span is long enough, of radical monstration, *idamvāda* undoing *ahamvāda*.

This scene, of claiming the brand of the owner as my own, to create in

19. Toni Morrison, *Beloved* (New York, 1987), p. 62; hereafter abbreviated *B*.

this broken chain of marks owned by separate white male agents of property an unbroken chain of rememory in enslaved daughters as agents of a history not to be passed on, is of necessity more poignant than, let us say, the wonderful Creole writer J. M. Coetzee's novel *Foe,* where Friday, the slave whose tongue has been cut off, actually writes something on his slate, "on his own," when the metropolitan anticolonial white woman wants to teach him writing. And when she, very anxious, wants to see it, he withholds it by rubbing it off, *idamvāda* as erasure.[20] And yet even Morrison's powerful staging, in a U.S. text in the tradition of the novel, is productive in a mode that the washed-up coastline of the southeastern edge of Bangladesh, the northern edge of the landmass off the coast in which you—the Singaporeans, if you've lost track of this identity-traffic—so successfully inscribe yourself, cannot share. Yet, I can hope, like Djebar's autobiographer-heroine Isma, to earn the right to be an ephemeral storyteller of this episode and arouse curiosity about the remote ancestors of the U.S. task force.

The scene in *Beloved* passes between mother and daughter and then the mother withholds the passing of it—because of course she cannot mark her child. In slavery and less extremely in migrancy, the dominant mark must be made by the master in order to be claimed as "my mark." The speaking in English in *Meeting Nasser,* the child turning forward and speaking in English—that mark is not given by the mother who speaks Arabic. This precarious moment in the scene of cultural translation, when it is suppressed or ignored, produces *at the other end* the performance of today's war, or the uncaring gift of the task force. This precarious scene of claiming the brand of the owner as my own, to create in this broken chain of marks owned by separate white male agents of property, an unbroken chain of rememory in enslaved daughters, teaches us the lesson that we must, as agents, *claim* that mark as Elizabeth Hassan is doing, as in a much more violent moment the slave mother is doing, as Guillermo Gomez Peña is doing. It is not a gift to be given. It is not a gift that you give at the end of a gun, or off a helicopter, and the other accepts with victory signs or an abject letter.

The lesson of the impossibility of translation in the general sense, as Toni Morrison shows it, readily points at absolute contingency. Not the sequentiality of time, not even the cycle of seasons, but only weather. Listen to this incredible passage and quietly relate this to the tedium of my first case: "By and by, all trace is gone. And what is forgotten is not only the footprints but the water too and what it is down there. The rest is weather. Not the breath of the disremembered and unaccounted for, but

20. For a longer discussion of this, see Spivak, "Versions of the Margin: Coetzee's *Foe* reading Defoe's *Crusoe/Roxana,*" in *Theory and Its Consequences,* ed. Jonathan Arac and Barbara Johnson (Baltimore, 1990), pp. 171, 173.

wind in the eaves, or spring ice thawing too quickly. Just weather" (*B*, p. 275).

That too is time. Geological time, however slow, is also time. One must not *make* history in a deliberate way. One must respect the earth's tone. One might be obliged to claim history from the violent perpetrator of it in order to turn violation into the enablement of *idamvāda*, but that is another story. After the effacement of the trace, there must be no project for restoring the origin. That is "just weather," here today as yesterday.

With this invocation of contingency, where nature may be the great body without organs of woman (that passage of Marx again), we can begin to see that the project of translating culture within the politics of identity is not a quick fix.

I want now to come to my closing case, both inside and outside whatever it might be a case *of*. I want now to read a little bit from Jacques Derrida's *Glas*.

When I talk about the postponement of eco-logic by positing land as the *da* of *da-sein*, or of the border art where Gomez Peña goes back and forth from Tijuana to San Diego, where Jamelie Hassan goes back and forth from the Islamic world to the world of eastern Canada, where Toni Morrison crosses through slavery from Africa into the United States—for this, the word Derrida would offer us is *navette*, a shuttle.

The book *Glas* is a kind of typographic miming. It is written in bits and pieces. On the left-hand side is the homoerotic traditional tale of Western philosophy, on the right-hand side the criminal male homosexual Jean Genet. As we read, we are obliged to be a *navette* between the two sides in order to find out what every extraordinary page might mean. Is this also the effort to learn a case of the institution or a historico-geographical moment in gay culture, a culture that cannot speak? "*Navette* is the word. . . . The word—*la navette*—is absolutely necessary. It will have had to be there. . . . It concerns a small metal vessel in the form of a boat. . . . And then the weaver's *navette*. . . . coming and going woven in a chain. The weave is in the *navette*. . . . Isn't elaboration [Derrida is using it in the expanded sense—*elaborare*, to work out] a weaver's movement?"[21]

But then Derrida stops. In Derrida's early work the text is one of the master metaphors: the text as textile, through the Latin *texere*, to weave. But here, in mid-Derrida—and Derrida's later work is again different—he temporarily gives up the metaphor of the text. The weaver's shuttle, the *navette* smoothly going back and forth between the two sides is not going to serve here.

The question/statement (half a quote from Genet) with which *Glas* begins, in the right-hand column, is: "'*what remained of a Rembrandt torn into small, very regular squares and rammed down the shithole*' is divided in

21. Derrida, *Glas*, trans. John P. Leavey, Jr., and Richard Rand (Lincoln, Nebr., 1986), pp. 207–8; hereafter abbreviated *G*.

two" (*G,* p. 1). What remains, what is the essence of art, or of identity, when it is torn up into a million ID cards and stuffed into English, divides (at least) into two. You cannot say that the result is a smoothly woven text: "Yet we have mistrusted the textile metaphor. This is because it still keeps . . . a kind of . . . naturality, primordiality, cleanliness [*propreté*]. At least the textile metaphor is still more natural, primordial, proper than the metaphor of sewing, of the seam [*couture*]" (*G,* p. 208). *Couture* carries the echo of the *coupure* or cut—the cut from the place of origin.

Derrida is learning this lesson by looking at the gay man's text. We are in the house of identity: what is the name of (the straight white) man? In the left-hand column Hegel is accusing Kant of being a fetishist because he does not introduce love into religion; and Freud is launching the fetish into indeterminacy by genuinely speculating with it. Again and again Derrida puts in *Glas* texts on the so-called African fetish found in Hegel to show that these people have not earned the right to speak of the fetish. The withheld translation of Africa has been suppressed (see *G,* pp. 207–11).

For Hegel the fetish is an animal substitute for the Eucharist: this notion is implicit when Hegel, Marx, and Freud use the fetish as an accusing concept in their text, even though Freud does unmoor it. For the notion of the fetish, it will not do simply to weave a *navette* between Marx, Hegel, Freud, Kant. Derrida is going to have to cut holes and put *their* fantasy of the African fetish, which one cannot restore in a text written in English, into French. He is going to have to patch it on the text to see what difference it makes.

Meanwhile, on the right-hand side Genet is in the harem of transvestites and criminal gay men. They are putting on all kinds of *fétiches,* dildos, grape clusters on the crotch, et cetera, as that text unfolds. Who is the authority for whom, and how is the *navette,* shuttling from Hegel and company to Genet and his accomplices, weaving anything at all? Derrida suggests that we will have to think *now,* rather than of textile—a weave—as in the old dispensation, of the kind of sewing and patching that betrays, exposes what it should hide, dis-simulates what it signals, makes the TV screen crap its pants.

Therefore he can do nothing other than cite: "Cit[ing], as perhaps you have just seen: only to displace the syntactic arrangement around a real or sham physical wound that draws attention to and makes the other be forgotten. . . . All the examples stand out, are cut out [*se découpent*] in this way. Regard the holes if you can" (*G,* pp. 215, 210).

This is not postmodern practice. There is none of that confident absolute citation where what is cited is emptied of its own historical texting or weaving. This is a citing that invokes the wound of the cutting from the staged origin. I harmonize with Djebar here: autobiography is a wound where the blood of history does not dry. Postmodernist practice manages the crisis of postmodernity—the end of the dream of modernization as the imperialist dream.

Where is the crisis of identity managed? If the rhetoric of woman's body and the claims of man's logic are both in shreds, if women and men in harems are subversive of identity, is there any comfort to be found? Is it only the abstraction of the law that must assume that all human beings are one? Is it all only "the blind spot of an old dream of symmetry?"[22]

To strain against these questions, Derrida breaks decorum. Derrida considered Joyce with Husserl, many years ago; and has more recently written on Joyce's Molly.[23] However deep he dives, Joyce's world is irreducibly gendered; Molly and Leopold digest separately. Anna Livia Plurabelle and H.C.E. remain distinguishable.

An unemphatic moment of embarrassing naïveté gives me another hint of the limits of ontology. The dream of a fundamental ontology is to precede cultural identity, but we know how much, in Heidegger's case, that dream was compromised by convictions of the special place of Greek and German. If we move from the mind to the body, the reproductive system is so thoroughly compromised in patriarchy that it will not show us a way out. In *Glas* Derrida circles around the question of the family, the mother, male homosexuality, the double bind of tumescence (in French, *bander* or to bind) and makes visible the inflexibility of this limit. Antigone is the only daughter there, and, in his problematic book around female homosexuality, he can claim nothing but a problematic *droit de regard* or right to watch.[24]

The digestive system is deeply, culturally marked. What are the limits to ontology here? *Glas* on the right-hand side starts with the shithole, as I have already remarked. The outer limits to Kant's sublime were long ago located in vomit.[25] Derrida's current work, once again around the Eucharist and that assimilated Creole Augustine, obstinately asks: "What is it to eat?" In this unemphatic moment in *Glas,* Derrida asks a question that causes embarrassment. I cannot include it in my staging of the fragments of identity-talk: Derrida's practice does not share in that crisis management.

Derrida suggests that the text, which was the privileged metaphor in his earlier dispensation—and will not be discarded—is a *navette* between

22. Irigaray, "The Blind Spot of an Old Dream of Symmetry," *Speculum of the Other Woman,* trans. Gillian C. Gill (New York, 1985), pp. 11–29.

23. See Derrida, "Ulysses Gramophone: Hear Say Yes in Joyce," trans. Tina Kendall and Shari Benstock, in *Acts of Literature,* ed. Derek Attridge (New York, 1992), pp. 256–307.

24. See Derrida, afterword, in Marie-Françoise Plissart, *Droit de regards* (Paris, 1985).

25. See Derrida, "Economimesis," trans. Richard Klein, *Diacritics* 11 (Summer 1981): 3–25.

Geist and *Gäschen,* between spirit and a fart, between the transcendent breeze and the wind that makes us embarrassed, which is marked by the body's materiality. Genet is talking about roses shooting whiff after whiff at our faces (the rose is a character in this gay brothel)—and Derrida, in the middle of one of these passages, comments, "The essence of the rose is its nonessence: its odor insofar as it evaporates. Whence its effluvial affinity with the fart [*pet*] or the belch: these excrements do not stay [*se gardent*], do not even take form" (*G,* p. 58). *Fart* in French is *pet,* so to repeat identically, absolute translatability becomes *ré-peter,* each fart different because of what the body must take in to live. A familiar case of the daily failure of the simplicity of ontology. Rather than the idea infinitely repeatable and therefore always identical, the repetition becomes something that cannot be caught. "How could ontology lay hold of a fart?" (*G,* p. 58). He rewrites the ontico-ontological difference by reminding us of the body's being: the ontic, which in Heidegger is the intimacy of being, to which the being is so proximate or close that no ontology can lay hold of it, in the late Heidegger becomes a certain kind of fetish. His politics change, he invokes an originary or primordial language.

What Derrida is looking at is the way we are when we are close to ourselves. *This* lecture—in Singapore—would have been an exercise in the discomfort of controlling flatulence if it had been an after-dinner lecture. And when one is alone and proximate to oneself, one finally gives way to the totally unembarrassing comfort of the signature of the body being itself (as it were)—nobody there to be embarrassed or repelled. It is simply the end of the public sphere, for the moment. It is really very difficult to hear this question: How can ontology—the *philosophy* of being—lay hold of a fart? There is none of the glamor of sexuality here, or of the so-called spectrum of sexual practices. How can ontology lay hold of a fart? An ontology can always put its hand on whatever remains in the john—the shit—but never on the whiffs let out by roses. So the text is a gas, the mark of the spirit in one's body. The text is an imperfect *navette* between *Geist* and fermentation, *Gäschen,* the little gas. The ontic as fart or belch, the signature of the subject at ease with itself decentered from the mind to the body, which writes its inscription. This also is the level at which war has no meaning, and indeed the embarrassment often offered by the subaltern victim in the flesh, scratching herself and picking her nose.

In this version of the ontic as such, to go back to the same bit of Marx, "to say that the human being's physical and mental life is linked to nature simply means that nature is linked to itself," breathing in and out, as it were.[26]

Marx puts it in the language of classical German philosophy, which Derrida takes to its limit. On that ground, there is no importance of any-

26. Marx, "Economic and Philosophical Manuscripts," in *Early Writings,* p. 328.

thing. But if you cannot catch it, how can ontology lay hold of it? This is not as glamorous as either mind or body, high-toned mind-talk or the highly attitudinizing body-talk; it is none of that. There is crisis, there is the long-haul politics of culture, but this rag-and-bone shop remains the counter-case of cultural institution, of indeed the philosophy of Being, highest talk of identity.

It is not possible to remain here. Zoom now to the other end of the spectrum. We have considered varieties of Creole and migrant art and theory, writing by a woman who takes the history of slavery seriously, responsibly, art and theory that try to cope with the problem of the politics of translation, the politics of culture, the politics of identity.

Now let us touch on the responsibility of the "national" artist seeking an international audience. I'm not speaking of the artist who is an immigrant, but the artist who has remained in decolonized space to represent that culture to the persons in metropolitan space eager for other cultures. This is a great narrative indeed, and upon this register I think that the national artist has a very strong responsibility not to take advantage of the sanctioned ignorance of the West.

Recently in Italy I saw a performance by a woman, an Indian artist, a dancer, which was broken up by an Italian director. What he was actually doing onstage (I was reminded of Olympia in Hoffmann's story, Freud's treatment of "The Sand-man") was actually making her do her classical dance and then asking her to break up her sequences, taking away her music, and then slowing the sequences down as much as possible, making her do 5 percent of the sequence and then putting other women—whom he no doubt treats the same way—together so they could do a peculiar kind of a dance together under his control. And in the representation of this happening—which filled me with terror, because that is how *we* were produced by assenting to imperialism—at a certain point, he makes her say that she had resisted him for a long time until she realized that he was not going to take away her style. When questioned by Trinh T. Minh-ha, as to how she believed that he would not take away her style she said confidently, he promised me nothing. I believed him.

We are afraid of this kind of seductive winning of the assent of the colonized, so that the result is a kind of ventriloquism that then stands in for free will. Our own complicity in our production is another kind of translation of cultures, access to a "museumized" identity, roots in aspic. The national artist in the Third World has a responsibility not to speak for the nation in response to a demand made by this craving for intercultural exchange. Everything is susceptible to exchange; but commodity is something *made* for exchange. Identity as commodity.

And so I would like to turn to the film *The Voyage Beyond*, by the Bengali filmmaker Gautam Ghosh. This is not a film about contemporary

India, but of India in the last century. It is the story of a very young girl being married off to a dying old man. They are in a burning ghat on the borders of the Ganges or Ganga. At a certain point the outcast, the Untouchable, wins her to sexuality. She is there because she's going to be *sati,* a widow who self-immolates. At the end, she is washed away in the waves of the Ganga, as is her dying husband.

This is basically the story. Actually the film engages in a peculiar species of auteurism by borrowing the proper name of a magisterial text of Bengali fiction, Kamalkumar Majumdar's *Antarjalīyātrā* (1961). The metropolitan viewer cannot know this. The result, in this particular case, is a sort of violation of the transcoding or translation between two media. (I know that films are not supposed to be faithful to novels, that is not my point.) I believe that it is this possibility of violating the particularity of *this* novel as historical icon that kept Satyajit Ray and Mrinal Sen from attempting its filming.

If in the context of the other cases I have said that sometimes it is necessary to withhold translation, as in the extreme case staged by Toni Morrison, here, turning 180 degrees, I am suggesting that in certain macrocontexts there is also room for a gesture of faithfulness to the original, if it is to be a faithfulness to the original considered as one case among many, not a case that should be idealized. In a certain historical conjuncture, when the West is avid for Third World culture, it sometimes becomes the appropriate case. Given the experimental verbal authority of this novel, no film using the title *Antarjalīyātra* can avoid auteurism. A new *Macbeth* is a new *Macbeth.*

I will not attempt to comment on the verbal experimentation of *Antarjalīyātra.* Let me, however, say a word or two about the general project of the book. It does have something to do with the question of identity. The idea of identity is often marked by the names of continents, huge chunks of the world: Asian identity, Third World identity. The author of the book attempts the nearly impossible task of grasping identity in the extremely proximate or close-up place—the place where, in postmodernity, Derrida locates the fart—where it has not yet reached the level of adjectival description. In the layer of its incessant and inchoate emergence, close to the body, if the body too is understood as a kind of shuttling, between bone and blood, nerve and twitching muscle. Kamalkumar chooses the liminal space of the burning of the body and three human beings relating differently to that event-to-come: an event that hangs over the text, but never happens. The dying brahmin, the woman in imminent death-in-life, and the Untouchable, who is the facilitator of the flame that consumes the body. Ghosh shatters this project by staging the burning ghat as a realistic referent carrying a realistic amount of local color, a stage for a broadly conceived psychodrama played out by easily grasped stock characters: the good and earthy Untouchable, the good, colonially touched doctor who is not quite good enough, the patriarchally oppressed woman awakening into struggling self-consciousness. Hinduism as precolonial superstition: a screen easy to work out from a base of minimal knowledge.

What the author of the novel is trying to do *takes as understood* a fully formed ideological subject, to whom the reader is invited to be ex-centric. In other words, Majumdar expects the reader to have enough internalized perception of a certain kind of Hinduism, as a heteropraxic cultural system, to have earned the right to be asked to consider the following question: How do the affects work when such extreme dispensations as *sati* and the caste system operate as a felt cultural norm? This kind of a question is extremely important today in my nation-state of origin where Hindu fundamentalism is violent, where even children and young girls are sometimes being convinced that to be a good citizen of India one has to internalize an absolute version of the majority religion, which cannot admit that it is a negotiated mistranslation. Again we have an attempt at the cultural or political translation of origins.

In this context, to redo the book for a national audience would have been quite different from doing it for an international audience. This is not the place to develop those suggestions.

Let us go back to the novel's project. His question: how do the affects work when such extreme dispensations as widow-burning and the caste system operate as a felt cultural norm? How could our mothers and grandmothers have assented to this, and remained human? There is no possibility here for the viewer to interpret the film from a position of cultural superiority. This is a question that can only be asked *by* us as Hindus, *of* ourselves. This text is exactly not for the outsider who wants to enter with nothing but general knowledge, to have her ignorance sanctioned.

Majumdar wants to avoid critical distance as far as possible because he knows it is not fully possible. He articulates the most extreme system of belief, not because he wants to give himself distance, but because he wants to acknowledge proximity, because he wants to get at that most difficult thing, perspectival normativity. In other words, he is not distancing himself by portraying these three people as "normal." He is trying to perspectivize the idea of normality as such by choosing the hardest possible case. He is perspectivizing all normality, yours and mine as well, not just "Asian" or "historical." *And*—this is a difficult point but I want to continue to emphasize it—the base of normality out of which normality in general is thus unmoored is a rather specific Bengali cultural base, a general "identity," if you like. From out of this base, presupposed only to be put under erasure, Kamal Majumdar seems to ask a question that I can, since I write in English, put to you almost exactly in the words of John P. Leavey, Jr., and Richard Rand as they have translated the French of Jacques Derrida: "How does one give the *seing* [a thumbprint as well as one's breast] to an affect?" (*G*, p. 42b).

It is easy to get information about the identity of an entire continent, or to put one's signature on a concept, support it or oppose it. But how does one claim the normality of an affect in extremis as one's own, in the place of the *seing* rather than the signature? One way is to unmoor affect from the natural person and place it in ideology—can this be done except from above?

Again, this is a question that I can neither not ask nor answer. Turning away from this limit, let us notice cruder ways of fabricating identity. Let us look at the way in which Ghosh changes the introductory verbal material from novel to film.

At the beginning of the film, Ghosh's subtitle writer takes a feeble whack at giving the viewer a bit of potted history. In 1829 Lord William Bentinck abolished the self-immolation of widows, echoed by Indian names like Ram Mohun Roy in the dialogue. In the Bengali film, there is nothing but the title and the opening credits. Let us now turn to some of the sentences in the preface of the book, dealing precisely with the identity or rather the subject-position of the assigned reader or viewer: "The affective-icon of this book is Ramakrishna's, the poetic icon Ramprasad's. . . . I am certain our country still thinks of the Ganga as its life, our country still touches immortality, everyone will understand our story. My profound respect to the reader."[27]

Who are these two named figures? Ramprasad Sen, an eighteenth-century clerk patronized by Raja Krishna Chandra Sen, is not exactly a figure unknown to the West. Some of his exquisitely and deceptively simple poetry in praise of Kali was translated into French fifty years ago. He is a constituent figure of Bengali culture. He is part of that great movement of reinscribing Kali into an affective goddess, both mother and daughter, violent only out of radical innocence, not malevolent but a punisher, in sheer childlike impatience with evil. This Kali is the book's icon, not the peculiarly monstrous figure behind the Untouchable in a sequence towards the end of the film, where he is talking to the young bride, reminiscent of nothing so much as Coppola's insensitive imaging of the Bodhisatva icon in *Apocalypse Now.*

Ramakrishna, a mystical visionary of the second half of the nineteenth century, is another constituent figure of contemporary Bengali culture who is not unknown to the West. Centers of the Ramakrishna mission began to be established in the West from the very beginning of the twentieth century. His conversations have been translated into English. Christopher Isherwood wrote a sympathetic biography about ten years ago. He is one of the most moving affective reformers of Hinduism, attaching himself to a Kali who closely resembles Ramprasad's beloved goddess. He is a perspectivist, attempting affectively to enter the subjectivity of a Muslim, a Christian, a woman. He is absolutely opposed to the caste system. This is not the place to comment on what has happened to

27. Kamalkumar Majumdar, *Antarjalīyātrā* (Calcutta, 1981), p. ix.

Ramakrishna's vision as it has become socially institutionalized. What is important for the question of the identity of the reader/viewer is that *this* figure is the affective icon of the book.

Majumdar writes, "the new Bengal has been created by remembering him, by keeping him in mind. He took away a bit of fear in the natural human being in the raw, from his own wakeful state by saying: 'is a human being a small thing, eh!' "[28]

The book's point of view is a certain Ramprasad's and a certain Ramakrishna's, without violence, without cruelty, without caste, and without addiction to flesh. Now suppose Gautam Ghosh had tried to transcode this complex micrological project into filmic idiom! Instead he appropriated, abdicated, banalized, putting the name of William Bentinck on the screen of Ramprasad Sen and Ramakrishna Paramahansa.

The Voyage Beyond is actually what is called a "topical" film. It is made in the atmosphere of great interest in *sati* following Rup Kanwar's self-immolation a few years ago. Feminist mobilization and resistance to *sati* on that occasion was widespread. In that legalized context, it was understandably not possible to approach gendered subjectivity with any subtlety. The movement had to remain on the level of female agency. A filmic representation of woman-in-*sati* is not confined to such restrictions. What does Gautam Ghosh do with the relative autonomy of this art form? There are at least five looks at different points of the film that consolidate the representation of the young bride Jashobati in the film:

a) an unconsummated look before the exchange of garlands that seals the marriage;

b) a look at the temple of the grotesque goddess asking for a repetition of the sexual encounter;

c) a rounded gaze at the stone printed with the palm mark of the burnt widow;

d) a look at the end with Jashobati pinned on the woodframe evocative of the seasonal status of goddesses regularly deposited in the river;

e) the visually exciting representation of the unfocused look of the eye painted on the boat.

The least convincing bit of liberated script, "Am I your plaything?" is not accompanied by any orchestration of the gaze.

Considerations of the first three should accompany a viewing of the film. I would like to point out here that Jashobati looking out of the disposable goddess-frame and the lovely boat with the pair of eyes that cannot gaze carry a heavy cultural message without cultural logic. The suspension of two particular deaths—the natural death of the old man and the forced unnatural death of the young wife—deaths that do not happen in the novel, is here recoded as a return to a cultural base without any cultural justification. To play thus with textual subtlety seems to me to

28. Ibid.

be an abdication of the responsibility of the national artist, trafficking in national identity (in the name of woman) for international consumption.

For it is *against* the grain of *this* responsibility of the national in the international that we feminist internationalists strain. I am thinking now of the worldwide group called Women Living under Islamic Law, extending all the way from North Africa to Indonesia with members from immigrant communities in the First World.[29] These feminist internationalists must keep up their precarious position within a divided loyalty: being a woman and being in the nation, without allowing the West to save them. Their project, menaced yet alive, takes me back to my beginning. It is in their example that I look at myself as a woman, at my history of womaning. Women can be ventriloquists, but they have an immense *historical* potential of *not* being (allowed to remain) nationalists; of knowing, in their gendering, that nation and identity are commodities in the strictest sense: something made for exchange. And that they are the medium of that exchange.[30]

When we mobilize that secret ontic intimate knowledge, we lose it, but I see no other way. We have never, to quote *Glas,* been virgin enough to be the Other. Claudine Hermann, a lawyer who has practiced both in Afghanistan and in France, gives me my closing words: We have always known how [in "culture"] "to see women through the eyes of men and, in life, to see men through the eyes of women." We have always known "how wide the gap is." We have always been "schizoid and we might add . . . hermaphrodite."[31] Not androgynous, but a bit of a hermaphrodite secure in the conviction that sex and gender are structurally not identical. Cultures are built violently on the enforced coercion that they are. War is its most extreme signature, and, like all signatures, patriarchal.[32] Our lesson is to act in the fractures of identities in struggle.

29. See Marie-Aimée Hélie-Lucas, "Women Living under Islamic Laws," *South Asia Bulletin* 10, no. 1 (1990): 73.

30. See Ted Swedenburg, "Palestinean Women Now: Tradition and Difference in the 1936–39 Revolt: Implications for the *Intifada,*" conference paper, "Marxism Now: Tradition and Difference," 2 Dec. 1989, University of Massachusetts. He makes this point for one of the most important global sites of contestation: Palestine.

31. Claudine Hermann, *The Tongue Snatchers,* trans. Nancy Kline (Lincoln, Nebr., 1989), p. 7.

32. For the patriarchality of signatures in identity, see Derrida on Nietzsche, "Logic of the Living Feminine," *The Ear of the Other: Otobiography, Transference, Translation*, trans. Peggy Kamuf (New York, 1985), pp. 3–19. It is this logic that we must ab-use as we act bits, talk identity.

The Empire Renarrated: *Season of Migration to the North* and the Reinvention of the Present

Saree S. Makdisi

> The old river in its broad reach rested unruffled at the decline of day after ages of good service done to the race that peopled its banks, spread out in the tranquil dignity of a waterway leading to the uttermost ends of the earth.
>
> —Joseph Conrad, *Heart of Darkness*

1

The serenity and the majesty of the Thames as it is described at the beginning of *Heart of Darkness* are only too appropriate for this waterway down which had sailed, long before Joseph Conrad's time, vessels carrying with them the seeds of the British Empire. Conrad's Thames flows in remarkable contrast to the Nile that rages through al-Tayyib Salih's *Season of Migration to the North* (1969). Far from resting in "tranquil dignity," the Nile and the people inhabiting its banks are shown undergoing violent

A shorter version of this paper was presented at the American Comparative Literature Association Conference held at Pennsylvania State University, 29–31 March 1990. I am indebted to Fredric Jameson, Richard Dienst, and Cesare Casarino for their helpful comments on earlier drafts of this essay.

All translations from the Arabic are mine unless otherwise noted.

This article originally appeared in *Critical Inquiry* 18 (Summer 1992).

transfigurations. If *Heart of Darkness* narrates the history of modern British imperialism from a position deep within its metropolitan center, *Season of Migration* presents itself as the counternarrative of the same bitter history. Just as Conrad's novel was bound up with Britain's imperial project, Salih's participates (in an oppositional way) in the afterlife of the same project today, by "writing back" to the colonial power that once ruled the Sudan.

But *Season of Migration* is also a radical intervention in the field of postcolonial Arab discourse, which has long been centered on the debate between "traditionalism" and "Westernism." This debate has its origins in the nineteenth century, when the ideology of modernity (which sustained the emerging European empires) began to be imposed on Arab social formations, in many cases long before the actual arrival of the European armies.[1] From the very beginning, this ideology had to compete with the residual (but still very powerful) ideological structures of traditionalism, and the interaction of these ideologies has shaped the whole process of modernization in Arab societies from the nineteenth century until the present day. Modernity, in the Arab world, has been inextricably associated with Europe itself.[2] In the face of this association, however, some Muslim and Arab intellectuals tried to reform the traditional structures of Islamic society in order to contest modernity as it was presented by Europe. Jamal al-Din Afghani and Muhammad Abduh, for instance, argued that Islam embodied the principles of modernity within its own doctrine and therefore that the confrontation between traditionalism and modernity was a false one since the latter is immanent

1. This is especially the case in the Levant. In North Africa, much of which came under direct rule earlier than the areas to the east, European empires often imposed their ideologies by force, as when the French tried to introduce private property in Algeria by forcibly breaking up and expropriating family-run farmland in 1873. This policy, according to one French deputy, was "but the crowning touch to an edifice well-founded on a whole series of ordinances, edicts, laws and decrees of the Senate which together and severally have as the same object: the establishment of private property among the Arabs" (quoted in Rosa Luxemburg, *The Accumulation of Capital,* trans. Agnes Schwarzschild [London, 1951], p. 380).

2. This is true not just of the Arab societies but also of the Ottoman Turks who ruled them and acknowledged what they saw as a need to "modernize." They tried to address this problem by turning to western European societies: the sultan opened embassies in Europe at the end of the eighteenth century, and a major bureau was opened in Istanbul to translate documents and cultural artefacts from western European languages. See Albert Hourani, *Arabic Thought in the Liberal Age, 1798–1939* (1962; Cambridge, 1983), pp. 40–49.

Saree S. Makdisi is assistant professor of English at the University of Chicago. He is preparing a book on the relationship between the cultures of imperialism and modernity in the British romantic period.

in the former.[3] Against this position, many other Arab intellectuals insisted on the absolute identity of modernity and Europe. Rifaah al-Tahtawi, whose work has had tremendous influence on cultural production in the Arab world, emphasized the role of science as the basis for modern civilization and insisted that Arabs could modernize their societies by "adopting" the European sciences. For Tahtawi, the European states (particularly France) became standards to which Arabs could aspire, although in order to "be modern," one had somehow to "become European." The goal of the process of modernization, as it was formulated by Tahtawi, is therefore impossible; it means becoming Other.

The ideology of modernity, following Tahtawi, is at the center of the movement in the Arab world that came to be called the *Nahda*—literally a rebirth or reawakening.[4] The crisis of modernization, as it was formulated immediately before the *Nahda,* has emerged as one of double alienation. Abdallah Laroui and others maintain that Arab intellectuals still experience this crisis; in addition to the obvious alienation from Western culture, Laroui argues, there is another form of alienation, more prevalent but veiled, due to the "exaggerated medievalization obtained through quasi-magical identification with the great period of classical Arabian culture."[5] The Lebanese-Syrian critic Adunis argues that the Arab cultural heritage has been projected as something "absolutely exemplary, timeless, and outside of history," and has been used as such to maintain what he identifies as a still-powerful "religiofeudal" social order that bases itself on this heritage, especially in religious terms.[6] Against this sort of traditionalism, which has been sustained by the educational and cultural policies of the Arab states, the Westernizing rationale of the *Nahda* has been adopted by many twentieth-century intellectuals. Taha Hussein, one of the most admired novelists in the Arab world, renewed many of the arguments that had been made in the previous century by Tahtawi, declaring that "we must follow the path of the Europeans so as to be their equals and partners in civilization, in its good and evil, its sweetness and bitterness, what can be loved or hated, what can be praised or blamed."[7] The adherents of

3. Jamal al-Din Afghani (1839–97) argued that Muslims should strictly obey the teachings of the Koran and follow the *Sunna* in order to revitalize the strength they had lost by straying off the Prophet's path. Muhammad Abduh (1849–1905) was an Egyptian student of his who elaborated some of his positions.

4. *Nahda* is thus used to describe the literary and cultural "renaissance" that took place in the Arab world in the nineteenth century and culminated in the movements of Arab nationalism. See George Antonius, *The Arab Awakening: The Story of the Arab National Movement* (Philadelphia, 1939). Even the term *Nahda,* however, derives from a European concept.

5. Abdallah Laroui, *The Crisis of the Arab Intellectual: Traditionalism or Historicism?* trans. Diarmid Cammell (1974; Berkeley, 1976), p. 156.

6. Adunis, *Al-thabat wa al-tahawwul: sadmat al-hadatha* (Beirut, 1979), p. 276.

7. Quoted in Hourani, *Arabic Thought in the Liberal Age,* p. 330. He goes on to say that "Egypt has always been part of Europe," and blames the four centuries of Ottoman rule for

Hussein's position have engaged traditionalism in cultural production and educational institutions throughout the Arab world.

A compromise has, however, been reached between these ideological positions, out of which has emerged an institutionalized Manichaeism. This bifurcation permits, on the one hand, the preservation of a certain social, cultural, and religious traditionalism, and, on the other, the adoption of certain "modern" principles, especially in science, technology, and economy. It is precisely this Manichaeism that has perpetuated the double alienation described by Laroui, which by now has institutionalized a permanent crisis of modernization in Arab societies.

2

If postcolonial Arabic discourse has been centered on the debate between traditionalism and Westernism, *Season of Migration to the North* shatters the very terms of this opposition and explodes the dualism developed before and during the *Nahda.* The novel lies between the traditional categories of East and West—that confusing zone in which the culture of an imperial power clashes with that of its victims—the antithetical relationship between which provides much of its driving force. This is the same dynamic that has generated many of the contradictions now characteristic of other postcolonial societies that manifest themselves in the clash between such categories as the "modern" and the "traditional," the new and old ways of life, and of course between Western and native cultures and values. Native intellectuals, as they have been called, often (though not always) feel trapped between some traditional culture (or its residual traces) and the now-dominant culture associated with imperialism, which forces itself on them.[8] In response to the alienation from the colonial and precolonial pasts there have been widespread efforts throughout the Third World at returning to and coming to terms with the past by revising it and renarrating it, often by literally rewriting the histories of imperialism.[9]

---

the fall of the Arabs behind the Europeans in terms of modernity (ibid.; Hourani is paraphrasing Hussein here).

8. See, for example, Eqbal Ahmad, "From Potato Sack to Potato Mash: The Contemporary Crisis of the Third World," *Arab Studies Quarterly* 2 (Summer 1980): 223–34; Ngũgĩ wa Thiong'o, *Homecoming: Essays on African and Caribbean Literature, Culture, and Politics* (London, 1972); Amilcar Cabral, "National Liberation and Culture," *Unity and Struggle: Speeches and Writings,* trans. Michael Wolfers (New York, 1979), pp. 138–54; and of course Frantz Fanon, *The Wretched of the Earth,* trans. Constance Farrington (1961; London, 1983), pp. 166–99.

9. See Edward W. Said, "Intellectuals in the Post-Colonial World," *Salmagundi,* nos. 70–71 (Spring-Summer 1986): 44–64, and "Third World Intellectuals and Metropolitan

Often, however, the engagement with imperialism by postcolonial intellectuals centers on a reaffirmation of the traditional cultures and ways of life that were disrupted by it. They are thus led in search of alternatives to the present dominant culture that exist only in isolated images or practices that are taken as reaffirmations of traditional, precolonial cultures. Opposition to imperialism can therefore be diverted into a futile search for traditions, through which the postcolonial intellectual attempts (if only symbolically) to reembrace his or her own people and "their" culture. Having adopted the vestiges (or outer trappings) of these traditions, these intellectuals soon discover their emptiness; having tried to grasp hold of "the people," they are left clutching the now-barren symbols of the past.[10]

Rather than groping blindly for what is gone, however, *Season of Migration* sprawls not only between the past, the present, and the future; it fans out, through and across the different registers of textuality, narrative, form, chronology, and history, none of which remain stable, and each of which is wrapped up in a series of endless and constantly expanding contradictions. It shuns the straightforward narratives taken by some of Salih's earlier works (such as *The Wedding of Zein*) and presents itself as the narrative of a vast puzzle of which it is also one small part, and its reader another; it is therefore a narrative that necessarily will be incomplete. *Season of Migration* should be seen as a highly complex and multilayered event rather than as a "simple" text.[11] It is caught in the turbulence that is at the heart of the contradictions it reflects not only in that it chronicles two attempts to resolve them (as we shall see), but above all in that it is itself composed of these contradictions. It does not pretend to propel its readers out of its own turbulent time; rather, it leaves us floating uneasily in the present, waiting for a resolution that does not come.

Culture," *Raritan* 9 (Winter 1990): 27–50. The Subaltern Studies project in India is also an excellent example of this; see *Selected Subaltern Studies,* ed. Ranajit Guha and Gayatri Chakravorty Spivak (New York, 1988). But "writing back" to the metropolitan centers, of course, goes beyond historical and political analyses and into fiction, drama, poetry, and so on. On this point see *The Empire Writes Back: Theory and Practice in Post-Colonial Literatures,* ed. Bill Ashcroft, Gareth Griffiths, and Helen Tiffin (London, 1989).

10. See Fanon, *The Wretched of the Earth,* p. 180.

11. To examine any aspect of this event necessarily involves unwrapping it, separating its elements, cutting it off from other aspects, and laying it in artificially reassembled fragments under close examination. My own analysis of *Season of Migration* will therefore require partial dis- and reassemblies of the text.

3

One of the threads around which the narrative is twined is the narrator's own attempt to close the gap between himself and his people, which had opened with his departure from the Sudan to study at a British university. The novel opens with his jubilant claim, "I returned to my people, gentlemen, after a long absence: seven years, to be precise, during which time I was studying in Europe."[12] Although he feels, at first, alienated from the other villagers, he eventually convinces himself that he has been able to reattach himself to his childhood roots. Having felt, while abroad, like a "storm-tossed feather," he now feels like "a being with an origin, roots, and a purpose" (*S*, p. 6). He reinforces this feeling with many visits to his grandfather, Hajj Ahmad, whom he upholds as the enduring image of an immutable past, "something stable in a dynamic world" (*S*, p. 52). Indeed, Hajj Ahmad becomes his link to a precolonial past that he tries to construct, and to which he would like to escape.[13] Having thus "secured" himself, the narrator renounces his immersion in British culture and tries to reengage his Arab heritage; although he had earned a doctorate in English literature, he goes to Khartoum to teach pre-Islamic Arabic poetry at the secondary school level. He tries to convince himself that the alternative heritage being presented to him and to his people through colonialism can simply be shrugged off. While he acknowledges the physical changes that have taken place in his village, he nevertheless reassures himself that "life is good, and the world remains the same, unchanged" (*S*, p. 6).

In making this claim, however, he does so not just for himself, but for all of his people. He assures himself in a key passage:

> I am from here, just like the palm tree planted in the courtyard of our house grew in our courtyard and did not grow in some one else's. And if [the British] came to our villages, I don't know why, does this mean that we must poison our present and our future? They will leave our country sooner or later, just as other people have left other countries throughout history. The railways and the ships, the hospitals and the factories, will be ours; and we will use their language without feeling guilt or gratitude. We shall be as we are: normal people; and if we shall be lies, we shall be lies of our own making. [*S*, p. 53]

12. Al-Tayyib Salih, *Mawsim al-hijra ila al-Shimal* [*Season of Migration to the North*] (1969; Beirut, 1987), p. 5; hereafter abbreviated *S*. The English translation is by Denys Johnson-Davies, under the title *Season of Migration to the North* (London, 1969).

13. The narrator says of his grandfather: his "thin tranquil voice forms a bridge between myself and that anxious time that has not yet been formed, the times whose events have taken place and passed, and become bricks in an edifice with dimensions and depth" (*S*, p. 77).

Unfortunately, the present and the painful realities of colonialism eventually intrude on the narrator's dream of a future devoid of the traces of British rule. A number of events (the disappearance of Mustafa Said, the discovery of his secret room, the murder of Wad Rayyes, and the suicide of Hosna Bint Mahmoud) precipitate his sudden awareness that things really have changed, and that he and his people remain fixed in the present. Even Hajj Ahmad, through whom he had tried to reattach himself to the past, suddenly seems less immutable. The narrator asks himself, "My grandfather, with his thin voice and that mischievous laugh of his when he is in a good mood, where is his place in all this? Is he really as I assert and as he appears to be? Is he above this chaos? I don't know" (*S,* p. 111). His doubts multiply, and, no longer able to maintain his construction of a past and future that bypass the present, his alienation returns. "No escape," he finally realizes, "no place of safety, no safeguard. My world had been wide on the outside: now it has collapsed on itself, so that I have become the world and there is no world other than me. Where, then, are the roots striking into the past?" (*S,* p. 135). He walks, stunned, down to the banks of the river, and starts swimming to the north shore (the village is situated, symbolically, at a bend, where, "after having flowed from south to north, [the Nile] suddenly bends at an almost right angle, and flows from west to east" [*S,* p. 66]). At a point halfway between north and south, he finds himself exhausted, unable to return and unable to continue. After almost losing hope, he finds strength:

> All my life I never chose or made decisions. Now I choose. I choose life. I shall live because there are a few people that I want to stay with for as long as possible, and because I have responsibilities to take care of. It does not matter to me whether life has meaning or not. If I cannot forgive, then I shall try to forget. I shall live by strength and cunning. And I moved my hands and feet violently and with difficulty, until my torso was above water. With all the strength remaining to me, I screamed, as if I were a comic actor acting on stage: "Help. Help." [*S,* p. 171]

The novel ends with darkness engulfing the narrator. Trapped between north and south and east and west, his screams for help are absorbed by the immensity of the Nile.

4

There is, however, another main character in *Season of Migration.* But while the narrator represses the realization and the knowledge that the precolonial world has been irrevocably changed, Mustafa Said acknowledges these changes and incorporates them into himself. If the narrator tries to retrieve the precolonial past while dreaming of the postcolonial future, Mustafa tries to bind together the past and the present. This leaves him in a closed circuit between the two, in which the possibility of an escape to the future is locked out.

Mustafa was born in Khartoum in 1898, the year of the bloody defeat of the Mahdist forces by Kitchener's army in the battle of Omdurman, which signalled the final collapse of Sudanese resistance to British encroachment.[14] Rather than passively accepting this defeat, however, Mustafa's life is spent trying to symbolically "reverse" the history of modern European colonialism. As a child he quickly absorbs a Western education, pursuing it from a local school in the Sudan, to a British school in Cairo, to a university in England. After his appointment as a lecturer in economics at the University of London, he begins his campaign to throw colonialism back on the colonizers.

Mustafa carries out this self-appointed mission by inflicting pain and suffering on British women. Just as imperialism had violated its victims, Mustafa violates his, and his unwitting lovers become sacrifices in his violent campaign. The acts of finding lovers and engaging with them sexually become scouting operations and skirmishes in a war fought on the personal level. The descriptions used by Mustafa for his conquests are couched not only in terms of military operations in general, but in terms of traditional *Arab* military campaigns in particular: going to meet new victims is described in terms of saddling his camels; the process of courtship is compared to laying siege, involving tents, caravans, the desert, and so forth. The imagery associated with sexual acts are those of battle: bows, axes, spears, and especially swords and knives. He compares his exploits to those of Tarik ibn-Ziyad, the commander of the Arab army that conquered Spain in the eighth century, as he tells the narrator, "I imagined the Arab soldiers' first meeting with Spain. Like me at this moment, sitting opposite Isabella Seymour, a southern thirst being quenched in the northern mountain passes of history" (*S*, p. 46).

Not satisfied with only reenacting the ancient Arab victory over Europeans, Mustafa sees himself undoing the modern European victory over the Arabs. He claims to be the diametrical opposite of Kitchener and Allenby, reversing or at least superceding Kitchener's victories at Omdurman and Atbara, and Allenby's at Jerusalem (see *S*, p. 97). He dreams of telling the English, "Yes, gentlemen, I have come to you as a conqueror within your very house, as a drop of the poison which you have injected into the veins of history" (*S*, p. 98). The connection in Mustafa's mind between his sexual actions and the fight against colonialism is thus all too clear; to several friends, he announces: "I'll liberate Africa with my ———" (*S*, p. 122).

14. See John Gallagher and Ronald Robinson, *Africa and the Victorians: The Climax of Imperialism in the Dark Continent* (New York, 1961), pp. 339–78.

Mustafa's campaign is not carried out strictly in terms of physical violence, however. Indeed, most of the damage he does is psychological, and he drives all but one of his victims to suicide (he murders the last, Jean Morris). At the same time, however, he does violence to himself, willingly becoming for his victims the incarnation of the great Orientalist myth-fantasy; and his apartment in London, packed with incense, Persian rugs, mirrors, ointments, and perfumes, becomes "a den of lethal lies." He weaves "intricate and terrifying threads of fantasy," so that each victim "would tell me that in my eyes she saw the shimmer of mirages in hot deserts, that in my voice she heard the screams of wild beasts in the jungles" (*S,* p. 147).[15] Soon, however, his lies turn into "truths" that he himself begins to believe, so that he gets caught in his own Orientalist phantasmagoria.

Mustafa starts living a lie, and in doing so he "becomes" a lie. There is an ongoing comparison in his own narrative between himself and Shakespeare's Othello, one of the best-known European literary misrepresentations of the Arab, as he alternately claims that "I am no Othello: I am a lie," and that "I am no Othello: Othello was a lie" (*S,* pp. 37, 98).[16] During his trial for the murder of Jean Morris, Mustafa is tempted to stand up and shout, "This Mustafa Said has no existence. He is an illusion, a lie. And I ask you to rule for the killing of the lie" (*S,* p. 36). He becomes, however, a bundle of contradictory selves, known to various people as Richard, Hassan, Charles, Amin, and Mustafa.

After serving seven years in jail (for the murder he committed and to which he confessed) and then traveling all over the world, Mustafa Said, the child of colonialism, returns to his native Sudan and takes up residence in the narrator's village. Here his contradictions no longer manifest themselves violently or openly, as they had done in England. To everyone in the village, he presents himself as he does to the narrator: "I am this person that is before you, as he is known to everyone in the village. I am nothing other than that, and I have nothing to hide" (*S,* p. 19). A lapse, however, reveals his hidden secrets. He drunkenly recites a poem in English, even though he denies any knowledge of the language of the imperialists.

His deepest, darkest secret, though, is his hidden room. This room, discovered late in the novel by the narrator, is a preserve for Mustafa's British self. It is a life-size replica of the salon in his London apartment,

15. Earlier we learn of his meeting with Isabella Seymour: "She asked me, as we drank tea, about my country. I told her that the streets of my country's capital were crowded with elephants and lions, and that crocodiles crawled through it during the afternoon nap-time" (*S,* p. 41).

16. Mustafa is, at another level, exactly like Othello. When Isabella Seymour asks him, "Are you African or Asian?" he responds, "I am like Othello: Arab-African" (*S,* p. 41). Moreover, the novel itself takes us back to *Othello* when a secret lover comes to Jean Morris's apartment and accidentally drops his handkerchief.

complete with fireplace, chairs, Persian rugs, and a vast library of books. When the narrator discovers the room, he is stunned:

> Imagine it—an English fireplace with all its accessories, above it a brass hood, and in front of it a square area tiled in green marble, with the mantelpiece of blue marble; on either side of the fireplace were two Victorian chairs covered in silk material, and between them was a round table with books and notebooks on it. [*S*, p. 137]

The bookshelf, not surprisingly, contains not a single Arabic book; even the Koran is in English. It does, however, hold a number of books by Mustafa (in English) on the economics of colonialism. The narrator is shocked by this, calling the library and the room itself "a graveyard. A mausoleum. An insane idea. A prison. A huge joke" (*S*, p. 139). The photographs scattered throughout the room preserve intact various times in Mustafa's British life:

> Mustafa Said laughing, Mustafa Said writing, Mustafa Said swimming, Mustafa Said somewhere in the country, Mustafa Said in cap and gown, Mustafa Said rowing on the Serpentine, Mustafa Said in a Nativity play, a crown on his head, as one of the Three Kings who brought perfumes and myrrh to Christ; Mustafa Said between a man and a woman. Mustafa Said had not let a moment pass without recording it for memory and history. [*S*, p. 140]

The bundle of contradictions that Mustafa had become ("normal" Sudanese peasant farmer on the outside, sophisticated London intellectual on the inside) cannot be undone. He disappears one day, presumably drowned in the Nile, either by accident or by suicide.[17] To the narrator and to those who will uncover his room, he leaves his "Life Story," which contains a one-line dedication: "To those who see with one eye, talk with one tongue, and see things as either black or white, either Eastern or Western" (*S*, p. 152).

5

Mustafa's life story is dedicated to a nonbeing, a being that could not possibly exist; and, indeed, the rest of its pages are entirely empty. To see the world in the way it prescribes would, precisely, require one to be entirely Eastern or entirely Western, entirely black or entirely white.

17. I've been told that if one keeps very careful account of the dates and time frames of the novel (which is very difficult to do), it emerges that Mustafa disappears at the age of fifty-eight, or in 1956, the year of Sudan's independence—that is, his life coincides with the period of direct British occupation of the Sudan.

Mustafa's problem—and the narrator's—is that they are neither black nor white, but grey; neither wholly Eastern nor wholly Western, neither completely European nor completely Arab (furthermore, given Sudan's situation, neither entirely Arab nor entirely African). They are trapped between cultures (and here, as intellectuals, they are not exceptions to a social norm; rather, the contradictions of the rest of society are made explicit and even brought to their logical extremes in Mustafa and the narrator). The narrator responds to the trap by trying, unsuccessfully, to wish it away. Having embraced British culture, he tries to abandon it and to reembrace his native culture, the culture of his childhood.[18] Mustafa's response is no more successful. Rather than simply wishing away his experiences, he tries to maintain them, while completely separating them from each other. He does so not by becoming entirely European or entirely Arab, but by becoming *both,* but never at the same time, in the same place, or with the same people.

The contradictions that mold the characters of the narrator and Mustafa are also evident in the structure and form of *Season of Migration to the North.* The narrative is presented through a number of often conflicting voices, which flow through an extremely unstable chronological framework, moving in quick and apparently random succession through the past, present, and future. Moreover, that the narrator is himself a main character in the novel also generates uncertainties; as the narrative voice breaks down, the reader is increasingly denied a stable reference point from which to assess other developments.

Even its form is a contradiction. As a novel, it has its origins in western Europe, but the style in which it is presented at the opening is that of the old *hakawati* of the Arabic oral tradition (it is addressed to an audience of "gentlemen"). However, it moves away from this rigidly defined style—and hence from all of its traditional components, including a resolution at the end of the tale—to an indeterminate ending more characteristic of European modernist novels.[19] *Season of Migration* makes constant reference, both in terms of content and of structure, to Western literary

18. His situation is strikingly similar to the native intellectual described by Fanon: "In the second phase we find the native is disturbed; he decides to remember what he is. . . . But since the native is not a part of his people, since he only has exterior relations with his people, he is content to recall their life only. Past happenings of the byegone days of his childhood will be brought up out of the depths of his memory; old legends will be reinterpreted in the light of a borrowed estheticism and of a conception of the world which was discovered under other skies" (Fanon, *The Wretched of the Earth,* p. 179).

19. *Heart of Darkness,* for example, closes as follows:

> Marlow ceased and sat apart, indistinct and silent, in the pose of a meditating Buddha. Nobody moved for a time. 'We have lost the first of the ebb,' said the director, suddenly. I raised my head. The offing was barred by a black bank of clouds, and the tranquil waterway leading to the uttermost ends of the earth flowed somber under an overcast sky—seemed to lead into the heart of an immense darkness. [Joseph Conrad, *Heart of Darkness* (1902; Harmondsworth, 1989), p. 121]

works—*Othello, King Lear, Heart of Darkness*—and deliberately confronts these texts from within. Barbara Harlow argues that the novel has many of the elements of the Arabic literary technique of *mu' arada,* which literally means opposition or contradiction, and which involves at least two writers, the first of whom writes a poem that the second will undo by writing along the same lines but reversing the meaning.[20] Salih's text, then, is and is not a novel; it is and is not a *hakawati* oral tale; it is like *Heart of Darkness* as much as it is unlike it; it draws its formal inspirations from Europe as much as it seeks to distort and undermine them; it remains, finally, an unstable synthesis of European and Arabic forms and traditions.

Rather than representing some imaginary resolution of the contradictions of form and content, *Season of Migration* leaves them gaping open. Ironically, it has been interpreted by many critics (particularly in the Arab world) as an affirmation of life, as a resolution of conflicts, as the representation of the final closure of imperialism. Such interpretations generally hinge on a positive reading of the closing chapter. Issa Boullata, for instance, concludes that

> gradually as [the narrator] is swimming across the river, he begins to feel he is being pulled downwards by the water and for an indeterminate period [surrenders] to its destructive force. Then suddenly he regains his desire for life, and for the first time in his life he chooses and he makes a decision. He fights the water and screams for help.
>
> With this affirmation of life, al-Tayyib Salih ends his novel.[21]

While the novel itself lacks any firm conclusion or resolution, these critics try—desperately and unconvincingly—to close it, to supply what is missing. They try to determine and fix those aspects of the plot, such as the fate of the narrator, that are left ambiguous by the flow of events through an unstable framework. While the novel gradually moves away from and

20. See Barbara Harlow, "Sentimental Orientalism: *Season of Migration to the North* and *Othello,*" in *Tayeb Salih's "Season of Migration to the North": A Casebook,* ed. Mona Takieddine-Amyuni (Beirut, 1985), pp. 75–79.

21. Issa J. Boullata, "Encounter between East and West: A Theme in Contemporary Arabic Novels," in *Critical Perspectives on Modern Arabic Literature,* ed. Boullata (Washington, D.C., 1980), pp. 56–57. Another example of this is from an essay on *Season of Migration* by Takieddine-Amyuni, in her analysis of the final few lines:

> Symbolically, the Narrator finds himself halfway between North and South, the river's destructive forces pulling him downwards. But life is stronger in the Narrator after all. He chooses it whether it has meaning or not, for he has duties to perform and people to love. His daughter is called "Hope" and he looks forward to the future. He has ceased to be the romantic young man we encountered at the beginning of the novel. He has grown into a realistic human being, fully aware of the mediocrity of his position in Khartoum and of all the pitfalls in which the newly independent Sudan was caught. [Takieddine-Amyuni, "Tayeb Salih's *Season of Migration to the North:* An Interpretation," *Arab Studies Quarterly* 2 (Winter 1980): 16–17]

See also Takieddine-Amyuni's introduction to *Tayeb Salih's "Season of Migration to the North."*

finally abandons the traditional *hakawati* style, such critics remain imprisoned by the limitations of this older form and the neat resolutions it offers. While it moves continually between different registers and frameworks, they try to reduce it to a one-dimensional narrative with a beginning, a middle, and an end. Its power as an ideological form is, ironically, demonstrated by these critics who try to supply it with a narrative closure that will "make sense" within a certain ideological framework marked and governed by the existence of fundamental categories and rigid absolutes.

6

But *Season of Migration* defies and deconstructs such categories as it undermines many of the traditional dualisms that are associated with postcolonial discourse. What appears at first to be neatly divisible into black and white is dialectically broken down and synthesized into an endless variety of shades of grey. The existence of pure and unaffected traditional cultures to which postcolonial intellectuals can "escape" is exposed as an illusion. Indeed, the very existence of any culture in some sort of absolute isolation from others is shown to be impossible in the postcolonial world; the very existence of *Season of Migration* is proof of this. The novel, in this sense, takes place in the twilight between cultures, for which the eerie dawn at the end of the narrative is a metaphor; the narrator is left not just between east and west and north and south, but also between day and night, so that "the objects on the two shores [are] half visible, appearing and disappearing, shimmering between light and darkness" (*S*, p. 168).

At the beginning, however, the narrator views his return to his people as a return to his proper place, the place to which he can be attached, and in relation to which his life has meaning. When he first meets Mustafa, his immediate reaction is curiosity: "Where is he from? Why has he taken up residence in this village? What is his story?" (*S*, p. 13). He is unable to place Mustafa, however, and hence unable to understand him; but he is amazed that Mustafa considers himself a part of the village and the narrator an outsider. Angered by the way Mustafa mocks his English degree ("we here

---

Joseph John and Yosif Tarawneh reach a similar conclusion:

> While, on the literal level, this statement [the narrator's last few words] denotes a sudden awareness of the need to strive for survival, at the symbolic level it is a re-enactment of his disengagement, his final liberation, from the ghost of Mustafa Sa'eed, laid to rest forever in the rectangular [secret] room. It is important to note that the river episode forms a richly symbolic finale to the narrator's moral pilgrimage. His final cry, "Help! Help!" is a resounding repudiation of the Sa'eedian world of death; it is his everlasting "yes" to life. [Joseph John and Yosif Tarawneh, "Quest for Identity: The I-Thou Imbroglio in Tayeb Salih's *Season of Migration to the North,*" *Arab Studies Quarterly* 8 (Spring 1986): 175]

have no need for poetry"), the narrator is outraged: "Look at how he says 'we' and does not include me, despite the fact that the village is my village, and it is he—not I—who is the stranger" (*S,* p. 13). Later, after Mustafa's disappearance, the narrator starts doubting his own position; "Is it possible," he asks himself, "that what happened to Mustafa Said could happen to me? He said that he was a lie. So am I also a lie?" He answers himself by insisting that "I am from here. Is that not sufficient truth? I too lived with [the British], but I lived with them superficially, neither loving nor hating them. I used to carry this small village within myself, seeing it with the eye of my imagination wherever I went" (*S,* pp. 52–53). But the novel unfolds with his gradual realization that he has lost his proper place, and indeed that there is no longer any place that can be sealed off from others so that people can be identified by it. The rigid distinction between East and West to which the narrator originally clings has eroded by the end of the novel.

The dualism (between Eastern and Western) developed by Abduh, Tahtawi, and others in the nineteenth century, is thus broken down and destroyed in Salih's novel. While such dualisms have led to a whole series of inescapable dilemmas, *Season of Migration* negates them as well as the ideological framework they represent. The colonial project, as Johannes Fabian has argued, developed a scale of "progress," so that "all living societies were irrevocably placed on a temporal slope, a stream of Time—some upstream, others downstream. Civilization, evolution, development, acculturation, modernization (and their cousins, industrialization, urbanization) are all terms whose conceptual content derives, in ways that can be specified, from evolutionary Time."[22] While the program of the *Nahda* was itself a formulation of this ideology, the world it mapped out is reconfigured in *Season of Migration.* If there is any sense of historical flow at all, as symbolized by the Nile itself, the crucial point is that, from the narrator's perspective at the end of the novel, the river's symbolic edges (north or south, east or west) are unattainable. There is no going north or west to become European, as Tahtawi and his followers would have insisted; and there is no going south or east to return to tradition, as Abduh would have had it.

Season of Migration points away from the traditionalism of the Arab past—as well as from the future that imperial Europe, through the ideology of modernity, once held out to its victims—and in an entirely new direction, finally escaping the narrow and tightly defined orbit of the debates surrounding the *Nahda.* Through this double negation, it offers tremendous liberating potential, allowing entirely new conceptualizations of social realities, and drawing an entirely different map of the present.

22. Johannes Fabian, *Time and the Other: How Anthropology Makes Its Object* (New York, 1983), p. 17.

7

In a certain sense, then, *Season of Migration* "reinvents" the present, bringing into sharp focus many of the issues that have long remained repressed in Arab cultural production. The ideological bulwark of religion, for instance, so prevalent in traditional writing, is absent here. If in *The Wedding of Zein,* one of Salih's earlier stories, the lives of the villagers center on the imam,[23] in the world of *Season of Migration* such a stable system of signification is inconceivable. Along with other novels of Arabic modernism—such as the later novels of Naguib Mahfouz (*Miramar,* for instance, or even *The Thief and the Dogs*), or the recent work of the Lebanese novelist Elias Khoury (such as *Little Mountain* and [forthcoming in English translation] *The Journey of Little Ghandi*), or that of the Palestinian Emile Habibi (author of *The Secret Life of Said, the Ill-Fated Pessoptimist*)—*Season of Migration to the North* challenges the literary and ideological principles of the *Nahda.*[24] Even beyond this, though, Salih, Khoury, Mahfouz, and others situate themselves in opposition to Arabic cultural and ideological production long preceding the *Nahda* itself.

In *Season of Migration* this is perhaps nowhere clearer than in the novel's gender dynamics. It is not, of course, a coincidence that Mustafa conducts his misogynistic campaign of revenge against colonialism in sexual terms. This opens up a new register through which the novel runs, and the intersection of gender, sexuality, violence, male hegemony, and colonialism is a central concern of this work. Even in Mustafa's narrative, such connections are revolutionary in terms of previous Arabic cultural production; *Season of Migration* brings them home much more forcefully in the violent and catastrophic clash between Hosna Bint Mahmoud and Wad Rayyes.

This clash forms the final blow for the narrator. If previously he had been able to convince himself that he could flee the contradictions of imperialism and modernity by clinging to his proper place, Hosna's murder and suicide drive home the realization that this place was never really what it had seemed. It is only after this double event that the narrator can say that "the world has suddenly turned upside down" (*S,* p. 135). Earlier,

23. Here, we are told, "the village was divided into clear camps in relation to the Imam (the villagers did not call him by name: he was, in their eyes, not a person but an institution)" (Salih, *'Urss al Zein* [Beirut, 1966], p. 75; trans. Johnson-Davies, under the title *The Wedding of Zein* [London, 1969].

24. To speak of an Arab "modernism" is not to imply that this in any way follows in the path of European modernism. If the term is to be used at all—and it already has been—it should be used guardedly. Even while drawing connections between present-day Arabic novels and European novels of seventy years ago, one must not posit any sort of scale of progress on which Europeans would be placed at a more advanced level than Arabs. Such a notion would be consistent not only with the program of the *Nahda,* but with the ideology of modernity itself. See Fabian, *Time and the Other,* p. 17.

when he questions whether Hosna wanted to be married to Wad Rayyes, Mahjoub cuts him off, saying, "You know how life is organized here. The woman belongs to the man, and a man is a man even if he gets old and decrepit." The narrator protests, "In this age . . . ," but Mahjoub cuts him off again, saying, "The world has not changed as much as you think" (*S*, pp. 102–3).

Later on, Hosna's own actions change the world, or, rather, change the villagers' awareness of their world. In defying her husband, Hosna defies tradition; in actually killing him, she aims her blows not only at Wad Rayyes as a person but at him as the embodiment of tradition. For if Hosna, as Mustafa's wife, had become in some measure Westernized through contact with him, Wad Rayyes, on the contrary, represents the extreme side of traditionalism.[25] While Mustafa's project of reversing colonialism, which had been encoded in sexual terms, serves in the novel as the first dramatic link between sexuality and violence, the marriage of Hosna and Wad Rayyes makes the connections even clearer. The villagers, however, are not willing to view Hosna's actions in terms of the tradition against which she rebels, but as a demented abberation that should never have happened; in this sense, they place the blame on her rather than on Wad Rayyes.[26] Even Bint Majzoub, the most important woman in the village, tells the narrator, "A person cannot speak easily of Bint Mahmoud's action. It is something the likes of which we have neither seen nor heard of in past times or present" (*S*, p. 126). The villagers bury the bodies of Hosna and Wad Rayyes before dawn on the night of the killings with no funeral and no mourning; as Bint Majzoub says, they bury the story along with the corpses. But the narrator knows that despite the village's continuing and seemingly timeless routine, "the world has changed" (*S*, p. 131). In making these connections in the way it does, *Season of Migration* goes against the standards and conventions of traditional Arabic literature; it comes as no surprise, then, that the original has only been published in Beirut.

8

Season of Migration to the North does not merely reinvent the present, it opens up new possibilities for the future. The process of cultural production not only shapes perceptions but constitutes a lived system of beliefs, values, and realities. Artists like Salih, in struggling to create a new

25. Their clash further problematizes the binary oppositions of East and West, colonizer and colonized, male and female, oppressor and oppressed, even as it binds them together.

26. Hosna, by the way, is usually identified in the novel as "Bint Mahmoud"—that is, the daughter of Mahmoud—so that her very being, her identity, is encoded in terms of a patriarchal structure.

culture, are at the same time, however gradually, creating new ways of seeing and feeling reality. In rewriting imperialism, Arab modernism, including *Season of Migration,* necessarily looks away not only from the premodern but beyond imperialism and toward some alternative future that it is in the process of inventing.[27] If, in other words, European modernism can be seen as the narration of imperialism from a European perspective, *Season of Migration* and other works of Arab modernism emerge as counternarrations of the thoroughly intertwined histories of imperialism and modernization from a non-European perspective, a "writing back" to Europe.

One cannot, however, as Fanon so brilliantly argues in *The Wretched of the Earth,* address imperialism only by addressing its victims, for in doing so one is already addressing the colonizers themselves.[28] In struggling for the creation of a postimperial Arab society, then, a novelist like Salih is struggling for the creation of a genuinely postimperial world. While Mustafa Said's life story is dedicated to a reader who could not possibly exist, *Season of Migration to the North* is dedicated to readers who do not yet exist: those who can simultaneously see with two eyes, talk with two tongues, and see things both as black *and* as white.

27. Fredric Jameson has argued that European modernism celebrates the premodern. See the conclusion to his *Postmodernism, or, The Cultural Logic of Late Capitalism* (Durham, N.C., 1991), pp. 297–318. Postmodernism arises, in Jameson's terms, out of a condition of completed modernization in which the premodern has finally been liquidated. In the situation of incomplete modernization in which the Arab world finds itself, the premodern has not yet been liquidated. One cannot speak of an Arab postmodernism in the same sense as Jameson speaks of, say, American postmodernism.

28. See Fanon, *The Wretched of the Earth,* p. 254.

What Is a Muslim? Fundamental Commitment and Cultural Identity

Akeel Bilgrami

1

In recent years, the concept of identity has had its corset removed and hangs loosely and precariously in the domain of culture and politics. This is largely a result of a gradual realization in theoretical work in these subjects that local contexts of study determine our individuation of cultural phenomena quite variously, and that it is much too tidy and distorting to

I should stress at the very outset that this essay, though in an important sense self-standing, is one of three essays on the subject of Islamic identity. The others, entitled "Intrinsic and Extrinsic Explanations of Islam" (forthcoming in *Transition*) and "Islamic Identity and Quotidian Institutions," address aspects of the subject that the present essay ignores. The first of these essays addresses issues in political economy and the political sociology of the state as they impinge on the question of religious identity. The second explores the role of mosques, prayer, alms collection, pilgrimage, and other such institutions in the sustaining of identity. The present paper's concern is more with underlying philosophical issues. (All three papers are written within the context of a question and concern for the prospects and possibilities of reform and modernization.) The reader is urged, therefore, not to assume that the points made here aim at anything approximating a comprehensive treatment of the subject. All the same, the sense in which the paper *is* self-standing is that there is nothing in the other two papers that seriously revises or qualifies the claims made in this one. See also footnote 7 for a more specific statement of this last point.

My thanks to G. A. Cohen, Ronald Dworkin, Charles Larmore, Isaac Levi, Thomas Nagel, Carol Rovane, Stephen White, Bernard Williams, the members of the New York University legal theory seminar, and the Fellows of the Whitney Humanities Center, Yale University, for comments and criticisms that have helped to improve this paper.

This article originally appeared in *Critical Inquiry* 18 (Summer 1992).

demand, or proceed as if there were, stricter criteria for their identification. The point cannot be dismissed as some arcane, postmodern development in the theory of culture. It accurately captures the experience of individuals and communities. I recall that some years ago in India, almost to my surprise, I heard the words "I am a Muslim" on my lips. It is not just to meet a theoretical demand that I had better specify the context. I was looking for paying-guest accommodation in a neighborhood with a predominantly lower-middle-class Hindu population, hostile to Muslims. A landlord who was interviewing me asked me what my religion was. It seemed hardly to matter that I found Islamic theological doctrine wholly noncredible, that I had grown up in a home dominated by the views of an irreligious father, and that I had then for some years adopted the customary aggressive secular stance of those with communist leanings. It still seemed the only self-respecting thing to say in that context. It was clear to me that I was, without strain or artificiality, a Muslim for about *five minutes.*[1] That is how negotiable the concept of identity can be.

Lying behind and consolidating the contextualization of identity is a somewhat more abstract point. Quine has argued that the concept of identity occupies the minds of theorists only in the primitive stages of inquiry.[2] In this phase one is prone to anxiety over one's lack of exact criteria of identity of given phenomena, anxieties that are often released in strict stipulations or in taxonomical theorizing, which one then sheds as investigations become more theoretically sophisticated. Quine was concerned primarily with the phenomena and concepts studied by natural science, but the point, it seems to me, is no less valid, for questions such as what is a Muslim? what is an Indian? and so on. As inquiry advances, the absence of

1. No suggestion here that my commitment to being a Muslim has not been more than five minutes long. There are several other contexts, and many more sustained contexts, in which someone with that background and those antitheological views could identify himself or herself as a Muslim. There is no particular list of *types* of such contexts for identification. If there were, it would undermine the very idea of locality since it would allow us to formulate the very sort of generalizations that stricter criteria of identity demand. Someone with no theological commitments might feel a sense of identity with Islam in contexts as diverse as: when he feels shame at the actions of Muslims—as say, the Muslim response to the publication of Rushdie's *The Satanic Verses;* when he feels concern about the future of Muslims in some hostile area—as say, in parts of India or England; or quite simply by an intellectual inheritance of public-mindedness from the fact that his family has been involved in Muslim politics for a very long time. There is no interesting common thread running through these different contexts. It is obvious of course that being born a Muslim is neither a necessary nor a sufficient condition for having a Muslim identity.

2. See W. V. Quine, *Word and Object* (Cambridge, Mass., 1960) and "Natural Kinds," *Ontological Relativity and Other Essays* (New York, 1969), pp. 114–38.

Akeel Bilgrami is professor of philosophy at Columbia University. He is the author of *Belief and Meaning* (1992) and *Self-Knowledge and Intentionality* (forthcoming).

strict criteria need no longer be seen as a sign of one's confusion. It is justified by the fact that the concept in question ("Muslimness," "Indianness," as it might be, or "electron," "the unconscious") is to be understood as having a place in a more or less systematic theory, with its own particular role in the inferences and transformations that the theory sanctions. This point is not the same as the point about the local and contextual nature of these concepts, but it allows one to embrace their locality with some methodological right. If, after all, these concepts depend on their place in a network of theory, then shifts in theory due to cultural difference or historical change will shift the inferential place and role of the concepts without any anxieties about losing our hold over them.

One might think that these methodological observations should have made us realize that our obsession with questions such as what is a Muslim? is irrational and, as with all neuroses, that that realization should by itself be the basis of cure. But things have not been that simple, and more work needs to be done to properly diagnose the persistence not merely of an intellectual yearning that such questions reveal, but also the social and cultural phenomena that these questions are undoubtedly tracking. One needs to explain our interest in these questions, not merely dismiss them. And, in any case, the best among those who have ushered in the localizing revolution would be the first to say, "Context is only the beginning of wisdom." It does not sweep conceptual problems away nor does it herald the end of theory; it merely removes the rigidities and reifications of a long-standing theoretical tradition.[3]

2

The context of my own interest in the question of Islamic identity is shaped by a prior political interest in the reform of Islam. The fate of a reformist movement within Islam depends on the extent to which Muslim populations will consider the details of their identification with Islam as negotiable in the face of other values that they also cherish. There may be some for whom Islam is nothing short of a monolithic commitment, overriding all other commitments, whenever history or personal encounter poses a conflict. But I think it is safe to say, despite a familiar tradition of colonial and postcolonial caricature in Western representations of Islam, that such an absolutist project is the exception in a highly diverse and internally conflicted religious community. For the most part, there is no

3. In saying this I am taking a stand against the more apocalyptic, theory-destroying view of the emphasis on context that is to be found in Richard Rorty's numerous recent writings on the effects of pragmatism. This disagreement may turn on the fact that pragmatism for him, but not for me, is mixed in with Kuhnian incommensurability and deconstruction.

reason to doubt that Muslims, even devout Muslims, will and do take their commitment to Islam not only as one among other values, but also as something that is itself differentiated internally into a number of, in principle, negotiable detailed commitments. If so, there is a pressing question that arises for anybody interested in the reform of Islam. What are the difficulties that recent absolutist assertions or reassertions of Islamic identity pose for the prospect of Islamic social and legal reform? Like most questions about the determinants of culture, this question can also be posed from the opposite direction: to what extent is the relative absence of reformist thinking among moderate Muslims responsible for the susceptibility of Islamic polities to constant threat from powerful minority movements that assert Islamic identity is, for the most part, nonnegotiable?[4]

The complexity of this pair of questions does not lie merely in the conflict between a minority of Islamic absolutists[5] (or "fundamentalists" as they are sometimes misleadingly called) and the far larger class of Muslim moderates who oppose their vision of an antisecular polity based on Islamic personal and public law (the *Sharia*). There is widespread today a more interesting conflict *within* the hearts of moderate Muslims themselves, a conflict made the more excruciating because it is not always explicitly acknowledged by them. This is the tension generated by their opposition to Islamic absolutism on the one hand and, on the other, their faith in a religion that is defined upon detailed commitments with regard to the polity, commitments that Islamic absolutists constantly invoke to their own advantage.[6] In the last few years it has become clear to me that this internal conflict within the moderate Muslim will not be resolved in favor of the former unless he or she sees through to the need for a reform of the faith.[7] But this requires a capacity to criticize one or another detail

4. The threat is very real and can be seen, not just in the spectacular developments in Iran during the 1980s, but also in the "Islamization" policies of Pakistani governments, in the complexion of powerful guerilla forces and political parties in Afghanistan and the Maghreb respectively, in the accelerating Islamist reaction in the Middle East to the recent Iraqi defeat, as well as, more generally, in the policy commitments in personal law, especially regarding the status of women, in many Muslim populations, even despite the fact of being under de facto secular governments. Recoil from "Orientalist" misrepresentations of Islamic countries should not blind us to the reality and threatening promise of these developments.

5. Though it will not be relevant to my concerns in this paper, it should be mentioned that the absolutist minority does not form a unified movement. There has, for some time, been division between the anti-imperialist Islamist groups and the Islamist groups who draw resources from and give allegiance to Saudi Arabia. There is partial coincidence of this division with the Shia-Sunni division because the anti-imperialist groups are inspired by the Iranian example, but it is only partial. This division is much more marked since the Gulf War for reasons that should be evident.

6. This internal conflict in the moderate Muslim is an essential stage in the dialectic of this paper. The paper's interest is to study what notion of reform and what extent of negotiation and transformation of identity is possible, once one records that there is this conflict.

7. There are two quite opposite theoretical tendencies that resist the idea of doctrinal

or even central features of one's fundamental commitments. It therefore requires a careful scrutiny—in part philosophical—of what the specific demands and consequences of one's particular commitments are in specific historical or personal circumstances.

There is a tradition of political and moral thought that attempts to finesse these detailed tasks because it assumes that philosophical truth is on the side of the secular and the liberal ideal, and that a full grasp of the objectivity of this ideal will itself provide the basis for a deep and destructive philosophical critique of absolutism. From this point of view, and to put it more crudely than it deserves, philosophical argument by itself will give one the right to describe the conflict within moderate Muslims as a conflict between moral truth and falsity.[8]

I have not yet come across the philosophical argument that would support this claim, and so will proceed on the assumption that liberal and secular values have no purely philosophical justification that puts them outside the arena of essentially contested substantive moral and political values. They happen to be my values and my commitments, but I will not pretend that philosophical ethics affords them a more objective status

---

reform. First, there is a tendency to think that if the doctrine, at least in its originary formulations in the Quran, is conceived of as the revealed word of God, no genuinely devout Muslim, however moderate, will tolerate its reform. Thus, it will be objected that I am, in emphasizing the need for doctrinal reform, unfairly imposing the theologically skeptical cast of my own mind—admitted to at the outset—on the *devout* moderate. See my remarks toward the end of the paper (and in footnote 27) about the noncodifiability of religious identity, which address precisely this objection. Second, there is a quite different tendency to think that a full and proper understanding of the underlying political, economic, and cultural conditions (the specific themes of the other two papers cited in the first footnote) relevant to the question of this conflict will undermine my claim (in this paper) about the necessity for *doctrinal* reform. The tendency is to think that changes wrought in these underlying conditions, without any need for doctrinal reform, would be sufficient to defeat the claims and the influence of absolutist movements. Such a view is usually the product of a fear that otherwise one would be endorsing simple-minded Western essentialist explanations of Islamic absolutism, where it is seen to be an intrinsic part of, or growth from, the doctrine and the faith itself. In the first of the two papers I mentioned at the bottom of p. 821, I try to demonstrate how many Islamic absolutist movements sustain themselves and thwart efforts to bring about such political, economic, and cultural changes by exploiting certain aspects of the doctrine. Thus doctrinal reform, I argue, must be a necessary part of the moderate Muslim's opposition to such movements. To that extent, and only to that extent, I think there is a kernel of truth to the idea of intrinsic or essentialist explanations of Islamic absolutism, over and above the extrinsic or nominalist ones invoking political, economic, and cultural causes.

8. There has also been a partially overlapping intellectual tradition, much less current, which adds to this, an a priori historical conviction that makes it an inevitable outcome of the progressive development of social, political, and economic formations that this liberal vision will take hold. This strand of argument has lost its strength in the last few decades, but the more purely philosophical claims are still the subject of interesting and lively dispute among philosophers.

than the values of those who reject them or other values that I myself espouse.

This position is, to some extent, a specific application of Bernard Williams's critique of some of the more ambitious claims of traditional Ethical Theory.[9] The targets of Williams's argument are philosophical theories (for example, utilitarianism, Kantian theories) which offer principles that stand outside a man or woman's fundamental projects and commitments (such as Islam, say, or even more immediate commitments to one's family, lovers, close friends, deep and driving intellectual or artistic interests), principles whose justification depends on considerations that make no specific reference to those commitments, principles that would in fact, when called on, be the basis for assessing and adjudicating between those commitments. Though I will not argue for it here, I believe that Williams is right in concluding that, on inspection, such principles are simply unavailable.

However, there is a tendency, present in Williams's own writing (and much more so in the writings of the existentialists who, I believe, are his philosophical antecedents in this critique of Ethical Theory), to conclude that what this leaves us with is a moral life filled with fundamental commitments, and no particular space to stand on from which they can be subject to our own moral criticism. Criticism requires a theoretical position outside the arena of these commitments, and that is exactly what the critique of Ethical Theory has removed. Thus when these fundamental commitments conflict, there is little scope for anything but moral "tragedy," something that apparently ancient Greek playwrights understood better than ancient Greek philosophers, or philosophers since. For those who have graduated from contempt and fear of the Islamic world to an alienated despair about it, this offers a cheap theoretical confirmation of their mood. Thus, in a curious way, in Williams's picture, identity remains nonnegotiable; its just that now a number of different nonnegotiable identities stand in (possibly) tragic conflict with one another.

But the picture is not compulsory, even if one accepts his skepticism about Ethical Theory.

9. I will continue to use the expression "Ethical Theory" with capital letters to mark that it is traditional moral philosophy which is the target of this critique. The critique may be found in a number of Williams's writings, including his contribution to J. J. C. Smart and Bernard Williams, *Utilitarianism: For and Against* (Cambridge, 1973). See also Williams, "Utilitarianism and Moral Self-Indulgence," *Moral Luck: Philosophical Papers, 1973–1980* (Cambridge, 1981), pp. 40–53. In more recent work Williams addresses Aristotelian ethical theory in some detail as well, and his relation to it is much more complex than to Kant and to utilitarianism. Since this paper is not intended primarily as a commentary on Williams, I will restrict my discussion to the points he makes in his earlier work, which I wish to exploit in the discussion of Muslims' fundamental commitment to their faith. I should also add that, in a letter to me, Williams quite rightly points out that in more recent work he is far less obviously the target of the criticisms I make of him in this paper. See particularly the postscript to his *Ethics and the Limits of Philosophy* (London, 1985).

Many have found the very idea of a fundamental commitment or fundamental project (an idea and phrase that goes back to Kierkegaard) obscure. They would have us simply think of them as values, adding perhaps that they are "thick" values, if that helps to bring out the particularistic nature of these commitments (not justice or goodness, which are "thin," but a whole variety of less abstract values ranging from properties of character such as kindness, detachment, sympathy, loyalty, to commitments that people might have, such as to religion or theatre).[10] To them there seems nothing distinctive about fundamental commitments over and above thinking of them as one among many others in this range of specific values.

But that is not my complaint against Williams in this discussion of Islamic identity. There very likely *is* something distinctive about a devout person's commitment to Islam, over and above its particularity. Though he never spells out explicitly and in detail what he has in mind by fundamental commitments, Williams says enough for us to infer that they lead up to the existentialist idea (and even perhaps ideal) of authenticity. And it is this connection between a person's fundamental commitments and the idea of the authentic self that explains the persistence of questions about identity (questions such as what is a Muslim?) despite an acknowledgement of the radical negotiability of the concept of identity.

A way to expound this theoretical connection is to look to the sorts of effects brought on a person by his or her abandoning—or the prospect of abandoning—such commitments. I once shared a flat with a close friend, who was an appallingly successful drug dealer. He had made far more money than I thought was decent, and it was money made on the steady destruction of people's lives, some of whom were talented, even brilliant, in the university. One day, while he was out, the police arrived at the door and asked me if I had any suspicion that he was a dealer. They said that they did not have sufficient evidence to produce a warrant and search the place, but they were morally certain that he was guilty, and all they needed was for his roommate to express the slightest suspicion. That would give them enough to legally search his premises. I had long quarrelled intensely with my friend about his cynical profiteering from drugs and had come to find him utterly reprehensible in this respect. But faced with the question from the police, I found myself turning them away.

Conflicts of this kind are not by any means unusual, nor is the sort of decision that I made. The right description to put on my decision, in the context of the present discussion, is that I could not abandon the fundamental commitment to friendship, even in the face of thorough and deep moral pressure from within my own moral values.

Here one finds oneself saying that what this amounts to is that I

10. This distinction may be found in Williams himself and is by now common in discussions of moral value.

placed the value of friendship over the sorts of values that made me disapprove of his drug dealing; and there is nothing false about saying it. But I suggest that it is not *all* that it amounts to.

The suggestion is not that one could never give up a fundamental commitment. That is not what is fundamental about it. One can imagine oneself allowing the police in, even if one had a fundamental commitment to one's close friends. What makes the difference is the kind of effect that the relinquishing of a commitment would have upon one. I think it would be fair to say that for many people, in such a conflict, their betrayal of friendship would amount, in their own self-conception, to something of a different order of wrong (though not necessarily moral wrong, certainly not wrong from the point of view of utilitarian principles) than a betrayal of the values that take profiteering from destructive drugs to be reprehensible. It is notoriously hard to describe why there is a different order that is at stake in the comparison rather than merely a difference in degree. But one thing to say is that if I had betrayed my friend, I would have felt a deep and *integrated* destruction of my self, which is missing from the more ordinary, though undoubtedly genuine and severe, bad feelings induced in me by my having failed to act on those other values. It is not merely that I would have had *more* such bad feelings or *worse* feelings. It is rather that I would have felt (and many people in my place would have felt) that I had lost something much more defining of what held my self-conception together. The existentialists described the source of this integrity of the self as *authenticity*, an obscure term no doubt, but examples like this help to convey what they intended.[11] The idea is delicate and difficult, but it is not incoherent nor irredeemably obscure.

So I am not balking at the very idea of fundamental commitment in Williams. On the contrary, even *moderate* Muslims may well have such a fundamental commitment to their religion, and I think it is important to acknowledge this, or else one might make things much too easy for oneself, in one's efforts to think of the way out of a state of conflict. It is partly (though, as we shall see, not by any means entirely) because the commitment to Islam has this deeper and more integrated place in the moderate Muslim's self-identity that the conflict seems so entrenched, that reform has been slow to come, and that absolutist minorities have gotten away with the sort of exploitative appeal they have. But, on the other hand, having acknowledged that there is this more fundamental level of commitment, there is still the danger that one might settle down with the idea of being locked helplessly in a conflict, a sort of tragic stasis; and that would make things too easy for oneself in another way—something akin to the familiar intellectual laziness that accompanies existential anguish. In

11. It is conceivable, though not perhaps routine, that people have fundamental commitments not to things like friendship and religion but to utilitarian and other sorts of principles of traditional moral philosophy that Williams is inveighing against.

short, in the study of Islamic identity and the conflict that it generates in moderate Muslims today, it would be premature either to dismiss the idea of a fundamental commitment or to rest with it in the form that Williams's own writings leave us with.

What is missing in Williams is any interest or effort to offer an explanation of what sort of animal any particular fundamental commitment is, what its origins are and what particular role or function it has in a person's or community's moral-psychological economy. Different kinds of fundamental commitment will naturally have very different roles, but one must pay attention to them to come to some understanding of what is particularly disabling about any particular conflict in which any such commitment figures, and what the rehabilitating elements might be. Once Williams abandons the pretensions of Ethical Theory, which would deliver from on high general principles with a power to criticize particular values and commitments on the ground floor, he does not return to focus on the theoretical possibility that one might, in the process of resolving conflicts between fundamental commitments, come to a fuller understanding of the critical power and generality that is *built into* the commitments on the ground floor.

I have made this last point with such abstractness that it might help here to repeat it with the aid of the more concrete theme of Islamic identity and conflict. Moderate Muslims, I have said, are conflicted, given their opposition to antisecular absolutist forces in their countries and their fundamental commitment to a religion whose Book speaks with detailed pretension to issues of the law and of state. They may often not perceive the conflict, but there is plenty of evidence for it in their own behavior.[12] Confronted with this conflict it is tempting, as I said, to think that this is like any ordinary conflict between any two sets of values (in this case modern and traditional) and that sooner or later the conflict will resolve itself, with one side victorious. Even if one discards the Whiggish tendency to think the modernist victory inevitable, there is this temptation to think that there is nothing particularly distinctive or difficult about the conflict and its eventual resolution. There is also the other temptation. Acknowledging that there is something special and difficult about this conflict, which traditional moral philosophers are especially blind to, one is tempted to say that moderate Muslims have a fundamental commitment to the conflicting values of Islam and of modernity and that it is the arrogance of abstract philosophy to think that it has anything specific and useful to say by way of diagnosis or cure about something so deep-going in a community's moral psychology. I have already said something to resist the

12. See my "Rushdie and the Reform of Islam," *Grand Street* 8 (Summer 1989): 170–84, and "Rushdie, Islam and Postcolonial Defensiveness," *Yale Journal of Criticism* 4 (Fall 1990): 301–11, where I cite and discuss this schizoid behavior, which would count as evidence for this conflict.

former temptation. In doing so I have registered sympathy with Williams's dissatisfactions with Ethical Theory. The latter temptation, I'm saying, issues from a lack in Williams's own approach to moral philosophy. It is a failure to give moral philosophy the task of mixing it up with (in this case) history in order to say something about the specific functional sources of given fundamental commitments (such as to Islam) and then, relatedly, a failure to consider a more bottom-up approach to the study of moral principles.

3

What, then, are the sources of a devout but moderate Muslim's fundamental commitment to Islam today?

In answering this sort of question, there is yet another temptation to which philosophers are prone: to make a general and ahistorical claim about the human need for some sense of identity that is not merely determined by their material and social circumstances. It is a Hegelian-derived acknowledgement that a long tradition of Marxist and Marxist-influenced social thought has neglected the sense of identity that spirit and nonmaterially determined consciousness has to offer. Here is G. A. Cohen, chiding his own earlier work for precisely such a neglect:

> In *Karl Marx's Theory of History* I said that for Marx, by contrast with Hegel, "the ruling interest and difficulty of men was relating to the *world,* not to the *self.*" I would still affirm that antithesis, and I now want to add that, to put it crudely, Marx went too far in the materialist direction. In his anti-Hegelian, Feuerbachian affirmation of the radical objectivity of matter, Marx focused on the relationship of the subject to an object which is in no way subject, and, as time went on, he came to neglect the subject's relationship to itself. . . . He rightly reacted against Hegel's extravagant representation of all reality as ultimately an expression of self, but he over-reacted, and he failed to do justice to *the self's irreducible interest in a definition of itself* [my emphasis; that expression is exploited crucially in my argument just below] and to the social manifestations of that interest.
>
> I refer to the social manifestations of the interest in self identification because I think that human groupings whose lines of demarcation are not economic, such as religious communities, and nations, are *as strong and as durable* [my emphasis] as they evidently are partly because they offer satisfaction to the individual's need for self identification. In adhering to traditionally defined collectivities people retain a sense of who they are.[13]

13. G. A. Cohen, "Reconsidering Historical Materialism," in *Marxist Theory,* ed. Alex Callinicos (Oxford, 1989), pp. 154–55.

I don't wish to enter into a discussion of the details of Marxist theory, and my interest in criticizing these remarks is not prompted by a desire to defend economic determinism or historical materialism. The issue between us is entirely over the question as to whether we should *rest* our analysis of the concept of religious identity with some primitive or irreducible interest in the definition of itself.[14] I think it both unnecessary and wrong to assign one's understanding of a particular community's religious commitments, in a particular historical and cultural context, to some unanalyzable need for self-identity. That would only distract us from what I really wish to emphasize, namely, the historical and functional determination of our fundamental commitments and the sense of identity they impart. I agree with Cohen that it is a crucial function of their commitment to Islam that it does indeed give Muslims a sense of autonomy and dignity, so I am not suggesting that there is a materialist dissolution of religious commitment. But that function is *itself* to be understood as a function of historical, social, and material circumstances in precisely the sense Cohen wishes to abandon for some concession to the subject's irreducible interest in the definition of itself. In explaining what he rightly notices as the strength and durability of religious and nationalist sentiment, Cohen swings from materialist prejudice to an equally unsatisfactory and unhelpful explanatory resting point.[15] It is not that he thinks religion (or nationalism) are irreducible needs; it is rather that he thinks that the need for a sense of identity is an irreducible need, and a fundamental commitment to religion (or nation) often fulfils that need. And my objection is that once one sees that these identity-constituting commitments have specific func-

14. I should stress that the question here is not primarily at the level of individual sensibility and psyche. When in this passage Cohen talks of the strength and durability of religious and nationalist sentiment, he is referring to a communal phenomenon. I think that despite his claim that the spiritual search for identity in the individual subject explains the communal phenomenon, Cohen would nevertheless say that these are different phenomena, irreducible to one another. What I say below, by way of disagreement with Cohen, obviously does not amount to a denial of the fact that individuals often have spiritual yearnings. Rather it amounts to a denial that this fact satisfactorily explains the phenomenon of communal religious identity as we find it in many Muslim countries today. That is, I deny that the phenomenon is, to use Cohen's words, merely a "social manifestation" of the "self's irreducible interest in a definition of itself." It has a quite distinct functional and historical explanation, about which more below.

15. Here I should add that, despite my opposition to Cohen's point, which is advertised by him as a point inspired by Hegel, the view I am promoting is perfectly in consonance with the aspect of Hegelian doctrine that precisely emphasizes historical conditioning of self-definitions. My complaint, then, is that Cohen's essay fails to think through the implications of the fully Hegelian doctrine. The idea of the "self's *irreducible* interest in a definition of itself," which Cohen is stressing in his essay, is at odds with the historically conditioned conception in Hegel. What I below describe as the rock-bottom attitude to what I call the "surplus phenomenology of identity," an attitude that Cohen, for all he says in that paper, can claim as his own, is just the attitude that escapes the historical conditioning. It is just the attitude that makes the phenomenology un-Hegelian.

tional roles in particular historical circumstances, the very idea of an underlying, explanatory, *irreducible* need for identity that they fulfil is undermined as superfluous and misleading in the study of identity. That different fundamental commitments constitute different identities under different historical circumstances does not at all imply that there is an irreducible need for identity that is anyway there, and that needs to be fulfilled by some sense of identity or other. There is simply no such irreducible need. To posit it is to posit an explanatory dangler.

In contemporary Islam, the further historically determined function is not hard to trace. It is hardly questioned by any but the most stubbornly resistant "Orientalist" that a good deal of Islamic revivalism in various countries in the Middle East, South Asia, and North Africa, not to mention some of the northern cities of England, is the product of a long colonial and postcolonial history, which has shaped a community's perception of itself in terms of the Other. It is a defensive reaction caused not only by the scars and memories of Western colonial rule but by the failure of successive governments to break out of the models of development imposed on them by a dominating neocolonial presence of the superpowers through much of the cold war, and even more so now with American interests more entrenched than ever in the Middle East after a humiliating war. The failure of Egypt under Nasser and of pan-Arab secular nationalism to provide leadership, and the general Arab failure to pressure the West to force Israeli compromise on the Palestinian issue have also contributed to the appeal that Islam holds as a source of dignity and autonomy in the face of what is perceived to be successive defeats at the hands of an omnipresent, controlling West. These points are familiar by now. I stress them here in order to say that if Islam is a fundamental commitment today, in the sense I had characterized earlier, it also has recognizable historical sources and has a vital function in a people's struggle to achieve a sense of identity and self-respect in the face of that history and the perceptions formed by it.[16] Hence the strength and durability of Islamic identity has a much more situated and local explanation than Cohen offers.

The issue between us is so large that it would be surprising if there were not problems remaining for my functional account. Though I cannot deal with them all here, it would be evasive not to, at least, mention the most obvious. A central problem with a functional treatment of identity, such as the one I'm proposing, is the tendency of some social and cultural phenomena (in the present case, conviction in a religious doctrine) to *exceed* what is required by their functions, and thereby to attain an independent phenomenological status in the communal psyche. Islamist senti-

16. I am not suggesting that this defensive function exhausts the functional explanation of Muslims' fundamental commitment to Islam. (In the papers cited on page 821, I consider other functional roles.) But it is the *central* function to fasten on when the task is to diagnose the failure to think one's way out of the present conflict. See below.

ment, like many nationalisms, in this way impresses an identity on many Muslim communities that outruns the sort of function we have diagnosed it to have. The source of the commitment may lie in its historically local function, but the commitment then acquires a momentum of its own that may survive even after the function has lapsed. I will call this phenomenon the "surplus phenomenology of identity." It is a surplus quite literally in the sense that it is more than the functional analysis can account for. It is an excess, a residue; and it is properly described as phenomenological precisely because it has no functional role in the psychological economy of the community. It is an experience without a point.

Now it is possible for Cohen to step in right here and claim that this is precisely what he intends by "the self's *irreducible* interest in a definition of itself." He says as much a little after the passage I have quoted: "people engage themselves with people and institutions *other* than to secure an identity, and then the engagement persists when whatever its original rationale was has gone, so that it becomes an identification ungrounded in further reasons."[17] In saying that identity can have phenomenological rather than functional status, I may have given the impression of a concession to this claim. But that impression would be wrong. It's not so much that I want to deny that these engagements might persist. I want to say rather that if they persist in a form that genuinely confers identity in the sense that I have defined above, if they persist in terms of authenticity and fundamental commitment as I have sketched them, then it cannot be that they are ungrounded in some further reasons in the way that Cohen allows. Conversely if they are now ungrounded, then they have lost their blue-chip, identity-imparting aspect, and they no longer count as fundamental commitments in the sense that this paper is concerned with. If they really are ungrounded in any important function, relinquishing these engagements and commitments (due to pressure from conflicting values and commitments) would no longer have the traumatic, authenticity-destroying or integrity-destroying effects on the psyche that is special to fundamental commitments, as I defined them earlier.

So, if these engagements persist as *fundamental* commitments and confer identity in the sense that is relevant to this paper's theme, then, I would argue, that it is only *in appearance* that this surplus commitment is ungrounded; it is only at first sight that it has a self-standing validity. In emphasizing the functional explanations of identity-forming fundamental commitments, in refusing to treat them as flowing from a primitive and unanalyzable need in our consciousness, I am insisting that this slide from the requirements of the function to a residual surplus phenomenology of identity is, from the point of view of *one* level of functional explanation, a form of communal irrationality. And like all irrational phenomena it

17. Cohen, "Reconsidering Historical Materialism," p. 157.

demands *another* level of functional explanation.[18] Neuroses, for example, are often identified as neuroses only because at the level they are being identified they do not seem to have a function; they do not fit in with the normal assignation of roles to mental states. This does not preempt there being another level of functional explanation of the behavior identified initially as neurotic. Indeed all of psychoanalytic theory is founded on this assumption.

Perhaps a better and closer analogy is with the phenomenon that T. S. Eliot located in much romantic poetry and other writing, and which he scathingly described as lacking an "objective correlative."[19] The sentimentality he noticed in such poetry—missing, in his opinion, in the finest examples of what he and others called metaphysical poetry—was the product of a surplus emotion, emotion that exceeded the demands of its ground or object. Here too it is possible for someone to reply that such excess sentiment is a primitive and unanalyzable fact in the poetic consciousness and in readers' responses, but that again seems to me to misdescribe the facts. Eliot's negative evaluation of the phenomenon depended precisely on its not having this sort of rock-bottom justification *within poetics,* that is, the phenomenon demanded another level of explanation in the poet or reader's person, which Eliot considered an irrelevant, egotistical intrusion into the poetic and critical tasks at hand. So also, what I have called the "surplus phenomenology of identity" is to be seen as an irrational tendency in the life of cultures and communities because it too outpaces the level of functional explanation we have offered and similarly demands a further, extrinsic level of functional investigation. There is no reason, therefore, to take a theoretical stance that would deny its irrationality and glamorize it with obscure, unanalyzable philosophical notions such as "the subject's irreducible interest in a definition of itself." It is true that it is not a form of irrationality that has been much studied by

18. An example may be helpful here. Take the survival of Hindu nationalism in India today. Its sources are usually analyzed in terms of the function it served in mobilizing the Indian masses against British colonial rule, but it is evident everywhere that the communal sentiment has survived that function since colonial rule ended. This would seem irrational from the point of view of that level of functional explanation of Hindu identity. Here too it would be quite wrong to say that, whatever its functional sources, once the sentiment comes into existence it gains a self-standing rationale in the subject's need for self-identification within itself. There clearly are *other* functions it now serves. See my "Cry the Beloved Subcontinent," review of *India: A Million Mutinies Now,* by V. S. Naipaul, *New Republic,* 10 June 1991, pp. 30–34, for an analysis of contemporary Hindu nationalism in terms of the function of creating a mythological Hindu unity in the face of recent efforts to expose the deeply divided nature of Hindu culture by the implementation of affirmative action policies.

19. See T. S. Eliot, "Hamlet and His Problems," *The Sacred Wood: Essays on Poetry and Criticism* (London, 1920), and *The Use of Poetry and the Use of Criticism: Studies in the Relation of Criticism to Poetry in England* (London, 1933). Obviously, I am only invoking Eliot's general idea here, not his particular literary critical judgements.

philosophical anthropologists or the theorists of culture.[20] But that may well be just *because* it is too often relegated to some rock-bottom need for self-identification, which then absolves these disciplines from further diagnostic work.

4

Let me return to how the identifying of the specific historical and functional sources of the commitment to Islam opens things up in the study of the conflict under discussion.

It is because their commitment to Islam today is to a large extent governed by a highly defensive function that moderate Muslims find it particularly difficult to make a substantial and sustained criticism of Islamic doctrine; and this, as I said, leaves them open to be exploited by the political efforts of absolutist movements, which exploit the doctrine for their own ends. Their defensiveness inhibits them with the fear that such criticism would amount to a surrender to the forces of the West, which have for so long shown a domineering colonial and postcolonial contempt for their culture. Thus it is that the historically determined function of their commitment, the source of their very self-identity, loops back reflexively on Muslims to paralyze their capacities for self-criticism.

That a fundamental commitment could be further diagnosed along these lines—something that Williams's theoretical framework has no particular place for or interest in—opens up various other lines for thinking about its "unsettleability" in the face of conflict. For it gives us space to examine whether there might be aspects of the commitment and its function in one's psychological economy that are superfluous or even incoherent. It thus gets us beyond the stultifying idea of being locked in a tragic and irresolvable conflict between such commitments. Let me pursue this general point further with the specific issue of Islam.

I think that it is possible to argue that critical reflection on the inhibiting effect of the defensive function of their contemporary commitment to Islam should lead Muslims to the conclusion that there is a simple but deep philosophical malaise at the heart of it; and that insight, in turn, should help them distinguish between different aspects of their faith in a way that allows for its doctrinal reform, and so eventually allows for the conflict they find themselves in to be resolved in favor of a more determined opposition to Islamic absolutism than they have been able to produce so far.

What do I mean here by a philosophical malaise? I have already granted that the contemporary reassertion of Islamist sentiment in many

20. Writings in these disciplines, to their detriment, do not mix it up enough with historical and political studies to develop theoretical (philosophical) treatments of this phenomenon of "surplus phenomenology."

countries as well as a good part of the moderate Muslim's own commitment to Islam is the product of a certain history of subjugation and condescension, which continues today in revised but nevertheless recognizable forms. Why, then, am I not showing the appropriate sympathy towards these defensive stances? It is in answering this question that the specifically abstract character of the malaise is revealed.

The answer is that Muslims themselves have taken the wrong attitude to this historical determination of their Islamist sentiments. Their own observation of the role of colonialism and the West in shaping their commitments and identity ought to—but, alas, *does not*—have a strictly limited and circumscribed role in their own self-conception. The acute consciousness of and obsession with the historical cause of their commitment has made them incapable of critical reflection about the commitment itself. For too long now there has been a tendency among Muslims to keep saying, "You have got to *understand* why we are like this," and then allow that frame of mind to dominate their future actions. This has destroyed their capacity for clearheaded, unreactive political thought and action.

There is an air of paradox in my claim: one's coming to an understanding of the historical source and function of one's commitments can put one in an unreflective and uncritical state of mind about those very commitments. But the paradox is only apparent. Understanding a phenomenon is something that occurs in the third person. And, of course, we do often take such a third-person stance toward *ourselves.* But to allow such a stance to develop into defensive and reactive commitments is to *rest* with a third-person conception of ourselves. It is to deny the first-person or agent's point of view. Thus (when considering the spread of absolutist sentiment in their countries) moderate Muslims are often heard to say, "This is how things are with us because of colonial and neocolonial domination." Or, to take another closely related recent example (when considering Palestinian support for Saddam), moderate Muslims are often heard to say, "This is how things are with us because of Israeli intransigence and America's refusal to come through with serious pressure on Israel." And so on. These remarks are impeccable. But they are bits of knowledge that one has when one takes a third-person stance toward oneself. And that stance, I'm saying, cannot be allowed to exhaust one's self-conception. On the lips of sympathetic others ("This is how things are with *them*") these remarks *are* the *only* stance to take. But on *our* lips, on the lips of Muslims, they cannot be the only remarks we make unless we treat ourselves as objects, unless we think of our future as we think of our past, as something that we cannot make a difference to. The philosophical malaise is quite simply that in allowing the third-person point of view to dominate our political responses we are failing to live up to the basic conditions of free agency.

This point echoes, in a much more specific and political context, a point made famous in the third section of Kant's *Grundlegung.*[21] In the form it occurs in Kant, the point's relevance to politics is not obvious; indeed, its relevance to anything outside the very general conditions for the possibility of agency is not obvious. The idea of seeing ourselves primarily as objects, the idea of taking an *exclusively* third-person point of view of ourselves, in that very general Kantian setting, should have the effect of making us altogether passive—extreme versions of the eponymous figure, Oblomov, in Goncharóv's novel. After all if one did not think that the future was *any* different from the past, why would one act at all? Though that is the extreme and logical end of taking such a perspective on oneself, my claim is that, when the concerns are not as purely general and metaphysical as they are in Kant's discussion, there are less extreme effects of adopting such a perspective—or at any rate of being dominated by this perspective—that consist, not in passivity, but in reactive and defensive actions, rather than fully autonomous actions.

A failure to see through the implications of their opposition to the absolutists, a failure to press for the reforms that will undermine the ground on which the absolutists stand, are just two among the many examples of such reactiveness and defensiveness on the part of moderate Muslims. Their sulking, censorious response to Salman Rushdie's book, which was blind to the book's own antiabsolutist polemic and importance, is another example, as is the constant disposition of moderate Muslims to lend silent support to third-rate, vainglorious leaders such as Qaddafi and Saddam, who offer instant autonomy and dignity in the face of Western domination with ineffectual warlike stances. Their understanding of themselves as the victims of a history of Western domination constitutes the third-person perspective that then perpetuates just these sorts of defensive actions. If this third-person point of view did not so overwhelm their vision of themselves, it would leave space for the *first*-person point of view, essential to the very idea of agency. The first-person point of view would not allow the context of understanding the colonial past to breed the defensiveness that weakens their opposition to the absolutists; it would not allow the Palestinians to give up the moral high ground by their self-destructive support of Saddam.[22]

I should add that this philosophical fallacy informs a great deal of defensiveness not only in the more obviously political arena, but in the academy as well. Recent powerful, trenchant, and much-needed critiques

21. See Immanuel Kant, *Foundations of the Metaphysics of Morals,* trans. Lewis White Beck (Indianapolis, 1983).

22. Incidentally, it should go without saying, but perhaps it will not, so I will say it: it is not a matter of the moral high ground for its own sake. The point is straightforwardly one of *self-interest.* If Machiavelli was given to advising displaced people rather than princes, he too would have said: Don't give up the moral high ground unless you are absolutely certain that this man in this real world of U.S. military domination will deliver you from displacement.

of Orientalism have forced scholars to shun the essentializing tendency in studies of Islam and the Third World, and they have taught scholars to pay attention to the detail and diversity of their subject.[23] This effect is laudable. But they have also created a bandwagon effect that inhibits self-criticism in the fear that one is playing into Western and "Orientalizing" caricatures of Islam and the Third World. Criticism and reform *do* mean abstracting from diversity and detail in order to identify a core doctrine or tendency to which one is opposed.[24] Indeed, as I argue in "Intrinsic and Extrinsic Explanations of Islam," it is not merely criticism and reform but even the very idea of *explanation* of social phenomena that requires such abstraction. This methodological ploy does not amount to essentialism or caricature, and we cannot afford to be tyrannized into thinking so by bandwagon intellectual trends. It is not essentialism because quite simply no social science, no historical understanding, no agenda for social and political change can afford to ignore this simple methodological canon.

Speaking initially in the third person, moderate Muslims might correctly say, "In the face of colonial history and in the face of recent frustrations and defeat, Islam has an appeal for us; it is grounded in a doctrine we embrace and which has comprehensive pretensions and claims on us, including—crucially—on our polities, and this gives us a sense of autonomy and identity." If I am right that this defensive attitude reflects a predominantly third-person perspective on ourselves, it will do no violence to the use of "us" and "we" here if we replace them with "them" and "they." This is, after all, the voice of a community's understanding of its own condition and its causes. It is the voice of the subject that takes itself to be an object.

But then, if I am right, there should be place and possibility for the switch to the first person, for the voice of the subject as agent to say, "This appeal of Islam is something we have uncritically and indiscriminately embraced out of demoralization and defeat, often allowing it to dominate our political actions, and it has gotten us nowhere; it is up to us to assess the relative merits of its diverse doctrinal commitments, up to us to work towards its reform, up to us to oppose the inviolability of the *Sharia,* to fashion a depoliticized Islam so that its appeal and relevance are spiritualist and universalist rather than to the polity, so that it does not remain perpetually exploitable by the fundamentalist political factions, whom we oppose." This is neither merely the passive voice nor the reactive voice. It is, bending language a bit, the active voice.

23. The *locus classicus* is, of course, Edward W. Said, *Orientalism* (New York, 1978).

24. Moreover almost every scholar on this bandwagon has (quite justly) abstracted from the diversity of the West to explain the West's colonial and neocolonial domination of these regions. It then seems methodologically inconsistent to discourage such abstraction from the diversity within the Islamic people and nations for particular contexts of explanation and of Islamic reform.

5

These are of course very general things to say about the need for reform, and they require detailed and specific study and analysis, as well as a systematic and strategic agenda for reformist political action. That is beyond the province of this paper.[25] But certain general lines of direction should flow obviously from points I have made so far. The idea of reform in the particular context of the conflict we have been discussing applies only to those portions of the Quran that speak to questions of the polity and to personal and public law. They leave intact the verses with the more purely universalist and spiritual claims and commitments. It is a well-known and highly significant fact that the early verses written in Mecca are all of the latter sort. Only some of the verses that follow from Muhammad's arrival in Medina make detailed claims about the state, the economy, inheritance, marriage, divorce, the status of women in the home and society, and so on. Once they have shed their defensiveness, it is possible for Muslims to argue that after the initial, deep, spiritual, defining pronouncements of the new faith in Mecca, the post-Medina verses were intended to address a very specific historical context in which conversion was paramount in the concerns of the prophet. Conversion was bound to be more effective if the faith addressed itself to a variety of social and interpersonal themes so that Islam could present itself as offering the (often nomadic) regional populations a hitherto unavailable sense of belonging to a unified community. It should also be possible for Muslims, therefore, to argue that since that historical context of seeking conversion has lapsed, the verses to be emphasized now are the Mecca verses that have no specific political commitments. This would indeed constitute an Islamic reformation. It would reopen the gates of *ijtihad* (reinterpretation of Islamic doctrine) that have been closed for centuries in the rigid readings of the *Sharia.*[26]

Notice that this conception of Islamic reform, and this argument for it, will not be overturned if it turns out that I'm wrong about the functional analysis of Islamic identity. That analysis was intended to counter an unnecessarily limited notion of fundamental commitment and an unmalleable notion of conflict that it generated. But the actual conclusions and argument about reform are independent of the analysis. Even if my functionalist claim (that a good deal of the moderate Muslim's fundamental commitment to Islam is out of a historically determined defensive-

25. I have written in more detail about the methodology and substance of this reformist agenda in "Intrinsic and Extrinsic Explanations of Islam."

26. In "Intrinsic and Extrinsic Explanations of Islam," I discuss more fully the place of the *Sharia* in our understanding of Islamic doctrine, and I disentangle the different aspects of doctrine (*Quran, Hadith, Sunna*) that are relevant to the question of the sort of reform that I have briefly gestured at here.

ness) is exaggerated, even if one emphasized the view I have downplayed (that their commitment is primarily out of the need for some purely spiritual basis for self-identification), the point of this reformist proposal for a depoliticized Islam, which stresses precisely the universal and spiritual commitments in the early verses of the Quran over many of the later verses, would still retain its validity.

My use of terms like *universalist* should not be made to carry more weight than is intended, so let me make the intention a little clearer. It may appear that in asserting the primacy of the Mecca verses and their universalist appeal, I think of reform as requiring an abandonment of what is specific and unique to Islam, leaving some deist core that is hardly recognizable as relevant to the subject of this paper, namely, *Muslim* identity. That appearance is not only not intended, but I would argue that it is conjured up only within a framework of thinking about communal identity that thoroughly misdescribes a community's psychology of identity. It is only if one saw communal identity as a highly codifiable phenomenon, that one would even be tempted to say that a relaxation or abandonment of some set of principles would have the effect of changing the subject. Though I won't argue for it here, I think it is an egregious misconception of religious identity to see it as a codifiable phenomenon.[27] The idea that without the specific doctrinal commitments of public and personal law, Islam would be indistinguishable from all other universal and spiritual claims would be, in the spirit of this codificatory misconception, to divorce the message of the Mecca verses from their origins and history, as well as the abiding set of specific Islamic institutions and practices of prayer, pilgrimage, the collection of alms (to name just a very few) that they have spawned. No such idea underlies my use of terms like *universalist* and *spiritualist* to characterize the message of these verses. Their use is meant merely to mark a contrast with the specific political and legal commitments that should be the targets of reformers today. Depoliticization, however, does not imply deracination. Thus, though such a transformation in Muslims' fundamental commitment to Islam would now leave no

27. Fazlur Rahman, who has written with learning and acuteness on these subjects, seems to be struggling to make this point in his plea for modernization in *Islam and Modernity: Transformation of an Intellectual Tradition* (Chicago, 1982), but botches it somewhat by describing the Quran as a *unity*. See pp. 159–61, and the introductory remarks on pp. 2–3. The suggestion of Quranic unity is precisely what intellectuals of the absolutist movements themselves invoke to resist reform, arguing that reform would undermine unity. The revealed word of God may tolerably be reformed precisely because the revealed word is not a unity. Different revelations can now be seen as indexed—even qua revelation—to different historical contexts. It is really the noncodifiability that Rahman should be stressing rather than unity, and not of the text but of the sense of identity in which the text has a place among other identity-shaping practices and institutions. The point about noncodifiability of identity should allow religious identity (of even a highly devout moderate Muslim) to take in stride the idea that some revealed verses may be stressed over others as historical contexts lapse.

particular doctrinal element that absolutists could invoke, nevertheless, it would be a transformation *within* a commitment to Islam. It would, therefore, still constitute an answer to the question, What is a Muslim?

But to return now to the larger point: for such reform not to seem to themselves a total surrender to long-standing, hostile, alien, cultural, and political forces, Muslims will have to take the first step in resolving the present conflict by overcoming their acute defensiveness, which, as I said, comes from taking an overwhelmingly third-person perspective on themselves. How a community acquires the alternative perspective (of autonomy) in specific historical contexts is a subject that I cannot address in this paper,[28] whose aim is merely to uncover the malaise that makes a conflict seem irresolvable. But I will say this: A failure to overcome the defensiveness, a failure to acquire the first-person perspective, will prove a point of the bitterest irony. A failure to come out of the neurotic obsession with the Western and colonial determination of their present condition will only prove that that determination was utterly comprehensive in the destruction it wrought. That is to say, it will prove to be the final victory for imperialism that after all the other humiliations it has visited on Muslims, it lingered in our psyches in the form of *genuine self-understanding* to make self-criticism and free, unreactive agency impossible.

6

An underlying theoretical point of this paper has been that if fundamental commitments and the questions of cultural identity that they bring with them (What is an *X*?) are understood in terms of functional analyses of the kind I have tried to give in the case of Islamic identity today, then there is scope to see these commitments as susceptible to various criticisms in the particular context of a conflict in which they might figure. All this seems to me to offer far more scope and interest to moral philosophy than Williams allows it, even after granting to Williams the validity of the central role he gives to the idea of fundamental commitment and the validity of his critique of traditional moral philosophy.

The paper has studied the question, What is a Muslim? in the dialectic of a conflict arising out of a concern for Islamic reform. The conflict is one that arises because of moderate Muslims' fundamental commitment to a doctrine that contains features that are often effectively invoked by

28. A first step would be to acknowledge the conflict itself, which for the most part lies hidden; such an acknowledgement might lead to processes of reflection that are necessary. The specific forms of reflection that underlie the first-person point of view is a large and important philosophical subject. See Thomas Nagel, *The View from Nowhere* (New York, 1986), chaps. 7, 9, and Isaac Levi, *Hard Choices: Decision Making under Unresolved Contact* (Cambridge, 1986), chap. 4, for interesting discussions of this problem.

the absolutists whom moderate Muslims fundamentally oppose. If a full analysis of the commitment reveals its defensive function, which has disabled Muslims from a creative and powerful opposition to the absolutists, and if, moreover, this function of the commitment is diagnosed as itself based on a deep but common philosophical fallacy, it should be possible then for moderate Muslims to think their way out of this conflict and to transform the nature of their commitment to Islam, so that it is not disabling in that way.

The question of identity—what is a Muslim?—then, will get very different answers before and after this dialectic has played itself out. The dialectic thus preserves the negotiability of the concept of identity and the methodological points I began with, at the same time as it situates and explains the urgency and fascination that such questions hold for us.

Nationalism and Social Division in Black Arts Poetry of the 1960s

Phillip Brian Harper

1

This essay begins with an epigraph, not its own, but one from a key publication in the history of black American poetry. Dudley Randall's anthology *The Black Poets,* published in 1971, is significant not so much for the texts it provides of folk verse and literary poetry from the mid-eighteenth through the early twentieth centuries; rather, its import derives from its participation in a contemporary process of canonization performed on poetry from the Black Arts movement. The concluding sec-

This essay has benefitted from the attention given to earlier versions of it by audiences at three different venues. For their helpful comments, criticisms, and suggestions, I would like to thank my colleagues at Brandeis and Harvard Universities and, especially, students and faculty in the English department at Johns Hopkins University. I am also grateful for the opportunity to reprint the following poems: "SOS" and "Poem for Half White College Students," by Imamu Amiri Baraka (LeRoi Jones). © 1969 by Amiri Baraka (LeRoi Jones), reprinted by permission of Sterling Lord Literistic, Inc.; "The True Import of Present Dialogue: Black vs. Negro," by Nikki Giovanni. From *Black Feeling, Black Talk/Black Judgment.* © 1968, 1970 by Nikki Giovanni, reprinted by permission of William Morrow & Company, Inc.; "Okay, 'Negroes,'" by June Jordan. © 1970 by June Jordan, reprinted by permission of the author; "Move Un-Noticed to Be Noticed: A Nationhood Poem," by Don L. Lee (Haki Madhubuti). From *We Walk the Way of the New World.* © 1970 by Don L. Lee (Haki Madhubuti), reprinted by permission of Broadside Press; "blk/ rhetoric," by Sonia Sanchez. © 1969, 1978 by Sonia Sanchez, reprinted by permission of the author; "chant for young / brothas & sistuhs," by Sonia Sanchez. © 1970 by Sonia Sanchez, reprinted by permission of the author.

This article originally appeared in *Critical Inquiry* 19 (Winter 1993).

tion of Randall's anthology is titled "The Nineteen Sixties," and it is introduced by the short poem "SOS" by Imamu Amiri Baraka (LeRoi Jones), which is printed not in the main text but on the title page for the section:

> Calling black people
> Calling all black people, man woman child
> Wherever you are, calling you, urgent, come in
> Black People, come in, wherever you are, urgent, calling
> you, calling all black people
> calling all black people, come in, black people, come
> on in.[1]

It seems reasonable to infer that, as it occupies an epigraphic position in Randall's compilation, Baraka's "SOS" can be identified as emblematic of the poetic project of many young black writers of the late 1960s. And it is not particularly difficult to identify exactly in what this emblematic nature might consist. We know, after all, that radical black intellectual activism of the late 1960s was characterized by the drive for a nationalistic unity among people of African descent. As Larry Neal put it in 1968 in his defining essay "The Black Arts Movement,"

> Black Art is the aesthetic and spiritual sister of the Black Power concept. . . . The Black Arts and the Black Power concept both relate broadly to the Afro-American's desire for self-determination and nationhood. Both concepts are nationalistic. One is concerned with the relationship between art and politics; the other with the art of politics.[2]

Addison Gayle also embraces the nationalist impulse in his conception of the movement, outlined in his 1971 introduction to *The Black Aesthetic.* According to Gayle, "The Black Aesthetic . . . is a corrective—a means of helping black people out of the polluted mainstream of Americanism."[3] And in 1972 Stephen Henderson elaborated the development of this

1. Imamu Amiri Baraka, "SOS," in *The Black Poets,* ed. Dudley Randall (New York, 1971), p. 181.

2. Larry Neal, "The Black Arts Movement," in *The Black Aesthetic,* ed. Addison Gayle, Jr. (New York, 1971), p. 257.

3. Gayle, introduction, *The Black Aesthetic,* p. xxii.

Phillip Brian Harper is associate professor at New York University, where he teaches in the department of English. He is the author of *Framing the Margins: The Social Logic of Postmodern Culture* (1994) and *Are We Not Men? Masculine Anxiety and the Problem of African American Identity* (forthcoming).

impulse through the late 1960s: "the poetry of the sixties is informed and unified by the new consciousness of Blackness. . . . a consciousness [that has] shifted from Civil Rights to Black Power to Black Nationalism to Revolutionary Pan-Africanism."[4] Thus do three of the Black Aesthetic's most prominent theorists conceive the importance of nationalist unity to the Black Arts movement.[5] For the moment, we can leave aside the various directions in which the nationalist impulse might develop as we attempt to identify its presence, in however rudimentary a form, in Baraka's poem.

In the introduction to their authoritative anthology, *Black Nationalism in America,* John Bracey, Jr., August Meier, and Elliott Rudwick assert that

> the simplest expression of racial feeling that can be called a form of black nationalism is *racial solidarity.* It generally has no ideological or programmatic implications beyond the desire that black people organize themselves on the basis of their common color and oppressed condition to move in some way to alleviate their situation. The concept of racial solidarity is essential to all forms of black nationalism.[6]

It is precisely this essential impulse to racial solidarity that is manifested in Baraka's "SOS." Considered with respect to nationalism, the political import of the poem inheres not so much in the stridency and exigency of its appeal but rather in its breadth, in the fact that Baraka's call apparently includes all members of the African diaspora, as it is directed explicitly and repeatedly to "*all* black people," thereby invoking a political Pan-Africanism posited as characteristic of the Black Arts project. Moreover, the enjambment of the last two lines and their modification of the injunction definitively transform the SOS from a mere distress signal into a general summons for assembly. What is striking about Baraka's poem, however, is not that it "calls" black people in this nationalistic way but that this is *all* it does; the objective for which it assembles the black populace is not specified in the piece itself, a fact I take to indicate fundamental difficulties in the nationalist agenda of the Black Arts poets, as we will soon see.

In the meantime, I think it is useful to consider Baraka's "SOS" as a

4. Stephen Henderson, introduction to sec. 3, in *Understanding the New Black Poetry: Black Speech and Black Music as Poetic References,* ed. Henderson (New York, 1973), p. 183.

5. For an overview of the development of black nationalism in the Black Arts movement, see Houston A. Baker, Jr., *The Journey Back: Issues in Black Literature and Criticism* (Chicago, 1980), esp. chap. 4, "In Our Own Time: The Florescence of Nationalism in the Sixties and Seventies," pp. 77–131.

6. John H. Bracey, Jr., August Meier, and Elliott Rudwick, introduction, in *Black Nationalism in America,* ed. Bracey, Meier, and Rudwick (Indianapolis, 1970), p. xxvi; hereafter abbreviated "I."

synecdoche for all of his poetic output of the 1960s, which constituted a challenge to other black poets to take up the nationalist ethic he espoused. Insofar as a significant number of black poets did heed his call, Baraka can certainly be seen as the founder of the Black Aesthetic of the 1960s and "SOS" as representative of the standard to which his fellow poets rallied. "SOS" is part of Baraka's collection *Black Art,* comprising poems written in 1965 and 1966 and published, along with two other collections, in the volume *Black Magic: Poetry, 1961–1967.*[7] Its message was subsequently engaged by other black writers from different generations and disparate backgrounds. In her 1972 autobiography, *Report from Part One,* Gwendolyn Brooks, who built her reputation on her expertly crafted lyrics of the 1940s and 1950s, makes Baraka's enterprise her own as she describes her new poetic mission in the early 1970s: "My aim, in my next future, is to write poems that will somehow successfully 'call' (see Imamu Baraka's 'SOS') all black people: black people in taverns, black people in alleys, black people in gutters, schools, offices, factories, prisons, the consulate; I wish to reach black people in pulpits, black people in mines, on farms, on thrones."[8] Sonia Sanchez, on the other hand, in her 1969 poem "blk / rhetoric" invoked Baraka's language to question what might happen after the calling had been done:

who's gonna make all
that beautiful blk / rhetoric
mean something.
                        like
i mean
        who's gonna take
the words
        blk / is / beautiful
and make more of it
than blk / capitalism.
                        u dig?
        i mean
                like who's gonna
take all the young / long / haired
natural / brothers and sisters
and let them
                grow till
                                all that is
impt is them
                selves
                    moving in straight /
revolutionary / lines
                        toward the enemy

7. See LeRoi Jones, *Black Magic: Poetry, 1961–1967* (Indianapolis, 1969).
8. Gwendolyn Brooks, *Report from Part One* (Detroit, 1972), p. 183.

(and we know who that is)
like. man.
who's gonna give our young
blk / people new heroes
(instead of catch / phrases)
(instead of cad / ill / acs)
(instead of pimps)
(instead of wite / whores)
(instead of drugs)
(instead of new dances)
(instead of chit / ter / lings)
(instead of a 35¢ bottle of ripple)
(instead of quick / fucks in the hall / way
of wite / america's mind)
like. this. is an S O S
me. calling. . . . .
calling. . . . .
some / one
pleasereplysoon.[9]

Sanchez's call—prefaced as it is by her urgent question and attended by the entreaty to her listeners in the final line—is more pleading than Baraka's, which is unabashedly imperative. I would suggest that the uncertainty that characterizes Sanchez's poem is the inevitable affective result of writing beyond the ending of Baraka's "SOS," which it seems to me is what "blk / rhetoric" does. By calling into question what will ensue amongst the black collectivity after it has heeded the general call—succumbed to the rhetoric, at it were—Sanchez points to the problematic nature of the black nationalist project that characterizes Black Arts poetry.

What remains certain, in Sanchez's rendering—so certain that she need not state it explicitly—is the identity of the "enemy" against whom the assembled black troops must struggle. While Sanchez's elliptical reference might appear somewhat ambiguous at this point, especially after the emergence in the early and midseventies of a strong black feminist movement that arrayed itself against patriarchal forces, it seems clear enough that in the context of the 1969 Black Arts movement the enemy was most certainly the white "establishment." But this is the *only* thing that is "known" in Sanchez's poem, and while the identification of a generalized white foe is a central strategy in the Black Arts movement's effort to galvanize the black populace, here it provides a hedge against the overall uncertainty that characterizes the rest of the poem—a definitive core on which the crucial questions about the efficacy of nationalist rhetoric can center and thus themselves still be recognizable as nationalist discourse.

9. Sonia Sanchez, "blk / rhetoric," *We a BaddDDD People* (Detroit, 1970), pp. 15–16.

With its counterbalancing of fundamental inquiries about the future of the black nationalist enterprise by recourse to the trope of the white enemy, Sanchez's "blk / rhetoric" verges on the problematic that I take to be constitutive of the Black Arts project. Insofar as that project is nationalistic in character, then its primary objective and continual challenge will be, not to identify the external entity against which the black masses are distinguished—this is easy enough to do—but rather to negotiate division within the black population itself. I specifically invoke *negotiation* here and not, for instance, *resolution* because I want to claim that the response of Black Arts nationalism to social division within the black populace is not to strive to overcome it but rather repeatedly to articulate it in the name of black consciousness.

2

It has been widely held that the fundamental characteristic of Black Arts poetry is its virulent antiwhite rhetoric. For instance, as Houston Baker has noted, the influential black critic J. Saunders Redding disparaged the Black Aesthetic as representative of a discourse of "hate," a "naive racism in reverse."[10] And it is true that Baraka himself became known for a generalized antiwhite sentiment, often manifested in highly particularized ethnic and religious slurs, especially anti-Semitic ones. His "Black Art" provides an exemplary litany, calling for

> poems that wrestle cops into alleys
> and take their weapons leaving them dead
> with tongues pulled out and sent to Ireland. Knockoff
> poems for dope selling wops or slick halfwhite
> politicians Airplane poems . . .
> . . . Setting fire and death to
> whities ass. Look at the Liberal
> Spokesman for the jews clutch his throat
> & puke himself into eternity . . .
> . . . Another bad poem cracking
> steel knuckles in a jewlady's mouth.[11]

"Black People!" calls for the "smashing [of] jellywhite faces. We must make our own / World, man, our own world, and we can not do this unless the white man / is dead. Let's get together and killhim."[12] Similarly, Nikki

10. Baker, *Afro-American Poetics: Revisions of Harlem and the Black Aesthetic* (Madison, Wis., 1988), p. 161.

11. Baraka, "Black Art," in *The Black Poets,* p. 224.

12. Baraka, "Black People!" in *The Black Poets,* pp. 226–27.

Giovanni, in a poem that we will soon consider more fully, inquires urgently of her black reader, "Can you kill . . . / . . . Can you poison . . . / . . . Can you piss on a blond head / Can you cut it off . . . / . . . Can you kill a white man."[13]

While the affective power of such antiwhite sentiment in much of the poetry certainly cannot be denied, it seems to me that the drama of interracial strife that this rhetoric represents also serves to further another objective of Black Arts poetry—the establishment of *intra*racial distinctions that themselves serve to solidify the meaning of the Black Aesthetic. In order to clarify this point, I would like to examine a few poems by key practitioners of the Black Aesthetic: Baraka, Sanchez, Giovanni, Haki Madhubuti (Don L. Lee), and June Jordan. These five poems have been widely anthologized as exemplary of the Black Arts project, yet I would argue that they are exemplary, not because they are *representative* of the poetics deployed in most Black Arts productions, but rather because they expose the logic of the Black Arts ethic that governs work from the movement generally, but whose operation is carefully suppressed in most of that material. I think that the strength of my claim will be augmented through the presentation of the complete poems, so I give the full texts here. First, Baraka's "Poem for Half White College Students":

Who are you, listening to me, who are you
listening to yourself? Are you white or
black, or does that have anything to do
with it? Can you pop your fingers to no
music, except those wild monkies go on
in your head, can you jerk, to no melody,
except finger poppers get it together
when you turn from starchecking to checking
yourself. How do you sound, your words, are they
yours? The ghost you see in the mirror, is it really
you, can you swear you are not an imitation greyboy,
can you look right next to you in that chair, and swear,
that the sister you have your hand on is not really
so full of Elizabeth Taylor, Richard Burton is
coming out of her ears. You may even have to be Richard
with a white shirt and face, and four million negroes
think you cute, you may have to be Elizabeth Taylor, old lady,
if you want to sit up in your crazy spot dreaming about dresses,
and the sway of certain porters' hips. Check yourself, learn who it is
speaking, when you make some ultrasophisticated point, check
yourself,

13. Nikki Giovanni, "The True Import of Present Dialogue: Black vs. Negro," in *The Black Poets,* pp. 318–19.

when you find yourself gesturing like Steve McQueen, check it out, ask
in your black heart who it is you are, and is that image black or white,

you might be surprised right out the window, whistling dixie on the way in[14]

Second, Giovanni's "The True Import of Present Dialogue: Black vs. Negro":

Nigger
Can you kill
Can you kill
Can a nigger kill
Can a nigger kill a honkie
Can a nigger kill the Man
Can you kill nigger
Huh? nigger can you
kill
Do you know how to draw blood
Can you poison
Can you stab-a-jew
Can you kill huh? nigger
Can you kill
Can you run a protestant down with your
'68 El Dorado
(that's all they're good for anyway)
Can you kill
Can you piss on a blond head
Can you cut it off
Can you kill
A nigger can die
We ain't got to prove we can die
We got to prove we can kill
They sent us to kill
Japan and Africa
We policed europe
Can you kill
Can you kill a white man
Can you kill the nigger
in you
Can you make your nigger mind
die
Can you kill your nigger mind
And free your black hands to

14. Baraka, "Poem for Half White College Students," in *The Black Poets,* p. 225.

strangle
Can you kill
Can a nigger kill
Can you shoot straight and
Fire for good measure
Can you splatter their brains in the street
Can you kill them
Can you lure them to bed to kill them
We kill in Viet Nam
for them
We kill for UN & NATO & SEATO & US
And everywhere for all alphabet but
BLACK
Can we learn to kill WHITE for BLACK
Learn to kill niggers
Learn to be Black men[15]

Third, Lee's "Move Un-Noticed to Be Noticed: A Nationhood Poem":

move, into our own, not theirs
into our.
they own it (for the moment): the unclean world, the
polluted space, the un-censor-ed
air, yr/foot steps as they
run wildly in the wrong
direction.
move, into our own, not theirs
into our.
move, you can't buy own.
own is like yr/hair (if u let it live); a natural extension of ownself.
own is yr/reflection, yr/total-being; the way u walk, talk,
dress and relate to each other is *own.*
own is you,
cannot be bought or sold
can u buy yr/writing hand
yr/dancing feet, yr/speech,
yr/woman (if she's real),
yr/manhood?
own is ours.
all we have to do is take it
take it the way u take from one another.
the way u take artur rubinstein over thelonious monk
the way u take eugene genovese over lerone bennett,
the way u take robert bly over imamu baraka,
the way u take picasso over charles white,

15. Giovanni, "The True Import of Present Dialogue: Black vs. Negro," in *The Black Poets,* pp. 318–19.

the way u take marianne moore over gwendolyn brooks,
the way u take *inaction* over *action.*
move. move to act act.
act into thinking and think into action.
try to think. think. try to think think think.
try to think. think (like i said, into yr/own) think.
try to think. don't hurt yourself, i know it's new.
try to act,
act into thinking and think into action.
can u do it, hunh? i say hunh, can u stop moving like a drunk gorilla?
ha ha che che
ha ha che che
ha ha che che
ha ha che che
move
what is u anyhow: a professional car watcher, a billboard for nothingness,
a sane madman, a reincarnated clark gable?
either you is or you ain't!

the deadliving
are the worldmakers,
the image breakers,
the rule takers: blackman can you stop a hurricane?

"I remember back in 1954 or '55, in Chicago, when we had
13 days without a murder, that was before them colored
people started calling themselves *black.*"
move.
move,
move to be moved,
move into yr/ownself, Clean.
Clean, u is the first black hippy i've ever met.
why u bes dressen so funny, anyhow hunh?
i mean, is that u, Clean?
why u bes dressen like an airplane, can u fly,
i mean,
will yr/blue jim-shoes fly u,
& what about yr/tailor made bell bottoms, Clean?
can they lift u above madness,
turn u into the right direction.
& that red & pink scarf around yr/neck what's that for, Clean,
hunh? will it help u fly, yeah, swing, swing ing swing
swinging high above telephone wires with dreams
of this & that and illusions of trying to take bar-b-q
ice cream away from hon minded niggers who
didn't event know that *polish* is more than a
sausage.
"clean as a tack,
rusty as a nail,

haven't had a bath
sence columbus sail."

when u going be something real, Clean?
like yr/own, yeah, when u going be yr/ownself?

the deadliving
are the worldmakers,
the image breakers,
the rule takers: blackman can u stop a hurricane, mississippi couldn't.
blackman if u can't stop what mississippi couldn't, *be it, be it.*
black man be the wind, be the win, the win, the win, win win:

woooooooooowe boom boom woooooooooowe bah
woooooooooowe boom boom woooooooooowe bah
if u can't stop a hurricane, be one.
woooooooooowe boom boom woooooooooowe bah
woooooooooowe boom boom woooooooooowe bah
be the baddest hurricane that ever came. a black hurricane.
woooooooooowe boom boom woooooooooowe bah
woooooooooowe boom boom woooooooooowe bah
the baddest black hurricane that ever came, a black
hurricane named Beulah,
go head Beulah, do the hurricane.
woooooooooowe boom boom woooooooooowe bah
woooooooooowe boom boom woooooooooowe bah
move
move to be moved from the un-moveable,
into our own, yr/self is own, yrself is own, own yourself.
go where you/we go, hear the unheard and do,
do the undone, do it, do it, do it *now,* Clean
and tomorrow your sons will
be alive to praise
you.[16]

Next, Sanchez's "chant for young / brothas
& sistuhs":

yall

out there. looooken so coool

in yo / highs.

yeah yall

16. Don L. Lee, "Move Un-Noticed to Be Noticed: A Nationhood Poem," in *Understanding the New Black Poetry,* pp. 340–43.

rat there

listen to me

screeaamen this song.

did u know i've

seen yo / high

on every blk / st in

wite / amurica

i've seen yo/self/

imposed/quarantined/hipness

on every

slum/

bar/ revolutionary / st

& there yall be sitten.

u brotha.

u sistuh.

listen to this drummen.

this sad / chant.

listen to the tears

flowen down my blk / face

listen to a

death/song being sung on thick/lips

by a blk/woman

once i had a maaan
who loved me so he sed
we lived togetha, loved togetha
and i followed wherever he led

now this maaan of mine

got tired of this slooow pace
started gitten high a lot
to stay on top of the race.

saw him begin to die
screeaamed. held him so tight
but he got so thin so very thin
slipped thru these fingers of might

last time i heard from him
he was bangen on a woman's door
callen for his daily high
didn't even care bout the score.

once i loooved a man
still do looove that man
want to looove that man again
wish he'd come on home again

need to be with that maaannn
need to love that maaaannnn
who went out one day & died
who went out one day & died.

yall

out there looooken so cooool

in yo / highs.

yeah. yall

rat there

c'mon down from yo / wite / highs

and live.[17]

And, finally, "Okay 'Negroes,'" by Jordan:

Okay "Negroes"
American Negroes
looking for milk
crying out loud
in the nursery of freedomland:
the rides are rough.
Tell me where you got that image
of a male white mammy.

17. Sanchez, "chant for young / brothas & sistuhs," in *The Black Poets*, pp. 240–42.

God is vague and he don't take no sides.
You think clean fingernails crossed legs a smile
shined shoes
a crucifix around your neck
good manners
no more noise
you think who's gonna give you something?

Come a little closer.
Where you from?[18]

These pieces, disparate as they are, share certain features. There are, to be sure, the disparaging references to white society—Jordan's "male white mammy," Sanchez's rendering of the heroin high, Baraka's invocation of film celebrities as representative of the shallowness of white culture—all of which fit neatly into characterizations of Black Arts poetry as essentially antiwhite. But while these works might engage conceptions of white America as a negative force, the rhetoric of the pieces is not addressed—not directly at any rate—to the white society that is the ostensible target of their wrath. Indeed, the thematic context of the poems and their employment of the second-person pronoun *you* are clearly meant to conjure a specifically black addressee and thus to give the impression that the poetic works themselves are meant for consumption by a specifically black audience. In other words, the rhetoric of Black Arts poetry, in conjunction with the sociopolitical context in which it is produced, works a twist on John Stuart Mill's proclamation that "poetry is overheard," as it seems to effect a split in the audience for the work. Because of the way the poetry uses direct address and thus invites us to conflate addressee and audience, it appears that the material is meant to be *heard* by blacks and *over*heard by whites. I think, however, that this is appearance only, and it will be the serendipitous consequence of my primary argument to show that, while Black Arts poetry very likely does depend for its effect on the division of its audience along racial lines, it also achieves its maximum impact in a context in which it is understood as being *heard* directly by whites and *over*heard by blacks.

Clarification of that point is forthcoming. In the meantime, it is necessary to acknowledge the substantial polemical effect that is achieved through the *presentation* of Black Arts poetry as meant for black ears only, for it is this presentation that commentators have seized on when they have characterized the Black Arts movement as representing a completely Afrocentric impulse. As Gayle, for instance, puts it in his introduction to *The Black Aesthetic,* the black artist of the 1960s "has given up the futile practice of speaking to whites, and has begun to speak to his brothers. . . .

18. June Jordan, "Okay 'Negroes,'" in *The Black Poets,* p. 243.

to point out to black people the true extent of the control exercised upon them by the American society."[19] Gayle's claim is, in itself, not earthshaking; it is typical of the contemporary conceptions of the Black Arts movement's significance in black cultural history. What *is* notable is that Gayle's statement, in positing the Black Arts strategy as historically unique, establishes itself as a historical repetition, insofar as, nearly fifty years before, a black theorist of the Harlem Renaissance made a very similar claim about the nature of that movement. In his 1925 article on the flowering of the Harlem Renaissance, "Negro Youth Speaks," Alain Locke insisted that, "Our poets have now stopped speaking for the Negro—they speak as Negroes. Where formerly they spoke to others and tried to interpret, they now speak to their own and try to express."[20] The full irony of this repetition lies in the fact that it is precisely on the basis of the perceived failure of the Harlem Renaissance to engage black interests that Black Arts theoreticians find fault with the earlier movement. Neal specifically charges that the Harlem Renaissance "failed" in that "it did not address itself to the mythology and the life-styles of the Black community."[21] Clearly, there is an anxiety of influence operative here, manifested in the powerful need among the Black Aestheticians to disassociate themselves from the Harlem Renaissance; and this disassociation will be based on the later movement's apparently uniquely effective manner of addressing itself to the interests of black people. By examining this strategy, we can see more clearly both how social division within the black community is fundamentally constitutive of Black Arts nationalism and, relatedly, why it *is* so difficult for the Black Arts movement to postulate concrete action beyond "black rhetoric," to project beyond the "call" manifested in Baraka's "SOS."

3

What is most striking about the way the poems under consideration —which I have suggested distill the logic of the Black Arts project— address themselves to the black community is their insistent use of the second-person pronoun. This aspect of the poetry is notable not only because it is the verbal indicator of the Black Arts poets' keen awareness of issues of audience and of their desire to appear to engage directly with their audience (both of which I have already alluded to), but because the *you* references also—and paradoxically, given the Black Aesthetic's nation-building agenda—represent the implication of intraracial division within its Black Arts strategy. It is clear, of course, that the use of the

19. Gayle, introduction, *The Black Aesthetic,* p. xxi.
20. Alain Locke, "Negro Youth Speaks," in *The Black Aesthetic,* p. 17.
21. Neal, "The Black Arts Movement," p. 273.

second-person pronoun of indefinite number implies less inclusiveness than would, say, the use of the first-person plural, *we*. What remains to be explored is exactly on what this apparent exclusivity—this implicit social division—is founded, both grammatically and historically, in order for us to grasp more fully the significance of Black Arts poetics.

The import of the second-person pronoun—both generally and in the specific context of Black Arts poetry—derives largely from its special grammatical status. Because *you* is a deictic, or shifter, whose reference varies among a multitude of different subjects, it is always necessary to anchor that reference before we can interpret any linguistic construction in which *you* appears. This would seem to be a relatively easy thing to accomplish, given that *you* is functionally fixed in a lexemic dyad through which its meaning is conditioned and focused. Émile Benveniste has elucidated the peculiar relation that obtains between the second-person pronoun and the first-person (singular) pronoun, emphasizing that "'you' is necessarily designated by 'I' and cannot be thought of outside a situation set up by starting with 'I.'"[22] Indeed, Benveniste suggests that these pronominal forms alone—exclusive of what we conventionally call the third-person pronoun—can properly be called personal because only the first and second persons are present in the discourse in which they are referenced. Having thus dismissed the genericized *he* as lacking this "sign of person," Benveniste then proposes a definition of *you* based on its inevitable relation to *I*, which itself always designates the speaking subject: "It is necessary and sufficient," he says, "that one envisage a *person* other than 'I' for the sign of 'you' to be assigned to that person. Thus every *person* that one imagines is of the 'you' form, especially, but not necessarily, the person being addressed 'you' can thus be [most accurately] defined as 'the non-*I* person.'"[23]

Once we specify the referential field for *you*, however, it becomes clear that the more problematic task is identifying the referent for any *I* with which we are confronted. For, while it may be true that *I* and *you* are defined against one another—with *I* representing the speaker of an utterance and *you* representing the "non-*I* person"—this mode of anchoring deictic reference is useful only for specifying the subject represented in discourse; it provides us with no information about the subject articulating that discourse, which is always only imperfectly identified with the former. As Antony Easthope puts it, deriving his formulation from Lacan, "the 'I' as represented in discourse . . . is always sliding away from the 'I' doing the speaking," which makes for a profound crisis of identity for the speaking subject, who constantly oscillates between identification with the *I* represented in discourse (the realm of the *imaginary* in Lacanian terms)

22. Émile Benveniste, *Problems in General Linguistics*, trans. Mary Elizabeth Meek (Coral Gables, Fla., 1971), p. 197.

23. Ibid., p. 201.

and recognition of the faultiness of such identification (the realm of the *symbolic*).[24]

Numerous commentators have discussed the ramifications of such post-structuralist theories of the subject for socially marginalized groups, whose political agendas have often been considered as based on a primary need to forge stable identities in the first place and not on the deconstruction of the possibility of such identity.[25] Certainly, the Black Arts movement can very readily be seen as representing the impulse to establish a positive black subjectivity—based on nationalist ideals—in the face of major sociopolitical impediments to its construction. But post-structuralism's positing of the always imperfect discursive constitution of the subjective *I* does not, I think, *prohibit* the Black Aesthetic's construction of a powerful black nationalist subject; it merely stipulates that such construction is possible only from a position externally and obliquely situated with respect to the discursive *I*. I *will* argue, however, that the disjuncture between this as yet unidentified position and the discursive *I* itself precludes the constitution of an effective black nationalist *collectivity*. This is because the strategy necessarily deployed by Black Arts poetry to establish a strong black nationalist subject—and through which it derives its meaning and power—is founded on the oppositional logic that governs the pronominal language characteristic of the work. That opposition is thematized in the poetry, not in terms of the us vs. them dichotomy that we might expect, however, with *us* representing blacks and *them* whites; rather, it is played out along the inherent opposition between *I* and *you*, both these terms deriving their referents from within the collectivity of black subjects. Thus, the project of Black Arts poetry can be understood as the establishment of black nationalist subjectivity—the forcible fixing of the identity of the speaking *I*—by delineating it against the "non-*I* person," the *you* whose identity is clearly predicated in the poems we are considering. So the *you* in Baraka's "Poem for Half White College Students" is the African-American who identifies with the Euro-American celebrity, against which the speaking *I* of the poem is implicitly contrasted. In Giovanni's and Lee's poems, *you* represents the Negro subject whose sense of self-worth and racial pride has yet to be proven. In Sanchez's "chant," *you* is the black junkie who finds solace in the "wite" high of heroin, clearly meant to be associated with Euro-American corruption. And in Jordan's "Okay, 'Negroes,'" *you* is the African-American who has not yet developed an understanding of the raciopolitical forces that impinge on black subjectivity. Clearly, I oversimplify to the extent that the referent of any given *you* might well vary even within a single poem. But my point is that

24. Antony Easthope, *Poetry as Discourse* (London, 1983), p. 44.

25. For example, Joyce A. Joyce objects to the use of post-structuralist theory in black literary criticism; see Joyce A. Joyce, "The Black Canon: Reconstructing Black American Literary Criticism," *New Literary History* 18 (Winter 1987): 335–44.

because, in spite of these shifts, the second person is much more readily identified than the speaking *I* for any utterance, any *you* that these Black Arts poets invoke can function as a negative foil against which the implicit *I* who speaks the poem can be distinguished as a politically aware, racially conscious, black nationalist subject. It seems to me that it is this intraracial division on which the Black Arts project is founded and not on any sense of inclusiveness with respect to the black community that we might discern in Baraka's "SOS."

Indeed, once we have clarified the *I-you* division that underlies the Black Arts concept of the black community, we can better understand the intraracial division that is implicit in movement references to the "black" subject itself. If it appears to us that Baraka's "SOS" embraces all members of the black diaspora, this is only because we are forgetting that the designation *black*, from the middle 1960s through the early 1970s, represented an emergent identification among nationalist activists and intellectuals and not a generic nomenclature by which any person of African descent might be referenced. Consequently, if Baraka is calling "all black people," he is already calling only those African-Americans whose political consciousness is sufficiently developed for them to subscribe to the designation *black* in the first place. All others—designated by *you* in the poems that utilize the pronominal rhetoric—will be considered as *negroes*, as in the titles of Giovanni's and Jordan's poems, a term that is intermittently transmuted into *niggers* in Giovanni's text.

4

Given these poems' authorization of their own black nationalist rhetoric, how then do we account for the historical and political factors in the movement's differentiation of the black body politic into disparate elements? Doesn't this division run counter to the solidarity we have taken to found black nationalism? Undoubtedly, a number of specific, local contingencies contributed to the development of the Black Arts movement's agenda and strategy. At the same time, it is possible, within the cultural-analytical context set up here, to identify a potential general motivation for the intraracial division so insistently deployed by Black Arts practitioners. That motivation is strongly related to the degree—noted above—to which Black Aestheticians of the 1960s sought to disassociate their movement from the Harlem Renaissance of the 1920s.

The Harlem Renaissance, apart from its evident cultural import, can be considered in sociopolitical terms as representing the culmination of a wave of black nationalist sentiment that lasted, according to Bracey, Meier, and Rudwick, from the 1880s until the onset of the Depression. During this period, they argue, "appeals to race pride and race unity became commonplace, and separate educational, religious, and economic institutions were more and more widely advocated" ("I," p. xl). On the other hand, they indicate the fundamentally ambiguous nature of this nationalist impulse by noting that these separatist appeals were mounted on behalf of a general accommodationist policy and not with a view toward ultimate black autonomy. They assert that while these separatist ideas "pervaded the spectrum of black social thought in the nineties and after the turn of the century . . . in general, they characterized the thinking of accommodators like Booker T. Washington more than that of protest leaders" ("I," p. xl). And they clarify further: "The ambiguous way in which nationalism has functioned in Negro thought was never more apparent than during this period. Almost always, except in the case of out-and-out colonization movements, separatism was advocated as a means of paving the way for full acceptance in American society" ("I," p. xli). To the degree that it conceived of this full acceptance as predicated on a Washingtonian *social* separatism (as opposed to the ostensibly empowering *political* and *economic* separatism espoused by the Black Power movement), and thus approximated alarmingly the agenda of segregationist whites, the racial solidarity impulse of the turn of the century would be entirely out of sync with the black nationalism of the 1960s, which was keenly sensitive to the possible cooptation of its agenda by white interests. Consequently, just as we can identify in the Black Arts movement the strong impulse to reject the cultural strategies of the Harlem Renaissance, so too was it characterized by a profound need to disassociate itself from the political objectives of the early black separatist movement. It intensely repudiated the influence of the elders.

Black Aestheticians also—as is already widely recognized—rejected the more immediate predecessor of the Black Power project, the Civil Rights movement of the 1950s and early 1960s. While the actual temporal relation between these two movements is more complex than that of mere consecutiveness—as is roughly emblematized in the overlap of the careers of Martin Luther King, Jr., and Malcolm X—Black Power has nonetheless consistently been represented as a radical *progression* from the less urgent strategies of civil protest. Thus the notion of historical advance strongly influenced the Black Power movement's sense of itself in relation to both turn-of-the-century and midcentury black political movements, and its need to present itself as historically distinct from these other movements can be discerned in the rhetoric of its poetic productions, the logic of which transmutes that historical differentiation into the highly self-defensive division of the contemporary black population into disparate segments.[26]

26. It is also possible that the intraracial division effected in Black Arts poetry is a function of the black community's status as a sort of mutated colonial entity. During the late 1960s, analyses of the colonialized nature of black communities in the U.S. were forthcoming from both social scientists and black activists. Indeed, in their introduction to *Black*

It is also true, to develop the point further and in a slightly different direction, that the identification and consequent strong rejection of a putatively ineffectual bourgeois accommodationism in whatever era of black social and political history must have been a necessary undertaking for a Black Arts movement characterized by an intense and potentially crippling middle-class *ressentiment.* The Black Aestheticians' strong consciousness of the need to appear rooted in the traditions of the folk was certainly not a new phenomenon among mass political movements, nor is it the case that movement intellectuals and the black masses were strictly dichotomized. Nevertheless, for a movement that emerged in opposition to nonviolent strategies that it represented as removed from the exigencies of everyday black existence, the threat of being perceived as similarly alienated loomed particularly large. It accounts, for instance, for the Black Aestheticians' characterization of the emergent black studies movement of the late 1960s and early 1970s as unacceptably "bourgie";[27] and the anxiety built up around this possibility is evident in Stokely Carmichael's injunction of 1966: "We have to say, 'Don't play jive and start writing poems after Malcolm is shot.' We have to move from the point where the man left off and stop writing poems."[28] Thus is made

---

Nationalism in America, the editors posit just such a conception of black America, citing as their justification some contemporary studies in sociology and political science. (See "I," p. lvi; among the material they cite, one article in particular clearly outlines the issues at stake in conceptualizing black communities as colonial entities. See also Robert Blauner, "Internal Colonialism and Ghetto Revolt," *Social Problems* 16 [Spring 1969]: 393–408.) Given this, it is interesting to note that Abdul R. JanMohamed has identified as one of the cultural manifestations of colonialism a mapping of the social entity along a Manichean duality that defines a morally "good" constituency—the colonizers, more often than not—against one that is seen as inherently "evil"—the colonized. See Abdul R. JanMohamed, *Manichean Aesthetics: The Politics of Literature in Colonial Africa* (Amherst, Mass., 1983) and "The Economy of Manichean Allegory: The Function of Racial Difference in Colonialist Literature," *Critical Inquiry* 12 (Autumn 1985): 59–87. While I do not believe that the situation of black Americans can be posited unproblematically as a colonial one, its historical sine qua non—the slave trade—can certainly be considered as a manifestation of the colonizing impulse. Consequently, it seems possible that, just as the economics of slavery developed in a particular manner after the initial appropriation of the "resources" from the African continent, there occurred concomitant mutations in the cultural realm in which we can still trace the remnants of an essential colonial logic. Thus, the *I-you* dichotomy that characterizes Black Arts poetry might represent the internalization within the black American community of the Manichean ethic that JanMohamed identifies with the colonial situation proper. It falls outside the scope of this essay to trace the various mechanisms through which this internalization might have been effected, but its possibility suggests a direction for further work on this topic.

27. A. B. Spellman, cited in James A. Emanuel, "Blackness Can: A Quest for Aesthetics," in *The Black Aesthetic,* p. 208.

28. Stokely Carmichael, "We Are Going to Use the Term 'Black Power' and We Are Going to Define It Because Black Power Speaks to Us" (1966), in *Black Nationalism in America,* p. 472.

clear the dominant sense of the suspect nature and relative ineffectuality of artistic and intellectual endeavors in the Black Power movement. It is a sense that is reiterated often in the poetry itself; for instance, Giovanni considers her inability to produce a "tree poem" or a "sky poem" in "For Saundra":

so i thought again
and it occurred to me
maybe i shouldn't write
at all
but clean my gun
and check my kerosene supply

perhaps these are not poetic
times
at all[29]

And, much less typically, Sanchez worries explicitly that black-power rhetoric will lead only to "blk / capitalism." It seems to me that it is the threatening unpredictability of exactly what will issue from nationalist organizing that accounts for Baraka's decision not to project beyond the call manifested in "SOS." The power of the work thus derives from the energy of the essential nationalist impulse itself and is not undermined by ambivalence regarding the different directions in which that impulse might develop.

Finally, I think that it is in order to quell such ambivalence that so much of the work employs a violent rhetoric, in which the mere repetition of references to killing the white enemy seems to be considered as the actual performance of the act. The positing of this violent rhetoric as performative language predicates the status of Black Arts poetry as being *heard* by whites and *over*heard by blacks. For if, in the performative logic of the Black Arts work, to be heard is to annihilate those persons who effect one's oppression, to be *over*heard is to impress upon one's peers just how righteous, how fearsome, how potently nationalistic one is, in contradistinction to those very peers who are figured as the direct addressee of the Black Arts works.

Which brings us back to where we began—with a consideration of conventional assessments of Black Arts poetry as primarily defined by its call for violence against whites. Clearly this rhetoric of violence, while certainly provoking various affective responses amongst white readers and auditors—responses that I don't pretend to address here—also represents the Black Arts movement's need to establish division *among blacks,* and, indeed, itself actually serves to produce such division. If we recognize

29. Giovanni, "For Saundra," p. 322.

the fundamental significance of this intraracial division to such black nationalism as is represented in the Black Arts project, then it seems to me that we are much closer to understanding the full social import of the nationalist imperative. Black Arts poetry can help us to do that because, as the most recent vital example of the nationalist impulse, it reflects the contradictions of the ideology in a particularly striking way. It behooves us to study those contradictions at this historical juncture as we begin to see in this country a new florescence of black nationalist consciousness whose cultural manifestations have yet to be fully realized and whose political ramifications have yet to be effectively theorized.

Black Writing, White Reading: Race and the Politics of Feminist Interpretation

Elizabeth Abel

1

> I realize that the set of feelings that I used to have about French men I now have about African-American women. Those are the people I feel inadequate in relation to and try to please in my writing. It strikes me that this is not just idiosyncratic.
>
> —Jane Gallop, "Criticizing Feminist Criticism"

Twyla opens the narrative of Toni Morrison's provocative story "Recitatif" (1982) by recalling her placement as an eight-year-old child in St. Bonaventure, a shelter for neglected children, and her reaction to Roberta Fisk, the roommate she is assigned: "The minute I walked in . . . I got sick to my stomach. It was one thing to be taken out of your own bed early in the morning—it was something else to be stuck in a strange place with a girl from a whole other race. And Mary, that's my mother, she was right. Every now and then she would stop dancing long enough to tell me something important and one of the things she said was that they never washed their hair and they smelled funny. Roberta sure did. Smell funny, I mean."[1] The racial ambiguity so deftly installed at the narrative's origin

1. Toni Morrison, "Recitatif," in *Confirmation: An Anthology of African American Women,* ed. Amiri Baraka (LeRoi Jones) and Amina Baraka (New York, 1983), p. 243; hereafter abbreviated "R." I am deeply indebted to Lula Fragd for bringing this story to my attention and to Toni Morrison for generously discussing it with me. I am also very grateful to Margaret Homans for sharing with me an early draft of "'Racial Composition': Metaphor

This article originally appeared in *Critical Inquiry* 19 (Spring 1993).

through codes that function symmetrically for black women and for white women ("they never washed their hair and they smelled funny") intensifies as the story tracks the encounters of its two female protagonists over approximately thirty years. Unmediated by the sexual triangulations (the predations of white men on black women, the susceptibility of black men to white women) that have dominated black women's narrative representations of women's fraught connections across racial lines, the relationship of Twyla and Roberta discloses the operations of race in the feminine.[2] This is a story about a black woman and a white woman; but which is which?

I was introduced to "Recitatif" by a black feminist critic, Lula Fragd. Lula was certain that Twyla was black; I was equally convinced that she was white; most of the readers we summoned to resolve the dispute divided similarly along racial lines. By replacing the conventional signifiers of racial difference (such as skin color) with radically relativistic ones (such as who smells funny to whom) and by substituting for the racialized body a series of disaggregated cultural parts—pink-scalloped socks, tight green slacks, large hoop earrings, expertise at playing jacks, a taste for Jimi Hendrix or for bottled water and asparagus—the story renders race a contested terrain variously mapped from diverse positions in the

and Body in the Writing of Race," which became central to my thinking on writing and race; and to Janet Adelman, John Bishop, Mitchell Breitwieser, Carolyn Dinshaw, Catherine Gallagher, Anne Goldman, Crystal Gromer, Dori Hale, Saidiya Hartman, Marianne Hirsch, Tania Modleski, Helene Moglen, Michael Rogin, Dianne Sadoff, Susan Schweik, Valerie Smith, Hortense Spillers, and Jean Wyatt for their helpful comments on this essay.

2. The intervention of white men in relationships between black and white women is repeatedly represented in slave narratives, best epitomized perhaps by Harriet Jacobs, *Incidents in the Life of a Slave Girl: Written by Herself* (1861); the intervention of white women in black heterosexual relationships is most fully explored in the civil rights fiction typified by Alice Walker, *Meridian* (1976). For a study of American literary representations of the relationships between black and white women in the nineteenth-century South, see Minrose C. Gwin, *Black and White Women of the Old South: The Peculiar Sisterhood in American Literature* (Knoxville, Tenn., 1985); for an optimistic characterization of interracial female friendships in recent American women's fiction, see Elizabeth Schultz, "Out of the Woods and into the World: A Study of Interracial Friendships between Women in American Novels," in *Conjuring: Black Women, Fiction, and Literary Tradition*, ed. Marjorie Pryse and Hortense J. Spillers (Bloomington, Ind., 1985), pp. 67–85.

Elizabeth Abel is associate professor of English at the University of California, Berkeley. She is the author of *Virginia Woolf and the Fictions of Psychoanalysis* (1989) and editor of *Writing and Sexual Difference* (1982). She is currently working on a book on race, gender, and representation.

social landscape. By forcing us to construct racial categories from highly ambiguous social cues, "Recitatif" elicits and exposes the unarticulated racial codes that operate at the boundaries of consciousness. To underscore the cultural specificity of these codes, Morrison writes into the text a figure of racial undecidability: Maggie, the mute kitchen worker at St. Bonaventure, who occasions the text's only mention of skin color, an explicitly ambiguous sandy color, and who walks through the text with her little kid's hat and her bowed legs "like parentheses," her silent self a blank parenthesis, a floating signifier ("R," p. 245). For both girls a hated reminder of their unresponsive mothers, Maggie is not "raced" to Twyla (that is, she is by default white); to Roberta, she is black. The two girls' readings of Maggie become in turn clues for our readings of them, readings that emanate similarly from our own cultural locations.

My own reading derived in part from Roberta's perception of Maggie as black; Roberta's more finely discriminating gaze ("she wasn't pitch-black, I knew," is all Twyla can summon to defend her assumption that Maggie is white) seemed to me to testify to the firsthand knowledge of discrimination ("R," p. 259). Similarly, Roberta is sceptical about racial harmony. When she and Twyla retrospectively discuss their tense encounter at a Howard Johnson's where Twyla was a waitress in the early 1960s, they read the historical context differently: "'Oh, Twyla, you know how it was in those days: black—white. You know how everything was.' But I didn't know. I thought it was just the opposite. Busloads of blacks and whites came into Howard Johnson's together. They roamed together then: students, musicians, lovers, protesters. You got to see everything at Howard Johnson's and blacks were very friendly with whites in those days" ("R," p. 255). In the civil rights movement that Twyla sees as a common struggle against racial barriers, Roberta sees the distrust of white intervention and the impulse toward a separatist Black Power movement: she has the insider's perspective on power and race relations.

It was a more pervasive asymmetry in authority, however, that secured my construction of race in the text, a construction I recount with considerable embarrassment for its possible usefulness in fleshing out the impulse within contemporary white feminism signalled by the "not just idiosyncratic" confession that stands as this paper's epigraph. As Gallop both wittily acknowledges the force of African-American women's political critique of white academic feminism's seduction by "French men" and, by simply transferring the transference, reenacts the process of idealization that unwittingly obscures more complex social relations, I singled out the power relations of the girls from the broader network of cultural signs.[3] Roberta seemed to me consistently the more sophisticated reader

3. *Transference* is Gallop's own term for her relation to black feminist critics. In her *Around 1981: Academic Feminist Literary Theory* (New York, 1992), esp. pp. 169–70, Gallop critiques the idealization and exoticization of black women, but she limits herself to making

of the social scene, the subject presumed by Twyla to know, the teller of the better (although not necessarily more truthful) stories, the adventurer whose casual mention of an appointment with Jimi Hendrix exposes the depths of Twyla's social ignorance ("'Hendrix? Fantastic,' I said. 'Really fantastic. What's she doing now?'" ["R," p. 250]). From the girls' first meeting at St. Bonaventure, Twyla feels vulnerable to Roberta's judgment and perceives Roberta (despite her anxiety about their differences) as possessing something she lacks and craves: a more acceptably negligent mother (a sick one rather than a dancing one) and, partially as a consequence, a more compelling physical presence that fortifies her cultural authority. Twyla is chronically hungry; Roberta seems to her replete, a daughter who has been adequately fed and thus can disdain the institutional Spam and Jell-O that Twyla devours as a contrast to the popcorn and Yoo-Hoo that had been her customary fare. The difference in maternal stature, linked in the text with nurture, structures Twyla's account of visiting day at St. Bonaventure. Twyla's mother, smiling and waving "like she was the little girl," arrives wearing tight green buttocks-hugging slacks and a ratty fur jacket for the chapel service, and bringing no food for the lunch that Twyla consequently improvises out of fur-covered jelly beans from her Easter basket ("R," p. 246). "Bigger than any man," Roberta's mother arrives bearing a huge cross on her chest, a Bible in the crook of her arm, and a basket of chicken, ham, oranges, and chocolate-covered graham crackers ("R," p. 247). In the subsequent Howard Johnson scene that Twyla's retrospective analysis links with the frustrations of visiting day ("The wrong food is always with the wrong people. Maybe that's why I got into waitress work later—to match up the right people with the right food" ["R," p. 248]) the difference in stature is replayed between the two daughters. Roberta, sitting in a booth with "two guys smothered in head and facial hair," her own hair "so big and wild I could hardly see her face," wearing a "powder-blue halter and shorts outfit and earrings the size of bracelets," rebuffs Twyla, clad in her waitress outfit, her knees rather than her midriff showing, her hair in a net, her legs in thick stockings and sturdy white shoes ("R," p. 249). Although the two bodies are never directly represented, the power of metonymy generates a contrast between the amplitude of the sexualized body and the skimpiness and pallor of the socially harnessed body. Twyla's sense of social and physical inadequacy vis-à-vis Roberta, like her representation of her mother's inferiority to Roberta's, signalled Twyla's whiteness to me by articulating a

---

the transference conscious rather than positing alternatives to it. In "Transferences: Gender and Race: The Practice of Theory," delivered at the University of California, Berkeley, 3 Apr. 1992, Deborah E. McDowell, who had inadvertently occasioned Gallop's comments about transference, deliberately spoke back from, and thereby exploded, the position of the transferential object.

white woman's fantasy (my own) about black women's potency.[4] This fantasy's tenaciousness is indicated by its persistence in the face of contrary evidence. Roberta's mother, the story strongly implies, is mentally rather than physically ill, her capacity to nurture largely fictional; Roberta, who is never actually represented eating, is more lastingly damaged than Twyla by maternal neglect, more vulnerable as an adult to its memory, a weakness on which Twyla capitalizes during their political conflicts as adults; the tenuousness of the adult Roberta's own maternal status (she acquires stepchildren, rather than biological children, through her marriage to an older man) may also testify figuratively to a lack created by insufficient mothering.

Pivoting not on skin color, but on size, sexuality, and the imagined capacity to nurture and be nurtured, on the construction of embodiedness itself as a symptom and source of cultural authority, my reading installs the (racialized) body at the center of a text that deliberately withholds conventional racial iconography. Even in her reading of this first half of the story, Lula's interpretation differed from mine by emphasizing cultural practices more historically nuanced than my categorical distinctions in body types, degrees of social cool, or modes of mothering. Instead of reading Twyla's body psychologically as white, Lula read Twyla's name as culturally black; and she placed greater emphasis on Roberta's language in the Howard Johnson scene—her primary locution being a decidedly white hippie "Oh, wow"—than on the image of her body gleaned by reading envy in the narrative gaze and by assigning racial meaning to such cultural accessories as the Afro, hoop earrings, and a passion for Jimi Hendrix that actually circulated independently of race throughout the counterculture of the 1960s; as Lula knew and I did not, Jimi Hendrix appealed more to white than to black audiences.[5] Roberta's coldness in this scene—she barely acknowledges her childhood friend—becomes, in

4. The "not just idiosyncratic" nature of this fantasy is suggested by Gallop's accounts in "Tongue Work" and "The Coloration of Academic Feminism" in *Around 1981,* pp. 143–76 and 67–74, and, by extension through the analogies she draws between constructions of race and class, in "Annie Leclerc Writing a Letter, with Vermeer," in *The Poetics of Gender,* ed. Nancy K. Miller (New York, 1986), pp. 137–56. In her analysis of the black woman's telling role in Joan Micklin Silver's film *Crossing Delancey,* Tania Modleski outlines an especially exploitative enactment of this fantasy; see Tania Modleski, *Feminism without Women: Culture and Criticism in a "Postfeminist" Age* (New York, 1991), pp. 129–30. In Richard Dyer, "Paul Robeson: Crossing Over," *Heavenly Bodies: Film Stars and Society* (London, 1986), Dyer succinctly summarizes the most pervasive, nongendered version of this fantasy: "Black and white discourses on blackness seem to be valuing the same things—spontaneity, emotion, naturalness—yet giving them a different implication. Black discourses see them as contributions to the development of society, white as enviable qualities that only blacks have" (p. 79).

5. On the general phenomenon of black innovation and white imitation in postwar American culture, see Kobena Mercer, "Black Hair/Style Politics," *New Formations* 3 (Winter 1987): 33–54.

Lula's reading, a case of straightforward white racism, and Twyla's surprise at the rebuff reflects her naivete about the power of personal loyalties and social movements to undo racial hierarchies.

More importantly, however, this scene was not critical for Lula's reading. Instead of the historical locus that was salient for me—not coincidentally, I believe, since the particular aura of (some) black women for (some) white women during the civil rights movement is being recapitulated in contemporary feminism (as I will discuss later)—what was central to her were scenes from the less culturally exceptional 1970s, which disclosed the enduring systems of racism rather than the occasional moments of heightened black cultural prestige. In general, Lula focussed less on cultural than on economic status, and she was less concerned with daughters and their feelings toward their mothers than with these daughters' politics after they are mothers.

When Twyla and Roberta meet in a food emporium twelve years after the Howard Johnson scene, Twyla has married a fireman and has one child and limited income; Roberta has married an IBM executive and lives in luxury in the wealthy part of town with her husband, her four stepchildren, and her Chinese chauffeur. Twyla concludes in a voice of seemingly racial resentment: "Everything is so easy for them. They think they own the world" ("R," p. 252). A short time later the women find themelves on opposite sides of a school integration struggle in which both their children are faced with bussing: Twyla's to the school that Roberta's stepchildren now attend, and Roberta's to a school in a less affluent neighborhood. After Twyla challenges Roberta's opposition to the bussing, Roberta tries to defuse the conflict: "'Well, it is a free country.' 'Not yet, but it will be,'" Twyla responds ("R," p. 256). Twyla's support of bussing, and of social change generally, and Roberta's self-interested resistance to them position the women along the bitter racial lines that split the fraying fabric of feminism in the late 1970s and early 1980s.[6]

Privileging psychology over politics, my reading disintegrates in the story's second half. Lula's reading succeeds more consistently, yet by constructing the black woman (in her account, Twyla) as the politically correct but politically naive and morally conventional foil to the more socially adventurous, if politically conservative, white woman (Roberta), it problematically racializes the moral (op)positions Morrison opens to revaluation in her extended (and in many ways parallel) narrative of female friendship, *Sula*.[7] Neither reading can account adequately for the text's

6. For a particularly powerful statement of the disenchantment bred among women of color by white women's opposition to bussing, see Nikki Giovanni, "Why Weren't Our 'Sisters in Liberation' in Boston?" *Encore,* 6 Jan. 1975, p. 20.

7. By tracing the course of a friendship from girlhood through adulthood, "Recitatif" filters the narrative of *Sula* (1973) through the lens of race, replacing the novel's sexual triangulation with the tensions of racial difference. It is hard for me to imagine that the critical question that Sula, Roberta's knowing, transgressive counterpart, poses to Nel—"How

contradictory linguistic evidence, for if Twyla's name is more characteristically black than white, it is perhaps best known as the name of a white dancer, Twyla Tharp, whereas Roberta shares her last name, Fisk, with a celebrated black (now integrated) university. The text's heterogeneous inscriptions of race resist a totalizing reading.

Propelled by this irresolution to suspend my commitment to the intentional fallacy, I wrote to Toni Morrison. Her response raised as many questions as it resolved. Morrison explained that her project in this story was to substitute class for racial codes in order to drive a wedge between these typically elided categories.[8] Both eliciting and foiling our assumption that Roberta's middle-class marriage and politics, and Twyla's working-class perspective, are reliable racial clues, Morrison incorporated details about their husbands' occupations that encourage an alternative conclusion. If we are familiar (as I was not) with IBM's efforts to recruit black executives and with the racial exclusiveness of the firemen's union in upstate New York, where the story is set, we read Roberta as middle-class black and Twyla as working-class white. Roberta's resistance to bussing, then, is based on class rather than racial loyalties: she doesn't want her (middle-class black) stepchildren bussed to a school in a (white) working-class neighborhood; Twyla, conversely, wants her (white) working-class child bussed to a middle-class school (regardless of that school's racial composition). What we hear, from this perspective, in Twyla's envy of Roberta, "Everything is so easy for them," and in her challenge to the status quo—it's not a free country "but it will be"—is class rather than (or perhaps compounded by) racial resentment, the adult economic counterpart to Twyla's childhood fantasy of Roberta's plenitude.

By underscoring the class-based evidence for reading Twyla as white, Morrison confirms at once my own conclusion and its fantasmatic basis. Morrison's weighting of social detail, her insistence on the intersections, however constructed, between race and class, are more closely aligned with Lula's political perspective than with my psychological reading, fueled by racially specific investments that the text deliberately solicits

---

do you know? . . . About who was good. How do you know it was you?"—could be translated, in "Recitatif," into a white woman's challenge to a woman of color (Morrison, *Sula* [New York, 1973], p. 146).

8. In this exchange (November 1990), Morrison provided a more detailed account of her intentions than she does in her only (and very recently) published comment on the story, in the preface to her *Playing in the Dark: Whiteness and the Literary Imagination* (Cambridge, Mass., 1992): "The kind of work I have always wanted to do requires me to learn how to maneuver ways to free up the language from its sometimes sinister, frequently lazy, almost always predictable employment of racially informed and determined chains. (The only short story I have ever written, 'Recitatif,' was an experiment in the removal of all racial codes from a narrative about two characters of different races for whom racial identity is crucial)" (p. xi).

and exposes. By both inviting and challenging racialized readings that are either "right" for the "wrong" reasons or "wrong" for the "right" ones, "Recitatif" focusses some questions to address to the massive, asymmetrical crossing of racial boundaries in recent feminist criticism. If white feminist readings of black women's texts disclose white critical fantasies, what (if any) value do these readings have—and for whom?[9] How do white women's readings of black women's biological bodies inform our readings of black women's textual bodies? How do different critical discourses both inflect and inscribe racial fantasies? What rhetorical strategies do these discourses produce, and (how) do these strategies bear on the value of the readings they ostensibly legitimate?

Black feminists have debated the politics and potential of white feminists' critical intervention, but they have not compared or critiqued specific reading strategies, which is perhaps more properly a task of white self-criticism.[10] This essay attempts to contribute to this task by examining signal moments, across a range of discourses, in the white critical texts

9. Although I realize that by isolating white / black dynamics of reading from white feminist readings of texts by other women of color I am reinforcing the unfortunate collapse of "color" and "black," encompassing such a diverse textual field within a single analysis would blur important differences. In contrast, for example, to black feminist complaints about the white feminist misrecognition of the politics and language of black feminism, Norma Alarcón protests the Anglo-American feminist resistance to granting theoretical status to the multiple-voiced subjectivity of women of color; see Norma Alarcón, "The Theoretical Subject(s) of *This Bridge Called My Back* and Anglo-American Feminism," in *Making Face, Making Soul: Haciendo Caras,* ed. Gloria Anzaldúa (San Francisco, 1990), pp. 356–69. For a different perception of white feminism's response to the multiple voicing characterizing texts by women of color, see Teresa de Lauretis, "Eccentric Subjects: Feminist Theory and Historical Consciousness," *Feminist Studies* 16 (Spring 1990): 115–50.

10. The strongest questions about, although not unqualified opposition to, white feminist readings of black women's texts have been posed by bell hooks. See, for example, bell hooks [Gloria Watkins], "Critical Interrogation: Talking Race, Resisting Racism," *Inscriptions* 5 (1989): 159–62, and "Feminism and Racism: The Struggle Continues," *Zeta* (July-Aug. 1990): 41–43; see also Patricia Hill Collins, "The Social Construction of Black Feminist Thought," *Signs* 14 (Summer 1989): 745–73. For some more positive perspectives, see Valerie Smith, "Black Feminist Theory and the Representation of the 'Other,'" in *Changing Our Own Words: Essays on Criticism, Theory, and Writing by Black Women,* ed. Cheryl A. Wall (New Brunswick, N.J., 1989), pp. 38–57; Hazel V. Carby, *Reconstructing Womanhood: The Emergence of the Afro-American Woman Novelist* (New York, 1987), chap. 1; Michele Wallace, "Who Owns Zora Neale Hurston? Critics Carve Up the Legend," in *Invisibility Blues: From Pop to Theory* (London, 1990), pp. 179–80; Barbara Christian, "But What Do We Think We're Doing Anyway: The State of Black Feminist Criticism(s) or My Version of a Little Bit of History," in *Changing Our Own Words,* pp. 67, 73; and hooks, *Talking Back: Thinking Feminist, Thinking Black* (Boston, 1989), chap. 7. For a trenchant black male critique of the racial privilege concealed behind the self-referential gestures of some white male commentators on African-American texts, see Michael Awkward, "Negotiations of Power: White Critics, Black Texts, and the Self-Referential Impulse," *American Literary History* 2 (Winter 1990): 581–606. See also Kenneth W. Warren, "From under the Superscript: A Response to Michael Awkward," and Awkward, "The Politics of Positionality: A Reply to Kenneth Warren," *American Literary History* 4 (Spring 1992): 97–109.

emerging with such volume and intensity within contemporary feminism. By "contemporary" I mean since 1985, a watershed year that marked the simultaneous emergence of what has been called postfeminism and, not coincidentally, of pervasive white feminist attention to texts by women of color.[11] This new attentiveness was overdetermined: by the sheer brilliance and power of this writing and its escalating status in the literary marketplace and, consequently, the academy; by white feminist restlessness with an already well-mined white female literary tradition; and by the internal logic of white feminism's trajectory through theoretical discourses that, by evacuating the referent from the signifier's play, fostered a turn to texts that reassert the authority of experience, that reinstate political agency, and that rearticulate the body and its passions. The end of the most confident and ethnocentric period of the second wave (roughly 1970–1985) has interestingly collapsed postfeminism and prefeminism as the ideological frameworks in which white women turn to black women to articulate a politics and to embody a discursive authority that are either lost or not yet found. Like Frances D. Gage's perception of Sojourner Truth rescuing the faltering 1851 Women's Rights conference in Akron through the power of her physical presence and resounding question, "A'n't I a woman?" which took "us up in her strong arms and

11. In "Feminism, 'Postfeminism,' and Contemporary Women's Fiction," in *Tradition and the Talents of Women*, ed. Florence Howe (Urbana, Ill., 1991), pp. 268–91, Deborah Silverton Rosenfelt proposes 1985 as the date of postfeminism's emergence and defines the phenomenon succinctly as the "uneven incorporation and revision [of feminism] inside the social and cultural texts of a more conservative era" (p. 269). For a more negative assessment of postfeminism, and a broader location of its origins in the mid-1980s, see Gayle Greene, *Changing the Story: Feminist Fiction and the Tradition* (Bloomington, Ind., 1991), esp. part 3. In selecting 1985 as the watershed year in white feminists' engagement with questions of racial location, I am building on Miller's suggestion in the conversation held between Miller, Marianne Hirsch, and Jane Gallop, published under the title "Criticizing Feminist Criticism," in *Conflicts in Feminism*, ed. Hirsch and Evelyn Fox Keller (New York, 1990), p. 359. In 1985 *Conjuring*, the first anthology of literary criticism coedited by a black woman and a white woman, was published. The same year *The Color Purple* was selected as the focus for a collective presentation at the sixth annual British conference on "Literature/Teaching/Politics"; this presentation culminated in several white feminist essays on the novel. This year also witnessed the first serious white British feminist response to critiques by women of color; see Michèle Barrett and Mary McIntosh, "Ethnocentrism and Socialist-Feminist Theory," *Feminist Review*, no. 20 (June 1985): 23–47; for four different responses to this essay, see Caroline Ramazanoglu, Hamida Kazi, Sue Lees, and Heidi Safia Mirza, "Feedback: Feminism and Racism," *Feminist Review*, no. 22 (Feb. 1986): 83–105, and Kum-Kum Bhavnani and Margaret Coulson, "Transforming Socialist-Feminism: The Challenge of Racism," *Feminist Review*, no. 23 (June 1986): 81–92. Another way to mark the shift occurring in 1985 is to contrast the semantic fields of two identical titles: *Between Women: Biographers, Novelists, Critics, Teachers, and Artists Write about Their Work on Women*, ed. Carol Ascher, Louise DeSalvo, and Sara Ruddick (Boston, 1984), about the enabling identification between women writers and the women about whom they write, and Judith Rollins, *Between Women: Domestics and Their Employers* (Philadelphia, 1985), about the conflicts between white women and the black women who work for them.

carried us safely over the slough of difficulty turning the whole tide in our favor"; or, in one of the generative contexts for the second wave of feminism, like Jane Stembridge's discovery of a miraculously unashamed mode of female speech in Fanny Lou Hamer's proud bearing and voice at a 1964 SNCC rally—"Mrs. Hamer . . . knows that she is good. . . . If she didn't know that . . . she wouldn't stand there, with her head back and sing! She couldn't speak the *way* that she speaks and the way she speaks is this: she announces. I do not announce. I apologize"; the postfeminist turn to black women novelists enacts an anxious transference onto black women's speech.[12]

As Valerie Smith has eloquently argued, the attempt to rematerialize an attenuated white feminism by routing it through black women's texts reproduces in the textual realm white women's historical relation to the black female bodies that have nurtured them.[13] This relation unfolds along a spectrum of materiality. More complex than its prefeminist analogue, contemporary white feminism invokes black women's texts not only to relegitimate the feminist agenda called into question by post-structuralism but also, paradoxically, to relegitimate post-structuralism by finding its prefiguration in black women's texts. Yet whether as a corrective difference or a confirming similarity, as a sanction for a renewed or a resuspended referentiality, black women writers are enlisted to bestow a cultural authority that derives in part from their enforced experience of embodiment.

To attempt to do justice to the spectrum of white feminist approaches, I have organized this study through three case studies that, although far from exhaustive, nevertheless offer a range of influential discourses: deconstruction, psychoanalysis, and cultural criticism. This sequence traces a trajectory from a strategy that seems able to escape my own fantasmatic production of an embodied other to one that unexpectedly reproduces it. My conclusion will turn to the conclusion of "Recitatif" to reopen the question of reading and race.

12. I am following Phyllis Marynick Palmer's wonderful reading of Sojourner Truth's role at the Akron Women's Rights convention in "White Women/Black Women: The Dualism of Female Identity and Experience in the United States," *Feminist Studies* 9 (Spring 1983): 151, 153. Palmer quotes from Frances D. Gage, "The Akron Convention," in *The Feminist Papers: From Adams to de Beauvoir,* ed. Alice Rossi (New York, 1974), p. 429. Paula Giddings cites Jane Stembridge's reaction to Fanny Lou Hamer in her *When and Where I Enter: The Impact of Black Women on Race and Sex in America* (New York, 1984), p. 301. For SNCC's complex role in catalyzing the second wave of a white feminist movement, see chap. 17, and Sara Evans, *Personal Politics: The Roots of Women's Liberation in the Civil Rights Movement and the New Left* (New York, 1979). In *Meridian* and in "Advancing Luna—and Ida B. Wells" (1977), Walker offers narrative accounts of white women's predatory relation to a movement that gave them the illusion of purposefulness.

13. See Valerie Smith, "Black Feminist Theory and the Representation of the 'Other,'" in *Changing Our Own Words,* pp. 38–57.

2

> The nonblack feminist critic/theorist who honestly engages his or her own autobiographical implication in a brutal past is likely to provide nuances such as that of the black feminist critic. What, however, are the preconditions and precautions for the nonblack feminist critic/theorist who dares to undertake such a project?
>
> —MAE G. HENDERSON, response to Houston A. Baker, Jr., "There Is No More Beautiful Way"

Through the exchanges between Derrida and Lacan, we have become familiar with the debate between deconstruction and psychoanalysis over the discursive construction of subjectivity. Recent work by two prominent white feminist theorists, Barbara Johnson and Margaret Homans, suggests how this debate plays out in the related question of the discursive construction of race: a question especially urgent for critics reading and writing across racial lines.

Because it directly poses the question of the white reader's relation to the African-American text and because it has widely influenced readings of Zora Neale Hurston in particular, and of race in general, "Thresholds of Difference: Structures of Address in Zora Neale Hurston" is an apt focus for a study of Barbara Johnson's textual strategies.[14] "Thresholds" mounts an enormously complex and brilliant critique of the belief in essential racial differences that for Johnson is the substance of racism. (Arguing that black representations of a black essence always operate within a "specific interlocutionary situation" and are "matters of strategy rather than truth," Johnson brackets the question of a possible black belief in, or desire for belief in, a black identity ["T," p. 285]). Through a read-

14. See Barbara Johnson, "Thresholds of Difference: Structures of Address in Zora Neale Hurston," *Critical Inquiry* 12 (Autumn 1985): 278-89; hereafter abbreviated "T." For evidence of this essay's influence, see Angela P. Harris, "Race and Essentialism in Feminist Legal Theory," *Stanford Law Review* 42 (Feb. 1990): 581–616; Priscilla Wald, "Becoming 'Colored': The Self-Authorized Language of Difference in Zora Neale Hurston," *American Literary History* 2 (Spring 1990): 79–100; Wallace, "Who Owns Zora Neale Hurston?" pp. 172–86; Tamar Katz, "'Show Me How to Do Like You': Didacticism and Epistolary Form in *The Color Purple*," in *Alice Walker*, ed. Harold Bloom (New York, 1989), esp. pp. 191–92. The race of the reader is not an issue in "Thresholds"'s companion piece, published the year before, "Metaphor, Metonymy, and Voice in *Their Eyes Were Watching God*," in *Black Literature and Literary Theory*, ed. Henry Louis Gates, Jr. (New York, 1984), pp. 205–15, in which gender performs a more critical role than race; similarly, in her "Apostrophe, Animation, and Abortion," *A World of Difference* (Baltimore, 1987), pp. 184–99, another outstanding essay on structures of address, differences in gender occlude racial differences, which are theorized for neither the poets nor the critic. In Johnson's other African-American essays, such as "Euphemism, Understatement, and the Passive Voice: A Genealogy of Afro-American Poetry" and "The Re(a)d and the Black," in *Reading Black, Reading Feminist: A Critical Anthology*, ed. Gates (New York, 1990), pp. 204–11 and 145–54, the racial position of the reader is similarly bracketed.

ing of three Hurston texts—"How It Feels to Be Colored Me" (1928); "What White Publishers Won't Print" (1950); and *Mules and Men* (1935)—Johnson maps the interlocutionary situations that generate Hurston's ambiguous and contradictory representations of racial identity and difference. Rather than a constant, color (which figures race for both Hurston and Johnson) varies with positions in discursive exchanges whose subversion of the difference between inside and outside, self and other, is detailed in Johnson's reading of Hurston's complex relation as a northern anthropologist to the southern black communities whose folklore (or "lies") she represents in *Mules and Men.* By anticipating and legitimating the project of dereferentializing race, and by relocating differences between the races as internal differences (as in her celebrated figure of resemblances among the heterogeneous contents of differently colored bags), Hurston—or the Hurston represented by these particular texts—is a deconstructive critic's dream.[15]

In the body of the essay, Johnson and Hurston seem to speak in a single voice, but the two voices occasionally diverge, and through their divergence the essay interrogates the politics of interracial reading. Paralleling the "multilayered envelope of address" with which Hurston frames the folktales of *Mules and Men,* Johnson frames her own readings with an analysis of her position as a "white deconstructor" interpreting a "black novelist and anthropologist" ("T," p. 278). As her language indicates, the frame deploys the rhetoric of racial essences the rest of the essay deconstructs. In addressing (as does Hurston's frame) the politics of a discourse on race, the frame also demonstrates their effects: the interlocutory situation of a white reading of a black text demands some acknowledgement of racial differences. The essay thus deploys a schizophrenic discourse, split between a first-person discourse on the politics of discourse across race and a third-person discourse on the discursive (de)construction of race. The discursive position of a "white deconstructor" of race is self-different, embracing both the assertion and the deconstruction of difference, positions the text constructs as white and black, respectively.

These positions, however, are themselves unstable. Through what

15. The Hurston represented by other texts fulfills other critical dreams. See, for example, Mary Helen Washington, foreword, *Their Eyes Were Watching God* (1937; New York, 1990), pp. vii–xiv, and Walker, "On Refusing to Be Humbled by Second Place in a Contest You Did Not Design: A Tradition by Now" and "Looking for Zora," in Zora Neale Hurston, *I Love Myself When I Am Laughing . . . and Then Again When I Am Looking Mean and Impressive: A Zora Neale Hurston Reader,* ed. Walker (New York, 1979), pp. 1–5, 297–313, and "Foreword: Zora Neale Hurston—A Cautionary Tale and a Partisan View," in Robert E. Hemenway, *Zora Neale Hurston: A Literary Biography* (Urbana, Ill., 1977), pp. xi–xviii. In *I Love Myself When I Am Laughing,* Walker describes "How It Feels to Be Colored Me" as "an excellent example of Zora Neale Hurston at her most exasperating" (p. 151). For a black feminist reading that is closer to Johnson's, but is routed through Bakhtin instead of Derrida, see Mae Gwendolyn Henderson, "Speaking in Tongues: Dialogics, Dialectics, and the Black Woman Writer's Literary Tradition," in *Changing Our Own Words,* pp. 16–37.

becomes an excess of politicized rhetoric in the frame, read retrospectively against the text's interior, the differences between outside and inside, first person and third person, white and black, collapse and with them the tension between politics and deconstruction. If the questioning of motive and audience in the frame's opening paragraph are to be taken straight, the response the next paragraph offers is far more problematic: "It was as though I were asking her [Hurston] for answers to questions I did not even know I was unable to formulate. I had a lot to learn, then, from Hurston's way of dealing with multiple agendas and heterogeneous implied readers" ("T," p. 278). The deference to Hurston seems as disingenuous as Hurston's comparably located and requisite expressions of gratitude to her white patron, Mrs. Osgood Mason; for as much as Johnson has to learn from Hurston about strategic discursive constructions of race, she has little to learn from her about strategies of discourse generally; far from a humble student or innocent reader with no anterior agendas of her own, she constitutes Hurston as much in her own deconstructive image as she is herself reconstituted by Hurston's texts.[16] Yet read in the context of Johnson's reading of *Mules and Men,* the dissembling rhetoric of the frame becomes a deliberate imitation of Hurston's imitation of the strategy of "lying" that she learns from the Eatonville residents who, weary of white folks prying into their ways, set verbal "'toy(s)'" "'outside the door[s]'" of their minds to distract and deceive their white investigators ("T," p. 286). If, as Johnson argues, "it is impossible to tell whether Hurston the narrator is *describing* a strategy [of lying] or *employing* one" since "Hurston's very ability to fool us—or to fool us into *thinking* we have been fooled—is itself the only effective way of conveying the rhetoric of the 'lie,'" Johnson's ability to fool us functions analogously as a rhetorical tool that, once we have understood its calculated impact, transports us along with both Hurston and Johnson from the outside to the inside of Eatonville's discursive universe ("T," pp. 286, 289).

The fluidity of this boundary transgression, however, conceals an important difference between Hurston crossing the boundaries between subject and object, North and South, literate and oral communities, and Johnson or her white readers crossing a racial boundary. In the course of Johnson's essay, a discourse on positionality comes to displace, as well as to produce, a discourse on race. As the frame slides into the interior, the questions it raises disappear. There is no further problem about a white deconstructor writing about, or writing as, a black novelist and anthropologist, since position has come to stand for race. This erasure of conflict is clear when the frame briefly returns at the end, merging Johnson's and Hurston's voices in the single conclusion that "the terms 'black' and 'white,' 'inside' and 'outside,' continue to matter" only as diversely inhab-

16. For a similar critique, see Tzvetan Todorov, "'Race,' Writing, and Culture," in *"Race," Writing, and Difference,* ed. Gates (Chicago, 1986), pp. 379–80.

ited and mutually constitutive positions on a signifying chain ("T," p. 289). By dislocating race from historically accreted differences in power, Johnson's deconstructive reading dovetails with Hurston's libertarian politics.[17]

In Johnson's discourse on gender, by contrast, her feminist politics enforce a distinction, political rather than metaphysical, between the positions inhabited by men and women: "Jacques Derrida may sometimes see himself as *philosophically* positioned as a woman, but he is not *politically* positioned as a woman. Being positioned as a woman is not something that is entirely voluntary." The shift from gender to race in the next sentence—"Or, to put it another way, if you tell a member of the Ku Klux Klan that racism is a repression of self-difference, you are likely to learn a thing or two about repression"—bypasses the racial analogy to the problematic masculine (= white) assumption of a figuratively feminine (= black) position to insinuate the reaction of the racist that places the white deconstructor in a position of vulnerability akin to (rather than politically distinct from) the black person's position.[18] Similarly, Johnson distinguishes more firmly between the figurative and the literal in relation to gender than to race: "the revaluation of the *figure* of the woman by a male author cannot substitute for the actual participation of women in the literary conversation. Mallarmé may be able to speak from the place of the silenced woman, but as long as *he* is occupying it, the silence that is broken in theory is maintained in reality."[19] Johnson's relentlessly deconstructive discourse on race subverts the equivalent gestures that would subject her own role as a white deconstructor to her critique of masculine deconstructions of gender. This difference within her practice of deconstruction, the undoing of a counterpart for race to the feminist resistance to deconstruction, facilitates the project of writing across race. The interlocutory situa-

17. Hurston's resistance to considering race a sociopolitical obstacle to success recurs throughout her writing. For example, she asserts: "I do not belong to the sobbing school of Negrohood who hold that nature somehow has given them a lowdown dirty deal and whose feelings are all hurt about it. . . . I have seen that the world is to the strong regardless of a little pigmentation more or less. No, I do not weep at the world—I am too busy sharpening my oyster knife" (Hurston, "How It Feels to Be Colored Me," *I Love Myself When I Am Laughing*, p. 153). Similar claims pervade her autobiography, *Dust Tracks on a Road* (1942). For an analysis of Hurston's racial politics, see Hemenway, *Zora Neale Hurston*, esp. chap. 11. For a different reading of Johnson's position in this essay, see Awkward, "Negotiations of Power," 603–4.

18. Johnson, introduction, *A World of Difference*, pp. 2–3.

19. Johnson, "Les Fleurs du Mal Armé: Some Reflections on Intertexuality," *A World of Difference*, p. 131. As the paragraph continues, Johnson qualifies, but does not undo, the figurative / literal distinction. The pressures created by Johnson's racial position are visible in her differences of emphasis from the Afro-Americanist whose position on race is closest, indeed very close, to her own: Henry Louis Gates, Jr.; see, for example, her response to Gates's "Canon-Formation, Literary History, and the Afro-American Tradition: From the Seen to the Told," in *Afro-American Literary Study in the 1990s*, ed. Houston A. Baker, Jr., and Patricia Redmond (Chicago, 1989), pp. 14–38, 39–44.

tion that requires the white critic to acknowledge racial difference also requires her to dissolve the tension between literal and figurative, political and philosophical, voluntary and involuntary modes of sameness and difference.

Johnson's essay first appeared in the 1985 special issue of *Critical Inquiry* entitled "*'Race,' Writing, and Difference,*" edited by Henry Louis Gates, Jr., whose position on the figurative status of race is signalled by the quotation marks with which he encloses the word; Johnson's essay conforms clearly to that volume's ideology. Gates has been criticized for the politics of his deconstruction of race, and some of the most passionate criticism has been launched by black feminists. Following one of these women, Joyce A. Joyce, Margaret Homans argues compellingly in a recent essay, "'Racial Composition': Metaphor and the Body in the Writing of Race," that Gates's, and thus by extension Johnson's, deliteralization of race is effectively a masculinist position.[20] The difference between Johnson and Homans derives to a significant degree from the shift from deconstruction to psychoanalysis and the consequent shift from the inside/outside opposition privileged by deconstruction to that between body and language, or the literal and the figurative, which psychoanalysis genders oppositely from deconstruction. Whereas for Johnson, playing primarily off Derrida, figuration enacts an emancipatory feminine displacement of phallogocentric reference, for Homans, playing off Lacan and Chodorow, figuration enacts a masculine displacement of the specifically female (maternal) body whose exclusion founds the symbolic register. Whereas for Johnson the figurativeness of race is enabling for all races, for Homans it enables only men, since women across race accede to figuration only by devaluing the femaleness that is culturally conflated with the body. Paradoxically, however, both positions serve to legitimate

20. "Racial Composition': Metaphor and the Body in the Writing of Race" was delivered as a talk at the conference on "Psychoanalysis in African-American Contexts" at the University of California, Santa Cruz, 23–25 October 1992; hereafter abbreviated "RC." Although my brief summary does not do justice to the altered version appearing in *Female Subjects in Black and White,* I have selected the earlier version because it offers such an illuminating counterpart to Johnson's essay. For some earlier examples of Homans's writing on African-American women's texts, see Margaret Homans, "'Her Very Own Howl': The Ambiguities of Representation in Recent Women's Fiction," *Signs* 9 (Winter 1983): 186–205, which is primarily concerned with negotiating tensions between Anglo-American and French feminist positions on language and women's experience, and which subordinates racial to gender differences; and "The Woman in the Cave: Recent Feminist Fictions and the Classical Underworld," *Contemporary Literature* 29 (Fall 1988): 369–402, which, by reading Gloria Naylor's *Linden Hills* with Luce Irigaray's *Speculum of the Other Woman,* also foregrounds the compatibility of French feminist discourse and fiction by African-American women. Juxtaposing "'Racial Composition'" and "Thresholds of Difference" exaggerates, perhaps, the differences between Homans and Johnson, who have both been influenced by both deconstruction and psychoanalysis; but the contrast also clarifies the ways each of these (internally heterogeneous) discourses informs the debate on the discursive construction of race.

white feminist readings of black women's texts: privileging the figurative enables the white reader to achieve figurative blackness; privileging the literal enables the white *woman* reader to forge a gender alliance that outweighs (without negating) both racial differences within gender and racial alliances across gender.

"'Racial Composition'" takes as its starting point the debate on black literary criticism carried out in four texts in a 1987 issue of *New Literary History:* the original essay by Joyce A. Joyce, "The Black Canon: Reconstructing Black American Literary Criticism," criticizing the deliteralization of race in Gates and Houston A. Baker, Jr.; the responses by Gates and Baker; and Joyce's response to them.[21] Building on her premises that "the position Gates inherits from post-structuralism identifies and celebrates the abstract as masculine and devalues embodiment as female," and that Gates "substitute(s), in the undesirable position of the referent or ground from which language differentiates itself, female for black," Homans deftly teases out a gendered subtext in the exchange ("RC," pp. 3–4).[22] In Joyce's critique of the assimilation of black literary criticism to the elite discourse of post-structuralism that, through its esoteric terminology and

21. See Joyce A. Joyce, "The Black Canon: Reconstructing Black American Literary Criticism," *New Literary History* 18 (Winter 1987): 335–44; Gates, "'What's Love Got to Do with It?': Critical Theory, Integrity, and the Black Idiom," *New Literary History* 18 (Winter 1987): 345–62; Baker, "In Dubious Battle," *New Literary History* 18 (Winter 1987): 363–69; and Joyce, "'Who the Cap Fit': Unconsciousness and Unconscionableness in the Criticism of Houston A. Baker, Jr., and Henry Louis Gates, Jr.," *New Literary History* 18 (Winter 1987): 371–84. In a recent interview with Charles H. Rowell ("An Interview with Henry Louis Gates, Jr.," *Callaloo* 14 [1991]: 444–63), Gates qualifies and clarifies the basis for his response to Joyce (pp. 451–52). For a different configuration of race, gender, and reading in the the *NLH* (and other) critical debates, see Awkward, "Race, Gender, and the Politics of Reading," *Black American Literature Forum* 22 (Spring 1988): 5–27. Rather than gendering the dispute between Joyce and Baker and Gates, Awkward allies Joyce's position on race with Elaine Showalter's position on feminism as reductively sociopolitical modes of criticism and contrasts both with the more fluid post-structuralist approaches represented by Baker and Gates, on the one hand, and by Mary Jacobus on the other. One uncomfortable consequence of Awkward's construction is that, by using white feminism as his frame of reference, he erases Joyce's participation in the discourse of black feminism. For yet another account of the *NLH* debate, see Diana Fuss's chapter, "'Race' under Erasure? Post-Structuralist Afro-American Literary Theory," *Essentially Speaking: Feminism, Nature and Difference* (New York, 1989), pp. 73–96; Fuss sides primarily with Gates and Baker and mentions the gender implications of the debate only in passing.

22. Homans focusses appropriately on Gates rather than Baker, since the label *post-structuralist* applies far more accurately to Gates. In "Caliban's Triple Play," Baker's response to Gates's special issue of *Critical Inquiry,* for example, Baker sounds at times uncannily like Joyce in criticizing Anthony Appiah, and implicitly Gates as well, for belittling the visible, biological signs of race that function so perniciously in the "real" political world; see Baker, "Caliban's Triple Play," in *"Race," Writing, and Difference,* pp. 381–95. For a critique of Baker's "essentialism," see Elliott Butler-Evans, "Beyond Essentialism: Rethinking Afro-American Cultural Theory," *Inscriptions* 5 (1989): 121–34. For a defense of Baker's "materialism," see Fuss, *Essentially Speaking,* pp. 86–93. Baker is definitely an "essentialist" when it comes to gender, as is clear in his recent book, *Workings of the Spirit:*

representation of race as a metaphor, severs its connections with the black reading community, with literary traditions rooted in the lived experience of black people, and with the concrete, sensuous features of black literary language, Homans sees a defense of the "body that is troped as female in post-structuralist theory and whose absence that theory requires" ("RC," p. 7). In the high-handed and patronizing responses by Gates and Baker, she uncovers these critics' sexualized self-representations as the saviors of a feminized black literary body in danger of a retrograde sensualization at the hands of black feminists. Homans then proceeds, via an analysis of the more egalitarian tone and terms of the debate on essentialism within black feminism, to a powerful analysis of the rhetoric of critical scenes in narratives by Alice Walker, Toni Morrison, and Maya Angelou, where the tension between (relatively) literal and figurative language constitutes the "rhetorical form in which the debate over racial and gendered 'essence' is worked out. The use or representation of a relatively literal language corresponds to and puts into practice a belief in the embodiedness of race and of gender . . . while the view that race is figurative coincides with and is performed as a celebration of language as figuration and a tendency to use conspicuous metaphors" ("RC," p. 5). While insisting on the necessity of maintaining, at different times, both positions, Homans calls attention to black women writers' continuing and complex commitment "to the body and to the literal," a commitment that contrasts in both its substance and its ambivalence with Gates's and Baker's unequivocal endorsement of the figurative, and that reiterates, within a different context, Homans's own perspective in *Bearing the Word* ("RC," p. 19).[23] As Johnson extends and reauthorizes deconstruction through Hurston, Homans extends and reauthorizes, primarily through Walker, a revaluation of the literal.

Like Johnson, Homans frames her argument by positioning herself in relation to black women's texts. Both frames incorporate acknowledgements of racial difference; but whereas Johnson becomes, in the course of her argument, figuratively black, Homans becomes more emphatically white: "Neither literally nor figuratively a black feminist, then (nor even figuratively literally), I would prefer, following bell hooks' recommendation, to identify my perspective clearly as that of a white feminist" ("RC," p. 38). Homans's feminist critique of the overvaluation of the figurative

The Poetics of Afro-American Women's Writing (Chicago, 1991), and from Henderson's response to Baker's essay, "There Is No More Beautiful Way: Theory and the Poetics of Afro-American Women's Writing," in *Afro-American Literary Study in the 1990s*, pp. 135–63. In her response to the panel on "Black Feminism" at the Wisconsin Conference on Afro-American Studies in the Twenty-First Century (Apr. 1991), Carby singled out for criticism Baker's idealization of black women writers and erasure of black feminist critics.

23. See Homans, *Bearing the Word: Language and Female Experience in Nineteenth-Century Women's Writing* (Chicago, 1986), especially chapter one, which juxtaposes Lacan and Chodorow to explore the association of the literal with the feminine.

demands that, in direct opposition to Johnson, she affirm the literalness of (at least her own) race.

This is a necessary conclusion, in the context of Homans's argument, and also a brave and a problematic one. By embodying her own whiteness, Homans contests the racialization that coexists with the more overt gendering of the symbolic register. In a white feminist counterpart to Gates's strategy of making blackness figurative and figuration black ("figuration is the nigger's occupation"), Homans insistently pinions (female) whiteness to literality, resisting through a different route the dominant culture's splitting of a white symbolic realm from a black materiality.[24] Homans affirms solidarity with black women by asserting a literal difference that is ultimately overridden by the sameness of literality: by the shared association with embodiment.

In resisting white patriarchal culture's dissociation from the body, however, Homans also implicitly resists a recurrent construction of whiteness by black women writers such as Walker who, in one of the scenes from *The Temple of My Familiar* that Homans analyzes from a different perspective, represents whiteness as the "hideous personal deficiency" of having no skin, of being "a ghost," the quintessence of lack, not only of color, but also of body itself.[25] The occasional and moving alliances between black and white women that Homans analyzes in texts by Walker and Morrison do not necessarily produce or reflect a shared experience of embodiment. Six months pregnant, beaten, "sweating" milk for the eighteen-month-old baby from whom she has been separated, torn between "the fire in her feet and the fire on her back," Sethe hears Amy Denver's "young white voice . . . like a sixteen-year-old boy's" before she sees the scrawny body with its "arms like cane stalks" (*B*, pp. 79, 31, 34, 32). Although she has been "'bleeding for four years,'" Amy "'ain't having nobody's baby'": the carmine velvet that constitutes the goal of *her* escape sublimates the repro-

24. For Gates's revision of the traditional saying "signification is the nigger's occupation" to "figuration is the nigger's occupation," see "Criticism in the Jungle" and "The Blackness of Blackness: A Critique of the Sign and the Signifying Monkey," *Black Literature and Literary Theory*, pp. 1–24, 285–321. For the cultural splitting of a disembodied white femininity from a black female materiality, see Christian, *Black Feminist Criticism: Perspectives on Black Women Writers* (New York, 1985), chap. 1, and Carby, *Reconstructing Womanhood*, chap. 2.

25. Walker, *The Temple of My Familiar* (San Diego, 1989), p. 360. This passage actually describes a white man, but the ghostliness and disembodiedness attributed to whiteness are typically applied to white women as well, not only throughout Walker's fiction, but also in the distinction she draws between (black) "womanist" and (white) "feminist": "Womanist is to feminist as purple to lavender" (Walker, *In Search of Our Mothers' Gardens* [New York, 1983], p. xii). Note the similarity between Walker's account of white people's skinlessness and Morrison's description of "the men without skin" who operate the slave ship in *Beloved* ([New York, 1987], p. 210; hereafter abbreviated *B*); or between Walker's account and, from a different ethnic perspective, the white "ghosts" of Maxine Hong Kingston, *The Woman Warrior: Memoirs of a Girlhood among Ghosts* (New York, 1976).

ductive female body into cloth (*B*, p. 83). As the midwife whose *last* name is conferred on Sethe's baby, Amy is affiliated as closely with the absent (and literate) father (with whom the baby will strongly identify) as with the birthing mother. By "reading" the scar inscribed on Sethe's back, Amy is positioned on the side of figuration vis-à-vis the massively embodied Sethe. By implying that the embodiment black and white women share is weightier than differences of color, Homans proposes a commonality often called into question by black women's texts.

More problematically, however, literalizing whiteness logically entails reliteralizing blackness as well, and an argument for the literalness of race (or sex) can be safely made only from the position of the subordinated race (or sex), which can define and revalue its own distinctiveness. Speaking for the literal from a position of dominance risks reinscribing the position of the dominated. Homans's position on figuration leads her to an impasse: as a woman she can't ally herself with a (masculine) position on the figurativeness of race; as a *white* woman she can't ally herself with black women writers' (ambivalent) adherence to the embodiedness of race without potentially reproducing the structure of dominance she wants to subvert. There are as serious, although very different, problems with revaluing the literalness of race as with asserting its figurativeness.

3

> I began to wonder whether there was any position from which a white middle-class feminist could say anything on the subject [of race] without sounding exactly like [a white middle-class feminist]. . . . The rhetorical predictability of it all. The political correctness. . . . In which case it might be better not to say anything.
>
> —NANCY K. MILLER, "Criticizing Feminist Criticism"

Different as are their consequences for the reading of race, deconstruction and psychoanalysis are both subjectivist critical ideologies that mandate a high degree of self-reflexiveness. Materialist feminisms, by contrast, which have always had priority within black feminist discourse, emphasize the political objectives (and objectivity) of the reading over the question of positionality.[26] Designed to disclose systematically (and ulti-

26. For an especially powerful and influential account of black materialist feminism, see The Combahee River Collective, "A Black Feminist Statement," in *All the Women Are White, All the Blacks Are Men, But Some of Us Are Brave: Black Women's Studies,* ed. Gloria T. Hull, Patricia Bell Scott, and Barbara Smith (Old Westbury, N.Y., 1982), pp. 13–22; see also Bonnie Thornton Dill, "Race, Class, and Gender: Prospects for an All-Inclusive Sisterhood," *Feminist Studies* 9 (Spring 1983): 131–50. For a warning against eclipsing the formal and imaginative qualities of literature by privileging sociopolitical analysis, see Christian, "But What Do We Think We're Doing Anyway."

mately to change) the intersecting axes of race, class, gender, and sexuality through which women are multiply and differentially oppressed, materialist feminisms, both black and white, have de-emphasized the reader's racial location. White readers within this discourse have paid only perfunctory (if any) attention to the problem of their own positionality, and black materialists have generally been hospitable to white women's readings of black texts.[27] It is not coincidental that Valerie Smith, who insists on the materialist orientation of black feminist theory, also redefines this theory to "refer not only to theory written (or practiced) by black feminists, but also to a way of reading inscriptions of race (particularly but not exclusively blackness), gender (particularly but not exclusively womanhood), and class in modes of cultural expression"; or that Hazel Carby, writing within the discourse of cultural studies, has become one of the most resolutely antiessentialist and politically exacting black feminist voices, calling into question simultaneously the presumption of interracial sisterhood and the presumption of seamless continuity between racial experience, discourse, and interpretation.[28] The de-essentialization of race among black feminists (in contrast to both white feminists and male Afro-Americanists) has occurred primarily through the intervention of material rather than textual differences, and under the aegis of Marxism and cultural studies rather than deconstruction.

Materialist feminism would appear to be the approach through which white critics could write about black women's texts with the least self-consciousness about racial difference and perhaps with the least difference. Yet white investments in some form of black cultural or social specificity, investments exempted from analysis under the banner of an interracial socialist feminist sisterhood, tend to intervene in white readings of black texts, substituting racial for class specificity rather than disrupting each with the other. Racial differences are visibly played out in the critical response to *The Color Purple.* Both black and white feminists from diverse critical schools have celebrated the text's subversive stance toward the narrative and rhetorical conventions of epistolary, sentimental, and

27. Two examples of white materialist feminist criticism that either do not consider the critic's racial position an obstacle, or consider it a readily surmountable obstacle, are Lauren Berlant, "Race, Gender, and Nation in *The Color Purple,*" *Critical Inquiry* 14 (Summer 1988): 831–59, and Anne E. Goldman, "'I Made the Ink': (Literary) Production and Reproduction in *Dessa Rose* and *Beloved,*" *Feminist Studies* 16 (Summer 1990): 313–30. For some examples of black materialist feminist willingness to entertain readings by white feminists, see Carby, *Reconstructing Womanhood,* chap. 1; Carby's argument that there are no "pure, autonomous cultures that belong to particular groups or classes of people" implicitly opens the analysis of cultural struggles and articulations to a diverse materialist readership (Carby, "The Canon: Civil War and Reconstruction," *Michigan Quarterly Review* 28 [Winter 1989]: 42). See also hooks, *Talking Back,* chap. 7, and Valerie Smith, "Black Feminist Theory and the Representation of the 'Other.'"

28. Valerie Smith, "Black Feminist Theory and the Representation of the 'Other,'" p. 39. See Carby, *Reconstructing Womanhood,* chap. 1.

realist fiction, and toward the sexual, domestic, and spiritual institutions of patriarchy.[29] But among materialist feminists race has made a difference in the assessment of the novel's politics. For example, bell hooks criticizes the novel for isolating individual quests and transformative private relationships from collective political effort, for celebrating the "ethics of a narcissistic new-age spirituality wherein economic prosperity indicates that one is chosen," and for breaking with the revolutionary impulse of the African-American literary tradition epitomized by the slave narrative; Cora Kaplan, in an essay entitled "Keeping the Color in *The Color Purple,*" defends the novel from accusations of bourgeois liberalism by British socialists who, she feels, have "bleached" the text into "an uncontentious, sentimental, harmless piece of international libertarianism" by failing to understand its relation to "a specifically racial set of discourses about the family and femininity." Kaplan revalues the novel through a black cultural context that hooks claims the novel has repudiated.[30] And whereas Hazel Carby criticizes the critics who, through their celebration of *The Color Purple* (and its line of descent from *Their Eyes Were Watching God*), indulge in a romantic vision of rural black culture that enables them to avoid

29. See, for example, Deborah E. McDowell, "'The Changing Same': Generational Connections and Black Women Novelists," *New Literary History* 18 (Winter 1987): 281–302; Henderson, "*The Color Purple:* Revisions and Redefinitions," *Sage* 2 (Spring 1985): 14–18, repr. in *Alice Walker,* pp. 67–80; Thadious M. Davis, "Alice Walker's Celebration of Self in Southern Generations," *Southern Quarterly* 21 (Summer 1983): 39–53, repr. in *Alice Walker,* pp. 25–37; Christian, "Alice Walker: The Black Woman Artist as Wayward" and "No More Buried Lives: The Theme of Lesbianism in Audre Lorde's *Zami,* Gloria Naylor's *The Women of Brewster Place,* Ntozake Shange's *Sassafras, Cypress and Indigo,* and Alice Walker's *The Color Purple,*" in *Black Feminist Criticism: Perspectives on Black Women Writers,* ed. Christian (New York, 1985), pp. 81–102 and 187–204; Katz, "'Show Me How to Do Like You'"; pp. 185–94; Jean Wyatt, "Eros as Creativity: The Extended Family in *The Color Purple,*" *Reconstructing Desire: The Role of the Unconscious in Women's Reading and Writing* (Chapel Hill, N.C., 1990), pp. 164–85; Molly Hite, "Romance, Marginality, Matrilineage: *The Color Purple,*" *The Other Side of the Story: Structures and Strategies of Contemporary Feminist Narrative* (Ithaca, N.Y., 1989), pp. 103–26. It is interesting to note, nevertheless, a difference in emphasis: some black feminists (preeminently McDowell) have emphasized the novel's subversion of the conventions of characterization and diction governing black literature, whereas most white feminists have located the novel in relation to the dominant traditions of white literature.

30. hooks, "Writing the Subject: Reading *The Color Purple,*" in *Alice Walker,* p. 223; Cora Kaplan, "Keeping the Color in *The Color Purple,*" *Sea Changes: Essays on Culture and Feminism* (London, 1986), pp. 182, 187. Focussing on twentieth-century black male discourses on gender and the family, Kaplan is foregrounding a different black literary tradition from hooks, yet, as the title of her essay indicates, she insists that the novel's value resides in its relation to specifically black cultural traditions. In Alison Light, "Fear of the Happy Ending: *The Color Purple,* Reading and Racism," in *Plotting Change: Contemporary Women's Fiction,* ed. Linda Anderson (London, 1990), pp. 85–96, the novel's "imaginary resolution of political and personal conflicts" (p. 87), which hooks protests in relation to a black audience, is endorsed in terms of the political importance of utopianism for a (white) feminist audience. Black discursive specificity enables Kaplan's rehabilitation of the text; white reading specificity implicitly enables Light's.

confronting the complex social crises in the urban black community, Susan Willis praises the novel for contesting industrial capitalism by resurrecting the homestead and cottage industry.[31] The representation of black social relations as utopian alternatives to industrial capitalism or to patriarchal nationalism has appealed more to white than to black materialist feminists.[32]

This appeal, and its problems, surface clearly in the work of Willis, who deserves special attention as the only white feminist author of a book on black women novelists and of an essay in Cheryl A. Wall's recent anthology of black feminist criticism, *Changing Our Own Words* (1989).[33] In *Specifying: Black Women Writing the American Experience* (1987), Willis maps the ways that twentieth-century black women novelists record through their narrative strategies and subjects the shift from a southern agrarian to a northern industrial economy. Suffused with nostalgia for an agrarian culture that in Willis's opinion supported a "noncommodified relationship" between an author, her language, and her audience, the book insists that "one of the major problems facing black writers today is how to preserve the black cultural heritage in the face of the homogenizing function of bourgeois society."[34] This romanticization of "the" black cultural heritage, whose truth resides in an uncontaminated past to which these novels' protagonists repeatedly return, becomes apparent through the contrast between Willis's study and Hazel Carby's *Reconstructing Womanhood: The Emergence of the Afro-American Woman Novelist,* published the same year, which situates nineteenth-century black women's cultural discourses in relation to hegemonic ideologies.[35] In her essay "I Shop There-

31. See Carby, "It Just Be's Dat Way Sometime: The Sexual Politics of Women's Blues," *Radical America* 20, no. 4 (1986): 11, and Susan Willis, *Specifying: Black Women Writing the American Experience* (Madison, Wis., 1987), chaps. 5 and 7.

32. The tendency toward idealization troubles even the most brilliant materialist reading of the text, Berlant's, "Race, Gender, and Nation in *The Color Purple.*" For although Berlant ultimately repudiates the novel's (in her view inadequate) "womanist" alternative to patriarchal nationalism, her struggle to endorse this alternative contrasts with her less ambivalently negative representation of white women's privatized cultural bonds and identifications in her essay "The Female Complaint," *Social Text,* no. 19–20 (Fall 1988): 237–59. Despite her political critique of Walker's text, Berlant is more sympathetic to it than either hooks or Carby.

33. See Willis, "I Shop Therefore I Am: Is There a Place for Afro-American Culture in Commodity Culture?" in *Changing Our Own Words,* pp. 173–95; hereafter abbreviated "I."

34. Willis, *Specifying,* pp. 16, 72.

35. See Carby, "Reinventing History / Imagining the Future," review of *Specifying,* by Willis, *Black American Literature Forum* 23 (Summer 1989): 381–87. In this detailed and largely favorable review, Carby criticizes only the romanticization of rural black folk culture, which for Carby typifies a misleading trend in contemporary Afro-American cultural history. Willis's book has received extensive and largely favorable reviews from black feminists. Although several have decried its arbitrary historical boundaries and selection of texts, they have mostly found her historically grounded readings provocative and illuminat-

fore I Am: Is There a Place for Afro-American Culture in Commodity Culture?" however, Willis begins to engage this relation by shifting from a strict economic reading of a discrete literary tradition to a more variegated account of African-American participation in the cultural arena produced by commodity capitalism. The essay, more than the book, positions Willis in a relation to Fredric Jameson analogous to that between Johnson and Derrida, and even more to that between Homans and Lacan, since Willis, like Homans, prioritizes what is unincorporated by a master system. "I Shop Therefore I Am" opens up the third term that Jameson brackets in "Reification and Utopia in Mass Culture," the term representing the possibility of "authentic cultural production" by marginal social groups that inhabit a position outside the dialectic of high culture and mass culture. More committed than Jameson to criticizing mass culture from a position of estrangement that tends in her work to devolve into a place of authenticity, Willis both racializes and genders a cultural exterior, relinquishing black men to an ambiguous dance of subversion and assimilation with mass culture while retaining black women as unambivalent voices of resistance.[36]

Willis answers her central question—whether it is possible for African Americans to participate in commodity culture without being assimilated to it—in gendered terms. The essay plays Toni Morrison, whose

---

ing. See, for example, Christian, "Connections and Distinctions," review of *Specifying,* by Willis, *The Women's Review of Books* 4 (July-Aug. 1987): 25–26; Wall, "Black Women Writers: Journeying along Motherlines," review of *Specifying,* by Willis, *Callaloo* 12 (1989):419–22; and McDowell, review of *Specifying,* by Willis, *Color, Sex, and Poetry: Three Women Writers of the Harlem Renaissance,* by Hull, and *The Character of the Word,* by Karla Holloway, *Signs* 14 (Summer 1989): 948–52. One critic with nothing good to say about this "odd Marxist colonization (domestication? deflowering?) of black women writers" is Wallace, "Who Owns Zora Neale Hurston?" p. 184.

36. Fredric Jameson, "Reification and Utopia in Mass Culture," *Social Text* 1 (Winter 1979): 140; Jameson devotes only a paragraph to this possibility. In his later essay, "Postmodernism, or, The Cultural Logic of Late Capitalism," *New Left Review* 146 (July-Aug. 1984): 53–92, he greatly complicates the position from which might emanate a political art no longer tied to cultural enclaves whose marginality is representable in two-dimensional space; there is no longer any position unincorporated within "the truth of postmodernism, that is, . . . the world space of multinational capital" (p. 92); Willis, however, is responding primarily to "Reification and Utopia in Mass Culture." For Willis, the utopian possibilities of marginal space are available to diverse groups. In her "Gender as Commodity," *South Atlantic Quarterly* 86 (Fall 1987): 403–21, for example, children play the role that black women writers play in "I Shop Therefore I Am"; in Willis, "*Fantasia:* Walt Disney's Los Angeles Suite," *Diacritics* 17 (Summer 1987): 83–96, the nature represented in the "Nutcracker" sequence images the utopian social relations of a space outside of capitalist production. In "*Fantasia,*" Willis begins with the perspective of historical estrangement that the film offers for critiques of contemporary mass culture but slides into the utopian position offered by the "Nutcracker" sequence. In her discourse on black women's writing, estrangement is consistently utopian.

Claudia in *The Bluest Eye* represents for Willis "the radical potential inherent in the position of being 'other' to dominant society" by repudiating the white-dominated culture industry epitomized by a Shirley Temple doll, against Michael Jackson, who "states himself as a commodity" through the vertiginous display of self-transformations and imitations that undo the possibility of authenticity ("I," pp. 174, 187). "*Moonwalker* suggests a split between contemporary black women's fiction, which strives to create images of social wholeness based on the rejection of commodity capitalism, and what seems to be a black male position which sees the commodity as something that can be played with and enjoyed or subverted" ("I," p. 195). Although Willis reluctantly admits the subversive possibilities of parody, represented in her essay by Jackson and by the black film and art critic Kobena Mercer, who argues that commodity culture heightens the radical potential of artifice, she clearly prefers the authenticity represented for her by Morrison and Walker, with whom the essay begins and ends. This preference incurs two penalties. First, Willis's analytical inventiveness and subtlety are most impressively released by untangling the contradictions of mass cultural figures: Michael Jackson and his conservative antitype Mickey Mouse, on whose genealogical descent from the tradition of black minstrelsy she brilliantly speculates in an epilogue to a slightly different version of this essay that was published in *New Formations.* The utopian pressures Willis levies on black women writers, by contrast, simplifies her interpretation. Moreover, by pitting black women novelists against black male cultural critics and performers, Willis sidesteps an encounter with the black feminist critics who have endorsed the position she characterizes as "black male." Although there is more of an encounter with black feminist criticism in the essay, where Willis acknowledges her differences from Carby, for example, but doesn't theorize them, than in the book, where she lists black feminists in a general bibliography rather than engaging with them individually, Willis still doesn't interrogate what fuels her own investment in black women writers' representation of "social wholeness," "the autonomous subject," and "fullness of . . . humanity" ("I," pp. 195, 174).[37]

The essay, however, does offer clues. In contrast to Homans, who invokes black women's representations of alliances with white women to underscore the prospects of reciprocity and commonality, Willis enlists

37. Willis's footnote to Carby painfully reveals her struggle to agree and disagree simultaneously rather than to analyze the sources of their differences. Carby's position in general is closer to Kobena Mercer's than to Willis's, calling Willis's gender analysis into question. Similarly, although Willis cites Sylvia Wynter's essay on minstrelsy as parody (see Sylvia Wynter, "Sambos and Minstrels," *Social Text* 1 [Winter 1979]: 149–56), she doesn't speculate about why Wynter is so much less ambivalent about the subversive power of parody than Willis is. Wallace's essay on Michael Jackson, "Michael Jackson, Black Modernisms and 'The Ecstasy of Communication'" (1989) (*Invisibility Blues,* pp. 77–90), which appeared about the same time as Willis's, is closer to Wynter's analysis than to Willis's, further

black women's representations of white women to suggest women's socially constructed differences. In *The Bluest Eye*'s characterization of "frozen faced white baby dolls" and in *Meridian*'s account of the mummified white female body exhibited for profit by her husband, Willis finds images of the reification white women suffer through immersion (both longer and deeper than black women's) in the culture of commodities. Haunting the white female consumer's version of the cogito, "I shop therefore I am" (parody is apparently a strategy available to white feminists if not to black), the spectre of the self's mortification as commodity drives the commitment to the difference of black women's texts, as the title of the other version of this essay indicates: "I Want the Black One: Is There a Place for Afro-American Culture in Commodity Culture?" Overtly, this title replaces the voice of the white female consumer whose identity is shopping with the voice of the black female consumer manipulated into buying black replicants of white commodities, Christie dolls instead of Barbies. Yet the overdetermined referent of the first-person pronoun betrays as well (and this is presumably why this title was not used for the version of this essay in Wall's anthology) the desire of the white feminist critic who also wants "the black one"—the text that promises resistance and integrity, the utopian supplement to her own "deconstruction of commodities."[38] White feminists, like the frozen or mummified white women represented in some black women's texts, seem in Willis's discourse to be corpses finding political energy through the corpus of black women.

Willis's essay brings us back, through a different route, to my reading of Roberta as a site of authority and plenitude figured as a vital, integrated body. In contrast to Johnson and Homans, who locate black and white women on the same (although opposite) sides of the symbolic register's divide, Willis and I operate from a model of difference rather than similarity. The claim for sameness is enabled by, and in turn reauthorizes, belief in a subversive feminine position in language (whether the subversion operates through figuration or literality); the argument for an idealized (biological, social, or literary) difference is fueled by the perception of an increasingly compromised white feminist social position drained by

---

problematizing the gender alliance across racial lines. About her resistance to grappling with individual black feminist critics in her book, Willis explains: "Taken as a whole, these [black feminist] books define the critical context for my thinking about the literature. None of these texts is directly cited in my interpretations because I chose not to speak to the criticism. Such a method would have produced a very different book" (p. 183). This "very different book" might have beneficially entailed some dialogue about differences rather than a construction of difference based on the desire for a vision of "transformed human social relationships and the alternative futures these might shape" (p. 159).

38. Willis, "I Want the Black One: Is There a Place for Afro-American Culture in Commodity Culture?" *New Formations,* no. 10 (Spring 1990): 96.

success of oppositionality. But whether argued in terms of sameness or of difference, or in terms of the symbolic or the social domains, these theorizations of reading across race are marked by white desires.

5

> The first thing you do is to forget that i'm Black. Second, you must never forget that i'm Black.
>
> —Pat Parker, "For the White Person Who Wants to Know How to Be My Friend"

How, then, should we evaluate this critical undertaking? The question incorporates two complexly interwoven ones, a hermeneutic question about difference and a political question about legitimacy, that I wish to (re)open briefly in my conclusion by returning to my starting point: reading "Recitatif."

To produce an allegory about reading and race, I omitted aspects of the story—most importantly, its own conclusion—that complicate the division between the characters and, consequently, between their readers. "Recitatif" ends with parallel recognitions by Twyla and Roberta that each perceived the mute Maggie as her own unresponsive, rejecting mother, and therefore hated and wanted to harm her. After dramatizing the differences produced by race and class, the story concludes with the shared experience of abandoned little girls who, in some strange twist of the oedipal story, discover that they killed (wanted to kill), as well as loved (wanted to love), their mothers (see "R," p. 261).[39] Sameness coexists with difference, psychology with politics. Race enforces no absolute distinctions between either characters or readers, all of whom occupy diverse subject positions, some shared, some antithetical.[40] By concluding with a psychological narrative that crosses differences (indeed, with a variant of *the* universalizing psychological narrative), "Recitatif" complicates, without cancelling, both its narrative of difference and the differences in reading that this narrative provokes.

Race enters complexly into feminist reading. The three case studies

39. I am borrowing, with thanks, Sue Schweik's insights and formulation.

40. For an powerful statement of a similar conclusion about race and reading, see Mary Helen Washington, "How Racial Differences Helped Us Discover Our Common Ground," in *Gendered Subjects: The Dynamics of Feminist Teaching,* ed. Margo Culley and Catherine Portuges (Boston, 1985), pp. 221–29. Washington decides: "I will never again divide a course outline and curriculum along racial lines (as I did in 'Images of Women') so that the controlling purpose is to compare the responses of white women and black women, because I see how much the class imitates the syllabus. I do not want to see black women in opposition to white women as though that division is primary, universal, absolute, immutable, or even relevant" (pp. 227–28).

examined in this essay do indicate certain pervasive tendencies among white feminists, who have tended to read black women's texts through critical lenses that filter out the texts' embeddedness in black political and cultural traditions and that foreground instead their relation to the agendas of white feminism, which the texts alter, or prefigure, but ultimately reconfirm. For despite Jane Gallop's account of the displacement of French men by African-American women as figures of authority for white feminists, the discourses produced by French (and German and American) men continue to shape the reading habits of white feminists, who are usually better trained in literary theory than in African-American cultural studies. There has been little in white feminism comparable to the detailed reconstructions of black women's literary traditions produced by Barbara Christian, Mary Helen Washington, Deborah E. McDowell, Gloria T. Hull, Nellie Y. McKay, or Margaret B. Wilkerson; or to the mapping of this literature's social and discursive contexts produced by Hazel Carby, Barbara Smith, Valerie Smith, bell hooks, Michele Wallace, Audre Lorde, or June Jordan.[41] Instead, we have tended to focus our readings on the "celebrity" texts—preeminently those by Hurston, Walker, and Morrison —rather than on "thick" descriptions of discursive contexts, and have typically written articles or chapters (rather than books) representing black women's texts as literary and social paradigms for white readers and writers. In these texts we have found alternative family structures, narrative strategies, and constructions of subjectivity: alternative, that is, to the cultural practices of white patriarchy, with which literature by white women

41. This is not an inclusive list of black feminist critical projects, practitioners, or texts; it merely calls attention to some influential examples of black feminist writing on, or collections of, black women writers, such as *Black Women Novelists: The Development of a Tradition, 1892–1976,* ed. Christian (Westport, Conn., 1980) and Christian, *Black Feminist Criticism;* Washington, *Black-Eyed Susans: Classic Stories by and about Black Women* (Garden City, N.Y., 1975), *Midnight Birds: Stories by Contemporary Black Women Writers* (Garden City, N.Y., 1980), and *Invented Lives: Narratives of Black Women 1860–1960* (Garden City, N.Y., 1987); McDowell, "New Directions for Black Feminist Criticism," in *The New Feminist Criticism: Essays on Women, Literature, and Theory,* ed. Elaine Showalter (New York, 1985), pp. 186–99, and *Slavery and the Literary Imagination,* ed. McDowell and Arnold Rampersad (Baltimore, 1989); the series, Black Women Writers (Boston, 1987–); Hull, *Color, Sex, and Poetry: Three Women Writers of the Harlem Renaissance* (Bloomington, Ind., 1987) and *Give Us Each Day: The Diary of Alice Dunbar-Nelson* (New York, 1984); *Critical Essays on Toni Morrison,* ed. Nellie Y. McKay (Boston, 1988); *Nine Plays by Black Women,* ed. Margaret B. Wilkerson (New York, 1986); Carby, *Reconstructing Womanhood;* Barbara Smith, "Toward a Black Feminist Criticism" (1977), in *All the Women Are White, All the Blacks Are Men, But Some of Us Are Brave,* pp. 157–75; Valerie Smith, "Black Feminist Theory and the Representation of the 'Other'" and *Self-Discovery and Authority in Afro-American Narrative* (Cambridge, Mass., 1987); hooks, *Ain't I a Woman: Black Women and Feminism* (Boston, 1981), *Feminist Theory from Margin to Center* (Boston, 1984), *Talking Back,* and *Yearning: Race, Gender, and Cultural Politics* (Boston, 1990); Wallace, *Invisibility Blues;* Audre Lorde, *Sister Outsider: Essays and Speeches* (Trumansburg, N.Y., 1984); and June Jordan, *Civil Wars* (Boston, 1981).

has come to seem uncomfortably complicit.[42] The implied audience for this critical venture has been white.

The critical picture is not, however, entirely black and white. As the work of Hortense J. Spillers demonstrates especially well, black feminists draw from, as well as criticize, a range of "high" theoretical discourses, including the psychoanalytic discourses that have functioned more prominently within white feminism.[43] As Deborah E. McDowell has powerfully argued, moreover, white feminist tendencies to construct black feminism as "high" theory's political "other" reinscribe, rather than rework, the theory/politics opposition.[44] White feminist criticism is itself fractured by class and generational differences that partially undo the racial divide. Some still-unpublished essays, particularly those by a new and differently educated generation of graduate students, and some essays that are published less visibly than those analyzed in this paper, more closely approximate the historical and political concerns of black feminist criticism. Yet however interwoven with and ruptured by other differences, race remains a salient source of the fantasies and allegiances that shape our ways of reading.

Difference, however, paradoxically increases the value of crossing racial boundaries in reading. Our inability to avoid inscribing racially inflected investments and agendas limits white feminism's capacity either to impersonate black feminism, and potentially to render it expendable, or to counter its specific credibility. More important, white feminist readings contribute, however inadvertently, to a project many black feminists endorse: the racialization of whiteness.[45] As masculinity takes shape in

42. For some recent white feminist accounts of the alternatives offered by black women's texts, see Elizabeth Abel, "Race, Class, and Psychoanalysis? Opening Questions," in *Conflicts in Feminism,* ed. Marianne Hirsch and Evelyn Fox Keller (New York, 1990), pp. 184–204; Hirsch, *The Mother/Daughter Plot: Narrative, Psychoanalysis, Feminism* (Bloomington, Ind., 1989), esp. pp. 176–99; Hite, *The Other Side of the Story,* pp. 103–26; Elizabeth Meese, *(Ex)Tensions: Re-Figuring Feminist Criticism* (Urbana, Ill., 1990), pp. 129–54 (and, for other women of color, chaps. 2 and 5); Roberta Rubenstein, *Boundaries of the Self: Gender, Culture, Fiction* (Urbana, Ill., 1987), pp. 125–63 (and all of part 2 for other women of color); and Wyatt, *Reconstructing Desire,* pp. 164–209.

43. For some examples of Spillers's revisionist use of psychoanalytic theory, see her "Interstices: A Small Drama of Words," in *Pleasure and Danger,* ed. Carol Vance (Boston, 1984), pp. 73–100, and "Mama's Baby, Papa's Maybe: An American Grammar Book," *Diacritics* 17 (Summer 1987): 65–81. Spillers's work productively complicates the distinction Susan Thistlethwaite draws in her *Sex, Race, and God: Christian Feminism in Black and White* (New York, 1989) between the psychological focus of white feminism and the sociopolitical focus of black feminism.

44. McDowell made this argument in a paper entitled "Residues," delivered at the Wisconsin Conference on Afro-American Studies in the Twenty-First Century.

45. Carby and hooks have both written pervasively and eloquently about this need; for some recent examples, see Carby, "The Politics of Difference," *Ms.* (Sept.-Oct. 1990): 84–85, and hooks, "Critical Interrogation." On whiteness as "the metaphor for the metaphorical production of the Subject as one devoid of properties," see David Lloyd, "Race

part through its constructions of femininity, whiteness—that elusive color that seems not to be one—gains materiality through the desires and fantasies played out in its interpretations of blackness, interpretations that, by making the unconscious conscious, supplement articulated ideologies of whiteness with less accessible assumptions. Reading black women's texts, and reading our readings of them, is one (although certainly not the only) strategy for changing our habitual perception that "race is always an issue of Otherness that is not white: it is black, brown, yellow, red, purple even."[46]

Articulating the whiteness implied through the construction of blackness approaches, through a different route, the goal of Toni Morrison's recent critical project: "to avert the critical gaze from the racial object to the racial subject; from the described and imagined to the describers and imaginers; from the serving to the served."[47] There is a significant political difference, of course, between Morrison analyzing European-American texts and white feminist theorists staking critical claims to the African-American texts that constitute a privileged and endangered terrain of black feminist inquiry.[48] The risks of this intervention have been circumscribed, however, by the effectiveness of black feminists in establishing the authority of their own positions and by the failure of "high" theory to secure some unproblematic grounding for white feminists by either resolving or displacing the politics of reading and race. If we produce our readings cautiously and locate them in a self-conscious and self-critical relation to black feminist criticism, these risks, I hope, would be counterbalanced by the benefits of broadening the spectrum of interpretation, illuminating the social determinants of reading, and deepening our recognition of our racial selves and the "others" we fantasmatically construct—and thereby expanding the possibilities of dialogue across as well as about racial boundaries.

---

under Representation," *Oxford Literary Review,* no. 1–2 (1991): 13. On the asymmetry of the system of racial marking, which "inscribes the system of domination on the body of the individual, assigning to the individual his/her place as a dominated person" while not assigning "any place to the dominator," who remains unmarked, see Colette Guillaumin, "Race and Nature: The System of Marks," *Feminist Issues* 8 (Fall 1988): 41.

46. hooks, "Critical Interrogation," p. 162.

47. Morrison, *Playing in the Dark,* p. 90.

48. In "The Race for Theory," *Cultural Critique* 6 (Spring 1987): 51–63, Christian powerfully demonstrates the distorting effects of literary theory's intervention in the reading of black women's texts. Although she does not hold white *feminists* responsible for this intervention, her argument clearly applies to white feminist (as well as masculinist) theoretical discourses.

The Erotics of Irishness

Cheryl Herr

Like all fields of inquiry, Irish studies has its own traditions, its own ways of organizing information. Even the most adventurous of the native practitioners tend carefully to maintain disciplinary boundaries when presenting evidence to sustain a thesis, and American scholars have used Irish practice as their frame of reference. This essay, which engages with the time-honored and increasingly vexed enterprise of defining "Irishness," introduces play into these traditions both in spirit and in methodology. An alternative approach to analyzing Ireland might foreground the underlying assumptions about social relations and historical patterns that link Irish art and writing across diverse fields of inquiry.[1] Exploring the many rhetorics of Ireland might make it impossible, for example, for those involved in the essential task of historical and scientific inquiry—the realm commonly construed as that of hard facts—to overlook the submessages of popular Irish representations.

I begin, obliquely, with a contrast between American and Irish

1. Richard Kearney has been by far the most successful organizer of multidisciplinary studies of Irish life. The authors in his recent collection of essays, *Across the Frontiers: Ireland in the 1990s* (Dublin, 1988), examine the place of Ireland in the 1992 Eurostate in ways that aggressively complicate cultural, political, and economic perspectives on contemporary Ireland. The volume, however, seeks more to initiate discussion than to produce an integrated analysis across various terrains. In terms of introducing an external perspective, many of the issues referred to in this essay receive much fuller consideration in my study in progress "Significant Space: Ireland by Design."

This article originally appeared in *Critical Inquiry* 17 (Autumn 1990).

FIG. 1.

censorship of music videos. My inquiry targets some fundamental differences between American and Irish appropriations of the body, from which the essay suggests symmetries between the psychological development of individuals in Ireland and one stage in what might be termed the psychohistory of Irish culture. As an experimental, semi-disruptive piece that challenges disciplinary lines in the field and introduces fresh theoretical categories, this essay reaches toward a new Irish studies.

Videologic in America

In 1984 Stuart Arbright, a musician based in New York, coproduced with feminist filmmaker Beth B a video of his successful cut

---

Cheryl Herr, professor of English at the University of Iowa, is the author of *Joyce's Anatomy of Culture* (1986), *For the Land They Loved: Irish Political Melodramas, 1890–1925* (1990), and *Critical Regionalism from Ireland to the Heartland* (forthcoming).

FIG. 2.

"The Dominatrix Sleeps Tonight" (figs. 1 and 2). Although the record and video alluded to sadomasochistic themes, Arbright and B had consciously worked toward what they called a "subtle," "conceptual" package.[2] On the evening that the video was to be aired on ABC's "Hot Tracks," Arbright and friends quickly realized that despite frequent teasers, the cut was going to be pulled. Following suit, MTV told B that the visuals were "too hot" and showed "too much skin." When Arbright and B refused to "tone down" the work, MTV continued their boycott. This action surprised Arbright. Yes, the video appears to be set in an urban jungle village populated by powerful women; yes, it toys with deprivation and sadism (the women keep their men locked up, comically, in a body shop and obviously have the upper hand when it comes to driving the cars that represent power in their social order). But Arbright insists that clubgoers did not pick up on the more sexually violent interpretive possibilities. When they discovered that the video's

2. Quotations in this paragraph and information in the following paragraph are from a telephone conversation with Stuart Arbright, 21 January 1988. My thanks to Arbright and Beth B for supplying the videotape of "The Dominatrix Sleeps Tonight" along with inside information about its history, and to Arbright for permission to reprint the stills. "The Dominatrix Sleeps Tonight": video coproduced by S. Arbright and Beth B, directed by Beth B. Dominatrix is (was) Stuart Arbright.

lead singer was a woman named Dominique, they asked the videomaker, "Are you Trix?" Arbright believes that, sadomasochism aside, it was actually "the idea of a woman being in power" that "freaked" network broadcasters.

In 1985, the Museum of Modern Art, New York, put on a music video retrospective. One of the thirty works chosen for exhibition, "Dominatrix" had found an audience far more exclusive than the one originally targeted; the work was displayed next to a Miles Davis cut. Soon after, Paris's Pompidou Center showcased "Dominatrix" while alluding to American commercial hypocrisy.[3] Widely distributed in England, the Netherlands, West Germany, and Ireland, this Arbright/B venture also won acclaim at the Berlin Film Festival.

Among the many things that one might say about this series of events is that the kind of censorship experienced by Arbright and B demonstrates a still-existing lag in America between legislative or everyday notions of what the body is and the digitized or cyborgian technobody, with its casual unity and its ready absorption into cartoon graphics. If videologists are at all correct in hailing the subsuming of our historical "event horizon"[4] into a world that could not exist outside of the small screen, the growing absurdity of much if not all censoring of video body images becomes apparent. But while MTV increasingly takes place on a two-dimensional, information-dense videoplane that insists on its self-referentiality, the audience and programmers sometimes still watch through a porthole framed by nostalgia.

Vivian Sobchack addresses this situation using a tripartite structure.[5] In our "moving image culture," we "live cinematic and electronic lives," she argues, complete with an appropriately altered "psycho-

3. It would seem that the Pompidou has become a place of imprimatur for works produced in the uncongenially censored settings outside of France. Gordon Lambert believes that despite setbacks in the past, the aesthetic "potential in Ireland is limitless," and notes, "We have come a long way from the conservative academic objection to a Henry Moore reclining figure, presented to the Dublin Municipal Gallery over two decades ago, to Nigel Rolfe's naked body performances in flour which have earned contemporary Irish art recognition in the Pompidou Centre!" (Gordon Lambert, "A Matrix of Contemporary Irish Visual Art," in *Ireland and the Arts,* ed. Tim Pat Coogan [London, 1983], pp. 204, 205).

4. See *The Event Horizon: Essays on Hope, Sexuality, Social Space, and Media(tion) in Art,* ed. Lorne Falk and Barbara Fischer (Toronto, 1987), which maps the world of video representation from several angles toward a utopianism based in representation.

5. The quotations from Sobchack in this paragraph are from the manuscript of an essay, forthcoming in *Post Script* (Autumn 1990), that was translated and first published in German. The English title is "Scene of the Screen: Toward a Phenomenology of Cinematic and Electronic 'Presence.'" The German version is "The Scene of the Screen: Beitrag zu einer Phänomenologie der 'Gegenwärtigkeit' im Film und in den elektron-

logic" and "bio-logic." The most extreme of these altered states is the electronic, for here we find a new sense of "presence" that incorporates users "in a spatially decentered, weakly temporalized and quasi-disembodied state" and subjects them to "the transmission of random information." It is this flattened, superficial, binary, antigravitational, electronic state that is not fully available—not *visible*—in certain under- or more recently developed countries. Before the electronic body, before the cinematic body, there was the photographic bio-logic, which rendered "a presence in the present that is always past," recording the traces of loss, death, and nostalgia that are neutralized in videophenomenology.

In many ways, the Ireland that produced *Finnegans Wake* seemed if not well on its way at least amenable to postmodernism (however restricted to the realm of "culture") and to deconstructive literary strategies, but despite the transnational status of patriarchy and profit motives, Ireland even now uneasily integrates first-world biotechnology and third-world politico-economics. Still battling the old cycle of poverty and emigration, Ireland stands *at* but definitely outside the threshold of postindustrial posthumanism—even while works like "The Dominatrix Sleeps Tonight" paradoxically play in Irish clubs without comment. What keeps Ireland keyed into the photographic dimension in most of its cultural registers? What keeps this video outside the current censorship-danger zone in Ireland? What determines an Irish version of the Dominatrix that is entirely different from Arbright/B's American woman?

By examining closely one moment in Irish art history and folding into its frame evocative materials from anthropology, literary criticism, and archaeology, I want to suggest the almost unthinkable (from the outside) gap separating Irish and American representations of body-experience. As we move in and out of a few select Irish spaces—an art museum, a rural village, the city of Dublin, and a prehistoric burial mound on the river Boyne—we see displayed the neutralization of the body in this island culture and some meanings of that desomatizing in Ireland's historical and current identity crisis.[6]

---

ischen Medien," in *Materialität der Kommunikation,* ed. Hans Ulrich Gumbrecht and K. Ludwig Pfeiffer (Frankfurt am Main, 1988). My thanks to Brooks Landon for suggesting that I read Sobchack's essay.

6. Although my comparison of Irish and American body images sometimes affirms the critique of institutionalized gender relations advanced by Irish feminists, my primary aim is not to criticize the pattern of relations in Ireland nor to promote the erotics of American society. I am much more interested in enhancing for international students of Irish studies the differences between the two cultures as a way of valuing the distinctiveness of Ireland and of the people who live there.

Irish Minds in Irish Bodies

> I didn't know I was Irish until I went to America.[7]
>
> —U2's Bono

Most writers on Ireland sooner or later put forward one trait that they see as definitive of the "Irish mind" or the "Celtic consciousness."[8] This characteristic is thought to reproduce itself throughout the cultural fabric across time and space. Hence, the Irish are variously linked to a fatal divisiveness and "emotional oscillation," a "split-mindedness" that becomes a genius for "dispersion and disconnexion" as well as an "incapacity to generalize."[9] Various forms of doubling are frequently put forward as somehow intrinsic to Irishness, as are a strong "sense of place"[10] and a "funerary" obsession.[11] How to read these efforts at self-definition without falling prey to essentialism or oversimplification is a critical question; that said, there is no doubt that Ireland is increasingly in the throes of what might be called an "over-identity crisis."[12]

But one feature that almost no one mentions is the relationship between the Irish mind and any kind of Irish body. The identity-obsession marks a social repression of the body on a grand scale. As I see it, the loss occurs on both individual and collective levels. Ireland has literally eroded, in the sphere of representations that constitute social identity, a comfortable sense of the body;[13] in traditional as well as in colonial and postcolonial Ireland, the body has frequently been asso-

7. Paul Hewson, "Bono: The White Nigger," in *Across the Frontiers,* p. 188. Hewson, a.k.a. Bono, is the lead singer of U2.

8. See *The Irish Mind: Exploring Intellectual Traditions,* ed. Kearney (Dublin, 1985), and *The Celtic Consciousness,* ed. Robert O'Driscoll (New York, 1981).

9. Sean O'Faoláin, *The Irish,* rev. ed. (1947; New York, 1969), pp. 19, 22, 31, 44, 54.

10. See Patrick Sheeran, "*Genius Fabulae:* The Irish Sense of Place," *Irish University Review* 18 (Autumn 1988): 191–206.

11. See Nina Witoszek, "Ireland: A Funerary Culture?" *Studies* 76 (1987): 206–15.

12. The Irish artist Pat Kennan used this phrase in a conversation with me about contemporary Irish life and art.

13. I am not suggesting that the actual physical experience of any individual in Ireland is or is not different from the sensory experience in other countries or that if this were the case, a non-Irish viewer would be able to detect this difference. Ethnographic studies (for example, see Nancy Scheper-Hughes's *Saints, Scholars, and Schizophrenics: Mental Illness in Rural Ireland* [Berkeley, 1979]; hereafter abbreviated *S*) lend some support to the possibility of censored sensation in certain parts of Ireland, but such conclusions are highly controversial. What I would rather direct attention to are the ways in which a collective Irish body text, composed of repeated descriptions and received ideas, implies the ongoing force of code-systems that appear to be uncharacteristic of body representations in the United States. This is a point that seems, judging from many discussions of body texts, *écriture feminine,* and the like, to be easily ignored or effaced.

ciated representationally with danger and has been scrutinized with an intensity that *stills* (photographically). And as I will try to show, the academic world's portrayal of a powerful prehistory dialectically replicates that situation in the framework of psychohistory. What is thought of as the "typically Irish" embracing of censorship (something that appears to but does not conflict with the acceptance of the Arbright/B video in Ireland) throughout modern history iterates these ideologically linked losses as a sign of cultural trauma or denial. Although this is not the place to go into detail, the arc of James Joyce's writing career shows his increasingly acute analysis of this social systematizing of repression, compensatorily troped as immobility. From his own experience of having *Dubliners* censored, Joyce produced both *Ulysses,* which centers on the suddenly unsuppressed Dominatrix (Molly's monologue hinting at a folklore-based Gea-Tellean power that Joyce apparently chose to honor at some level), and *Finnegans Wake,* which reclaims the prehistoric, evaded moment that it calls the "annadominant."[14] Tracing the sources and meanings of his pain, anger, exile, and dualism took Joyce unerringly along the channels of Irish psychohistory—back to the most obvious feature of Ireland-as-body: the mounds, cairns, tumuli, and generally massive circular field monuments visually organizing large portions of Irish geography. In the *Wake* Joyce allows these womb-grave-body-parts to stand in for a missing link in Irish identity, the moment that might replace the perception of paralysis with a celebration of movement.[15]

Let me note here that the sort of interpretation that I have in mind veers away from the often fruitful but to me unwieldily universal

14. James Joyce, *Finnegans Wake* (New York, 1967), p. 14; hereafter abbreviated *FW.* Several commentators on Joyce have moved in various ways and degrees toward accounting for the portrayal in the *Wake* of the archaic "annadominant" but without fully considering the highly contextual and psychohistorical motivation for Joyce's quite remarkable inquiry into Irish prehistory. More important, the connection between Joyce's inquiry and the larger patterns of Irish discourse and Irish censorship has not been pursued. See Bonnie Kime Scott, *Joyce and Feminism* (Bloomington, Ind., 1984), chap. 2, and *James Joyce* (Atlantic Highlands, N.J., 1987), chap. 4; John Bishop, *Joyce's Book of the Dark, "Finnegans Wake"* (Madison, Wis., 1986); and Margot Norris, *The Decentered Universe of "Finnegans Wake": A Structuralist Analysis* (Baltimore, 1976).

15. When Julia Kristeva talks about Joyce (see her essay, "Joyce 'The Gracehoper' or the Return of Orpheus," in *James Joyce: The Augmented Ninth,* ed. Bernard Benstock [Syracuse, N.Y., 1988], pp. 167–80), she claims that he deliberately opened himself to multiple identities in an attempt to backtrack, to understand the identification process with all of its ambiguities. She traces processes of individual psychosocial development as that development relates to the production of literature. Always there is the surfacing of the maternal and archaic in displaced ways that have aesthetic outcomes. It is interesting that Kristeva entertains what this process might have looked like on the purely social level and sees the two processes as congruent. The moment of retrieval of the archaic aligns, I think, with the moment in which the Prankquean appears. She takes on the role of condenser, displacer, and irrepressible feminine principle. Knocking at the door, she is

attempts to reclaim the "goddess" in any given cultural setting. We're moving more in the direction of Julia Kristeva's *abject,* of an excess that speaks and threatens and suffers repression in an endless micro-macro cycle. In my consideration of Irish culture, I call this conceptual space the *arkhein.*[16] *Arkhein* is, conveniently, a bracketed term in the *American Heritage Dictionary*'s list of Indo-European roots. It is a Greek verb "of unknown origin" meaning to begin, to rule, to command. Its derivatives include *archaic* and *archive.* Given that the *AHD* presents the Indo-European roots as the "prehistory" of English, *arkhein* seems to me a suitably remote, uncertain, and gender-free term to signify elements that might be variously expressed through ideas such as Kristeva's *abject* or *semiotic* or *chora,* Freud's Minoan moment, the primarily filmic sense of a nonpatriarchal imaginary, a (m)other tongue, the speaking of Luce Irigaray's "two lips," any version of a pre-Oedipal semiotic (in Kristeva's sense) that sweeps up the possibility of segueing into a matri-symbolic or alternative primary code. (Although most of these terms are woman-identified and although the ideological positioning of women in Ireland lends support to my argument, I would suggest that the projected category be taken as a fluidly ungendered alternative to the symbolic as we know it.) As I think will become clear, interpreting the Arbright/B video might send me for analytic tools to post-structuralist theorists, to Jane Gallop, Angela Carter, and the post-Freudian literature on phallic mothers, but I have to go through different frames of reference to draw forth Ireland's Dominatrix-Body—as arkhein, as Kathleen Ni Houlihan, as Queen Medb, as the formidably misunderstood Irish Mother, as a pervasive Irish resistance to achieving cultural identity in the terms that those outside of Irish society often deem necessary.[17]

---

the domineering, primitive Kathleen Ni Houlihan, refusing to be deterred in her quest but, as yet metaphorically presymbolic, unable to express the quest very clearly. It is, like Ireland's own quest, a search for identity. The *Wake* signals in many ways the site of a loss that is associated with lack of movement and of erotic pleasure.

16. Arkhein echoes the Heideggerian *arche* or ground, but the arkhein has less to do with Being than with a specifically cultural archaic. As a bracketed root, *arkhein* carries the connotation of being constructed, projected backward into a linguistic prehistory that is highly fluid and open to meanings, pregendered, presymbolic, alternative. I prefer the more aggressively manufactured root to describe the presymbolic zone in Irish history.

17. Many commentators appear to conduct their research on Ireland with a preconceived notion of what the Irish should do and, as an implied corollary, what Irish identity ought to look like. This is true of writers who are Irish as well as of those who are not. Most often, those who are in varying degrees outsiders (including many Irish-Americans) tend to have a nostalgic sense of Irish culture that privileges old ways and communicates a desire for the old ways to be reclaimed. Another example of kindly bias comes forward in Elizabeth Shannon's *I Am of Ireland: Women of the North Speak Out* (Boston, 1989), in which she argues that Irish women, north and south, should band together under the banner of feminism, refuse to cooperate in the masculinist conflicts that she finds at the heart of the political crisis. Shannon discerns in that ongoing conflict an Irish male compensation for a history of unemployment and emotional insecurity. One prob-

FIG. 3.—Micheal Farrell, *Madonna Irlanda or "The Very First Real Irish Political Picture,"* 1977. 73 × 68 in. Hugh Lane Municipal Gallery, Dublin. Photograph by kind permission of the artist.

Madonna Irlanda

Which brings us to Micheal Farrell, one of Ireland's foremost contemporary visual artists, a painter who reminds many Americans of Larry Rivers. His painting, *Madonna Irlanda or "The Very First Real Irish Political Picture"* (fig. 3),[18] iconographically reinscribes, some fifty years after the fact, Joyce's highly charged analysis of the Irish annadominant

---

lem with such an argument is that Shannon tends to discount the opinions of Irish women with whom she disagrees. Another problem is the peculiarly one-dimensional and nondynamic nature of the feminism that she espouses. It is difficult to imagine how her proposed solution could be put into practice across the incredibly complex field of Irish life in the two countries.

18. For discussing Farrell's painting with me, I want to thank the group of scholars at University House (University of Iowa) during the summer of 1989, especially Abby Zanger (Harvard University) for sharing her knowledge of French art history. University House, under the direction of Jay Semel with the help of Lorna Olson, kindly provided

and emotional reinvestment in the arkhein. Because Farrell's career mapped, prior to *Madonna Irlanda,* his own movement from an international style to a concern with native tradition—particularly motifs that privilege swirling, circularity, and concentricity in the manner of Celtic brooches and prehistoric burial mounds[19]—it is at first all the more surprising that the artist's announced formulation of an alternative style cycled him into what seems like a predictable stasis; the painterly persona warily approaches the Irish body (always construed as threatening domination, however mildly disposed) through a dense visual program. The painting is at once a gathering of contemporary Irish icons, a history of perspectival Western art, and a self-portrait of the artist. In the work, Farrell himself stares hostilely at his own semi-discarded pictorial modes, the traces of Celticism popularly attributed to the Irish mind, and a space that Irish art has left mostly vacant through the centuries (akin to that abysmal dream-space that Freud detected, a possibly Minoan and unrepresentable pre-Oedipality). Farrell's change of style or heart found expression in the Miss O'Murphy series, of which *Madonna Irlanda* is a major example.

The series involves various takes on the nudes of the eighteenth-century French painter François Boucher. Why Boucher rather than Rubens or Ingres or Picasso? A 1978 lithograph by Farrell provides one answer; it depicts a Boucher nude outlined on a smeared and blotched background, with the printed title in the upper left corner, "LES NOUVELLES COUPES DE BOUCHERIE A LA MODE IRLANDAISE." Farrell labeled the young woman's body to designate the appropriate political cuts—"gigot," "le cul," "fourquarters," "kneecap" (especially important to Northern political groups). Butchered by the history of Irish politics, she rests there, sanctified in the public eye by her own willingness not to know her violation. The picture perfectly extends the plan of Jonathan Swift, Boucher's Irish contemporary, whose modest proposal still finds in Ireland the occasional reader who cannot see the point.[20]

But there is more to this series of paintings than such an obvious satiric pun. Boucher (1703–70) sums up perfectly the century in which he reigned as court painter for Louis XV, its comfortable decadence, its intrigues and careful avoidance of distressing immediacies. He chroni-

---

the space and quiet in which I wrote this essay. I am also grateful to Ruth Salvaggio of Virginia Tech for discussions about feminism and archaeology.

The Howard Foundation of Brown University supported through a generous fellowship the research on which this essay is based.

19. See Cyril Barrett, *Micheal Farrell* (Dublin, 1979), pp. 6–7.

20. See Rosita Sweetman, *On Our Backs: Sexual Attitudes in a Changing Ireland* (London, 1979). She provides evidence to this effect, demonstrating that sectarian divisions in Ireland still can make insensitive use of Swift's satire.

cled prerevolutionary France, excelling in the portrayal of naked bodies in putatively mythical situations, resisting the rigors of Dutch realism in favor of an "erotic body" that promulgates an ersatz dehistoricity. While Norman Bryson eloquently defines Boucher's role in producing this body capable of being "consumed in the moment of the glance,"[21] Boucher's nudes strike many critics more as brimming with health than as inspiring possessive desire; they seem too impersonal to be at all scandalous, too benign to be censorable (despite the historical rumor that the king's mistress commissioned Boucher to paint these nudes for Louis's personal "musée secret"),[22] too limp to engage, in fact. These cherubic bodies yield most to the pressures of rococo design, floating through scene after scene of emotional detachment, rarely making eye contact. Their gazes go inward, with the look we find in small children, in baby ducks.

Boucher's *Blonde Odalisque* (fig. 4), to which *Madonna Irlanda* directly alludes, has this tensionless, fluid, generic attitude. An Irish artist would likely be drawn to the *Odalisque* because of the story that Boucher used for his model a fourteen-year-old Irish courtesan, "Mademoiselle O'Murphy," of whom Casanova speaks approvingly in his memoirs and who was briefly the paramour of Louis XV.[23] Farrell provides his own discursive analysis of the Miss O'Murphy phenomenon; he uses the pictures to "'make every possible statement on the Irish situation, religious, cultural, political, the cruelty, the horror, every aspect of it.'" Why Mother Ireland? he was asked. "'Because she is a whore.'"[24]

Lest I get sidetracked in Stephen Dedalus's generic, "all-too-Irish" preoccupation with the cult of the virgin, which contains its own deconstructive underside (or in the many analyses across cultures of the virgin-whore dichotomy to which women have so often been subjected),[25] I want to keep the focus on how art historians have viewed Boucher's lady and what in Farrell's own gaze belongs to the system of meanings called "Irishness." In the outdated but classic *The Nude: A*

21. Norman Bryson, *Word and Image: French Painting of the Ancien Régime* (Cambridge, 1981), p. 92.

22. See Paul Frankl, "Boucher's Girl on the Couch," in *Essays in Honor of Erwin Panofsky*, ed. Millard Meiss, 2 vols. (New York, 1961), 1:151.

23. For details on Casanova, Boucher, and Miss O'Murphy, see Alastair Laing, "Catalogue of Paintings," in *François Boucher: 1703–1770* (exhibition catalog, Metropolitan Museum of Art, New York, 17 Feb.–4 May 1986), pp. 259–62.

24. Quoted in *Contemporary Irish Art*, ed. Roderic Knowles (Dublin, 1982), pp. 56, 57.

25. For an excellent analysis of the virgin-whore dichotomy, see Coppélia Kahn, "The Hand that Rocks the Cradle: Recent Gender Theories and Their Implications," in *The (M)other Tongue: Essays in Feminist Psychoanalytic Interpretation*, ed. Shirley Nelson Garner, Claire Kahane, and Madelon Sprengnether (Ithaca, N.Y., 1985), pp. 72–88.

FIG. 4.—François Boucher, *Blonde Odalisque,* 1752. Oil on canvas. 23¼ × 28¾ in. Alte Pinakothek, Munich. Photograph courtesy of Alte Pinakothek.

Study of Ideal Form, Sir Kenneth Clark picks up the tone of much of this criticism:

> Freshness of desire has seldom been more delicately expressed than by Miss O'Murphy's round young limbs, as they sprawl with undisguised satisfaction on the cushions of her sofa. By art Boucher has enabled us to enjoy her with as little shame as she is enjoying herself. One false note and we should be embarrassingly back in the world of sin.[26]

Similarly, Paul Frankl's famous meditation on the *Odalisque* begins, "Boucher's painting . . . can be smilingly enjoyed as one enjoys a rosebud which needs no interpretation,"[27] and he is seconded by Bryson, who, though deep in the throes of deconstructing the myth of a seamless and triumphant quattrocento space, pauses to point out that Boucher gives us what "the erotic gaze most desires . . . simply, posture."[28] This consensus is striking because the viewpoint these critics

26. Kenneth Clark, *The Nude: A Study in Ideal Form* (New York, 1956), pp. 149–50.
27. Frankl, "Boucher's Girl on the Couch," p. 138.
28. Bryson, *Word and Image,* p. 95.

share (a viewpoint that in Boucher's own time worried Diderot) is simply not available for the representative persona adopted in this painting by Farrell, whose experience of classic art history and obvious mastery of its terms does not invade in any way the sinister social *méconnaissance*—the routine emptiness and orthopedic futility—of the female body in much Irish self-representation. From the upper right-hand corner of *Madonna Irlanda,* Farrell's self-portrait gazes on Miss O'Murphy with the face that occupies other paintings of himself; he tends to look as though he has stepped out of a painting by Hockney or Fischl—jaded, a little flabby, detumescent.

Frankl's analysis of Boucher must be used for one other point; he hypothesizes that O'Murphy became the prototype for Boucher's many nudes whose mythic narrative situation insists that they be *swimming.* The possibly skewed relationship between her body and the couch (they could well exist on slightly separated planes) suggests that Boucher recognized this further use of her figure as he was painting her. Frankl concludes that in "the swimming pose Boucher picked out one of the unstatic movements which are completely in harmony with the essence of the rococo. . . . Stern morality is static and firmly grounded, the morality of the rococo swims."[29] Farrell pictorially exploits this elegant point to insist on O'Murphy's *motionlessness.* Held in place by halo on the left and burning buttocks on the right, slowly turning from living flesh (Boucher was famous for his flesh tones, his rosy knees and buttocks) to statuary marble, she is cut free from the rococo world of pleasant motion and hooked into a profound stasis produced from ambivalence about the female body, about the body in general as eternal threat to the other half of the Cartesian scale.

Stasis and Censorship

The Irish of the last seven centuries have always been the victims of some kind of censorship, finally extricating themselves in the south from English rule only to impose there a complex and repressive internal censorship code, one result of which is putatively the radical underdevelopment of visual art education in Ireland. To say that the Catholic church (in complicity with English Victorian mores) *produced* this aspect of Irishness, as most historical analysts of Irish censorship have, is to miss the main event: a reflexive and widespread resistance to *seeing* movement, to recognizing its necessity, and ultimately to sanctioning radical changes of posture. Similarly, one way to read the famous ambiguity and obliquity of English-as-it-is-spoken-in-Ireland involves noticing the protective coloration involved; the discourse

29. Frankl, "Boucher's Girl on the Couch," p. 151.

swims with possibilities while bodies are imaged as changeless—inert, Finn MacCoolian masses on the verge of reabsorption into the landscape.

As I see it, then, censorship in Ireland is not really a political or legislative issue at heart; it is a symptom of a specific kind of psychological development on individual and group levels. (This is one reason that a video like "The Dominatrix Sleeps Tonight" was, according to its producers, never censored in Ireland as it was in the U.S.—it is simply irrelevant to indigenous experience, with its huge American cars and Victoria's Secret underwear, its promise of upward mobility in a markedly lesbian world; a Dominatrix is different and threatens more subtly on this island.)

For example, violate the introjected command to remain in place, and you risk the fate of Cuchulain, Ireland's Oedipus-in-reverse, who not only spends much of his brief heroic life doing battle because of the ultra-dominant Queen Medb but also murders his only son, goes mad, and spends himself battling the sea. The motility feared in Farrell's world connects with resistance to the suppressed arkhein that Joyce's ALP embodies as "the language of flow." Hence, the problems aired by *Madonna Irlanda* include not only the difficulty of keeping virgin-whore stereotypes strictly in place but also the grotesque social cost involved. From retrograde constitutional referenda banning abortion and divorce in the Republic (1983, 1987) to the dynamics of terrorist vision in the North, such terrible tensions are represented in the painting, as will become clear, through inner details and outer frame.

Miss O'Murphy safely pinned down, the male body also has its place in *Madonna Irlanda.* The composition forces the outsider's eye into peripheral motions that sweep us, on the one side, to Leonardo's Vitruvian man, and on the other, to the artist's self-portrait. This balance between reference to the spatial paradigm of the Italian Renaissance and reference to a disembodied head insists that we remove the body from material existence and codify it in art historical terms. A theoretical question posed by this compositional strategy is how to sustain a relationship between the iconography of the Celtic head cult and the self-castration signing the projected universal "castration" of the woman as she modulates into a specifically Irish form of suppression.

Head Cult

The Celts took to heart the early European belief that the head is "the source of spiritual potency."[30] When Cuchulain undergoes heroic

30. Proinsias MacCana, "The Cult of Heads," in *Louis le Brocquy and the Celtic Head Image* (exhibition catalog, New York State Museum, Albany, 26 Sept.–24 Nov. 1981), p. 11.

empowerment, he generates a heroic halo to mark this site of power—a piece of pagan information with which we can qualify the heavy irony of Miss O'Murphy's BVM headgear. This ideology of the head suggests that one kind of energy expresses itself through the face, another through the body, a severing that Farrell transcribes through the benign irrelevance of Boucher's odalisque as she looks into nothingness. Her orientation is important; where the face looks *matters,* at least in the Celtic frame of reference, in which stone godheads were placed on hills to keep an eye on the terrain.[31] So common are these field monuments that Irish children have been surprised "not to find them everywhere" in other countries.[32] Part of the landscape, these heads are neither male nor female—although they assimilate to discussion under the rubric of "the gods." Neutered and possibly neutralized by their symbolic value, they are panoptical beings ironically less powerful than the landscape-as-deity they survey.[33] The virgin land, much raped and pillaged by the likes of Neolithic tribes, Celts, Vikings, and Englishmen, lies immobile, passive, blindly inattentive to itself, projecting the otherwise powerful Dominatrix's privilege of vision (Ireland as a woman who fixes you with her gaze) onto neuter heads that disregard their ambiance. Miss O'Murphy's eye-power is syphoned off into the official elsewhere.

Farrell's own head iterates the attitude customary in his self-portraits of sullen disregard; his face displays a reluctance to look at the

31. See ibid., p. 14.

32. Anne Crookshank, "Louis le Brocquy," in *Louis le Brocquy and the Celtic Head Image,* p. 22. Crookshank is a professor of art history at Trinity College, Dublin, and her comments bear quoting at length:

> To those of us with an Irish childhood, accustomed from our earliest days to picnics beneath high crosses, by ruined abbeys, or at ancient sites, the idea of the head image is an ingrained part of our visual memory. Like round towers and bogs, it comes as a surprise not to find them everywhere. These grey stone faces look solemnly down at us, the sole inhabitants now of isolated, grass covered places once the centre of religious ceremonies. Very difficult to date, some of them may have been carved during the late Middle Ages so that the ancient tradition has continued in a small way for a long time. [P. 22]

33. Louis le Brocquy is the contemporary Irish artist most clearly indebted to the Celtic head cult, although many artists experiment with images of masked and travestied visages. An interesting feature of le Brocquy's aesthetic obsession with the head is his emphasis on the masculine face, the masculine Look. His heads pointedly portray a number of well-known Irishmen—Wolfe Tone, Robert Emmet, Yeats, Joyce, Beckett—usually in multiple versions or impressions; for example, le Brocquy produced 120 takes on Joyce's head. He has also portrayed a cluster of non-Irish men—August Strindberg, Federico García Lorca—and he has done some female studies—"Study of a Girl's Head," "Image of Anne," "Caroline." The 1981 exhibit of his work at the New York State Museum (the catalog for which is *Louis le Brocquy and the Celtic Head Image*) carefully plots this tendency to heroize, etherealize, and particularize the men of his country and to generalize the women. In fact, most portraits of women date from before his 1960s enthusiasm for the Celtic head cult. Le Brocquy instinctively accedes to the preference in Ireland for male viewers and the relative inattention to women's physicality—this against the grain of Western art's love affair with the female face and form.

body before him. My students have commented on the oddity of his look—why does this man not strike us as a voyeur? Why is he not attracted to the body that titillated Casanova, Boucher, Louis XV, and Sir Kenneth Clark? Of course, though she looks vaguely continental, this is his mother, and his mother appears to him to be a whore. And so he fears her to the point of bodilessness in her presence? He becomes "adipose rex," as the *Wake* would have it (*FW*, p. 499)? She becomes the phallus embodied, albeit flaccidly, and lying on a sofa? Whatever the case, needing her to be his body—to access all of the somatic energy that the head cult suppresses in favor of eye-control—he hates her, the dominating ingenue who maps his world. He looks at her with the authoritarian intensity and puritanical commitment of a Provo guerrilla,[34] provisional especially in his willingness to gaze at the mother repressed into passivity and codified into self-destroying contradiction. But Miss O'Murphy does not *appear* to care. She looks off into a middle distance that he cannot occupy. Her line of vision potentially spies only the Vitruvian man on a trompe l'oeil curtain.

Poor Visibility, Celtic Twilight

Leonardo's man in a circle (fig. 5) illustrates Vitruvius's "code of human proportions,"[35] the ideal body of a certain historical moment. Vitruvius felt that designs of buildings and other artifacts should draw their proportionality from the relationships among body units, chin to crown of head, navel to extended arm, and so on. Oddly disproportionate, Leonardo's version of this concept looks severe if not disgusted by the whole project, "devoid of volume." Only ten years later, Leonardo would himself outmode this sense of the human figure.[36] Of course, he epitomized the intellectual and visual force of his historical period much as Boucher did for the late eighteenth century. He worked with linear perspective and with how the eye operates; he respected the sense of sight above all others,[37] but at the time that he drew the Vitruvian man, Leonardo had not yet arrived at these studies or performed the anatomical work for which he became famous. The space he represented in 1485 was much flatter, a system of planes that isolated figures and pinned them, each to separate walls, like moths who had died blind and vaguely disgruntled. It is to this space and look, but without postmodern motivation, that Farrell recurs in his own

34. See Ken Heskin, "The Psychology of Terrorism in Northern Ireland," in *Terrorism in Ireland,* ed. Yonah Alexander and Alan O'Day (London, 1984), pp. 88–105.

35. A. E. Popham, *The Drawings of Leonardo da Vinci* (New York, 1945), p. 61.

36. Carlo Pedretti, *Leonardo: A Study in Chronology and Style* (Berkeley, 1973), p. 79.

37. See Ritchie Calder, *Leonardo and the Age of the Eye* (New York, 1970), p. 69.

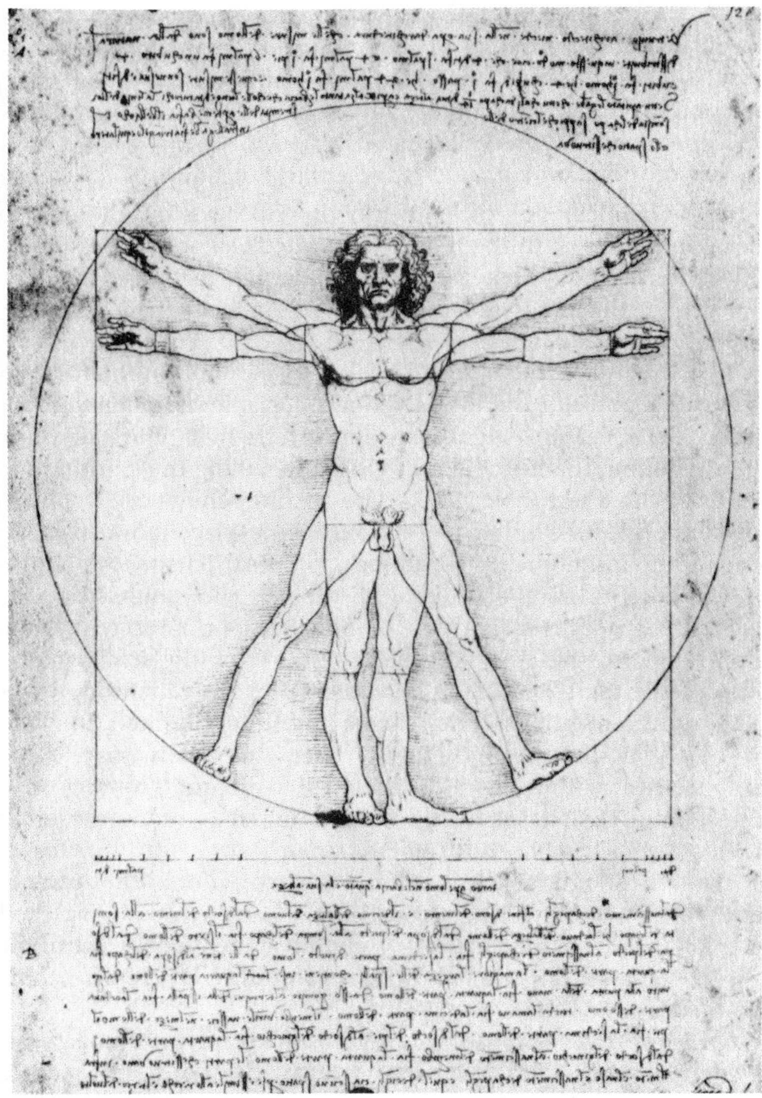

FIG. 5.—Leonardo da Vinci, "Le proporzioni del corpo umano." Photograph courtesy of Elemond, Milan.

composition. What we notice, even in a reproduction of *Madonna Irlanda*, is that the Vitruvian model has been fractured by the curtain—actually, by being part of the curtain that is a faux frame.

The introduction of a trompe l'oeil effect works much as Jean Baudrillard claims in his essay on this device. Understandably, he finds this style of painting simulacral, "highly ritualised," flat. "Trompe-l'oeil," he claims, "forgets all the grand themes and distorts them by means of the minor figuration of some object or other." The emphasis in Baudrillard falls heavily on forgetting, loss of memory, denial of history, the hauntedness that trompe l'oeil objects convey. In their opposition to "the whole representative space elaborated by the Renaissance," these objects "preserve the . . . fantastic pregnancy—that of the discovery of the mirror image by the child. Something, that is, like an immediate hallucination of its own body as preexisting the perceptual order." In reference to the individual and collective suppression of the erotic-maternal body that we are triangulating through Farrell's self-portraiture, the investment of trompe l'oeil in forgetting speaks volumes.[38]

The semantics of loss that Farrell charts installs in the foreground of individual and cultural identity a particular developmental moment. What is *Madonna Irlanda* if not, at some level, a metaphorically "mirror-staged" painting that uses lines of vision (including the painting's many eyes, even the amorphous "frog" eye—a Frenchified viewpoint from the Irish perspective of hard moral outlines?—placed toward the lower frame) not to install the universal space of linear perspective but rather to point out the parallel fields indicated by viewpoints that cannot cohere, the spaces flattened not by Sobchackian movement from the photographic to the cinematic-electronic but by the steady plod of a culture dedicated to *méconnaissance* and skilled in generating its visual style out of suppressions? The space in question is lighted, for Baudrillard, by a glow that he finds "mysterious," sourceless, surrealist. The Irish have been known to call it the Celtic twilight. The very shadowlessness Baudrillard speaks of reveals the fear of movement that Farrell's depicted view confirms and then frames with dimensionless drapery—as though (and this seems pure projection) if he were not to keep an eye on her and box her in, Miss O'Murphy would lose the halo and engulf him. That she is shown as limply benign speaks to this point; she is underplayed in a denial of fear and power. The entire composition accedes to her loss of energy.

On that curtain is yet another sign of the emptying of meaning that is elsewhere anxiously constructed; against the head cult's values we find posed the Vitruvian man's caricature head, which looks very like the ape-Irish stereotypes used by the English from the thirteenth century to the present (fig. 6). Instead of defining the circle of his existence, Farrell's Paddy lowers his arms to cover his genitals, more interested in protecting himself than in claiming his corporeal integrity as the measure of all things.[39] This is the boy who would "enjoy

38. Jean Baudrillard, "The Trompe-L'oeil," in *Calligram: Essays in New Art History from France,* ed. Bryson (Cambridge, 1988), pp. 53, 54, 56.

39. In my fall 1989 Irish studies course at the University of Iowa, I asked my undergraduate students to interpret the "Vitruvian man's" posture in Farrell's painting. The

FIG. 6.—Matt Morgan, *The Irish Frankenstein,* 1869. Reproduced from Liz Curtis, *Nothing But the Same Old Story: The Roots of Anti-Irish Racism* (London, 1985).

Invisibility"[40]—especially when confronted by Miss O'Murphy. More than just a threatening female body forcing him into predictable castration anxiety, Miss O'Murphy is the dominatrix who compels even without knowing it. She is the figure, ground, and trompe l'oeil frame; an unthinkable presymbolic undoing of the Name of the Father transposed into a realm of pure silence; a cliché; a saint who is absent in her own violation; a body that conforms to so overdetermined an iconographic program that transparency and presence are not available even as myths; the Irish arkhein; the mirror moment when linguistic prehistory torques into the obliquities of Irish discourse. Her attributes are not coincident, of course; they cannot integrate but instead flip through their contradictory modes before the rewinding that in Irish circles looks like the latest Celtic "renaissance." By mentioning the prehistoric and the pre-Oedipal, I am not gesturing toward a Jungian racial unconscious but rather toward a quasi-Lacanian formulation, the collective mind in its most bodily condensation, which turns out to be structured like a prehistoric language banned from official registers of Irish self-representation but still capable of emitting signals into the symbolic. In the negative space mapped by this painting lies a potential for certain kinds of movement, connection, process that have yet to be produced in an Ireland seemingly poised these many years at the brink of paradigmatic change.

Given that, as I show below, institutional perspectives underplay the possibility of a matriarchal society predating patriarchy and symmetrically resist legitimating varieties of female power, it is worth asking how individual modern Irish women figure in this analysis. To what extent is their experience swept up in Farrell's arch aesthetic interrogation of Irish social traditions?

Herotica

> "People may fuck a lot but they still don't even bare their bodies" (Marianne, age 20, Ireland, 1979).
>
> "The trouble with a lot of women is they're putting up a front, doing things to make others happy. All giggling . . . then rape you when you're on your own" (Nato, age 21, Ireland, 1979).
>
> "The nuns told us girls were always to blame for arousing men" (Rosemary, age 21, Ireland, 1979).
>
> "Our whole formation as priests, it wasn't exactly anti-women,

American students were unsure whether he was masturbating or protecting himself. The one Irish student in the class, Ray Ryan, immediately quipped that masturbation and self-protection are "the same thing."

40. James Joyce, *Ulysses* (New York, 1984), p. 9.

but it didn't help us relate to them in any way" (Father Quinlan, Dublin, 1979).

"When you talk of Ireland, you talk of a uniquely damaged culture" (Ivor Browne, department of psychiatry, University College, Dublin, 1979).

"You can be naked in Ireland; you just can't be doing anything" (Pat Murphy, Irish filmmaker, 1988).

"We used to get lectures (I haven't written about this because it is not really believable) that since we had a steady salary we would be an enormous source of sexual excitement; that girls might be prepared to do certain things because of our position and that it was our duty to restrain these women" (John McGahern, Irish novelist, 1987).[41]

One convenient text for approaching popular images of the body is Nancy Scheper-Hughes's *Saints, Scholars, and Schizophrenics.* This ethnographic study, like others done in Ireland, has been controversial, especially among the Irish. In her second edition of the book, Scheper-Hughes herself documents the degree of outrage expressed by the people she had lived among after they had read her book. Several years later, Scheper-Hughes returns to this topic and draws some different lines to describe her current anthropological practice, the reduced degree to which she probes secrets and exposes her informants to discomfort.[42] Although the book received reasonably good reviews in social science journals when it appeared,[43] the passage of years has cast into relief a number of methodological issues. In particular, a reader has to question the value of evidence gained when an anthropologist administers psychological diagnostic tests that are themselves of debatable reliability. There is a good deal of the self-fulfilling prophecy about Scheper-Hughes's inquiry, and yet *Saints, Scholars, and Schizophrenics* usefully documents prominent aspects of Irish self-representation. The evidence that she provides for a lowest common denominator of traditional beliefs about body and mind in

41. The first five quotations here are from Sweetman, *On Our Backs,* pp. 43, 47, 55, 82, and 90. I quote Pat Murphy from her comments at the Contemporary Irish Film Festival held at the New School for Social Research, New York, 15 Mar. 1988. The McGahern quotation is from John Devitt, "Education in the Land of a Nod and a Wink," review of *Education Policy in Twentieth Century Ireland,* by Séamus O'Buachalla, *A Troubled Sky: Reflections on the Irish Educational Scene, 1957–1968,* by Sean O'Connor, and *Education and the Arts,* ed. Daniel J. Murphy, *Irish Literary Supplement* 8 (Fall 1989): 17.

42. See Scheper-Hughes's sensitive article, "The Best of Two Worlds, the Worst of Two Worlds: Reflections on Culture and Field Work among the Rural Irish and Pueblo Indians," *Comparative Studies in Society and History* 29 (Jan. 1987): 56–75.

43. For a cogent and critical review, see Sidney Callahan, "An Anthropologist in Ireland," *Commonweal,* 25 May 1979, pp. 310–11. My own assessment is that Scheper-Hughes does not demonstrate the multivalent immersion in Irish life at large that would lend to her fieldwork in Ireland the interpretive nuance that it deserves.

rural Ireland has profound implications echoed by Farrell and other artists.

Beginning from the often-adduced point that the Republic has "the highest hospitalization treatment rate for mental illness in the world" and that "schizophrenia is the core problem" (*S*, p. 3), Scheper-Hughes explores the genetic, biochemical, and environmental explanations for this situation. She did her fieldwork in a small community in Kerry, reconstructing the ethnohistory of the area and talking with both "normal" and hospitalized residents. Ambivalence, ambiguity, irony, evasion, conflict—all of these traits and more are given deep resonance in this study. She tries to define Irish identity according to a model that explains its etiology, persistence, and chained cause-effects.

Scheper-Hughes focuses on celibacy norms, asceticism, resistance to being touched, and sexual repression as well as less obvious phenomena such as the then putatively widely dispersed ignorance of orgasms among Irish countrywomen or the taboo on breast-feeding (considered by some a violation of body boundaries).[44] She gathers impressive evidence that in rural areas the Irish body is or was construed as worthless, endangering, and constantly threatened. The typical reader of this situation would attribute such body coding to the impact of the Catholic church on the "peasant mind," but Scheper-Hughes's evidence takes us much further.

Consider that she presented normal adolescents and those diagnosed as mentally ill with Thematic Apperception Test cards. One such card pictures a woman lying face up in bed with a sheet over her lower body but with her breasts exposed; standing up and facing away from her is a fully dressed man, who covers his eyes with his upraised arm (fig. 7). According to Scheper-Hughes, responses to this card displayed the alacrity with which normal young people censored from their interpretations "sexual love or intimacy themes." In place of "romance or marriage stories," these adolescents tried collectively to "defuse or desexualize situations in which the sexes are in proximate contact" (*S*, p. 125). Half of the normal respondents read the card as a death scene. On the other hand, the diagnosed schizophrenics (and Scheper-Hughes claims to have compared these Irish diagnoses with nonnative doctors' readings to insure a measure of "objectivity") did not deflect the sexual content of the scene, insisting on the place of romance and erotic physicality in their interpretations.

Reading Scheper-Hughes's study of rural Ireland in tandem with a work like Rosita Sweetman's *On Our Backs,* a series of interviews with Dubliners, is troubling. (The two books share a 1979 copyright.) Emphatically concerned with the official blindness in Irish institutions

44. See *S*, pp. 119, 122. Scheper-Hughes presents these beliefs as traditional ideas that remained active during the period of her fieldwork, 1974, and following.

FIG. 7.—Thematic Apperception Test Card 13 MF. Reprinted by permission of the publishers from Henry A. Murray, *Thematic Apperception Test*, Cambridge, Mass.: Harvard University Press. © 1943 by the President and Fellows of Harvard College. © 1971 by Henry A. Murray.

to the suffering caused by sexual ignorance and dysfunction, Sweetman presents a fascinating if skewed portrait of how urban Ireland thought, in the seventies, about the body. She shows us what she calls a "hidden aspect" of Ireland,[45] which finds best expression in the votes for continued constitutional bans on abortion and civil divorce. Populating this invisible Eire, whose children are now reaching middle age, are the abused orphan, the prostitute, the "Irish macho," the irresponsible and alcoholic father still dominated by his doting mother, the ignored wife who repeats history by adoring her son while refusing to tell him the facts of life, the priests who counsel their male charges against the evils of women wearing backless dresses, the convent girls so terrorized by the nuns' violent response to their becoming women that they cease menstruation. Again and again, Sweetman suggests that not just marital dissatisfaction but also the turmoil of Irish history is illogically laid, by

45. Sweetman, *On Our Backs*, p. 11.

both genders, at the feet of Irish women. The tension that this attribution both masks and reveals has to do with myths of matriarchal dominance in Ireland. Although it is demonstrable that the Irish mother has a good deal of influence within many homes, especially in the minds of her sons, and although Ireland itself is generally thought of as a woman who demands and gets considerable sacrifice,[46] the actual power exercised by Irish women is severely constrained to a certain familial and ideological zone that does not disarm the more powerful patriarchal syntax of the culture. That the diffuse agents of patriarchy resist reverse domination and stylize socially produced ideologies of the body to compensate for perceived danger is precisely to the point of the symmetries that this essay charts.

The Arkhein

> Is dads the thing in such or are tits the that?
>
> —JAMES JOYCE, *Finnegans Wake*

The varied, traditional, and ongoing repression of the represented body that Joyce, Scheper-Hughes, Sweetman, and others document goes hand in hand with the socially *systematic* constructions of Irish identity, and this complex system is folded into Farrell's self-portrait. That Farrell (however archly) defines his own pictorial subjectivity in these terms is disturbing. Equally unsettling is the fact that institutional archaeology in Ireland, apparently governed by symmetrical stylizations, reads out of the official story a great deal of female-identified content that could be useful to Irish feminists and others interested in claiming alternative somatic and social texts.

The Irish archaeological enterprises that are probably best known worldwide today involve the excavation of Neolithic structures, including what have been called passage tombs, court tombs, cairns, mounds, and tumuli. Many of these structures have been categorized according to internal design, but most of them appear similar from the outside; they are large circular mounds of earth and stone often found on hilltops overlooking attractive vistas. Lest my connection of the rhetoric of Irish art with the rhetoric of Irish archaeology seem tenuous, I should add that these structures are the earliest ones remaining in Ireland, dating from four thousand or more years ago, and have been consid-

46. The 1988 video entitled "Mother Ireland," directed by Anne Crilly and produced by Derry Film and Video with support from Britain's Channel Four, explores and explodes many myths surrounding the figure of Ireland as woman. In Irish studies circles, this video has been enormously influential in bringing to the fore women's voices and attitudes about the terms in which they are persistently stereotyped. The Mother Ireland myth does show remarkable resilience, even in the face of ongoing critique.

ered a nominal point of origin for an indigenous identity, the prehistoric architecture of Irishness. The country, north and south, hosts about 1,400 megalithic mounds as well as other circular structures (the count varies, depending on one's source and assumptions about whether to incorporate a projection for now-destroyed monuments), including some of the largest and most spectacular tombs in Europe. They are high-profile aspects of the Irish setting. Farrell's early art, which self-consciously grounds itself in Irish motifs, exploits the designs characteristic of these ancient structures. More to the point, the Neolithic passage graves frequently symbolize Ireland in the media; as Luke Gibbons has pointed out, the best known of these mounds have been portrayed "not only in IDA [Industrial Development Authority] brochures but also in the Bank of Ireland's publicity material."[47] Gibbons suggests the ironies of such commercial appropriation of these structures to further a made-up prehistory that suits the purposes of the corporate world, but the fact remains that the Neolithic passage graves are among the best-known identifiers in Ireland for Ireland.

Three major mounds cluster in the Boyne valley, about twenty-five miles from Dublin. Newgrange (fig. 8), a popular tourist site, has been described in print since the seventeenth century. Knowth, under excavation for the past twenty years, has much to tell us about Neolithic society, information embodied in George Eogan's elegant and authoritative book *Knowth and the Passage-Tombs of Ireland.* Having been to Newgrange, Knowth, and various cairns throughout Ireland, I find Eogan's report an excellent field in which to explore the disciplinary decorum of archaeology in relation to larger cultural patterns in Ireland.

Eogan describes Neolithic society in the Boyne valley as focused on a cult of the dead and as divided into a hierarchy of workers. Evidence for social stratification comes from the mounds themselves; to build Knowth required construction skills that it is rather difficult to project back into that dim period occupied in *Finnegans Wake* by the character Mutt, whose (m)other lingo the invader Jute attributes to a speech impediment. For the most part, Eogan's book sustains a rigorously nonspeculative mode. As a careful scientist, he presents the facts, particularly the measurements relevant to his project of excavation and preservation. This scientific perspective stands at odds with a great deal of depiction that I would call "mound art" and that includes painters' and sculptors' uses of passage-grave decorative motifs, poems that refer to the mounds, stories set near prehistoric spots, folklore about these sites, straightforwardly antiestablishment theories about Irish prehistory (such as those sometimes put forward by antiquarians and

47. Luke Gibbons, "Coming Out of Hibernation? The Myth of Modernity in Irish Culture," in *Across the Frontiers,* p. 213.

FIG. 8.—Newgrange. Reproduced from Benedict Kiely, *The Aerofilms Book of Ireland from the Air* (London, 1985), by permission of Hunting Aerofilms.

psychics), and the occasional scholarly flight of informed speculation about the early society in question and its uses of these locations. Some of these aesthetic responses to the mounds point in the direction of local assessments: as far as I have been able to determine from recorded ethnographic anecdote, people living near the tumuli have consistently overlaid onto the cairns their own meanings, assigning to them a powerful charge and imagining them as having been the dwellings of female-identified supernatural beings such as the Tuatha De Danaan. Given the option to walk over a mound or around it, locals often walk around. Today, many scholars and all archaeologically oriented feminists that I am aware of claim the cairns and their decorations as evidence for widespread European worship of a primary goddess (either in the Neolithic period or in later uses of these sacred sites) and for a corresponding social register of matriarchal power.[48]

Following the specific mores of his discipline, Eogan is thorough and impeccable in describing the site, and he does not linger on the folklore that has accumulated around the mounds, the art inspired by them, or the more speculative side of the archaeological project. He describes the designs found in these mounds as nonrepresentational and geometric, without recoverable meaning. Within this context, the way in which Eogan describes his initial entry into Knowth is of remarkable interest. First, he tells the story of his discovery of the apparent "guardian" of the inner chamber, an orthostat depicting "what seemed to be an anthropomorphic figure with two large, staring eyes" (fig. 9).[49] His narrative continues:

> At a point which would prove to be about a third of the way in, we came upon a well-preserved stretch and felt growing excitement.

48. See Scott, *Joyce and Feminism,* chap. 2; Lucy Lippard, *Overlay: Contemporary Art and the Art of Prehistory* (New York, 1983); Marija Gimbutas, *The Gods and Goddesses of Old Europe: 7000 to 3500 BC Myths, Legends, and Cult Images* (Berkeley, 1974); Máire and Liam de Paor, *Early Christian Ireland* (London, 1978); and Helen Lanigan Wood, "Women in Myths and Early Depictions," in *Irish Women: Image and Achievement,* ed. Eiléan Ní Chuilleanáin (Dublin, 1985), pp. 13–24.

In a review of Lippard's work on prehistoric and contemporary art, Irish art historian Dorothy Walker states unequivocally, "I am . . . quite convinced, although I can quote no archaeologist to support my view, that the great tumulus at Newgrange, one of the earliest stone structures in the world, while certainly used as a tomb, was originally built as a womb of the Mother Goddess, receiving the shaft of the rising sun directly into the spiral-carved interior at the winter solstice every year. This solar mating has survived 5000 years of successive cultures" (Dorothy Walker, review of *Overlay: Contemporary Art and the Art of Prehistory,* by Lippard, *Irish Literary Supplement* 3 [Fall 1984]: 44–45).

49. George Eogan, *Knowth and the Passage-Tombs of Ireland* (London, 1986), p. 32. The photograph that Eogan provides of the "guardian" elicits some viewers' readings of the eyes as breasts, surmounted by a smaller head stone and positioned over an elaborate spiral design that suggests a pregnant belly carrying a fetus.

FIG. 9.—Orthostats inside passage-tomb at Knowth. Reproduced from George Eogan, *Knowth and the Passage-Tombs of Ireland* (London, 1986), by kind permission of the author.

> Soon we were on hands and knees again. . . . My course sloped gradually upwards, then stopped as if in mid-air. Before me in the lamp's beam was the most amazing sight of my life. About 2.5 m below lay a large chamber, whose great corbelled roof rose around me [fig. 10], spanned by a single capstone up to 4 m above. My 'passage' over the orthostats was roofed by vast lintels, some of which were decorated. After a while I dropped down into the chamber, noticing its cruciform plan with a number of decorated orthostats. The right-hand recess in this plan was 'guarded' by two large jambstones. Looking between them, I saw a uniquely ornamented stone basin, with horizontal and vertical scorings on the outside and, just opposite the recess opening, a composition of concentric circles with flankers at the bottom. . . . What a structure and what a surprise! . . . And, having wriggled through some difficult parts in the passage on my way in, my presence alone in the tomb—despite its massiveness—gave me a sense not of isolation, but of security.[50]

Despite the claims made on his consciousness and procedures by the scientific enterprise of institutional archaeology, Eogan generously chronicles his entry in a kind of counternarrative to the rest of his writing. The securely enwombed archaeologist, caught up in his wonderful experience of a tumulus "revirgined" by a centuries-long removal from curious eyes, spontaneously appreciates the sight. I would say that Eogan's writing projects his experience of an energy excess (communicated by Neolithic design), of the primeval arkhein that, built around a uterine space and also panoptically surveying the surrounding landscape, framed the society's experience and organized its identity in terms of somatic power. The architecture reconveyed to him some of its structural meaning before disciplinary codes of operation intervened to deflect that information in the more formal portion of his report.[51] Eogan's portrayal of his personal experience aligns him with many

50. Ibid., pp. 34–35.

51. Lippard cites numerous examples worldwide of male archaeologists effacing evidence of female-identified cultures and quotes Aubrey Burl's dissatisfaction with the concept of a goddess cult in Ireland (Lippard, *Overlay*, p. 65). Whether or not a goddess cult existed seems less interesting than the rhetoric of contemporary Irish archaeology and the responses of scholars outside the archaeological profession to that rhetorical position. A case in point is the artist Martin Brennan, whose discussion of Knowth bears repeating:

> Knowth is strictly in the domain of archaeologists. It is completely sealed off from the enquiring eyes of independent researchers by a high fence topped with barbed wire. Inside, the mound is in the process of being cut apart like a layer cake, while its magnificent art treasures lie covered up under sheets of black plastic. Perhaps the comparative obscurity of megalithic art today is due to the fact that at Knowth

FIG. 10.—Corbelling inside the passage-tomb at Knowth. Reproduced from Eogan, *Knowth and the Passage-Tombs of Ireland,* by kind permission of the author.

other writers on the mounds who have been deeply moved by visual or tactile experience of them. It could be argued that the institutionally necessary rhetorical shift in Eogan's report from personal experience to archaeological specificities repeats a gesture of neutralization that we have seen before and that we can profitably examine in the pursuit of a crossdisciplinary understanding of Irish culture.

My point here is not that the Irish should reach back to the Neolithic past for a sense of identity—an impossible gesture to carry through and a sentimental journey as fraught with difficulties as a social praxis based on Deleuzian schizoanalysis. Rather, I think that the authorized interpretation of visual materials from that overwhelmingly female-identified past (or at least a past whose remains generations have read in "somatomorphic" terms) has tended to ensure a flattened appropriation of them, a reluctance to connect issues of shape and structure with cultural dialogue and possibility, and an unwillingness to recover at any level the physicality of the body in other than the most destructive and threatening sense. There is a prevailing institutional taboo against imagining what Irish prehistory was like, against allowing competing visions to converse. Disciplinary boundaries overrule consideration of the many ways the body can be represented and set in motion; these blockages chart a meaning-charged relationship. So it is that in my reading of Irish self-representation, the undoing by his discipline of an archaeologist's personal sensory responses metaphorically doubles the treatment of Miss O'Murphy, for whom an experience of her own violation is not available. The redounding of her anaestheticization, art historical and otherwise, in Farrell's pictorial disembodiment speaks to more than just the castration fears that Farrell sees in his world; we enter here a realm of internal censorship that traverses genders and ricochets into a shared obsession with defining the collective mind. Literally and broadly out of touch with its bodies, that mind produces an aesthetics of denial that is uncomfortable appropriating multidimensionally the design of its environment. Again, we're talking about *1,400* megalithic mounds plus other related field monuments that Irish people have gone to for childhood picnics as Pennsylvanians would go to Valley Forge or Gettysburg (Ireland is about the size of Pennsylvania).

> some of its greatest examples remain quite literally cloaked in secrecy. [Brennan, *The Stars and the Stones: Ancient Art and Astronomy in Ireland* (London, 1983), p. 56]

Brennan favors a representational status for Neolithic art. It is worth noting that in 1980 he and Jack Roberts confirmed previous reports that various cairns in Ireland constitute a massive and precise system for charting astronomical movements. According to Brennan, this discovery was ignored by the Irish archaeological establishment even though the Irish press headlined the story. The layman in these issues is likely to be intrigued by Brennan's book, which is exciting and elegant.

Side by side with this denial is the work of a filmmaker like Pat Murphy, who specifically attempts to access a feminist perspective in her analyses of Irish life and who finds these monuments a potential source of enrichment that Irish men and women have been taught to discount.[52] Consider the untutored comment of a local woman who, when asked by Scheper-Hughes what some fieldstones meant, replied, "'Those were the kinds of altars we used to have before the priests made them flat'" (*S*, p. 23). (This flattening is not the sort that Sobchack analyzes; her videologic would be relatively invisible or nonsignifying in this field.) At the level of collectivity, the cairns might operate as mediators to a register of meaning that accommodates a concept of other symbolic orders, an alternativity, a visual semiotic that could foster new ways of looking and moving.

Terrible Beauty

Take the mounds as a Rorschach test. Consider that looking closely at Newgrange and at Miss O'Murphy continues to produce not sensuous significance but a loss of vitality that instantiates a primal anti-erotic gaze. When a certain kind of institutional Irish eye looks at women, it sees a rather daunting witch, a voracious female. How did that arkhein which promotes an archaeologist's feelings of security become the represented-as-grimly-dominant Irish mothers of the past two centuries? A shorthand answer suggests itself in Patrick J. Keane's study of Yeats and Joyce. His work is grounded in the varied identifications of Ireland with a woman (Kathleen Ni Houlihan, the Poor Old Woman) who compels young men to die for her. Keane feels honorably and passionately that violence is not the answer to Ireland's political and economic problems, but in place of an analysis of this lived history and of the relationship of art to it, he loosely connects some references to Bloody Sunday and English shoot-to-kill policies to the many allusions in Irish writing to an evil hag. Thus he suggests that a commitment to the vicious service of the mythical Mother Ireland is *the cause* of ongoing bloodshed.

I see these relationships differently. The argument that the myth of Ireland as a woman motivates the endless sacrifice of her sons and lovers runs counter to the actual situation, in which a prevailing refusal of official sanction for Ireland's female-identified prehistory feeds the unbalanced negativity that many writers have indeed exploited. Representative of a whole school of thought about Ireland, Keane's book demonstrates the hazards that attend a failure to approach Irish icons

52. Conversation with Pat Murphy, Dublin, 21 Aug. 1989.

through an analysis of the complex systems of Irish "identity" and psychohistory.[53] The type of work that deplores violence in moralistic terms alone cannot explain why it is that the oppressions of invading forces have been stylized through the centuries and introjected as the Dominatrix-Mound-Mother's putative pleasure in the death of her sons. Nor can it explain why that supposed voracity has led to a certain neutralizing of sexuality, let alone of *écriture feminine,* in Ireland. Or why an admittedly skewed gene pool has produced not just high levels of schizophrenia but schizophrenia that speaks in the voice of the body-censor. Or finally, why voyeurism appears to find its most powerful native expression not in Peeping Tomism or in art history but in the covert optics of guerrilla warfare.

Surely a different reading of Irish bodies and Irish social patterns must be generated if we are to understand the continued power of traditional images, myths, and gestures. This alternative reading would attend to the degree to which the represented body has become an anti-fetish in Ireland, a turnoff, the presumed source of whatever it is that makes Joycean paralysis the safe choice; so it is that the learned eye stills the body at which it gazes while simultaneously screening out both movement and messages that would dislodge this visual-hermeneutic circuit. While the need for a certain stillness remains projected onto the body, preferably the body of a woman or a landscape figured as female, the authorized centers of meaning in the society discover again and again that their own ability to move has been impeded.

That the power of an alternativity or matri-symbolic (again, projected here in the most nonliteral terms imaginable) still has cultural force is expressed in many aspects of Irish life, including Farrell's choice of the Madonna Irlanda figure for his series of political paintings. Having in earlier days worked through the available international modes and spiraled back to the interesting shapes of Neolithic and Celtic art, he became sufficiently aware of some threatening or disturbing element—what I locate in the trope of a repressed prehistory—to retreat ironically into the sanctioned, universal visual language of Western art history. Looking for an Irish body, he thus went with conscious irony to Boucher and Leonardo. Like Joyce ransacking the Western world not for "universality" but for moral support in approaching a crucially identifying unknown that has taken shape in Ireland as a feared Dominatrix, Farrell appropriated the double-speak, puns, wit, bitter irony, allegorical iconography, and the other displacing figures often seen as typical of Irish discourse. This fallback position we "recognize" as Irish; it is the form of choice for expressing

53. See Patrick J. Keane, *Terrible Beauty: Yeats, Joyce, Ireland, and the Myth of the Devouring Female* (Columbia, Mo., 1988).

anxiety over the inability to block awareness of the arkhein sedimented into certain visual registers. As Ellie Ragland-Sullivan notes, quoting Jacques Lacan, "'In our relationship to things, as constituted by the path of vision and ordered in the figures of representation, something glides, passes, transmits itself from stage to stage, in order always to be in some degree eluded there.'"[54] One sense that this comment could take on in the current discussion is to describe the self-replicating twist at the heart of Irish self-representation. Around the neutralized body, a complex system of social identification resists postmodernism and all that we associate with it even while allowing the texts of an American present to enter its ports. There are thus profound disjunctions in Ireland today between traditions of collective identity and the kinds of information, ancient and videological, that are available. How the culture proceeds to negotiate its constitution of an Irish mind in the midst of these material changes may well tutor us all in the possibilities and means of social transformation.

54. Ellie Ragland-Sullivan, *Jacques Lacan and the Philosophy of Psychoanalysis* (Urbana, Ill., 1986), p. 44.

Diaspora: Generation and the Ground of Jewish Identity

Daniel Boyarin and Jonathan Boyarin

> In the field of rational analysis, a feeling of recognized kinship is more desirable than nationalism.
>
> —Gayatri Chakravorty Spivak[1]

Group identity has been constructed traditionally in two ways. It has been figured on the one hand as the product of a common genealogical origin and, on the other, as produced by a common geographical origin. The first has a strongly pejorative value in current writing—having become tainted with the name *race* and thus racism—while the second has a generally positive ring. One of the reasons for this split in values is undoubtedly the unfortunate usages to which the term and concept of

Some of the material in this paper is taken from the final chapter of Daniel Boyarin's forthcoming book, *A Radical Jew: Paul and the Politics of Identity.* Other material is from Jonathan Boyarin's "Der Yiddisher Tsenter; or What Is a Minyan?" and Jonathan Boyarin and Greg Sarris, "Jews and Native Americans as Living Voice and Absent Other," presented at the MLA convention, December 1991. We wish to thank Harry Berger, Jr., Stephen Greenblatt, and Steven Knapp, none of whom necessarily agrees (and one of whom necessarily disagrees) with the claims being made but all of whom made vitally significant interventions.

All biblical translations are our own.

1. Gayatri Chakravorty Spivak, "Acting Bits/Identity Talk," p. 150. Paradoxically, Spivak means "recognized kinship" and even "family resemblance" that have nothing to do with genealogy, thus inscribing herself inevitably in a Pauline descent according to the spirit. Perhaps "in the field of rational analysis" is meant exactly as an ironic—or even satiric—distancing from that field.

This article originally appeared in *Critical Inquiry* 19 (Summer 1993).

race in the sense of genotype has been put in Europe since early modern times.[2] Another source, however, of our cultural disdain for genealogy as a value is undoubtedly the sustained attack on it that lies at the fountainhead of Christendom, the Letters of Paul. In this paper, we would like to interrogate the Pauline sources of Western discourse about generation, space, and identity, along with the rabbinic Jewish counterdiscourse around these terms. We will trace this fault line into the present as well, confronting claims of "pure theory" with our own discourses of critically grounded identity, speaking about paradoxes of individual and collective identity with reference to Jean-François Lyotard, Jean-Luc Nancy, and Walter Benn Michaels.

1

> פּאָולוס איז געווען דער ערשטער באָלשעוויק
> [Paul was the first Bolshevik.]
>
> —Hillel Kempinsky[3]

In early patristic writings and again in many quarters since the mid-nineteenth century, Paul's project has been understood as one of universalizing the Torah, breaking through the "particularism" of the Jewish religion. Galatians 3:26–29 is taken as the moral center of Paul's work: "For as many of you as were baptized into Christ have put on Christ [saying]: 'There is neither Jew nor Greek; there is neither slave nor free-

2. It was not, of course, always used that way. Symptomatic perhaps of this shift is the following statement from Dio Cassius: "I do not know the origin of this name [Jews], but it is applied to all men, even foreigners, who follow their customs. This race is found among Romans" (quoted in John Gager, *The Origins of Anti-Semitism: Attitudes toward Judaism in Pagan and Christian Antiquity* [New York, 1983], p. 91). We see from this quotation that race once had much suppler and more complex connections with genealogy, cultural praxis, and identity than it has in our parlance.

3. Oral communication to Jonathan Boyarin. Hillel Kempinsky ז"ל was the archivist of the Jewish Workers' Bund in New York.

Daniel Boyarin is Taubman Professor of Talmudic Culture at the University of California, Berkeley. He is the author of *Intertextuality and the Reading of Midrash* (1990), *Carnal Israel* (1993), and *A Radical Jew: Paul and the Politics of Identity* (1994). **Jonathan Boyarin** is a student at Yale Law School. His books include *Polish Jews in Paris* (1991), *Storm from Paradise: The Politics of Jewish Memory* (1992), and the forthcoming *Palestine and Jewish History* and *Thinking in Jewish*. He is also editor of *Remapping Memory: The Politics of TimeSpace* (1994).

man; there is no male and female. For you are all one in Christ Jesus.' If, however, you belong to Christ, then you are Abraham's offspring, heirs according to the promise."

Paul cites the baptismal formula that the Galatians themselves recited or heard recited at the time of their baptism: "There is neither Jew nor Greek."[4] He interprets the text, and thus baptism itself, in the following fashion. The rite consists of a new birth that is understood as substituting an allegorical genealogy for a literal one. In Christ, that is, in baptism, all the differences that mark off one body from another as Jew or Greek (circumcision is considered a "natural" mark of the Jew [Rom. 2:27]), male or female, slave or free are effaced, for in the Spirit such marks do not exist.

Accordingly, if one belongs to Christ, then one participates in the allegorical meaning of the promise to the "seed of Abraham," an allegorical meaning of genealogy that is already hinted at in the biblical text itself, when it said that in "Abraham all nations would be blessed" (Gen. 12:3) and even more when it interpreted his name as "Father to many nations" (Gen. 17:5). The individual body itself is replaced by its allegorical referent, the body of Christ of which all the baptized are part.[5] This is what the "putting-on" of Christ means, which is certainly a reference to the topos of the body as a garment.[6] Paul is the vehicle of a certain distrust of corporeality that is characteristic of Christian culture as well as of the Western critique of ethnicity since his text is the material base of much of the discourse on ethnicity in Christian culture. Things of the body are less important than things of the spirit. The physical connection of common descent from Abraham and the embodied practices with which that genealogy is marked off as difference are rejected in favor of a connection between people based on individual re-creation and entry de novo into a community of common belief. Charles Mopsik has recently glossed the cultural effect of Paul's works as "the persistence of a split opened two millennia ago by the ideological victory over one part of the inhabited world of the Christian conception of carnal relation—and of carnal filiation—as separate from spiritual life and devalued in relation to it."[7]

In his authentic passion to find a place for the Gentiles in the Torah's

4. See Dennis Ronald Macdonald, *There Is No Male and Female: The Fate of a Dominical Saying in Paul and Gnosticism* (Philadelphia, 1987) and the classic paper by Wayne A. Meeks, "The Image of the Androgyne: Some Uses of a Symbol in Earliest Christianity," *History of Religions* 13 (Feb. 1974): 165–208.

5. The parallel citation of the formula in 1 Corinthians 12:13 makes this even more explicit: For in one spirit we were all baptized into one body.

6. As in the dominical saying identified plausibly by Macdonald as the source of the baptismal formula itself: "when ye trample on the garment of shame, when the Two become One, and Male with Female neither male nor female." See also Jonathan Z. Smith, "The Garments of Shame," *History of Religions* 5 (Winter 1966): 217–38.

7. Charles Mopsik, "The Body of Engenderment in the Hebrew Bible, the Rabbinic Tradition and the Kabbalah," in *Fragments for a History of the Human Body*, ed. Michel Feher (New York, 1989), p. 49.

scheme of things and the brilliance of the radically dualist and allegorical hermeneutic that he developed to accomplish this purpose, Paul had (almost against his will) sown the seeds for a Christian discourse that would completely deprive Jewish ethnic, cultural specificity of any positive value and indeed turn it into a "curse" in the eyes of Gentile Christians.[8] Elizabeth Castelli has focussed most sharply on the extent to which the drive for sameness was constitutive of Pauline discourse by analyzing the function of imitation and its political effects in his letters:

> the language of imitation, with its concomitant tension between the drive toward sameness and the inherent hierarchy of the mimetic relationship, masks the will to power which one finds in Pauline discourse. Paul's appropriation of the discourse of mimesis is a powerful rhetorical move, because this language identifies the fundamental values of wholeness and unity with Paul's own privileged position vis-à-vis the gospel, the early Christian communities he founded and supervises, and Christ himself. *Here is precisely where he makes his coercive move. To stand for anything other than what the apostle stands for is to articulate for oneself a place of difference, which has already implicitly been associated with discord and disorder.* To stand in a position of difference is to stand in opposition, therefore, to the gospel, the community, and Christ.[9]

8. This is not to deny the radically progressive intent nor even the radically progressive effect of Paul's utterance. Indeed, one of the larger points of Daniel Boyarin's forthcoming book *A Radical Jew: Paul and the Politics of Identity* is to show precisely that ideals of universal human equality that have given rise to the French Revolution, the emancipation of slaves, and the feminist movement also flow from the fountainhead of Galatians 3:28–39. For the nonce, see Daniel Boyarin, "Paul and the Genealogy of Gender," *Representations,* no. 41 (Winter 1993), in which this argument is expressly made. As Boyarin writes there:

> In any case, if on the one hand, Wire points to the devastating history of male oppression of women in the name of Paul, one can also cite at least a nascent discourse and real history of chastity as female autonomy also carried out in his name in what is, after all, the Acts of Paul and Thekla for notable example. Similarly with regard to the parallel issue of slavery. Philemon has been used (maybe misused) as a text in the service of slavery. It is just as true, however, that Galatians 3:28 has been mobilized in anti-slavery discourses. The failure of consistency here does not involve Paul's aspirations but his achievements. Others who come after may indeed be able to put into practice that which in Paul is fraught with contradiction. I think that the ultimate elimination of slavery in all of the Christian world is an eloquent case in point, although it took nearly two thousand years for Paul's vision to be realized here. [Pp. 32–33 n. 91]

Indeed, if anything, the ultimate point of the present paper is that the progressive elements of that Western universalism that we are locating in Paul are inescapably bound up in their very problematic coerciveness. If, as Etienne Balibar argues (see n. 23 below), the very discourse of "the Rights of Man" provides the form for a particularly French racism, this does not mean that the world would be better off not having had those principles articulated.

9. Elizabeth A. Castelli, *Imitating Paul: A Discourse of Power* (Louisville, Ky., 1991), p. 87; emphasis added.

Castelli describes the personal will to power implicit in the Pauline rhetorical drive toward sameness. The same analysis can be applied, however, to the politics of group relations even after the apostle's death. We suggest that as Paul gradually became not an embattled apostle for one kind of Christianity contending with others but the source of Christianity *tout court,* and as so-called pagans faded from the scene, the function of those who "stand in a position of difference" came to be filled almost exclusively in the discourse by the Jews, and the "coercive move" toward sameness came to be directed at the Jews.[10] The place of difference increasingly becomes the Jewish place, and thus the Jew becomes the very sign of discord and disorder in the Christian polity. That this is so can be shown from the fact that as other "differences" appear on the medieval European scene (the Lollards, for example), they are figured in literature as "Jews."

It is, however, important to emphasize that Paul is not "anti-Semitic" or even anti-Jewish. From his perspective, the drive toward sameness was precisely to be understood as the fulfillment of Judaism, for "true" Jewishness was not an affair of descent "according to the flesh" (Gal. 4:21–31); nor was it an affair of practice according to the flesh, like circumcision (Rom. 2:28–29).[11] True Jewishness lay, according to Paul, precisely in renunciation of difference and entry into the one body of Christ. Anyone at all can be Jewish, and those who "call themselves Jews" are not necessarily Jewish at all.

This double reading of the sign *Jew* by Paul as both signifier of unruly difference and symbol of universalism has had fateful consequences for the Jews in the Christian West. Once Paul succeeded, "real Jews" ended up being only a trope. They have remained such for European discourse down to the present and even in the writings of leftists whose work is *explicitly* opposed to anti-Semitism—and even in the writings of Jews. Although well intentioned, any such allegorization of *Jew* is problematic in the extreme for the way that it deprives those who have historically grounded identities in those material signifiers of the power to speak for themselves and remain different. In this sense the "progressive" idealization of *Jew* and *woman,* or more usually, *jew* and *Woman,* ultimately deprives difference of the right to be different.

2

Sometimes the reference to the allegorized Jew is implicit or made in passing; in other recent works it is an explicit and central trope. An exam-

10. At least until new "pagans" were discovered in the early modern period.

11. For a full discussion, see Daniel Boyarin, "'This We Know to Be the Carnal Israel': Circumcision and the Erotic Life of God and Israel," *Critical Inquiry* 18 (Spring 1992): 474–506.

ple of the former is contained in Jean-Luc Nancy's recent *The Inoperative Community.* Nancy's central problem in that work is to formulate a notion of community that will not violate the standard of noncoercion. That standard holds that community is "the compearance [*comparution*] of singular beings." For Nancy, such singularity and the simultaneity that is a condition of it appear to imply an evacuation of history and memory. So many brutalities, so many violations of any notion of humanly responsible community have been carried out in the name of solidary collectives supposed to have obtained in the past, that Nancy seems to have renounced any possible recourse to memory in his attempt to think through the possibility of there ever being community without coercion. Of there ever *being:* the only community that does not betray the hope invested in that word, Nancy argues, is one that resists any kind of stable existence.[12]

The problem is that Nancy has in fact attempted a generalized model of community as *nonbeing*. Hence any already existing "community" is out of consideration by its very existence, relegated through philosophical necessity to a world we have lost or that never existed. Following Nancy's rhetoric, the only possible residues of that lost world are false community appearing as a serial, undifferentiated collective in the same analytic category as the fascist mass or, alternatively, an assemblage of unrelated individuals. The individual in turn "is merely the residue of the experience of the dissolution of community," and furthermore, "the true consciousness of the loss of community is Christian" (*IC,* pp. 3, 10).

Although Nancy is silent on the relations among history, memory, and community, he considers at some length the apparently tortured relation between "myth" and community. For Nancy, myth—that necessary fiction that grounds the insistent specialness of the existent communal group—is an irreducible component of community and at the same time is necessarily pernicious in its effects. Therefore Nancy asserts a search not for the eradication of myth but rather for its "interruption": "The interruption of myth is therefore also, necessarily, the interruption of community" (*IC,* p. 57). In a footnote, Nancy elaborates on a comment made in 1984 by Maurice Blanchot:

> "The Jews incarnate . . . the refusal of myths, the abandonment of idols, the recognition of an ethical order that manifests itself in respect for the law. What Hitler wants to annihilate in the Jew, in the 'myth of the Jew,' is precisely man freed from myth." This is another way of showing where and when myth was definitively interrupted. I would add this: "man freed from myth" belongs henceforth to a community that it is incumbent upon us to let come, to let write itself. [*IC,* p. 162 n. 40]

12. Jean-Luc Nancy, *The Inoperative Community,* trans. Peter Connor et al., ed. Connor (Minneapolis, 1991), p. 58; hereafter abbreviated *IC.*

We want to press, in a sense by literalizing, the opening offered here. The quote from Blanchot seems ambiguous if not contradictory: do the Jews literally "incarnate the refusal of myths," or is that one of Hitler's myths? Let us first pursue the first reading, which is both the more flattering and the more dangerous. This reading would tell us that community without myth was once the special possession of the Jews. Nancy's "addition" would then explore the consequences of the release of that secret to "us" as a result of the genocide. What else, after all, can *henceforth* mean? We deeply respect the fact that this and other work of Nancy's is explicitly motivated by the desire to understand and "unwork" the complicity between philosophy and twentieth-century violence.[13] Nancy would doubtless be horrified and/or furious at the suggestion that his rhetoric is complicit in perpetuating the cultural annihilation of the Jew, yet it seems clear that this is one potential accomplishment of his further allegorization of Blanchot. *That which the Jew represented before "he" was annihilated is that which "we" must let come, must let write itself.* The word *henceforth* indeed implies that the secret of freedom from myth has passed from the Jews to a community that does not exist, that is only imaginable in and by theory. The secret becomes potentially available to all who await a second coming of this sacrificed Jew. We insist that this plausible yet "uncharitable" reading cannot be stretched to an accusation of anti-Judaism. On the contrary, it is clear that Nancy and thinkers like him are committed to a sympathetic philosophical comprehension of the existence and annihilation of the Jews. Our claim is rather that within the thought of philosophers such as Nancy lies a blindness to the particularity of Jewish difference that is itself part of a relentless penchant for allegorizing all "difference" into a univocal discourse.

Now let us pursue the alternate reading of Blanchot, and of Nancy's gloss. Its implications are both more modest and more conducive to our project. According to this second reading of Blanchot, the Jews' freedom from myth was primarily, if not exclusively, significant as a myth that murderously irritated Hitler. Nancy would then be saying not that "we" have inherited the secret of the Jews but rather that it is incumbent upon us—the pronoun this time not excluding in any way Jews living after the Nazi genocide—to assume the challenge of the myth of freedom from myth, to let come a community that is free from myth. We will suggest below that living Jews may have a particular contribution to make to that general effort, especially in the experience of Diaspora that has constrained Jews to create forms of community that do not rely on one of the most potent and dangerous myths—the myth of autochthony.

The critical text that has gone furthest in employing "the jew" as an

13. See Philippe Lacoue-Labarthe and Nancy, "The Nazi Myth," trans. Brian Holmes, *Critical Inquiry* 16 (Winter 1990): 291–312.

allegorical trope for otherness is Jean-François Lyotard's recent *Heidegger and "the jews."* The title tells the story: *Heidegger* gets a capital *H,* but *the jews* are in lowercase. This is done, as the back cover blurb explains, "to represent the outsiders, the nonconformists: the artists, anarchists, blacks, homeless, Arabs, etc.—and the Jews."[14] The Jews are doubtless chosen as exemplary both because the voices of some Jews are so prominent in European modernism and because of the enormous challenge of Nazi genocide to Enlightenment thought. But the name as used here is *essentially* a generic term standing for the other. And indeed Lyotard's book is all about the danger of forgetting that one ("one" in a position of relative power, that is) has always already forgotten the Other.

But why does Lyotard feel free to appropriate the name *the jews?* What does it mean for David Carroll, the author of the introduction to the English translation of Lyotard's book, to write in reference to Lyotard's citation of "Freud, Benjamin, Adorno, Arendt, Celan" that "these are ultimately 'the jews' we all have to read and even in some sense to become, 'the jews' we always already are but have forgotten we are, 'the jews' that Heidegger forgets at great cost for his thinking and writing" (*H,* p. xxiv)?

What Lyotard refuses to forget, remembering the negative example of Heidegger, is not so much upper- *or* lowercase Jews as Christian European crimes against humanity. In other words, Lyotard takes history seriously as an implication of philosophy, doubtless a vital exercise. This sketch of a critique, therefore, is not intended as an exposé of Lyotard but as a further implication of the universalizing, allegorizing traditions of Hellenistic philosophy as absorbed in Christian culture.

Lyotard basically repeats Sartre's thesis about the production of the Jew by the anti-Semite: "What is most real about real Jews is that Europe, in any case, does not know what to do with them: Christians demand their conversion; monarchs expel them; republics assimilate them; Nazis exterminate them. 'The jews' are the object of a dismissal with which Jews, in particular, are afflicted in reality" (*H,* p. 3). Let us pause at the first words here and test a paraphrase. How would it work if a man or a woman said, "What is most real about real women is that men continually try to dominate them"? The condescension of Lyotard's statement immediately becomes evident.

It would have been quite different if Lyotard had written rather, "What matters most to me here about those usually called 'Jews' is that Europe does not know what to do with them." There is no gainsaying the power of his insight. Europe indeed does not know what to do with "real Jews." But what of European philosophy? Is Lyotard not Europe here? Might we not fairly say, "Europe does not know what

14. Jean-François Lyotard, *Heidegger and "the jews,"* trans. Andreas Michel and Mark S. Roberts (Minneapolis, 1990); hereafter abbreviated *H.*

to do with them," "philosophers allegorize them," and so on? To which one might comment that in doing so, they continue another particularly Christian practice with regard to uppercase Jews, one that begins with Paul.

Here we can see more analytically what is wrong with Carroll's rhetoric about us all becoming once again "the jews we always already are but have forgotten we are." We must resist the seduction of these sentiments, for like Paul's writing they deny, they *spiritualize* history. For some contemporary critics—indeed, those most profoundly concerned with the lessons of the encounter between Jewish identity and European self-adequation—it seems that the real Jew is the non-Jewish Jew. What does this say about the "reality" of those Jews—most of those who call themselves Jews, of course, are the untheorized, unphilosophical, unspiritualized Jews—who would think the phrase "non-Jewish Jew" to be nonsense? Is it politically correct, that is, ethical, to "forget" them and to fashion an imaginary dialogue with the other who is, in fact, the already sanctioned, official model of the "non-Jewish Jew," the Franz Kafkas and Walter Benjamins? For as we know, the vast majority of the Nazis' Jewish victims were unredeemed, "real" Jews.[15]

Against this incipient critique stands precisely the force implicit in Lyotard's act of allegorizing the name *jew.* Radiating out from the sun of philosophy, remembering the other by writing the "jew," Lyotard challenges all those who would fetishize their particular difference, insisting that we learn how to imagine ourselves as blacks, as Arabs, as homeless, as Indians. This is a political challenge, but Lyotard does not suggest how those who are themselves "real Jews" could respond to it. Indeed, he explains that one reason for his avoidance of the proper noun, of the uppercase "Jews," is to make clear that he is not discussing a particularly Jewish political subject, which he identifies as Zionism (*IC,* p. 3). We want to insist in response to Lyotard that there is a loss and a danger either in allegorizing away real, uppercase Jews or in regarding them primarily as a problem for Europe. Our claim entails in turn a responsibility to help articulate a Jewish political subject "other" than that of Zionism, which in fundamental ways merely reproduces the exclusivist syndromes of European nationalism. Zionism itself is predicated on a myth of autochthony. We will suggest that a Jewish subject-position founded on generational connection and its attendant anamnestic responsibilities and pleasures affords the possibility of a flexible and nonhermetic critical Jewish identity.

15. Lest there be confusion, we of course endorse Isaac Deutscher's actual point that modern Jewish radicals who do not practice the Jewish religion nevertheless can represent an appropriate way of enacting Jewishness in the contemporary world. See Isaac Deutscher, *The Non-Jewish Jew and Other Essays* (New York, 1968).

3

In a recent essay, Walter Benn Michaels criticizes the notion of a cultural retentionism that is not "race"-based. His text is of extraordinary theoretical importance for the analysis of both the ancient dialectic between Paul and the Rabbis on the status of Jewish ethnicity, as well as for the current debate over ethnicity and multiculturalism in the United States. Michaels argues that all conceptions of cultural ethnicity are dependent on prior and often unacknowledged notions of race. In a series of examples, including the work on African-American culture of anthropologist Melville Herskovits and a novel of Oliver La Farge, Michaels argues that although they insist they are only talking about culture and not something that is biologically innate, they nevertheless assume that someone who does not "have" the culture of his or her "People" is in some sense lacking something and that the lack can be repaired.[16] Michaels questions this assumption: if they do not already observe the practices of that culture, in what sense other than "racial" can it be said to be theirs? His conclusion is, "This is not to say, of course, that all accounts of cultural identity require a racial component; it is only to say that the accounts of cultural identity that do any cultural work require a racial component" (p. 59). By this Michaels means that one is already either doing "Navajo things" or not. If one is doing them, then there is no cultural work to be done; they are one's culture already. If one is not already doing them, then it can only make sense to call them one's culture that one ought to be doing on the basis of an assumed or imputed biological identity as Navajo. He concludes that "the modern concept of culture is not, in other words, a critique of racism; it is a form of racism" (p. 60).

Michaels's argument that any identification of culture with ethnicity is logically dependent on a genealogical connection for it to work at all seems correct. Yet by glossing as "racist" all claims for group identity based on genealogy (whatever the posture of that genealogy, rhetorical or biological, might be), he inscribes a particular ideology as natural. The residue of Michaels's critique of genealogically based identity as "racist" is a radically individualist, voluntaristic, and attenuated notion of something that can only with difficulty be called "identity." This valorization of any kind of elective and affective connection between people over against the claims of physical kinship is deeply embedded in the Platonic value system Europe has largely inherited from Paul. In opposition to a traditional Jewish culture, which, in virtually all of its varieties, considered literal descent from Abraham and thus physical kinship as of supreme value in establishing identity, Paul preached kinship in the spirit as the mark of identity. Secondly, where other Jewish groups insisted on the value of doing tradi-

16. See Walter Benn Michaels, "Race into Culture: A Critical Genealogy of Cultural Identity," pp. 56–57.

tional Jewish things—the Law—as the practice of Jewish identity, Paul asserted the doing of new things, "better" things, baptism for instance, as the marker of Christian identity. Both of these moves are, moreover, crucially founded on the hierarchical dualism of spirit and flesh, with anything having to do with flesh implicitly and explicitly devalued.

The attenuation of memory in Michaels's residual account of identity is shown by his remarks on Herskovits. Herskovits had argued that African practices were retained by house slaves who had been acculturated into the white culture through a process of "reabsorption" of "Africanisms." To this Michaels reacts, "if you were trained as a house slave, why would absorbing Africanisms count as reabsorbing them?" (p. 56). The function of this claim for Herskovits, as Michaels correctly argues, is precisely to avoid the necessity for assuming any "innate endowment" of cultural traits in order to bolster his argument for the African component of African-American culture. At this point, however, Michaels jumps from here to the following:

> To make what *they* did part of *your* past, there must be some prior assumption of identity between you and them, and this assumption is as racial to Herskovits as it is in Cullen or La Farge. The things the African Negro used to do count as the American Negro's past only because both the African and the American are "the Negro." Herskovits's anti-racist culturalism can only be articulated through a commitment to racial identity. [P. 57]

Indeed. But this demonstration, repeated over and over in Michaels's essay, does not in any way imply that cultural practices are "innately endowed," as racialist (and racist) theories of cultural differentiation had been wont to do before the intervention of culturalists like Franz Boas and his followers, whose work, as we have said, had been largely accomplished by the 1920s.[17]

Let us think for a moment how Herskovits's "house slaves" might have come to feel a sense of identity with the field slaves who had not been acculturated to the white norm. First of all, they might indeed have managed to *remember*—simply not forget—that their immediate ancestors had been Africans in Africa. Secondly, their bodies were marked as being different from the other people doing "white" things. Third, they shared a slave status with the field hands. Fourth, the notion of complete separation followed by reestablished contact is a pure fiction. Much more plausible would be a model of acculturation whereby these house slaves had been exposed to the culture of the other slaves that they had partially forgotten during the process of (presumably) early childhood "acculturation" to the house culture and that indeed they might reabsorb as adults.

17. For W. E. B. DuBois on this, see Anthony Appiah, "The Uncompleted Argument: DuBois and the Illusion of Race," *Critical Inquiry* 12 (Autumn 1985): 30–32.

Identity is not only reinvented, as Michaels would have it; it is at least partially given for different people in different ways and intensities. Bodies are marked as different and often as negatively different to the dominant cultural system, thus producing a dissonance or gap between one's practices and affects. Partly assimilated, partly repressed, early childhood acculturation reasserts itself as a sense of dissonance, or guilt, as well. Contact with other people who share the name of a given identity and seem to feel organically connected to a community can produce a sense of nostalgia even in one who has never been near the things that that community does. Michaels obscures all of this by eliding racism—the idea of an innate capacity or tendency for certain practices—and generation understood as a kinship with other people who happen to do certain things. Versions of this same argument can be constructed for all of Michaels's deconstructions of culturalism.[18]

Michaels's text thus implicitly inscribes as natural another characteristically Protestant theme, a radical individualism, in which a person sufficiently makes her- or himself. For Michaels, apparently belonging to a culture cannot determine a life trajectory. There can be no "mark of identity that transcends one's actual practices and experiences. . . . The fact . . . that something belongs to our culture, cannot count as a motive for our doing it since, if it *does* belong to our culture we *already* do it and if we don't do it (if we've stopped or haven't yet started doing it) it doesn't belong to our culture" (pp. 58 n. 36, 59–60). Does this apply to children? Is there no model of *learning* or *transmission* here? What happens if we substitute *language* for *culture?* Should we say that it is racist to speak of teaching children "their language" because "their language" is what they know already, so there is no reason for parents to speak a different language than that of the majority to small children in order that they will know "their" native language as well as the dominant one? What about a thirteen-year-old child whom we have allowed until now to concentrate on learning the language/culture of the dominant group? Is it racist to send him or her to a school to learn "our" language? What about a thirty-year-old long-lost cousin who wants to reconnect with his or her "roots"? Michaels's individualism allows him to slip in the problematic pronoun *our,* which he employs in fact to mean not only each and every one of us, separately, but—as this quote shows—each and every one of us separately from any possible identity with ourselves yesterday or tomorrow because that would be to prescribe in a racist way what "our" identity is, separately from anything that happened before we, as particular organisms, were born.

18. We do mean deconstruction precisely in the technical sense in which one of the terms of a binary distinction, in this case between race and culture, is shown to be dependent on that which it seeks to exclude. Once again, Michaels has indeed shown the weakness of notions of "culture" dependent on their assumption of binary opposition to a pernicious and discredited account of race.

Male Jewish circumcision provides a particularly sharp disruption of Michaels's statement that no "mark of identity . . . transcends one's actual practices and experiences," for it certainly can be a mark that transcends one's actual practices and (at least remembered) experiences, yet it is a mark that can reassert itself, and often enough does, as a demand (almost a compulsion) to reconnect, relearn, reabsorb, and reinvent the doing of Jewish things.[19] Indeed, one could understand circumcision precisely as the cultural construction of a genealogical differentiation, as a diacritic that symbolizes the biological status of Jewishness—not in the sense of a biological difference between Jews and others but in the sense of the biological connection that filiation provides. Further evidence that this connection has nothing to do with racism per se is the fact that one not Jewish can indeed adopt Jewish identity by taking on Jewish practices and through symbolic rebirth (and for men, physical marking) as a member of the Jewish People. It is thus not quite as obvious as Michaels claims it to be that a New York Jew cannot become a Mashpee Indian (p. 57 n. 36). Certainly a Mashpee Indian can become a Jew. Those Jewish subcultures that do promulgate racist or quasi-racist notions of Jewishness have great theological difficulty with conversion and ultimately retreat to the same kind of dualism of bodies and souls that characterizes Paul.

More revealingly, however, the convert's name is changed to "ben Avraham" or "bas Avraham," son or daughter of Abraham. The convert is adopted into the family and assigned a new "genealogical" identity, but because Abraham is the first convert in Jewish tradition, converts are his descendants in that sense as well. There is thus a sense in which the convert becomes the ideal type of the Jew. We not only do these things because we are this thing, but we are this thing because we do these things.

Michaels also marginalizes the political dimensions of cultural retention and loss: "Without race, losing our culture can mean no more than doing things differently from the way we now do them and preserving our culture can mean no more than doing things the same—the melodrama of assimilation disappears" (p. 62). He allows only that "the situation is entirely different with respect to compulsory assimilation; what puts the pathos back is precisely the element of compulsion" (p. 62 n. 41). However, as Michaels surely knows, power operates in many ways other than the exercise of actual compulsion. Ideological state apparatuses and discourses all press mightily on different identities to assimilate to the dominant culture. The pathos of notions such as assimilation, cultural demise, and cultural survival grows precisely out of the ways in which they are embedded in political processes of domination and exploitation. The insistence on the value of bodily connection and embodied practice that is

19. See the analysis of the function of Daniel Deronda's circumcision in Sander Gilman, "'I'm Down on Whores': Race and Gender in Victorian London," in *Anatomy of Racism,* ed. David Theo Goldberg (Minneapolis, 1990), pp. 162–63.

emblematic of Judaism since Paul thus has significant critical power vis-à-vis the isolating and disembodying direction of Western idealist philosophies.

4

> This feeling of identity between self and body, which, naturally, has nothing in common with popular materialism, will therefore never allow those who wish to begin with it to rediscover, in the depths of this unity, the duality of a free spirit that struggles against the body to which it is chained. On the contrary, for such people, the whole of the spirit's essence lies in the fact that it is chained to the body. To separate the spirit from the concrete forms with which it is already involved is to betray the originality of the very feeling from which it is appropriate to begin.[20]

Levinas's statement here is extremely significant. If, as he claims, writing in 1934, the philosophy of Hitlerism is a reaction to German idealism with its disembodied notions of universal spirit, then we have a startling and troubling analogy with the reaction of rabbinic Judaism to similar philosophical developments in the Rabbis' world, a reaction that also rejected the notion of "the duality of a free spirit that struggles against the body to which it is chained." Levinas argues that the philosophy of Hitlerism consists precisely of a struggle against this flight from the body so characteristic of Western culture, a protest against the disgust with corporeality that makes one ashamed of having parents, genealogical connections, or a native country. Like white cells gone wild and destroying healthy tissue, this reaction turned into the most destructive horror that human beings have ever invented. With a terrifying irony, then, the rabbinic reaction against dualism in late antiquity bears strong analogies to this modern one. If Lyotard continues Paul, does Heidegger continue the Rabbis?

The reaction against such idealism and disembodiment in "the philosophy of Hitlerism" produced the worst violence that human beings have ever perpetrated against each other, but Judaism, in a similar reaction, did not. The most violent practice that rabbinic Judaism ever developed vis-à-vis its Others was spitting on the floor in the synagogue or walking around the block to avoid passing a pagan or Christian place of worship. Something else was needed for the potential negative implications of the culture to become actualized. That necessity is power over others. Particularism plus power yields tribal warfare or fascism.

20. Emmanuel Levinas, "Reflections on the Philosophy of Hitlerism" (1934), trans. Seán Hand, *Critical Inquiry* 17 (Autumn 1990): 68–69.

Christianity plus power has also yielded horror. If particularism plus power tends toward fascism, then universalism plus power produces imperialism and cultural annihilation as well as, all too often, actual genocide of those who refuse to conform. Our thesis is that Judaism and Christianity, as two different hermeneutic systems for reading the Bible, generate two diametrically opposed and mirror-image forms of racism—and also two dialectical possibilities of antiracism.[21] The genius of Christianity is its concern for all the peoples of the world; the genius of Judaism is its ability to leave other people alone.[22] And the evils of the two systems are the precise obverse of these genii. The genies all too easily become demons. Christian universalism, even at its most liberal and benevolent, has been a powerful force for coercive discourses of sameness, denying, as we have seen, the rights of Jews, women, and others to retain their difference. As Etienne Balibar has brilliantly realized, this universalism is indeed a racism:

> This leads us to direct our attention towards a historical fact that is even more difficult to admit and yet crucial, taking into consideration the French national form of racist traditions. There is, no doubt, a specifically French brand of the doctrines of Aryanism, anthropometry and biological geneticism, but the true "French ideology" is not to be found in these: it lies rather in the idea that the culture of the "land of the Rights of Man" has been entrusted with a universal mission to educate the human race. There corresponds to this mission a practice of assimilating dominated populations and a consequent need to differentiate and rank individuals or groups in terms of their greater or lesser aptitude for—or resistance to—assimilation. It was this simultaneously subtle and crushing form of exclusion/inclusion which was deployed in the process of colonization and the strictly French (or "democratic") variant of the "White man's burden."[23]

21. Etienne Balibar, in a quite different historical context, writes: "In fact racism figures *both* on the side of the universal and the particular" (Etienne Balibar, "Racism and Nationalism," trans. Chris Turner, in Balibar and Immanuel Wallerstein, *Race, Nation, Class: Ambiguous Identities* [London, 1991], p. 54).

22. Paula Fredriksen cites abundant evidence to the effect that in antiquity Jews permitted Gentiles to attend the synagogue without conversion and even if they continued to worship idols! See her *From Jesus to Christ: The Origins of the New Testament Images of Jesus* (New Haven, Conn., 1988), pp. 149–51.

23. Balibar, "Is There a 'Neo-Racism'?" in *Race, Nation, Class,* p. 24; hereafter abbreviated "I." To be sure, there are those who would locate the origins of this "universal mission to educate the human race" in the "imperialist" monotheism of the Hebrew Bible, and ultimately, of course, the Hebraic and Hellenic sources of Christianity cannot be neatly separated out. There are aspects of both the Israelite history and of the prophetic discourse that could give rise to such a reading. Rabbinic Judaism and Christianity—in their relation to peoplehood and universalism—are interpreted by us, in a sense, as mutual thesis and antithesis within the biblical system. See further discussion below, as well as our reach for a synthesis.

Thus paradoxically and tragically, at the very heart of those most truly progressive discourses of Europe, including Marxism, the inability to accommodate difference provides a fatal flaw. This inability was characteristic of German liberalism, as Marc Shell points out,[24] and still persists in the United States of today in such "liberal" expressions as "too Jewish."[25] Shell documents such notions in the discourse of the contemporary Russian ideologue Igor Sharevich, who argues that Jews must abandon their difference if they wish to be full citizens of Russia.[26] The paradox in such discourse is that nearly always, as Shell emphasizes, the justification for coercing Jews to become Christian Russian citizens of the world is the alleged intolerance of the Jews. The parallels between this modern liberal discourse and that of Paul seem obvious.

The Rabbis' insistence on the centrality of peoplehood can thus be read as a necessary critique of Paul, for if the Pauline move had within it the possibility of breaking out of the tribal allegiances and commitments to one's own family, as it were, it also contains the seeds of an imperialist and colonizing missionary practice. The very emphasis on a universalism expressed as the concern for all of the families of the world turns very rapidly (if not necessarily) into a doctrine that they must all become part of our family of the spirit with all of the horrifying practices against Jews and other Others that Christian Europe produced. The doctrine of the Apostle of the Free Spirit can be diverted, even perverted, to a doctrine of enslaving and torturing bodies. Paul had indeed written, with notorious ambiguity, "For though absent in body I am present in spirit, and if present I have already pronounced judgment in the name of the Lord Jesus on the man who has [lived with his father's wife]. When you are assembled and my spirit is present, with the power of our Lord Jesus, you are to deliver this man to Satan for the destruction of the flesh, that his spirit may be saved in the day of the Lord Jesus" (1 Cor. 5:3–5). It is surely Paul's own sense of self, divided into body and spirit so that this spirit can be where his body is not—and he means this literally—that permits him to suggest (if that is what is meant) and his followers to practice torturing and killing bodies to save the souls. As Henri Baudet has remarked concerning

24. "Moses Mendelssohn in his *Jerusalem* tried to steer the ideology of a universalist Enlightenment . . . away from what he took to be its probably inevitable course towards barbarism. . . . In the Germany of his day Jews were pressured to renounce their faith in return for civil equality and union with the Christian majority. The pressure was kindly, but it was also a form of intolerance towards non-kin" (Marc Shell, "Marranos [Pigs], or From Coexistence to Toleration," *Critical Inquiry* 17 [Winter 1991]: 331).

25. On this point see Gilman, *The Jew's Body* (New York, 1991), pp. 25–27. At Oxford University, the Centre for Advanced Hebrew Studies holds its dinners on Friday night (even though many of its participants cannot, therefore, attend) because "we are not a Jewish institution; we are an Oxford institution." This is, we submit, an example of the internalization of the racist demand for universalism.

26. See Shell, "Marranos (Pigs)," p. 332 n. 84.

late fifteenth-century Portugal, "although the bodies of Negroes might be held captive, this very fact made it possible for their souls to achieve true freedom through conversion to Christianity. And so the enslavement of Negroes took on a kind of missionary aspect. It was in keeping that christened Negro slaves should enjoy certain small privileges above their fellows."[27] Disdain for the bodies of others combined with concern for the souls can thus be even more devastating than neglect. From the retrospective position of a world that has, at the end of the second Christian millennium, become thoroughly interdependent, each one of these options is intolerable.

Critics of Zionism, both Arab and others, along with both Jewish and non-Jewish anti-Semites, have often sought to portray Jewish culture as essentially racist. This foundational racism is traced to the Hebrew Bible and is described as the transparent meaning of that document. Critics who are otherwise fully committed to constructionist and historicist accounts of meaning and practice abandon this commitment when it comes to the Hebrew Bible—assuming that the Bible is, in fact and in essence, that which it has been read to be and authorizes univocally that which it has been taken to authorize. Frederick Turner writes, "But the distinctions raised in the covenant between religion and idolatry are like some visitation of the khamsin to wilderness peoples as yet unsuspected, dark clouds over Africa, the Americas, the Far East, until finally even the remotest islands and jungle enclaves are struck by fire and sword and by the subtler weapon of conversion-by-ridicule (Deuteronomy 2:34; 7:2; 20:16–18, Joshua 6:17–21)."[28] The historically and materially defined local practices of a culture far away and long ago are made here "naturally" responsible (like the khamsin, the Middle Eastern Santa Ana) for the colonial practices of cultures entirely other to it simply because those later cultures used those practices as their authorization.[29] One effect of this sudden dehistoricization of hermeneutics has been an exoneration of European

27. Henri Baudet, *Paradise on Earth: Some Thoughts on European Images of Non-European Man,* trans. Elizabeth Wentholt (New Haven, Conn., 1965), p. 30. In California, certain missionaries had thousands of Indian babies killed so that their souls would be saved before their bodies could sin.

28. Frederick Turner, *Beyond Geography: The Western Spirit against the Wilderness* (New York, 1980), p. 45. In his book, *Storm from Paradise: The Politics of Jewish Memory* (Minneapolis, 1992), p. 134 n. 13, Jonathan Boyarin has provided a summary critique of Turner's book. See also on this theme Regina Schwartz, "Monotheism, Violence, and Identity," in *Religion and Literature,* ed. Mark Krupnick (forthcoming).

29. A particularly extreme and explicit version of this naturalizing and dehistoricizing move vis-à-vis biblical hermeneutics is found in Donald Harman Akenson, *God's Peoples: Covenant and Land in South Africa, Israel, and Ulster* (Ithaca, N.Y., 1992), who writes, "For certain societies, in certain eras of their development, the scriptures have acted culturally and socially in the same way the human genetic code operates physiologically. That is, this great code has, in some degree, directly determined what people would believe and what they would think and what they would do" (p. 9).

Christian society that has been, after all, the religious hegemonic system for virtually all of the imperialist, racist, and even genocidal societies of the West, but not, of course, Judaism. There were no Jewish missionaries in the remote islands and jungle enclaves. It is not the Hebrew Bible that impels the "Societies for the Propagation" but rather Pauline rhetoric like "For as in Adam all men died, so in Christ all men shall be made alive" (1 Cor. 15:22). Jews and Jewish culture will have to answer for the evil that we do (especially to the Palestinians), but it is absurd for "the Jews" to be implicated in practices in which they had no part and indeed have had no part even until now: forced conversion, deculturation, genocide.[30] Even the primitive command to wipe out the peoples of Canaan was limited by the Bible itself to those particular people in that particular place, and thus declared no longer applicable by the Rabbis of the Talmud.[31] It is precisely the very literalism of rabbinic/midrashic hermeneutics that prevented a typological "application" of this command to other groups. It should be clearly recognized, then, that the attempt of the integrationist Zionist Gush Emunim movement to refigure the Palestinians as Amalek and to reactivate the genocidal commandment is a radical act of religious revisionism and not in any way a continuation of historical rabbinic Judaism.

Does this mean that rabbinic Judaism qua ideology is innocent of either ethnocentric or supremacist tenets? Certainly not. What it argues is rather that Jewish racism, like the racism of other peoples, is a facultative and dispensible aspect of the cultural system, not one that is necessary for its preservation or essential to its nature. Perhaps the primary function for a critical construction of cultural (or racial or gender or sexual) identity is to construct it in ways that purge it of its elements of domination and oppression. Some, however, would argue that this is an impossible project not because of the nature of Jewishness but because any group identity is oppressive, unless it is oppressed.

In a recent Marxian analysis of both race and racism, Balibar has argued that "racism" has two dissymmetrical aspects. On the one hand, it constitutes a dominating community with practices, discursive and otherwise, that are "articulated around stigmata of otherness (name, skin colour, religious practices)." It also constitutes, however, "the way in which, as a mirror image, individuals and collectives that are prey to racism (its 'objects') find themselves constrained to see themselves as a community." Balibar further argues that destruction of racism implies the

30. See Shell, "Marranos (Pigs)," for the argument that Jewish reluctance to convert others is built into the system and not merely a result of later material and historical conditions. We think, however, that Shell underestimates the potential for grounding racist thought in other aspects of biblical discourse.

31. See Jonathan Boyarin, "Reading Exodus into History," *New Literary History* 23 (Summer 1992): 523–54.

"internal decomposition of the community created by racism," by which he means the dominating community, as is clear from his analogy to the overcoming of sexism that will involve "the break-up of the community of 'males'" ("I," p. 18). This is, however, for us the crucial point, for the question is, obviously, if overcoming sexism involves the breaking up of the community of males, does it necessarily imply the breaking up of the community of females? And does this, then, not entail a breaking up of community, *tout court?* Putting it another way, are we not simply imposing a more coercive universal? On the other hand, if indeed the very existence of the dominant group is dependent on domination, if identity is always formed in a master-slave relationship, is the price not too high? What we wish to struggle for, theoretically, is a notion of identity in which there are only slaves but no masters, that is, an alternative to the model of self-determination, which is, after all, in itself a Western, imperialist imposition on the rest of the world. We propose Diaspora as a theoretical and historical model to replace national self-determination.[32] To be sure, this would be an idealized Diaspora generalized from those situations in Jewish history when Jews were both relatively free from persecution and yet constituted by strong identity—those situations, moreover, within which Promethean Jewish creativity was not antithetical, indeed was synergistic with a general cultural activity. Another way of making the same point would be to insist that there are material and social conditions in which cultural identity, difference, will not produce even what Balibar, after P. A. Taguieff, has called "differentialist racism," that is,

> a racism whose dominant theme is not biological heredity but the insurmountability of cultural differences, a racism which, at first sight, does not postulate the superiority of certain groups or peoples in relation to others but "only" the harmfulness of abolishing frontiers, the incompatibility of life-styles and traditions; in short, it is what P. A. Taguieff has rightly called a *differentialist racism.* ["I," p. 21]

To our understanding, it would be an appropriate goal to articulate a theory and practice of identity that would simultaneously respect the irreducibility and the positive value of cultural differences, address the harmfulness, not of abolishing frontiers but of dissolution of uniqueness, and encourage the mutual fructification of different life-styles and traditions. We do not think, moreover, that such possibilities are merely utopian. We would certainly claim that there have been historical situations in which they obtained without perfect success in this radically imperfect

32. To the extent that this diasporic existence is an actual historical entity, we ourselves are not prey to the charge of "allegorizing" the Jew. It may be fairly suggested, however, that the model is so idealized as to be in itself an allegory.

world. The solution of Zionism—that is, Jewish state hegemony, except insofar as it represented an emergency and temporary rescue operation—seems to us the subversion of Jewish culture and not its culmination. It represents the substitution of a European, Western cultural-political formation for a traditional Jewish one that has been based on a sharing, at best, of political power with others and that takes on entirely other meanings when combined with political hegemony.

Let us begin with two concrete examples. Jewish resistance to assimilation and annihilation within conditions of Diaspora, to which we will return below, generated such practices as communal charity in the areas of education, feeding, providing for the sick, and the caring for Jewish prisoners, to the virtual exclusion of others. While this meant at least that those others were not subjected to attempts to Judaize them—that is, they were tolerated, and not only by default of lack of Jewish power—it also meant that Jewish resources were not devoted to the welfare of humanity at large but only to one family. Within Israel, where power is concentrated almost exclusively in Jewish hands, this discursive practice has become a monstrosity whereby an egregiously disproportionate measure of the resources of the state is devoted to the welfare of only one segment of the population. A further and somewhat more subtle and symbolic example is the following. That very practice mentioned above, the symbolic expression of contempt for places of worship of others, becomes darkly ominous when it is combined with temporal power and domination—that is, when Jews have power over places of worship belonging to others. It is this factor that has allowed the Israelis to turn the central Mosque of Beersheba into a museum of the Negev and to let the Muslim cemetery of that city to fall into ruins.[33] Insistence on ethnic speciality, when it is extended over a particular piece of land, will inevitably produce a discourse not unlike the Inquisition in many of its effects. The archives of the Israeli General Security Services will one day prove this claim eminently, although already we "know" the truth.

We are not comparing Israeli practice to Nazism, for that would occlude more than it reveals and would obscure the real, imminent danger of its becoming the case in the future; the use of *Lebensraum* rhetoric on the part of mainstream Israeli politicians and the ascent to respectability and a certain degree of power of fascist parties in Israel certainly provide portents of this happening. Our argument is rather for an as yet un-

33. A highly ingenuous, or more likely egregiously disingenuous, claim by Abba Eban is given the lie in every page of Israeli history, particularly the last ones. Beersheba may have been "virtually empty," but that is little consolation to the Bedouin who were and continue to be dispossessed there and in its environs. And the refugees in camps in Gaza, as well as the still-visible ruins of their villages, would certainly dispute the claim that Arab populations had avoided "the land of the Philistines in the coastal plain . . . because of insalubrious conditions" (Abba Eban, letter to W. D. Davies, in Davies, *The Territorial Dimension of Judaism* [1982; Minneapolis, 1992], p. 76; hereafter abbreviated *T*).

realized but necessary theoretical compatability between Zionist ideology and the fascism of state ethnicity. Capturing Judaism in a state transforms entirely the meanings of its social practices. Practices that in Diaspora have one meaning—for example, caring for the feeding and housing of Jews and not "others"—have entirely different meanings under political hegemony. E. P. Sanders has gotten this just right:

> More important is the evidence that points to Jewish pride in separatism. Christian scholars habitually discuss the question under the implied heading "What was wrong with Judaism that Christianity corrected?" Exclusivism is considered to be bad, and the finding that Jews were to some degree separatist fills many with righteous pride. We shall all agree that exclusivism is bad when practiced by the dominant group. Things look different if one thinks of minority groups that are trying to maintain their own identity. I have never felt that the strict Amish are iniquitous, and I do not think that, in assessing Jewish separatism in the Diaspora, we are dealing with a moral issue. (The moral issue would be the treatment of Gentiles in Palestine during periods of Jewish ascendancy. How well were the biblical laws to love the resident alien [Lev. 19:33–34] observed?)[34]

The inequities—and worse—in Israeli political, economic, and social practice are not aberrations but inevitable consequences of the inappropriate application of a form of discourse from one historical situation to another.

For those of us who are equally committed to social justice and collective Jewish existence, some other formation must be constituted. We suggest that an Israel that reimports diasporic consciousness—a consciousness of a Jewish collective as one sharing space with others, devoid of exclusivist and dominating power—is the only Israel that could answer Paul's, Lyotard's, and Nancy's call for a species-wide care without eradicating cultural difference.[35] Reversing A. B. Yehoshua's famous pronouncement that only in a condition of political hegemony is moral responsibility mobilized, we would argue that the only moral path would be the renunciation of Jewish hegemony qua Jewish hegemony.[36] This would involve first of all complete separation of religion from state, but even more than that the revocation of the Law of Return and such cul-

34. E. P. Sanders, "Jewish Association with Gentiles and Galatians 2:11–14," in *The Conversation Continues: Studies in Paul and John in Honor of J. Louis Martyn,* ed. Robert T. Fortna and Beverly R. Gaventa (Nashville, Tenn., 1990), p. 181.

35. See Jonathan Boyarin, "Palestine and Jewish History," chap. 7 of *Storm from Paradise.*

36. Shell argues, following Spinoza, that temporal power is necessary for toleration ("Marranos [Pigs]," p. 328 n. 75). We are suggesting the opposite, that only conditions in which power is shared among religions and ethnicities will allow for difference with common caring.

tural, discursive practices that code the state as a Jewish state and not a multinational and multicultural one. The dream of a place that is ours founders on the rock of realization that there are Others there just as there are Others in Poland, Morocco, and Ethiopia. Any notion, then, of redemption through Land must either be infinitely deferred (as the Neturei Karta understands so well) or become a moral monster. Either Israel must entirely divest itself of the language of race and become truly a state that is equally for all of its citizens and collectives or the Jews must divest themselves of their claim to space. Race and space together form a deadly discourse.

Genealogy and *territorialism* have been the problematic and necessary (if not essential) terms around which Jewish identity has revolved. In Jewish history, however, these terms are more obviously at odds with each other than in synergy. This allows a formulation of Jewish identity not as a proud resting place (hence not as a form of integrism or nativism) but as a perpetual, creative, diasporic tension. In the final section of this paper, then, we would like to begin to articulate a notion of Jewish identity that recuperates its genealogical moment—family, history, memory, and practice—while it problematizes claims to autochthony and indigenousness as the material base of Jewish identity.

5

> The Tanak and other sources of Judaism reveal certain ideas concerning The Land that reflect, or are parallel to, primitive Semitic, other Near Eastern, and, indeed, widespread conceptions about the significance of their land to a particular people. Israel is represented as the center of the Earth. . . . The religious man desires to live as near to this sacred space as possible and comes to regard it, the place of his abode, his own land, as the centre of the world. [*T,* p. 1; see also p. 87]

There are two diametrically opposed moments in the Jewish discourse of the Land. On the one hand, it is crucial to recognize that the Jewish conception of the Land of Israel is similar to the discourse of the Land of many (if not nearly all) "indigenous" peoples of the world. Somehow the Jews have managed to retain a sense of being rooted somewhere in the world through twenty centuries of exile from that someplace (organic metaphors are not out of place in this discourse, for they are used within the tradition itself).

It is profoundly disturbing to hear Jewish attachment to the Land decried as regressive in the same discursive situations in which the attachment of native Americans or Australians to their particular rocks, trees, and deserts is celebrated as an organic connection to the Earth that "we" have lost.[37] The uncritical valorization of indigenousness (and particularly the confusion between political indigenousness and mystified autochthony) must come under critique, without wishing, however, to deny the rights of native Americans, Australians, and Palestinians to their Lands precisely on the basis of real, unmysterious political claims. If, on the other hand, Jews are to give up hegemony over the Land, this does not mean that the profundity of our attachment to the Land can be denied. This also must have a political expression in the present, in the provision of the possibility for Jews to live a Jewish life in a Palestine not dominated by one ethnic group or another.

On the other hand, the biblical story is not one of autochthony but one of always already coming from somewhere else. As Davies has so very well understood, the concept of a divine promise to give this land that is the land of Others to His People Israel is the sign of a bad conscience for having deprived the Others of their Land (see *T*, pp. 11–12).[38] Thus at the same time that one vitally important strain of expression within biblical religion promotes a sense of organic, "natural" connectedness between this People and this Land—a settlement in the Land—in another sense or in a counterstrain, Israelite and Jewish religion is perpetually an unsettlement of the very notion of autochthony.

Traditional Jewish attachment to the Land, whether biblical or postbiblical, thus provides a self-critique as well as a critique of identities based on notions of autochthony. Some myths about "the tree over there from which the first man sprung," along with European nationalist myths about Atlantis,[39] have been allowed to harden into a confusion of "indigenous" (the people who belong here, whose land this rightfully is—a political claim, founded on present and recently past political realities) and "autochthonous" (the people who were never anywhere else but here and

37. An aboriginal Australian recently began her lecture at a conference with greetings from her people to the indigenous people of the United States, of whom there were two representatives in the audience and whom she addressed by name. Much of her lecture consisted of a critique of the rootlessness of Europeans. Daniel Boyarin had a sense of being trapped in a double bind, for if the Jews are the indigenous people of the Land of Israel, as Zionism claims, then the Palestinians are indigenous nowhere, but if the Palestinians are the indigenous people of Palestine, then Jews are indigenous nowhere. He had painfully renounced the possibility of realizing his very strong feeling of connection to the Land (this connection having been co-opted by the state) in favor of what he and Jonathan Boyarin take to be the only possible end to violence and movement toward justice. Are we now to be condemned as people who have lost their roots?

38. Davies remarks that this sense of "bad conscience" can be found in texts as late as the first century B.C.E. We think he underestimates this. The classical midrash on Genesis, Bereshith Rabba, a product of the fourth and fifth centuries C.E., begins with the question, "Why does the Torah open with the creation of the world?" It answers, "So that when the Nations will call Israel robbers for their theft of the Land, they will be able to point to the Torah and say: God created the earth and can dispose of it at his will!" (our trans.).

39. See Pierre Vidal-Naquet, "Atlantis and the Nations," trans. Janet Lloyd, *Critical Inquiry* 18 (Winter 1992): 300–326.

have a natural right to this land). The Jewish narrative of the Land has the power of insisting on the connection without myths of autochthony, while other narratives, including the Zionist one, have repressed memories of coming from somewhere else. The confusion between indigenousness and autochthony is of the same kind as the confusion in Michaels's text between any kind of genealogically based racism belonging to a people and modern scientific racism.

These very conflations are complicitous with a set of mystifications within which nationalist ideologies subsist. Harry Berger argues that "the alienation of social constructions of divinity and cosmos by conquest groups resembles the alienation of socially constructed kinship and status terms from domestic kin groups to corporate descent groups—in anthropological jargon, from the ego-centered kinship system of families to the more patently fictional ancestor-centered system of lineages."[40] Distinguishing between forms of "weak transcendence" and "strong transcendence," Berger argues that "family membership illustrates weak kinship; tribal membership, strong kinship." Strong transcendence is more aggressive because it is more embattled and does more ideological work, that is, according to Berger, serves to justify land control. "Status that depends on land is generally more precarious and alienable than status inscribed on the body; mobile subsistence economies tend to conceptualize status in terms of the signifying indices of the body—indices of gender, age, and kinship—rather than of more conspicuously artificial constructions, and are closer to the weak end of the weak-to-strong scale" ("L," p. 121). The place of the first of these alienations can, however, be taken by the alienation of a socially constructed connection to a land by myths of autochthony and the unique belonging of this land to a people, an alienation that can serve the interest of conquerors, as easily as by the transcendental legitimation of kings. Thus if Berger, following Walter Brueggemann, contrasts two covenants, one the Mosaic, which rejects "the imperial gods of a totalitarian and hierarchic social order" ("L," p. 123), and one, the Davidic, which enthrones precisely those gods as the one God, we could just as well contrast two trajectories, the one toward autochthony and the one against it, in the same way. The first would support the rule of Israelite kings over territory; the second would serve to oppose it.[41]

40. Harry Berger, Jr., "The Lie of the Land: The Text beyond Canaan," *Representations,* no. 25 (Winter 1989): 121; hereafter abbreviated "L."

41. For an even more nuanced reading of tensions within the Davidic stories themselves, see Schwartz, "Nations and Nationalism: Adultery in the House of David," *Critical Inquiry* 19 (Autumn 1992): 142. Schwartz's forthcoming book will deal with many of the themes of identity in the Bible that this essay is treating, albeit with quite different methods and often with quite different results.

> The dialectical struggle between antiroyalism and royalism persists throughout the course and formative career of the Old Testament as its structuring force. It sets the tent against the house, nomadism against agriculture, the wilderness against Canaan, wandering and exile against settlement, diaspora against the political integrity of a settled state. ["L," p. 123]

Our argument, then, is that a vision of Jewish history and identity that valorizes the second half of each of these binary systems and sees the first as only a disease constitutes not a continuation of Jewish culture but its final betrayal.

Berger, however, has also implicated "ancestor-centered systems of lineages" as ideological mystifications in the service of the state power of conquest groups while we have held up such an organization as one feasible component of an alternative to statism. Empirically, tribal organization, with its concomitant myths of the eponymous ancestor, is nearly emblematic of nomadic peoples. Berger's own discourse, however, is inconsistent here, for only a page later he will refer to the premonarchic period of Israel ("roughly from 1250 to 1000 B.C.") as a sociological experiment in "the rejection of strong transcendence in favor of a less coercive and somewhat weaker alternative, the tribal system that cuts across both local allegiances and stratificational discontinuities" ("L," p. 123). Thus Berger first puts tribalism on the side of "strong transcendence" and then on the side of "weak." Against Berger's first claim on this point and in favor of his second, we would argue that talk of the eponymous ancestors, of the patriarchs, is conspicuously less prominent in the "Davidic" texts of the settlement than in the "Mosaic" texts of the wandering. As Berger himself writes, David "tried to displace the loyalties and solidarity of kinship ties from clans and tribes to the national dynasty" ("L," p. 124). We suggest that descent from a common ancestor is rather an extension of family kinship and not its antithesis and thus on the side of wilderness and not on the side of Canaan. Even the myth of descent from common ancestry belongs rather to the semantic field of status through the body and not to the semantic field of status through land. Diaspora, in historical Judaism, can be interpreted then as the later analogue to nomadism in the earlier set of material conditions and thus as a continuation of the sociological experiment that the Davidic monarchy symbolically overturns.[42] With the

42. It is important to emphasize that this analysis is indifferent to the historical question of whether there were nomadic Israelite tribes to begin with or the thesis (made most famous by the work of Norman K. Gottwald, *The Tribes of Yahweh: A Sociology of the Religion of Liberated Israel, 1250–1050 B.C.E.* [Maryknoll, N.Y., 1979]) that ascribes them to a "retribalization" process taking place among "native" Canaanites. For a discussion of this thesis, see "L," pp. 131–32. For our purposes, the representations of the tribes as nomadic and the ideological investments in that representation are indifferent to the "actual" history.

rabbinic "invention" of Diaspora, the radical experiment of Moses was advanced. The forms of identification typical of nomads, those marks of status in the body, remained, then, crucial to this formation. Race is here on the side of the radicals; space, on the other hand, belongs to the despots.

One modernist story of Israel, the Israeli Declaration of Independence, begins with an imaginary autochthony—"In the Land of Israel this people came into existence"—and ends with the triumphant return of the People to their natural Land, making them "re-autochthonized," "like all of the nations." Israeli state power, deprived of the option of self-legitimation through appeal to a divine king, discovered autochthony as a powerful replacement. An alternative story of Israel, closer, it would seem, to the readings of the Judaism lived for two thousand years, begins with a people forever unconnected with a particular land, a people that calls into question the idea that a people must have a land in order to be a people. "The Land of Israel was not the birthplace of the Jewish people, which did not emerge there (as most peoples have on their own soil). On the contrary it had to enter its own Land from without; there is a sense in which Israel was born in exile. Abraham had to leave his own land to go to the Promised Land: the father of Jewry was deterritorialized" (*T,* p. 63).[43] In this view, the stories of Israel's conquest of the Land, whether under Abraham, Joshua, or even more prominently under David, are always stories that are compromised with a sense of failure of mission even more than they are stories of the accomplishment of mission, and the internal critique within the Tanakh (Hebrew Bible) itself, the dissident voice that is nearly always present, does not let us forget this either. Davies also brings into absolutely clear focus a prophetic discourse of preference for "exile" over rootedness in the Land (together with a persisent hope of eschatological restoration), a prophetic discourse that has been totally occluded in modern Zionist ideological representations of the Bible and of Jewish history but was pivotal in the rabbinic ideology (see *T,* pp. 15–19).

The Rabbis produced their cultural formation within conditions of Diaspora, and we would argue that their particular discourse of ethnocentricity is ethically appropriate only when the cultural identity is an embattled (or, at any rate, nonhegemonic) minority. The point is not that the Land was devalued by the Rabbis but that they renounced it until the final redemption; in an unredeemed world, temporal dominion and ethnic particularity are impossibly compromised. Davies phrases the position just right when he says, "It was its ability to detach its loyalty from 'place,'

43. Also: "The desert is, therefore, the place of revelation and of the constitution of 'Israel' as a people; there she was elected" (*T,* p. 39). Davies's book is remarkable for many reasons, one of which is surely the way that while it intends to be a defense and explanation of Zionism as a deeply rooted Jewish movement, it consistently and honestly documents the factors in the tradition that are in tension with such a view.

while nonetheless retaining 'place' in its memory, that enabled Pharisaism to transcend the loss of its Land" (*T*, p. 69).[44] Our only addition would be to argue that this displacement of loyalty from place to memory of place was necessary not only to transcend the loss of the Land but to enable the loss of the Land. Political possession of the Land most threatened the possibility of continued Jewish cultural practice and difference. Given the choice between an ethnocentricity that would not seek domination over others and a seeking of political domination that would necessarily have led either to a dilution of distinctiveness, tribal warfare, or fascism, the Rabbis chose ethnocentricity. Zionism is thus a subversion of rabbinic Judaism, and it is no wonder that until World War II Zionism was a secular movement to which very few religious Jews adhered, seeing it as a human arrogation of a work that only God should or could perform.[45] This is,

44. We think that Davies occasionally seems to lose his grip on his own great insight by confusing ethnic identity with political possession (see *T*, pp. 90–91 n. 10). The same mixture appears also when he associates, it seems, deterritorialization and deculturation (p. 93). It is made clear when he writes, "At the same time the age-long engagement of Judaism with The Land in religious terms indicates that ethnicity and religion . . . are finally inseparable in Judaism" (p. 97). We certainly agree that ethnicity and religion are inseparable in Judaism, but we fail to see the necessary connection between ethnicity, religion, and territoriality. Moreover, a people can be on their land without this landedness being expressed in the form of a nation-state, and landedness can be shared in the same place with others who feel equally attached to the same land. This is the solution of the Neturei Karta, who live, after all, in Jerusalem but do not seek political hegemony over it.

45. Davies states that "for religious Jews, we must conclude, The Land is ultimately inseparable from the state of Israel, however much the actualities of history have demanded their distinction" (*T*, p. 51). Yet clearly many religious Jews have not felt that way at all. Although we do not deny entirely the theological bona fides of religious Zionism as one option for modern Jewish religious thought, the fact that they are the historical "winners" in an ideological struggle should not blind us to the fact that their option was, until only recently, just one option for religious Jews, and a very contested one at that. Even the theological "patron saint" of religious Zionists, the holy Rabbi Loewe (Mahara"l) of Prague, who, as Davies points out, "understood the nature and role of nations to be ordained by God, part of the natural order," and that "nations were intended to cohere rather than be scattered"; even he held that "reestablishment of a Jewish state should be left to God" (*T*, p. 33). Rabbi Nahman of Bratslav's desire to touch any part of the Land and then immediately return to Poland hardly bespeaks a proto-Zionism either (ibid.). Davies nuances his own statement when he remarks, "Zionism cannot be equated with a reaffirmation of the eternal relation of The Land, the people, and the Deity, except with the most cautious reservations, since it is more the expression of nationalism than of Judaism" (*T*, p. 64). Davies is right, however, in his claim that J. J. Petuchowski's statement—that there can be a "full-blooded Judaism which is in no need to hope and to pray for a messianic return to Palestine" (J. J. Petuchowski, "Diaspora Judaism—An Abnormality?" *Judaism* 9 [1960]: 27)—is missing something vital about historical Jewish tradition. The desire, the longing for unity, coherence, and groundedness in the utopian future of the messianic age is, as Davies eminently demonstrates, virtually inseparable from historical Judaism (*T*, p. 66). There is surely a "territorial theological tradition." At issue rather is its status in premessianic praxis.

moreover, the basis, even to this day, for the anti-Zionist ideology of such groups as Neturei Karta.

The dialectic between Paul and the Rabbis can be recuperated for cultural critique. When Christianity is the hegemonic power in Europe and the United States, the resistance of Jews to being universalized can be a critical force and model for the resistance of all peoples to being Europeanized out of particular bodily existence. When, however, an ethnocentric Judaism becomes a temporal, hegemonic political force, it becomes absolutely, vitally necessary to accept Paul's critical challenge—although not his universalizing, disembodying solution—and to develop an equally passionate concern for all human beings. We, including religious Jews—perhaps especially religious Jews—must take seriously the theological dimension of Paul's challenge. How could the God of all the world have such a disproportionate care and concern for only a small part of His world? And yet, obviously, we cannot even conceive of accepting Paul's solution of dissolving into a universal human essence, even one that would not be Christian but truly humanist and universal, even if such an entity could really exist.[46] Somewhere in this dialectic a synthesis must be found, one that will allow for stubborn hanging-on to ethnic, cultural specificity but in a context of deeply felt and enacted human solidarity. For that synthesis, Diaspora provides a model, and only in conditions of Diaspora can such a resolution be even attempted. Within the conditions of Diaspora, many Jews discovered that their well-being was absolutely dependent on principles of respect for difference, indeed that, as the radical slogan goes, "no one is free until all are free." Absolute devotion to the maintenance of Jewish culture and the historical memory was not inconsistent with devotion to radical causes of human liberation; there were Yiddish-speaking and Judeo-Arabic-speaking groups of Marxists and anarchists, and some even retained a commitment to historical Jewish religious practice.[47] The "chosenness" of the Jews becomes, when seen in this light, not a warrant for racism but precisely an antidote to racism. This is a Judaism that mobilizes the critical forces within the Bible and the Jewish tradition rather than mobilizing the repressive and racist forces that also subsist there and that we are not denying.

Within conditions of Diaspora, tendencies toward nativism were also materially discouraged. Diaspora culture and identity allows (and has historically allowed in the best circumstances, such as in Muslim Spain),

46. Judith Butler asks, "How is it that we might ground a theory or politics in a speech situation or subject position which is 'universal' when the very category of the universal has only begun to be exposed for its own highly ethnocentric biases?" (Judith Butler, "Contingent Foundations: Feminism and the Question of 'Postmodernism,'" *Praxis International* 11 [July 1991]: 153).

47. Lenin's minister of justice, I. N. Steinberg, was an orthodox Jew.

for a complex continuation of Jewish cultural creativity and identity at the same time that the same people participate fully in the common cultural life of their surroundings. The same figure, a Nagid, an Ibn Gabirol, or a Maimonides, can be simultaneously the vehicle of the preservation of traditions and of the mixing of cultures. This was the case not only in Muslim Spain, nor even only outside of the Land. The Rabbis in Diaspora in their own Land also produced a phenomenon of renewal of Jewish traditional culture at the same time that they were very well acquainted with and an integral part of the circumambient late antique culture. Diasporic cultural identity teaches us that cultures are not preserved by being protected from "mixing" but probably can only continue to exist as a product of such mixing. Cultures, as well as identities, are constantly being remade. While this is true of all cultures, diasporic Jewish culture lays it bare because of the impossibility of a natural association between this people and a particular land—thus the impossibility of seeing Jewish culture as a self-enclosed, bounded phenomenon. The critical force of this dissociation among people, language, culture, and land has been an enormous threat to cultural nativisms and integrisms, a threat that is one of the sources of anti-Semitism and perhaps one of the reasons that Europe has been much more prey to this evil than the Middle East. In other words, diasporic identity is a disaggregated identity. Jewishness disrupts the very categories of identity because it is not national, not genealogical, not religious, but all of these in dialectical tension with one another. When liberal Arabs and some Jews claim that the Jews of the Middle East are Arab Jews, we concur and think that Zionist ideology occludes something very significant when it seeks to obscure this point. The production of an ideology of a pure Jewish cultural essence that has been debased by Diaspora seems neither historically nor ethically correct. "Diasporized," that is, disaggregated, identity allows the early medieval scholar Rabbi Sa'adya to be an Egyptian Arab who happens to be Jewish and also a Jew who happens to be an Egyptian Arab. Both of these contradictory propositions must be held together. Similarly, we suggest that a diasporized gender identity is possible and positive. Being a woman is some kind of special being, and there are aspects of life and practice that insist on and celebrate that speciality. But this does not imply a fixing or freezing of all practice and performance of gender identity into one set of parameters. Human beings are divided into men and women for certain purposes, but that does not tell the whole story of their bodily identity. Rather than the dualism of gendered bodies and universal souls, or Jewish/Greek bodies and universal souls—the dualism that the Western tradition offers—we can substitute partially Jewish, partially Greek bodies, bodies that are sometimes gendered and sometimes not. It is this idea that we are calling diasporized identity.

Crucial to this construction of Jewish history and identity is the simple fact, often consciously or unconsciously suppressed, that Diaspora is not the forced product of war and destruction—taking place after the downfall of Judea—but that already in the centuries before this downfall, the majority of Jews lived voluntarily outside of the Land.[48] Moreover, given a choice between domination by a "foreign" power who would allow them to keep the Torah undisturbed and domination by a "Jewish" authority who would interfere with religious life, the Pharisees and their successors the Rabbis generally chose the former (see *T,* p. 68).[49]

The story we would tell of Jewish history has three stages. In the first stage, we find a people—call it a tribe—not very different in certain respects from peoples in similar material conditions all over the world, a people like most others that regards itself as special among humanity, indeed as the People, and its land as preeminently wonderful among lands, the Land. This is, of course, an oversimplification because this "tribe" never quite dwelled alone and never regarded itself as autochthonous in its Land. In the second stage, this form of life increasingly becomes untenable, morally and politically, because the "tribe" is in cultural, social, and political contact with other people. This is, roughly speaking, the Hellenistic period, culminating in the crises of the first century, of which we have read Paul as an integral part. Various solutions to this problem were eventually adopted. Pauline Christianity is one; so perhaps is the retreat to Qumran, while the Pharisaic Rabbis "invented" Diaspora, even in the Land, as the solution to this cultural dilemma.

The third stage is diasporic existence. The rabbinic answer to Paul's challenge was to renounce any possibility of domination over Others by being perpetually out of power:

> Just as with seeing the return in terms of the restoration of political rights, seeing it in terms of redemption has certain consequences. If the return were an act of divine intervention, it could not be engineered or forced by political or any other human means: to do so would be impious. That coming was best served by waiting in obedience for it: *men of violence would not avail to bring it in.* The rabbinic aloofness to messianic claimants sprang not only from the history of disillusionment with such, but from this underlying, deeply engrained attitude. It can be claimed that under the main rabbinic tradition Judaism condemned itself to powerlessness. But recognition of powerlessness (rather than a frustrating, futile, and tragic resistance) was effective in preserving Judaism in a very hostile Christendom, and therefore had its own brand of "power." [*T,* p. 82]

48. Davies is one scholar who does not suppress this fact but forthrightly faces it. See *T,* p. 65.

49. Once again, the Neturei Karta, in their deference to Palestinian political claims on the Land of Israel, are, it seems, on solid historical ground.

As before, our impulse is only slightly to change the nuance of Davies's marvelously precise reading. The renunciation (not merely "recognition") of temporal power was to our minds precisely the most powerful mode of preservation of difference and, therefore, the most effective kind of resistance. The Neturei Karta, to this day, refuse to visit the Western Wall, the holiest place in Judaism, without PLO "visas" because it was taken by violence.

This response has much to teach us. We want to propose a privileging of Diaspora, a dissociation of ethnicities and political hegemonies as the only social structure that even begins to make possible a maintenance of cultural identity in a world grown thoroughly and inextricably interdependent. Indeed, we would suggest that Diaspora, and not monotheism, may be the most important contribution that Judaism has to make to the world, although we would not deny the positive role that monotheism has played in making Diaspora possible.[50] Assimilating the lesson of Diaspora, namely that peoples and lands are not naturally and organically connected, could help prevent bloodshed such as that occurring in Eastern Europe today.[51] In Eastern Europe at the turn of the century, the Jewish Workers' Bund, a mass socialist organization, had developed a model for national-cultural autonomy not based on territorial ethnic states. That program was effectively marginalized by the Bolsheviks and the Zionists. Diaspora can teach us that it is possible for a people to maintain its distinctive culture, its difference, without controlling land, a fortiori without controlling other people or developing a need to dispossess them of their lands. Thus the response of rabbinic Judaism to the challenge of universalism that Paul, among others, raised against what was becoming, at the end of one millennium and the beginning of the next, increasingly an inappropriate doctrine of specialness in an already interdependent world may provide some of the pieces to the puzzle of how humanity can survive as another millennium draws to a close with no messiah on the horizon. The renunciation of difference seems both an impoverishment of human life and an inevitable harbinger of oppression. Yet the renunciation of sovereignty (justified by discourses of autochthony, indigenousness, and territorial self-determination), combined with a fierce tenacity in holding onto cultural identity, might well have something to offer to a world in which these two forces, together, kill thousands daily.

50. Sidra Ezrahi has recently argued that monotheism and Diaspora are inextricably intertwined (oral communication with Daniel Boyarin).

51. Our point is not to reallegorize the Jew as wanderer but simply to point to certain aspects of the concrete realities of Jewish history as a possible, vital, positive contribution to human political culture in general. The implicitly normative call on other Jews to participate in our image of Jewishness is, we admit, ambivalent and potentially coercive, but how could it be otherwise? Even coercions can be ranked.

Appendix: Statement of the Neturei Karta[52]

We the Neturei Karta (Guardians of the City—Jerusalem), presently numbering in the tens of thousands, are comprised of the descendants of the pioneer Jews who settled in the Holy Land over a hundred years before the establishment of the Zionist State. Their sole motive was to serve G-d, and they had neither political aspirations nor any desire to exploit the local population in order to attain statehood.

Our mission, in the capacity of Palestinian advisers in this round of the Middle East Peace Conference, is to concern ourselves with the safeguarding of the interests of the Palestinian Jews and the entire Jewish nation. The Jewish people are charged by divine oath not to seek independence and cast off the yoke of exile which G-d decreed, as a result of not abiding by the conditions under which G-d granted them the Holy Land. We repeat constantly in our prayers, "since we sinned, we were therefore exiled from our land." G-d promised to gather in the exiled Jews through His messiah. This is one of the principles of the Jewish faith. The Zionist rebelled against this divine decree of exile by taking the land away from its indigenous inhabitants and established their state. Thus are the Jewish people being exposed to the divine retribution set down in the Talmud. "I will make your flesh prey as the deer and the antelope of the forest" (Song 2:7). Our advice to the negotiating contingent of the Palestinian delegation will remain within the framework of Jewish theology.

Zionist schoolings dictate a doctrine of labelling the indigenous Palestinian population "enemies" in order to sanction their expansionist policies. Judaism teaches that the Jew and non-Jew are to coexist in a cordial and good neighbor relationship. We Palestinian Jews have no desire to expand our places of residence and occupy our neighbors' lands, but only to live alongside non-Jewish Palestinians, just as Jews live throughout the world, in peace and tranquility.

The enmity and animosity toward the non-Jewish population, taught to the Zionist faithful, is already boomeranging. King Solomon, in Parables 27:19, describes reality "as one's image is reflected in water: so one's heart toward his fellow man"—so an enemy's heart is reflected in his adversary's heart. The Intifada is "exhibit A" to this King Solomon gem of wisdom. We hope and pray that this face-

52. This statement was made by the Palestinian Jewish (Neturei Karta) members of the Palestinian delegation to the Middle East Peace Conference in Washington, D.C., 1992, and has been translated here from the New York Yiddish weekly *Di yidishe vokhnshrift,* 4 Sept. 1992. We are not including this statement with our essay in order to advance Neturei Karta as an organization, nor are we members of Neturei Karta, some of whose policies we are in sympathy with and others of which we find violently objectionable. We include it because we consider it to be eloquent evidence of the kind of radical political rhetoric available within a highly traditional diasporic Jewish framework and in particular for its insight into what could be called the construction of the demonized Other.

to-face meeting with imagined adversaries will undo the false image created and that both Jew and Arab in Palestine can once again live as good neighbors as was the life of yesteryear, under a rule chosen by the indigenous residents of the Holy Land—thus conforming with G-d's plan for the Holy Land.

Inchallah![53]

Three members of the Neturei Karta posing with Hanan Mikhail Ashrawi (left), head of the Palestinian delegation to the Middle East peace talks. Photo: *Di yidishe vokhnschrift,* 4 Sept. 1992.

53. The word is the traditional Muslim prayer, "May it be God's [Allah's] will."

The Time of the Gypsies: A "People without History" in the Narratives of the West

Katie Trumpener

Ahead was a light cart, driven by a man, and trudging along at the side was a woman, sturdy and elderly, with a pack on her back. . . .

The road was narrow. Leo sounded the horn sharply. The man on the cart looked round, but the woman on foot only trudged steadily, rapidly forward, without turning her head.

Yvette's heart gave a jump. The man on the cart was a gipsy, one of the black, loose-bodied, handsome sort. . . . his gaze [was] insolent in its indifference. . . . Leo honked the horn again, imperiously. . . . But still [the gipsy] did not pull aside.

Leo made the horn scream, as he put the brakes on and the car slowed up near the back of the cart. . . .

"Get out o' the way then!" yelled Leo. . . .

"Don't the pretty young ladies want to hear their fortunes?" said the gipsy on the cart, laughing except for his dark, watchful eyes,

I owe great thanks to Ian Hancock for his encouragement and for a constant stream of primary sources; to Ronald Lee, Alaina Lemon, Loren Kruger, Nancy Glazener, Shamoon Zamir, Russell Berman, Terry Castle, David Wellbery, Norma Field, and Michael Geyer, and to the Interdisciplinary Perspectives on the Study of Europe (IPSE) Workshop at the University of Chicago for their help in articulating the thrust of these arguments; to Gary Finder, Sabine Golz, Elizabeth Heckendorn Cook, Deidre Lynch, Laura Rigal, and Elizabeth Helsinger for valuable leads and sources; and finally to the Free University of Berlin, the University of Chicago Humanities Institute, the Mellon Foundation, and the University of Pittsburgh for fellowship support that made this research and writing possible.

All translations from the German are mine unless otherwise noted.

This article originally appeared in *Critical Inquiry* 18 (Summer 1992).

which went from face to face, and lingered on Yvette's young, tender face. . . .

"Oh yes! let's!" cried Lucille at once.

"Oh yes!" chorused the girls.

"I say! What about the time?" cried Leo.

"Oh bother the old time! Somebody's always dragging in time by the forelock," cried Lucille.

"Well, if you don't mind *when* we get back, *I* don't!" said Leo heroically.

—D. H. Lawrence, *The Virgin and the Gipsy*

"Gypsies are great thieves. They have an uncanny ability to con their way into people's homes and then to find exactly where their valuables are. It's almost like they can smell it. They're uncanny.

"One of the worst days in the police department is Good Friday. An awful lot of Gypsies steal on Good Friday. What's taught to the young Gypsy kids is that when Christ was put on the cross, they had four nails to nail him to the cross. A Gypsy kid came by and stole one of the nails. That's why, on the crucifix, Christ's feet are nailed with one nail and the other two are in the hands.

"That's passed down from generation to generation. So, according to Gypsy lore, Christ on the cross is supposed to have said, From now and forevermore, Gypsies can steal and it's not a sin.

"Good Friday's a big day for them. When I was working the Gypsies, we worked them for ten years, we would never take Good Friday off because it was a day we'd have to get up early and be on the run with them because they would be everywhere."

—Connie Fletcher, *What Cops Know*

During a wave of Norwegian patriotism in the 1880s, Lillehammer dentist Anders Sandvig began, on annual dental tours of duty through the surrounding region, to collect folkloric artifacts and became concerned that ancient buildings were being demolished or were falling into disrepair. By 1904, when (amidst the rising nationalism that a year later would secure Norway's independence from Sweden) the Maihaugen Open Air Museum was opened in Lillehammer to house Sandvig's collection, it included a manor house, parish church, and six whole farm buildings rescued and reassembled from various sites throughout the area. Only the museum itself, however, gave cumulative meaning to Sandvig's isolated

---

Katie Trumpener is associate professor of Germanic studies and comparative literature at the University of Chicago. She is author of *Bardic Nationalism: The Romantic Novel and the British Empire* (forthcoming). She is currently working on the nanny as a figure of cultural memory in European modernity.

acts of surgical extraction and architectural restoration: traversing regional distance, freezing historical time, reconciling political and class divisions, the museum created a bounded, timeless Norwegian folk community, and a new kind of nationalist rhetoric. The official two-day opening celebrations themselves, described in Sandvig's memoirs, became an extended holiday that brought together the whole population of Lillehammer, garbed in national costume: feasting, dancing, speeches to the fatherland ("Norway, Awaken!"), repeated group singing of the national anthem, and, filling the second day, an allegorical procession welcoming the "Maihaug people" (the costumed site interpreters) into Lillehammer, while costumed "trolls" and other "hill people" who "might protest against the new inhabitants" were seen fleeing back into the surrounding hills. As the Maihaug people took up their new residences, spectators could watch the "farmers' families" performing chores while speaking authentic local dialect, listen to the saga recitations of Maihaugen's resident *skald,* and see the visibly growing restlessness of Peer Gynt in his cottage, as he quarreled with Åse and flirted with female visitors. Finally, during the last hours of the festivities, a family of Gypsies arrive as well to set up their tent on the grounds of Maihaugen:

> On occasions where many people [*mennesker*] are gathered together, those sorts of people [*folk*] will usually turn up suddenly. They had a horse and wagon and were equipped the way travelling people usually are. Even the dog wasn't missing. . . . Their leader was a horsetrader and a watch-trader. . . . The wife read palms and predicted the fates of young men and women. . . . Another, who smoked a chalk pipe, was a specialist in laying the cards but her payment had to be made ahead of time. . . . A younger pair of siblings, a temperamental woman and her brother, took people by storm with their musical abilities. The fortuneteller, with baby on her back, attracted attention everywhere. She possessed brilliant powers of speech and had a pair of dangerous eyes. When she came into the rectory and noticed the empty cradle in the bedroom, she took her child and placed it without hesitating into the crib. She lit her chalk pipe and began to rock the cradle, while she crooned and sang.
>
> At precisely that moment, Director Grosch came in with several others; appalled, he clapped his hands together and shouted indignantly:
>
> —No, this is the most brazen thing I've ever seen.
>
> Remarkably enough, there wasn't anyone except those in the know who realized that the whole thing was a staged feature of the evening's festivities. Everybody believed that they were genuine gypsies [but they were in fact well-known townspeople]. They were costumed so well, and everyone played his role so brilliantly that thus the masquerade was carried out.[1]

1. Anders Sandvig, *I praksis og på samlerferd* [*At Work and on Collecting Journeys*] (Oslo,

At the culmination of the nationalist celebration stands a ritualized expulsion of "the Gypsies" from the consecrated folkloric space of patrimony. When a national culture stops to celebrate and take stock of itself, it is only the "Gypsies" who keep moving and who persist as interlopers. Long after the Maihaug people have settled into their rightful places, and long after other threats to community (the trolls and hill people) have been chased off, it is "Gypsies" (characteristically given, it is believed, to stealing children from their homes) who attempt to usurp the cradle—preserved on behalf of the Norwegian people as a symbol of their own origins—to fill it instead with their own offspring.

As "the Gypsies" seize center stage, furthermore, Sandvig's own account undergoes a subtle shift in perspective and tone. The procession of events comes to a halt and the other displays seem robbed of their previous interest as the spectators turn to watch performed tableaux of Gypsy life. By the time this performance reaches its climax in a side room of one building, it is as if the whole assembly is crowded in there watching, and as if only the museum director's outraged shout can break the spell that has fallen over Maihaugen. Sandvig's account stresses at once the utter legibility of the "Gypsy scene" and the seeming spectatorial passivity or paralysis that attends it until its denouement. In retrospect, of course, the performance's hypnotic predictability derives from its careful scripting and staging, and "the Gypsies'" strange yet oddly familiar exoticism comes from the fact they are actually disguised townspeople. Indeed, as the culmination and summary of the Maihaugen festivities, the episode provides a final, piquantly transgressive illustration of how the whole museum, in assembling a national heritage, blurs the boundaries between literary, historical, and "representative" figures, as it does between its self-consciously stylized staging of traditional activities and its simple distillation of everyday life with its mixture of settled routine and contained restlessness.[2]

Played out in the drama at Maihaugen, in effect, is much of the ideological ensemble surrounding the cultural construction of "the Gypsies" in the Western imagination.[3] This essay follows several strands in succession

---

1943), pp. 183–84. I am indebted to Mark Sandberg for directing me to this passage and for the translation, as well as for the inspiration of his ground-breaking work on modernist institutions and relations of the visible (including a lengthier consideration of Sandvig and the open-air museum); see Mark Sandberg, "Missing Persons: Spectacle and Narrative in Late Nineteenth-Century Scandinavia" (Ph.D. diss., University of California, Berkeley, 1991).

2. For a comparable, contemporaneous cataloging of "Gypsy life" as plot, see also A. Khanzhonkov's comments about his "Drama in a Gypsy Camp near Moscow," in *Silent Witnesses: Russian Films 1908–1919,* ed. Paolo Cherchi Usai et al. (London, 1989), p. 48. "Gypsies" are omnipresent characters in film narratives from Georges Méliès, Cecil Hepworth, and D. W. Griffith onwards.

3. The question of nomenclature for the people popularly known as Gypsies remains

(the Gypsy encounter as set piece; the conflation of the Gypsies' literary and historical status; the freezing of time at the Gypsies' approach; the unmasking of their "character" as Western projection), its recurrent motif—as the epigraphs suggest—the ascribed relationship of Gypsies to Western temporality, and its consequences for the development and non-development of Western political discourse about Gypsy life.[4] Thus D. H. Lawrence's typical account of first contact stresses the nonsynchronicity with which the Gypsies in their cart and a carful of bored young white Europeans move through time; at first threatening to flatten whatever impedes their progress, the young people capitulate to Gypsy seductions by the very decision to abandon their usual timetables.[5] The related invo-

---

vexed. The mainly pejorative associations surrounding the term (and that it is not a self-designation but a Western coinage based on false surmises about the group's race and place of origin) lead European activists to insist on its replacement with the self-given tribal names of the various postdiasporic groupings (the Sinti and Roma in Germany, the Vlax in the Balkans, and so on) or (as in Britain) with the nonracial designation of "travellers," although this, too, risks fixing as *the* defining cultural characteristic a mode of life forced on the group only by historical circumstance and economic necessity—and indeed today many Gypsies in the English-speaking world no longer "travel," but have fixed homes and jobs. For an excellent discussion of the political stake of nomenclature, the nature of ethnic diversity among the Gypsies, and the ongoing economic basis of Gypsy "nomadism," see Thomas Acton, *Gypsy Politics and Social Change: The Development of Ethnic Ideology and Pressure Politics among British Gypsies from Victorian Reformism to Romany Nationalism* (London, 1974), esp. pp. 14–23, 53–96, 189–218, 245–70.

None of these designations, for the following reasons, seem suitable for all of the situations analyzed here: given the general focus on a period antedating the modern rights movement and on repetitive Western fantasies in which individual or historical differences of experience within "the Gypsy camp" are left deliberately undifferentiated and unexplored; given the primary focus on fictitious and even dress-up "Gypsies" rather than on real members of a particular postdiasporic group; and given, finally, the piece's recurring reference to the North American situation, in which immigration from all parts of Europe and the pressures facing the ethnic group as a whole make the use of subdesignations difficult and unhelpful. The essay has been forced, therefore, into somewhat eclectic practices: where the "Gypsies" are literally only costumes with white Europeans encased in them, that fact has been signalled by quotation marks; "ordinary" cases of fictionalization appear simply as Gypsies; and in passages stressing the distinction between such projections and the actual ethnic group, the latter appear (in a somewhat homogenizing collective term) as "Romani."

4. On time and historylessness, see Johannes Fabian, *Time and the Other: How Anthropology Makes Its Object* (New York, 1983); Hermann Bausinger et al., *Grundzüge der Volkskunde* (Darmstadt, 1978), esp. pp. 141ff.; Reinhart Koselleck, *Futures Past: On the Semantics of Historical Time,* trans. Keith Tribe (Cambridge, Mass., 1985); M. M. Bakhtin, *The Dialogic Imagination: Four Essays,* trans. Caryl Emerson and Michael Holquist, ed. Holquist (Austin, Tex., 1981); *Chronotypes: The Construction of Time,* ed. John Bender and David E. Wellbery (Stanford, Calif., 1991); and Bruce Robbins, *The Servant's Hand: English Fiction from Below* (New York, 1986), esp. the preface and chap. 1.

5. Already in George Borrow's 1857 *Romany Rye* the Gypsies are cast as spokesmen for cultural conservatism, lamenting the advent of the railroads, and the displacement of one kind of wandering with mass transportation; by 1908, when a speeding motorcar in

cation, by a resident "Gypsy expert" with the Chicago Police Department, of a mythic Gypsy time of legend, curse, and prophecy ("from now and forevermore") to justify current police procedures (by which Gypsy citizens continue, Good Friday or not, to be questioned, harassed, and even framed solely on racial grounds) suggests the continuing historical consequence of Western "Gypsy" fantasies for the actual shape of Romani lives in Europe and North America today.

Although over the last twenty years (in conjunction with Romani lobbying for international recognition as a people without a country) a growing body of historical, anthropological, and polemical writing has addressed Romani experience, there has, to date, been little corresponding literary, cultural, or political analysis of the racism and Orientalism historically surrounding the Western construction of the "Gypsy Question," despite the allure and the obvious centrality of the topic; this essay thus represents a preliminary, tentative attempt to open up a field of theoretical and literary inquiry.[6] The focus of its first section is on ideological forms; drawing on a range of material to illuminate the role that Germans, in the shadow of the Third Reich, assign to the Gypsies in constructing their own relationship to non-German cultures, it links the static display of "the Gypsies" as visual spectacle and a complicated, if equally static, politics of cultural memory and amnesia. The second half, centered on the post-Enlightenment literary canon and on Britain, sketches the historical

---

Kenneth Grahame's *The Wind in the Willows* collides with a wandering Gypsy cart, it destroys not only the cart but the whole wandering way of life it represents.

6. The most useful overviews (written by Gypsy rights activists and aimed at a broad audience) are Acton, *Gypsy Politics and Social Change; In Auschwitz vergast, bis heute verfolgt: Zur Situation der Roma (Zigeuner) in Deutschland und Europa,* ed. Tilman Zülch (Hamburg, 1979); Ian Hancock, *The Pariah Syndrome: An Account of Gypsy Slavery and Persecution* (Ann Arbor, Mich., 1987); Donald Kenrick and Grattan Puxon, *The Destiny of Europe's Gypsies* (London, 1972); Puxon, *On the Road* (London, 1967) and *Rom: Europe's Gypsies* (London, 1973). David Mayall's *Gypsy-Travellers in Nineteenth-Century Society* (Cambridge, 1988) provides the best history of the Gypsies in Britain (including an appendix listing all major legislation affecting Gypsies, 1530–1908) while Alaina Lemon's "Performance, History, and Becoming Civilized: Roma (Gypsies) in the USSR and the Moscow Teatr 'Romen'" (Ph.D. diss. in progress, University of Chicago) promises the most sophisticated account to date of Roma self-construction. On Central Europe in particular, see Joachim S. Hohmann, *Geschichte der Zigeunerverfolgung in Deutschland* (Frankfurt, 1981); Bálint Sárosi, *Gypsy Music,* trans. Fred Macnicol (Budapest, 1971); Michael Zimmermann, *Verfolgt, vertrieben, vernichtet: Die nationalsozialistische Vernichtungspolitik gegen Sinti und Roma* (Essen, 1989); Romani Rose and Walter Weiss, *Sinti und Roman im Dritten Reich: Das Programm der Vernichtung durch Arbeit* (Göttingen, 1991); Selma Steinmetz, *Österreichs Zigeuner im NS-Staat* (Vienna, 1966); Georg von Soest, *Zigeuner zwischen Verfolgung und Integration: Geschichte, Lebensbedingungen und Eingliederungsversuche* (Weinheim, 1979); *Eigensinn und Hilfe: Zigeuner in der Sozialpolitik heutiger Leistungsgesellschaften,* ed. Reimer Gronemeyer (Giessen, 1983); Luise Rinser, *Wer wirft den Stein? Zigeuner sein in Deutschland* (Stuttgart, 1985); and Lea Rosh's 1985 film, *Das lustige Zigeunerleben—Sinti und Roma in der BRD.*

evolution of an overtly political account of the "Gypsies" into a literally autonomous literary one. This process of "literarization," the increasingly powerful Western symbolism developed around the Gypsies, and their discursive placement ever further outside of the national teleologies or cumulative time of history, leads simultaneously to a progressive dissociation and conflation of literary traditions with living people. At the Nürnberg trials, for example, an SS leader justified the Nazi persecution of the Gypsies by citing Schiller's literary descriptions of the Thirty Years War in much the same way that a legend of the Crucifixion was still being invoked in 1990 to justify the anti-Gypsy policies of American police forces.[7]

The coda, finally, centers on one of the most important pieces of Romani writing to date, Ronald Lee's *Goddam Gypsy* (1970), a militant autobiography that (setting its tale of ethnic coming-to-consciousness in the Montréal of the late sixties against rising French- and English-Canadian nationalism) poses the question of what future Gypsy representation, political or literary, can have in a West still dominated by the rhetoric and narratives of nationalism. Twenty years later, the political marginality of Gypsies in North America remains virtually unchanged: nineteenth-century bans of Gypsy immigration remain informally in place, as do police "Gypsy" experts officially; and despite the fact that it's unconstitutional, "Gypsies remain the only American ethnic minority against whom laws still operate, and who are specifically named in those laws."[8] In the depictions of the press and of mass culture, in literature written for children and in school textbooks, Gypsies continue (long after political pressure has forced out analogous generic characterizations of African Americans, Jews, or women) to appear as stereotypical figures of magic and menace; what is involved here is not only ignorance, a failure to realize that the Gypsies are a real and sizable population living as a still-threatened minority in Europe and North America, but also a refusal to give up a powerful set of cultural myths for their sake.[9] The steadily deter-

7. SS leader Otto Ohlendorf's testimony is cited in Bernhard Streck, "Die 'Bekämpfung des Zigeunerunwesens': Ein Stück moderner Rechtsgeschichte," in *In Auschwitz vergast, bis heute verfolgt,* pp. 64–65. The Gypsies have been mythologically linked to the Nativity as well as the Crucifixion; thus we have in "The Madonna and the Gipsy" (*Roadside Songs of Tuscany,* trans. Francesca Alexander, ed. John Ruskin [London, 1885]) a Gypsy woman who grants shelter to the Holy Family on their flight to Egypt and foretells the entire course of Jesus' life. But see also the anti-Gypsy "carols" from Spain, Provence, and Greece quoted by Kenrick and Puxon, *The Destiny of Europe's Gypsies,* pp. 26–27.

8. Hancock, *The Pariah Syndrome,* p. 105. The American office of the International Romani Union (headed by Hancock in Manchaca, Texas, 78652, tel. [512] 282-1268), continues to lobby for improved civil rights for the hundreds of thousands of Romani living in the United States.

9. The pervasiveness of "casual" American racism about the Gypsies even today may be suggested by two throwaway metaphoric references recently come across on the same day. The first is a letter to the editor of *Lingua Franca.* The author is a self-announced "gypsy

iorating legal status of Romani across Europe as well, in the wake of rapid political and economic changes, resurgent nationalisms, and neofascisms (repeated political and physical attacks on Gypsy groups in Rumania, Poland, Yugoslavia, Germany, and Hungary, revelations of unauthorized sterilization of Gypsy women in Czechoslovakia, and increasing official indifference or hostility towards Gypsy refugees throughout Western Europe) have only made Lee's concerns more urgent than ever.[10]

---

scholar . . . in the history business" who has taught at seven schools over the last sixteen years and who reports an experiment in "sexy" dressing-up for the classroom on the last day of her most recent contract. She ends her letter by moving back from the constraining semiotics of gender to her own precarious, if freewheeling, professional standing, a transition she effects by "tying *gypsy* and *clothing* together," and reporting on a childhood "gypsy Halloween costume" her grandmother made for her. "I'm going to look in a trunk right now to see if I still have it. Once a gypsy, always a gypsy" (Elisabeth A. Weston, letter to the editor, *Lingua Franca* 1 [June 1991]:3).

The other article, the cover story in the house organ of Pittsburgh's natural history and art museums, mobilizes a long-standing vocabulary of Gypsy parasitism, in part under the subheading "Voracious Immigrants from Europe," and throughout under the implicit threat of wholesale "extermination":

> A band of immigrants, taken forcefully from Europe, escapes its captors and finds freedom in America. . . . Despite the best efforts of their enemies who try to destroy them, they continue to grow and spread out across the land, leaving their mark wherever they settle. This would be a wonderful story, one we might even identify with our own forefathers, if the band of immigrants weren't the dreaded gypsy moths, and the mark they left wasn't acre after acre of barren and dying trees. . . . Considering these questions may lead to a final, effective solution to the gypsy moth problem. . . . Even the most adamant environmentalist couldn't be blamed for wishing for the total extinction of the monsters who ravaged his yard. This makes it difficult to look at the wider picture of the gypsy moth—the picture of an insect out of its natural environment. . . . "Once the gypsy moth invades an area, the forest will never be the same." [Anatole Wilson, "The Gypsy Moths Are Here," *Carnegie Magazine* 60 (May-June 1991): 12–18]

These are, of course, precisely the same metaphors used to condemn the Gypsies in eighteenth-century Europe. Joseph Addison referred to them as "this Race of Vermin . . . this idle profligate people . . . [that] infest all the Countries of *Europe,* and live in the Midst of Governments in a kind of Commonwealth by themselves" (Joseph Addison, *The Spectator,* no. 130, 30 July 1711, in *The Spectator,* ed. Donald F. Bond, 5 vols. [London, 1965], 2:17). And a 1787 aphorism of a Lithuanian minister claims that "Gypsies in a well-ordered state are like vermin on an animal's body" (cited in Kendrick and Puxon, *The Destiny of Europe's Gypsies,* p. 28).

10. See for instance the overview of Gypsy struggles in contemporary Europe in Bernd Dörler, "All hassen die Zigeuner," *Der Spiegel,* 3 Sept. 1990, pp. 34–57, and also the report, a year later and markedly more racist in tone, of growing tensions between Gypsy refugees and the residents of a working-class Hamburg neighborhood in Ariane Barth, "Hier steigt eine Giftsuppe auf," *Der Spiegel,* 14 Oct. 1991, pp. 118–43.

1

A picture in an old family album: two Gypsy girls, standing in the yard in ragged clothing, come to the house to sell their wild strawberries. As they look into the camera they are smiling, with shyness and—if family story is to be believed—with the sheer pleasure of having their picture taken for the first time. Taken during the 1920s, in the Bukovina district of Rumania, by a German woman, my grandmother's cousin Hetti, the photograph forms part of an extensive collection of domestic and "exotic" subjects: a bourgeois interior whose decor mixes German Biedermeier and Rumanian folklore; Hetti's three daughters bathing, dressing themselves up in borrowed peasant "costume," and sightseeing at nearby pilgrimage churches; travelling Gypsies with their wagons, a nomadic culture come to rest in a well-kept German backyard. So while this particular picture conveys freshness and spontaneity—the first picture ever taken of the two girls, a first contact between trusting Gypsies and sympathetic if curious Germans—the album as a whole and the handwritten annotation under this particular picture ("lustiges Zigeunerpack"; merry pack of Gypsies) suggests that the encounter is overlaid with a tradition of projection, prejudice, longing, and suspicion. The picture itself shows no high-spirited revelry. Nor do the two girls, with their polite, half-apprehensive smiles, form a literal mob or rabble: the word *Pack,* in German as in English, describes animal rather than human groups, implying that Gypsy social organization is primitive or subhuman, perhaps inherently criminal as well. If the photograph records a rapprochement, dissolving the social space separating the photographer and her subjects, the two words of the caption reestablish ironic or contemptuous distance, insisting on Gypsy life as debased and backward in character in order to forestall its unsettling allure.[11]

At the time the picture was taken, in fact, the notion of a carefree Gypsy existence had special appeal for someone in the photographer's particular historical and political situation, as a German colonist uneasily "occupying" part of an increasingly nationalist and xenophobic Rumania. As a young woman, Hetti had come to Bucharest during the final phase of World War I, literally part of the German occupation forces, to work in a female morale-boosting unit that ministered not only to German officers but also to German settlers just released from Rumanian

11. For the problem of "meaning" and "context" in photography, see Allan Sekula, *Photography against the Grain* (Halifax, 1984); Martha Rosler, *Three Works* (Halifax, 1981); Hans Haake, *Framing and Being Framed: 7 Works, 1970–75* (New York, 1975); John Berger, *About Looking* (New York, 1980); Berger and Jean Mohr, *Another Way of Telling* (New York, 1982); Pierre Bourdieu et al., *Eine illegitime Kunst: Die sozialen Gebrauchsweisen der Photographie* (Frankfurt, 1983); Malek Alloula, *The Colonial Harem* (Minneapolis, 1986); and Abigail Solomon, *Photography at the Dock: Essays on Photographic History, Institutions and Practices* (Minneapolis, 1991).

internment. At one of their folkloric "*Heimat* Evenings," Hetti fell in love with one of these newly released German prisoners, deeply moved (as she wrote home in a letter announcing her marriage) by all he had suffered during his captivity. At the end of the war, when the Rumanian government expelled the German forces, Hetti too was threatened for a time with deportation. Eventually permitted to remain, she settled with her husband in a German village in Bukovina, a former Austro-Hungarian territory newly ceded to Rumania after prolonged fighting between Rumanian and Ukrainian troops. Long a contested border region and part of the Ottoman Empire until the late eighteenth century, the area remained strikingly multiethnic, even by Austro-Hungarian standards.[12] Yet although ethnic Germans made up only one tenth of the population, Bukovina's cultural life had been dominated by Vienna since the nineteenth century, and its many German enclaves (some dating back to the thirteenth century) boasted their own schools, newspapers, and theaters. For fifteen years, Hetti's family became part of this "German" community, as her husband built up a prosperous small business exporting local wood to piano manufacturers in Germany. By the mid-thirties, however, their situation had worsened so dramatically (under the economic pressures of the worldwide depression and the political pressures of a growing, explicitly anti-German, Rumanian nationalism, which from 1922 onwards had increasingly forced the closure of German institutions and eventually began forcing Germans out of public life as well) that the family emigrated back to Berlin. Now, decades later, Hetti's daughters say they were equally dissatisfied with the fascist nationalism that awaited them in Germany. Yet when they refer today to their traumatic uprooting from Rumania, long ago, they appropriate highly charged nationalist rhetoric, still quoting the imperative phrase Adolf Hitler had used, during the same era, to justify his annexations of German-speaking territories and his forced repatriation of ethnic Germans: "Heim ins Reich"—brought back home into the Reich.

Here as everywhere, family stories intersect continually with political history. Yet the family mythology rests on elegiac nostalgia and historical forgetfulness, a cult presided over by the photograph of the Gypsy girls and by Hetti's handwritten caption. In the wake of military, colonial, and cultural defeat, as borders are being redrawn and identities officially redesigned, a dislodged bourgeoisie that sees itself as the recurrent victim

12. See Amy Colin, *Paul Celan: Holograms of Darkness* (Bloomington, Ind., 1991), introduction and chap. 1; Sophie A. Welisch, "The Bukovina-Germans in the Interwar Period," *East European Quarterly* 14 (Winter 1980): 423–37; Wolfgang Miege, *Das Dritte Reich und die Deutsche Volksgruppe in Rumänien 1933–38: Beitrag zur nationalsozialistischen Volkstumspolitik* (Bern, 1972); and Gregor von Rezzori, *Memoirs of an Anti-Semite* (New York, 1991), an autobiography concerned with German life in interwar Bukovina.

of history longs for the loss of time, converting the historical, political, and ethnic complexities of their own situation into an idealizing envy of a Gypsy life seemingly outside of history and beyond the reach of the authorities. The dream of historylessness, the longing for historical oblivion, takes historical forms and has historical ramifications, however, in its very attempt to banish history from a world it recreates as idyllic. Now far away and lost from sight, the Gypsies are remembered as insouciantly happy. Nomadic and illiterate, they wander down an endless road, without a social contract or country to bind them, carrying their home with them, crossing borders at will. Hetti's daughters still remember vividly how afraid they were, as children, of their mother's threats that Gypsies would come and steal them away. When they reminisce today about Bukovina, however, quoting their mother's phrase, such fears no longer seem present to them in the moment of quotation. Left in their place is a generalized memory of well-being, homage to their long-dead mother and to the aptness of her phrase to encapsulate aspects of their own experience of Rumania, as small children allowed to swim naked and play in the mud and dress up in the costume of peasants.

The daughters seem, in other words, to remember themselves as that *lustiges Zigeunerpack,* still half-animal, half-savage, dirty, and happy. The function of nostalgia is to restore innocence, by covering over other memories, harsher realities of tension and hostility and fear: the mother's fear of expulsion, the father's memories of prison, the children's terror of being stolen away, never to be returned, their identity, memory, language lost forever. The picture, the caption, and the quotation turn that terror around and turn the viewer into a happy Gypsy. But to do so they must erase both the identities of the girls being photographed and the historical reality of Gypsy life, a story over the last millennium of persecution, expulsion, and prison sentences as much as carefree wandering. In much of present-day Rumania, in fact, Gypsies were held as slaves and serfs for several centuries, officially emancipated only in the 1850s. In Weimar Germany, during the decade in which the photograph itself was taken, a 1929 law made it a punishable offense for Gypsies to travel or live "as a horde"—that is, in any group larger than a nuclear family. And during the late 1930s, while Hetti's family struggled in a Berlin suburb to adjust to their new life in Germany (reminiscing over their old photograph albums), the Nazi government organized the large-scale internment, sterilization, deportation, and finally "extermination" of Gypsies throughout Central, Eastern, and Southeastern Europe, resulting by 1945 in at least six hundred thousand deaths, nearly one-third of all the Gypsies in Europe. Beginning in 1939, all the Gypsies in Germany were interned in regional labor and concentration camps, and in 1943 moved on to Auschwitz-Birkenau, where a special, separate "Gypsy family camp" housed Gypsies from eleven countries; by 1944, when the camp was dissolved at the approach of the Russian army, half of its inmates had already died of hunger, exhaustion, and disease, and most of those who remained were sent to the gas chambers.[13]

During the initial roundup of German Sinti and Roma, no attempt seems to have been made to keep the fact or the purpose of the internment camps secret from anyone; they were reported on, editorialized, even joked about in local newspapers. One major internment camp, Marzahn, was established only twenty kilometers from Hetti's new home, on the outskirts of the capital city itself, its convenient location facilitating visits from psychologists and social workers who not only "studied" Gypsy life at close range, but even filmed emaciated Gypsy children at play on the grounds of the camp.[14] Gypsy faces preserved forever as images and icons, although their actual bodies may soon be starved, sterilized, or gassed: in an idyllic interlude in Traugott Müller's 1942 film *Friedemann Bach* (loosely based on Albert Emil Brachvogel's mid-nineteenth-century novel of the same name, and shot simultaneously with the building of the special Gypsy camp at Auschwitz), the genial eighteenth-century composer who cannot find a place for his music in the courtly and ecclesiastical institutions of his time discovers solacing, if irresponsible freedom among a group of itinerant Gypsies as the last refuge of genius. Like Orpheus playing for the wild animals, Friedemann Bach even performs the music of his father, Johann Sebastian, to a spellbound Gypsy audience appreciative of the music's sheer brilliance at a time in which the rest of Germany has forgotten Bach's greatness. In its utopian invocation of a carefree and genial Gypsy existence circulating outside of history and transcending political and institutional constraints, the movie itself attempted to move its own war-worn German audience temporarily outside of their increasingly demoralized historical moment, during which, as it happens, the Nazis themselves were actively engaged in eliminating Gypsy freedom of movement. In a careful division of labor and an equally careful synchronization between the Third Reich's linked apparatuses of repression and representation, the two halves of the post-Enlightenment ideology of Gypsy alterity—feared as deviance, idealized as autonomy—are played out simultaneously but separately, making visible all its internal contradictions.

For if "the primitive person does not change and does not allow himself to be changed," as Robert Ritter argued in 1940 in favor of Gypsy sterilization, Nazi racialists were at once fascinated and threatened by

13. See Zimmermann, *Verfolgt, vertrieben, vernichtet,* pp. 18–39.

14. I owe much of this information to *Ich bin kein Berliner: Minderheiten in der Schule,* an excellent 1987 exhibit at the West Berlin Arbeitsgruppe Pädagogisches Museum. The Gypsies of Berlin had already been interned in Marzahn once before, for the entire duration of the 1936 Olympic Games. See Kenrick and Puxon, *The Destiny of Europe's Gypsies,* p. 71. See also Zimmermann, *Verfolgt, vertrieben, vernichtet,* pp. 18–39.

such "essentialism."[15] "In contrast to the case of the Jews, mixed-blooded Gypsies were seen as socially 'inferior' to those of 'pure race'"; while the "mixed" group (some ninety percent of German Gypsies) were believed inherently criminal, beyond any social integration, the intact endogenous kinship organization of the "pure" nomadic Gypsies was held up as a *völkisch* ideal of cultural autonomy and racial segregation.[16] The Nürnberg Racial Laws, and the first German wildlife protection laws, both enacted in 1935, were imbued with related thinking, as Himmler's initial plans for the Gypsies make clear, for they involved the simultaneous incarceration and sterilization of "mixed" Gypsies and the group resettlement and species preservation of "pure" Gypsies on special protected preserves.[17] While most of these plans were never implemented (and different "categories" of Gypsies merged during the course of incarceration), the separate Gypsy camp within Auschwitz deliberately assigned the "work-dodging" Gypsy prisoners to the most debilitating labor details, while at the same time maintaining somewhat protected living conditions for them. Unlike any other prisoner group, they were not forced to have their heads shaved or to wear prison uniforms; they were allowed to remain in family groups and to keep their possessions—in short, to live, until 1944, some very distant semblance of their ordinary lives. In genocidal captivity, in the midst of a death camp, subject at will to medical experimentation, and prior to their own mass execution, Gypsies thus found themselves compelled to live out German fantasies of autonomy in ways only more concrete, more perverse, and much more painful than usual.[18]

Both in underlying premises and specific tactics, Nazi Gypsy policies show unmistakable continuities, up to the mouth of the gas chambers, with the "ordinary" persecutions of pre- and postwar European police procedures. Proposals for mass Gypsy internment, deportation, and eugenics were developed already in the late nineteenth century—as were

15. "The further birth of primitive asocials and members of criminal families should be stopped by the separation of the sexes or sterilization" (Robert Ritter, "Primitivität und Kriminalität," *Monatsschrift für Kriminalbiologie und Strafrechtsreform* 9 [1940]; quoted in Kenrick and Puxon, *The Destiny of Europe's Gypsies,* p. 66).

16. Streck, "Die 'Bekämpfung des Zigeunerunwesens,'" p. 77. See also Jercy Ficowski, "Die Vernichtung," in *In Auschwitz vergast, bis heute verfolgt,* pp. 91–112, and Zimmermann, *Verfolgt, vertrieben, vernichtet,* esp. pp. 40–42. Kenrick and Puxon discuss related 1937 German proposals for Gypsy deportations to Abyssinia or Polynesia (*The Destiny of Europe's Gypsies,* p. 64).

17. For the parallels between the Nürnberg laws and the Nature Protection Laws (*Naturschutzgesetze*) see Streck, "Die 'Bekämpfung des Zigeunerunwesens,'" pp. 83, 87. Zimmermann points out, however, that the Nature Protection Laws simultaneously criminalized parts of the traditional Gypsy economy, since the raw materials for Gypsy basket-making, for instance, formerly had been taken from now-protected trees (Zimmermann, *Verfolgt, vertrieben, vernichtet,* p. 19).

18. On the complicated considerations behind the special conditions of the Gypsy family camp, see Zimmermann, *Verfolgt, vertrieben, vernichtet,* pp. 75–81.

various criminological specialties and institutions for "fighting the Gypsy pestilence," which (unlike many of their objects of study) survived in many cases, until well into the postwar period, virtually unchanged in method or in personnel. (Established in 1898, the Central Office for Combatting the Gypsy Menace, for instance, continued to function under that name until 1970. A number of German Gypsies who survived the camps of the Third Reich but whose identity papers were lost or impounded there, were ruled officially "stateless" by the *postwar* West German government, while a 1956 decision of the West German Supreme Court, declaring the Sinti Gypsies to be a criminal organization rather than an ethnic minority, implicitly justified the initial Nazi-era internments on criminological grounds.)[19] Romani organizations are still fighting for official recognition of the Nazi persecution itself, whether in Germany for the same war crimes reparations long extended to members of other affected groups or, in the United States, for inclusion in the U.S. Holocaust Memorial.[20] If the initial Nazi roundups of the Gypsies met with indifference or approval from the public at large, the postwar revelation of their mistreatment, starvation, and massacre has still had remarkably little impact either on public attitudes or even on public policy.

During the Third Reich itself, while the Nazis had the power to stage their cultural fantasies quite literally, as living tableaux and as macabre theme parks, those without such means, officially on the "other side" of the war, or even caught themselves within the Nazi penal system, still could and did frame their own rhetorical equivalents. German-Jewish poet Gertrud Kolmar, assigned to forced labor in a factory along with Gypsies and other prisoners (and later to die in Auschwitz herself) thus writes in a 1941 letter of an uplifting "encounter" with a Gypsy coworker:

19. See Sozialdienst Katholischer Männer, "Bei Hitler waren wir wenigstens noch Deutsche," in *In Auschwitz vergast, bis heute verfolgt,* pp. 237–40; Rosh, *Das lustige Zigeunerleben;* Hancock, *The Pariah Syndrome;* and, more generally, Rainer Hehemann, *Die "Bekämpfung des Zigeunerunwesens" im Wilhelminischen Deutschland und in der Weimarer Republik, 1871–1933* (Frankfurt, 1987). In Switzerland, the Protestant organization Pro Juventude carried out the forcible "socialization" of Romani children from the 1920s to the mid-1970s. The children were literally kidnapped from the parents, impressed with the information that their parents had died or abandoned them, and raised as orphans. See Mariella Mehr, "Jene, die auf nirgends verbriefte Rechte pochen: Zigeuner in der Schweiz," in *In Auschwitz vergast, bis heute verfolgt,* pp. 274–78.

20. Hancock chronicles the long struggles of Gypsy representatives with the governing board of the U.S. Holocaust Memorial Council both over "whether Gypsies really did constitute a distinct ethnic population" and over whether, as Elie Wiesel claimed, the Holocaust was "'essentially a Jewish event . . . the Jewish people alone were destined to be totally annihilated, they alone were totally alone'" (Hancock, *The Pariah Syndrome,* pp. 81, 80). While in absolute terms, a much smaller number of Gypsies than Jews were killed in Nazi camps, Hancock points out that the relative proportion of each population killed was approximately the same.

> A brief little incident was recently of help to me. In the locker room during the breakfast break . . . I sat all alone on a bench with a young Gypsy woman, who did nothing, said nothing, only gazed unmoving out into the desolate factory yard. . . . I watched her, she didn't have that sharp Gypsy face with the restless, gleaming eyes; her features were soft, more Slavic, she was also relatively light skinned. . . . And on her face lay not just the apathy, the acquiesence of animals, of old draught-horses, that certainly, but also much more: an impenetrable closedness, a silence, a distance, which could not be reached by any word, any glance from the outside world. . . . And I recognized that this is the thing I always wanted to have, and yet didn't quite, because if I did, nothing and no one besides me could affect me.[21]

The effect of this description is to transform a fellow prisoner into a living allegory of an alterity both resistant and subhuman. Kolmar represents the Gypsy's mode of suffering as simultaneously stolid and stoical, a full, uncomprehending surrender to the crushing conditions of capitivity ("did nothing, said nothing, only gazed unmoving . . . the apathy, the acquiesence of animals") and a complete mastery of them, a deliberate and unbreakable dignity ("an impenetrable closedness, a silence, a distance, which could not be reached by any word"). In the meantime, of course, Kolmar's process of idealization excludes any reciprocity as well as any expression of solidarity; the rhetorical framing of this encounter prevents it precisely from becoming an actual encounter at all. The still of the locker room cannot be broken; the Gypsy woman "could not be reached by any word," even if one were to be uttered. Kolmar's description transforms the Gypsy woman into a dumb animal, whose strength lies in her oblivion and in her silence. And it isolates her and removes her from a common captivity, in order to put her into a separate Gypsy camp, where the spectacle of her exemplary fortitude under suffering becomes a source of strength and inner liberation for the spectator. Like the caption of Hetti's picture, Kolmar's description makes visible a microracism; the fact that its process of objectification is bound up in simultaneous idealization does little to obviate the immediate or enduring consequences of the distance it reinforces.

Idealization, objectification; sympathetic picture, denigrating caption; exemplary autonomy, feared alterity: what constitutes the mythology of Gypsy life is the tension between two simultaneous, mutually contradictory yet continually coexisting moments—memory and amnesia. Even the most comprehensive postwar attempt to come to terms with the legacy of German racism, East German writer Franz Fühmann's 1962 autobiography, *Das Judenauto: Vierzehn Tage aus zwei Jahrzehnten* [*The Jew Car: Fourteen Days from Two Decades*], proves to be built on a displacement

21. Gertrud Kolmar, letter of 23 Oct. 1941, *Weibliches Bildnis: Sämtliche Gedichte* (Munich, 1987), pp. 778–79.

and specularization of Gypsy life. In every other respect the book is without precedent in German letters for its intense, precise attention to German history as colonial domination, to the micropolitics of historical consciousness and historical denial, and to the political and historical supports of the *Bildungsroman* as genre. His life story begins by linking the rise of anti-Semitic mythologizing among schoolchildren in 1929 to the effects of the worldwide depression, and goes on to analyze the German "liberation" of the Sudetenland (*Heim ins Reich*), the invasion of the Soviet Union, and the German occupation of the Ukraine. Held in 1945 as Soviet prisoners of war and confronted with the defeat of a German imperialism that has become the ground of their identity, Fühmann and his fellow prisoners declare their intention to retreat from all politics completely and forever, "with great radicalness jumping out of history itself."[22] Yet the book ends by describing a political reeducation through which Fühmann embraces a Marxist conception of history, the book itself becoming, in retrospect, a model for this process as it works through and discards a series of static, racist myths to embrace a new, teleological model of development from the first memories of infancy towards political consciousness.

Fühmann's own earliest memories, which opened the book, are of the Gypsies—or rather almost of them, for he strains to remember:

> How far back does remembering go? A warm green, that must be the earliest picture in my memory: the green of a tile stove, around whose upper rim the relief of a Gypsy camp is supposed to have run; but I only know that from my mother's tales, no effort of the brain will bring this picture back to me. But I have retained the green, a warm bottle green with a dull gloss. Whenever I summon this green before my eyes I can feel myself hanging in the air high above the floor: I could, Mother has told me, only see the Gypsies when Father lifted me, a two year old boy, up into the air.[23]

22. Franz Fühmann, *Das Judenauto: Vierzehn Tage aus zwei Jahrzehnten* [*The Jew Car: Fourteen Days from Two Decades*] (1962; Leipzig, 1987), p. 138.

23. Ibid., p. 5. Although a famous contemporary East German novel, Johannes Bobrowski's 1964 *Levins Mühle* [*Levin's Mill*], makes more satisfactory use of Gypsy material in developing new ways to analyze racist formations in general and German imperialism in particular, the rhetorical opposition between teleological progression and the anarchic isolationism of Gypsy society continued to be a commonplace of political discourse in the GDR as in the West. Thus in the most famous East German socialist realist "production novel," Erik Neutsch's *Spur der Steine* [*Path of Stones*] (Halle, 1964), a key argument between the Party secretary and a resisting farmer about the need for agricultural collectivization turns on a metaphoric opposition between Gypsies and Communists; those isolated by their own animal regressiveness and those who advance material progress for all (pp. 346–47). The contrast between those who circulate endlessly and those who through their own labor create a lasting place for themselves is in many ways the structuring opposition of the book as a whole. The *Bildungsroman* of an itinerant construction worker whose pride in his craft and anarchic political attitudes yield to socialist goals and activist accomplishments, *Spur*

In a book otherwise so self-consciously and panoramically about the history and the psychology of political persecution, this is the sole mention of the Gypsies. Fühmann's placement of the Gypsies as the limit case of psychopolitical working-through, as the point at which political memory continually fails and is continually grasped at, is both highly poignant and highly problematic: his own book has both given them pride of place and almost forgotten their inclusion. Given the chronological, cumulative structure of the book, Fühmann's opening passage (with its Gypsies glimpsed travelling along the stove's border) represents the primal scene of European historical memory and the foundational moment in the history of European racism as well. But the memory of the Gypsies also marks for Fühmann the beginning and the end of the earliest phase of psychological and social development, which must be strained at to be remembered at all: the earliest blurred phase of undifferentiation ("a warm green") and the first ontological awareness of separation and autonomy, as the infant is lifted up above the family, suspended above the familiar room. Bukovina is here lost and found all over again, as the Gypsy frieze reflects one's own face and as an autonomy gained through displacement is conflated with the historical origins of human memory in an inchoate animal existence. Lifted up and out of history, the Gypsies themselves are reinstated only as a memory problem: the strength of forgetfulness, the struggle to remember.

2

> Among the peoples of Europe there is one which rose up quite suddenly one day, without anyone being able to say exactly where it had sprung from. It descended upon our continent without evincing the slightest desire of conquest; and without even demanding any right of permanent residence. It had evidently no desire to appropri-

---

der Steine takes its metaphoric title phrase from its hero's realization that his years as a peripatetic journeyman working on construction sites across the country in fact add up to a commitment and contribution to the rebuilding of East Germany. Random wanderings become in retrospect a teleological path towards political engagement; worthless Gypsy becomes value-producing Red.

Even as late as Christoph Hein's 1985 novel *Horns Ende* (in which the yearly arrival of a band of Gypsies to winter in a small East German town, the yearly attempts of local officials to make them move on, and their eventual permanent departure become the means of reconstructing a sketchy but implicitly critical account of postwar social and political dynamics) the Gypsies serve a mainly metaphoric function, both as place markers in the town's political chronicle and as catalysts for the town's plots and self-examinations. Indeed although the book repeatedly draws attention to the fact that the Gypsies suspended their visits to the town during the war years, the fact of their persecution and internment under the Nazis is never made explicit; instead, the novel's "official" victims of the Third Reich are a family affected by its euthanasia laws.

> ate one single inch of land; but, on the other hand, it set its face completely against the grant of an hour's service to anyone. Without any idea of subjugating others, it would not itself be subjugated. . . . It neither looked back to any remembrance, nor forward to any hope. It refused all possible benefits which might attach to colonisation; and was apparently too vain of its sad race to condescend to mingle with any other.
>
> It seems only to continue to exist because it absolutely refuses to cease to do so; refusing also to be anything but what it is actually, and permitting no influence, no prescription, no persecution, and no instruction either to modify, dissolve or extirpate it.
>
> To our eyes this people seems to lead what is practically an animal existence; in the sense that it has neither any knowledge nor interest in anything beyond itself. Ages may come and go, the world may travel on, the countries which shelter it may be either at war or at peace, they may change their masters or transform their customs; but to all these events it remains impassible and indifferent.
>
> It is one which does not itself know either whence it came or whither it is going . . . preserving no tradition and registering no annals. A race having neither any religion nor any law, any definite belief or any rule of conduct; holding together only by gross superstition, vague custom, constant misery and profound abasement; yet obstinately persisting, in spite of all degradations and deprivations, in keeping its tents and its rags, its hunger and its liberty.
>
> It is a people which exercises on civilised nations a fascination as hard to describe as to destroy; passing, as it does, like some mysterious legacy, from age to age; and one which, though of ill-repute, appeals to our greatest poets by the energy and charm of its types.
>
> —Franz Liszt, *The Gipsy in Music* (1859)

Decades after the persecution of the Gypsies under the Third Reich, Gypsy life remains in the popular imagination as a carefree, defiant, disruptive alternative to a Western culture at once humanized by its history and restrained by the discipline of its own civilization. Moving through civil society, the Gypsies appparently remain beyond reach of everything that constitutes Western identity, as Franz Liszt's influential mid-nineteenth-century summary suggests: outside of historical record and historical time, outside of Western law, the Western nation state, and Western economic orders, outside of writing and discursivity itself. All the Gypsies have, all they need, all they know is their own collectivity, which survives all odds and persecutions, as if their identity inheres in their very blood. Despite their self-containment, paradoxically, the Gypsies' wildness is highly contagious, as their arrival in a new place initiates and figures a crisis for Enlightenment definitions of civilization and nationalist definitions of culture. Here, in the Gypsy camp, is a culture without "culture," transmission without "tradition"—self-knowledge and collective amnesia side by side. Anchored themselves in an eternal present, a self-continuity that transcends context and time, they seem able to remove and replace the memory of others at will. Those who join them—whether as stolen children, "scholar-gypsies," or willing or resistant fellow travellers—seem not only to forget who they are but to lose all sense of time; indeed what literary characters who meet the Gypsies seem to notice first is that time immediately slows down or stands still.

Compact, transportable, self-perpetuating, the tropes of racism express the same essentializing beliefs again and again in widely diverging situations and for a whole range of reasons; they are historically charged and fraught even as they enact a denial of history. The specifics of the Gypsy ideology in post-Enlightenment Europe both problematize and reinforce traditional theorizations of ideology itself. The static resting point suggested by Marx's camera obscura does not capture the diffuse location of the ideology *in* Hetti's picture, at once utopian photograph, cynical caption, and a practice of citation both historically inflected and resistant to all historical pressures. At the same time, Western thinking about the Gypsies manifests itself quite literally as false consciousness: an obsession with memory is visible mainly as amnesia, a need for continuity staged as moments of frozen suspension. The difficulty is to give an account that addresses both the stasis and fluidity of an ideology, the obviousness and subtlety of its logic, its monolithic instantiations and its quotidian performance, its continuities and transformations over time.

"He who wants to enslave you," a Romani proverb runs, "will never tell you the truth about your forefathers."[24] One of the far-reaching consequences of the European myth of the Gypsies—on several levels about the erasure of history and the struggle to preserve memory—has been the obliteration of a people's actual and tragic history. Its reconstruction now remains daunting, both from factual and formal points of view. As Gilles Deleuze and Félix Guattari remind us, "History is always written from a sedentary point of view and in the name of a unitary State apparatus, at least a possible one, even when the topic is nomads. What is lacking is a Nomadology, the opposite of a history."[25] But while in many ways the point is admirably appropriate for the Gypsies, theirs is also a case in which an articulated unitary history remains largely missing, while all too many nomadologies have already been attempted. If the account that follows—assembling and piecing together dispersed materials on the one hand, and on the other retelling familiar political and literary histories from the perspective of the Gypsy ideology—aims only at characterizing generalizations, it is framed in the hope that such basic work may make possible far more adequate accounts and perhaps, finally, true nomadologies as well.

24. Cited by Hancock, *The Pariah Syndrome,* p. 2.

25. Gilles Deleuze and Félix Guattari, *A Thousand Plateaus: Capitalism and Schizophrenia,* trans. Brian Massumi (Minneapolis, 1987), p. 23.

The Romani left northern India, Ian Hancock has argued, between 800 and 950, probably as soldiers, camp followers, or prisoners of war; moving through Byzantium, they settled in the Balkans after 1100. In the fourteenth century, Gypsy slavery was instituted in Moldavia and Wallachia, and at least half the Romani were enslaved. Behind the much-metaphorized phenomenon of Gypsy nomadism lies this history of Gypsy slavery, for the rest escaped bondage only by entering into a repeated diaspora and an increasingly nomadic existence throughout northern, central, and southern Europe.[26] Continually held to be marauding Tartars, Muslims, or Turkish spies, and feared for their skin color, unfamiliar language, and customs, they encountered persecution and pogroms virtually wherever they travelled or tried to settle. Officially banished from Spain at the end of the fifteenth century (as they were repeatedly from England, France, and a host of Italian and German states up through the sixteenth century), transported Romani were among early settlers of the European colonies in North and South America, the West Indies, Africa, and even India itself. As late as 1802, French authorities in the Basque region organized a mass expulsion of Romani to the coast of Africa. If the racial and cultural alterity of the Gypsies continued, for white Europeans, to embody the threat of the non-West, it also helped to provide a practical rationale for imperialist expansion as well, as new colonies immediately became dumping grounds for undesired peoples.[27]

In many parts of Germany, the Romani continued to stand under automatic sentence of death until well into the eighteenth century, and they were, in isolated instances, still being hunted for sport as late as the 1830s. In Hungary a group of forty Gypsies, groundlessly accused of murdering and cannibalizing several dozen peasants, were tortured and executed in 1782, only to be exonerated posthumously by Joseph II himself. By the 1760s and 1770s, indeed, the enlightened despotism of Austria-Hungary's rulers included attempts to mandate the forced settlement and assimilation of Gypsies into the empire and its labor force through laws forbidding traditional language, dress, diet, and occupations, and mandating conscription, religious training, settlement in permanent dwellings, and the removal of Romani children from their parents to be raised as "New Hungarian" agricultural workers. Underfunded and meeting with sustained resistance, both from the Gypsies themselves and from the people they were to settle among, the program (like parallel attempts in Germany and Spain) failed almost completely.[28]

26. See Hancock, *The Pariah Syndrome,* pp. 7-36.

27. See Hancock, *The Pariah Syndrome;* Hohmann, *Geschichte der Zigeunerverfolgung in Deutschland;* and Sárosi, *Gypsy Music,* pp. 11–22.

28. See Sárosi, *Gypsy Music,* pp. 18ff. Kenrick and Puxon report similar cannibalism charges brought in 1927 against a group of Slovakian Gypsies and eventually, after the group had been brought to trial, dismissed as without foundation. See Kenrick and Puxon, *The Destiny of Europe's Gypsies,* p. 33. See also Hohmann, *Geschichte der Zigeunerverfolgung in*

In Britain, similarly, judiciary and constabulary worked systematically until the late eighteenth century to "eradicate Gypsies from [the] country by transportation, banishment and execution," with a collective public hanging in 1780 serving as a "symbolic watermark that signalled the end of the excessively severe persecution."[29] Thereafter, David Mayall argues, state and church began more pragmatic attempts to contain, reform, or assimilate a population increasingly accepted as an inevitable social burden. As late eighteenth-century literature records with almost seismographic precision, it is at this historical and political juncture—as overt hunting-down gave way to less lethal forms of social control—that the social "meaning" of the Gypsies rapidly acquired new contours and density, attracting increased attention with every decade.

In the prior literary depictions of the seventeenth and early eighteenth centuries, Gypsies appear as good-hearted if ingenious thieves, as "band[s] of lawless vagrants" and a "race of vermin," as Joseph Addison put it, and as fortunetellers delivering messages of questionable import and motive.[30] In the world of the picaresque, of course, the Gypsies are only one among many groups of travellers, most similarly dependant on various forms of petty crime. Through the mid-eighteenth century (when the narrator of the "autobiographical" *Apology for the Life of Bamfylde-Moore Carew, King of the Gypsies* [1745] claims not only to have joined the Gypsies but to have been chosen as their leader) they are seen as a racially and culturally cohesive group that nonetheless welcomes all seeking initiation; indeed, they are of particular interest to Carew as to Henry Fielding (in *Tom Jones* [1749]) for their democratic social organization, led by elected, not hereditary, leaders.

Deutschland, pp. 52ff. for the eighteenth-century settlement attempts in Austria-Hungary and Germany.

29. Mayall, *Gypsy-Travellers in Nineteenth-Century Society,* p. 97. Hohmann makes a similar point about early nineteenth-century German policy, which shifted, he argues, from *Verfolgung* [persecution] to *Fürsorge* [social programs]. See Hohmann, *Geschichte der Zigeunerverfolgung in Deutschland,* p. 52.

30. Addison, *The Spectator,* no. 130, 2:17. See Gil Vicente, *Auto das Ciganas* (1521); Miguel Cervantes, "La Gitanilla," in *Novelas Exemplares* (1613); Ben Jonson, *The Gypsies Metamorphos'd* (1621); Thomas Middleton and Nicolas Rowley, *The Spanish Gipsy* (1623); Samuel Pepys's diaries of the 1660s; Molière, *Le Mariage forcé* (1664); Johann (Hans) Jakob Christoffel von Grimmelshausen, *The Runagate Courage* (1670); John Gay, *The Shepherd's Week* (1714); Daniel Defoe, *The Life, Adventures, and Piraces of the Famous Captain Singleton* (1720); Samuel Richardson, *Pamela; or, Virtue Rewarded* (1740); Voltaire, *Essai sur les moeurs et l'esprit des nations* (1756); and Oliver Goldsmith, *The Vicar of Wakefield* (1766). For overviews of the literature on the Gypsies in Eastern and Western Europe, see Sárosi, *Gypsy Music;* Marilyn Brown, *Gypsies and Other Bohemians: The Myth of the Artist in Nineteenth-Century France* (Ann Arbor, Mich., 1985); Hohmann, *Geschichte und Geschichten der Zigeuner* (Darmstadt, 1981); and *The Wind on the Heath: A Gypsy Anthology,* ed. John Sampson (London, 1930).

Already in Fielding's "Inquiry into the Causes of the Late Increase of Robbers" (1751), however, the free movement of Gypsies and other itinerants has come to seem irreconcilable with their legal accountability; in his capacity as magistrate, Fielding ends his discussion "Of Laws Relating to Vagabonds" with the ambivalent recommendation that the poor be forced to remain in place, compelled "to starve or beg at home; for there it will be impossible for them to steal or rob without being presently hanged or transported out of the way."[31] If the subsequent rise of European nationalisms, in identifying peoples in historical relationship to place, would redefine civil society to exclude Gypsies from being part of the nation or forming a distinct nation themselves, already these earlier reconsiderations of the poor laws, reacting to the large-scale social displacements of enclosure, gave renewed stress to the indigent's place of origin. As the poor were thus forcibly reanchored, the anomalous social position of the Gypsies began to seem to be the result both of their mysterious collective origin in the non-West and of the birth of individual Gypsies in transit, where they remained uncounted by parish records. From the standpoint of an emerging bureaucracy, the Gypsies' perennial "homelessness" thus became at once an innate failing and a virtually irreparable state.

In the wake of Enlightenment policing and *grandes enfermements,* the Gypsies were left one of the few groups still travelling, and they struck settled men-of-letters with increasing, confused distaste as willfully deviant. William Cowper's account in *The Task* (1785) of the "vagabond and useless tribe" thus moves from the opacity of their origins ("a tawny skin / The vellum of the pedigree they claim") to moralize what he sees as their choice of a fundamentally unproductive life:

> Strange! that a creature rational, and cast
> In human mould, should brutalize by choice
> His nature; and, though capable of arts
> By which the world might profit, and himself,
> Self-banish'd from society, prefer
> Such squalid sloth to honourable toil![32]

The 1775 letter on the periodic visits of "two gangs or hordes of gypsies which infest the south and west of England" in Gilbert White's *The Natu-*

31. Henry Fielding, "Inquiry into the Causes of the Late Increase of Robbers," sec. 6, "Of Laws Relating to Vagabonds," *Works,* ed. Leslie Stephen, 10 vols. (London, 1882), 7:241. This new view of the Gypsies does not immediately displace the previous one, of course. Thus while Charles Johnstone's *Chrysal, or the Adventures of a Guinea* (1760) initiates a new phase in the picaresque's obsession with circulation (here juxtaposing monetary, social, and sexual circuits), the Gypsies still appear quite neutrally and nonethnically, merely part of the vast throng of travellers and transmitters.

32. William Cowper, "The Task," bk. 1, ll. 559, 568–69, 574–79, *The Poetical Works of William Cowper,* ed. H. S. Milford, 3d ed. (Oxford, 1926), p. 141.

ral History of Selbourne is similarly preoccupied by the place "those peculiar people" occupy between the categories of history and of nature, then undergoing mutual revision in White's hands as in European culture at large. The Gypsies' "harsh gibberish" seems to bear "amidst their cant and corrupted dialect many mutilated remains" of an Egyptian or possibly Greek origin. Yet if they may, amazingly enough, be descended from the classical civilizations of the Mediterranean, "these sturdy savages" insist on leading an existence as close as possible to that of the animals, as proven by the young girl who horrifies White by giving birth out-of-doors, in his own rain-drenched garden.[33]

Until the mid-eighteenth century, the Gypsies presented not only a social policy problem for European magistrates but also (like the "Persians" or "Chinese" beloved of the period's utopian satire) an interesting alternative form of political and social organization. For a late eighteenth century that ranked cultures by hierarchized developmental stages, the Gypsies were, instead, a people who insisted, inexplicably, on remaining "nature" rather than entering "history." Agreed in reading the Gypsies as more deliberate agents and their acts as self-conscious refusals of state authority, the romantics and other early nineteenth-century authors bifurcate, along predictable political lines, between those who still seem to harbor eighteenth-century fears for the forces of civilization—contact creating contagion—and those who celebrate in the Gypsies a community united by a love of liberty and a tradition of political resistance.[34] In

33. Gilbert White, *The Natural History of Selbourne,* ed. Richard Mabey (1788; Harmondsworth, 1977), p. 179.

34. For early nineteenth-century anxieties about Gypsies as a social force, see for instance William Wordsworth, "Beggars" (1802), Hannah More, "Tawney Rachel, or the Fortune Teller" (1797), Achim (Ludwig Joachim) von Arnim, *Isabella von Ägypten: Kaiser Karl des Fünften erste Jugendliebe* (1812), and George Crabbe, "The Lover's Journey" (1812). For parallel idealization or political championing of the Gypsies, see Washington Irving, *Bracebridge Hall* (1822); John Galt, *Sir Andrew Wylie of That Ilk* (1822); Mary Russell Mitford, *Our Village: Sketches of Rural Character and Scenery,* 5 vols. (1824–32); William Hazlitt, "On Manner" (1815), "On Going on a Journey" (1822), and "On Personal Identity" (1828); Nicolaus Lenau, "Die Drei Zigeuner" (1838), and John Clare's numerous Gypsy poems, which span his writing life, from "The Gipsies Evening Breeze" in the 1810s, "The Gipseys Camp" and "The Gipsey" of 1820, and "The Gipsy Camp" (1840) to the late poems ("The Camp," "The Gipsy Lass," and "The Bonney Gipsey") written from Northampton Asylum, from whose captivity, as Clare reports in a journal of 1841, some Gypsies offer to help him escape. If a Gypsy chorus, singing a Christopher Marlowe song, forms the idyllic background to Clare's most self-consciously literary work, the Elizabethan pastoral "Excursion with 'the Angler,'" with its cameo appearances by Isaak Walton, Sir Walter Raleigh, John Donne, George Herbert, Richard Hooker, et al., ethnographic passages in Clare's *Autobiography* also record sustained friendships with Gypsy travellers, observations about their cultural values, and a stinging condemnation of their treatment at the hands of the British judiciary. Percy Bysshe Shelley's equally sympathetic personal encounters with Gypsies are recorded in Thomas Jefferson Hogg, *Life of Shelley,* 2 vols. (1855; London, 1933), 1:144–47. See also Thomas Moore's drama, *The Gypsy Prince* (1801); Ruskin, "The Gipsies" (1837); and Ralph Waldo Emerson, "The Romany Girl" (1853).

Wordsworth's 1807 "Gypsies," the narrator (passing at evening the same encampment as at morning) thus anxiously moralizes a now-familiar contrast between the static, "torpid life" of the "outcasts of society" and his own productive use of time.[35] John Clare's 1825 "The Gipsy's Song," in contrast, presents "gipsy liberty" both as a spontaneous Jacquerie opposing the disciplining mechanisms of the modern state and as insistence on a traditional liberty still inhering in the English landscape despite all attempts at enclosure:

> We pay to none or rent or tax,
> And live untithed and free. . . .
>
> Bad luck to tyrant magistrates,
> And the gipsies' camp still free . . . .
>
> And while the ass that bears our camp
> Can find a common free,
> Around old England's heaths we'll tramp
> In gipsy liberty.[36]

If until now the Gypsies have been used to allegorize alternative state forms, archaic stages of society, or specific political struggles, Walter Scott and Jane Austen's contrasting approaches to Gypsy material together inaugurate new kinds of social allegory, with wide-ranging political and aesthetic implications. In Scott's *Guy Mannering* (1815), incidents of violence perpetrated on and then by Gypsies generate a parable of tradition and modernity, in whose course concrete political anxieties about enclosure and the expansion of state authority are displaced into a myth of lost

35. On Wordsworth's "Gipsies" see David Simpson, *Wordsworth's Historical Imagination: The Poetry of Displacement* (New York, 1987), esp. pp. 44–47, but also Hazlitt's comical invective against the poem's hypocrisy, by linking Gypsy and poetic license:

> Mr Wordsworth, who has written a sonnet to the King on the good that he has done in the last fifty years, has made an attack on a set of gipsies for having done nothing in four and twenty hours. . . . We did not expect this turn from Mr Wordsworth, whom we had considered as the prince of poetical idlers, and patron of the philosophy of indolence, who formerly insisted on our spending our time 'in a wise passiveness. . . .' [T] he gipsies are the only living monuments of the first ages of society. They are an everlasting source of thought and reflection on the advantages and disadvantages of the progress of civilisation: they are a better answer to the cotton manufactories than Mr. W. has given in the *Excursion*. [Hazlitt, "On Manner" (1815), *Complete Works of William Hazlitt* (New York, 1967), 4:45–46 n. 2]

36. Clare, "The Gipsy's Song," *Selected Poems* (London, 1975), pp. 208–10. Clare's *Autobiography* is equally explicit in linking enclosure and the fate of Gypsy life: "There [are] not so many of them with us as there used to be. The Enclosure has left nothing but narrow lands where they are ill-provided with a lodging" (*The Prose of John Clare,* ed. J. W. and Anne Tibble [London, 1951], p. 38). On Clare's relationship to enclosure more generally, see John Barrell, *The Ideal of Landscape and the Sense of Place 1730–1840: An Approach to the Poetry of John Clare* (Cambridge, 1972).

social origins, imagined contradictorily as consisting both in a state of free circulation and in the sustaining bonds of feudal alliances. In Austen's *Emma* (1816), in contrast, a violent incident perpetrated by Gypsies inaugurates a meditation on authorial and literary memory in whose course social anxieties about Gypsy alterity are displaced into a textual register where they linger as problems of transmission and narration. Between these two poles, social fable and textual trace, the Gypsies turn into their own memory problem.

Guy Mannering announces the derivation of its Gypsy plot from a "true" historical incident at the threshold of the Enlightenment: Adam Smith's near-kidnapping in infancy by strolling tinkers, before a rescuing uncle proved himself "the happy instrument" (as Smith's late eighteenth-century biographer Dugald Stewart formulates it) "of preserving to the world a genius, which was destined, not only to extend the boundaries of science, but to enlighten and reform the commercial policy of Europe."[37] In Stewart's 1795 account, the Gypsies are still simply a force of social regression that can barely be prevented from carrying off, in the person of Smith, the future history and progress of Europe. In Scott's novel, however, Gypsies kidnap a young lord only in revenge for his father's "improvements" and enclosures which (synchronous and parallel, as the subplot makes clear, with the consolidation of British conquest in India) have intensified the gap between property holders and the propertyless, and effected the eviction or *enfermement* of the whole folk community. Thus the subsequent attempts of the Gypsy captors to erase the identity and memory of their aristocratic hostage are depicted as a reaction to a prior aristocratic loss of memory, a deliberate, cynical amnesia about feudal obligations that made drastic repressions possible. In *Guy Mannering*, the forced wandering and antisocial behavior of the Gypsies thus comes to figure as the original displacement, and first price, of modernity. As Peter Garside argues, it figures simultaneously as the original dislocation of imperialism, since the novel's Indian subplot brings together linguists' dawning realization of the Gypsies' Indian origin, and contemporary political debate over the deleterious social and economic consequences of the Western property laws forcibly introduced into British-ruled Bengal.[38] If for Smith and Stewart, the Gypsies represent a force of histor-

37. Dugald Stewart, "Account of the Life and Writings of Adam Smith, LL. D." (1795), ed. J. S. Ross, in Adam Smith, *Essays on Philosophical Subjects,* ed. W. P. D. Wightman and J. C. Bryce, vol. 3 of *The Glasgow Edition of the Works and Correspondence of Adam Smith,* ed. D. D. Raphael and A. S. Skinner, 6 vols. (Oxford, 1980), p. 270. A comparable French legend reports that seventeenth-century engraver Jacques Callot ("Bohemians on the March," ca. 1622) had briefly lived with the Gypsies as a child. See *The Wind on the Heath,* p. 340 n. 100.

38. See Peter Garside, "Meg Merilees, India and the Gypsies," paper delivered at the International Sir Walter Scott Conference, Edinburgh, 16 Aug. 1991. Sárosi (*Gypsy Music,* p. 12) gives a summary history of the scholarly investigation, from the 1770s onwards, into the links between Gypsy and Indian cultures, a link that Hazlitt also suggests in "On Man-

ical regression, for Scott they come to represent both the traditional and the colonial unconscious of an industrializing, imperialist Europe—the trace memory of the traumatic cost of improvement and expansion.[39]

Austen glosses and reworks a different facet of late eighteenth-century Gypsy reception: its almost hysterical moralism in the face of Gypsy intransigence. In the brief but famous episode in *Emma,* a group of Gypsy children, on a lonely stretch of road, harass a young "gentlewoman," herself made socially vulnerable by her somewhat mysterious provenance. The actual danger presented by contact with the Gypsies passes almost immediately; the woman is rescued by an acquaintance who happens to be passing, his timing at once "a most fortunate chance" and anchored in a myriad of everyday habits and errands. But the episode continues to color everyday perception long after it is over, lingering obsessively in the memory of a few characters until it threatens their trust in memory itself:

> The gipsies did not wait for the operations of justice; they took themselves off in a hurry. The young ladies of Highbury might have walked again in safety before their panic began, and the whole history dwindled soon into a matter of little importance but to Emma and her nephews:—in her imagination it maintained its ground; and Henry and John were still asking every day for the story of Harriet and the gipsies, and still tenaciously setting her right if she varied in the slightest particular from the original recital.[40]

In the wake of the Gypsies' disruptive passage, special care must be taken to hold on to a history that exists only as an oral tradition: the psychic trauma of social violence is subsumed into a narratological compulsion to repeat. And the movement here from Gypsies who appear as actual (if threatening) characters to a lingering narrative anxiety about the Gypsies as shadowy, haunting discursive figures parallels the main shift of "Gypsy" literature in the nineteenth century from political allegory into memory problem and from self-contained social group into self-contained literary

---

ner" through his juxtaposition of Gypsies and "Hindoos." See *Complete Works of William Hazlitt,* 4:45–46.

39. For nineteenth-century reaction to and rewriting of Scott's Gypsy plot, see the intense discussion of Gypsy origins, life-style, and crimes throughout the first year of *Blackwood's Edinburgh Magazine* (Apr. 1817–Apr. 1818); see also John Keats, "Old Meg She Was a Gypsey" (1818), and Ruskin, "Notes upon Gipsy Character" (1885).

40. Jane Austen, *Emma* (1816; Harmondsworth, 1966), p. 333. See also the related passages from the 1836-37 diaries of the future Queen Victoria, in which she details her sentimental encounters with "such a nice set of Gipsies, so quiet, so affectionate to one another . . . so discreet, not at all forward or importunate . . . and *so* grateful," and concludes with a vow that "the place and spot may be forgotten, but the Gipsy family Cooper will *never* be obliterated from my memory!" (*The Wind on the Heath,* pp. 322-23).

chronotope, as overt meditations on progress give way to ever more oblique reflections on literary form and literary autonomy.

From the beginning of the nineteenth century, the Gypsies are, for instance, a mainstay of the new genre of the fantastic, with its pivotal tension between enlightened and superstitious worldviews and its own habitual specularization of political anxieties into epistemological ones. In Jan Potocki's 1803 *The Saragossa Manuscript* (which for Tzvetan Todorov is the "book which magisterially inaugurates the period of the fantastic narrative" and the genre's quintessential example),[41] detailed encounters with Spanish Gypsies, like parallel encounters with Jews and Arabs, will prove literally phantasmagoric; the specters of three cultures long since expelled as infidel return not as political ghosts but as epistemological uncertainty, the vehicles—or mirages—of diabolical forces. And if, in 1773, Goethe's *Götz von Berlichingen* already seeks in the Gypsy camp a temporary respite from the world-historical clashes and transformations that the rest of this ground-breaking "historical drama" is intent on mapping, the appearance of the Gypsy fortune-teller in Heinrich von Kleist's *Michael Kohlhaas* (1808) interrupts the historical chronicling of a populist campaign against despotic civil authority to shift *the tale itself* into the different generic mode of the fairy tale. The illusion of progression through historical time is broken by a figure who lives outside of history, and who brings magical timelessness with her into the narrative.[42]

So if the Gypsies are increasingly reduced to a textual effect, their chronotope increasingly exerts a decisive power over the temporal cohesion of the text itself. Everywhere the Gypsies appear in nineteenth-century narratives, they begin to hold up ordinary life, inducing local amnesias or retrievals of cultural memory, and causing blackouts or flashbacks in textual, historical, and genre memory as well. Such "time-banditry" will find one terminus, at the end of the century, in Hanns Gross's foundational text of central European criminology. Gypsies plan-

41. Tzvetan Todorov, *The Fantastic: A Structural Approach to a Literary Genre,* trans. Richard Howard (1970; Ithaca, N.Y., 1975), p. 27; Potocki is also the book's most frequently cited example.

42. For the later literary descendants of Kleist's fortune-teller—Gypsy figures whose prophecies break through historical time into myth, or conversely, who bring historical perspectives or innovations with them into the mythic time of a closed community—see Joseph Roth, *Tarabas, A Guest on Earth* (1934); Gabriel García Marquez, *A Hundred Years of Solitude* (1967); Robertson Davies, *The Manticore* (1972) and *World of Wonders* (1975). It could be argued that such tensions also structure Ronald Florence's 1985 page-turner, *The Gypsy Man:* a driven, glamorous American woman lawyer is derailed from her high-powered career path by the erotic and mystical allure of a Gypsy man she meets on vacation. He is accused—and finally, with her assistance, cleared—of the long-premeditated murder of a Gypsy-phile ethnographer who, it emerges, played an auxiliary role in the Nazi internment and extermination of the Gypsies at Auschwitz. It is the book's increasingly documentary structure that finally undoes its own opening romanticization of Gypsy life; at the same time, it mobilizes the whole modern history of a people to effect a change in life in a single yuppie protagonist.

ning to burglarize unsuspecting households begin with a kind of time surgery, breaking through the ordinary laws of time encasing household routines:

> Things never noticed by the servant after years of residence in the house, or by the neighbor after decades of living adjacent to it, the old Gypsy woman who comes begging, fortunetelling or selling potions has noticed and figured out so precisely within a few minutes that the most complicated thefts can be conducted on the basis of her perceptions.[43]

Items detached from their usual temporality by the mere fact and perspicacity of the Gypsy gaze will soon vanish from the household altogether. Gross's description both makes visible, in slow motion, the process of Gypsy "autonomization" and underscores the poignant fragility of "normal life"; the Gypsies are imagined dogging the steps of bourgeois order and its realist epistemology, reconstructing the detailed property inventories that are its stock-in-trade to turn them against their proper owners.

But the antagonistic relationship between the Gypsy life and bourgeois life can also be given the opposite emphasis in the nineteenth century, as a self-consciously embattled authorship seeks in the Gypsy camp a last refuge from the political and social pressures of bourgeois norms, and the only remaining site of cultural autonomy.[44] In Pushkin's *Tsygany* (1824), ethnographic detailing merges with timeless intertextuality as the Gypsy tribe harboring the poem's nineteenth-century hero proves also to have sheltered Ovid long ago in his political exile, and received his Orphic songs in return; parallel to and as metaphor for art itself in the post-Enlightenment period, the Gypsies come to embody the simultaneity of internal cohesion within a tradition and separation from the social and historical world. At the same time, a whole succession of Central European composers use Gypsy music to theorize the relationship of genial invention to musical tradition, taking the repertoire of wandering Gypsy musicians either to cosmopolitanize and contaminate the pure source of national folk music or, conversely, to function as a kind of time capsule, removing currently unfashionable parts of the national heritage from the currents of historical change and storing them intact for future retrieval.[45]

43. Hanns Gross, *Handbuch für Untersuchungsrichter als System der Kriminalistik,* 3d ed. (Graz, 1899), p. 338; my translation; trans. and ed. J. Collyer Adam, under the title *Criminal Investigation: A Practical Handbook for Magistrates, Police Officers and Lawyers* (London, 1924), p. 247.

44. See for instance Robert Browning, *The Flight of the Duchess* (1845); Matthew Arnold, "The Scholar-Gipsy" (1853); George Meredith, *The Adventures of Harry Richmond* (1871); and Leo Tolstoy, *The Live Corpse* (1900).

45. See for instance Robert Schumann, "Zigeunerleben" (1840); Richard Wagner,

The contradictions between these various memory functions (and their subterranean relationship to anxieties about cultural transmission and the maintenance of class and imperial power) are particularly evident in the contrast of two famous midcentury novels, written during the same year and in the same household. Before Charlotte Brontë's *Jane Eyre* (1847) confronts the specter of an imprisoned colonial and then the prospect of missionary work in British India, a "Gypsy" fortune-teller (Mr. Rochester in disguise) appears as a recording angel and the cumulative memory of the narrative up to that point, holding up for Jane Eyre's inspection the past and present as they reveal the outlines of her own character.[46] The Gypsy in Emily Brontë's *Wuthering Heights* appears in contrast as a demonic figure for the countercolonization of memory and the erosion of Western identity under "native" influence. Appearing out of nowhere, without a name, age, or history, Heathcliff is given the name of a dead son, but goes on to become the "usurper of his father's affections and his privileges," a mistreated foundling who turns changeling, an "incarnate goblin," "not a human being." A "mad dog . . . [not] a creature of my own species," he swallows the family inheritance with "sharp cannibal teeth," "poisoning" the family's existence and (keeping its descendants in a state of dependence and almost animal ignorance) nearly succeeds in erasing their humanity as well as their family identity.[47]

In their efforts to stave off such Gypsy threats of primeval violence

---

"Eine Pilgerfahrt zu Beethoven" ["On the Way to Beethoven"] (1840); Franz Liszt, *The Gipsies and Their Music in Hungary* (1859); Johannes Brahms, *Zigeunerlieder* (1887); Albert Emil Brachvogel, *Friedemann Bach* (ca. 1858); and the ethnomusicological writings of Béla Bartók and Zoltán Kodály. On the nationalist controversies surrounding Liszt's book, see Sárosi, *Gypsy Music,* pp. 141–50; on the replaying of the Liszt debate in the work of Bartók and Kodály, see my "The Voice of the Past: Anxieties of Cultural Transmission in Post-Enlightenment Europe" (Ph.D. diss., Stanford University, 1990), chap. 3.

46.

> One unexpected sentence came from her lips after another, till I got involved in a web of mystification; and wondered what unseen spirit had been sitting for weeks by my heart, watching its workings and taking record of every pulse. . . . Where was I? Did I wake or sleep? Had I been dreaming? Did I dream still? The old woman's voice had changed: her accent, her gesture, and all, were as familiar to me as my own face in a glass—as the speech of my own tongue. [Charlotte Brontë, *Jane Eyre* (1847; Harmondsworth, 1966), pp. 228, 231]

On the colonial framework of Brontë's novel, see Susan Meyer, "Colonialism and the Figurative Strategy of Jane Eyre," in *Macropolitics of Nineteenth-Century Literature: Nationalism, Exoticism, Imperialism,* ed. Jonathan Arac and Harriet Ritvo (Philadelphia, 1991), pp. 159–83.

47. Emily Brontë, *Wuthering Heights* (1847; New York, 1981), pp. 34, 156–57, 147, 162, 157; for a twentieth-century recasting, see Margery Sharp, *The Gipsy in the Parlour* (1953). Elizabeth Helsinger has suggested in conversation that the imperialist subtext in *Wuthering Heights* is supported by a conflation of Gypsy and Irish cultural markings, amnesias, and cannibalisms in the way Heathcliff is drawn (and in the fact that his only traceable point of origin is Liverpool, the debarkation port for the Irish ferry).

and cultural cannibalism, the protagonists of the most famous nineteenth-century fictional encounters with Gypsy life—George Borrow's *Lavengro* (1851) and *Romany Rye* (1857), and George Eliot's *The Mill on the Floss* (1860)—invoke previous accounts of colonial conquest and the civilizing force of literature itself. Borrow's influential, semiautobiographical novels (based on repeated contact, as Bible translator and proselytizer, with Gypsies in Spain, in England, and in Wales) sparked renewed ethnographic interest in "Gypsy lore" throughout Europe, and still offer an unusually panoramic survey of nineteenth-century Britain's heterogeneous subcultures. Yet the novels habitually frame their examinations of present-day cultural forms as a quest for lost linguistic and literary origins. In plot and narrational style, the novels search for the lost picaresque forms, Newgates, and ramblings of the eighteenth-century novel. And their linguist narrator ("Lavengro," master of words, as the Gypsies name him) searches at once for the key to all languages and the linked key to the Gypsies' historical origin, finally hypothesizing their descent from the founders of ancient Rome, and thus their unwitting embodiment of the whole history of the West, just as he finds their language to contain traces of all Western languages. Lavengro's encounters with these unlikely repositories of Western culture are therefore heavily overlaid with intertextual and imperial echoes: when he meets Gypsies for the first time, and they threaten him with physical violence, he calms them by reading them a passage from *Robinson Crusoe* in which Crusoe hears mysterious noises and fears the approach of the cannibalistic savages who haunt his island, only to find that the sounds emanate, instead, from a dying animal. The logic of Borrow's passage—with its taming movement from violence to literature, cannibals to animals, threatening noise to interpretable sound—is that of the imperial encounter, the first of many efforts in studying Gypsy culture to assimilate it to the narrative of Western civilization.[48]

During Maggie Tulliver's comparable encounter in *The Mill on the Floss* with the Gypsies (whom she had planned to run away with, tell stories to, educate, and eventually rule as their queen), the reality of their distressing poverty, strangeness, and diffuse hostility makes her cling to her meager stock of book knowledge, an imperfectly recollected *Catechism of Geography* and the exemplary history of Columbus serving as temporary barrier against more primeval fears of cannibals, devils, and monsters. In Eliot's ironic rewriting of Borrow, putative masters of words find themselves taking refuge behind the ineffectual bulwark of textual and intertextual memory against an overwhelming yet mundane strangeness that both exceeds and does not fill its exoticizing descriptive tradition (a tradi-

48. See for instance Michael de Certeau, "Ethno-graphy, Speech, or, the Space of the Other: Jean de Léry," *The Writing of History,* trans. Tom Conley (New York, 1988), pp. 209-43.

tion to which Eliot herself would subsequently contribute with the publication in 1867 of "The Spanish Gipsy," an ill-fated long poem obsessed with the question of cultural identity).

If in the course of the nineteenth century the Gypsies became increasingly stylized, exoticized, "generic" figures of mystery, adventure, and romance, they also become intimately identified, on several different levels, with the formation of literary tradition itself, acting as figurative keys to an array of literary genres and to the relations between them.[49] By the fin de siècle, the Gypsies thus figure prominently in a whole series of new genres derived from earlier aestheticist, pastoralist, and fantastic forms. In detective stories and in sensation fiction, the Gypsies play their old chronotopically anachronistic parts, as figures of magic and malevolence, in order precisely to measure their new genres' derivation and distance from older, more straightforwardly "magical," genres.[50] At the same time, a symbolism and aestheticism fascinated with the mysterious origins of art claims the mystery and magic of the Gypsies as an emblem for their own bohemianism, aesthetic autonomy, and artistic alchemy.[51] Finally, both simultaneously and in contrast to the growing folkloric study of Gypsy life, the Gypsies become central to a new writing of racial essentialism, including both Celtic twilight mysticism and new forms of nationalist idyll rooted in natural history (culminating, finally, in the pastoral reportage of

49. In France alone, see Victor Hugo, *Notre-Dame de Paris* (1831); Eugène Sue, *Plik et Plok* (1831); Théophile Gautier, *Voyage en Espagne* (1845); Prosper Mérimée, *Carmen* (1847); George Sand, *La Filleule* (1853); and Edmond de Goncourt, *The Zemganno Brothers* (1879), as well as related uses of Gypsy material by authors from Flaubert to Nerval and Zola. Brown's *Gypsies and Other Bohemians* also discusses the fascination with Gypsy life by French painters from Daumier and Courbet to Manet, Renoir, Van Gogh, and Henri Rousseau (as indeed for European painters from Joseph Turner to Otto Muller).

50. See for instance Charles Dickens, *The Mystery of Edwin Drood* (1870); Arthur Conan Doyle, "The Adventure of the Speckled Band" (1892); and George du Maurier, *Trilby* (1894), all picking up on the tradition of Gypsy Gothic established by William Harrison Ainsworth, *Rookwood* (1834). During the 1850s, anxious articles on the recent emancipation of the Vlax Gypsies in the Balkans began appearing in Victorian periodicals. See for instance "The Gipsy Slaves of Wallachia," in Dickens's magazine *Household Words* 7 (1854): 139–42. It might be argued, indeed, that renewed Western European fears of Gypsy "invasion" and "parasitism," following reports of extreme poverty among the freed slaves and the migration of some away from the site of their captivity, inform not only the wave of literary and ethnographic writing about the Gypsies in the 1860s and 1870s, but also remain latently present in the vampire story, with its Balkan setting; Bram Stoker's *Dracula* itself, which relaunches the genre in 1897, thus portrays Gypsy life as part of the sinister ambiance of Transylvania. On the concurrent waves of anti-Gypsy agitation and the rise of Gypsy nationalism and political organization in Britain, see Acton, *Gypsy Politics and Social Change*, p. 101, and Mayall, *Gypsy-Travellers in Nineteenth-Century Society*, chaps. 6 and 7.

51. See, for instance, Charles Baudelaire, "Bohemiens en voyage," *Les Fleurs du mal* (1852); the numerous "Gypsy" writings of Arthur Symons and Sacheverell Sitwell; Aleksandr Blok, "The Camp Moved" (1898) and "Lower the Faded Curtain" (1908); Thomas Mann, *Tonio Kröger* (1903); and Ezra Pound, "The Gipsy" (1912), as well as the general discussion of bohemianism in Brown, *Gypsies and Other Bohemians*.

W. H. Hudson's 1910 *A Shepherd's Life,* in which Gypsies appear literally as wild animals).[52]

If at the end of the nineteenth century, apparently disparate branches of literary production are thus peculiarly connected by their common fascination with Gypsies' "primitive magic," the longer list of authors and literary forms preoccupied with Gypsy life is, as the preceeding pages have suggested, virtually synonymous with the modern European literary canon—and is synonymous as well, if the many thousands of popular novels, poems, songs, operettas, paintings, and films featuring Gypsies are added to it, with European (and North American) cultural literacy more generally. Over the last two hundred years, European literary and cultural mythology has repeatedly posed the Gypsy question as the key to the origin, the nature, the strength of cultural tradition itself. It could be argued, indeed, that as the Gypsies become bearers, par excellence, of the European memory problem in its many manifestations, they simultaneously become a major epistemological testing ground for the European imaginary, black box, or limit case for successive literary styles, genres, and intellectual moments. Thus for neoclassicism they are there to symbolize a primitive democracy; for the late Enlightenment, an obstruction to the progress of civilization; for romanticism, resistance and the utopia of autonomy; for realism, a threat that throws the order and detail of everyday life into relief; for aestheticism and modernism, a primitive energy still left beneath the modern that drives art itself; and for socialist and postcolonial fiction, finally, a reactionary or resistant cultural force that lingers outside of the welfare state or the imperial order.[53]

52. For the new Gypsy "folklore," see Charles G. Leland, *The English Gipsies and Their Language* (1873); Francis Hindes Groome, *In Gipsy Tents* (1880); and the *Journal of the Gypsy Lore Society,* founded in 1888. For the multiplicity, political context, and address of these studies, see Mayall, *Gypsy Travellers in Nineteenth-Century Society,* esp. pp. 97–149, and Acton, *Gypsy Politics and Social Change,* esp. pp. 104–18. For a Gypsy-inflected Kailyard that sentimentalizes Ainsworth, see James Barrie, *The Little Minister* (1891); for a more grandiose and sensationalist Gypsy Celticism, see Theodore Watts-Dunton, *Aylwin; or, The Renascence of Wonder* (1898) and *The Coming of Love* (1898), which juxtapose "Cymric" and Gypsy "ancestral voices of the blood" and explore in parallel plots Gypsy prophecy and nervous hysteria treated by magnetism. For Edwardian Gypsy pastoralism, see John Masefield, "Vagabond" (1902) and "At Heaven's Gate" (1911); Grahame, *The Wind in the Willows;* W. H. Hudson, *A Shepherd's Life* (1910); Edward Thomas, "The Gypsy" (1915); and Edmund Blunden, "The Idlers" (1922).

53. For socialist attempts to come to terms with Gypsy culture, see John Arden's controversial *Live Like Pigs* (1958); the East German literature (both socialist-realist and intending in its own way to be postcolonial) mentioned above in n. 23; Puxon, "Roma heute: Zur Situation der europäischen Zigeuner," in *In Auschwitz vergast, bis heute verfolgt,* pp. 29–63, which is a dossier on the spectrum of pro- and anti-Gypsy policies implemented by the former Communist governments in Eastern Europe, and by the non-Communist European countries as well; and, on their political legacy, Nicolae Gheorghe, "Roma-Gypsy Ethnicity in Eastern Europe," *Social Research* 58 (Winter 1991): 829–44. In the West, the traditional rhetoric of left-wing parties seems to have excluded Gypsy concerns fairly completely, since

Commissioned in October 1939, Virginia Woolf's "Gipsy, the Mongrel" represents a quintessentially modernist resorting of a long tradition of "Gypsy literature" as well as an ambivalent historical document preoccupied with yet occluding Gypsy sufferings. As the story begins, two couples sit talking late one night about old friends:

> "She had such a lovely smile," said Mary Bridger, reflectively. . . . Helen Folliott, the girl with the lovely smile, had vanished. None of them knew what had happened to her. She had come to grief somehow, they had heard, and, they agreed, each of them had always

---

Gypsies have been seen either as migrant "non-workers" existing outside of political, economic, and class struggles altogether, or else as embodying the wrong kind of reaction to political oppression. In *Die Gefährten* [*The Comrades of the Road*], Anna Seghers's 1932 novel about the political persecution and diaspora of the left following the defeat of the Hungarian and German revolutions, the struggles of the "politicals" in a Polish prison to be put into a cell of their own is concretized by the fact that they are placed, initially, with Gypsies (who are accused of murder) and other common criminals. The contrast here is precisely between a politically motivated diaspora and an ethnically motivated one, between political "crimes" and the real crimes of the Gypsies. On the final page of Antonio Gramsci's "The Modern Prince" (1930-34), the metaphors of "gypsy bands or nomads" appears repeatedly and pejoratively to describe voluntarist or opportunistic "mass" parties (Antonio Gramsci, "The Modern Prince," *Selections from the Prison Notebooks,* trans. and ed. Quintin Hoare and Geoffrey Nowell Smith [New York, 1971], pp. 204-5). And when Alfred Döblin, a German-Jewish and leftist novelist, visits Poland in 1925 and is informed in Vilnius (Wilno) that Gypsy refugees, fleeing the Bolsheviks, have been arriving there from Russia, he contradicts the report out of hand, on two different grounds: "'They're not fleeing the Bolsheviks, my son. When poor people come to power, they strike only at the rich. The gypsies always flee, or rather, they do not flee, they wander.' I impress the word 'wander' on my companion" (Alfred Döblin, *Journey to Poland,* trans. Joachim Neugroschel, ed. Heinz Graber [1925; New York, 1991], p. 96). Although he has spent most of his trip reflecting on the intricate relationships in Eastern Europe between nationalism, fundamentalism, Zionism, and anti-Semitism, Döblin clearly disbelieves the possibility of a Bolshevik threat to ethnic minorities, while the fact that Gypsies are always "wandering" anyway, putting themselves completely outside of the political process, makes it equally impossible that they can ever be seen as refugees.

Michael Denning's sympathetic discussion of Frederick Whittaker's 1881 *Nemo, King of the Tramps; or, The Romany Girl's Vengeance: A Story of the Great Railroad Riots,* however, implies that in popular political culture, at least, "Gypsies" (in this case, he argues, "a synecdoche for immigrant workers") can at moments become rallying figures for many disenfranchised groups simultaneously (Michael Denning, *Mechanic Accents: Dime Novels and Working-Class Culture in America* [New York, 1987], p. 152). There seems to be some evidence for this in European working-class and mass culture as well: the strong identification of many French proletarian cigarette smokers, for instance, with the Gitane brand—including homemade tattoos based on its trademark Gypsy dancer—imply identification as well with notions of political defiance and utopian strivings for freedom (chosen in lieu of the more straightforwardly patriotic connotations of Gallois, the other inexpensive brand). See, relatedly, Acton's account both of the traditional indifference of the British Labour party to the persecution of Gypsies, and of grass-roots support for the tactics of the Gypsy civil rights movement there (Acton, *Gypsy Politics and Social Change,* chaps. 11–14).

known that she would, and, what was odd, none of them had ever forgotten her.

"She had such a lovely smile," Lucy Bagot repeated.

And so they began to discuss the oddities of human affairs—what a toss up it seems whether you sink or swim, why one remembers and forgets, what a difference trifles make, and how people, who used to meet every day, suddenly part and never see each other again.

Then they were silent. That was why they heard a whistle—was it a train or a siren?—a faint far whistle that sounded over the flat Suffolk fields and dwindled away. The sound must have suggested something. . . . for Lucy said, looking at her husband, "*She* had such a lovely smile." He nodded. "You couldn't drown a puppy who grinned in the face of death," he said. It sounded like a quotation. The Bridgers looked puzzled. "Our dog," said Lucy.[54]

A dog story follows, about a mongrel of "remarkable character" and "indescribable charm" ("GM," p. 274). Hearing a Gypsy whistle one night, a farmer arms himself with a dog whip and sets off into the snow to whip the Gypsies off his property. They have already broken camp but have left behind them a puppy. Intending to drown this unwanted dog, the farmer is won over by a grin on her face, and spares her. But she proves "a regular gipsies' dog" and makes "his life a burden to him," chasing hens, worrying sheep, killing the cat:

> "A dozen times he was on the point of killing her. Yet he couldn't bring himself to do it—not until she'd killed the cat, his wife's favourite. It was the wife who insisted. So once more he took her out into the yard, stood her against the wall, and was about to pull the trigger. And again—she grinned; grinned right into the face of death, and he hadn't the heart to do it." ["GM," p. 274]

Adopted by the Bagots, Gipsy gradually "'convert[s] the old Tory'" Hector (their well-behaved purebred dog "'with a pedigree as long as your arm'") to her own "vagabond," misbehaving ways, and although the fond Bagots know "'it was all her doing,'" they are so attached to her that they give Hector away instead ("GM," pp. 278, 275, 278). Now Gipsy herself goes into a decline, remorseful at having "done a good dog out of a home." Her owners anxiously sense that something is wrong but cannot find a means of reassuring her.

> "Dogs can't talk. But dogs . . . remember."
>
> "If only she could have spoken! Then we could have reasoned with her, tried to persuade her. . . . There was something she tried to

54. Virginia Woolf, "Gipsy, the Mongrel," *The Complete Shorter Fiction,* 2d ed., ed. Susan Dick (New York, 1989), p. 273; hereafter abbreviated "GM."

> resist, but couldn't, something in her blood so to speak that was too strong for her." ["GM," p. 279]

Finally, the couple sit with Gipsy on a snowy night like the one when the story began:

> "One could hear footsteps retreating. Everything seemed to be vanishing away, lost in the falling snow. And then—we only heard it because we were listening—a whistle sounded—a long low whistle—dwindling away. Gipsy heard it. She looked up. She trembled all over. Then she grinned. . . . Next morning she was gone."
>
> There was dead silence. They had a sense of vast empty space round them, of friends vanishing for ever, summoned by some mysterious voice away into the snow.
>
> "You never found her?" Mary Bridger asked at length.
>
> Tom Bagot shook his head.
>
> "We did what we could. Offered a reward. Consulted the police. There was a rumour—someone had seen gipsies passing."
>
> "What do you think she heard? What was she grinning at?" Lucy Bagot asked. "Oh I still pray," she exclaimed, "that it wasn't the end." ["GM," p. 280]

That is the end of the narrative. Gipsy vanishes as she came, leaving only the memory of her grin and the pieces of her story. Except that in the course of its telling, Mary Bridger realizes it is a love story, that Tom Bagot has been in love with Helen Folliott, "the girl with the lovely smile," whom he associates with his grinning dog, also lost, also missed, also come to a preordained bad end. "'Aren't all stories connected?' she asked herself" ("GM," p. 275).

"There is nothing like a dog story for bringing out people's characters" (ibid.). In Woolf's hands, the brief tale not only reveals the characters of tellers and listeners but meditates on loss and retrieval, the "race memory" in Gipsy's mongrel blood and the mediated recollection of lost loves, the way their brave smiles and "inexplicable charms" linger on, linked forever to everyday sights, sounds, and stories. A lost woman cannot be talked about except indirectly, as a silence, as an inability to keep narrating, as a story about something else. Vast empty space, friends vanishing forever, summoned away into the snow by a police whistle, a siren, the whistle of a train: written a month into the war, "Gipsy" is centrally concerned with disappearances and absences. To the modern reader, the story's mood and imagery, its evocation of the inchoateness of memory in the face of loss, seem to inaugurate both the thematics and the techniques of a "poetry after Auschwitz." But the story's historical prescience is matched by its historical oblivion. At a moment when Gypsies are being subjected, on racial grounds, to a mass internment in which they will be operated on, sterilized, kept or killed like animals, Woolf writes "Gipsy, the Mongrel" as a dog story. Displacing the supposedly characteristic features of "Gypsies" themselves (barnyard thefts and vagabond habits, the call of the open road in their blood, and their famous insouciance, even in the face of deserved execution) onto a dog, human fates onto those of animals, the story implicitly moralizes disappearance as an inexorable destiny to which the fallen woman and the mongrel are called alike by their own blood under the false promise of freedom.

Along with its historical circumstances, of course, what shapes the story's logic is its pedigree as a Gypsy story, a literary inheritance that it at once reiterates, ridicules, and reanchors. In a simultaneous process of literalization and allegorization, the tale plays out the Gypsy mythology as tragicomic low style in the central narrative (in a parodic replay of *Wuthering Heights, Carmen,* and *A Shepherd's Life,* a Gypsy foundling of "enormous charm" tempts a pedigreed companion to join her in a life of animal abandon and ends up doing "a good dog out of a home") while its underlying concerns about identity, causality, and memory, shifted into both the framing narrative and the narrative form itself, are elevated to the status of philosophical questions. "It sounded like a quotation": what joins the frame narrative to the dog story, Woolf's story to the long tradition of paranoid and often racist narratives about Gypsy life, is not only its intertextual plot and obsession with narrative memory but (for all its explorations of the boundaries and infinities of recollection) the textualist limits of its consciousness. For Woolf as for Liszt, what "Gipsy" represents is a "fascination as hard to describe as to destroy." But in an era that actually threatens the genocidal destruction of Gypsy life (a destruction echoed within Woolf's tale in the repeated threat of execution) the story's real interest remains why and how a Gipsy should be so hard to describe. The story's intense focus on one set of literary problems—the vicissitudes of memory; the interrelationship of narration, silence, and interpretation; the impossibilities of conveying character except through indirection—occludes its own reliance on politically brisant materials, its own procedures of allegorization, its own blurring of the boundaries between the animal and the human, its own internal need for silence and ambiguity at the heart of the Gipsy story:

> "I don't believe in stories. A dog has a character just as we have, and it shows itself just as ours do, by what we say, by all sorts of little things."
>
> "Yes . . . she taught us a lesson. I've often wondered . . . what she was thinking of us—down there among all the boots and old matches on the hearthrug? What was her world? Do dogs see what we see or is it something different?"
>
> They too looked down at the boots and old matches, tried for a moment to lie nose on paws gazing into the red caverns and yellow

> flames with a dog's eyes. But they couldn't answer that question. ["GM," pp. 277–78]

Far from constituting a trivial genre, the dog story (like the "Gypsy narrative") proves a testing ground for human epistemology, a limit case of narration itself, but only when it stops its momentary gazing from the hearthrug, ceases to be centrally about dogs at all, and becomes instead a medium "for bringing out people's characters," for narrators who lose themselves in memory or betray their most hidden emotions, for listeners who make stray connections across levels of narration. The dog ostensibly at the story's center in fact figures mainly as a site of investment and interpretation, displacement and paradigm sorting. Unable to speak for herself, her own actions and motivations remain uninterestingly mysterious, irrecoverable even as the tellers and listeners around her accumulate psychological complexity. While the other, human characters reveal layer after layer of developmental history, she remains within a compass of emotion so small it appears as strength of character—she smiles even in the face of death. While they mourn and guess and remember, she continues to be steered, silently and enigmatically, by older, simpler, deeper things: a whistle barely perceptible even in the silence, the conflicting voices of a mongrel blood. "Dogs can't talk. But dogs remember": race memory is reinvented here as a foil for a psychology that can manifest itself only in and as narrative.

"For as long as I could remember," writes Andrea Lee in "Gypsies," the fourth chapter of her 1984 novel, *Sarah Phillips,* "the civil rights movement had been unrolling like a dim frieze behind the small pleasures and defeats of my childhood: it seemed dull, a necessary burden on my conscience, like good grades or hungry people in India."[55] Periodically, Sarah Phillips's father ventures forth from Franklin Place, a street through a peaceful, middle-class, black Philadelphia suburb "with the constrained slightly unreal atmosphere of a colony or a foreign enclave" (*SP,* p. 39), to join dangerous civil rights marches through a hostile South. For his seven-year-old daughter that outside world remains distant, until one day a family of Gypsies drives into the neighborhood to sell handmade, rickety lawn furniture from the back of their rusty truck:

> The man behind the wheel had dark skin but was not a Negro; he looked a bit like one of the Indians we saw constantly defeated in TV westerns. . . . Beside him was a woman. . . . There was something frightening and wild . . . about the woman herself; she grinned at us, and we saw that one of her front teeth was broken in half. [She had]

55. Andrea Lee, *Sarah Phillips* (New York, 1984), pp. 39–40; hereafter abbreviated *SP.*

> small dark eyes that had the same glistening brightness, the jumpy intensity, of the eyes of a crow that had once alighted for an instant on my bedroom windowsill. [*SP*, pp. 42–43]

The Gypsies' bearing conveys both envy at the neighborhood's affluence and pity for the "colored" who are forced to live in segregation. "'Well, everybody's got . . . to . . . feel . . . better . . . than . . . somebody,'" Sarah's father puts it that evening, "drawling his words out progressively slower until they were as slow and exaggerated as the Uncle Remus record we had. . . . 'Most of the world despises Gypsies, but a Gypsy can always look down on a Negro'" (*SP*, p. 44). In the Gypsies' wake, the furniture they have sold to Sarah's family and neighbors immediately collapses, and her mother makes "a few quips about the 'Romany spell' that must have been cast to get her to buy something so worthless. . . . It was the same for the rest of the neighborhood; stories of the ephemeral tables and chairs that fell apart during thunderstorms or barbecues became standard jokes" (*SP*, pp. 45–46). But Sarah herself remains under the "Romany spell," with lingering Gypsy nightmares:

> It was not that I had really feared being stolen; it was more, in fact, that they seemed to have stolen something from me. Nothing looked different, yet everything was, and for the first time Franklin Place seemed genuinely connected to a world that was neither insulated nor serene. [*SP*, p. 46]

Arriving in an enclave of nonwhite Americans, themselves the survivors of diaspora and slavery, the Gypsies this time bring with them a memory of poverty and oppression, history rather than forgetfulness, a connection *back* to the outside world. Yet the narrator insists on that knowledge as a theft of innocence, on the lawn furniture as bewitched, on the Gypsies as inscrutable, frightening, animal-like. "Everybody's got to feel better than somebody": even a nonwhite writer attempting to write about minority experience in America cannot resist the temptation to invoke a racist mythology one more time, as shorthand for questions of identity and developmental memory. Andrea Lee's "Gypsies" suggests, in fact, that Gypsy alterity, cultural cohesion, and "race memory," so long a threat to the narratives of European nationalism, are equally threatening, for somewhat different reasons, to the self-conception of an emerging black nationalism as well, struggling against its own diasporic history and its own forced suppression of memory. What this has meant in practice, unfortunately, is that the Romani of North America, a much smaller and more dispersed group than African Americans, have been forced to mount a separate civil rights movement of their own.

Ronald Lee's *Goddam Gypsy* both laconically foretells this final instance of Romani exclusion even from "revolutionary" ethnic struggles, and at the same time recounts a rather different sort of story, with a ray of hope for new, postnational coalitions. Set on the margins of an ostensibly pluralist and multicultural Canada, the novel chronicles a "struggle to find recognition and equality in the land where I was born. I failed in both these aims and this is the story of that failure."[56] Adopted into a white foster family late in his childhood, Yanko (the Ronald Lee figure) grows up "white" and integrated into the Canadian mainstream; he attends university, marries a non-Gypsy, and works in an office. After the marriage founders, however, he takes to the road, meets up with other Gypsy ethnics, and recovers his cultural identity. The autobiography opens with this ethnic coming-to-consciousness, then describes at length the community of outcasts Yanko gradually gathers around him in Montréal: Gypsies still recovering from the Nazi persecution that drove them to Canada and suffering anew from the prejudice of the white community there, which categorically closes to them all legal employment and all neighborhoods save the slums; young native women from the reservation and a French-Canadian prostitute, both trying in vain to find a foothold in the city; a Black Muslim expatriate from the American South; legal and illegal immigrants full of nationalist nostalgia for their own Serbian, Greek, and Turkish cultures and deep-rooted hatred for each other's; angry young French and English Canadians, dislocated intellectuals dreaming of a revolution that is separatist, socialist, or both.

The novel ends, in fact, with Expo 67 (the Montréal World's Fair in the year of the Canadian centennial and an important symbol for Canada's emergence as a postcolonial nation) and with the rise of militant separatism in Québec, a moment at which the dreams of both Canadian and Québecois nationalists seem on the verge of being realized. But this is also, not by coincidence, the moment at which Yanko and his native wife decide to emigrate to Europe, to join the Romani activist movement then getting under way. In Canada, in Québec, Yanko predicts, the situation of the underclass, of native peoples, of the "unassimilatable" nonwhite and non-Western minorities, is bound to get worse than it was before, since *they* are not the groups that the new nationalist governments will speak to or for. Throughout the novel his own attempts to raise political awareness among his people and win public recognition for their plight have failed repeatedly. The months spent helping the last Gypsy patriarch compile the first Romani dictionary prove time wasted. For other national groups in the past, the publication of a vernacular dictionary had marked an important milestone in the group's self-definition and in its quest for credibility as a nation in the eyes of the world; indeed, given the historical absence of a written language and written records, a dictionary is the only possible one of the traditionally efficacious "national monuments" that

56. Ronald Lee, *Goddam Gypsy: An Autobiographical Novel* (Montréal, 1971), p. 8; hereafter abbreviated *GG*.

Rom intellectuals like Lee can use to stake a claim for Gypsy nationhood. But in the Canada of the late 1960s (in a publishing market notoriously unable to hold its own against American competitors) the publishers have little enough interest in English-Canadian fiction, let alone a Romani dictionary. The media is similarly indifferent—or worse, seeks yet another occasion to sensationalize Gypsy life, playing down its poverty and pariah status in favor of the same tired clichés.

Yanko's attempts to support his family "as a Gypsy" and by noncriminal means are similarly disastrous, despite his university education. Forced by economic pressures into a variety of semilegal scams, he longs for more respectable work that will engage his artistic and intellectual talents. In fact, he is a self-trained expert in the miniature reconstruction of historical ships, using extensive archival research and painstaking craftsmanship. But official curatorial work remains closed to someone so literally a gypsy scholar, and his only career break in this line comes as "someone who knows and understands animals": a job as theme director of an Expo wildlife pavilion, sponsored by a shadowy group of big-game hunters:

> They wanted to set up a privately sponsored, unofficial exhibit dedicated to the preservation of our Canadian wildlife. . . .
>
> "We must preserve, at all costs, this great national heritage of ours." . . .
>
> "Many species of animals are being forced into extinction today and we must do everything possible to save them. Others are being decimated and driven out of their natural habitat by predators. Animals that have developed certain habits and instincts cannot survive if they are suddenly and ruthlessly transplanted into a foreign environment or if they are struck by disease from man's pollution."
>
> Listening, I felt suddenly indignant as I thought of my wife and family, the Gypsies, Indians, and all the poor in the slums.
>
> [The exhibit] would consist of stuffed animals in their natural surroundings, in large, plexiglass cases. . . . life-size dioramas, store dummies dressed as hunters, trappers or anglers set in typical single or group scenes. [*GG,* pp. 178–79]

The episode has many layers of irony. From behind the scenes, the opening of Expo (and the opening salvo of the new Canadian nationalism, announcing itself to the world) appears as farce: to get one prize-winning caribou into its glass case, Yanko's crew lops off part of its antlers, and when it is pointed out that the deer "couple" in another case is actually two males, the crew quietly castrates one of the two stuffed stags. In some sense, this is what world's fairs, natural and national history museums, indeed nationalist movements themselves, have long been about: an unself-conscious "nature" is neutered, embalmed, displayed in a glass case, killed in order to support the claims for a living culture, their "great national heritage." The novel as a whole suggests clear parallels between the dismantling and reassembling of animal bodies to make them fit their cases and labels, the psychological bludgeoning and symbolic castration that Gypsies, native peoples, and other "wildlife" undergo in their respective ghettos and reservations. Yanko details case after case of friends who become alcoholic, impotent, abusive in response to the prejudice, poverty, and degradations of daily life; the more deadened and narcotized they become, of course, the more they confirm the ethnic stereotypes.

Far from breaking this vicious circle, Yanko suggests presciently, the nationalist movements of both English and French Canada will reinforce inequality for all groups save their own. Indeed their effect on their own culture can be destructive even as it is curative: they will inevitably need to freeze culture in order to preserve it. Ronald Lee's own book represents the attempt to develop a different, internationalist, strategy for representing cultural diversity. In a way, the autobiography manages to become the narrative equivalent of one of the ships Yanko painstakingly reconstructs, detail for detail, until the finished piece stands as a metonymic model for a whole historical epoch: in its anecdotal fashion, the book presents one of the most compact, panoramic, and biting social visions in Canadian literature (perhaps the reason it is virtually unknown in Canada today). And yet its presentation is completely casual, vernacular, seemingly haphazard and unstudied: an endless stream of impressions, chance conversations, political aperçus, overheard voices. Lee's autobiography in fact attempts to create itself as precisely what Canada is not: as a utopian Romanestan, as a polyglot, dialogic space in which travellers with different languages and cultural experiences can interact freely with each other, tracing family connections and comparing notes. But it is a book he can write only from memory, as an expatriate, from Europe:

> Jimmy and I had one last drink in the house. I took my glass and threw it against the wall where it smashed into fragments.
>
> "To hell with Canada, Long live Romanestan."
>
> Jimmy looked at me, only half understanding. He had heard of the proposed Gypsy state, a parallel to Israel, to be set up by the United Nations at the insistence of Gypsy leaders in Europe, educated men like me, who had found that they had no place as Romanies in their countries of birth. . . .
>
> We drove along Sherbrooke Street on the way to the ship. . . . separatists, students and anarchists were holding a sit-in and a demonstration. . . . The Canadian and Quebec provincial flags had been hauled down. . . .
>
> "*Magnifique,*" Etien was excited. . . . "*Formidable, on les aura.* It had to come. It's got to be that way, separation, *il faut en finir.*"
>
> Yes, I thought, there must be an end to it somewhere. Will the French-Canadians be allowed to find their own destiny as a separate nation in North America or will they go down in an orgy of blood and

> terrorism? Who knows? But they can't keep on going the way they are, losing their language, culture and self-respect. . . .
>
> "*Vive le Québec libre!*" he smiled, "*En avant aux barricades.*"
>
> "*Vive le Canada libre,*" I replied. It wasn't quite the same thing. [*GG*, pp. 236–37][57]

There must be an end to it somewhere. The problem for Ronald Lee is the way the rhetoric of nationalism and the model of cultural legitimation it establishes reinforce the division between the domains of ethnography and history, spectacle and narrative, between timeless "natural" cultures, locked into themselves, changeable only when disrupted, and culture-bearing, narrative-bearing nations, moving purposefully through history towards geographical and ethnic self-realization. In an epoch shaped by nationalist rhetoric, those peoples who do not claim a land and a written tradition for themselves, who cannot or do not claim a history, are relegated to nature, without a voice in any political process, represented only in the glass case of the diorama, the dehumanizing legend of the photograph, the tableaux of the open-air museum.

57. Acton's discussion of Gypsy nationalism and the politics of the Gypsy Council reports obliquely on Lee's subsequent involvement with British activism, identifying him, somewhat surprisingly, with an "ultra-nationalist" position (Acton, *Gypsy Politics and Social Change*, p. 230).

Critical Response

I

White Philosophy

Avery Gordon and Christopher Newfield

> The court acted like a philosopher who wanted to know positively whether a cat was on the mat in Mashpee.
>
> —James Clifford, *The Predicament of Culture*

1. Racism and the "Appeal to Race"

Liberal racism has recently been attracting the attention it deserves. Its defining feature is an antiracist attitude that coexists with support for racist outcomes. Liberal racism rejects discrimination on the basis of race or color and abhors the subjection of groups or individuals on racial grounds. But it upholds and defends systems that produce racializing effects, often in the name of some matter more "urgent" than redressing racial subordination, such as rewarding "merit" or enhancing economic competitiveness.

A particularly powerful form of liberal racism displays two additional features that will be especially important here. First, rather than explicitly rationalizing racism, it treats the categories through which racism operates, is felt, and is addressed as conceptual errors. It thus directs less attention to the histories, current forms, and social effects of racism (though it agrees racism is a problem) than to the problems of race and racial identity, categories it considers politically troubling and intellectually flawed. Liberal racial thinking seeks to go "beyond race" and does

This article originally appeared in *Critical Inquiry* 20 (Summer 1994).

not support racialized perspectives on racism on the grounds that they are a kind of reverse racism. Second, it seeks to describe its own move beyond race as part of reason rather than of history; the move is not, in other words, a racial ideology in its own right, with a genealogy that links the gesture to the social positions and racial interests of white progressives, but an expression of the rational truth about race.

It is one of the virtues of Walter Benn Michaels's essay "Race into Culture: A Critical Genealogy of Cultural Identity" (pp. 32–62) that it focuses attention on liberal racism, particularly the kind that appears in cultural pluralism. We have learned a great deal from his insistence that racism is not an accidental by-product of the liberal reforms that replaced the appeal to race with the appeal to culture but is part of the structure of such reforms. We have benefitted from his unveiling of racialization where it is most often invisible and his outline of racism's historical persistence through major intellectual watersheds. It is one of the symptoms of the times, however, that Michaels's essay locates the racism of cultural pluralism in its use of racial and cultural identity rather than in the liberal racism with which pluralism coexists. Writing in a period when a post–civil rights liberalism has been accumulating increasing political and intellectual influence, Michaels's call for an America "without race" does not get beyond the white moderate position on race but furnishes it with a philosophical rationale.

This ascendent race liberalism thrives on a contemporary debate about whether racism or race consciousness is the greater social problem. Where race consciousness involves a sense of links between one's social position and historical patterns of racialization, is it racist to be conscious of one's "racial" identity?[1] Or is racial identity (including its deployment) the result of racism? These questions—starkly polarized here—have become especially confusing at the present time, when signs of racial progress and racial regression exist side by side and can be difficult to tell

1. Gary Peller offers an analysis of the "racial compromise" by which "the price of the national commitment to suppress white supremacists would be the rejection of race consciousness among African Americans" (Garry Peller, "Race Consciousness," *Duke Law Journal* [Sept. 1990]: 760).

Avery Gordon teaches sociology at the University of California, Santa Barbara. She is the author of *Ghostly Matters* and coeditor, with Christopher Newfield, of *Mapping Multiculturalism* (both forthcoming). **Christopher Newfield** is associate professor of English at the University of California, Santa Barbara. He is the author of *The Emerson Effect: Individualism and Submission in America* (1995) and coeditor of *After Political Correctness* (1995).

apart. Biologically defined racism appears very much on the wane, and color-blind hiring practices are a presumed norm; at the same time, racially patterned inequality has not only persisted but has gotten worse. The idea that we are "post" civil rights suggests the period of civil rights protest to have been a success but also a failure. It has produced indications that the genuine progress represented by civil rights has not been enough to withstand embedded institutional and psychological resistances like the white backlash against affirmative action programs or unabating white anxiety about the presence of social and political actors who insist on the continuing significance of racism. The changing U.S. economy has intensified the attention paid to the multiracial composition of the workforce, but this has encouraged an ambiguous stress on higher productivity through cultural sensitivity *and* the rejection of race politics. Many experience all this as a dilemma: should racism—as a mode of hierarchical social differentiation—be granted ongoing social significance, or is racial identity itself an obstacle to progress?

The latter response has been especially influential in the political realm, for it locates the solution to racism in color blindness and the end of race consciousness.[2] The New Democrats, for example, have argued that too much emphasis on minority (especially African American) concerns for equity has itself been responsible for the racial setbacks of the Reagan-Bush era. In analyses made most prominent by liberals like Thomas Byrne Edsall, Mary Edsall, and E. J. Dionne, and put into practice by Bill Clinton, the persistence of racial inequality gets blamed not on white racism but on the invocation of race.[3] They regard the *explicit* appeal to race as separable from the racist past and present in which the appeal has most often been made.[4] Once the appeal to race is seen analytically, free of the context of racism, the usual causality becomes reversed: racism does not make people talk about race; talk about race sustains racism. One overriding characteristic of post–civil rights is a spurious equalizing effect: uses of race are the same regardless of the

2. See, for example, Kimberlé Williams Crenshaw, "Race, Reform, and Retrenchment: Transformation and Legitimation in Antidiscrimination Law," *Harvard Law Review* 101, no. 7 (1988): 1331–87, and Neil Gotanda, "A Critique of 'Our Constitution is Color-Blind,'" *Stanford Law Review* 44 (Nov. 1991): 1–68.

3. See Thomas Byrne Edsall and Mary D. Edsall, *Chain Reaction: The Impact of Race, Rights, and Taxes on American Politics* (New York, 1991), and E. J. Dionne, Jr., *Why Americans Hate Politics* (New York, 1991).

4. Such writers are themselves making an appeal to race in their address to the middle class as a supposedly inclusive and populist political category in the United States, but this appeal, though racially encoded as white, is not explicit. In this context, the concept of white supremacy is preferable to that of racism, which remains popularly conceived as intentional, psychological, and attitudinal, as a problem that minorities—those who are overtly racialized—create for those who are not, that is, whites. White supremacy, by contrast, views whiteness as a constitutive dimension of complex relations of governance in continual negotiation with other (and overlapping) governance systems.

race of the user; discrimination is no worse than reverse discrimination. In short, these analyses replace the race *problem* with the *"race"* problem.

This of course undoes civil rights era common sense, in which the more basic problem was considered to be racism itself. That sensibility promotes discussion of racism in all of its forms, particularly in its friendlier modern ones, like institutional racism. It asks for increased use of the category of race not because race is a biological fact or even because it defines one's intrinsic personal or cultural identity but because it is one of the most important principles by which U.S. social relations are organized. This is something like the way scholars who are interested in gender relations can speak about the impact of the American sex/gender system without believing that this system produces its effects biologically. These writers, while expressing a considerable range of views, generally regard race *"as an unstable and 'decentered' complex of social meanings constantly transformed by political struggle,"* a changing complex that nonetheless has decisive racializing effects.[5] They hold that it is racism and racialization that keep race alive.[6]

How has this idea gotten completely turned around? How has the turnaround endowed white racial moderates with a political influence they have not enjoyed in years? Part of the answer is of course that many have become persuaded that it was too upsetting to talk about America as an apartheid state; it was too offensive to talk about who continues to benefit; it was too disruptive to talk about pointed remedies. So they have offered an effective pragmatic argument that good coalition politics requires working around the racial resentments of white voters offended by the old Democrat social agenda; lessened race consciousness would lessen racism. But for this position to succeed, it requires a more complete reengineering of the terrain of racial common sense; nothing less will keep this river flowing upstream. Too much in the American world says that race consciousness largely issues from racism to make it easy to show the reverse. The reversal, racism from race, requires bigger upheavals in the old terrain. Ideally, such an upheaval would dwarf empirical and sociological conditions like white racial backlash, where racism is too inextricably mixed in with appeals to race to allow the elimination of racism as a major social cause. It would be better to be able to show that the appeal to race is the prior problem on grounds that *it is itself intrinsi-*

5. Michael Omi and Howard Winant, *Racial Formation in the United States: From the 1960s to the 1980s* (New York, 1986), p. 68.

6. Racialization and racism operate autonomously but rarely alone. Understanding the intersections among race, class, and gender dynamics—three of the most important modern social determinants—has been a major preoccupation of scholars for decades. It is unfortunately beyond the scope of this paper to pursue this, but it may suffice to note that pluralist racism evades consideration of gender altogether and tends to use a specifically American-style understanding of class to chart the declining significance of race.

cally racist, solid gold racism, too much the fountainhead of racism to have received racism from any lesser source.

Such a demonstration appears in "Race into Culture." Our next section considers the construction of this demonstration—the reasons Michaels offers for shifting from criticizing a history of veiled white racism to criticizing the appeal to race. This shift hinges on Michaels's categorical association of race consciousness with essentialist identity practices. The final section describes three undesirable outcomes of the type of racial management that Michaels's work implies (irrespective of his undoubtedly antiracist personal intentions), and sketches an alternative.

2. *Making Racial Ontology*

> Q.: If you were telling them about it, it would be because they didn't know about it, isn't that right?
> A.: Not at all times, no.
>
> —RAMONA PETERS under cross-examination from James St. Clair, *Mashpee Tribe* v. *New Seabury et al.* (1977)

Michaels's genealogy of U.S. cultural identity offers an extremely important general conclusion: "Our current notion of cultural identity both descends from and extends the earlier notion of racial identity" (p. 35). Cultural identity is "the project of lining up [one's] practices with [one's] genealogy" (p. 56). Lest one doubt the ongoing relevance of this description of certain cultural critics, *Time*'s recent special issue on America as the "world's first multicultural society" pictures multi*culturalism* as technologized color blending of the facial characteristics of seven ethnic types of both genders.[7] Michaels concludes that "the modern concept of culture is not . . . a critique of racism; it is a form of racism" (p. 60). To the extent that they have rested on the category of "cultural" identity, even liberal, progressive positions like cultural pluralism, positions that formally repudiate racism, have done little more than "rescue . . . racism from racists" (p. 61 n. 40).

But what is it about cultural identity that is racist? Is it that a certain group, like the white-acculturated corporate media professionals at *Time,* deploys cultural identity for its own interests or from its own exclusionary perspective? Or is something wrong with cultural identity itself, an inherent flaw that renders irrelevant historical or political distinctions among different uses? To polarize the issue again, does the problem lie in racist uses or in the appeal to race itself?

The former belief would lead to answers like this: the architects of

7. *The New Face of America: How Immigrants Are Shaping the World's First Multicultural Society,* special issue of *Time* (Fall 1993).

pluralist identity held milder, more sophisticated, more culturalized but nonetheless deep-rooted views about white superiority. Pluralism would then be racist because it articulates a complex white supremacism. But Michaels's essay does not trace racist pluralism to the history of progressive white racial thought. It traces it to the presence of racial ontology in all uses of culture. His conclusion expands the source of the race problem from racial identity to cultural identity but retains the causal claim of the post–civil rights liberalism noted earlier: "It is only the appeal to race that makes culture an object of affect and that gives notions like losing our culture, preserving it, stealing someone else's culture, restoring people's culture to them, and so on, their pathos. . . . Without race, losing our culture can mean no more than doing things differently from the way we now do them and preserving our culture can mean no more than doing things the same" (pp. 61–62). Michaels is suggesting that, without race, the deprivations and dominations linked to racism would disappear.[8] Free of cultural identity, we will be able to treat people as people rather than as races. This ideal has strong appeal in a variety of racialized communities—if we could all stop talking race, then we would have a chance to get along. When Michaels exclaims, "But why does it matter who we are?" the question harbors an insistent entreaty: our dealings with one another can ignore the conflicts and coercions, the innumerable interdependent historical circumstances that make us who we are in the first place (p. 59).

We agree with Michaels that replacing racial with cultural identity fudges the central questions about what the invocation of identity means. But the tangled relations between cultural and racial identity do not necessarily point to their union in racial ontology, as Michaels suggests. How does he demonstrate that "accounts of cultural identity that do any cultural work require a racial component" (p. 59)? How does he show that liberal racism consists of the appeal to race rather than, for example, to an investment in a (gentler) regime of racial inequality?

The answer lies in his argument that any invocation of identity is a form of racial ontology.

> But why does it matter who we are? The answer can't just be the epistemological truism that our account of the past may be partially determined by our own identity, for, of course, this description of the conditions under which we know the past makes no logical difference to the truth or falsity of what we know. It must be instead the onto-

8. Michaels appends a disclaimer to his text: "Needless to say, the situation is entirely different with respect to compulsory assimilation; what puts the pathos back is precisely the element of compulsion" (p. 62 n. 41). This suggests that he regards cultural relations and compulsion as usually separable things, that he thinks that appeals to race are not generally produced or even coexistant with the compulsions of racism. In spite of his conclusion, this merely brackets rather than resolves the causal connection between them.

> logical claim that we need to know who we are in order to know which past is ours. The real question, however, is not *which* past should count as ours but why *any* past should count as ours. . . .The history we study is never our own; it is always the history of people who were in some respects like us and in other respects different. When, however, we claim it as ours, we commit ourselves to the ontology of "the Negro," to the identity of "we" and "they," and the primacy of race. [P. 59]

Michaels distinguishes between studying history and studying "our" history. The introduction of a connection between history and identity makes even a social or historical question about one's placement, one's power, and so on a question about one's essence—about biology, ancestry, or similarly determinate and constitutive cultural traditions. Michaels rejects the possibility that identity questions are about one's historical and social relations to others who "were in some respects like us and in other respects different." Nonessentialist history, for Michaels, avoids identity questions because it knows that "the conditions under which we know the past," our social position, can "mak[e] no logical difference" to historical knowledge. Identity questions and historical questions are essentially different, and the former are always ontological. *All* identity questions are about this because, logically, none are embedded in collective history: "The real question" is "why *any* past should count as ours." Cultural identity is ontological, the ontology refers to a prehistorical essence, and this essence is the idea of race.

What does it mean for Michaels to reduce group histories to racial identity? Taking this citation by itself, it appears that Michaels achieves his reduction of identity questions to racial ontology by proposing an essentialist definition of genuine knowledge of the past—such knowledge has no "logical" connection to the position of the person creating the knowledge. "What we know" is independent of who we are and what made us this way.[9] Another factor may be his apparent indifference to a major development in cultural theory in the past decade, the attempt to

9. At the essay's pivotal junctures, Michaels imputes essentialism to identity as used by others: all uses (that do cultural work), and particularly pluralist uses, require "us to be able to say who we are independent" of what we do; "instead of who we are being constituted by what we do, what we do is justified by who we are" (pp. 60–61 n. 39, 60). In general, Michaels's antiessentialism works through a supplementary cultural *individualism*. Antiessentialism says only that we should not derive what we do from who we are in the sense in which "who we are" is logically prior to and undetermined by what we do. We agree with this sociological commonplace. It is *individualism* that allows us to ignore that what we do or who we are is always imposed and chosen within determinate social relations. Cultural studies must be antiessentialist to be *social* studies in the first place. We hope to be lending an air of gratuity—even of conformity—to the project that makes antiessentialism the vanguard of individualism. Daniel Boyarin and Jonathan Boyarin link Michaels's view of cultural identity to his individualsim in "Diaspora: Generation and the Ground of Jewish Identity" (pp. 305–37).

render the use of individual and group identity fully antiessentialist *and* social. Antiessentialist uses of identity have been pioneered by feminist thought, race and postcolonial studies, and lesbian and gay studies, to name some of the most active fields. Writers such as Norma Alarcón, Gloria Anzaldúa, Homi Bhabha, Ed Cohen, Diana Fuss, Giles Gunn, Stuart Hall, Donna Haraway, June Jordan, Duncan Kennedy, Ernesto Laclau, Lisa Lowe, Wahneema Lubiano, Kobena Mercer, Chantal Mouffe, Gayatri Chakravorty Spivak, and Patricia J. Williams have emphasized the variable, indeterminate, shifting boundaries of any group identity. Many commentators on identity politics have lived through the abundant political failures of essentialism and have retained the use of *social* identities even as they have repudiated—with a passion born of disappointed hopes—a dream of sharing essences. Much of this work, though of course not all, has been associated with scholars of color. When Michaels proceeds without engaging the work that challenges his claim that identity is always essentialist, he is reproducing a "color line" in cultural studies.

These are some odd liabilities for Michaels's demonstration that racism is the appeal to race, but we do not think they mean that Michaels "really" possesses essentialist or racist intentions; we presume he harbors neither of these. We see these features as signs of a broader discourse in play—a liberal racial common sense that transcends the present effects of racism by minimizing history. We will spend some time on Michaels's attempt to bring a nonliberal description of cultural identity into his orbit. We do this to suggest that the apparently plausible color-blind outcome depends heavily on an implausible dehistoricization of culture. This dehistoricization wreaks havoc on descriptions of commonplace U.S. racial divisions and does so through a philosophy that, historically speaking, is white.

Michaels makes his most sustained argument against identities in his discussion of James Clifford, who, in a two-page footnote, is joined to a cultural theorist that Michaels shows to harbor racialist thoughts.[10] Clifford's account of a federal trial, *Mashpee Tribe* v. *New Seabury et al.*, argues for the kind of strongly historical contextualization of the uses of culture that Michaels denies. The Mashpee, as Clifford tells it, went to trial in order to determine whether they were legally a tribe under federal statute. Were they able to prove tribal status, the Mashpee would have been

10. This writer is Melville Herskovits. Andrew Apter offers a critique of Herskovits's antiessentialism that leads to a different outcome from Michaels's. Trying to avoid the "double bind" in which "either we essentialize Africa or renounce it" (the latter being Michaels's solution to any "cultural identity"), Apter suggests a focus on cultural practices "as strategies of appropriation and empowerment" within "relations of domination." His use of phrases like "inner logic of syncretic practices," however, would be grist for Michaels's mill, and the confusions in our vocabularies about culture suggests the heuristic value of Michaels's criticisms (Andrew Apter, "Herskovits's Heritage: Rethinking Syncretism in the African Diaspora," *Diaspora* 1 [Winter 1991]: 251).

able to use the Non-Intercourse Act of 1790 to recover some land that had been sold to non-Indians, since the act prohibited such "alienation" of Indian land without the approval of the federal government. For Clifford, "Identity in Mashpee" makes sense only in relation to "'complex historical processes of appropriation, compromise, subversion, masking, invention, and revival'" (p. 57 n. 36). He explicitly criticizes the court's incomprehension of these processes and traces the Mashpee's defeat to the court's demand for an essential group identity, which effectively erased the contingencies of the group's actual history. Clifford also sees the court's position as reflecting a highly politicized Euro-American view of identity whose emergence cannot be separated from the history of interracial relations in the colonization of the New World. For Clifford, the appeals to identity on both sides of this case emerge from the history of colonization and of race as a mode of social organization. Given all this, Michaels will need to work hard to show that Clifford's use of cultural identity as a historical dynamic is actually an appeal to racial identity.

Michaels makes an argument that, as we read it, consists of four separate claims: (1) For Clifford, Mashpee tribal status turns on the existence of Mashpee identity. (2) Mashpee identity is expressed by the possession or recovery of a Mashpee cultural practice like drumming. (3) Any cultural identity that involves "'remembering'" as well as "'reinvention'" must rest on an appeal to a continuous, inherent, precultural identity, one that exists prior to the cultural practice (p. 57 n. 36). (4) This noncultural identity is racial identity. Taking these claims in turn, it becomes apparent that they reflect and defend current liberal racial common sense rather than describe Clifford's actual deployment of cultural identity.

1. *Tribal status, which involves cultural practices, is about cultural identity rather than social relations.* To the contrary, Clifford describes the Mashpee as attempting to establish a valid *tribal* rather than cultural identity; culture comes up as the demand of the court. The tribe is a political entity; the reason there is a question about Mashpee identity in the first place has nothing to do with anyone's confusion over whether drumming makes you an Indian or being an Indian makes you drum but over the way to retain some control over land use around the town of Mashpee. The Mashpee had political independence until the 1960s, "when local government passed out of Indian control, perhaps for good, and . . . the scale of [white land] development increased."[11] The recovery of legal status as a tribe would restore to the Mashpee a town government that they felt had been seized by absentee developers; the Mashpee do not seek to affirm the racial or cultural integrity of this government so much as to make the government again responsive to the political wishes of the ma-

11. James Clifford, *The Predicament of Culture: Twentieth-Century Ethnography, Literature, and Art* (Cambridge, Mass., 1988), p. 280; hereafter abbreviated *PC*.

jority of the town's historical inhabitants. Clifford makes his endorsement of Mashpee identity talk contingent on the legal and historical context of their petition for tribal status: "I concluded that since the ability to act collectively as Indians is currently bound up with tribal status, the Indians living in Mashpee and those who return regularly should be recognized as a 'tribe'" (*PC,* p. 336). Clifford's use of phrases like "act collectively as Indians" refers to relations both chosen and imposed within the history of power relations between different social groups. The most obvious sign of the Mashpee's identity as Mashpee is that they are on trial to see whether they are tribe enough to go on trial. *Culture* is one word for group agency; rather than express established identity, it is part of the process that creates it. In its complicated relation to tribal status, culture does not show that one is now or already was or can now become a Mashpee but that one has the right to petition a state apparatus for political sovereignty.[12]

In separating cultural identity from the history of intergroup conflict, Michaels approximates the epistemology of the federal court. It was the court that demanded cultural continuity as proof of valid tribal exis-

12. The Mashpee case was one chapter of the long and unfinished story of U.S. efforts to supersede the sovereignty of American Indian nations. The United States possesses title to its own land mass entirely because of land it acquired through treaties with Indians; American identity depends on this history of expropriation, and, for Americans, "Indian" identity existed and exists only within this history. The essentializing identity claims come most powerfully from the state's laws governing Indian identity. One native organization, Native American Consultants, Inc., summarizes the effect of the statutes this way:

> 1. An Indian is a member of any federally recognized Indian Tribe. To be federally recognized, an Indian Tribe must be comprised of Indians.
> 2. To gain federal recognition, an Indian Tribe must have a land base. To secure a land base, an Indian Tribe must be federally recognized. [Quoted in M. Annette Jaimes, "Federal Indian Identification Policy: A Usurpation of Indigenous Sovereignty in North America," *The State of Native America: Genocide, Colonization, and Resistance,* ed. Jaimes (Boston, 1992), p. 133]

The Mashpee trial took place within federal identity designations that, on top of the catch-22 quality Jaimes observes, determine whether any Indian or group of Indians can hold land independently of the white property system that has been swallowing their land for centuries. The question of Indian identity has a long and violent political history. It ranges from the 1887 General Allotment Act, which established Indian identification according to the "blood quantum" or "degree of Indian blood"; the aim here was to transform collective land holdings into individual private property. The Indian Citizenship Act of 1924 endowed Indians or groups of Indians with American identity (as U.S. citizens) regardless of their wishes. The 1934 Indian Reorganization Act overrode existing Indian governing councils in favor of more pliable councils modelled on corporate boards. The Indian Reorganization Act of 1972 appeared to abandon the "blood quantum" standard of Indian identity in favor of "self-identification," only to be evaded by the Reagan Administration's attempt to "enforce degree-of-blood requirements for federal services, such as those of the Indian Health Service." Most recently, the Indian Arts and Crafts Law (1990) restricted "definition of Indian artists to those possessing a federally issued 'Certificate of Degree of Indian Blood'" (pp. 130–31). At no point can Indian identity be distinguished from struggles over Indians' right to collective self-governance.

tence (see *PC,* pp. 320–25, 333–35). Clifford insists that identity is social and historical, discontinuous and changing; he holds that a proper historical awareness of cultural practices around Mashpee would show that "often the 'tribe' in Mashpee was simply people deciding things by consensus, in kitchens or at larger ad hoc gatherings where no records were kept. . . . The 'tribe' in Mashpee was simply shared Indian kinship, place, history, and a long struggle for integrity without isolation" (*PC,* p. 310). The court eclipses Mashpee history with Mashpee culture and in so doing successfully ignores Mashpee sovereignty while *also* evading the federal role in regulating it for two hundred years. The problem of cultural identity comes up in the context of domination. The Mashpee are trying to *avoid* American-style cultural identity: "Identity as an American meant giving up a strong claim to tribal political integrity in favor of ethnic status within a national whole. Life as an American meant death as an Indian" (*PC,* p. 341).[13] Tribal status would allow the Mashpee to avoid pregiven, ethnic identity in favor of the ongoing group agency made possible by national sovereignty (see *PC,* p. 280).

2. *Cultural identity is constituted by the possession or repossession of cultural practices.* Michaels writes that Clifford's "appeal to memory makes it clear that the resumption of a discontinued Indian practice cannot in itself count as a marker of Indian identity; going to powwows, taking up drumming, and starting to wear 'regalia' wouldn't turn a New York Jew into a Mashpee Indian" (p. 57 n. 36). "If, then," he concludes, "the criteria of Mashpee identity are drumming, dressing in 'regalia,' and so on, it should be the case that anyone who meets these criteria counts as a Mashpee" (p. 58 n. 36). In fact, however, drumming and dressing are not the criteria of Mashpee identity, which is only as mysterious as there being more to an engineer than wearing a pocket protector.

Michaels offers no evidence that Clifford reduces group identity to the pursuit of stereotypical activities. Mashpee cultural practices include whatever engages the ordinary and extraordinary historical convergences of coercive force and attempted self-direction. What makes the Mashpee different are the different details of these convergences: the Mashpee are subject to the racial, cultural, political, and economic forms of subordination American Indians experience generally, yet they are not governed by the Indian Reorganization Acts of 1934 and 1972 as admin-

13. Clifford is by no means entirely consistent on this and other points. Elsewhere he says, "The individuals of Indian ancestry from Mashpee who filed suit in 1976 were American citizens similar to Irish- or Italian-Americans with strong ethnic attachments." They were taking "advantage of the latest wave of pan-Indian revivalism" (*PC,* p. 301). Such an inconsistency might be explained through the many differences among the Mashpee involved in the suit, as one might expect of the individuals of any group. In any case, the point of reading Clifford, for us, is to continue to explore the complexities of radically discontinuous American sociocultural life by working through his contradictions and ambiguities rather than to use them to deny the major issue he addresses.

istered by the federal Bureau of Indian Affairs; they had controlled local politics in Mashpee until the mid-1960s; they are more assimilated into Euro-American society than many Native groups; and they retain a certain ideological and political solidarity in spite of this relatively greater assimilation. These five of the most obvious and outsider influences on their experience could reasonably be supplemented by dozens of others, and they can only arbitrarily be reduced to the simplistic culturalism of "drumming, dressing in 'regalia,' and so on."

The Mashpee themselves attempt to evade this drumming standard of culture when the court tries to apply it to them.[14] They display no anxiety about the markings of continuous cultural identity. They regard regalia as something you use, that you invoke "as long as needed" and for contingent reasons ("when my hair was long enough"). The meaning of bandannas and drums must be sought in the framework of multiple, varying, and conflicting social determinations.

3. *All forms of cultural identity that "do any cultural work" rest on a personal identity that "runs much deeper than culture"* (pp. 59, 58 n. 36). Having claimed that culture is about identity and that attitudes toward identity can be evaluated by the drumming standard, Michaels says that Clifford grounds cultural identity in an appeal to a continuous, inherent, precultural identity:

> Clifford rejects culture as a mark of identity because culture tolerates no discontinuities. But he himself can tolerate discontinuity only if it is grounded in a continuity that runs much deeper than culture: drumming will make you a Mashpee not because anyone who drums gets to be a Mashpee but because, insofar as your drumming counts as remembering a lost tradition, it shows that you already *are* a Mashpee. [P. 58 n. 36]

Michaels's second and third claims set up this binary choice for a member of a group: either you perform stereotyped activities associated with a group and this makes you a member *or* you are a member ontologically.

14.

Q. (St. Clair): I notice you have a headband and some regalia?
A.: Yes.
Q.: How long have you been wearing such clothing?
A.: Oh, I have been wearing a headband as long as needed, when my hair was long enough.
Q.: How long has that been?
Judge: That which you have on there, is that an Indian headband?
A.: It is a headband.
Judge: It has some resemblance to an ordinary red bandanna?
A.: Right, that's what the material is, yes.
Judge: A bandanna you buy in the store and fold up in that manner?
A.: Yes. ["Chiefy" Mills under cross-examination from James St. Clair, *Mashpee Tribe* v. *New Seabury et al.*, quoted in *PC*, p. 346]

If you are Chicano, this is either because you wear a T-shirt and khakis while driving a lowered Chevy *or* because you think *Chicano* describes your identity at birth. If you are not already doing Chicano things but think you "are" Chicano, then you must be assuming a biological identity with Chicano traditions. Either your connection to the status of Chicano consists of a set of existing behaviors or it is an essentialist and hence racial tie.

Why are these the two choices for the basis of group identity? The sentence that Michaels invokes in support of this reading says, "But is any part of a tradition 'lost' if it can be remembered, even generations later, caught up in a present dynamism and made to symbolize a possible future?" (*PC,* pp. 341–42). Clifford has just rejected the "either-or" choice posed by the face-off between plaintiffs and defendants—either continuous or wholesale assimilation. Both narratives are wrong for him, and "identity," both "real yet essentially contested," re-created yet potentially authentic, is precisely that which the "either-or" logic of the court is unable to capture (*PC,* pp. 341, 340). Identity involves culture and "tribal institutions," the history of events, conflicts, defeats, and resistances that are put together, dismantled, and reassembled by the ongoing process of collaborative narrativization. The tradition once lost and now and again, here and there remembered is *knowledge of history* rather than interior identity, and it is used in the present, continually changing situation and redefined by the living in relation to a "possible future."[15] Clifford sees "Identity in Mashpee" as "relational and political" and, rather than posit its continuity, argues that it can be discontinuous with its previous forms and *unbaffled by this changeability.* In fact, he suggests that identity is always discontinuous since change constitutes the social and political dimension of collective life. Remembering consists of all of the stories, social relations, personal ties, "changing federal and state policies and the surrounding ideological climate" that make up what you could and could not do, what you have and have not done, and what you can and cannot

15. Michaels offers similar arguments for racial essentialism at various points in the essays. His other contemporary example concerns Arthur Schlesinger, Jr., and this statement in particular: "We don't have to believe that our values are absolutely better than the next fellow's or the next country's, but we have no doubt that they are better *for us,* reared as we are—and are worth living by and worth dying for" (quoted p. 60). Michaels notes that if these values "are not just better but are just better 'for us,' then our reason for holding them can only be that they are ours." Schlesinger's use of the word *ours,* Michaels argues, rests on "something stronger than the claim that . . . they are the beliefs we actually hold"; to be "ours," these beliefs must be connected to an "essentialist assertion of identity," of "who we are" (p. 60). But it may be that Schlesinger means to say that our beliefs are better for us for a whole host of historical and cultural reasons. For example, we may think they are better for us because we read our sociocultural experience as saying that we are better off because of our beliefs, or because we have read a lot of books like Schlesinger's. Again, this separation of question of identity from questions about history and society has more to do with individualism than with antiessentialism.

do now. Remembering, in Clifford's account, describes past social possibilities and is often invoked to imagine a different future through the collaborative destruction and invention of cultural processes. Mashpee memory is not deeper than culture but is culture, the historical narrative of a society.[16]

4. *The noncultural continuity that Clifford purportedly invokes is racial identity.* Having affirmed that Clifford's notion of cultural identity is rooted in something "beyond" culture, Michaels's next sentence defines what that beyond must be. Clifford winds up believing, as Michaels sees it, that since "your drumming counts as remembering a lost tradition, it shows that you already *are* a Mashpee"; thus "his rejection of cultural identity gets him no further away from racial identity than does the more usual insistence on cultural identity." This is true but only because, for Michaels, no amount of historical and social relations gets any discussion of culture away from racial identity. He offers no evidence to support his claim, and since everything Clifford says, inconsistencies and all, does in fact lead away from both racial and narrowly cultural identity toward some conjuncture like historical socioculture, Michaels backs away: "The point here is not that Clifford is secretly depending on some notion of racial identity" (p. 58 n. 36). This too is true: Michaels's point is less to detect proof of biological racial meaning than to discredit claims that a differential identity is also historical and political. Once again, Mashpee

16. Reflecting an indifference to this kind of depth, Mashpee witnesses, when asked in court about the source of their Mashpee identity, say they are Mashpee because other people have always thought they were, because they think they are, because they say they are.

> Q.: How do you know you're an Indian?
> A.: My mother told me. [quoted in *PC*, p. 301]
>
> Q.: How do you know your ancestors?
> A.: My mother, grandparents, word of mouth. [quoted in *PC*, p. 287]

The witness knows she is an Indian because she trusts her mother. The verification of identity is an interpretive decision made within a group. Identity emerges from the history of stories that members of a group tell to each other. The witness knows her ancestors not because they are already "hers" or are culturally "her" but because of stories told about them. Some come from family, some come from no specific source, and none lay claim to legal or ontological authority. None establish an identity of the kind a contractual, property-owning society would recognize.

> Q.: How was your youth different from that of any small-town youth?
> A.: We were different. We knew we were different. We were told we were different. [quoted in *PC*, p. 281]

The identity is in the experiencing and the hearing, the accepting and the telling. Mashpee on the stand, and against their best interests, do not claim to be Mashpee prior to the stories told to them. They reverse Michaels's dictum: "who we are" turns out to come from "what we do," most of us together, and in conjunction with what has been done to us.

identity in Clifford's texts leads a very different life, a life involving the dynamic of the Mashpee's relations to those that had long lived among them without racial or ethnic connection.[17]

Michaels's assimilation of cultural identity to racial essentialism lends an air of credibility to an analysis that would otherwise be more readily seen to reflect the perspective of historically white interests. This perspective denies its own historical presence in the creation of cultural relations and diverts attention from an ongoing struggle for power under conditions of inequality. It further avoids a reckoning with the fact that the moments of nearest approach between culture and race are, in U.S. history, those most likely to be utterly inseparable from power struggles. The Mashpee trial, where the state demands identification, is an example of the inappropriateness of this separation.

But we do not regard Michaels's reading as an individual mistake. When an analyst of his acuity draws such conclusions, some larger forces are affecting the instruments. We think these forces, to repeat, consist of post–civil rights race moderation, which makes certain arguments seem implausible and impractical. It is to these forces, their content and aims, that we now turn.

17.

Q.: And now, before you went away to school—Incidentally, is that a private institution, if you know?
A.: Private?
Q.: Is it owned and operated by the state or federal government or is it owned and operated on a private basis, if you know?
A.: Private.
Q.: Do you know or are you guessing?
A.: I am not sure what they call themselves, Daughters of American Revolution and some Christian organizations involved in it.
Q.: Let's see, the Daughters of the American Revolution is not an organization that you would associate with Indians, is it?
A.: In our history, yes.
Q.: Pardon?
A.: I said in our history, yes. Wampanoag history—Mashpee Wampanoag history.
Q.: Daughters of the American Revolution, in your understanding of what you say is your history, have an Indian origin?
A.: It is not our history, but we were involved with that revolution and 149 of our Mashpee people died in that fighting for your independence.
Q.: Fighting for what?
A.: Independence.
Q.: But is it your understanding that the Daughters of the American Revolution have an Indian origin or are in some way related to persons of Indian descent?
A.: They embrace me as a member.
Q.: Pardon?
A.: I said the women that I met that were involved with the Daughters of American Revolution felt a kinship with me because of the Mashpee Wampanoags that had died in the war. [Ramona Peters under cross-examination from St. Clair, quoted in *PC,* pp. 316–17]

3. Postpluralism and the New Supremacism

> The question of my "identity" often comes up. I think I must be a mixed-blood. I claim to be male, although only one of my parents was male.
>
> —JIMMIE DURHAM, a Cherokee, quoted in *The State of Native America*

Race moderation remains largely in the hands of cultural pluralism. Though pluralism takes a variety of forms, a diffusely evangelical type has recently become influential through high-profile works like Arthur Schlesinger, Jr.'s, *The Disuniting of America*. Michaels explicitly rejects Schlesinger's pluralism by suggesting that it rests on the same racial essentialism it attacks in Afrocentrism. This distinction between essentialist and antiessentialist views, even assuming its validity here, should not obscure the extent to which Schlesinger and Michaels are pressed in a similar direction by the same general structure of liberal racial thought. Michaels's position repudiates Schlesinger's cultural pluralism while preserving important aspects of its project. We will briefly survey what we regard as the negative aspects of this "beyond race" liberalism and, in closing, suggest some features of a more desirable white racial outlook.

Cultural pluralism may frequently reflect democratic expectations, but it harbors other features that become especially prominent in times of perceived threat. First, it regards race as consciousness rather than as a mode of social power and as *false* consciousness at that. Race refers to *identity* rather than to cultural or social relations, and this view, which prevails in most officially color-blind institutions, builds on the longstanding ethnicity paradigm which, since the 1920s, has assumed that "racial and ethnic groups are neither central nor persistent elements of modern societies. . . . Racism and racial oppression are not independent dynamic forces but are ultimately reducible to other causal determinants, usually economic or psychological."[18] Second, cultural pluralism sees racial or cultural differences as properly subordinate to common culture and shared social institutions. Schlesinger, for example, calls for a return to George Washington's ideal of a "'new race'" forming "'*one people*'" in the

18. Robert Blauner, *Racial Oppression in America* (New York, 1972), p. 2. Nathan Glazer and Daniel Patrick Moynihan offered such an influential version of this thesis because they acknowledged the persistence of "the ethnic group" even as they declined to allot race, as distinct from white ethnicity, any reality apart from—and any superior importance to—a whole range of factors like "history, family and feeling, [political] interest, formal organization life" (Nathan Glazer and Daniel Patrick Moynihan, *Beyond the Melting Pot: The Negroes, Puerto Ricans, Jews, Italians, and Irish of New York City* [Cambridge, Mass., 1963], p. 19).

New World.[19] Third, this cultural pluralism does not mean cultural equality but a putatively nonracial Western supremacism. As Schlesinger puts it, "Whatever the particular crimes of Europe, that continent is also the source—the *unique* source—of those liberating ideas of individual liberty, political democracy, the rule of law. . . . There is surely no reason for Western civilization to have guilt trips laid on it by champions of cultures based on despotism, superstition, tribalism, and fanaticism" (*DA*, pp. 127–28). Schlesinger's pluralist sense that there are indeed other systems of values that might be (or might seem to be) better for other people easily coexists with his general belief that ours really is better. The payoff of this strain of cultural pluralism is that it combines tolerance and hierarchy, difference and inferiority, into pluralist, democratic supremacism.

These features of pluralism form the influential background for Michaels's efforts to reject pluralism, whose gravitational field is difficult to escape. For our present purposes we will call this postpluralism, without meaning by this term to designate various nonpluralisms in existence and under development. We mean instead a position that opposes pluralism's use of identities, particularly group identity, while retaining other features of a pluralist project.

On the first issue, Michaels separates race from its social dynamics by defining it as a concept of biological identity; he pulls the ostensibly more social category of culture into the same biologistic system. Rather than traditional pluralism's empirical or sociological arguments against the significance of race, Michaels sidesteps the social environments in which racism and race get deployed. His position excludes social relations not only from the analysis of racialized culture but also from any methodological discussion of the legitimacy of this exclusion. One need not make a historical or sociological case for the exclusion of history and society in this or that particular cultural system, a process that of course involves precisely those elements. One can offer instead reasons of philosophy, which perform clean separations of domains. The distinction between essentialist and antiessentialist uses of identity is itself a *historical* question, but Michaels uses the distinction to render history and politics irrelevant to the evaluation of cultural identity.

In this way, a controversial subject like race can be protected from the realm of politics and power without this protection being itself a political issue. The "truth" of race will then not vary depending on where the analyst stands in a network of racializing systems. With conventional cultural pluralism, these different political positions and interests are

19. Quoted in Arthur M. Schlesinger, Jr., *The Disuniting of America* (New York, 1992), pp. 24–25; hereafter abbreviated *DA*. Horace Kallen's pluralism offered a far more tolerant celebration of the commerce in difference, but it too looks toward "unity . . . [as] a future formation we desirefully steer our present imaginations toward" (Horace Kallen, *Cultural Pluralism and the American Idea: An Essay in Social Philosophy* [Philadelphia, 1956], pp. 47–48).

bound up with any discussion about overcoming them. A cultural pluralist usually starts by conceding that racial reality looks different to Asian Americans and Chicanos and must then make some kind of ethical, historical, or social case for conceiving of race as an identity that should be set aside. Within the domain of philosophy, the question of power and society need not even arise.

Equally important, ahistorical antiessentialism allows the analyst to disavow his or her own social position. The analyst exists in a field of reason rather than a discontinuous terrain of social antagonisms. It is not surprising, then, that philosophy would come to the fore in the analysis of race issues at a time when pluralism itself is under more scrutiny as the racial ideology of a minority white culture than at any time since the zenith of black nationalism twenty years ago. For unlike pluralism, which has a racial history into which it drags its adherents, philosophy is, to itself, never white.

Second, while Schlesinger's nationalist "'American Creed'" (*DA*, p. 27) visibly demands compliance with some substantive principles, the postpluralist produces a common culture through constitutive rules.[20] While pluralists like Schlesinger write as though there is a common culture—whose core beliefs form a creed by which any group can be judged according to its adherence or rejection of these beliefs—the postpluralist establishes boundaries between legitimate and illegitimate uses of social identity. The mode here is not to suggest that a person or group's practices and beliefs place them on the margins of Western values but that a person's individual or group identity corrupts reason. The postpluralist need not contest the Afrocentric's interpretation of the race record of U.S. democracy but only say that the Afrocentric's constitutive sense of racial difference prevents his or her views from counting as genuine knowledge. "Common culture" is translated into the zone of rational discourse or public reason; it excludes certain factors not because they differ from white or Western beliefs but because their belief in difference violates a criterion of reason.

In Michaels's essay, that criterion is antiessentialism. While pluralists might have judged a group according to its espousal of a unifying value like representative democracy, Michaels writes as though a group can be judged by its relation to an antiessentialism that remains unaffected by cultural, ideological, or historical differences. Individuals and groups as otherwise dissimilar as Oliver La Farge, James Clifford, Melville Herskovits, the Mashpee, and a scrivener for the Klan can be tested for essentialism and assimilated via the presence of that quality. If they are found to be essentialist, they can be excluded not from Americanness but from

20. Michael Hardt has described how contemporary liberalism, as represented by John Rawls, defines the boundaries of political communities by constituting the rules of public rationality in "Les Raisonnables et les différents: Le Libéralisme politique de Rawls," *Futur antérieur* (forthcoming 1994).

the sphere of reason itself. Those who consider racial or cultural identity an asset, a liability, a source of social knowledge, or any combination of these, can, under postpluralism, be shown *not* violating nationalistic ideals like a unified "'new race'" but violating contemporary standards of valid reasoning. Racialized experience becomes irrelevant to and indeed obstructive of authentic knowledge, knowledge of the kind that can legitimately be applied to social and political disputes. A common culture stripped down to what are presented as the minimum requirements of knowledge avoids Schlesinger's philistine assimilationism while excluding the identity talk that allows what opposes assimilation to enter into negotiation.

But is the postpluralist also a supremacist? Although reason seems to be an equal opportunity operation, and though it avoids oafish chauvinism and unprofessional derogations of others' beliefs, the kind of race philosophy we have been discussing assumes the power of epistemology to make the rules for political or ethnographic arguments. This superiority of the epistemological is not directly argued in Michaels's text, but it presumes its ability to settle the rules of discourse and judgment. Such a tacit supremacism easily coexists with political liberalism, flexibility, inclusion, and generosity; it consists of the quiet expectation that its procedures and standards will be taken as a dispute's rules of arbitration—that its concerns count the most.[21] This supremacism need never appear as an obviously rude insistence. When distinctively white philosophy criticizes someone for essentialism, it can work simply by taking for granted that people will care; it can proceed by assuming that the confusing intricacies of historical cases will have less weight. It knows that a Mashpee's indefiniteness about the status of a bandanna will not seem brilliant, not compared to, say, the claim that a position secretly rests on its apparent opposite. The taste culture addressed by such assumptions is also white in a sociocultural sense, and postpluralism can assume that this fact about its audience's group identity will seem less important within this group than the exposure of logical inconsistency. Schlesinger, still an old-fashioned pluralist, thinks he must openly state his belief that the West is the best and then marshall evidence for this belief. The postpluralist works with more pervasive and invisible presumptions that are not explicitly defended: the difference between essentialism and antiessentialism is independent of historical context; analysis of identity as a logic "knows" more than remembering a grievance, and so on. Postpluralist supremacism appears delicately, coasting on the historical prestige, the

21. Cheryl I. Harris importantly describes socially defined "whiteness" as the power to make rules *and* as the "settled expectation" that whites will face no "undue" obstacles. Of particular importance here is her claim that "whiteness as property is also constituted through the reification of expectations in the continued right of white-dominated institutions to control the legal meaning of group identity" (Cheryl I. Harris, "Whiteness as Property," *Harvard Law Review* 106, no. 8 [1993]: 1761).

institutional investments, and the economic and social superiority of the generally white powers with which it shares its modes. Lately, color blindness has been on the economic rise, and epistemology's assumption of the irrelevance of its social connections to the interests and history of this ideology, its irrelevance in creating the superiority of epistemological over political or identity claims, is itself a symptom of its assumed supremacy.

The pluralist's carefully relativized claims to his or her culture's superiority give way to the postpluralist's (perfectly liberal) discrediting of the modes by which a group's superiority might be overcome. Regardless of the postpluralist use of antiessentialism, many racialized groups know that their identity is bound up with their subordination and their pursuit of sovereignty; the Mashpee trial exemplifies this common phenomenon. Supremacism is maintained not by affirming the supremacy of one's own values but by defining contestations of the existing rules as irrational.

Postpluralism defines the most basic racism as the appeal to race. It says, in effect, that if you believe in a society beyond racism (meaning, it believes, beyond race), you must expose cultural difference as racialist pathos. This rejection would not appear to reflect your racialized political agenda but simply your enlightened, postessentialist philosophy. Postpluralism, shorn of pluralism's more obvious supremacist outbursts, would take over its role as racial management. It would never need to say, It doesn't matter who you are, I don't care who you are, or I don't like who you are. It would only ask, whenever racial hierarchy comes up, "But why does it matter who we are?" (p. 59). Around race, the artificial separation of cultural processes from politics enables such containment, intended or not.

We have been trying to make more explicit the reasons why evangelical pluralism *and* postpluralism can be regarded as liberal racism—not because their advocates hold racist attitudes but because they support the dehistoricization, the monopolized rule making, and the subtle supremacism that allow democratic institutions to produce nuanced but still racially discriminatory effects. Indirect, contemporary forms of racial subordination receive (often unintended) support from the opposition to race.

Rather than go down Michaels's particular path of postpluralism, we would suggest taking his important insights into pluralist racism in a different direction. For white Americans, particularly professionals, this starts with avoiding postpluralism's "'bad'. . . utopianism," which "grabs instantly for a future, projecting itself by an act of will or imagination beyond the compromised political structures of the present."[22] It involves

22. Terry Eagleton, "Nationalism: Irony and Commitment," in *Nationalism, Colonialism, and Literature,* ed. Eagleton, Fredric Jameson, and Edward Said (Minneapolis, 1990), p. 25.

reconceiving postpluralism through the rejection of the three prominent features we have discussed.

First, this redefined white nonpluralism must refuse to associate the advent of reason with the white version of cultural separatism—the belief that culture can be cleansed of political history. It is especially important to evade the pull of cultural separatism around the study of race by acknowledging that the appeal to race cannot be separated from the endurance of racism. If we do not grant the presence of conflict and contestation, of politics and history, of context and determinations in the study of culture, we are not avoiding politicization, but we are avoiding cultural knowledge itself. Second, the common culture formed by portable antiessentialism should be replaced with negotiation across perceived boundaries. This will require granting the existence of such boundaries when one party declares them and avoiding the impulse to simply assert a principle of reason to rule all domains in the same way. It will involve white Americans in repudiating the protective and legislative power of both the "'American Creed'" *and* its color-blind philosophies. Finally, it means that white Americans must reject the forms of pluralism discussed here as liberal racism—as cultural racism, in Michaels's useful concept—not because cultural pluralism rests on an essentialist notion of racial identity, Michaels's problematic, but because it is white/West supremacist and remains so in ever more objectivist and managerially abstract guises. A better future for race relations will require supporting ongoing race consciousness as the basis of negotiated group identities, intergroup equality, separatism, and autonomy. The democratic solution entails more careful and complex race consciousness rather than less. And this will require cultural studies to respond more fully to its history of using pluralism as racial management.

Critical Response

II

The No-Drop Rule

Walter Benn Michaels

In the final section of my essay "Race into Culture: A Critical Genealogy of Cultural Identity" (pp. 32–62), I criticize the idea of antiessentialist accounts of identity, which is to say that I criticize in particular the idea of cultural identity as a replacement for racial identity. My central point is that for the idea of cultural identity to do any work beyond describing the beliefs people actually hold and the things they actually do, it must resort to some version of the essentialism it begins by repudiating. Thus, for example, the idea that people can lose their culture depends upon there being a connection between people and their culture that runs deeper than their actual beliefs and practices, which is why, when they stop doing one thing and start doing another, they can be described as having lost rather than changed their culture. This commitment to the idea that certain beliefs and practices constitute your real culture, whether or not you actually believe or practice them, marks the invention of culture as a project (you can now *recover* your culture, you can *struggle to preserve* your culture, you can *betray* your culture, and so on), and it marks also the return to the essentialism that antiessentialists mean to oppose. For insofar as your culture no longer consists in the things you actually do and believe, it requires some link between you and your culture that transcends practice. That link, I argue, has, in the United States, characteristically been provided by race. Thus, I conclude, cultural identity is actually a form of racial identity.

This article originally appeared in *Critical Inquiry* 20 (Summer 1994).

Daniel Boyarin and Jonathan Boyarin in this essay "Diaspora: Generation and the Ground of Jewish Identity" (pp. 305–37) and Avery Gordon and Christopher Newfield in their essay "White Philosophy" (pp. 380–400), criticize this argument. They offer counterexamples to my notion that in order to make possible the kinds of projects mentioned above (preserving your culture, and so on) identity claims must be essentialist, and they deny that the only coherent alternative to essentialism is pure description. They also offer, respectively, a socioreligious reading of my argument (the Boyarins identify it as a form of the "radical individualism" that can be described as a "characteristically Protestant theme" [p. 316])[1] and a sociopolitical reading of it (according to Gordon and Newfield, my argument is an example of "liberal racism" in its "postpluralist" phase [pp. 380, 396]).[2] Finally, Gordon and Newfield identify my argument with

1. Gordon and Newfield repeat this criticism and link it to my supposed refusal to acknowledge that "what we do or who we are is always imposed and chosen within determinate social relations" (p. 386 n. 9). But my argument that only what people actually do and believe determines their identity is indifferent to the question of how many people share certain beliefs or practices and to the question of how they acquired those beliefs and practices. My point is only that their cultural identity cannot be determined by anything other than those beliefs and practices, however widely they are shared and however they were acquired.

2. Their idea here is that the question "'But why does it matter who we are?'" is a Rodney King-style plea for all of us to just "get along," to "ignore the conflicts and coercions, the innumerable interdependent historical circumstances that make us who we are" (p. 385). A critique of Gordon and Newfield's piety about "history" (it "make[s] us who we are") is beyond the scope of the current essay, but the idea that criticizing antiessentialist racism is a way of ignoring conflict and coercion merits some notice. How, exactly, does the refusal to deploy cultural identity as an explanation of the difference between someone living on welfare and, say, a middle-class English professor count as a way of *ignoring* conflict? The truth is just the opposite; it is the redescription of economic differences as racial that makes them tolerable. The current university commitment to curing middle-class white students of racial prejudice is exemplary in this regard since as long as we preach respect for the culture of others as the cardinal virtue, we will be able to regard economic inequality with our customary equanimity. Which is only to say that it's the pluralist discourse of race, not its critique, that makes getting along the great desideratum. (And which is also why Gordon and Newfield's complaint about pluralism—that it's a "milder, more sophisticated" form of "white supremacism" [p. 385]—is just that it isn't pluralist enough.)

Walter Benn Michaels is professor of English and the humanities at The Johns Hopkins University. He is author of *The Gold Standard and the Logic of Naturalism* (1987) and *Our America: Nativism, Modernism, and Pluralism* (1995). His previous contributions to *Critical Inquiry* include "Against Theory" and "Against Theory 2," both written in collaboration with Steven Knapp.

a form of thinking that they call "white philosophy" and that they associate (pejoratively) with "reason" and "logic." This is what they call "reproducing the existence of a 'color line'" (p. 387)—although they think that I'm the one who has done the reproducing. In any event, what their responses make clear is that the commitment to antiessentialist identitarianism is undiminished and that the question of whether and where to draw the color line remains crucial.

The Boyarins believe that Jewish identity constitutes a counterexample to my argument, and they instance male Jewish circumcision as "a particularly sharp disruption" of my effort to define identity in terms of "'one's actual practices and experiences,'" remarking that the fact of being circumcised "can reassert itself, and often enough does, as a demand (almost a compulsion) to reconnect, relearn, reabsorb, and reinvent the doing of Jewish things" (p. 317). But, setting aside the bizarre use of "re" (if, because you've been circumcised, you go to Hebrew school and learn "Jewish things," in what sense are you *re*learning them?) and setting aside also the even more bizarre idea that it's *circumcision* that compels you toward "Jewish things" (think of the millions of circumcised men not so compelled, that is, not Jewish), what's truly remarkable here is the idea that being circumcised should be presented as the mark of identity that trancends "'one's actual practices and experiences.'" Indeed, the Boyarins themselves appear to realize that circumcision obviously doesn't do this; they describe it as "a mark that transcends one's actual practices and (at least remembered) experiences" (p. 317). But while I do argue (in "Race into Culture" and elsewhere) that you can't remember or forget experiences you didn't have, I don't, of course, argue that you can't remember or forget experiences you *did* have. Indeed, insofar as Jewish identity is crucially dependent upon circumcision, it is crucially dependent precisely upon one's actual experience.

This is why the Boyarins' suggestion that it is "not quite as obvious" as I claim that "a New York Jew cannot become a Mashpee Indian" and their insistence that "a Mashpee Indian can become a Jew" makes my point rather than theirs (p. 317). The Mashpee Indian who became a Jew would do so by altering his or her actual practices and experiences, by getting circumcised, by observing the Jewish holidays, by learning (not relearning or remembering) "Jewish things." His or her Jewish identity would depend *entirely* on his or her actual practices and beliefs, and the minute the Mashpee stopped practicing and believing Jewish things he or she would cease to be a Jew. But insofar as being a Mashpee is different, under U.S. law, from being a Jew, it's because being a Mashpee does *not* depend simply on believing and doing Mashpee things. Tribal status cannot, in other words, be earned by conversion, and in describing the convert as "the ideal type of the Jew" the Boyarins commit themselves to a model of identity that reiterates rather than refutes the primacy of actural practices and experiences (p. 317).[3] Indeed, insofar as conversion is equivalent to assimilation (they both involve exchanging one set of beliefs and practices for another), the Boyarins' hymn to the former simply repeats my paean to the latter.[4]

For Gordon and Newfield, it is not the Jew but the Mashpee Indians, as discussed by James Clifford, who provide a counterexample to my analysis. In a footnote, I criticized Clifford's claim to be offering an ac-

3. My point here is not, however, that the Boyarins simply give the same account of identity that I do and just fail to realize it. For their discussion of cultural and linguistic transmission does suggest the possibility in their view of a certain discrepancy between at least the language children actually speak and the language that will count as theirs. "What about a thirteen-year-old child whom we have allowed until now to concentrate on learning the language/culture of the dominant group?" they ask. "Is it racist to send him or her to a school to learn 'our' language?" (p. 316). Obviously it isn't wrong to want one's child to learn a new language, but, of course, teaching a child a new language is not the issue. The issue is whether "our" language should count as the child's, whether a culture in which the child has not (according to the terms of the example) been instructed should count as his or hers. If my parents can speak Hebrew as well as English, but I am raised (until thirteen) speaking only English, in what sense is the Hebrew language mine? It will, of course, *become* mine if I learn it, but to say that the motive for learning a language is to make the language mine is obviously different from saying that the motive for learning it is that it already is mine.

The point of my criticism of cultural identity was that the concept of culture could not coherently provide us with such motives, could not, that is, provide a link that would enable us to describe languages we don't speak as in some sense ours. If I grow up speaking Hebrew and always regard it as my native language and my children grow up speaking English and always regard it as their native language, they will no more have lost their cultural identity than I will have lost mine; our identities will just be different. Indeed, if I myself eventually stop speaking Hebrew altogether and speak only English, I will still not have lost my cultural identity, for why should what I used to do (speak Hebrew) determine my identity in a way that what I now do (speak English) does not? The point here is not that nothing has been lost or even that nothing of value has been lost; my ability to speak Hebrew has been lost, and insofar as that ability was valuable, I have lost something of value. But I have not lost my culture; I have not lost my identity. Indeed, if everyone who spoke Hebrew stopped doing so and everyone who practiced "Jewish things" also stopped doing so, *no one* would lose his or her cultural identity. Cultural identity can't be lost.

4. This bears also on their reminder—with respect to my criticism of "compulsory assimilation"—that "power operates in many ways other than the exercise of actual compulsion" (p. 317). Insofar as this is true, it is true for conversion as well, but I leave it to others to decide when conviction becomes compulsion and note here only that "the ideal type of the Jew" has presumably been convinced rather than compelled and thus that, at least according to the Boyarins, the difference between the two survives. It may be worth noting, however, that if we were to accept the idea that *all* cultural practices were the results of something like compulsion, then the projects of cultural survival defended by the Boyarins and Gordon and Newfield would become utterly incomprehensible. These projects depend upon the idea that some beliefs and practices are linked to our identity in such a way as to make them ours even if we don't believe and practice them. But if *all* our beliefs and practices are the products of compulsion, why should some seem more ours than others? Why wouldn't the compulsory replacement of one set by another simply count as the replacement of an old tyranny by a new tyranny?

count of Mashpee identity that did not rely on what he calls the "organicist" criterion of cultural "continuity." Pointing out that participation in "traditional" Mashpee practices had been "intermittent," Clifford denied that Mashpee culture had, in the usual sense, "survived" but insisted that, nevertheless, Mashpee identity had not been "lost," since "any part of a tradition" that can be "remembered, even generations later," cannot be understood as "lost."[5] What's wrong with this account, I argued, is that in recasting the historical past as the remembered past and so redescribing the person who does Mashpee things for the first time (the Boyarins' convert) as a person who remembers the Mashpee things he used to do, it restores the "continuity" Clifford claims to repudiate and restores it at a level deeper than culture. For the invocation of memory makes the person who now does Mashpee things, "even generations later," the same as the person who used to do them, generations before. According to Gordon and Newfield, however, "Mashpee memory" (as Clifford describes it) "is not deeper than culture but is culture, the historical narrative of a society" (p. 393). My effort to link Clifford's account of Mashpee identity to what Gordon and Newfield call "interior identity" rather than "*knowledge of history*" is rejected by them with the assertion that the Mashpee are "indifferen[t] to this kind of depth" (pp. 392, 393 n. 16). When "asked in court about the source of their Mashpee identity," Gordon and Newfield write, the Mashpee "say they are Mashpee because other people have always thought they were, because they think they are, because they say they are." When asked, "How do you know you're an Indian?" the Mashpee makes no appeal to "interior identity" (which is to say, to the essentialist categories I describe); instead she replies, "My mother told me" (p. 393 n. 16).

But why should we understand this question—"How do you know you're an Indian?"—as a question about the "source" of Indian identity? For, after all, the epistemological question of how you know you're a Mashpee is not the same as the ontological question of what it takes to make you a Mashpee, which is only to say that there's a difference between the source of your identity and the source of your knowledge of your identity.[6] And, although Gordon and Newfield may be confused on

5. James Clifford, *The Predicament of Culture: Twentieth-Century Ethnography, Literature, and Art* (Cambridge, Mass., 1986), pp. 341, 342; hereafter abbreviated *PC*.

6. It's interesting that Gordon and Newfield continually double their cultural geneticism with an epistemological geneticism, insisting that what they call "reasons of philosophy" be subordinated to the "interests" those reasons are judged to "reflect," and suggesting that my reasons in particular "reflect the perspective of historically [a nice touch] white interests" (p. 394). If there were any merit to this geneticism, it would, in my view, work against the defense of racial identity since racial identity was, in the U.S., invented by whites and enforced upon blacks. But, of course, there isn't any merit to it. The commitment to disinterestedness—which is to say, the commitment to the idea that the validity of our beliefs depends upon the conditions in which we come to hold them—is simply reproduced here as the commitment to interest—which is to say that Gordon and Newfield have missed the point of

this point, the Mashpee clearly aren't: when asked the ontological question, "What does it take to be a member of the Mashpee tribe?" their medicine man replies, "Tracing ancestry back to your great-grandfather or great-grandmother" (*PC,* p. 292). You may *know* you're a Mashpee because your mother tells you you are, but you *are* a Mashpee because you have Mashpee ancestors. So if converted Jews cannot exemplify an antiessentialism that goes beyond the description of actual beliefs and practices because their identity as Jews is *entirely determined* by their actual beliefs and practices, then the Mashpee cannot exemplify an antiessentialism that goes beyond the description of actual beliefs and practices because there is *nothing antiessentialist* about the way they determine their identity. My original point in discussing Clifford was to show that his account of a Mashpee identity that stayed the same despite numerous changes in Mashpee beliefs and practices could only be defended by the appeal to what another interested anthropologist called "a traceable heritage to aboriginal ancestors" (*PC,* p. 321). And while almost everyone involved in the trial agreed that insistence on "'some fairly high degree of blood quantum'" (*PC,* p. 326) would be unfair, the history of race in the United States has conclusively proven that—for the purposes of racial classification—only one drop is needed.

Gordon and Newfield acknowledge that there are some "inconsistencies" in Clifford's discussion of Mashpee identity, but they insist nevertheless that everything he says "does in fact lead away from both racial and narrowly cultural identity toward some conjuncture like historical socioculture" (p. 393). And it is, of course, perfectly true that everything Clifford says is *meant* to lead away from race and toward "some conjuncture like historical socioculture," which seems to be enough for Gordon and Newfield. Making good on their suggestion that, with respect to identity, "remembering a grievance" counts more than exposing a "logical inconsistency" (p. 398), they reject the idea that people could be mistaken about the direction of their own thought; indeed, they seem unhappy with the idea of mistakes altogether, associating my claim that the defenders of antiessentialist accounts of racial identity are mistaken about their antiessentialism with "white philosophy"'s valorization of "contemporary standards of valid reasoning" (p. 398) and with "liberal racism"'s interest in "conceptual errors" (p. 380).[7] Thus the fact that "many commentators

---

the critique of objectivity and that they continue to think that the truth of people's views should be determined by reference to a causal account of how they came to hold them.

7. Gordon and Newfield assert that the Mashpee are somehow indifferent to "conceptual errors," but the closest they come to demonstrating this claim is with quotations like the one reproduced above in which a young woman says she knows she's an Indian because her mother told her, and as we've already seen, the only conceptual error here is Gordon and Newfield's. In any event, it's hard to see why the defense of identity claims should involve any less logic than the critique of them, and harder still to accept the kind of primitivism implied by Gordon and Newfield's racialization of "logic."

on identity politics" have repudiated racial essentialism but "have retained the use of *social* identities" is itself a liability for my argument because, presumably, one can say of these commentators what, as it turns out, one cannot say of the Mashpee, that they really have given up on essentialism (p. 387). At least according to Gordon and Newfield, these "scholars of color," if asked what it takes to be a scholar of color, would not reply, "Tracing ancestry back to your great-grandfather or great-grandmother." So what does it take to make a scholar a scholar of color? How does race without biology work in the United States today?

That the commitment to race without biology, to what Michael Omi and Howard Winant call "race as a social concept,"[8] is widespread cannot be questioned. Writers like Omi and Winant are hostile to the explanation of behavior by appeal to a biology of race and criticize more generally efforts to give the concept of race a "scientific meaning" (*RF,* p. 68), but they decline to abandon the concept of race as such. On the contrary, regarding race as "a pre-eminently *social* phenomenon" (*RF,* p. 90), they celebrate what they call "the forging of new collective racial identities during the 1950s and 1960s," arguing that "the racial subjectivity and self-awareness which [were] developed" have taken "permanent hold" in American society (*RF,* p. 91). And this commitment to racial identity without biology certainly does extend beyond the writings of social scientists like Omi and Winant or Gordon and Newfield and clearly has become what Gordon and Newfield say it is, "one of the most important principles by which U.S. social relations are organized" (p. 383). In a widely noticed racial identity case in Louisiana, for example, the Fourth Circuit Court of Appeals, remarking (like Gordon, Newfield, and others) that "the very concept of the racial classification of individuals . . . is scientifically insupportable,"[9] ruled that Susie Phipps, "who had always thought she was white, had lived as white, and had twice married as white,"[10] was not in fact white because her parents, who had provided the racial information on her birth certificate, had thought of themselves and of her as "colored." "Individual racial designations are purely social and cultural perceptions" (*JD,* p. 372), the court said; the relevant question, then, was not whether those perceptions correctly registered some scientific fact (since the court denied there was any relevant scientific fact) but whether they had been "correctly recorded" at the time the birth certificate was issued. Since in the court's judgment they had been, Phipps and her fellow appellants remained "colored."

8. Michael Omi and Howard Winant, *Racial Formation in the United States* (New York, 1986), p. 60; hereafter abbreviated *RF.*

9. *Jane Doe* v. *State of Louisiana, through the Department of Health and Human Resources, Office of Vital Statistics and Registrar of Vital Statistics,* 479 So. 2d 372 (1985); hereafter abbreviated *JD.*

10. F. James Davis, *Who Is Black?* (University Park, Pa., 1991), p. 10; hereafter abbreviated *W.*

Because Phipps was by credible evidence at least one-thirty-second black, commentators like Omi and Winant cite this case as an example of racial biologism and F. James Davis in his important book *Who Is Black?* describes the Phipps case as confirming the legality of the one-drop rule.[11] This rule had, of course, a biological meaning. In older racist texts like Robert Lee Durham's *The Call of the South* (1908), the justification for counting as black anyone with a traceable amount of black blood is the conviction that this trace will at some point manifest itself, as when the savagery of his African grandfather emerges in the quadroon Hayward Graham and he rapes his white wife: "With a shriek of terror she wildly tries to push him from her: but the demon of the blood of Guinea Gumbo is pitiless, and against the fury of it, as of the storm, she fights and cries—in vain."[12] The idea, then, is that black blood makes a difference to the intrinsic identity of the person, and even if this difference is ordinarily invisible (even if the person characteristically looks and acts even more white than Hayward Graham who is "unobtrusively but unmistakably a negro"),[13] at some point his blackness will show itself. The reasoning, in other words, depends on a commitment to the biology of race. But it turns out that the designation of people who neither look nor act black as nonetheless black does not necessarily depend on the idea that their blackness might actually show itself or might even be the sort of thing that could in principle show itself, which is to say that it's a mistake to see that biological account of race confirmed in the Phipps decision. On the contrary, the court, as I have noted, firmly insists that "racial designations are purely social and cultural perceptions." Phipps is "colored" not because of her traceable amount of black blood but because her parents said she was.[14]

The rule the court enforces here is the rule that Gordon and Newfield imagine for the young Mashpee woman, Vicky Costa: "Q.: How do you know you're an Indian? A.: My mother told me" (*PC*, p. 301). "The witness," Gordon and Newfield remark, "knows she is an Indian because

11. Noting that both the Louisiana Supreme Court and the United States Supreme Court refused to review the decision of the court of appeals, Davis argues that "the highest court in the United States saw no reason to disturb the application of the one-drop rule" (*W,* p. 11). Although, as will become clear below, I do not entirely agree with Davis's interpretation of *Jane Doe* v. *State of Louisiana* (which is how the Phipps case was filed), I have learned a great deal from his history of the one-drop rule and from his comparison of racial practices in the United States to racial practices elsewhere.

12. Robert Lee Durham, *The Call of the South* (Boston, 1908), p. 290.

13. Ibid., p. 7.

14. When the Phipps case went to trial, a 1970 statute declaring that anyone with "one thirty-second or less Negro blood" could not be counted as black was still in effect. But by the time the case reached the court of appeal, that statute had been repealed and the court, since it based its own decision on "social and cultural perceptions," declared that it was, in any event, "not relevant." The statute that replaced it, according to Davis, explicitly gives "parents the right to designate the race of newborns" (*W,* p. 10).

she trusts her mother" (p. 393 n. 16). The court requires that Phipps, like Costa, trust her mother. And, in the spirit of Gordon and Newfield, what this produces is not a one-drop rule but a no-drop rule, the legal equivalent of the social scientist's "*social* phenomenon." It solves the problem of the scientific establishment of racial identity by denying that racial identity is anything more than a question of "social perception." But, of course, this solution is accompanied by a problem. If racial identity is no longer understood to have anything to do with "blood," what are we to imagine that Phipps's parents were thinking when they thought of themselves and of her as black? If their criteria for racial identity were the same as the state's criteria, they weren't thinking that she had some proportion of black blood; according to the court, "purely social and cultural perceptions," not blood, determine racial identity. But they could not be thinking of her as someone who was *perceived* by them as being black; that is, they could not think that their perception of her as black was what made her black because to think that would be to beg the question why they perceived her as black in the first place. The perception of blackness, in other words, may be enough to make someone black in the eyes of the state, but it isn't enough to explain what blackness is. (And, of course, her behavior couldn't do this either since, as a newborn, she presumably didn't talk in an imaginably black dialect or exhibit any of the forms of behavior that might conceivably be associated with the cultural behavior of blacks.) What, then, is the perception of blackness a perception of?

The standard interpretation of this case is, as we have seen, that it restored the one-drop rule; since everybody agreed that Phipps did have *some* black ancestry, she counted as black. But, despite this ancestry, if her parents had perceived themselves and her as white, she would—even acknowledging this very small proportion of black blood—have counted as white. Louisiana law, in other words, as articulated by the majority in this decision, insists on the "subjective nature of racial perceptions" and takes no account of the ancestry. Perhaps one could argue that Louisiana doesn't go far enough in discounting ancestry; after all, why should her *parents'* perception of her racial identity be determining? Gordon and Newfield point out that "the Indian Reorganization Act of 1972 appeared to abandon the 'blood quantum' standard of Indian identity in favor of 'self-identification,' only to be evaded by the Reagan Administration's attempt to 'enforce degree-of-blood requirements'" (p. 389 n. 12). Maybe the injustice in the Phipps case is that the wrong social perceptions were enforced; Phipps should be white because even though her parents perceived themselves and her as black, she perceived herself as white. It is, as Omi and Winant say, her "racial self-awareness" that should be respected. But, of course, this doesn't solve the problem posed by the parental perception of her as black; it just relocates it: what's her perception of whiteness a perception of?[15] When Phipps looks back on the little baby that her parents perceived as black, what makes her perceive it as white?

The truth is that Louisiana law, acknowledging no biological basis for the determination of racial identity and therefore refusing to establish a biological standard for the law, has decided instead to establish not biology but people's mistaken accounts of biology as the legal standard. In other words, the fact that Phipps had at least one black ancestor could not make her black under the law, but the fact that her one black ancestor made her parents perceive her as black *did* make her black under the law. The biological determination that the state itself regards as "scientifically unsupportable" nonetheless counts as determining as long as the determination isn't made by the state. Refusing itself to apply the one-drop rule, the state chose instead to enforce Phipps's parents' application of the one-drop rule. What it means, then, to accept the idea of racial identity as a function of "purely social and cultural perceptions" instead of as biology is to accept the idea of racial identity as the codification of people's mistakes *about* biology. In a way, then, Davis is right to assert that some version of the one-drop rule is being enforced under current Louisiana law, but what is being enforced is not the claim that one drop of black blood makes a person black; what's being enforced is the claim that the *perception* that one drop of black blood makes a person black makes a person black. Everything the court says, as Gordon and Newfield might put it, leads away from race and "toward some conjuncture like historical socioculture." And everything in "historical socioculture" leads right back to race.

According to Louisiana law, Phipps was passing, pretending to be white when she was, in fact, black. Both the law and the very idea of passing require that there be some fact of racial identity, a requirement that was easily met as long as there could be some appeal to science but that the repudiation of scientific racism has made more difficult. The requisite fact must now be social or cultural rather than biological. Thus, in a recent and powerfully written essay called "Passing for White, Passing for Black," Adrian Piper denies that there is any "set of shared physical characteristics" that "joins" her "to other blacks" because, she says, "there is none that all blacks share."[16] What makes blacks black is rather "the shared experience of being visually or cognitively *identified* as black by a white racist society, and the punitive and damaging effects of that identification" ("PW," pp. 30–31). This is the Louisiana standard: if you're per-

15. The problem with self-identification from the standpoint of racial essentialism is that you can't trust people to tell the truth; the problem with self-identification from the standpoint of racial *anti*essentialism is that you have no idea what criteria might help you to determine the truth and so no reason to believe that there is any truth.

16. Adrian Piper, "Passing for White, Passing for Black," *Transition,* no. 58 (1992):30; hereafter abbreviated "PW."

ceived as black, you are black. But Piper's account of her own experience makes the incoherence of this standard even more obvious than it is in the Phipps case. For Piper describes herself as so light skinned that she is constantly (both by people whom she identifies as black and by people whom she identifies as white) being treated as if she were white. She is thus made to feel that she is passing for white, and since passing for white seems to her "a really, authentically shameful thing to do" ("PW," p. 10), she is led into strenuous efforts to identify herself as black. (The irony that produces her title is that these efforts lead her to be accused—again by both whites and blacks—of passing for black.) But what consequences must these efforts have for her nonbiological definition of racial identity? The point of that definition is that being black means being identified by a white racist society as black. On what grounds, then, can someone who is *not* identified by that society as black be said to be black?

Piper makes this dilemma even clearer by going on to remark that she has "white friends who fit the prevailing stereotype of a black person" and thus have "experiences" "similar" to the ones that make blacks black ("PW," p. 31). If they really do have such experiences, what can she mean by calling these friends "white"? That they can be white even if they are treated as black; that she can be black even if she is treated as white—these facts are tributes to, not critiques of, racial essentialism. The very idea of passing—whether it takes the form of looking like you belong to a different race or of acting like you belong to a different race—requires an understanding of race as something separate from the way you look and the way you act. If race really were nothing but culture, that is, if race really were nothing but a distinctive array of beliefs and practices, then, of course, there could be no passing, since to believe and practice what the members of any race believed and practiced would, by definition, make you a member of that race. If race really were culture, people could change their racial identity, siblings could belong to different races, people who were as genetically unlike each other as it's possible for two humans to be could nonetheless belong to the same race. None of these things is possible in the U.S. today. And, were they to become possible, we would think not that we had finally succeeded in developing an antiessentialist account of race but that we had given up the idea of race altogether.

On rehearing, the Louisiana court took the opportunity to remind the appellants that we can't afford to give up the idea of race, that the accumulation of "racial data" is "essential" for "planning and monitoring public health programs, affirmative action and other anti-discrimination measures" (*JD,* p. 374). Or, as Gordon and Newfield put it, race "is one of the most important principles by which U.S. social relations are organized" (p. 383). My point in this response has not been simply to argue that these claims are wrong for, at least in one sense, they are obviously right: U.S. social relations have been and continue to be organized in part by race. My point has been to assert that this organization is the consequence of a mistake, and that antiessentialist defenses of race amount to nothing more than new ways of making the mistake. As absurd as the one-drop rule of Jim Crow is, the no-drop rule of antiessentialism is even more absurd. Omi and Winant cite two "temptations" that they believe must be resisted in thinking about race: the first is the temptation "to think of race as an *essence,* as something fixed, concrete and objective"; the second is "to see it as a mere illusion" (*RF,* p. 68).[17] Their point, of course, is that in seeing race as a social construction we can avoid both temptations. But if, as I have argued, to see race as a social construction is inevitably (even if unwillingly and unknowingly) to essentialize it, then race really is either an essence or an illusion. The two "temptations" are the only choices we have.

17. From the standpoint of antiessentialism, in other words, what's wrong with the idea of race is that it's essentially essentialist or, to put the point a little more precisely, what's wrong with it is that there can be no coherent antiessentialist account of race. It may be worth wondering, however, why this should count as a problem. Those who believe that individual racial identity is a biological reality don't need an antiessential account of race; those who don't believe individual racial identity is a biological reality don't need one either, unless, of course, their commitment to the category of race is so complete that they understand themselves to be required to maintain it at all costs. And this does seem to be the point of the whole debate over racial essentialism, the point, that is, of insisting that the problem with the biology of individual racial identity is that it's *essentialist* rather than *false.* Transforming the question of whether or not there is such a thing as individual racial identity into the question of whether or not race is an "essence" and thus deploying race as the grounds of the question rather than as its object, this debate reinvigorates and relegitimates race as a category of analysis. If, then, racial antiessentialism is a mistake, it is, at least, a mistake with a purpose, and if race is, as Gordon and Newfield say, "one of the most important principles by which U.S. social relations are organized," then racial antiessentialism turns out to be one of the ways in which U.S. intellectuals can make their own modest contributions to the maintenance of that most important principle.

Critical Response

III

Fashionable Theory and Fashion-able Women: Returning Fuss's Homospectatorial Look

Molly Anne Rothenberg and Joseph Valente

Politically activist postmodern theory has tended to define its project in aporetic terms. Postmodern forms of feminist, postcolonial, and queer theory have deployed a radical social constructivism in order to challenge existing normative hierarchies by showing their underlying categories of intelligibility to be fundamentally arbitrary, invidious, and unstable. But they do so in the name and in the interest of social collectivities whose integrity and whose standing in the political dialogue depend, at some point, upon the existence of the taxonomy to be discredited. Hence, these theories have waged a contest against the operative structure of group identities on behalf of group identities instituted by and within that structure, thus perpetuating the social grammar they aimed to undo. Recognition of this problem, tacit and expressed, has led to a subtle but significant shift in the basic distinctions with which such postmodern theories conjure toward an even "purer" form of constructivism. Instead of seeking to counter the natural with the social, as the primary formative dimension, they seek to counter all formative causality, natural or social, with figurative activity—the given with the assumed, the constructed with the performed, primacy politics with parody politics, the typologies of identity with the tropologies of identification.

But this paradigm shift has serious problems of its own. Turning as it does upon a cardinal principle of psychoanalysis, *identification,* it cannot but draw upon and recycle the essentialist attitudes and assumptions of

The authors wish to thank Barbara Herrnstein Smith, Jonathan Riley, Geoffrey Harpham, and the participants in the Theory Workshop at the University of Colorado in May 1994 for helpful criticism. We also thank the participants in the Mellon Summer Seminar in Critical Theory at Tulane in 1991 for opportunities to discuss issues relevant to this essay. Responsibility for all views expressed remains ours.

that mode of discourse even as it denies its (af)filiation with them—disavowing psychoanalysis in the psychoanalytic sense. That is to say, in formally freeing postmodern theory of its residual essentialism, this new trend risks consolidating that essentialism in less visible but more substantive terms.

Just how insidious this danger is may be seen in the recent work of Diana Fuss, which senses these problems and yet exemplifies them. In her article "Fashion and the Homospectatorial Look" (pp. 90–114), Fuss makes this instructively contradictory observation: "the restless operations of identification [are] one of the most powerful but least understood mechanisms of cultural self-fashioning" (p. 93). And yet by her own admission Fuss draws for her pictorial exegesis on existing, and so presumably *inadequate,* explanations of the mechanisms of identification, instead of advancing some new and more answerable hypothesis of her own:

> The project of this essay is to begin to decode the complicated operations of identification and desire, of being and having, that are at work in the social production of female spectatorial subjectivity. In an attempt to account psychoanalytically for the enduring fascination that commercial fashion photography holds for its female viewers, I will draw on Freud's theories of primary and secondary identification, Lacan's readings of specularity and subjectivity in relation to the preoedipal mirror stage, and Kristeva's notions of abjection and the "homosexual-maternal facet." [P. 93]

Accordingly, her entire essay can be seen to beg the question upon which it is implicitly founded: How do we know identification is one of the most powerful mechanisms of cultural self-fashioning so long as it remains one of the least understood?

Surely the first step in making the dynamic of identification understood lies precisely in determining whether it possesses any effective force of its own, or whether it operates as a mere extension of preexisting—if historically contingent—social identities and the desires and interests they inscribe or reflect. Fuss underlines the importance of just such a task

---

Molly Anne Rothenberg is associate professor of English at Tulane University and a candidate at the New Orleans Psychoanalytic Institute. Her most recent book is *Rethinking Blake's Textuality* (1993). **Joseph Valente** is assistant professor of English at the University of Illinois, Champaign-Urbana. His most recent book is *James Joyce and the Problem of Justice: Negotiating Sexual and Colonial Difference* (1995). They are coauthoring *Raising the Unreal: A Post-Lacanian Approach to Cultural Analysis* (forthcoming).

in her summary:

> One question I have not addressed is how lesbian viewers might consume these images. What is at issue in this reading [of identification] . . . is not "homosexual" versus "heterosexual" spectatorship but the homosexualization of the viewing position itself as created by the contemporary codes of women's fashion photography. . . . It is the enculturating mechanisms . . . that instantiate and regulate these differences in the first place. [Pp. 113–14]

Her essay, Fuss seems to contend, upholds the relative autonomy of the identification process ("the homosexualization of the viewing position itself") as opposed to its dependence upon pregiven states of being ("'homosexual' versus 'heterosexual' spectatorship"). Yet in pausing at the end of an article on lesbian viewership to explicitly announce that she has sidelined the question of "how lesbian viewers might consume these images," she implicitly acknowledges that the preexisting economies of erotic desire make all the difference, that issues of "'homosexual' versus 'heterosexual' spectatorship" give her project its definition.[1]

According to Fuss, heterosexual women come to desire other women by means of "lesbian-looks coded by fashion photography" wherein the photocultural apparatus itself positions the viewer so as to rearrange her sexual identity:

> The lesbian-looks coded by fashion photography radically de-essentialize conventional notions of the identity of the viewing subject that posit desire in the viewer, prior to any operations of spectatorial identification. We need to theorize "homoerotic looks" not in terms of anything inherent to the viewing subject but in terms of a visual structuring and identification that participates in organizing the sexual identity of *any* social subject. [P. 113]

In her effort to produce a purely constructivist version of subjectivity, to "de-essentialize conventional notions of . . . identity," Fuss implicitly posits the desiring capacity of the viewing subject *at any given point* as a tabula rasa, a site of absolute lability. Granting the photocultural apparatus virtually dictatorial power to order the "sexual identity of *any* social subject," independently of prior sexual identity, Fuss must treat desire as wholly and uniformly prey to any stimuli that this mechanism *intentionalizes* as erotic. This is why, despite Fuss's professed constructivism, she goes on to give a formalist reading of each of her fashion photos, paying little

1. By recommending Danae Clark's essay, "Commodity Lesbianism," *Camera Obscura* 25–26 (Jan.–May 1991): 181–201, Fuss tacitly concedes that her own analysis of the way enculturating mechanisms sexualize "the viewing position itself" does not apply to "*any* social subject," as she claims in her conclusion, but only to already heterosexual(ized) women (p. 113).

consideration to the different subject-positions of her magazine readers. One might say that Fuss's argument marks the point at which a radical constructivism passes into a reductive essentialism.

Because Fuss's argument relies on the absolute plasticity of desire, it also requires her to suppose that desire conforms in every instance and in predictable ways to the photocultural apparatus, which is to say that desire always finds its structure, its identity, reified in that apparatus. "To look straight *at* women," Fuss remarks, "straight women must look *as* lesbians," and she expressly locates the coercive power conveyed by the imperative "must" in various institutions of "visual structuring" (p. 91). Presumptively heterosexual women will desire other women, in this account, because their libido is entirely controlled by the photoideological apparatus, irrespective of prior constraints on their sexual makeup. But in thus positing a univocal female response and similarly univocal cultural codes, Fuss effectively implies the uniformity of women's erotic propensities. The absolute lability of indigenous desire turns out to be the absolute stability of alienated desire.

The specific incoherence of Fuss's model—its interpretation of desire as both a fixed structure and a fugitive impulse—marks its adherence to the performative school of gender studies. The central concept of this school, "primary mimetism," holds that acts of identification precede and constitute the economies of desire that have generally been taken to animate them.[2] In executing this reversal of commonsense logic, primary mimetism can rightfully pretend to be a fully and distinctively postmodern theory of gender development, perhaps the first such theory. But that by itself is no warrant of its viability. For the mimetic account cannot tell us what, in the absence of desire as such, could motivate identification in the first place, nor how identification would determine its object, directionality, or telos, nor even where the object or motive of identification could be located if not in an a priori structure of identity, an inference that ties this most postmodern of gender narratives to its premodern antitypes.

It is precisely owing to these deficiencies in the performative model of subjectivity that Fuss must rely upon the photocultural apparatus to give the act of identification its impetus, its trajectory, and its ends. In

2. The performative school of gender studies has been championed most prominently by Judith Butler; see her *Gender Trouble: Feminism and the Subversion of Identity* (New York, 1990), *Bodies That Matter: On the Discursive Limits of "Sex"* (New York, 1993), and "Imitation and Gender Insubordination," in *Inside/Out: Lesbian Theories, Gay Theories,* ed. Diana Fuss (New York, 1991). Butler herself traces the derivation of her ideas to Mikkel Borch-Jacobsen's revisionary analysis of Freud and to Ruth Leys's adaptations of it; see Mikkel Borch-Jacobsen, *The Freudian Subject,* trans. Catherine Porter (Stanford, Calif., 1988), and Ruth Leys, "The Real Miss Beauchamp: Gender and the Subject of Imitations," in *Feminists Theorize the Political,* ed. Butler and Joan W. Scott (New York, 1992), pp. 167–214. For an extended criticism of this model as it appears in Butler's work, see our chapter, "The Wages of Performativity," *Raising the Unreal: A Post-Lacanian Approach to Cultural Analysis* (forthcoming).

effect, she purports to explain the complicity of magazine consumers in their own manipulation by reducing subjectivity itself to a reflex of a larger social machine:

> This is not to deny that more work needs to be done on how spectators from different gendered, racial, ethnic, economic, national, and historical backgrounds might appropriate or resist these images, but only to insist that if subjects look differently, it is the enculturating mechanisms of the look that instantiate and regulate these differences in the first place. [Pp. 113–14]

Fuss begins here by acknowledging that "different . . . backgrounds" condition diverse responses to the "enculturating mechanisms of the look" but concludes by judging all such differences to be realized "in the first place" by these same mechanisms. This type of *petitio principii* underlies Fuss's every consideration and her every intimation of the issue of social causality. She cannot, for example, explain how "enculturating mechanisms" could ever induce different effects, or the effects of difference, in a prospectively homogeneous population, without resorting to the idea that comparatively localized cultural instruments can actually create ex nihilo the culturally significant differences they require.

Paradoxically, instead of securing her argument within its self-appointed limits, Fuss's ruling *petitio principii* marks the point at which her constructivism supports and collapses into essentialism. For in denying the fashion-able subject any pre- or paracultural difference, Fuss robs the photocultural apparatus of any structured site of intervention and so forfeits her own ability to explain the particular means whereby that apparatus performs its regulative functions. She leaves a theoretical vacuum in which constructivist notions themselves come to play an ontological role; socially fabricated fixity and primacy amount to fixity and primacy as such if their conditions of existence go unspecified.[3] Sure enough, in keeping with this script, Fuss winds up according gender, race, ethnicity, class, and nationality the very kind of essentialist status that she is in the midst of repudiating. The last quotation invites other scholars to investigate the experience of different groups of people to see

3. Walter Benn Michaels has the relevant argument here:

> There are no anti-essentialist accounts of identity. The reason for this is that the essentialism inheres not in the description of the identity but in the attempt to derive the practices from the identity—we *do* this because we *are* this. Hence anti-essentialism with respect to cultural identity must take the form not of producing more sophisticated accounts of identity (that is, more sophisticated essentialisms) but of ceasing to explain what people do or should do by reference to who they are and/or what culture they belong to. (Needless to say, and for the same reason, making the *culture* more complex, contradictory, discontinuous, and so on is also just another turn of the essentialist screw.) [Walter Benn Michaels, "Race into Culture: A Critical Genealogy of Cultural Identity," p. 61 n. 39]

how their encounters with "enculturating mechanisms" enroll them in their respective identity categories, only to turn around and treat the same categories as prior constraints on people's experience of these mechanisms. What makes this maneuver *profoundly* essentialist is Fuss's failure to acknowledge in a theoretically meaningful way that because gender, race, and so on are never fixed by any stable set of cultural forces, they factor differently from one individual, or even one situation, to another, depending upon the specific economy of relevant social determinants in force. However finely she calibrates the relevant background factors and their operation, her analysis still presumes their more or less uniform impact upon the individuals possessing them and hence their practical autonomy and self-identity.

The essentialist aspect of Fuss's thought takes over in the second phase of her argument where she tries to defend the unlikely proposition that heterosexual women, whose sexual identity has been (re)oriented to the homoerotic, nonetheless return to homosocial (heterosexual) identification by means of the *very* photographic image that "homosexualized" them in the first place:

> Fashion photography works to ensure the formation of a subject's heterosexual object-choices through the stimulation and control of its "homopathic" identifications; the same-sex desire one might imagine to be triggered by the erotically charged images of women's bodies is sublimated into the camera's insistence on same-sex identification (being rather than having the woman). [Pp. 109, 111]

As Fuss sees it, fashion photography both produces homoeroticism, by encoding certain images that solicit women's homoerotic cathexes, *and* transmutes those cathexes into heterosexual object-choices, by actuating a mysterious process of "homopathic" identification. In using the language of psychoanalysis to link "sublimation" to the camera's "insistence," Fuss suggests that the photographic apparatus itself provides the necessary and sufficient conditions for the sublimation (de-eroticization) of the very images it has eroticized. But without a cultural or technological account of this itinerary of desire, Fuss must presume, as the fashion industry itself presumes, a unanimously and, more to the point, a univocally heterosexual viewership. While Fuss generalizes the camera's "insistence" to "*any* social subject," the camera could only produce this effect by way of the presumptive—and presumptively uncomplicated—heterosexuality of a female viewer, as Fuss would have recognized had she applied her constructivist model to other subject-positions. For if photographic codes direct sexual identification unilaterally and without reference to the subject's prior sexual orientation, as Fuss asserts, lesbians would follow the same trajectory of desire as heterosexual women, *forsaking* same-sex cathexis in order to arrive at same-sex identification, ending up with a different sexual organization than they had before encountering these omnipotent coded images—that is, becoming heterosexual in the process. By the same token, the heterosexual male's cathexis of fashion models would be a mere way station on the road to his cross-sexual identification with them; he would, in effect, desire "to be" rather than "to have" women because the camera "insists" upon it.

Fuss only avoids the conclusion that all heterosexual men would identify with women's images "at the camera's insistence" by drawing a developmental contrast disparaging to women. Conflating Freud and Kristeva, she argues that women are "always imperfectly oedipalized" and therefore rehearse an earlier homosexual cathexis to the mother when viewing these images:

> Through *secondary* identification(s) with the sequence of images that fashion photography serially displays, the female subject is positioned by the photographic codes of framing, color, lighting, focus, and pose to rehearse repetitiously the introjection of the (m)other's imago, which is itself a complex rehearsal of the infant's primary identification or absorption with the (m)other. [Pp. 104, 95]

Here Fuss has misconceived the role of iteration in the oedipal conflict, for in fact the "resolution" of this conflict in both genders consists *only* in the incessant rehearsal—an always differential repetition—of the gendered options provided by the oedipal imperative. In suggesting that men somehow *resolve,* while women only *rehearse,* their oedipalization, Fuss reproduces the infamous Freudian grounds of female inferiority and thereby causes her theory to stagger under an unlooked-for political burden: either men identify as women, or women are inferior to men.

What is more, Fuss's argument does not have the warrants in psychoanalytic theory that she claims for it. Her profile of Freud's theory of primary and secondary identification, in which "primary identification . . . signifies the child's preoedipal state of nondifferentiation with the mother, and secondary identification . . . signifies the child's oedipal introjection of the imago of the same-sex parent," bears little resemblance to his actual position (p. 95 n. 4). "Primary identification" in the Freudian corpus refers to the "earliest emotional ties" of the child with the *father* and, in any event, has nothing to do with nondifferentiation from the mother, who only enters Freud's analysis when he explains that children of both sexes will identify—both negatively and positively—with both parents.[4] Then, ostensibly on Kristeva's authority, Fuss goes on to argue

4. Freud tells us that the earliest identification with the father might more properly be "'with the parents'; for before a child has arrived at a definite knowledge of the difference between the sexes . . . it does not distinguish in value between its father and its mother" (Sigmund Freud, *The Ego and the Id,* in *The Standard Edition of the Complete Psychological Works of Sigmund Freud,* trans. and ed. James Strachey, 24 vols. [London, 1953–74], 19:31 n. 1). Freud makes it clear that he is referring to female as well as male children by using an example of a young woman to clarify what he means by a primary identification with the

that "primary identification" actually refers to "primary narcissism," thereby collapsing the psychoanalytic concepts of nondifferentiation, primary identification, and primary narcissism in order to set up her assertion that all women rehearse their "homosexual" identifications with their mothers.[5] Kristeva, however, is well aware that "primary identification" refers to identification with the father; she writes of "a trait indicated by Freud under the name of *primary identification* with the 'father in the personal prehistory,' . . . a degree zero of identification which mobilizes affects, instincts and a certain image of the body."[6]

More importantly, Fuss follows Kristeva's importation of oedipal processes back into the preoedipal phase so that she can go on to treat the earliest stage of development in diametrically opposed ways: as a stage of "nondifferentiation" from the mother (a pregendered condition) and as a stage of primary homosexual cathexis (a gendered condition). In so doing, she tacitly smuggles gender identities into the pregendered conditions of gender itself; ultimately, by affirming that women are "always imperfectly oedipalized," condemned to "rehearsing" their identifications with the mother, Fuss has to assume that the identification at the preoedipal stage was made *on the basis of the mother's gender* (p. 104).[7] Thus, for her, secondary identifications are paradoxically both *definitive* in establishing gender identities and, insofar as women only "rehearse" the libidinal dynamics of Fussian primary identification, *unnecessary*, for those gender identities must already have been in place. This double move provides a putative principle to describe heterosexual women as always already homosexual *in* their heterosexuality; in fact, it defines heterosexuality itself as crypto-homosexuality.

---

father; see ibid. We are not making any claims for the validity of Freud's theory; rather, we are pointing to the inaccuracy of Fuss's representation of a theory she herself presents as valid at this juncture in her argument.

5. Fuss writes, "for Kristeva. . . . in the pre-mirror stage, the still to be gendered pre-subject is 'face to face with primary narcissism,' . . . caught in a primary identification with the mother that, for the girl, positions her . . . on a homosexual continuum" (p. 98). Although Kristeva does indicate that at the mirror stage the child has an unstable identity, calling it a "narcissistic instability" in which the child questions its own identity and "sometimes" confuses itself with its mother, she does not equate "primary identification" with "primary narcissism" (Julia Kristeva, "A Question of Subjectivity—An Interview," *Women's Review* 12 [1986]: 20).

6. Kristeva, "Identification and the Real," in *Literary Theory Today*, ed. Peter Collier and Helga Geyer-Ryan (Ithaca, N.Y., 1990), p. 167. Kristeva goes on to indicate distinctions among primary identification, narcissistic identification, hysterical identification, ego-ideal, and so forth—the very sorts of distinctions Fuss fails to sustain in her own essay.

7. According to Fuss's argument that the child's nondifferentiation from the mother is equivalent to its "primary identification" with her, the male child too must enact a primary identification with the mother so that the male viewer looking at female bodies presumably would also "rehearse" that primary identification in a secondary identification, necessarily desiring to be, rather than to have, the woman. Male heterosexual voyeurism would be entirely precluded on such a model.

Despite her earlier reliance upon Freud, Kristeva, and Lacan, Fuss concludes her argument with a repudiation of them, signalling as her own original contribution to psychoanalysis the discovery that "the desire to be *like* can itself be motivated and sustained by the desire to *possess*," a formulation she figures as the "lesbian vampire" (pp. 107, 114).[8] At this point, Fuss (mis)represents Freud's proposition—that identification is a desire to be and object-choice is a desire to have—as though it were a fixed and absolute antinomy. She argues that any communication between these states would be a "structural impossibility": the Freudian "symmetrical, rigid, chiasmatic relation between terms," Fuss asserts, must be corrected by showing "the ways in which any identification *with* an other is secured through a simultaneous and continuing desire *for* that other" (p. 114). But Freud does in fact insist that identification and object-choice are indistinguishable at the root, that is, in the preoedipal stage of development.[9] Fuss here confuses the mutual implication of identification and desire, which is a staple of standard psychoanalytic theory, with a simple metaphorical equivalence between these states, which is what she wishes to advance. Her claim, reductive in our view, is that one identifies *only* with that which one desires, that the desire to be (like) a person is directed by sexual liking for that person, so that one's identificatory models are determined univocally by the gender of one's object-choices. Having argued that where identification was, there desire shall be—in keeping with the dictates of primary mimetism—Fuss now maintains that where desire is, there identification must be.[10] In either case, gender is

8. See Freud, *Group Psychology and the Analysis of the Ego,* 18:38.

9. See Freud, *The Ego and the Id,* 19:28–29. Freud further indicates that this indistinguishability is a sine qua non for any ego development at all:

> It may be that this identification is the sole condition under which the id can give up its objects. . . . Especially in the early phases of development [this identification] is a very frequent one, and it makes it possible to suppose that the character of the ego is a precipitate of abandoned object cathexes and that it contains the history of those object-choices. [19:29]

In other words, while Freud distinguishes wanting to be and wanting to have as analytical constructs, he shows that these modes of desire are necessarily implicated in one another in the formation of subjectivity. Far from being a "structural impossibility" in Freud, the recognition of simultaneous identification with and desire for a same-sex object is the key to numerous Freudian case analyses, as the Wolf Man clearly demonstrates. A crucial moment in the Wolf Man's therapy comes when Freud realizes that the Wolf Man's obsessive pathology, which involves a taboo desire for the mother, is overdetermined by a hysterical identification with her. Freud goes on to hypothesize that all obsessive neuroses contain a kernel of such hysterical identification. See Freud, *From the History of an Infantile Neurosis,* in *Standard Edition,* 17:76–78.

10. Fuss's disavowal concentrates itself in the sentence, "This becoming [the mother] is presumed to erase all desire, or rather to reroute the desire toward a wholly different love object" (p. 114). In fact, we would submit that Freud's own original contribution was his insistence that the displacement of desire follows a rigorously logical, if complex, economy of *substitution.* Contrary to Fuss's assertion, "rerouting" entails not the erasure of desire,

imported as both a motive and a determinant of supposedly pregendered beings.

What is at issue in Fuss's failed efforts to claim an original contribution to psychoanalysis is nothing less than the *political import* of her analysis of fashion photography—her argument for the ostensible primacy of the homosexual. Two paradoxes (unremarked by Fuss) expose the costs of this approach at the political level. In the first, Fuss apparently universalizes the lesbian viewpoint—but only by refusing to take the lesbian viewer into account. In the second, she propounds a constructivist notion of sexual identity—but only by positing the *essence* of heterosexual women as their homosexuality. Despite Fuss's constructivist assertions, it is obvious that the photocultural apparatus does not have unilateral sexualizing, or even eroticizing, effects; it always works with and against a certain resistance exerted by a previously defined sexual position. Fuss reduces social subjects—but in particular heterosexual women—to undifferentiated psyches that passively await libidinal definition from any stray object, a traditional and notoriously sexist description of female sexuality.[11] But because Fuss must rely upon the resistance of prior identities even as she attempts to theorize it out of existence, she treats her viewers both as originarily heterosexual women, unwittingly homosexualized by the photocultural apparatus, and as always already homosexual, perpetually rehearsing identifications with the lost maternal object. Taken together, these gestures frame heterosexual women as the ideal targets of Madison Avenue manipulation. For if, as Fuss suggests, lesbianism occupies the psychic recesses of *all* women, then differences between homo- and heterosexual orientation must really index relative degrees of self-consciousness: the female heterosexual is tacitly represented as being in the thrall of false consciousness, unaware of her true nature and thus vulnerable to the machinations of consumer culture.

Finally, when Fuss defines female heterosexuality as uniform but always already homosexual, she engages in the classic double game of othering, a colonizing strategy endemic to patriarchy: deny women's claims to individuated subjectivity by representing them as all "alike" in their otherness, but also deny women's possession of some unmasterable difference or independent standard of value by troping their otherness as

---

which is indestructible in any case, but its repetition elsewhere under the pressure of resistance. Fuss's idea of a "wholly different love object" has no place in psychoanalysis whatsoever. Substitute love objects are always in some unconscious way the same as the love objects they replace.

11. That Butler makes a similar point in a discussion of Irigaray demonstrates the fundamentally antifeminist stance that an argument such as Fuss's entails—woman finds her essence only in her amenability to outside form. See the section entitled "Irigaray/Plato," in Butler, *Bodies That Matter,* pp. 27–55. Significantly, Fuss herself has written in support of Irigaray in order to controvert this very conclusion; see her *Essentially Speaking: Feminism, Nature, and Difference* (New York, 1989).

merely deficient versions of the judging subject. In this case, given that heterosexual women (not lesbians, presumably) fall prey to the intentionalizing effects of the photocultural apparatus due to their inferior oedipal status and their lack of authentic consciousness, lesbians are positioned as the full, original, and autonomous subjectivity from which heterosexual women deviate. Hence, in Fuss's theory, lesbianism stands in an imperialistic relation to heterosexual women. On this score, her lesbian commitments lapse into patriarchal complicities.

Critical Response

IV

Look Who's Talking, or If Looks Could Kill

Diana Fuss

"Fashion and the Homospectatorial Look" is not an essay I would write again. In my mind, this early attempt to utilize psychoanalysis in the service of an antihomophobic politics takes Freud's description of the mechanisms of identification and desire at face value, overlooking the ideological production of the concepts themselves. Yet my own concerns about this essay differ antithetically from Molly Anne Rothenberg and Joseph Valente's. Whereas for them "Fashion and the Homospectatorial Look" (pp. 90–114) is not psychoanalytically orthodox enough, for me it is far too orthodox, far too uncritical of the discourse from which it sprang, particularly on the subject of identification. In the following essay I will sketch out a few other ideas on identification. But first I wish to address what I take to be the central claims put forward by Rothenberg and Valente's severely normative critique, a critique, moreover, that is unapologetically waged in the interest of defending and strengthening a domain of heterosexual presumption and privilege putatively threatened by recent lesbian theory.

Nowhere in "Fashionable Theory and Fashion-able Women: Returning Fuss's Homospectatorial Look" (pp. 413–23) do the authors name their own speaking position. This omission is not, of course, mere oversight; the use of an objective, moralizing, and universal voice is one of the standard tropes of homophobic discourse. Rothenberg and Valente assume the authoritative prerogative of heterosexual speech that never has to declare itself as such.[1] By conducting their critique from this un-

1. For a more detailed treatment of the politics of heterosexuality's privileged invisibility, see David Halperin, "The Queer Politics of Michel Foucault," *Saint Foucault: Towards a Gay Hagiography* (New York, 1995), pp. 15–125.

marked position (presumptively straight and critically dishonest) they foreclose all scrutiny of the political determinations and the ideological investments of their "return look." To immediately challenge the privilege accorded to heterosexuality's cultural invisibility, we might well ask, When this straight couple looks at "the lesbian," what do they imagine they see?

The first thing that Rothenberg and Valente see is a failed constructionist. The new trend in "postmodern forms of feminist, postcolonial, and queer theory," the authors claim, is towards a "radical social constructivism" that reconsolidates the very essentialism it sought to displace (p. 413). The attempt to de-essentialize identity, they argue, "marks the point at which a radical constructivism passes into a reductive essentialism" (p. 416). This is a curious line of argument to take in light of my own position, detailed in *Essentially Speaking,* that anti-essentialism never escapes the pull of essentialism, that staking out a "pure" constructionist position reinscribes an essentialist logic, and that constructionists, by assuming that essentialism is always already reactionary, need to be wary of acting as if essentialism has an essence.[2] The charge that I am myself guilty of the very thing that I criticize is a deeply disingenuous one if it does not simultaneously acknowledge the complex and difficult ways that all such critiques are compromised from the start by that from which they seek to escape. What, then, is to be gained by Rothenberg and Valente's triumphant unmasking of the irreducible essentialism at the heart of lesbian constructionism?

The straight couple's strategy of exposing the essentialism in lesbian theory, outing the closet essentialist in the "professed constructivis[t]" (p. 415), strikes me as a return to a particularly spurious and hypocritical mode of discourse in which the label *essentialism* is wielded as a ready or convenient term of derogation and dismissal. Relegating lesbian theory to the theoretical wastebin of error, deviation, and falsehood, Rothenberg and Valente deploy essentialism as the weapon of choice, seeking to identify, classify, abjectify, and finally contain the encroaching threat at the borders of heterosexual privilege. There may, in fact, be no better illustration than Rothenberg and Valente's response of what lesbian theorists in particular have long been troubled by—the realization that "what motivates the suspicion . . . of a fantom feminist essentialism, may be less the risk of essentialism itself than the further risk which that entails: the risk

2. See my *Essentially Speaking: Feminism, Nature, and Difference* (New York, 1989).

Diana Fuss is associate professor of English at Princeton University. She is the author of *Essentially Speaking: Feminism, Nature, and Difference* (1989) and *Identification Papers* (1995), and the editor of *Inside/Out: Lesbian Theories, Gay Theories* (1991) and *Human, All Too Human* (1995).

of challenging directly the social-symbolic institution of heterosexuality."[3] Rothenberg and Valente's work represents an attempt to revive the essentialist label in the interests of shoring up the integrity and inviolability of a discrete and self-contained "heterosexual" identity, erecting a cordon sanitaire that strives to insulate and to protect it from the taint of "homosexuality."

In their insistence on a pure, precultural, presymbolic heterosexuality, finally untouched by the predations of its monstrous other, Rothenberg and Valente participate in an essentialism more thoroughgoing and more absolute than Freud's. Yet the problem is not so much the authors' invocation of an essentialist discourse as their persistent and unprincipled refusal to read the politics of its deployment. Rothenberg and Valente want to have it both ways, discharging essentialism as a mode of aggressive assault while simultaneously occupying it as a self-defensive bulwark. Taking their homophobia seriously therefore involves asking what work the charge of essentialism is doing in their essay and exactly what it seeks to safeguard. For the authors, what are the intellectual remunerations, and the political returns, in vilifying (not to say stigmatizing) lesbian theory?

Ultimately, Rothenberg and Valente are securing, through their own canny essentialist moves, the right of the heterosexual couple to regulate and to control all the discourses about it. "Fashion and the Homospectatorial Look" is used as an instrument in a polemical battle waged over the very right of lesbian theory to exist at all. That feminist theory might have something to learn from lesbian theory, that it might even be another name for it, is the fear that motivates and sustains this couple's most quarrelsome and defensive diatribes.[4] Ultimately, Rothenberg and Valente's essay is not an argument *with* lesbian theory but an argument *over* it, a defiant and hostile challenge to the very idea of lesbian theory as such.

The authors' main criticism strikes a familiar refrain. It is not only that in aspiring to a radical constructionism lesbian theory (which, in their view, is exemplified in its most "insidious" form in my own work) has fallen back into a reductive essentialism, but also that such "lesbian commitments lapse into patriarchal complicities" (pp. 414, 423). There is more going on here than simply a Paglia-esque effort to discredit "radical" lesbian constructionists by rooting out the patriarch in the feminist,

3. Teresa de Lauretis, "The Essence of the Triangle, or Taking the Risk of Essentialism Seriously: Feminist Theory in Italy, the U.S., and Britain," *Differences* 1 (Summer 1989): 32. See also Ellen Rooney, "In a Word: *Interview,*" interview with Gayatri Spivak, *Differences* 1 (Summer 1989): 124–56. These essays have been reprinted in book form in *The Essential Difference*, ed. Naomi Schor and Elizabeth Weed (Bloomington, Ind., 1994).

4. It is by no means clear to me what Rothenberg and Valente understand in their essay by *feminist*. It is only clear that for them feminism does not include lesbianism, any more than heterosexuality, in their view, incorporates homosexuality.

the erotophobe in the lesbian, the essentialist in the anti-essentialist, and so on. The real force of the charge derives from the pervasive rhetoric of "lapsing" that evokes perhaps the most dangerous psychoanalytic typology of all: the lesbian as fallen woman, the figure of psychosexual failure who, after a series of developmental miscarriages, lapses back into a state of regression.[5] Rothenberg and Valente's response repeatedly draws, for its censorious effect, on the psychoanalytic paradigm that brands lesbianism as a reversion, a backsliding, a lapse. This allegory of a fall into patriarchal essentialism is further couched in an all too painful and recognizable rhetoric of the professed and the disavowed, the explicit and the implicit, the open and the tacit, the acknowledged and the disclaimed—those well-worn binaries without which the very distinction of homo and hetero would lose its classificatory coherence and threaten to dissolve altogether. It is the aim of Rothenberg and Valente's intellectual project to keep the homo and the hetero from ever overflowing the prescribed boundaries of their established cultural containers.

Thus, when the authors undertake to "return [my] homospectatorial look," they are actually proposing to return the homospectatorial look *to me,* to the place where it first issued and where it must be safely reinstated. What most disorients and disturbs Rothenberg and Valente is how my argument apparently "defines heterosexuality itself as crypto-homosexuality" (p. 420). Putting aside for the moment the questionable phrase "heterosexuality *itself*" and the interesting choice of the word "crypto," it is fair to ask why the authors read the political deconstruction of sexuality as lesbianism's seditious attempt to "colonize" female heterosexuality. What is at stake in the fear of domination by the lesbian? Why does the mere specter of the homo in the hetero terrify? Why does the suggestion that it is heterosexual, and not homosexual, women who may "deviate" provoke such a deeply phobic response?[6]

If there is any deviation going on in "Fashion and the Homospectatorial Look," the authors insist, it is my own wayward departure from the canonical Freud. Claiming privileged access or entitlement to Freud's "actual position," Rothenberg and Valente chastise me for deliberately "misconceiv[ing]" Freud's theory of identification (p. 419). Once again drawing on the corrective and patronizing tone of official psychoanalytic doctrine, the authors take this lesbian theorist to task for willfully refusing

5. I have discussed at length the psychoanalytic trope of falling that Freud deploys to pathologize lesbian identity in my essay "Freud's Fallen Women: Identification, Desire, and 'A Case of Homosexuality in a Woman,'" *Yale Journal of Criticism* 6 (Spring 1993): 1–23.

6. My intent has obviously never been to set up lesbianism as the norm and heterosexuality as the deviation, but rather to call decisively into question the entire psychoanalytic vocabulary of norms and deviations. Rothenberg and Valente's critical misreading of my project is thus an instructive one, for the *fear* of the pathologization of heterosexuality is a particularly telling indicator of the high level of anxiety that direct challenges to traditional narratives of normative sexuality can produce.

to get it straight. Such contests over the real meaning of Freud are, in my mind, intellectually suspect and politically bankrupt. In the present instance, quarrels over Freud's "actual" position on identification obscure the far more interesting and difficult questions one might ask about this complicated and often contradictory notion, namely, Where does Freud's theory of identification come from, what work is it doing, and what is its theoretical and political yield? Indeed, what is missing from the debate at large is a wider historical, political, and intellectual frame in which to read the concept of identification, a frame whose contours I would like to signal, however briefly, in the space remaining.[7]

Freud's papers on identification begin as early as the correspondence with Wilhelm Fliess in the late 1890s and conclude forty years later with a posthumously published journal note. In a professional career comprising several hundred published pieces, ranging from letters, reviews, and prefaces to scientific abstracts, case histories, and analytical papers, Freud never allocated to identification a book or monograph of its own (Lacan was later to devote a whole seminar to the problem). Its most sustained treatment comes in chapter 7 of *Group Psychology and the Analysis of the Ego* (1921),[8] but, even in this focussed investigation of group ties, what may be psychoanalysis's most original idea commands far less rigorous attention than a host of other familiar Freudian concepts fundamentally dependent upon it, concepts including oedipality, fantasy, repression, castration, and ambivalence. The theory of identification, one of Freud's most important contributions to twentieth-century thought, is also one of the most imperfectly understood—not least of all by Freud himself.

In perhaps its simplest formulation, identification is the detour through the other that defines a self. This detour follows no predetermined developmental path, nor does it travel outside history and culture. Identification names the entry of history and culture into the subject, a subject that must bear the traces of each and every encounter with the external world. Identification is, from the beginning, a question of *relation,* of self to other, subject to object, inside to outside. Every relation, most especially the self-relation, is a response to the call of the other—the other who always exceeds me, the other who withdraws me from myself.

This paradox of approximating identity through the retreat of iden-

7. I address these issues at considerably greater length in my book *Identification Papers* (New York, 1995), from which the following remarks are drawn. In writing their response, Rothenberg and Valente did not consult my other published work on identification, including not only "Freud's Fallen Women," but also "Monsters of Perversion: Jeffrey Dahmer and *The Silence of the Lambs,*" in *Media Spectacles,* ed. Marjorie Garber, Jann Matlock, and Rebecca L. Walkowitz (New York, 1993), pp. 181–205 and "Interior Colonies: Frantz Fanon and the Politics of Identification," *Diacritics* 24 (Summer–Fall 1994): 20–42.

8. See Sigmund Freud, "Identification," chap. 7 of *Group Psychology and the Analysis of the Ego,* in *The Standard Edition of the Complete Psychological Works of Sigmund Freud,* trans. and ed. James Strachey, 24 vols. (London, 1953–74), 18:105–10; hereafter abbreviated *SE.*

tity is a recurrent theme in the philosophical discourse on the problem of alterity. In the wake of Hegel, philosophers of modernity repeatedly return to the question of whether the other as other can be grasped at all and whether the self is always only a substitute for the other that cannot finally be known. Some of the most radical work on the problem of the other can be found in twentieth-century French intellectual thought, where the topic of alterity enters the philosophical conversation most directly through the influence of Alexandre Kojève's lectures on Hegel's *Phenomenology of Spirit*.[9] This tradition of French Hegelianism—which includes contemporary thinkers as diverse as Philippe Lacoue-Labarthe, Jean-Luc Nancy, Emmanuel Levinas, Luce Irigaray, René Girard, Mikkel Borch-Jacobsen, Maurice Blanchot, Hélène Cixous, and Jacques Derrida—provides a larger philosophical framework in which to understand psychoanalysis's continued interest in the problem of identification. While the concept of identification holds a status specific to the intellectual tradition of psychoanalysis,[10] the longer history of philosophical work on the question of otherness clarifies the central problematic involved: How is it that it is only through the other that I can be myself, only in the place of the other that I can arrive at a sense of self?

One of Rothenberg and Valente's concerns is that my original essay fails to adhere to the precise critical distinctions psychoanalysts posit between various kinds of self-other identifications. But what interests me more is the very fact of their multiplication. Identification, broadly defined as the internalization of the other, itself eludes the analytic desire for possession and appropriation. The psychoanalytic literature on identification is littered with taxonomic qualifiers that seek to identify, with greater and greater precision, modes and types of identifications: primary and secondary, feminine and masculine, imaginary and symbolic, maternal and paternal, idiopathic and heteropathic, partial and total, centrifugal and centripetal, narcissistic and regressive, hysterical and melancholic, multiple and terminal, positive and negative. This often incongruous proliferation of kinds of identifications points to a theoretical difficulty psychoanalysis must routinely confront in laying hold of its object, a difficulty, that is, in identifying identification. How can the other

9. See Alexandre Kojève, *Introduction to the Reading of Hegel*, trans. James H. Nichols, Jr. (New York, 1969). Mikkel Borch-Jacobsen analyzes at length the importance of Kojève and his teaching for postwar French thought in *Lacan: The Absolute Master*, trans. Douglas Brick (Stanford, Calif., 1991). For more on the influence of Hegel on contemporary French philosophy, see Judith P. Butler, *Subjects of Desire: Hegelian Reflections in Twentieth-Century France* (New York, 1987), and Michael S. Roth, *Knowing and History: Appropriations of Hegel in Twentieth-Century France* (Ithaca, N.Y., 1988).

10. Identification is only one philosophical approach among many to the problem of alterity. It would be a useful project to track the many different treatments of otherness outside the tradition of psychoanalytic thought, an enterprise that may belong more properly to a sociology of knowledge. Such a study might begin by looking to the work of Pierre Bourdieu.

be brought into the domain of the knowable without annihilating the other *as other*—as precisely that which cannot be known?

Freud begins from the assumption that the other can at least be approximated, if not fully incorporated; he attributes the failure of earlier attempts to think the otherness of the other to a historical privileging of imagination over reason. Previous models that seek to conceptualize the influence of other on self—demonic or ecstatic possession, contagious passion, animal magnetism, mesmerism, hypnosis—all represent otherness in mystical rather than rational terms, subsuming science into religion. Freud presents his theory of psychical identification specifically as a corrective to the figurative excesses of nineteenth-century psychology. Identification replaces "sympathy," "imagination," and "suggestion" to describe, in more "scientific" fashion, the phenomenon of how subjects act upon one another. In light of Rothenberg and Valente's cursory dismissal of what they call "figurative activity" and the "tropologies of identification" (p. 413), we might turn our attention to Freud's ambivalent disavowal of the literary in his abandonment of previous philosophies of the other, his own substitution of a "factual" for a "figural" logic.

On the one hand, Freud is unusually attentive to the power of language and to the priority of the textual in his highly analogical descriptions of psychoanalysis. For Freud it is not only the case that creative writers discovered psychoanalysis first, but also that psychoanalysis operates as a form of creative writing or literary mythology.[11] Freud's most direct acknowledgment of the figurative nature of scientific discourse comes in *Beyond the Pleasure Principle* (1920), where he notes that he is "obliged to operate with the scientific terms, that is to say with the figurative language, peculiar to psychology." Replacing "psychological terms by physiological or chemical ones" would fail to extract from scientific language its rhetorical sediment, for "they too are only part of a figurative language."[12] Moreover, psychoanalysis, often understood as a form of narratology,[13] closely identifies with the literary insofar as it has already been anticipated by it, compromised from the start by the necessity of travelling though language and texts.

On the other hand, Freud also insists that psychoanalytic case histories are scientific documents, not literary exercises. Any reader expecting to find a "*roman à clef*" in the documentation of his analytic treatments,

11. In "Why War?" (1933), Freud writes to Albert Einstein: "It may perhaps seem to you as though our theories are a kind of mythology and, in the present case, not even an agreeable one. But does not every science come in the end to a kind of mythology like this?" (Freud, "Why War?" *SE,* 22:211).

12. Freud, *Beyond the Pleasure Principle,* in *SE,* 18:60.

13. The interpretation of psychoanalysis as narratology is a position generally associated with the work of Peter Brooks. See Peter Brooks, *Reading for the Plot: Design and Intention in Narrative* (New York, 1984) and *Body Work: Objects of Desire in Modern Narrative* (Cambridge, Mass., 1993).

Freud warns, can be assured that every precaution has been taken to guard against the encroachments of the rhetorical into the "purely scientific and technical."[14] The psychoanalyst is a "medical man" not a "man of letters," and psychoanalytic writing is science not fiction.[15] Psychoanalysis erects itself, as a science, *against* the literary. It seeks to establish its own truth claims on the basis of the repudiation of the power of figuration.[16]

It appears that psychoanalysis can turn against tropes only by invoking them. Freud's scientific theory of identification is entirely predicated on a logic of metaphoric exchange and displacement. Metaphor, *the substitution of the one for the other,* is internal to the work of identification. Freud's concept of self-other relations fundamentally presupposes the possibility of metaphoricity—of iterability, redoubling, translation, and transposition. The Greek *metaphora,* meaning transport, immediately implicates the transferential act of identification in the rhetorical process of figuration. Psychoanalysis, at least where its theory of identification is concerned, can actually be understood as a scientific discourse on the very problem of metaphorization. Our aim then might be not to reintroduce metaphor into a psychoanalysis that calls itself a science but rather to read the traces of a figurative logic already at work within a psychoanalysis that repeatedly and symptomatically forgets its metaphorical history.

There are many questions we might ask about the psychoanalytic figuration of identification. Are identifications conscious or unconscious? active or passive? immediate or belated? creative or lethal? These largely unresolved tensions in the psychoanalytic literature on identification continue to structure the various contemporary usages of the term, usages that cover the widest possible spectrum of critical interpretations. Some theorists view every identification as a cross-identification, while others read cross-identification as less a psychological given than a social mandate; some see identification as already in play and therefore relatively effortless, while others see identification as dangerous and difficult; some understand identification as a form of regressive nostalgia, while others view identification as a means of achieving real psychological change; and some highlight identification's tendency to align and to shore up identity, while still others emphasize identification's capability for dislocation and destabilization. Such pervasive contradictions are telling, for the very notion of identification (a process of substitution and displacement) puts these divisions into question. Identification is both voluntary and involuntary, necessary and difficult, effectual and dangerous, naturalizing and denaturalizing. Identification is the point where the psychical/social distinction becomes impossibly confused and finally untenable.

Accordingly, any politics of identity needs to come to terms with the

14. Freud, *Fragment of an Analysis of a Case of Hysteria,* in *SE,* 7:9, 8.

15. Ibid., 7:59.

16. I would suggest that the same is true of Rothenberg and Valente's own attempts to authorize their critique of queer theories of performativity by discrediting the power of

complicated and meaningful ways that identity is continually compromised, imperiled, one might even say *embarrassed* by identification. For example, how might it change our understanding of the political, of the very nature and significance of the social tie, to know that every identity claim ("I am not another") is based upon an identification ("I desire to be another")? How might it change our understanding of identity if we were finally to take seriously the poststructuralist notion that our most impassioned identifications may incorporate nonidentity within them and that our most fervent disidentifications may already harbor the very identity they seek to deny? How, finally, might it change our understanding and practice of identity politics if the "identity" in question is always already an "improbable" one, always already an "eccentric . . . distorted (displaced, dissimulated) subject in all sorts of identificatory roles and figures"?[17]

Identification has a history, a philosophically consequential history; it carries with it a host of theoretical problems, ideological incoherencies, and conceptual difficulties. One such conceptual difficulty is the long-standing confusion surrounding the question of identification's relation to its theoretical other, desire. "Fashion and the Homospectatorial Look" concludes by questioning Freud's assumption that to desire and to identify with the same person at the same time is a theoretical impossibility. I would take this challenge much farther now, insisting that psychoanalysis's basic distinction between wanting to be and wanting to have the other is a precarious one at best, its epistemological validity seriously open to question. Speaking of Freud's first full-length case history of hysterical identification, Parveen Adams questions whether it is really possible to deduce so readily from Dora's identifications whom she might desire, or, conversely, whether Dora's sexual object-choices tell us much of anything at all about how she might identify. Why assume, in other words, that any subject's sexuality is structured in terms of pairs?[18] Even Freud is unable to keep desire and identification completely straight. In "Mourning and Melancholia" (1917) Freud defines identification as a form of desire, "a preliminary stage of object-choice . . . the first way."[19] Isn't it finally worth exploring whether the critical displacement of the identification/desire opposition might open up a new way of thinking about the complexity of sexual identity formations outside the rigid thematics of cultural binaries?

Given the fundamental indissociability of identification and desire,

---

figuration; interestingly, for the authors, there is something decidedly queer and unsettling about "figurative activity" and its undercover operations.

17. Borch-Jacobsen, *The Freudian Subject,* trans. Catherine Porter (Stanford, Calif., 1988), p. 54.

18. See Parveen Adams, "Per Os(cillation)," *Camera Obscura* 17 (May 1988): 7–29.

19. Freud, "Mourning and Melancholia," *SE,* 14:249.

the question that insistently poses itself is why Freud works so hard to keep them apart in the first place. To answer this question, we need to look at those specific textual instances where Freud calls up the notion of identification as well as to examine closely the changes this notion undergoes from its earliest appearance in the correspondence with Fliess to its last invocation in Freud's journal notes. I have attempted this project elsewhere, tracking along the way the precise metaphorizations Freud invokes to fashion identification into a rigorous "scientific" concept.[20] Attending to the changes in figuration that mark the evolution of the theory of identification over a forty-year period might tell us much about the institutional process of constructing an epistemological object of inquiry (in this case, "sexuality") and about the challenges psychoanalysis inevitably faced in attempting to account, scientifically, for the complexities of human relations by adopting a tropological model.

The psychoanalytic notion of identification has indeed emerged for "politically activist postmodern theory" as a pressing theoretical question. Its deconstruction has profitably opened up new avenues of research and innovative rethinkings of the political. While I would argue that identification is neither an innocent nor a neutral concept,[21] I would also suggest that it is too early to foreclose on its political usages. Vigorous and responsible critiques of current theories of identification are important and necessary. But certainly lesbian theory deserves better than what Rothenberg and Valente have to offer. It deserves, at the very least, a second look.

20. Freud develops his theory of identification through three principal figures: falling, ingestion, and infection. I discuss each of these figures in turn in *Identification Papers*.

21. A theorist like Frantz Fanon, for example, asks us to remember the violence of identification, the material practices of exclusion, alienation, appropriation, and domination that transform other subjects into subjected others. Identification is not only how we accede to power, it is also how we learn submission. In colonial relations, identification can operate at once as the ontological privilege of the colonizer and as the subjugated condition of the colonized. Racial identity and racist practice alike are forged through the bonds of identification. Thus we need not only to place the psychoanalytic concept of identification within colonial history, but also to study how colonial history shapes the very terms in which psychoanalysis comes to understand the process of identification. See my "Interior Colonies."

Critical Response

V

Response to *Identities*

Michael Gorra

One of the most extraordinary passages in V. S. Naipaul's oeuvre is an account, in *An Area of Darkness,* of the way he melts into an Indian street:

> And for the first time in my life I was one of the crowd. There was nothing in my appearance or dress to distinguish me from the crowd eternally hurrying into Churchgate Station. In Trinidad to be an Indian was to be distinctive. To be anything there was distinctive; difference was each man's attribute. To be an Indian in England was distinctive; in Egypt it was more so. Now in Bombay I entered a shop or a restaurant and awaited a special quality of response. And there was nothing. It was like being denied part of my reality. Again and again I was caught. I was faceless. I might sink without a trace into that Indian crowd. I had been made by Trinidad and England; recognition of my difference was necessary to me. I felt the need to impose myself, and didn't know how.[1]

He becomes invisible. Yet it's not the invisibility of which Ralph Ellison writes, in which an individual cannot be seen because all that can be seen of him is the fact of his skin, of his membership in one racial group or another. No, Naipaul's own invisibility stands as the antithesis of Ellison's. He has been made by Trinidad and England, where his individual identity is predicated on his racial difference from most of the people around him. But in India that identity remains invisible precisely because that difference is not only unseen but nonexistent. He misses that "special quality of response," the quality that has always marked his difference from other people; and indeed to lose that racial distinctiveness is for

1. V. S. Naipaul, *An Area of Darkness* (1964; New York, 1981), pp. 45–46.

Naipaul to lose his self, to watch it "sink without a trace." For that identity of skin is also, in Naipaul's case, a lie. He's not an Indian, he only looks like one, and though melting into the crowd entails a loss of individuality, that loss itself provides a reminder of the history that has taken him from the landscape his ancestors hymned.

Yet insofar as the self that India threatens grows out of his distinctiveness, his very individuality depends on his membership in a racial group, one from which he remains separated by both his family's migration and the trajectory of his own life but that nevertheless determines how he is, quite literally, seen. So India becomes for Naipaul both definitive and yet impossible, inescapable and yet irrelevant. And the implication is that there's no way to escape one's origins. It is as if the formation of the writer's identity, which depends on his difference from those around him, stands as but an extreme form of the process through which a child separates himself from his family. Losing himself in the crowd suggests the degree to which the process of individuation, of creating a self, must remain always incomplete. For his work, whose subject has always been "the worlds I contained within myself," depends on this paradox: the self is the same as the group.[2] More: the self he has made depends on his membership in a group that others, that British imperialism, have defined as marginal and powerless. His material—and therefore, as a writer, his very individuality—lies in the forces that would militate against the creation of an autonomous self, in a simultaneous acceptance and rejection not only of his own group but of the terms in which the colonial master has seen him.

I could say more about Naipaul's sense of the dialectics of identity; about, for example, the inevitability of mimicry in a world where individuation remains always unfinished. But perhaps I've said enough to suggest why I thought so often of this passage in looking over the essays in this volume. There's much to praise here: Gananath Obeyesekere's superb account ("'British Cannibals': Contemplation of an Event in the Death and Resurrection of James Cook, Explorer," pp. 7–31) of the way in which discourse, sometimes, produces the behavior it purports to describe; Sara Suleri's negative capability in pointing to tensions in our understanding of identity as a concept without feeling the need to square all theoretical circles ("Woman Skin Deep: Feminism and the Postcolonial Condition," pp. 133–46). I admire the historical density of Katie Trumpener's work ("The Time of the Gypsies: A 'People without History' in

2. Naipaul, *The Enigma of Arrival* (New York, 1987), p. 147.

Michael Gorra teaches English at Smith College and has recently finished a book-length manuscript on postcolonial fiction. He is the author of *The English Novel at Mid-Century: From the Leaning Tower* (1990).

the Narratives of the West," pp. 338–79). But I kept returning to two of these essays, drawn by what I can only describe as their quality of moral gravity. Because even as we argue on behalf of identity's contingent nature, more and more people in what we call—in this case justifiably—the real world insist on its absolute and peremptory claims, an insistence that makes our work seem at once necessary and feeble. In their very different ways both Akeel Bilgrami and Walter Benn Michaels know this. For they each seem to recognize the ways in which identity is both constructed and yet essential. Or rather they acknowledge the awful power of that moment when one persuades oneself that identity is indeed essential, that there are clear and unequivocal grounds for distinguishing between the self and the other.

We are all going to die; we have all had parents. Those are the two essential facts about us. Yet, having had parents, we know that we haven't had the makings of ourselves, that we're marked by our birth, by the shape of the nose or the color of the skin. Marked too by the perceptions of those whose parents aren't (or maybe sometimes are) our own, for whom we are each other's hated other. Michaels's essay, "Race into Culture: A Critical Genealogy of Cultural Identity" (pp. 32–62) has a dizzying argument in which the Bad Guys are always in the process of turning into the Good Guys, and vice versa. White Southern racism as the origin of American anti-imperialism? The notion of pluralism as dependent on "an unmeasurable and hence incomparable racial essence"—so that what we think of as tolerance becomes at the very least racialist and perhaps racist as well (p. 46)? The model of race Michaels draws from Frank Hankins seems to leave one no option but to be either a separatist or a supremacist, until one notes its barely spoken and untenable assumption that in a biological sense there are indeed different races. Yet while race doesn't exist as a genetic fact it does as a social one, and for Michaels it remains inextricable from our conception of culture. Indeed, his essay is most suggestive when it demonstrates that an idea of culture that valorizes the analysis of practices over heritable physical characteristics nevertheless depends upon an "earlier notion of racial identity" (p. 35).

Michaels argues that racialist thinking begins at the moment when culture becomes not simply descriptive but normative, when it provides a model not of what one does but of who one is. For in defining who one is, "authenticity becomes . . . crucial." "The attractions of Navajo things . . . consist in the fact of their being Navajo" (p. 50). But Navajo things aren't simply what the Navajo do. They must also be things that *only* the Navajo do: pure, untouched by the practices of some other people. In consequence the concept of authenticity comes into being only when it no longer exists, when some kind of continuity has been broken. It is an attempt to recover the past, to do what one's grandparents did. Or, as Michaels puts it, the project of authenticity in *Laughing Boy* is "made possible only by the fact that there's a sense in which Slim Girl isn't a Navajo and made fulfillable only by the fact that there's a sense in which" her ancestry means she already is (p. 50).

So culture becomes "a way of continuing rather than repudiating racial thought" (p. 61). And in consequence, any challenge to racialist thought must be willing to give up on the idea of authenticity as well, the idea of any cultural practice whatsoever belonging to any one group or person more than it does to any other. It must instead work toward something like the culture of Shakespeare readers that Michaels imagines—open to anyone who picks up a book. (Leave aside the fact that historically the culture of those who read Shakespeare has *not* functioned in quite that way.) Authenticity is a ghetto. In fact Michaels's argument makes me wonder about the usefulness of the term *multiculturalism,* in any of its various meanings. For at the very least the term implies that even if our influences and sources are multiple we can nevertheless tell where one culture leaves off and another begins, that they remain separate in essence.

And yet, and yet. Michaels's argument depends on an unacknowledged homology between the genetic unity of *Homo sapiens* and, if not a unity, then at least a universal accessibility of cultural practice. And that argument—and in places I have difficulty reading his tone—points to a fissure in our thought and forces us to recognize the costs and the consequences of our own anti-essentialism. For we also value authenticity, value it especially as an alternative to the homogenizing tendency of modernity. So much of humankind's murderous and yet enlivening diversity of cultures depends on the practitioners' belief that there is indeed some essential difference between their own people and those outside. Without that belief might not that diversity someday disappear?

At this point I'd like to turn to Bilgrami's essay, "What Is a Muslim? Fundamental Commitment and Cultural Identity" (pp. 198–219). In his functionalist analysis of Islamic identity today, and in particular of what he calls Islamic absolutism, he denies the claim—"to which philosophers are prone"—that there is an ahistorical "human need for some sense of identity that is not merely determined by their material and social circumstances" (p. 207). He argues instead that the function identity serves is itself "a function of historical, social, and material circumstances," though he does add that admitting that does not necessarily negate the strength of one's "fundamental commitments and the sense of identity they impart" (p. 208). Nevertheless the identity thus produced seems for Bilgrami so overdetermined, so much to "*exceed* what is required by [its] functions . . . [as] to attain an independent phenomenological status in the communal psyche" (p. 209). This "surplus" stands behind the "non-negotiable" terms of that identity and seems parallel to the insistence on authenticity that for Michaels undergirds the link between race and culture (pp. 210, 201). Yet while Bilgrami goes on to analyze the function of that surplus, he doesn't provide an explanation for it, doesn't explain why and how it comes into being. It remains for him a "communal irrationality" (p. 210).

Understanding that irrationality could, for Bilgrami, lead to a reform of Islam's current absolutism. But let me ask another question: Could an identity founded on religious belief be anything but excessive? For one who believes in a revealed religion cannot fully justify or explain his belief through an appeal to history alone, precisely because that belief must be held to transcend history, to reflect a divine order. A religious identity *needs* that quality of overdetermination if it's to do the cultural work required of it. Barthes puts it well in the preface to *Mythologies,* speaking of the "mystification" through which a historically contingent identity makes a bid for universality;[3] so the very excess of identity is a function of the degree to which one needs to hide—or hide from—that history. And perhaps that could be said for "culture" as well.

At times it seems as if we want to believe that because some things clearly *are* heritable, everything is: noses, beliefs, a set of skills with pots and pans. That's especially true for those who've suffered because of that inheritance—Do I at least get some solidarity in return? Or maybe nothing gets passed on and we create ourselves; that's a mythology, too. But the box on the census form of the self does need to be checked, if only to make sure there's someone at home. And it would be better if you could always do it yourself, but too often other peoples' pencils get there first. Our case studies of identity are often subtle, learned, and even sometimes wise. Yet more and more I am convinced that we have been looking to logic and theory to do the work of metaphor, and so our conceptions of identity remain both impossibly delicate and impossibly crude. They are scalpels and crowbars at once—even, or especially, as they attempt to fix the ways in which the borders of identity can't be fixed. They leave us stranded and alone; like Naipaul, we are never more solitary than when we are one with the crowd.

3. Roland Barthes, *Mythologies,* trans. Annette Lavers (New York, 1971), p. 9.

Critical Response

VI

Collected and Fractured: Response to *Identities*

Judith Butler

In the last several years a shift in public discourse has taken place. From the preoccupation with "identity" in the singular has emerged a complicated effort to think plurality. And yet, the plural form, "identities," would have to mark something other than a sequential multiplication of identities to constitute a shift of some significance. If the multiplication of identity becomes the way in which plurality is configured, then identity remains the fundamental term of the analysis, and it has not been displaced as the focus of political reflection. If identity becomes the unit that is multiplied, then the principle of identity is repeated—and reconfirmed—without ever yielding to another set of terms. And yet, the shift to the question of plurality seems to be mobilized by a desire for a more inclusive theoretical frame even as it belies a certain anxiety about that very project. We know that identities, however they are defined, do not belong to a horizontal sequence, separated and joined by a kind of conceptual neighborliness. But the problem of interrelation is almost impossible to think outside the frame of sequence and multiplication once we begin with "identity" as the necessary presupposition.

When I first received the request to contribute a response to this volume, I thought that the title was already anachronistic, that public discourse had already shifted, and that the pluralization of identity has now given rise to a general reflection on the conditions and limits of pluralism, multiculturalism, the parameters of public space, and the prospects for a more expansive sense of democratic community.

Within certain contemporary political vocabularies, the efforts to seek recourse to the notion of a subject-position as a legitimating ground place limits on our ability to think through the more urgent questions of difference and democracy. One finds, for instance, a continued emphasis on the language of "positions" and a recourse to an inarticulate map of social power on which various subjects are said to be placed—or "positioned." Subjects are said to speak "from" these positions, and these positions are conceptually fixed in ways that persistently pose the risk of cultural solipsism. In such a view, a position precedes the act of speaking and remains that which is "reflected" in and by that speaking. Speaking itself is paradigmatically an act of self-representation; it remains unclear to whom the speech is directed, whether it can be heard, whether the subject who speaks and the one who listens are transformed or transformable through such speech, and whether the context for speech is communicative or dialogic in any sense.

That the unmediated first-person voice is offered as the final phenomenological legitimation for a political claim may well attest to the requirements of political rhetoric rather than to any exigencies of truth. And it makes sense to ask, To what kinds of cultural effects do we seek recourse when we seek to ground ourselves in a subject-position? What any of us speak "of" is, unsurprisingly, our "position," and so speaking becomes the delivery of a report on my "position," a term that signals a historical restriction of the Marxist term *condition*.

If we begin with the requirement for such grounds, then pluralism emerges as an epistemological problem of how to surmount the solipsism that follows definitionally from this view. What form does listening take when the presumption is that "the position" from which one listens precludes the possibility of listening? Can the exchange of speech or writing be the occasion for a disruption of the social ontology of positionality? I will return to this question soon.

The notion of identity carries several burdens: the meaning of culture (recently argued by Kwame Anthony Appiah);[1] the problem of historical formation and contextualization; the possibility of agency, social transformation, representability, and recognizability in both linguistic and political terms. But why has it become the locus of so much intellectual discussion? It is not that identities constitute the only items historically formed and contextualized, and it cannot be that all that we mean

1. See Kwame Anthony Appiah, "Culture, Subculture, Multiculturalism," Bohen lecture, New York, 4 Mar. 1994.

Judith Butler is professor of rhetoric and comparative literature at the University of California at Berkeley. She is most recently the author of *Gender Trouble: Feminism and the Subversion of Identity* (1990) and *Bodies That Matter: On the Discursive Limits of "Sex"* (1993). She is at work on a manuscript on injurious language.

by historical formation and contextualization is covered by *identity* or by the anxious multiplication of the term through the term *identities* (anxious precisely because we know that a simple reduplication of the initial term does not suffice as an analysis of the social and political meaning of plurality). Above all, we might expect from the consideration of identity a sense of cultural specificity, and we may turn to identities to deliver that specificity in order to counter certain false and exclusionary generalizations of "man."

But here we tend to run into another quandary, for it seems that what we expect from the term *identity* will be cultural specificity, and that on occasion we even expect *identity* and *specificity* to work interchangeably. Whereas some would then claim that "identity" marks "difference," where difference is understood as cultural specificity—that is, as what is culturally different about a given subject—others would see "difference" as precisely that which thwarts the full constitution of the subject as any identity. In the former view, identity becomes synonymous with difference, and both mean cultural specificity; in the latter view, which might be described as poststructuralist, difference is that which both conditions and contests the postulation of identity in thoroughgoing ways. Identity is only constituted through the foreclosure of a field of possibilities, a field that nevertheless conditions that identity in absentia. To the extent that that field is constitutive (there can be no constitution of identity without the foreclosure of that field), every identity is implicitly or potentially contested by that field.

The poststructuralist view appears to enjoy the advantage of remaining above the fray of cultural specificities and historical formations, of being able to describe, without recourse to culture or history, what "every" and "any" postulation of identity might entail. But this logical domain, I would argue, is itself the distillation of a social organization occluded by the logic of the claim itself. Indeed, this account of the suppression of difference can only proceed through a suppression of difference of which it cannot take account. It would be a sad irony to replace the false generalizations of "man" with an analysis that falsely generalizes the operation of "difference" using a putative logic that governs "any" and "every" identity.

And, yet, the poststructuralist analysis offers an important counter to those moves that would ground and legitimate only those positions that conform successfully to the requirements of a full and transparent self-representation. Indeed, in the work of thinkers as diverse as William Connolly, Kendall Thomas, Drucilla Cornell, and Luce Irigaray, that emphasis on difference is the occasion for an ethical stance of openness, one that counters the closed circuitry of the subject-position and its self-referential declarations.

Diana Fuss ("Fashion and the Homospectatorial Look," pp. 90–114) reads the difference that constitutes the homospectatorial fashion gaze as culturally instructive, suggesting that homosexuality, in these practices of looking, is to be found less in the self-sufficient identity of the spectator than in the very vacillations of the gaze between identification and desire. The restriction of feminine identification to a nondesirous mimeticism misreads the lability of lesbian desire in which being and having an object are not necessarily mutually exclusive. On Fuss's reading, it would be impossible to locate the lesbian subject at one site along the trajectory of this vacillation, for in an important sense a certain version of lesbianism is constituted through that vacillation, one that is consistently misread by those who seek to distribute the being/having distinction along the heterosexual matrix. Fuss's important contribution to reformulating the Lacanian scheme runs the risk of restricting lesbianism to an identificatory process that takes the place of sexual acts, thus showing how lesbian desire is *contained* through the resolution of desire in identification. As a result, Fuss illustrates the furtive, unacted, and contained life of lesbian desire in the visual processes of identification central to feminine identification within an apparently heterosexual frame.

The tenuousness that identification introduces into the notion of identity can be mapped in other ways. There are various important efforts to situate and reformulate the poststructuralist contention about the tenuousness of identity within other terms of the social fray, the different workings of power relations through time and space. What might constitute the specificities of the tenuous in the field of identities, and how might such tenuous sites become the occasions for significant social analyses and possible transformations? Such questions, with their expectations, are at a critical distance from the position that would insist on an ontological self-sufficiency of subject-positions from the start.

This latter view is often expressed through the imperative to mark one's position, where "self-marking" is taken to be the ultimate ethical achievement of political responsibility, often referred to as "accountability." According to this language of "political moralism,"[2] to mark oneself is to take account, to give account, and, hence, implicitly, to answer to a charge and seek exoneration. The moral horizon of guilt and innocence frames such an imperative from the start. And when politics is reduced to political moralism of this sort, the self-referential declaration of identity is elevated to the status of an ethical imperative, restricting the field of public discourse to individualist declarations or to claims first grounded in such declarations.

Sara Suleri ("Woman Skin Deep: Feminism and the Postcolonial Condition," pp. 133–46) takes clear aim at those who would offer an

2. See Wendy Brown, *States of Injury: Power and Freedom in Late Modernity* (Princeton, N.J., 1995).

unmediated presentation of self as a "legitimating" move, although Gayatri Spivak argues that such assertions, erroneous as they are, retain a political necessity ("Acting Bits/Identity Talk," pp. 147–80). In a grammar that asserts and undoes the grammar of collectivity at once, Spivak insists that "our lesson is to act in the fractures of identities in struggle" (p. 180). In apparent opposition to this position, Elizabeth Abel's article "Black Writing, White Reading" (pp. 242–70) insists on the political importance of generalizing blackness and whiteness. Abel, however, does not ask how that binary framing might refuse (and require the refusal of) the field of "fractured" identities to which Spivak refers. To conceive of racism primarily as a problem of psychic projection requires that dyadic structure by which a dominant subject projects and a subordinated Other is projected upon. But the complex distribution of institutional processes of racialization and racism are not simply matters of psychic projection; the racialization of the subject requires an account of subject formation through the terms of race,[3] but this account could not take place within the terms of an analysis in which a subject-status were taken for granted as a "ground" or "presupposition." Moreover, the dyadic frame cannot account for the myriad racialized identities that are neither white nor black, nor constituted simply in a dyadic relation to one other race.

A recent formulation of political responsibility, however, appears to require that we speak of and as monolithic identities. This view tends to conflate a political analysis of race with a self-referential discourse of ethical responsibility. According to this view, taking responsibility first takes the form of marking oneself, and within feminist frameworks, where appropriate, that would mean marking oneself as a "white feminist." This deliberate act of self-totalization is offered as an important counter to the invisible and insidious operations of a hegemonic writing that appears to lay claim to an "aracial" perspective. Taking account of race is thus equated with a reduction of the critic to a racial position. This willful act of self-reduction is sanctified as public self-declaration, and this culminates, paradoxically, in the production of the saintly white person, the responsible white person, the politically accountable white subject. In the place of a thoroughgoing analysis of race or racialization, we witness—obscenely—yet another self-glorification in which whiteness is equated with moral rectitude, an equation that not only reproduces racialism (the reduction of a subject to his or her race) but a significant historical strand in U.S. racism whereby whiteness and moral purity are repeatedly interlocked. Played out in the context of feminism, the figure of white femininity is resaturated with moral purity, a production with serious racist consequences for women of color who come to stand once again, by implication, for the morally impure.

3. See Michael Omi and Howard Winant, *Racial Formation in the United States: From the 1960s to the 1980s* (1986; New York, 1994).

Crucial to this position of the "white feminist" is the existence of white women who get it wrong; the ritual denunciations of other white women—or the denunciatory production of "white feminism"—become the ways in which the morally righteous white feminist critic acquires her sanctity through the moralizing repudiation of others. The project thus remains enmeshed in the problematic of a white guilt, and white guilt is, finally, a form of negative narcissism and quite useless as a resource in building a political community organized by an affirmative struggle against racism. Thus, the effect of white guilt is to forfeit the opportunity for a critical engagement with questions of race in favor of a self-referential drama of confession, repudiation, and exoneration, a drama that consistently resolves political questions into the negativity of moralism. To take the marking of a subject-position as the ground (not to be confused with a point of departure) and as the goal of feminist analysis reifies—in the very act of self-grounding—precisely those social effects that are most urgently in need of a critical genealogy. Consider the impossibility of a study such as Harryette Mullen's "Optic White" if whiteness is taken to be without a history, reduced to the static social mark of a subject.[4]

This kind of argument not only reduces the political and social analysis of race to an ethical framework indissociable from moralism, but restricts as well the possibilities of self-referential and autobiographical writing to the moral requirements of declarative confession and self-marking along with its self-sanctifying consequences.

Consider, though, that not all self-referential claims take the form of the moral sanctification of a fixed subject-position. Akeel Bilgrami ("What Is a Muslim? Fundamental Commitment and Cultural Identity," pp. 198–219) insists that central to the meaning of Islamic identity is the first-person active voice, one that is not linked to a declarative mode of speech, but that is, rather, tied to historical self-reflection, self-criticism, and agency. Because Islamic identity cannot be derived from a set of religious strictures or codes, it ought to be understood as dynamic, temporally expansive, centrally concerned with self-revision. Relying on the existential notion of a "fundamental project" (p. 204), Bilgrami insists that the continuous and active voice of Islam is committed both to a critique of imperialism and to self-reform. Here one might understand Islamic identity to be a process of critique and self-transformation orchestrated and conditioned by a set of religious practices and writings that are neither determining in their effects nor arbitrary in their meaning.

This emphasis on the historical formation and formative power of

4. See Harryette Mullen, "Optic White: Blackness and the Production of Whiteness," *Diacritics* 24 (Summer–Fall 1994): 71–89.

identity coincides with Hazel Carby's view ("Policing the Black Woman's Body in an Urban Context," pp. 115–32), although Carby emphasizes that historical self-reflection takes place through available cultural representations. Her analysis suggests that one might read in the gaps of the cultural construction of the blues artist as a wandering black male a less legible tradition of strong black women blues artists. For these black women artists to constitute the occasion for an empowering representation for black women of freedom and desire, they must become culturally legible. And Carby, as literary historian, works to render that representation legible through her own historiographic practice. That this tradition is in need of historical retrieval suggests that contemporary historical self-reflection requires vigilant historiographic work to reconstitute such occasions for an empowering historical self-reflection. Interestingly, the literary or cultural historian must recover and, to a degree, produce that occasion for self-reflection. I take it, then, that racial identity is not a given in such a view but a historical formation that is in the process of being given, being rendered, by those critics committed to expanding the historical occasions of mediated self-recognition for black women.

Walter Benn Michaels ("Race into Culture: A Critical Genealogy of Cultural Identity," pp. 32–62) offers the provocative suggestion that contemporary appeals to cultural pluralism presuppose a notion of culture that has served the function of consolidating racialism. He remarks: "culture has turned out to be a way of continuing rather than repudiating racial thought. It is only the appeal to race that make culture an object of affect" (pp. 61–62). The strength of his remarks, as I understand them, is that he insists that there is a genealogy to the notion of culture and that positions that seek to defend "culture" or "cultures" as a legitimating ground of argumentation may well be reproducing racialism precisely through such appeals. Michaels's counsel to engage in historical self-reflection on the racialist formation of certain notions of "culture" gives good grounds for entertaining political caution regarding the implicit presumptions of contemporary political vocabularies. And, yet, there is a problematic slide in his argument in which culture is first figured as "*a* way of continuing . . . racial thought" and then figured as exercising its affective force "*only*" as a concealed appeal to race (my emphasis). For culture to derive its affective force *only* through its tacit appeal to racialism, culture must be understood as singly and unilaterally an effect or metonymy of race. And though Michaels makes the case that culture is *a* way of continuing racial thought, he does not offer evidence for the claim either that culture is nothing other than the continuation of racial thought or that race is the sole determinant of contemporary notions of culture. Indeed, it seems right that the term *culture* has in fact presupposed racialism in part, but that is not to account for contemporary invocations and resignifications of the term that counter or diverge from its animating intentions. Indeed, it would be as mistaken to freeze the notion of "culture" in one phase of its history as it would be to sanctify the "subject" as an ahistorical ground of politics.

Phillip Brian Harper's essay ("Nationalism and Social Division in Black Arts Poetry of the 1960s," pp. 220–41) argues that the unified representation of black identity in the Black Arts project in the late 1960s is importantly confounded through considering poetic language as a form of address. Whereas it might appear that the poems from this period are idealized self-representations, promoting a powerful black nationalist subject, Harper argues that the implied or stated "you" in several poems is constituted at a distance from the speaking "I" and its self-representation. As a result, he argues, the poems appear to represent a subject of black national solidarity but enforce a set of intraracial divisions in the process. To the extent that the poems engage a rhetoric of violence against whites, they perform an interracial violence as well. Thus, these poems document the failure to produce a unified nationalist subject, a failure that is to be savored precisely for the critical readings it now affords and for the differentiated, non-nationalist sense of community toward which it gestures.

If one could ground a reading in a subject-position, then there would be no need to ask how such subject-positions are formed and with what kind of legacy they arrive on the contemporary political scene. And, yet, to read from above the fray is equally impossible. Although the move from identity to identities appears to undermine the regime of the singular subject, making identity plural may do no more than reiterate that subject if relationality is conceived of as neither quantitative nor homologous. Pluralization disrupts the social ontology of the subject itself when that relationality is understood not merely as what persists *among* subjects, but as the internal impossibility of the subject as a discrete and unitary kind of being. Identity as effect, as site, as dynamic, as simultaneously formed and formative is not equivalent to the notion of identity as *subject* and *ground*. Reading identities as they are situated and formed in relation to one another means moving beyond the heuristic requirement of identity itself.

And what takes the place of the subject's cultural solipsism is the task of translation, not only as an act that takes place between subjects, but as a movement among languages that sets in crisis the notion of the subject itself. Even within translation there remains the risk that a subject might reconsolidate itself through the appropriation or refusal of alterity. But there is also the possibility of a movement through the temporal and textual distance between what is written and what is read where difference is neither foreclosed nor domesticated. It is this sort of exchange that also poses a question for thinking the pluralization of community along non-nationalist and nonseparatist lines, as collected and fractured at once.[5] If adequate translation is no longer possible, it is because assimilation to the available norms is no longer politically viable. And if translation remains a necessity, then this act will be one that works precisely through failing to establish a radical commensurability between the terms it seeks to relate. To resist the lure of particularism, however, translation remains a movement that must be attempted and whose failure is to be valued. It is this kind of impossibility and necessity that constitutes the kind of reading that does not always return us to the ground we already knew. The rift in the subject is paradoxically its capacity to move beyond itself, a movement that does not return to where it always was, identity as movement in the promising sense.

5. See William E. Connolly, *The Ethos of Pluralization* (Minneapolis, 1995), on the tension between pluralism and pluralization.

Index